DECORATING WITH
FABRIC
LIBERTY
STYLE

CHARMIAN WATKINS

CONSULTANT EDITORS

OLIVER STEWART-LIBERTY
JOHN LAFLIN

SIMON AND SCHUSTER
NEW YORK

CARE OF LIBERTY FURNISHING FABRICS

Do not use bleaching agents when cleaning or washing printed furnishing fabric. The possibility of shrinkage should also be considered when making loose covers and curtains and it is recommended that a shrinkage allowance of 5% should be made.

CHINTZ	Dry clean, or hand wash only (40°C/104°F). Do not twist or rub, and keep fabric flat. Rinse in warm water, drip dry, then iron with a medium iron whilst the fabric is still slightly damp, to retain the sheen which may be reduced by washing or dry cleaning. Do not spin dry. Chintz has been used in this book for upholstery. If you are expecting a particular item to have heavy wear, cotton or union will stand up better.
COTTONS	Dry clean, or hand wash only in 40°C/104°F warm water. Rinse in warm water, drip dry, then iron on the right side with a medium iron. Do not spin dry.
COTTON AND FLAX UNION	Dry cleaning only is recommended.
TANA LAWN (PIMA COTTON)	This is not classed as a furnishing fabric, but may be used in very lightweight articles as illustrated here. Hand wash in warm water (40°C/104°F) using soap powder rather than detergent. Most modern detergents contain optical brightening agents which, because of their whiter than white effect, can easily swamp the subtle colours of some of the prints, especially the commonly used cream background tints. Dry away from direct sunlight to avoid fading. Iron when still slightly damp.

Text copyright © 1987 by Charmian Watkins
Illustrations copyright © 1987 by The National Magazine Company Ltd.

Published by Simon and Schuster
A Division of Simon & Schuster, Inc.
Simon & Schuster Building, Rockefeller Center
1230 Avenue of the Americas, New York, New York 10020
SIMON AND SCHUSTER and colophon are registered trademarks of Simon & Schuster, Inc.

Published in Great Britain by Ebury Press.
Filmset by Advanced Filmsetters (Glasgow) Ltd.
Printed and bound in Italy by Arti Grafiche Amilcare Pizzi S.p.a. Milan

1 3 5 7 9 10 8 6 4 2
Library of Congress Cataloging-in-Publication Data

Watkins, Charmian.
    Decorating with fabric Liberty style.
    Includes index.
    1. Textile fabrics in interior decoration.
2. Liberty & Co. 1. Title.
NK2115.3.F3W38 1987   747′.9   87-4451
ISBN 0-671-61864-4

Project Editor: Suzanne Webber
Editors: Penny Lane, Gillian Haslam
Art Director: Frank Phillips
Designer: William Mason
Photographer: Jon Bouchier
Stylist: Cathy Sinker
Step-by-step illustrations: Jane Cradock-Watson
Colour illustrations: Susan Robertson
Consultant for sewing projects: Sandy MacCaw
Researcher: Julia Wigg

ONTENTS

INTRODUCTION	6
COOL CHINTZ	8
MORECAMBE BAY	12
A RARE PANELLED BEDROOM	16
LE BUNGALOW	20
CAPRICCIO KITCHEN	23
SWEET PEAS	26
FEMININE DRESSING	30
BATHROOM SPLENDOUR	33
HOSHI	36
STANDEN	40
CONSERVATORY CHIC	44
DRINKS IN THE GARDEN	48
THE CHELSEA ARTS CLUB	51
ARTIST'S BEDROOM	55
ESSENCE OF THE ORIENT	58
COUNTRY PATCHWORK	62
TEENAGE STUDIO	66
ASCOT BOX	70
ALGONQUIN SUITE	73
COTTAGE SEWING ROOM	76
CONTEMPORARY KITCHEN	78
OAK PANELLED OFFICE	80
A BOY'S BEDROOM	82
MARBLED BATHROOM	84
BABY BLUES	86
THEATRICAL BACKDROP	88
EASTERN PROMISE	90
AN ATTIC WINDOW	92
SEWING PROJECTS	93
SEWING TECHNIQUES	139
INDEX	143

INTRODUCTION

Liberty prints have held a continuing fascination for woven and printed textile lovers since they were first produced in the latter part of the last century. They are particularly interesting in that they encapsulated several decorative movements developing at the time of the foundation of Liberty's shop in Regent Street, London and that they employed in their design some of the finest talents of the time.

One major creative movement was gaining impetus in England when Arthur Lasenby Liberty set up East India House in 1875: that of the Arts and Crafts. The Arts and Crafts movement took its inspiration from an idealized notion of medieval life, but there were other influences on decorative and design ideals as well. Oriental pieces had been filtering slowly through to Britain but with the lifting of all commercial restrictions between Japan, Britain and America after 1868, goods began flooding into Europe.

With three assistants, Arthur Liberty began selling oriental silks in glowing soft colours unlike any available in Europe. Instant success followed and within eighteen months he had expanded the shop to include many things oriental: vases, screens, embroidery, lacquer, Buddhas, Japanese gods, cloisonné enamel and much else. William Morris, Alma Tadema, Oscar Wilde, Rossetti and Burne-Jones were frequent visitors to the shop and it quickly became a fashionable meeting place with well-to-do customers queuing on occasion, waiting for consignments to be unpacked.

Having established reliable sources for oriental silks which were printed in England, Arthur Liberty persuaded British firms to experiment with eastern dyeing techniques and weaves. He set up in cooperation with dyers and printers Thomas Wardle of Leek, Staffordshire who were already working with William Morris, in order to develop the soft hues called 'Liberty Art Colours'. Textiles printed in these colours were sold in vast amounts for the delicate draping and festooning of interiors.

Edmund Littler's works at Merton Abbey, on the site of a pre-Reformation priory and later bought by Liberty, were used to produce most of the prints, the River Wandle having been in use since the mid-eighteenth century by silk and calico printers because of the soft quality of its water.

By 1890 Arthur Liberty felt the need for a new approach to design. Although enjoying great success with his oriental imports, Indian-inspired fabrics and interior decoration contracts, he had become involved in the Arts and Crafts movement with its abhorrence of extraneous decoration—'fitness for purpose' and 'truth to nature' and a loyalty to purer form being its maxims. Generally disliking many of the excesses of continental Art Nouveau, Liberty promulgated a return to a solid, simple craft ideal incorporating simply stylized plant and geometric decorative forms and Celtic images of the middle ages but, unlike the Arts and Crafts movement, he encouraged the use of machinery to make available this purified form of Art Nouveau to a wider market.

Several eminent artist-craftsmen were commissioned to develop Liberty's design ideal in furnishing fabric, Cymric silver and Tudric pewter ware, enamel and copper work, jewellery, Clutha glass and furniture, including Archibald Knox, Dr Christopher Dresser, Jessie M King, Olive Baker, Bernard Cuzner, John

Pearson and William de Morgan. Arthur Liberty formed lasting friendships with many of these designers and with them he achieved the definitive style that became known as The Liberty Style.

Arthur Liberty became a member of many influential societies and in 1913 received a knighthood for his services in the field of applied and decorative arts. It was not standard policy at that time to name designers and he was more concerned to develop a Liberty identity or image, but working for him on textile design during this period were Lindsay P Butterfield, C F A Voysey, Frank Miles, Arthur Wilcock, J M Doran, Edgar L Pattison, Arthur Willshaw and Sidney Mawson. During the 1920s and 30s many Liberty designs, still on sale today, were bought from the Silver Studios, the Peacock, Peony and Pheasant designs being bestsellers. Designers there included Arthur Silver, his sons Rex and Harry, and Harry Napper. Sidney Haward, who lived at Bedford Park, the first garden suburb of London, also contributed greatly towards the Liberty design style; a brilliant draughtsman, his work still holds good today.

By the mid 1950s block printing had become so expensive that it was decided to record all Liberty block designs on paper. Many of the original blocks were subsequently sold, but the traditional designs are still produced with variations in colour. However, while keeping its distinct identity, Liberty design has stayed abreast of the times and the company has shown a creative approach to marketing.

In 1958, for example, William Poole, fabric and colour design consultant at Liberty, had a collection of fabrics designed to coincide with the opening of the 1960 exhibition of Art Nouveau in New York. In 1966 an Art Deco exhibition in Paris was planned to include original Sonia Delaunay designs from 1925, so Bernard Nevill, who took over William Poole's place in 1962, planned new designs to match. Susan Collier, in the same position in 1972, felt a strong shift towards the 1930s and produced a 'Fauviste' inspired range of fabric designs. This tradition continues today under the direction of John Laflin with the consultancy help of set designer Richard Peduzzi, whose work includes the sets for Lulu and The Ring at Bayreuth and whose theatrical and operatic designs are exhibited at Gare d'Orsay in Paris.

Liberty has had an inestimable influence on British and European printed textile design since the shop's inception and continues to be unique in its championing of British designers. It is our wish to show you how these prints can be used for decorating in many different settings in the hope that they will inspire and provoke you to experiment. The rooms on the following pages have not been set up for the book; they are very much in use in lived-in homes. You will find instructions for making the various furnishings in the second part of the book, and I am sure the book as a whole will encourage you to make use of one of the most interesting collections of decorating fabric designs available today.

COOL CHINTZ

An Edwardian terraced house in the heart of London, with large, high-ceilinged rooms and well-proportioned windows, is an ideal setting for the elegant chintzes featured here. Oliver Stewart-Liberty, Managing Director of Liberty of London Prints Ltd, and his wife Catherine have lived in this house for two years with their two children, and wanted a change from the mixture of styles already in place.

The owners were anxious to keep the sand coloured carpet in their drawing room and to avoid repainting. Catherine Stewart-Liberty loves light coloured prints and wanted to emphasize the airiness of the room while creating a warm surrounding to its north east facing windows. With the help of John Laflin, design director of Liberty of London Prints, she chose an oriental flower print together with a coordinating stripe from the East India Collection.

The Madison print used for the cartridge pleat curtains, Austrian blinds and assorted cushions was inspired by Chinoiserie flower forms of the eighteenth century, and was re-introduced from an earlier collection of Liberty designs into the East India Collection, so called because the main store building in Regent Street used to be called East India House. The sophisticated stripe Capriccio, a glazed cotton which was designed specifically to complement all the oriental chintzes, is employed here to cover the sofa in the same shades of yellow, cream, soft green and grey-blue and gently emphasizes the soft buttery yellow of the walls.

A comfortable, larger sofa kept its original butter yellow covering, and this colour is reflected in the bound edges of the feminine, bowed tiebacks behind it.

A beautifully proportioned window is enhanced by a very pretty Austrian blind with matching cartridge pleat curtains suspended from a brass pole

Rosette trimmed tiebacks add interest to the curtains at French windows in the opposite corner, their bound edges picking up the warm yellow theme.

Ruffling at the base of the Austrian blind is repeated along ruffled edges of the cushions below it, and by the ruffled edge of the fitted tablecloth.

This is a gently relaxing drawing room, which Catherine Stewart-Liberty says has delighted all her friends. It is stylish without being over designed, and shows how a new environment can be created while retaining many of the room's original furnishings and paintwork.

Main scheme fabric

Madison from the East India Collection
Design no 1143005D, 135/138 cm (53/54 in) wide
100% cotton glazed chintz, pattern repeat 64 cm (25¼ in)
Capriccio from the East India Collection
Design no 1143004G, 135/138 cm (53/54 in) wide
100% cotton glazed chintz, pattern repeat 32 cm (12½ in)

Although Capriccio has been used here for loose covers, this fabric is only suitable for light domestic use.

───── ALTERNATIVE SCHEME ─────
Trent from the Chesham II Collection, a William Morris design, gives a more traditional, though still light and airy, feel to the room.

Alternative scheme fabric for curtains, cushions and tiebacks only

Trent from the Chesham II Collection
Design no 1066010K, 135/138 cm (53/54 in) wide
100% cotton, pattern repeat 32 cm (12½ in)

Instructions

Curtains with locked-in lining (*see page 97*) with cartridge pleat heading (*see page 96*)
Stiffened tieback with contrast edging and rosette (*see page 108*)
Bow tieback with contrast lining and edging (*see page 107*)
Round fitted tablecloth with gathered skirt, piping and double ruffle (*see page 124*)
Lined Austrian blind with ruffle (*see page 112*)

Capriccio stripe has been used to cover this sofa, featuring the same shades as those picked out in the Madison print curtains behind it

A close-up view of the tieback and rosette holding back the curtains at the French windows, showing the plain glazed cotton centre of the rosette and the contrast binding of the tieback

Round box edged cushion cover with piping (*see page 120*)
Round cushion cover (*see page 118*) with double ruffle (*see page 142*)
Square cushion cover (*see page 117*) with double ruffle (*see page 142*)
Scroll-armed sofa cover with piping and kick-pleated skirt (*see page 113*)

Madison

Capriccio

Trent

MORECAMBE BAY

An old rambling farmhouse, nestling in a small village set on the edge of Morecambe Bay in Lancashire, is at present being sensitively redecorated throughout by its present owners, a married couple. The area is one of outstanding natural beauty, wild and empty sand flats stretching away into the distance at low tide, and the mountains of the Lake District just fifteen minutes away by car.

They first moved to this peaceful and slightly forgotten area fifteen years ago, taking a cottage and then converting a barn. In the three-hundred-year-old farmhouse, set at the end of a lane with its orchard and gardens extending down to the sea, they have found an idyllic home. Spectacular views over the neighbouring National Trust farm to the sand flats beyond, the nearby bird sanctuary with its wild geese and resident herons, all contribute to the feeling of peace and country living.

The village, though small, is an active one, and in the local market and nearby auction rooms the owner does much of her antique collecting . Her husband is responsible for the printing of the Liberty wallpapers, so it was an obvious choice to make use of one of the prints in the bedroom shown here. Although the house itself is south facing, this high-ceilinged room is situated on the far corner of one of the extensions to the house, and needed to be warmed.

The choice of the turn-of-the-century Penelope print of foxgloves, butterflies and old English flowers from the Cotton Collection for both wallpaper and fabric has brought a warmer, prettier, and

Home dried and fresh flowers enhance the flowered wallpaper on walls and ceiling. The bedspreads were bought locally

more countrified feel to the room, emphasized by the view from the windows of the orchard, filled with aconites, crocuses, daffodils and many shades of bluebell every Spring.

Ruffles were added to soften the edges of curtains, tablecloths, chair and cushions. The plain binding matches the carpet and tones with the fabric and wallpaper. Two bunches of dried flowers purchased from the local antique shop augmented her own ongoing collection of home-grown flowers for a lovely finishing touch to the top of the cupboard, further enhancing the flowers on the fabric and wallpaper. She particularly loves to dry the tiny, old-fashioned roses which she says seem to be unobtainable nowadays, simply by cutting them just before full flower and hanging them upside-down in small bunches to dry out.

Main scheme fabric/wallpaper
Penelope from the Cotton Collection
   Design no 1063664A 135/138 cm (53/54 in) wide
   100% cotton, pattern repeat 54 cm (21¼ in)

(Right) A short, circular tablecloth provides a very pretty covering for an antique folding table

(Below) The occasional brown in the Penelope print perfectly matches the rich brown of the corner cupboard

——— Alternative scheme ———
Santana from the East India Collection of Chintzes, a print adapted from a seventeenth century Edo period Japanese screen, gives a more elegant, less English country garden, feel to the room. The ceiling is left plain.

Alternative scheme fabric/ wallpaper
Santana from the East India Collection
   Design no 1143008C 135/138 cm (53/54 in) wide
   100% cotton glazed chintz, pattern repeat 64 cm (25¼ in)

Instructions
Ruffled curtains with sewn-in lining and contrast piping (*see page 97*)
Piped pelmet (cornice) with lined contrast-edged ruffle (*see page 106*)
Round tablecloth with bound and headed ruffle (*see page 124*)

Penelope

Santana

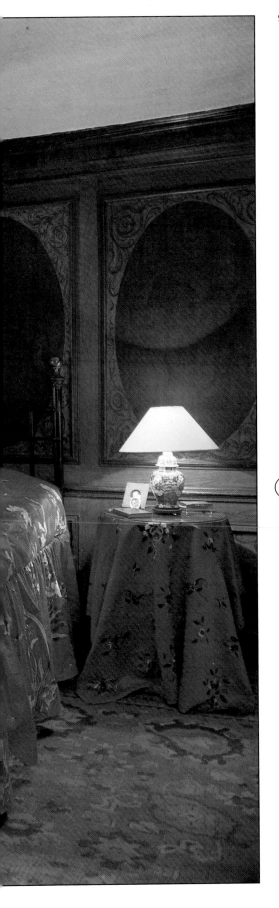

A RARE PANELLED BEDROOM

When Jane and Jerry Scott, owners of an old manor house steeped in history, chose to redecorate their bedroom, it was with a design inspired by Chinoiserie flower forms of the eighteenth century on a deep, lacquer red background. The result is a spectacularly successful combination of oriental design and fine, seventeenth century craftsmanship.

The owner's ancestor, Sir John Fowler, a merchant from Islington in London, was responsible for the building of the manor house in 1637. It was sited on an estate in Kent passed on to him by Sir Martin Bowes, another ancestor, who had been granted it after the attainder or trial without jury and execution of the previous owner Thomas Cromwell, by Henry VIII in 1540. The manor house and its land continued to be passed down through the family to its present owners. Sir Martin Bowes was one of the family of goldsmiths from which the Queen Mother is descended.

The room featured here was originally a drawing room, situated on the east side of the house and was therefore a shady room within which to protect the very pale English skins so prized at that time. Although another drawing room still remains on the first floor of the house, primarily because of its views, this room has now been turned into a bedroom, its beautiful panelling being its predominant feature. The panelling is of Virginian pine which was first imported into

Madison is a successful foil to the rare, painted panelling of this seventeenth century Kent manor house

A nineteenth century embroidered Chinese chairback is draped imaginatively over a bedside table to tone with the Madison print bedcover. It is set with a ginger jar lamp in the same colourways

England in the seventeenth century. It is handpainted to resemble four different woods: cherry, walnut, rosewood and mahogany. It is a very rare piece of painted panelling of this period, a like example being found at the Victoria and Albert Museum in Kensington. A marbled wood fireplace stands opposite the ornate five-foot wide brass bedstead, together with an important walnut dresser and Chinese silk screen of river scenes.

Madison from the East India Collection was chosen to enhance the rich browns of the panelling, to tone with the existing carpet with its faded reds and to add an exotic oriental feel to the room. The Orient is further emphasized by the Chinese ginger jar lamps at each side of the bed, and by a nineteenth century embroidered Chinese chairback. The whole exudes a rich warmth which delights the owners.

Main scheme fabric
Madison from the East India Collection
 Design no 1143005B, 135/138 cm (53/54 in) wide
 100% cotton glazed chintz, pattern repeat 64 cm (25¼ in)

ALTERNATIVE SCHEME

Two different shades of Keswick from the East India Collection would make a radical alternative to the lacquer red shown in the picture, the dark colouring to be used for the bedcover and the paler background for curtains and valance (dust ruffle). The stylized arrangement of anemones, primulas, peonies and old-fashioned roses set on a background of japonica-like twigs, taken from an early nineteenth century chintz design, would form a complete contrast to the main scheme and create a restful atmosphere.

Alternative scheme fabric
Keswick from the East India Collection
 Bedcover and tablecloth design
 no 1143007A, curtains and valance (dust ruffle) 1143007E, 135/138 cm (53/54 in) wide
 100% cotton glazed chintz, pattern repeat 64 cm (25¼ in)

Instructions
Lined bedspread (*see page 125*)
Split valance (dust ruffle) with contrast-bordered top (*see page 129*)
Curtains with locked-in lining (*see page 97*) with cartridge pleat heading (*see page 96*)

Madison

Keswick

*L*E *B*UNGALOW

A turn-of-the-century English colonial bungalow set within a glorious English country garden on the edge of the Seine at Mesnil-le-Roi is the setting for a celebration of one fabric, used to create a little piece of England in France.

he story of 'le Bungalow' is an interesting one. Madame Pauwels, once a comedy actress with the Jean Louis Barrault company, and her husband, a celebrated novelist and editor of *Le Figaro* magazine and *Madame Figaro*, have lived here happily for over thirty years. Her grandfather, having married an Englishwoman and wishing to make her more at home in France, purchased the bungalow in prefabricated form in 1905, from the firm of Boulton and Paul in Norwich. Its pine and thatch construction was shipped back to France where it is now set on a gentle incline overlooking a panoramic view of meadows, amid a beautiful and extensive garden containing many English plant varieties.

Wishing to extend the garden into the house, Madame Pauwels was immediately delighted with the soft honeysuckle blues and muted leafy greens of this William Morris design, not least because it was also very much in period with the bungalow and its furniture, and English style. The Arts and Crafts Movement so strongly championed by Morris made much of the nostalgic 'back to nature' ideal of innocent rustic living.

The backgrounds of Morris's designs were often dark and heavy, which although fashionable for that period, needed lifting and lightening for wider appeal. This Liberty did, and the soft

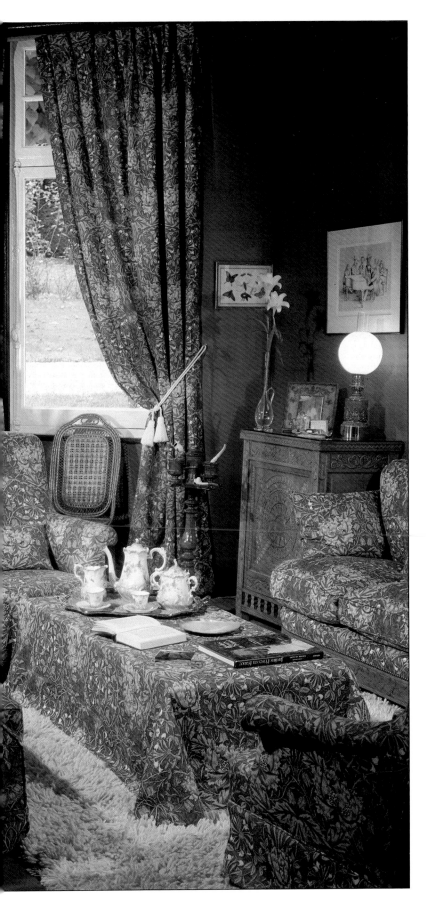

light browns of the Honeysuckle design from the Cotton Collection proved a perfect match for the mid browns of the 1880s bamboo furniture. It complemented the darker brown walls and reflected, to Madame Pauwels' particular delight, the muted earthy brown of the existing carpet. Here she has made full use of the fabric for curtains, lampshades, upholstery, tablecloth, box and scatter cushions.

Main scheme fabric
Honeysuckle from the Cotton Collection
  Design no 1069681E, 135/138 cm (53/54 in) wide
  100% cotton, pattern repeat 51 cm (20 in)

—— ALTERNATIVE SCHEME ——
The alternative fabric Lodden from the Chesham Collection is similar in style and period, but would create a lighter, more summery feel within a rather dark room. Here the print would be used for curtains, chairs and lampshade, together with a plain cream cotton glazed chintz tablecloth.

Alternative scheme fabric
Lodden from the Chesham Collection
  Design no 1069622B, 135/138 cm (53/54 in) wide
  100% cotton, pattern repeat 49 cm (19¼ in)
Plain 100% cotton glazed chintz, design no 1150001M, 135/138 cm (53/54 in) wide

Instructions
Curtains with locked-in lining (*see page 97*)
  with cartridge pleat heading (*see page 96*)
Simple rectangular tablecloth (*see page 124*)
Rectangular box edged cushion cover with piping (*see page 119*)
Rectangular cushion (*see page 117*) with piping (*see page 141*)

Alternative scheme illustrated overleaf

A William Morris design in soft blues, leafy greens and light browns emphasizes the soft, earthy browns of the carpet and darker walls, while providing a near perfect period match with an early prefabricated English bungalow in a French setting

Honeysuckle

Alternative scheme for Le Bungalow

Lodden

CAPRICCIO KITCHEN

A town house in London is the setting for the versatile and countrified kitchen, which to the owner Sandy MacCaw is the focal point of the house. As a self-employed person running two businesses from her home, she is more aware than most of the importance of her domestic surroundings and of the need for space and light.

When Sandy bought her house thirteen years ago, the kitchen was decorated a cheap and cheerful orange. Her criteria were that it should be a pleasant and comfortable eating place, somewhere to sit with friends, but that it should double at times as a work area. Sandy runs a successful soft furnishings business, working mainly for private clients decorating their homes. While concentrating on heavy silks used as an increasingly fantasy style of decoration, she believes firmly that soft furnishings should form the background for lovely objects or paintings.

In time the orange kitchen palled and a neutral background was chosen against which colour could glow. A café feel was envisaged, so natural pine units were fitted with white tiled work-surfaces

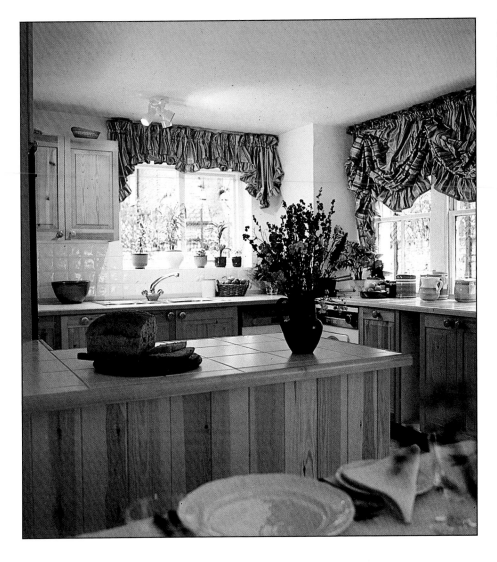

A richly ruffled and striped Austrian blind with contrasting apple green binding matches the Capriccio stripe of the ruffled valance to bring life and warmth to a town house kitchen

A luxuriously gathered Austrian blind softens the line of kitchen door and window, the green of the Capriccio print, its contrast piping and binding emphasizing the foliage beyond

interspersed with white handmade tiles in relief patterns of fruit and flowers, as were the white tiled walls. The use of Capriccio cotton glazed chintz from the East India Collection, with its marvellous striped shades of apple green, tomato, tangerine, china blue and grey on a cream ground, was chosen to liven up natural pine, the tomato giving warmth to what could be a cold and dark-looking kitchen, the green leading the eye outwards towards a patio filled with pots of flowers and greenery. The purchase of red pots and pans to echo the red of blinds has proved a very simple and successful way of pulling together the look of the room. The ruffled valance provides a soft contrast to the hard angles of the surrounding units.

Main scheme fabric
Capriccio from the East India Collection
Design no 1143004F, 135/138 cm (53/54 in) wide
100% cotton glazed chintz, vertical stripe, pattern repeat 32 cm ($12\frac{1}{2}$ in)

—————— ALTERNATIVE SCHEME ——————

In Hedgerow from the Chesham II Collection, originally a Sixties design and one of the few Liberty prints on a white background, fruits and berries emphasize the country feel of the kitchen, complementing the relief patterned tiles on the walls.

Alternative scheme fabric
Hedgerow from the Chesham II Collection
Design no 1066014F, 135/138 cm (53/54 in) wide
100% cotton, 64 cm ($25\frac{1}{4}$ in) half drop repeat

Instructions
Unlined Austrian blind (*see page 111*)
Curved valance with ruffled piped edge (*see page 100*)

Capriccio

Hedgerow

SWEET PEAS

When Victoria Sykes visited the home of John Laflin, Design Director of Liberty of London Prints Ltd, and saw the sponged walls, she immediately wanted to update her own bedroom in the same way. Since her bed and its coverings were beginning to look a little scruffy, it was obvious that they also had to be changed.

The seventeen-year-old daughter of Valerie Goad (who runs a thriving business designing children's clothes using Liberty Tana lawns extensively), Victoria is an extremely vital, erudite teenager with an avid interest in the arts.

The bedroom was sponged by Victoria in pink and blue on a white background using small, natural sponges and the finished effect delighted her: 'like waking up each morning in pink and white clouds,' she says. The very pretty and sophisticated Sweet Pea design on a creamy white ground, from an original drawing by the flower artist and textile designer Sidney Haward, was chosen to tone with the walls. Haward, who owned a garden full of flowers and worked closely with Liberty in the years around the turn of the century, produced many successful designs for the firm.

The print was used to cover both head- and footboards of a lovely old bed which had been given to Victoria by her grandmother five years previously, as well as for the scalloped fitted bedcover, split-cornered valance (dust ruffle) and washstand curtain. Her aunt helped her in the re-covering of the bed boards, which were already well padded, the Sweet Pea fabric being stretched evenly across the existing chintz. Tiny ornamental boxes from her collection are

The turn-of-the-century design Sweet Pea by Sidney Haward proves the perfect choice for a seventeen-year-old's bedroom

Delicate bamboo furniture perfectly complements the Sweet Pea fabric used for the washstand and window curtains, while a picture of Victoria Sykes' twin sister, photographed by Snowdon, takes pride of place on the little table

arranged on the bookshelf together with old scent bottles from the 1920s. Victoria, like her mother, who collects Clarice Cliff ceramics from the 1930s, loves a bargain, and the occasional rummage in the family furniture store produces alternative pieces of furniture.

Main scheme fabric
Sweet Pea from the Cotton Collection
   Design no 1061613B, 135/138 cm (53/54 in) wide
   100% cotton, pattern repeat 64 cm (25¼ in)

—— ALTERNATIVE SCHEME ——
The busier more cottage print Briarwood, also from the Cotton Collection, a design of dog roses, violets and birds in the William Morris style, could be chosen as a contrast to the more sophisticated Sweet Pea.

Alternative scheme fabric
Briarwood from the Cotton Collection
   Design no 1069674A, 135/138 cm (53/54 in) wide
   100% cotton, pattern repeat 20 cm (8 in)

Instructions
Re-covering head- and footboards (*see page 138*)
Lined fitted bedspread with pillow gussets and scalloped edge (*see page 126*)
Split valance (dust ruffle) with contrast-bordered top (*see page 129*)
Square cushion (*see page 118*) with knife-pleated ruffle (*see page 142*)

Sweet Pea

Briarwood

FEMININE DRESSING

Valerie Goad lives with her husband Mark and their five children in a lovely old red brick Kent farmhouse near Sevenoaks, from which they run a children's design and clothing company which makes good use of the Tana lawns so recognizable as Liberty's for their tiny sprig, flower and geometric designs.

Their bedroom contains quite beautiful French Provincial furniture from the late eighteenth and early nineteenth centuries, collected by his family in Wiltshire about forty years ago. The chest of drawers features many different birds including beautifully inlaid mother-of-pearl storks in full flight, peacocks, water fowl and birds of prey set round with roses, peonies, the branches of fir trees and other vegetation.

Handpainted roses, hollyhocks and fuchsia are among the varieties found in a design of flowers in an ornate vase at the centre of the bedhead, while gold scrolling picks out the shaped top and base of the headboard. In choosing a covering for such a bed, Valerie Goad decided upon the palest shades of Liberty Tana lawns which were made up by her old nannie into a diagonally stitched and quilted bedspread to give a very feminine but traditional look, which enhances rather than detracts from the ornate furniture. Five classic print designs were chosen which were used on their wrong sides to produce a more faded antique look to the covering.

Antique lace was gathered in layers to make flounces around the base of the bed, while ruffled antique lace cushions were piled at its head. Softly draped lace curtains, held in place with creamy-white satin ribbons, complete an overtly feminine and pretty bedroom of great style.

Main scheme fabric
A selection of classic Tana lawns
90 cm (35 in) wide
100% cotton lawn

Softly faded shades of
Tana lawns enhance
superb French Provincial
furniture of the late
eighteenth and early
nineteenth centuries

——— ALTERNATIVE SCHEME ———

Opium from the East India Collection
makes a complete contrast to the Tana
lawns, a design of golden dragons on
black background with lacquer red
border taken from a Coromandel incised
lacquer screen design of the late seventeenth century. The colours match those
of the ornate French bed. This fabric
would be better made up into a simple
throwover bedspread, rather than quilted.

Alternative scheme fabric

Opium from the East India Collection
  Design no 1143002A, 135/138 cm (53/54 in)
  wide
  100% cotton glazed chintz, pattern repeat
  64 cm (25¼ in)

Instructions

**Patchwork bedspread with diagonal
  quilting (*see page 127*)**
Alternative scheme illustrated overleaf

Opium

Alternative scheme for Feminine Dressing

BATHROOM SPLENDOUR

A warm cosy bathroom in shades of blue and filled with paintings, antique furniture and interesting objects was the image the owner had in mind when choosing a new print for curtains, valance and blinds.

Liz Stewart-Liberty and her husband share a mock Tudor Buckinghamshire house dating from 1913, when it was built as a wedding present for her in-laws. With its 'joke-oak' design it has been lived in by her husband's family since it was built, so it is very much a family home. 'I hope it is welcoming, warm, pretty and comfortable,' she said. 'Everything in it has a meaning for my husband and myself, having been inherited or collected over a number of years. I should like to think that all the bits and pieces hang together to give an impression of a comfortable jumble.'

Colour, warmth and masses of flowers

are her 'worst and most serious indulgence'. She is a talented painter of flowers, butterflies and birds, with a finely developed sense of colour and a free and semi-abstract style. Having already had three shows in as many years of painting, she works almost every day in one of the bedrooms. Her husband also has an office at home. In this change of curtains and blinds she broke with the household tradition of light-coloured prints and plumped immediately for Bladon from the East India Collection on a dark blue background, which tones perfectly with the blue walls and carpet. Her one decorating maxim is that one strong pattern is enough in a room and that fabric should be cheap and luxuriously full rather than expensive and skimpy.

The dark blues, reds and peach colourings of this Bladon design, adapted from a late nineteenth century design which shows both Indian calico print and Chinoiserie influence, matches the nearby comfortable sofa. The tiebacks and valance are bound in a coordinating red glazed cotton. Original wrought iron finials and square curtain rail have been retained and the curtains are fixed, their floor length adding a living room feel to the room and the Roman blind providing privacy.

In a perfect world, Liz Stewart-Liberty says, she would like to think that her house reflected her personality, and was a welcoming place to return for warmth, comfort and pleasure. This bathroom certainly fulfils her wish.

Main scheme fabric
Bladon from the East India Collection
   Design no 1143003B, 135/138 cm (53/54 in) wide
   100% cotton glazed chintz, pattern repeat 64 cm (25¼ in) half drop

────── ALTERNATIVE SCHEME ──────
Mariana, a strongly stylized print of Empire feel adapted from a seventeenth century silk damask in shades of mid blue, red and peach gives a lighter, fresher look which also matches the blues and reds of the room.

The design of a decorative white-painted wrought iron finial is echoed in the bamboo leaf detail of the oriental print Bladon

Bladon is gathered into contrast-bound tiebacks by silky cord threaded through buttonhole openings

Alternative scheme fabric
Mariana from the East India Collection
   Design no 1143009B, 135/138 cm (53/54 in) wide
   100% cotton glazed chintz, pattern repeat 64 cm (25¼ in)

Instructions
Roman blind (*see page 109*)
Combined curtain and valance (*see page 100*)
Lined tieback with cord and contrast edging
   (*see page 107*)

Luxuriously gathered curtains, valance and tiebacks create a warm and welcoming room in which antique furniture, objects and the owner's own paintings are found in happy combination

Bladon

Mariana

HOSHI

The Salcombe Estuary stretching from Kingsbridge to Salcombe bar is the home of the very beautiful and prized Hoshi, a 1909 gaff-rigged schooner of 25 metres (72 feet), with a heavy bowsprit, which has been owned since 1952 by the Island Cruising Club. The estuary is one of the finest in Britain for both high and low tide sailing, and the surrounding coastline, stretching past the Devon cliffs to Cornwall, makes glorious viewing from the sea.

Hoshi was built by Camper and Nicholson in Gosport as a private yacht for a Scot by the name of J Oswald. She is a classic Edwardian sailing ship that continues to win many important international races, amongst them the 1970 Tall Ships Race to Lisbon with an all-female crew. Her frame is of oak, her hull a Honduras mahogany, the deck is teak and the mast and boom are pine. She was rebuilt, rigged and decked in the original woods in 1933. Although her sails used to be of cotton, harder wearing terylene sails now replace them which last up to seven years.

A vinyl coated piped box edged cushion in Salazar print, with lockers behind and below, doubles as a single berth down one side of the main saloon

(Far right) The main saloon of mahogany, oak and pine showing the bunk base in its resting position as a seat back. On the table sit a chart of Port St Malo and approaches, brass and steel dividers, parallel rules, binoculars and skipper's watch while on the shelf behind rest a brass fog horn and hand-held compass. The wooden door knob is carved in the shape of a rope knot, while the plaques on the wall are for international races won between 1964 and 1984

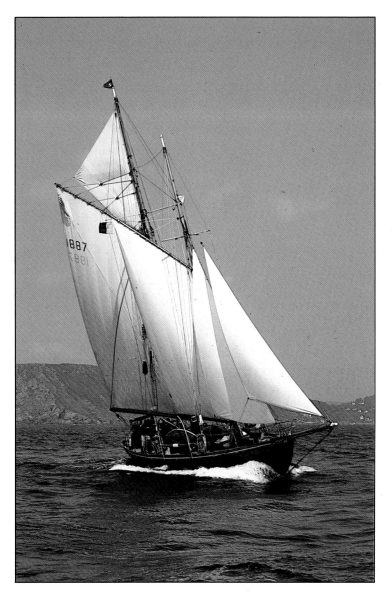

The 1909 gaff-rigged schooner Hoshi in full sail, a glorious sight on a summer's day

to Gothenburg. STA rules demand that at least fifty per cent of the crew be under the age of twenty-five, so the opportunity for younger people is tremendous. She returns home by way of the Orkneys and the Isle of Man, taking in many beautiful and unspoilt Irish harbours.

Because of the high percentage of young people working the ship, the fresh young Salazar design, with a tough vinyl coating, from the Chesham II Collection, was chosen for both the cushions and the bunk bed base in the main saloon. The vinyl coating of the print was absolutely essential given that the saloon and its occupants are very often damp; ordinary cotton covers would soon be rotted by sea water. Salazar was chosen especially since it is a modern design compatible in colour to the interior, yet its broken stripe will suit any period. Here it blends beautifully with the mahogany panelling, oak beams and pine floor, adding a masculine modern feel to the saloon.

Main scheme fabric
Salazar from the Chesham II Collection
    Design no 1066003A, 135/138 cm (53/54 in) wide
    100% cotton, vinyl coated to order at Liberty, pattern repeat 32 cm (12½ in)

────── ALTERNATIVE SCHEME ──────
Clementina from the Chesham II Collection, an 1890s design from the Liberty archives, is a period match with the schooner. It gives a more ornate sophisticated feel to the main saloon and complements the mahogany brown of the panelling.

Alternative scheme fabric
Clementina from the Chesham II Collection
    Design no 1066013N, 135/138 cm (53/54 in) wide
    100% cotton, pattern repeat 27 cm (10½ in)

Instructions
Rectangular box edged cushion with piping
    (*see page 119*)
Bunk cover (*see page 122*)

The Island Cruising Club, with a fleet of nearly one hundred yachts and day boats, runs cruises on Hoshi with a permanent crew of qualified skipper, mate and cook together with a crew of nine from the age of fifteen upwards, who cover both watches and washing up. Her sailing season lasts from May to October and she completes many one-week, cross-Channel cruises taking in the Channel Islands and Brittany, whilst some 10-day and fortnight cruises range further afield.

During July and August of each year Hoshi enters the Sail Training Association's Tall Ships Race, cruising up to the starting point at Larvik, situated at the entrance to the Oslo fiord, and racing

Salazar

Clementina

STANDEN

Standen is one of the few Victorian houses owned by the National Trust, and is situated just south of East Grinstead in West Sussex. It was based on a collection of primarily medieval farm buildings and was designed by the architect Philip Webb (1831–1915) for James Beale, a successful solicitor, and his family as an unpretentious and comfortable country retreat for weekends, holidays and for their eventual retirement.

Philip Webb was a lifelong friend of William Morris, the champion of nineteenth century artistic reform, and they worked on many projects together. Although both were committed socialists, looking forward to an age of simple values and beliefs unfettered by capitalism, their own work was ironically beyond the means of most people.

Standen is the remaining intact example of Webb's mature work, and much of its interior, furniture and metalwork are his own designs. In the dining room seen here, the original blue-green paint of the panelling has faded a little with time and the dresser, designed by Webb, houses the type of blue and white porcelain of which Webb and Morris were particularly fond. Also on the dresser can be seen a teapot and stand and water jug, both by W A S Benson, together with an unusual muffin dish by C R Ashbee. The glass claret jug with silver mounts is by Christopher Dresser. The curtains are the original Peacock and Dragon design by William Morris in heavy wool tapestry. They are set against the same dark panelling framing Georgian-style windows overlooking a large sloping garden partly designed by G B Simpson, which stretches towards beautifully clear views of the Medway valley.

Original dark blue-green
panelled walls by the
architect Philip Webb
are lightened by the
softer green background
of the William Morris
tapestry curtains. A fine
Liberty Guild oak table is
surrounded by turn-of-
the-century oak chairs
with drop-in seats
covered in the period
design Ianthe

The dining table and chairs, from the Liberty Guild are still produced today. They are part of a collection of hand-crafted solid oak furniture inspired by the Arts and Crafts Movement and made in England. The fine oak table is a copy of a 1900 original by Liberty. On the table is a Tudric pewter bowl filled with fruit, supported by four cabriole legs with a stylized leaf decoration made by Liberty in 1902. A pair of Liberty Tudric pewter candlesticks, pierced central stems decorated with leaves and berries on tendrils were probably designed in 1905 by Archibald Knox, who worked closely with the store.

The oak chairs from the Liberty Guild Collection have drop-in seats which obviously had to be covered in fabric true to the period. Ianthe from the Chesham Collection, a popular pattern created in about 1900 by an unknown designer, was the ideal choice.

Main scheme fabric

Ianthe from the Chesham Collection
Design no 1069604K, 135/138 cm (53/54 in) wide
100% cotton, pattern repeat 31 cm (12¼ in)

—— ALTERNATIVE SCHEME ——

The best-selling peacock feather print Hera, from the Cotton Collection, is the natural alternative choice for the seat coverings. The design is by Arthur Silver, who was the founder of the Silver Studio and an important designer of Liberty textiles, silver and pewter, and dates from 1887. Its dark green background perfectly matches the painted wall panelling, the lighter green of the feathers emphasizing the soft green background of the William Morris curtains.

Alternative scheme fabric

Hera from the Cotton Collection
Design no 1069635A, 135/138 cm (53/54 in) wide
100% cotton, pattern repeat 36 cm (14¼ in)

Instructions

Drop-in chair seat cover with double piping and box edged sides (*see page 137*)

The faded blues and maroons of Ianthe perfectly complement those of the carpet beneath and the glowing, mid-browns of the oak table, chair and wooden floorboards are enhanced by the brown tendrils of the print

Ianthe

Hera

CONSERVATORY CHIC

Stone Green Hall is a hotel set in a little village in the Kent weald near Ashford. The present owners, who have lived at the Hall for seven years, have totally transformed a huge chilly looking conservatory into a sub-tropical garden for summer drinks and dining.

James and Ingrid Kempston bought the hall at Mersham although they originally intended to buy a house in East Anglia. But when they found Stone Green Hall (the main part of which is Queen Anne, built around a seventeenth century Cromwellian farmhouse) their plans rapidly changed.

Neither Mr or Mrs Kempston had any training in hotel management, but a measure of their success is that they have never needed to advertise. The house is run as a private one and a guest could find himself in a bedroom whose walls are lined with Williamsburg fabric added early in the house's history, with 1820s silk damask, or in panelling.

The large conservatory shown here was built by a previous owner, the late Peter Wilson, then chairman of Sotheby's, who was an enthusiastic gardener. In this large airy L-shaped space a mixture of bentwood and wickerwork, antique oak, modern beech and white gloss-painted furniture has been pulled together by the use of one fabric from Liberty's East India Collection, Santana.

This marvellous chintz is adapted from a Japanese screen, one of a panel of six, dating from the seventeenth century Edo period, and has been used here for table-cloths bound in a toning rose-coloured glazed chintz, which has also been used for the napkins. The softly faded wood

A view of one end of the conservatory, showing piped chintz cushions with ties, tablecloth and napkins

The modern beech director's chair shows how covering plain canvas with the right print can transform a relatively ordinary piece of furniture into something special

and brick-tiled floor are enhanced by the stippled and burnished background of the print, whose sun-washed reds are matched by a magnificent rank of exotic camelia trees, planted thirty years ago by the previous owner, and by the stronger reds of the geraniums. The result is a spectacular example of one fabric effecting a total mood change, making the conservatory a wonderful place in which to relax.

Main scheme fabric
Santana from the East India Collection
Design no 1143008A, 135/138 cm (53/54 in) wide
100% cotton glazed chintz, pattern repeat 64 cm (25¼ in)
Plain cotton glazed chintz, design no 1150001F, width as above

───── ALTERNATIVE SCHEME ─────
The stripe Capriccio, from the East India Collection, offers a more modern approach picking up the red and green tones of the plants.

Alternative scheme fabric
Capriccio from the East India Collection
Design no 1143004G, 135/138 cm (53/54 in) wide
100% cotton glazed chintz, vertical stripe, pattern repeat 32 cm (12½ in)
Plain cotton glazed chintz, design no 1150001H, width as above

Instructions
Round tablecloth with bound edge (*see page 123*)
Napkins (*see page 139*)
Fabric-covered director's chair (*see page 136*)

Santana

Capriccio

DRINKS IN THE GARDEN

The five acre gardens surrounding Stone Green Hall, a small hotel near Ashford in Kent, are based on similar grounds in Hidcote, Gloucester. They were developed within the last thirty-five years by a previous owner of the house and keen horticulturalist, Peter Wilson, who laid them out in the grand manner to complement the Queen Anne period of the building.

Superb yew hedges form thick high walls which enclose amongst others a rose garden, a herbaceous garden, and a pond with gazebo—wonderful private places for assignations. The yew hedges surrounding the grass tennis court are over four metres (twelve feet) high, and in one of the walled gardens the owner, James Kempston, tends an impressive array of the herbs required for the excellent hotel restaurant for which he does all the cooking. His wife Ingrid gathers masses of fresh flowers every day from the various gardens with which to decorate the guest rooms.

These living walls create mysterious and secret environments, each with a different character. Randomly laid bricks and stone flags provide connecting pathways. Other paths have been laid to grass, flanked on the one side by yew walls and on the other by old fashioned pink and white roses. The eye is led naturally to a small white latticed gazebo set at one end of one of the paths against a copse of mature trees and guarded by dumpling shaped yew bushes. In other areas the yews have been clipped to form grand buttresses.

A small corner of the garden can be seen here, set with simple garden furniture in natural beech against a backdrop of wisteria and ball shaped yew bushes. The original canvas of the deckchairs has been covered in the fresh and pretty print Hedgerow, a 1960s design from the Cotton Collection. The lounger cushion, covered in the same print, is backed with a matching green towelling (terrycloth).

Main scheme fabric
Hedgerow from the Chesham II Collection
  Design no 1066014B, 135/138 cm (53/54 in) wide
  100% cotton, pattern repeat 64 cm (25¼ in) half drop

Modern natural
beechwood deck chairs
and a lounger covered in
the Hedgerow design in a
private corner of the yew
walled gardens of a
seventeenth century
Queen Anne hall

—— ALTERNATIVE SCHEME ——

A cooler, more sophisticated effect is created by the use of Tambourine from the Chesham Collection, an ikat design dating from the 1970s in muted shades of dark green, blue and brick to blend in with the colours of the garden and pathway.

Alternative scheme fabric
Tambourine from the Chesham Collection
   Design no 1064637D, 135/138 cm (53/54 in) wide
   100% cotton, pattern repeat 46 cm (18 in)

Instructions
Fabric-covered deckchair (*see page 136*)
Buttoned lounger cushion (*see page 121*)

Alternative scheme illustrated overleaf

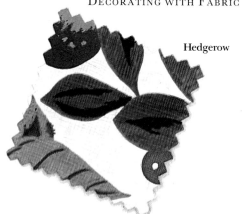

Hedgerow

Alternative scheme for Drinks in the Garden

Tambourine

THE CHELSEA ARTS CLUB

The club in London was founded in 1891 by Sterling Lee, Frank Brangwyn, George Clausen, James McNeil Whistler and Wilson Steer. Its aim was to provide a private club in which its members, originally from the painting, sculpting or architectural disciplines, would be able to relax in pleasant and congenial surroundings.

Eight years ago, although its rules remained intact, the membership of the Club had become seriously depleted and its marvellous old building, set in large grounds in Old Church Street in the heart of Chelsea, was in a very sad state of repair. It was then that Dudley and Mirjana Winterbottom, who owned and ran the Cherwell Boathouse Restaurant in Oxford, were invited to take over the running of the Club with which they fell in love.

The main club room is an enormous space with a gallery to one side reached by a narrow, winding staircase. Deep creamy yellow walls are hung with large canvases lent in an experimental three monthly exhibition by Royal Academicians, while two huge billiard tables straddle the parquet flooring. New cur-

Dark green carpeting in the gallery overlooking the club room is picked out in the green velvet piping of the cushions, providing a calm corner in which to read or play the piano

tains with matching self-piped tiebacks were chosen in the muted tones of Zebak from the Chesham Collection, blending beautifully with the old rugs, green baize and creamy walls of the room. Huge bay windows overlooking a garden complete with resident tortoise and frequented by Orlando, the Club's large ginger cat, are flanked with window seats covered in box edged cushions. Dark green velvet-piped scatter cushions are found in the green carpeted gallery above, which provides a cosy and comfortable hideaway where members can read or play the piano.

The use of the print Zebak has proved very successful: it does not detract from the paintings, it blends beautifully with the rugs and older furniture because of its traditional shapes, and looks wonderful in the soft evening glow of the table lights. Transformed by the Winterbottoms, the club now has the ambience of a large and relaxed household in which everyone comfortably co-exists.

Main scheme fabric
Zebak from the Chesham Collection
Design no 1064645A, 135/138 cm (53/54 in) wide
100% cotton, pattern repeat 64 cm (25¼ in)

—————— ALTERNATIVE SCHEME ——————
Burnham, a pattern from the 1890s to 1900s, origin unknown, is a magnificent large scale print of leaves, grapes and flower heads in shades of burgundy, brown, navy and soft turquoise on a peach coloured background. Printed on heavyweight Union, it makes a spectacular alternative in this large room.

Alternative scheme fabric
Burnham from the Union Collection
Design no 1095107A, 135/138 cm (53/54 in) wide
53% linen, 35% cotton, 12% nylon, pattern repeat 46 cm (18 in)

Instructions
Curtains with locked-in lining (*see page 97*) with cartridge pleat heading (*see page 96*)
Shaped interlined tieback (*see page 109*)
Rectangular box edged cushion with piping (*see page 119*)
Roman blind (*see page 109*)
Alternative scheme illustrated overleaf

A huge bay window curtained in Zebak, a print inspired by the folded edges of kelims piled high one on top of the other

Zebak

Alternative scheme for Chelsea Arts Club

Burnham

ARTIST'S BEDROOM

The very pretty Sweet Pea print from an original drawing by the textile designer and flower artist Sidney Haward, who worked closely with Liberty around the turn of the century, is used here on a China blue background to decorate one of the thirteen guest bedrooms in the Chelsea Arts Club in London. Each bedroom is decorated differently and in this double bedded room overlooking beautiful gardens at the back of the building, curtains, blinds, tiebacks, and a covered curtain pole complete a coordinated look.

Paintings belonging to the Club and the work of members both past and present (club rules dictate that seventy per cent of its members must practise art of some form) are hung at every opportunity up the staircases and along the landings leading off to the bedrooms, one whole corridor being given over to the work of its photographer members. In the hall downstairs a monthly exhibition is held of members' work, each exhibition having a different theme, and all the work is for sale. In the large dining room overlooking the garden, which contains a fountain in the last stages of restoration, further canvases are hung; this room is filled by an enormous wooden dining table at which everyone sits for breakfast.

The Sweet Pea design in this bedroom was chosen to coordinate with the deeper blue carpet already in position, and to bring freshness to the room. The fitted and gusseted bed covers are piped in the darker blue of the carpet. The curtains have a cased heading and the pole is covered to match. The metal arms fixed to each side of the window to hold the curtains in place are covered with a matching fabric casing to complete the look. The window recess holds a ruffled Austrian blind which softens the window and detracts from its height. Members are delighted with the finished effect, which shows how easily a quite ordinary room can be transformed into a pretty and welcoming one, by the use of one well-chosen print.

Main scheme fabric
Sweet Pea from the Cotton Collection
   Design no 1061613D, 135/138 cm (53/54 in) wide
   100% cotton, pattern repeat 64 cm (25¼ in)

Sweet Pea print is used to cover pole, pole ends and to provide cased, fixed curtains. It prettifies an essentially plain bedroom and provides softened, diffused light through unlined Austrian blinds set in a recessed window

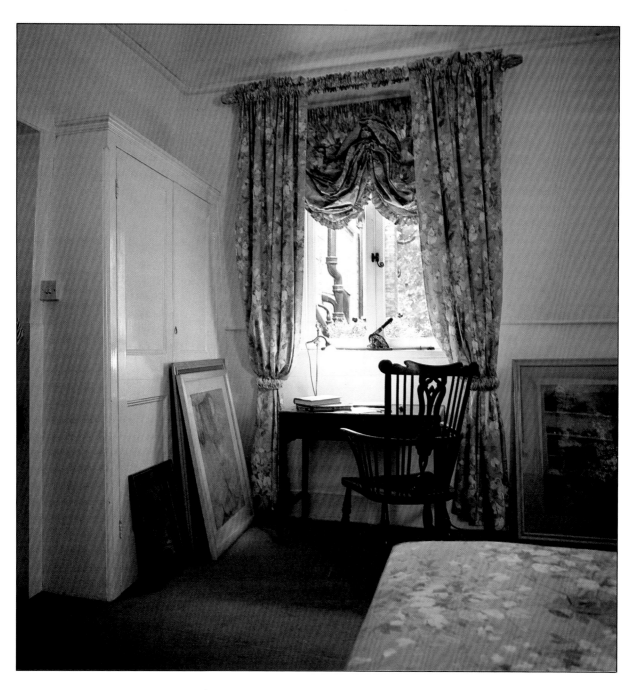

A ruffled Austrian blind
set in the window recess
directs the light
downwards to give a
gentle diffused glow

────── ALTERNATIVE SCHEME ──────

Willow from the Cotton Collection, a
flowing design of pale blue and white
adapted from a William Morris print, is
a pretty alternative to Sweet Pea. The
blue of the print tones with the carpet and
provides softness in a white-walled room.

Alternative scheme fabric
Willow from the Cotton Collection
Design no 1069620L, 135/138 cm (53/54 in)
wide
100% cotton, pattern repeat 32 cm (12½ in)

Instructions
Fixed curtains (*see page 99*)
Ruffled casing for metal arm (*see page 106*)
Unlined Austrian blind with double ruffle
(*see page 111*)
Fitted and piped bedspread with pillow
gussets and kick pleats (*see page 125*)
Pole cover (*see page 139*)

Sweet Pea

Willow

ESSENCE OF THE ORIENT

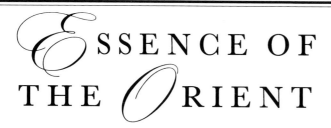

A Coromandel incised lacquer screen of the late seventeenth century is the inspiration behind the marvellously designed chintz fabric and wallpaper set in the living room of its designer, David Haward, in a large and spacious house in Strawberry Hill on the outskirts of London.

consultant designer for Liberty of London Prints Ltd and great-nephew of Sidney Haward, David runs an independent fabric design studio from his home, a business which also services other large furnishing fabric companies. His creative sources are varied. David Haward's collection of old Poole pottery formed the basis of a design story sold in the States and many of his designs, taken from seventeenth and eighteenth century Eastern screens, are in the East India Collection of fabrics.

Choosing one of his own designs for his

The elegant china blue print of Suki chintz with its matching wallpaper and border, is shown in luxurious relief in swags and lined tails (jabots) draped in sculpted folds across a bay window

Cartridge pleat curtains in Suki chintz from the East India Collection are lined and interlined to give a rich warm feel to the lounge. Small tails (jabots) punctuate the lush swags between them and the matching wallpaper and border pick out the soft faded pink of both prints, further emphasized by the Moorcroft ceramic pieces beneath living room, the designer went for the smokey blue-grey chintz of Suki from the East India Collection which one might have thought would look cold. On the contrary, it provides an oasis of peace, warmth and elegance which tones beautifully with the deep blue-grey of the ceiling. Two Moorcroft pieces can be seen on the small side table. Paintings by Allingham, a turn-of-the-century artist whose work was found in David's father's attic during a move, every canvas incidentally having been used as a palette on its wrong side, are now restored and hung, depicting scenes from a small area of Normandy. The Persian is one of an extended family of six cats that share the house, having full rein in the studio. An old sofa not in the picture is the designer's only bugbear. It remains undecorated until exactly the right fabric is found for it, but of course, once finished, the room will no longer be a challenge or give the excitement it now does, as there will be nothing left to improve or create anew.

Main scheme fabric
Suki from the East India Collection
Design no 1143001E, 135/138 cm (53/54 in) wide
100% cotton glazed chintz, pattern repeat 64 cm (25¼ in)

—— ALTERNATIVE SCHEME ——
Melbury from the Chesham II Collection, the original design of which is in the Victoria and Albert Museum, Kensington, provides a total contrast in soft faded shades of fawn, brown and china blue against walls painted a plain cream.

Alternative scheme fabric
Melbury from the Chesham II Collection
Design no 1066009E, 135/138 cm (53/54 in) wide
100% cotton, pattern repeat 51 cm (20 in)

Instructions
Swags and tails (jabots) for a bay window (*see page 102*)
Interlined curtains with handmade triple cartridge pleat heading (*see page 98*)
Shaped interlined tieback (*see page 109*)

Suki

Melbury

COUNTRY PATCHWORK

A Tana lawn patchwork bedspread in random log cabin design makes an ideal bedcovering in a late sixteenth century red brick country farmhouse set amongst four hundred acres of Kent farmland. Flower printed curtains carry through the country theme.

The bedroom came as a complete surprise to the wife of the owner, as he organized its redecoration in her absence. The pinch pleat curtains are made up in the design Petronella from the Chesham II Collection and the peach, pink and beige shades tone with the wood panelling and the bedspread. The patchwork is made up to gentle effect in a selection of Tana lawns.

Tana lawn was introduced to Liberty in the 1920s by a former cotton buyer and later director of Liberty, William Haynes Dorrell. An enormous amount of preparation goes into the weaving and finishing of this fine quality cloth made from Egyptian and Peruvian yarn, which is printed predominantly in England, each design being carefully colour matched to provide a colour story within the context of a whole range.

To complete the decoration of the room, a Victorian firescreen of berries and autumn leaves is set in an old brick fireplace above which is hung one of a number of Victorian watercolours of country scenes collected by the owners.

Main scheme fabric
Petronella from the Chesham II Collection
Design no 1066007C, 135/138 cm (53/54 in) wide
100% cotton, pattern repeat 46 cm (18 in) half drop

A Tana lawn patchwork bedspread in log cabin design forms the central focus of this sixteenth century farmhouse bedroom, decorated in shades of pale peach to complement the Petronella floral design of the pinch pleat curtains

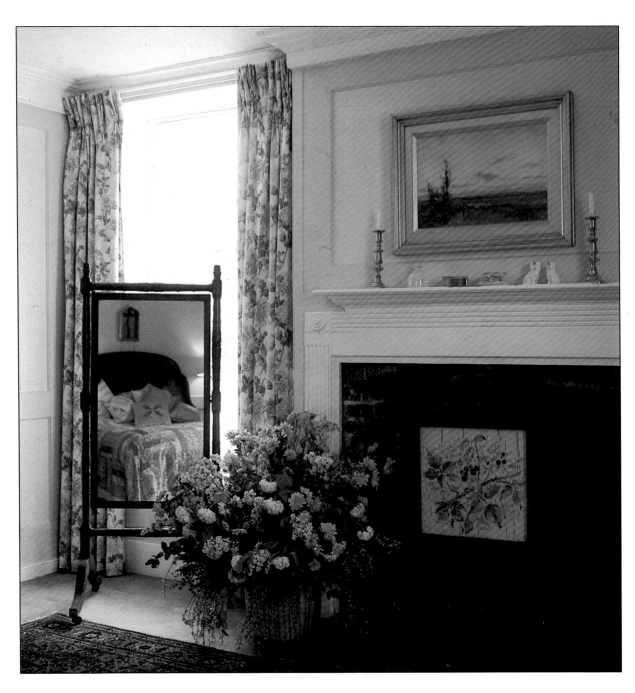

The soft peach and pink curtain shades of an original design from the turn of the century by flower artist and textile designer Sidney Haward, who worked closely with Liberty, are picked out in the panelling

——— ALTERNATIVE SCHEME ———
Hermia, a print of faded brown roses and pale grey wisteria set against muted shades of grey and blue-green foliage and pale oak lattice work, blends unobtrusively with the bedspread and harmonizes with the soft tones of the bedroom.

Alternative scheme fabric
Hermia from the Chesham II Collection
   Design no 1066005A, 135/138 cm (53/54 in)
   wide
   100% cotton, pattern repeat 64 cm (25¼ in)

Instructions
Patchwork bedspread (*may be bought at Liberty*) (*see page 128*)
Square patchwork (make as above) cushions (*may be bought at Liberty*) (*see page 128*)
Curtains with locked-in lining (*see page 97*) **with pinch pleat heading** (*see page 96*)

Petronella

Hermia

*T*EENAGE *S*TUDIO

The prime need of a seventeen-year-old girl must be for a place of her own. In the large and airy room featured here, parental inspiration is behind a well organized decorative theme, which has been created with a minimum of fuss and expense.

*B*eige carpeting, cream walls and white gloss woodwork provide an ideal backdrop for colour. With the addition of a lined throwover bedspread and large piped floor cushion together with a few smaller scatter cushions in the strong print Zebak from the Chesham Collection, in a colourway that ties up with the reds and blues of the prints and divan surround and the existing blue floor cushion, the whole is lifted and pulled together for minimal expenditure.

The print design Zebak is a new one, launched in 1984. It was developed by John Laflin, Design Director of Liberty of London Prints Ltd. On walking through the oriental carpet department on the third floor of the Liberty store in Regent Street, London, he noticed how beautiful the edges of the stacked kelims looked in combination. Their colour tones and varied designs blended so well that he took some colour photos of the stacked rugs, with the result that Zebak was born, a ten-colour print of immense character that lends itself as easily to a modern studio as to an old wood panelled room.

In this room the intention was to create a strong, cleanly modern look by using very simple, easily-made furnishings which could be changed at will to create another totally different feel to the same backdrop, and which would also be ideal for rented accommodation.

The narrow stripes of
modern aluminium
blinds echo the wider
stripes of the Zebak
printed floor cushion

A simple lined bedspread with matching scatter cushions in the kelim-inspired print Zebak, creates instant design impact in a teenager's studio

Main scheme fabric

Zebak from the Chesham Collection
Design no 1064645A, 135/138 cm (53/54 in) wide
100% cotton, pattern repeat 64 cm (25¼ in)

Alternative scheme fabric

Scherzo from the Chesham II Collection
Design no 1066001C, 135/138 cm (53/54 in) wide
100% cotton, pattern repeat 64 cm (25¼ in) half drop

—— ALTERNATIVE SCHEME ——

The print Scherzo, from the Chesham II Collection, a tongue-in-cheek paisley design, provides a lively modern feel to the room while blending in with the reds and blues of the prints and divan surround.

Instructions

Square cushion (*see page 117*) with piping (*see page 141*)
Lined bedspread (*see page 125*)

Zebak

Scherzo

ASCOT BOX

The walls of most boxes at this world-renowned racecourse in the Berkshire countryside are hung with the obligatory racing prints, but in this box, seating ten people, a quite different and totally refreshing effect has been achieved by the imaginative use of three fabrics.

The oriental pavilion featured here belongs to Liberal MP Clement Freud, the writer, broadcaster and culinary expert, who is also a racing enthusiast. His choice of brilliant lacquer reds in such an enclosed space may at first seem startling, but the overall result is quite spectacular. He loved the bright, racy red of the oriental print Bladon from the East India Collection, adapted from a late nineteenth century design showing the influence of both Indian calico print and Chinoiserie design, which he felt would counteract the dungeon-like qualities of the box. One wall was lined with mirrored glass in order to give the illusion of space and Bladon was used to make pinch pleat curtains, which are lined in a strong green matching the leaf colouring in the print.

Contrast-piped and shaped tiebacks sporting neat rosettes hold the curtaining in place, while the dark understair alcove is made cosy by a fabric covered wall, richly gathered and slung between three poles, in the Tana lawn print Mayfair. This paisley print is used again for the contrast-piped cushions set behind a black sofa, lightened by further cushions in Bladon and its coordinating stripe Capriccio, also from the East India Collection.

Crowning the box hangs a lush tented ceiling that uses over 33 metres (36 yards) of fabric. The use of the Capriccio stripe lifts the eye upwards, giving an illusion of height. The 'central' point of

A flamboyant oriental
pavilion, the perfect
setting for watching the
Ascot races

A warm and cosy corner is created by covering an alcove wall in lavishly gathered paisley print Mayfair from the Tana Lawn Collection, matched by plump piped cushions

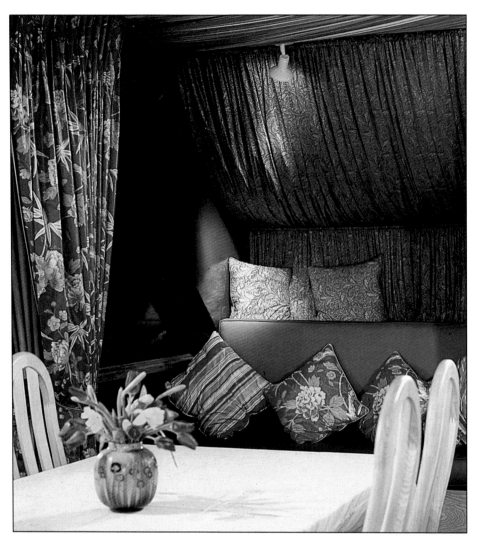

the ceiling, the gathered choux, is butted up to the mirror which reflects the half ceiling to create a full square. Covered fillets in the Bladon print neatly finish the tent edges.

Natural beech furniture and beige carpet form a calm focal point for the eye and the whole exudes a flamboyant and happy feeling of exotic warmth and comfort which makes the business of the race more exciting, the day a more special outing.

Fabric

Bladon from the East India Collection
Design no 1143003C, 135/138 cm (53/54 in) wide
100% cotton glazed chintz, pattern repeat 64 cm ($25\frac{1}{4}$ in) half drop

Capriccio from the East India Collection
Design no 1143004F, 135/138 cm (53/54 in) wide
100% cotton glazed chintz, vertical stripe, pattern repeat 32 cm ($12\frac{1}{2}$ in)

Mayfair from the Tana Lawn Collection
Design no 3336040B, 90 cm (35 in) wide
100% cotton lawn

Instructions
Gathered tented ceiling (*see page 132*)
Curtains with locked-in lining (*see page 97*)
    with triple pinch pleat heading (*see page 96*)
Gathered fabric wall (*see page 133*)
Square cushion cover (*see page 117*) with piping (*see page 141*)

ALGONQUIN SUITE

The Algonquin Hotel at 59 West 44th Street in New York, long a favourite for its literary history and friendly atmosphere, contains two suites decorated in Liberty fabrics which were originally refurbished at the time of the Festival of Britain in the United States, and entitled 'Festival' suites.

The Algonquin rise to fame as a literary watering-hole began in about 1914 with the patronage of the iconoclast, lexicographer and newspaperman H L Mencken. It was frequented by such luminaries as William Faulkner, James Thurber, Gertrude Stein, Graham Greene, Tennessee Williams and F Scott Fitzgerald. In 1919, Robert Benchley and Dorothy Parker took part in the meetings of the Round Table club. This 'inner circle' progressed through the Thanatopsis Poker and Literary Club to become the Thanatopsis Poker and Inside Straight Club, and it was as a result of these meetings at the hotel that Harold Ross created the *New Yorker* magazine to encapsulate the humorous outpourings of his friends.

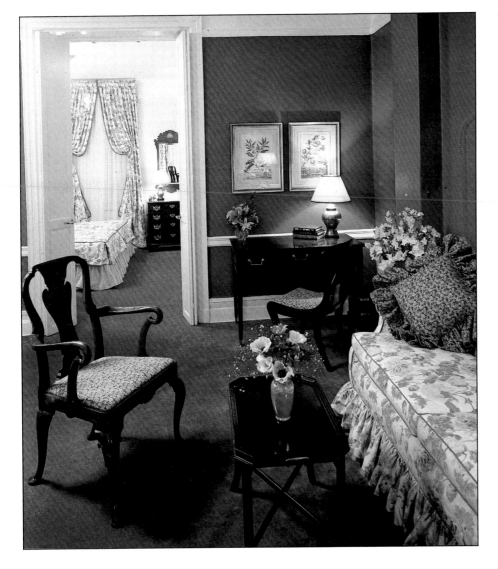

Quilted and piped bedspreads are matched by cased curtains, which are bound in the green of the carpet, providing a link between sitting room and bedroom in this American interpretation of British style

The Algonquin's rooms have now been restored to their original casual sophistication, and its lobby, lounge and restaurant are still a favourite and fashionable haunt of many literary and theatrical personalities. During a celebration of all things British, Liberty fabrics were used in the redecoration of the two 'Festival' suites, in an American interpretation of comfortable 'English country home' style.

The walls of the sitting room pictured here have been decorated in British racing green eggshell paint in a shade darker than that of the carpet, and this background colouring provides a warm and comfortable setting for the stylish Petronella from the Chesham II Collection, a design of peonies in frilly full bloom. Its peach shades are offset by dark green foliage, and curtains have been lined and bound to match.

Similar treatment has been given to the quilted bedspreads, which are lightened by the use of paler green valances (dust ruffles), while a very pretty, classic armchair has been covered in the totally contrasting print Terrace from the Cotton Collection, a simple geometric design. Ruffled cushions and the chair with its drop-in seat in Tana lawn were bought rather than made and introduce a third print reflecting the peach of the large-flowered Petronella.

Fabric

Petronella from the Chesham II Collection
Design no 1066007C, 135/138 cm (53/54 in) wide
100% cotton, pattern repeat 46 cm (18 in) half drop

Terrace from the Cotton Collection
Design no 1069657G, 135/138 cm (53/54 in) wide
100% cotton, pattern repeat 6 cm (2½ in)

Instructions

SITTING ROOM:
Curtains with locked-in lining (*see page 97*) **with cartridge pleat heading** (*see page 96*)
Piped pelmet (cornice) with lined contrast edge ruffle (*see page 106*)
BEDROOM:
Fitted quilted bedspread with contrast piping (*see page 130*)
Ruffled valance (dust ruffle) (*see page 129*)
Curtains with sewn-in lining and contrast piping on inner edges (*see page 97*)

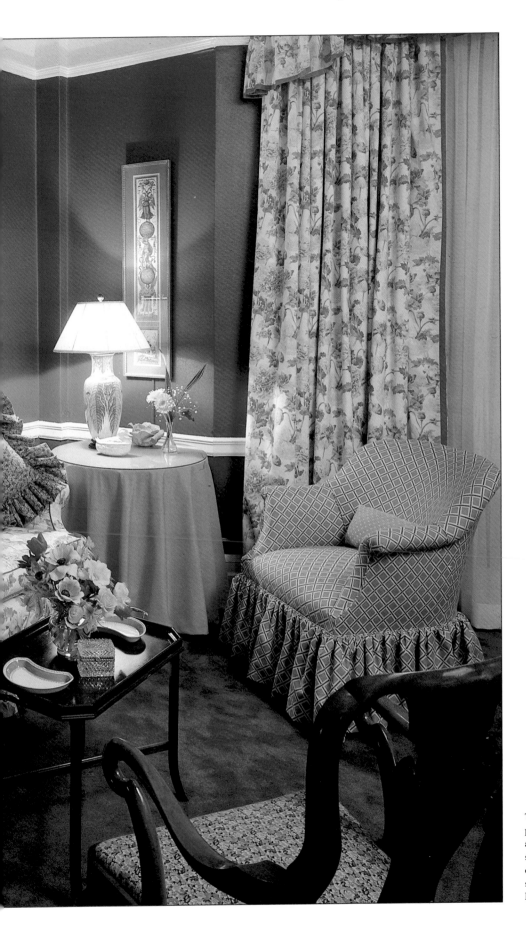

The turn-of-the-century
print Petronella provides
a pretty and
sophisticated focus in
one of the 'Festival'
suites at the Algonquin
Hotel, New York

COTTAGE SEWING ROOM

The village of Westerham in Kent is set among open farmland near Chartwell, home of the late Sir Winston Churchill. It is also the setting for several Tudor cottages built around 1540 during the last few years of the reign of Henry VIII.

At the turn of the century three of these cottages were converted into one larger, L-shaped house, now owned by the cookery writer Susanna Tee and her husband. It is a listed building and the house still retains its original timber framing and low beams. The house boasts several inglenook fireplaces, a bread oven, four attic rooms each of which is reached by a separate staircase from the first floor, small leaded light windows and a wealth of character.

Susanna's sewing room, in what would have been a bedroom in the original cottage, is a private wood-beamed room in which she can tuck herself away. At the end of a sewing session she can leave the sewing machine in position ready for the next bout and close the door on the piles of fabric, half-finished dresses and trails of threads which are the hallmark of a home dressmaker. She thinks of this room as a luxury and, being an avid collector of Liberty fabric, fell in love with the Clandon print from the Chesham II Collection which she felt matched the cottagey feel of the room.

The use of smocked tape as a heading for the curtains and as a means of gathering the stool cover works well in the

Smock-headed curtains in Clandon print, a mass of Spring flowers, provide the perfect match for the sewing room of a 1540s timber-framed Tudor cottage

context of this rustic room, as do the wooden rings and pole which enhance the period and the feel of the room. The deep blue colouring of a mass of narcissi, daffodils, freesia and tulips shot through with dusky pink, red and wine complement the dark beams and leaded windows perfectly.

Fabric
Clandon from the Chesham II Collection
Design no 1066008E, 135/138 cm (53/54 in) wide
100% cotton, pattern repeat 31 cm ($12\frac{1}{4}$ in) half drop

Instructions
Curtains with locked-in lining (*see page 97*) with smocked heading (*see page 94*)
Smocked stool cover (*see page 137*)
Smocked tieback (*see page 107*)

CONTEMPORARY KITCHEN

A terraced cottage in London is the setting for this spacious kitchen-cum-dining room where the choice of the vinyl coated print Bauhaus from the Chesham Collection in vivid shades of green, blue, red, pink, maroon and yellow provides a strong focal point to the room.

The wooden cupboards of the kitchen have been transformed by dark green lacquer coach paint and bright red handles into a stylish range of units. The clever use of original green enamelled 1920s schoolhouse lightshades gives a period feel to the room and the primary colours of the tablecloth and chair cushions work particularly well in a kitchen that has to be both a functional and pleasant sit-down area.

The Bauhaus print is adapted from an original tapestry designed by Gunta Stölzl, of the Bauhaus school, in 1926/27. Although commonly assumed to be a design movement of the 1920s and 1930s, Bauhaus was in fact an art school founded in Dessau, East Germany by the architect Walter Gropius and employing as staff some of the foremost painters, architects and designers of the time. This school was seen as the essence of the Modern Movement, yet it adopted many of the ideals of the Arts and Crafts Movement, such as simplicity of design, but unlike the practitioners of Arts and Crafts the Bauhaus did not disdain machines. The approach to design was to stress aesthetic fundamentals and to strive for geometrically pure forms. Since the school's closure in 1933, Bauhaus has become synonymous with the machine age in art and design, and its influence is felt here in this print.

A Bauhaus print, taken from an original tapestry of the Twenties by Gunta Stölzl is used here in vinyl coated form for a round tablecloth and knife-edged chair cushions

Fabric

Bauhaus from the Chesham Collection
Design no 1069663B, 135/138 cm (53/54 in) wide
100% cotton, PVC coated to order, pattern repeat 64 cm (25¼ in) half drop

Instructions
Round vinyl coated tablecloth (*see page 123*)
Square cushion cover (*see page 117*)

OAK PANELLED OFFICE

Rich dark oak panelling lines the walls of an old farm office from which a four hundred acre farm is managed. This panelling dates from the building of the farmhouse in 1637 and provides a wonderfully warm and cosy environment in which to work.

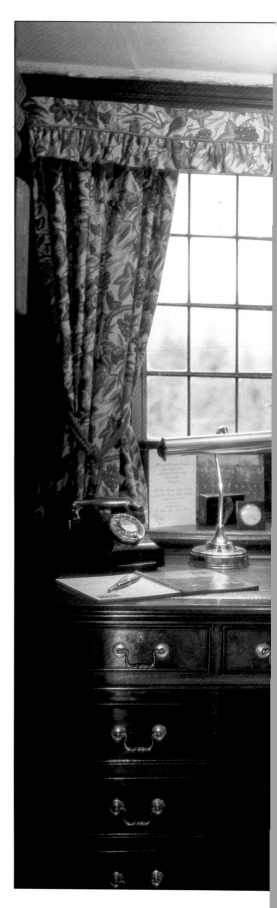

The print chosen for the pinch pleat curtains at the window and for the ruffled pelmet (cornice) is Melrose from the Chesham Collection. Its sophisticated yet homely design of vines, grapes, tropical fruit and exotic birds sporting important tail feathers, together with an occasional brightly coloured butterfly, furnishes a celebration of colour in this tiny room.

The curtains have been lined in the lighter, soft rose colouring of the tropical fruit, whilst the deeper maroon-brown of the grapes, which so richly complements the woodwork, is matched by silky tasselled cord tiebacks for a period touch. A simple terracotta pot of red geraniums picks out the scarlet colouring of the riper fruit, also reflected in the bright red neck feathers of the birds and the contrast piping on the pelmet (cornice). A well filled, box edged cushion with contrast piping is attached by ties of scarlet to the struts of a comfortable office chair.

Furnishing the office, an inlaid mother-of-pearl Victorian letter rack holds urgent post, files are set in matter-of-fact manner to one side of the recess, and a large metal spike holds paid bills firmly in position. A standard 1929 General Post Office desk telephone, a British design discontinued in 1936, is set at one side of the desk top. A small Edwardian glass shade gives unobtrusive light from above, while the brass handles of the desk are reflected in a brass desk lamp. High on a corner shelf, old leather bound volumes are a reminder of the age and history of the farm. The overall feeling of this small room is one of durability and practicality.

Fabric
Melrose from the Chesham Collection
    Design no 1069679A, 135/138 cm (53/54 in) wide
    100% cotton, pattern repeat 36 cm (14¼ in)

Instructions
Curtains with locked-in lining (*see page 97*)
    with pinch pleat heading (*see page 96*)
Pelmet (cornice) with piping and double
    ruffle (*see page 105*)
Round box edged cushion (*see page 120*) with
    contrast piping (*see page 141*)

The rich and glowing print Melrose, a celebration of vines, tropical fruit and birds, is employed here to complement seventeenth century oak panelling in the small office of a Kent farmhouse

A Boy's Bedroom

The decoration of a nine-year-old boy's bedroom which will stand the test of the years into his teens may seem an impossible goal to achieve. However, for Charlie, living with his family in London, a happy solution has been found which pleases him and his mother equally.

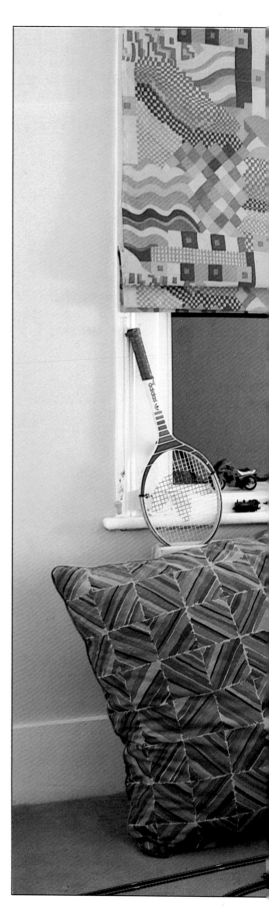

Charlie is a boisterous youngster who, when his turn came to choose fabric for the redecoration of his room, voiced a strong preference for red. His mother, however, realizing that he would quickly tire of a very bright colour, encouraged him towards the more muted shades of Bauhaus and Kasak, whose detailed designs would disguise the effects of dirty fingers. These he was very pleased with; they toned well with his soft beige carpet and fitted in nicely with the dark wood colouring of his desk and chair.

A Roman blind was made up in Bauhaus from the Chesham Collection in shades of grey, air force blue, muted navy, dulled rusts and peaches, the abstract design and masculine colouring of which he approved. Bauhaus is complemented by the design Kasak, also from the Chesham Collection, a design by Susan Collier inspired by the work of Sonia Delaunay, who was a pioneer of abstract painting from the early part of this century.

The floor cushion made up on one side in the print Kasak and on the other, Bauhaus in the same shades provides useful additional seating for Charlie, who spends much of his spare time developing the tracking of his train set. These prints will also take a fair amount of hard wear before beginning to look grubby. Since this picture was taken, Charlie's padded headboard has been recovered in the same Bauhaus print. His mother has also made up a throwover bedspread in Bauhaus, with which she is delighted, and the colours of the print together with the carpet and contrasting cushion result in a happy and practical solution for a growing boy's bedroom.

Fabric
Bauhaus from the Chesham Collection
   Design no 1069663F, 135/138 cm (53/54 in) wide
   100% cotton, pattern repeat 64 cm ($25\frac{1}{4}$ in) half drop

Kasak from the Chesham Collection
   Design no 1069624F, 135/138 cm (53/54 in) wide
   100% cotton, pattern repeat 41 cm ($16\frac{1}{4}$ in)

Instructions
Roman blind (*see page 109*)
Square cushion cover (*see page 117*) with
   piping (*see page 142*)

**A geometric design suits
the neat tailored lines of
a Roman blind**

MARBLED BATHROOM

Pale grey Carrara marble from the hills of North West Italy has been used throughout this bathroom to line the walls and floor and gives a modern clean impression to the room.

Against this quiet backdrop hangs a Liberty print roller blind in the design Kasak from the Chesham Collection. This was introduced in the early 1970s and has been used here in shades of pale and darker greys, fawn, taupe, muted grey-green and brown interspersed by the occasional splash of black against a background of pinky beige. It is a painterly design which works perfectly in very modern surroundings, giving a warm glow to this small room. The grey marbling in this bathroom encourages a feeling of spaciousness and is, of course, immensely practical to maintain.

In the rest of this London home, grey-stained floors and white walls throughout provide an exciting and serious backdrop for the owner's collection of contemporary paintings and for important pieces of furniture. The use of white, grey and other neutrals in the house creates a feeling of continuity and peace which extends into the bathroom.

Fabric
Kasak from the Chesham Collection
   Design no 1069624F, 135/138 cm (53/54 in) wide
   100% cotton, pattern repeat 41 cm ($16\frac{1}{4}$ in)

Instructions
Roller blind (*see page 112*)

Kasak is used in shades
of grey, fawn, muted
green and brown to
warm the pale grey tones
of Carrara marble in this
modern bathroom

ℬABY ℬLUES

A Moses basket (bassinet) is an ideal light-weight carrycot for a small baby, and the basket shown here is particularly prettily decked out. One of the very soft Tana lawn prints has been used to make its lining and coverlet, and the lining for the basket that holds the baby's essentials.

ana lawn has been printed by Liberty since the 1920s, when it was made of long staple cotton, grown near Lake Tana in Ethiopia, hence its name. Many of the beautiful little floral, geometric and paisley prints were taken from old block impressions in books. Other prints originated from bunches of flowers picked from around the studio in Merton Abbey, but nowadays screens have surplanted the blocks, some of which are in the Victoria and Albert Museum and others in private collections.

The sides of the Moses basket (bassinet) have been lined with one particularly pretty print which has been quilted to make it beautifully soft and cosy. This quilting is attached to an unquilted base, on top of which sits a fitted baby mattress with a washable cover. A deep ruffle has been added to the top of the quilting, split open at each side to allow the handles of the basket to protrude and coordinating ribbons tie the opening at the handles together.

Broderie anglaise (eyelet edging) is the ideal finishing touch for the ruffle edging, a detail which extends to the quilted coverlet. A smaller basket has been lined in matching quilted lawn, with a gathered broderie anglaise (eyelet edging) ruffle around its rim. Two blue

A lined, ruffled and
quilted Moses basket
(bassinet) with matching
coverlet provides a safe,
comfy and pretty
environment for a small
baby

and white teddies, one older and more
loved than the other, complete this
charming picture.

Fabric

Classic Tana lawn
   Design no 3336031B, 90 cm (35 in) wide
   100% cotton lawn
   It should be borne in mind that Tana
lawn is *not* suitable for furnishing but
appeals to those who like the typical Liberty
floral look.

Instructions

**Quilted Moses basket (bassinet) with
      matching coverlet (*see page 134*)
Basket with quilted lining (*see page 136*)**

THEATRICAL BACKDROP

Dramatic curtaining frames one of the tall windows of an Eaton Terrace home acquired by its owner some three years ago, and now undergoing stage-by-stage refurbishment. The houses of this area of central London were built between 1830 and 1840 and possess lofty, spacious rooms which give plenty of scope for decoration.

Since the owner of this house is an avid collector of tapestries, rugs and antique wall hangings, he has a strong preference for white walls and neutral carpets which form a plain backdrop. Anatolian kelims from the mountainous Asian region of Turkey feature strongly in the collection, as do Chinese opera robes and Thai wall hangings. It was felt that the richness of this collection would be best enhanced by the use of a richly coloured, plain fabric.

The plain gunmetal grey glazed chintz decided on for the cartridge pleat curtains are lined and interlined to make them drape well. The curtains drape on to the carpet for dramatic effect and are held in place with tasselled cord tiebacks. Swag and tails (jabots) are lined in contrasting bois-de-rose glazed cotton.

Fabric

Design no 1150001A (gunmetal grey) and 1150001N (bois-de-rose), 135/138 cm (53/54 in) wide
100% cotton glazed chintz

Instructions

Interlined curtains with triple pinch pleat heading (*see page 98*)
Swag and contrast-lined tails (jabots) (*see page 104*)

Heavy cartridge pleat
glazed cotton curtains
with matching bois-de-
rose lined swag and tails
(jabots) look timelessly
elegant and blend with
an eclectic collection of
kelims, wall hangings
and Chinese opera robes

EASTERN PROMISE

A spectacular quilted and lined bedspread featuring Chinese dragons, clouds and border print, makes a stunning addition to a lovely antique bedstead found discarded at the back of a country antique store.

The designer, whose bedroom this is, was originally inspired by a similar quilt made for the launch in March 1984 of the Liberty chintz range of furnishing fabrics entitled the East India Collection. He found the quilt 'totally over the top', had to have it, and was reduced to ordering the fabric and having a similar one made.

This type of one-off design will certainly become one of the antiques of the future. The bedspread is made from Opium, a fabric design adapted from a Coromandel incised lacquer screen of the late seventeenth century, and reversed with Suki, a design of oriental flowers in bowls from the same source and period. It makes stunning use of the borders of the Opium print, which are cut out to make four long panels of dragons with surrounding clouds. The border sections of the fabric are set at each side of the quilt and form dividing lines between each panel. A smaller strip using up the remaining border print is set at top and bottom of the covering. The panels are backed with wadding (batting) and each of the dragons, their flames, legs, claws and clouds are stitched round, giving them a three-dimensional effect. The panels are joined down the length to make a complete bedspread. Left-over areas of the central print designs of both Suki and Opium are made use of in scatter cushions in square, round and heart shapes, which are piled high on the bed, while the soft deep blue of the ceiling creates an exotic oriental night sky.

The origin of the Chinese lacquer screen from which these designs come takes its name from the Coromandel Coast along the Bay of Bengal in South East India, where a great deal of trading both by the East India Company and by others from Holland, France and Denmark, took place throughout the seventeenth, eighteenth and nineteenth centuries. A modern Japanese six-panelled and mother-of-pearl inlaid screen, one of a selection at Liberty, beautifully emphasizes the oriental ambience of the room, while a Tiffany-style lamp, also from Liberty, gives a warm feeling to the bedroom.

Fabric

Opium from the East India Collection
Design no 1143002A, 135/138 cm (53/54 in) wide
100% cotton glazed chintz, pattern repeat 64 cm (25¼ in)

Suki from the East India Collection
Design no 1143001A, 135/138 cm (53/54 in) wide
100% cotton glazed chintz, pattern repeat 64 cm (25¼ in)

Instructions

Lined bedspread with quilted dragon panels (*see page 131*)
Square cushion cover (*see page 117*) with piping (*see page 142*)
Square cushion cover (*see page 117*) with double ruffle (*see page 142*)
Heart-shaped cushion cover with double ruffle and piping (*see page 119*)

A spectacular quilted bedspread with Chinese dragons, clouds and strong border design is piled high with matching ruffled and piped scatter cushions to provide a rich oriental covering for an antique wooden bedstead

AN ATTIC WINDOW

Many attic bedrooms now have modern windows inserted in the pitched roof to provide extra light. Because of the simplicity of this spare bedroom, recently decorated in pale shades of blue and white to emphasize the lightness of the room, the owners of this London house wanted a fresh and pretty print for the roller blind that was to be set at the window.

A basic roller blind kit and three wooden slats were purchased. One of these slats was inserted through a casing at the base of the roller blind. As the slat protrudes at either side it could be slotted into grooves cut in the remaining slats that were cut and fixed at each side of the window, giving different positions of closure. The lower edge of each side slat was rounded off so that the bottom of the blind would slot easily into position and then painted to match the surrounding frame.

The blind was made up in the usual way, tensioning it higher than normal to prevent it sagging at this unusual angle. The cool blue colourway of the Willow print from the Cotton Collection was used for the blind, a lovely flowing print of willow leaves adapted from a design by William Morris which fits in well with the modern surround of the window. Light filtering into the room through so pale a print gives a soft diffused glow.

Houses on the Peterborough Estate in Fulham, where this one is situated, were built in the 1890s for skilled artisans and their families and sport stone lions on the parapets of their roofs. A guest in this house, therefore, pulling open the blind in the morning, is treated to a little of London's history at a closer angle than would otherwise have been possible.

Fabric
Willow from the Cotton Collection
   Design no 1069620L, 135/138 cm (53/54 in) wide
   100% cotton, pattern repeat 32 cm (12½ in)

Instructions
Roller blind (*see page 112***)**

Willow design from the Cotton Collection is the very pretty flowing print used here in the simple but successful treatment of a slanting attic bedroom window

SEWING PROJECTS

In Sewing Techniques (*see page 139*) I have included all the stitches, seams and finishes you will need to recreate the projects in this book. I have explained each task in the most straightforward way possible for the achievement of professional results.

The projects vary in ease of make. I would suggest that beginners gain confidence in sewing simple piped cushions, tablecloths or throwover bedspreads before attempting loose covers or the lined bedspread with quilted dragon panels, tempting though these may be. You will find that the same techniques are applied throughout so by the time you have made up some of the more simple ideas, you should have gained sufficient expertise to tackle any Decorating with Fabric project.

CURTAINS

Here the various aspects of curtain design, construction and hardware are explained in a step by step progression, from simple unlined curtains to interlined curtains with a handmade heading and swags and tails (jabots).

HEADINGS

The decorative finish—or heading—at the top of a curtain can be handmade or produced by attaching a commercial ready-made tape. The latter are strips of strong fabric that have slots for the hooks that attach the curtain to the runners on the track or pole. These tapes either have strings that are drawn up to form a gathered or pleated heading or, in the case of pinch pleated tape, special pronged hooks are inserted along the length of the tape to form single, double or triple pleats, according to your use of the prongs. Some tapes are more suited for use on lighter curtains. Check the appropriateness of the tape for the weight and type of your curtain fabric before you buy. Headings also come in different depths; choose a depth that is proportionately appropriate to the curtain length.

As a general rule, even if the curtains are to be set under a pelmet (cornice), a handmade pleated heading produces the most professional finish on interlined curtains, particularly if the drop is substantial. Although making this type of heading is time consuming, the result is a beautifully hung and folded curtain.

When making divided curtains, it is important that pleat groups should be evenly spaced across the divide. A flat section should also be left at the outer edge of each curtain; this should be long enough to cover the return if there is one. You also need to consider how widely spaced pleating will affect patterned fabric. It could give a pattern flattering emphasis or produce an annoying optical effect. The type of heading you choose should complement the curtain fabric.

Not all curtains have to be suspended by hooks from a track or pole. When positioning fixed curtains, either in a recess or in front of a window, a quick method is to slot a rod or wire through a channel stitched in the top of the curtain; this is called a casing. A casing is usually positioned a little way down from the curtain top so that the fabric gathers into a ruffle above it.

Different headings gather up different amounts of fabric. The varying degrees of fullness required by each heading are given under the illustrations. The width of fabric needed for a window is calculated by multiplying the fullness required by a chosen heading by the track or pole length (*see page 95* for details on calculating curtain size).

TRACKS, POLES AND ACCESSORIES

The track or pole you choose should be strong enough to bear the weight of the finished curtains. It should also be long enough to ensure that the curtains do not obscure the window when they are pulled back. How much you extend the track or pole either side of the window depends on the thickness of the curtain fabric and curtain width—and of course the space available.

Triple pinch pleat heading

Triple pinch pleat heading tape

Triple pinch pleat heading tape showing pronged hooks

Smock heading

Cartridge pleat heading

Cased heading

Pencil pleat heading tape

Locking device

Pole with rings and decorative end

Steel pin for hand pinch pleat

Smocking tape hook

Track with integral hooks

Hooks for handmade triple pinch pleats

Weights

If a track is going to show, choose one that is unobtrusive or a decorative one that blends in with the curtaining. Some tracks can be painted or covered with fabric. Poles are meant to be displayed, the curtains hanging below from wooden or brass rings.

There are many types of track and pole to choose from. Large department stores often have displays of curtain hardware where you can compare prices and functions. Flexible tracks will bend easily if you are making curtains to fit round a curved window; wooden poles can be mitred to fit round bays. Tracks are usually sold with runners. Most poles are packed complete with rings, brackets, screws and finials, and some are extendible. If you are making heavy curtains, buy a track or pole with an integral cording set to making drawing easy. Some manufacturers also offer curtain and valance tracks combined in one fitting.

Hooks for use in draw-string heading tape are made in metal or plastic, have a double bend and are threaded through the slots in the tape. Those used for hand-pleated headings are pronged and are pushed into the slots along the back of the tape to make groups of pleats. Hooks used for handmade headings are either the steel pin variety that are stabbed into the back of the heading to secure them or they are sewn on by hand. Both pin and pronged hooks come with long and short necks so the curtain can hang below a pole or the heading extend above a track. Match the hook to the track or pole used and allow one hook and runner to every 8 cm ($3\frac{1}{4}$ in) of curtain, plus one for each end.

Lead weights can be inserted in the hems of curtains to make them hang better. These are stitched into the mitre at each corner. Weighted tape can also be bought by the metre (yard) and laid along the base of the curtain hem.

LININGS, INTERLININGS AND STIFFENINGS

Linings ensure that curtains drape well, giving them body and fullness; they protect the fabric from light, noise and dirt and help insulate the room.

Most linings are made from 100 per cent cotton sateen and are available in a range of colours, besides the usual beige, which is also generally the cheapest. Choose the best lining you can afford because a poor one will wear out long before the curtains. Lining sateen is very closely and unevenly woven, so do not try to tear it when preparing lengths.

Detachable linings can be used for lightweight or open-weave curtains. They do not drape as well, but are easily removed for washing and can be detached during warmer months. They are made up in the same way as an unlined curtain (*see page 96*). Special heading tape for detachable linings enables you to hang the lining on the same hook as the curtain.

An interlining is the extra layer that can be stitched between the curtain fabric and the lining. Besides giving the curtain a plump luxurious look, it cuts out light and provides insulation. Soft and loosely woven, it comes in several thicknesses. In the UK bump is the thickest, and looks like a fleecy blanket; domette is a finer fluffy fabric suitable for interlining less heavy curtains. Both are cotton. In the USA flannel and flannelette are usually used. Both are lighter than bump and domette. There are also synthetic interlinings, which drape well and don't produce fluff or stretch when handled, but they do not block out light as effectively.

When hand-making headings for curtains you will need to use a buckram stiffening. This can be purchased in depths of 10 cm (4 in), 12 cm (5 in) or 15 cm (6 in) and it is attached to the back of the curtain top.

MEASURING FOR CURTAINS

Always measure for curtains with the track or pole in position (cased curtains are dealt with separately on page 99). These can be mounted within the window recess or extend either side of the window frame so that there is enough room for the curtains to be pulled back from the window. The height of the track above the window will

Fig 1 Overlap allowance
Sill length
Floor length

depend on the visual effect you want your curtains to make. Between 7.5 cm (3 in) and 12 cm (5 in) above the window is usual (fig 1).

1 | Measure the length of the track or pole. Multiply this figure by the heading fullness required (*see page 94*). To this amount add 5 cm (2 in) for each side hem. Add an allowance for the overlap if you have a track with an overlap arm.

2 | Divide this total by one fabric width (usually 122 cm/48 in or 137 cm/54 in), rounding up this calculation to the nearest width. (Unless you are making curtains for a very narrow window you will have to join widths to make up each curtain and you should therefore allow an extra 1.5 cm/$\frac{5}{8}$ in for each seam allowance.)

3 | For divided curtains halve this amount to get the number of widths needed per curtain. Position any half widths at outer edges of each curtain.

4 | Next measure off the desired length of the curtain from the rings on the track runners or from just under the pole.

5 | Add the top hem/heading allowance. Allow a 3 cm ($1\frac{1}{4}$ in) top hem for a handmade or ready-made heading if you are hanging the curtain from a pole. To cover a track, curtains should hang from the middle or lower row of slots on ready-made heading tape. Measure from the top of these slots (the point at which the curtains are suspended) to the top of the tape and add this

distance plus 3 cm ($1\frac{1}{4}$ in) to the length measurement (fig 1). Allow sufficient heading above the suspension point on a hand-pleated or handmade heading to cover the track. Add this measurement plus 3 cm ($1\frac{1}{4}$ in) top hem to the length.

6 | Add a 10 cm (4 in) base hem allowance to the overall length. Then deduct 1 cm ($\frac{3}{8}$ in) for floor- and sill-length curtains. Add at least an extra 7.5 cm (3 in) for curtains to drape on to the floor.

7 | Multiply the length by the number of widths needed for the curtains to get the total amount of fabric.

8 | Patterned fabric should be matched across seams and at the centre of a pair of curtains when closed. This demands extra fabric. To calculate the amount, measure the length of the pattern repeat by measuring the distance between the beginning of a pattern and the beginning of the next identical section. Add one of these lengths to the total amount for every width of fabric needed.

9 | You will need to buy approximately the same amount of lining and interlining as for the curtains, minus any extra that has been added to the top fabric for matching patterns. (See individual instructions for any disparities in widths and lengths.) You will also need the same amount of heading tape as the heading width of your curtains and seam allowances at each side of 2.5 cm (1 in).

10 | Allow extra fabric if you are adding ruffles and/or piping to curtains (*see pages 142 and 141*).

CUTTING OUT

You will need
Fabric
Lining (optional)
Interlining (optional)
Metre/yard stick
Set or L-square
Tailor's chalk

It is extremely important that curtain ends are cut

straight (the bottom and top edges must be at right angles to the selvedges). If the crosswise threads (the weft) appear to be straight, cut into the selvedge and gently pull out a thread across the fabric. This will leave a clear cutting line.

If the crosswise grain doesn't appear to be straight, use a set or L-square to achieve a straight edge, lining up one corner of the set or L-square with the fabric selvedge. Alternatively use a sheet of newspaper, lining up an edge with the selvedge. Further sheets can then be pinned in position to give a straight line across the fabric.

Cut out curtain widths on a large table or clear an area of floor where you won't be disturbed. Check that you always cut printed fabric with the design running in the same direction. There are usually arrows on patterned furnishing fabric selvedges that indicate the top.

1 *Plain fabrics only.* Straighten the edge of the first curtain length by the methods mentioned above. Measure off the first length and, using a set or L-square and rule, mark a straight line across the curtain width with tailor's chalk. Cut, using long firm scissor strokes to prevent a ragged edge. Repeat to cut the remaining lengths.

2 Cut any half widths by folding the fabric in half lengthways, lining up the selvedges and then carefully cutting up the fold of the fabric.

3 To prevent puckering at the seams, cut off the selvedges if they are tightly woven. Otherwise snip into them at 5 cm (2 in) intervals to release the edges.

4 Repeat steps 1 to 3 for the optional lining and interlining.

5 *Patterned fabric lengths only.* Mark a straight line across the fabric where a row of design repeats begin. This will form the hem foldline. Measure the length of the curtain up from this line and add the hem allowance below it (fig **2**). Cut across the fabric at the top and bottom of the curtain and

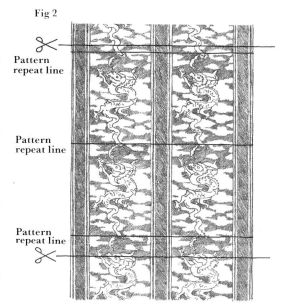

Fig 2

Pattern repeat line

Pattern repeat line

Pattern repeat line

identify the top end with a mark if necessary.

6 Locate the next line of pattern repeats. Draw a straight line across the fabric. Measure and cut the next curtain width as before, cutting away any waste material below the hem allowance. Continue until all the curtain lengths have been cut out.

UNLINED CURTAINS

You will need
Fabric
Heading tape
Matching thread

Making up

1 Refer to the measuring and cutting out sections and then cut out the curtain lengths. Stitch widths of fabric together if necessary to make up each curtain, positioning any half widths at the outer edge (fig **3**). Use a flat seam if stitching together selvedges or edges that can be neatly finished off. To hide raw edges use French seams (*see page 140*). Press.

2 If the fabric is patterned, it should be matched across seams. Press under the seam allowance along one of the edges to be joined and place it over the seam allowance of the other unfolded edge so that the pattern matches exactly (fig **4**). Pin in place. To make the pattern match exactly all

the way up the curtain, you may have to ease the fabric lengthways as you pin.

3 Next ladderstitch across the join (*see page 139*) and fold the fabric with right sides together. Stitch the fabric pieces together and neaten seams. Press. To conceal raw edges, use a flat fell seam (*see page 140*). The topstitching will be hidden by the pattern.

4 On both patterned and unpatterned curtains, press 6 mm ($\frac{1}{4}$ in) to the wrong side down the side edges

Fig 3

Outer edge

Half width

Whole width

Inner edge

Fig 4

of the curtain. Turn under 4.5 cm ($1\frac{3}{4}$ in), pin and press, leaving the bottom 10 cm (4 in) free. If you are using a sheer fabric, turn under 2.5 cm (1 in) then 2.5 cm (1 in) again to make a double hem down each side.

5 Turn up 5 cm (2 in) twice along the base to make a double hem and press, folding the corners into mitres (*see page 141*). Slipstitch (*see page 140*) the edges of the mitre together.

6 Slipstitch the hem in place along the base and sides of the curtain. Sheer fabrics look better machine stitched.

7 Measure off the finished length of the curtain from the base and mark a straight line across the curtain top. Press the excess fabric to the wrong side.

8 Cut a length of heading tape to the curtain width plus 10 cm (4 in). If you are using a pinch pleat heading check the positioning of the pleats when gathered up (*see page 99*) before you cut. If a triple or cartridge pleat falls at an edge you can cut the cords at the back to release.

9 At the tape end that will lie at the inner edge of the curtain, free the cords from the underside by 4 cm ($1\frac{1}{2}$ in) and knot. Trim the

Pencil pleat heading tape

Fig 5

Fig 6

Pencil pleat heading tape attached to curtain

tape to within 6 mm ($\frac{1}{4}$ in) of the knots and turn under 1.5 cm ($\frac{5}{8}$ in) so the knots are at the back (fig **5**). At the other end of the tape free the cords for 6.5 cm ($2\frac{1}{2}$ in) on the top side but do not knot. Trim the tape to within 12 mm ($\frac{1}{2}$ in) of the cords and turn under 6 mm ($\frac{1}{4}$ in).

10 With wrong sides together, line up the tape end with the loose cords against the outer curtain edge. Pin, then baste the tape to the curtain 3 mm ($\frac{1}{8}$ in) from the curtain top. Machine the heading tape to the curtain along all edges, being careful not to catch in the loose cords. Stitch both long edges in the same direction as this will prevent puckering while sewing.

11 Pull on the heading tape cords until the curtain is the correct width. Knot them neatly together, or wrap round a cord tidy (fig **6**). Do not cut the cords as the heading will need to be released when the curtains are cleaned. Thread curtain hooks through the heading tape at about 7.5 cm (3 in) intervals with a hook positioned at each end.

RUFFLED CURTAINS WITH SEWN-IN LINING AND CONTRAST PIPING ON INNER EDGES

This method of sewing in a lining gives a neat finish down the curtain sides and is suitable for light- to medium-weight curtains. Should you wish to leave out the ruffles and piping, allow the usual amount (see step 1, measuring for curtains) for each side turning on the curtain fabric, but cut the lining 7 cm ($2\frac{3}{4}$ in) less than the *finished* curtain width. (The lining length remains the same as given below.) For binding on inner edge omit steps 3, 4 and 5 and insert steps 2, 3 and 5 of the bound tablecloth (*page 123*) after step 10.

You will need
Fabric inclusive of ruffle (see step 1 for ruffle fabric allowance)
Lining
Heading tape
Matching thread
Enough contrasting covered piping (*see page 141*) or

binding to equal the length of one side of the curtain plus 3 cm ($1\frac{1}{4}$ in)

Making up

1 Measure for the curtains (*see page 95*), this time allowing 2.5 cm (1 in) for each side turning. The lining should be equal to the *finished* curtain width and 7.5 cm (3 in) shorter than the unfinished length. Cut the curtain and lining lengths (*see page 95*). Cut a strip of fabric for the ruffle 17 cm ($6\frac{3}{4}$ in) wide times twice the finished length of the curtain plus 3 cm ($1\frac{1}{4}$ in). From the contrast fabric cut enough bias strips to equal the length of one side of the curtain when joined plus 3 cm ($1\frac{1}{4}$ in).

2 Stitch curtain and lining fabric widths together as necessary, matching patterned fabric across seams (see unlined curtains, step 2).

3 Fold the ruffle strip in half lengthways and turn in 1.5 cm ($\frac{5}{8}$ in) along the short ends. Slipstitch (*see page 140*) to close. Gather the ruffle (*see page 142*) to equal the finished curtain length.

4 With raw edges even, baste the piping to the ruffle, leaving loose ends of 1.5 cm ($\frac{5}{8}$ in) at the top and bottom to tuck in to the curtain seam allowance. To avoid bulky seams, push back the piping covering from these ends and cut away the cord.

5 Measure off the finished length of the curtain from the hem foldline, marking the hem and heading foldline on the *inner* side edge of the curtain. With raw edges even and unpiped side of the ruffle uppermost, baste the ruffle/piping section to the right side of the curtain fabric between the marked points, taking a 1.5 cm ($\frac{5}{8}$ in) seam allowance.

6 Lay the curtain flat, right side uppermost. Lay the lining over it, wrong side uppermost, matching the top and side raw edges. Stitch the lining to the curtain fabric down the sides to within 6.5 cm ($2\frac{1}{2}$ in) of the hem foldline, using a zipper foot when stitching the piped side (fig **7**). As the lining is

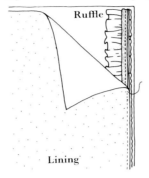

Fig 7 Ruffle **Piping** Lining

narrower than the curtaining, allow the top fabric to form slight folds beneath it.

7 Snip into the seam allowances at 10 cm (4 in) intervals. Turn the curtain right sides out. Press the inside ruffled seam so that it lies at the curtain edge. Now press the other side of the curtain; the top fabric will be drawn round to the wrong side, forming a 3 cm ($1\frac{1}{4}$ in) margin down the side edge.

8 Turn up 5 cm (2 in) twice along the base edge of the curtain to make a double hem, folding the hem diagonally at the unruffled corner and neatly covering the ruffle/piping seam allowances at the other side. Slipstitch the hem in place.

9 Turn up 2.5 cm (1 in) twice along the base edge of the lining. Press and machine stitch. Stitching on the underside of the lining, backstitch along the open part of the piped seam just above the hem to close. Slipstitch the remaining unstitched sections of the lining side edges to the curtain to finish.

10 Baste the lining to the curtain fabric along the top edge. Press the surplus fabric to the wrong side at the curtain top and attach the heading tape (see unlined curtains, steps 8 to 11).

CURTAINS WITH LOCKED-IN LINING

Lockstitching is a method of joining the curtain fabric and lining loosely together at intervals down the curtain length. It gives a professionally made look to large curtains and it helps them hang beautifully and evenly.

You will need
Fabric
Lining
Heading tape
Matching thread
Tailor's chalk
Metre/yard stick

Making up

1 Measure for the curtains and cut out curtain and lining widths (*see pages 95 and 96*). Cut the lining to the same width as the curtains, but 8 cm ($3\frac{1}{4}$ in) shorter in length.

2 Stitch together the curtain and then the lining widths, matching any pattern (see unlined curtains, step 2).

3 Press 5 cm (2 in) to the wrong side down each side of the curtain. Turn up and press a 10 cm (4 in) single hem along the base edge, folding mitred corners (*see page 141*). Slipstitch (*see page 140*) the edges of the mitres together.

4 Herringbone stitch (*see page 139*) along the raw side and hem base edges, picking up just a thread on the main fabric so the stitches will not show on the right side.

5 Curtain weights (*see page 95*) can be added to the base hem at this stage. Circular weights are stitched inside each mitre and at fabric joins (fig **8**). Lengths of weighting are laid inside the hem and caught in place at evenly spaced intervals.

6 Lay the curtain out flat with the wrong side uppermost and begin marking the lockstitching rows. First, using a metre (yard) stick, mark down the centre of the curtain from the top to just above the hem edge. Working from this line outwards, mark parallel lines at about 30 cm (12 in) apart.

Fig 8

Fig 9

Lockstitching lines

7 With wrong sides facing, match the central line on the wrong side of the fabric with the centre of the lining. Pin the lining to the curtain fabric down the centre line and fold it back against the line of pins. Lockstitch (*see page 140*) the lining to curtain fabric beginning 10 cm (4 in) from the top raw edges and finishing 2.5 cm (1 in) from the curtain hem.

8 Pin the lining and curtain fabric together at the next marked line, then fold back the fabric and lockstitch together in the same way. Repeat at each marked line until the lockstitching is completed, working outwards both ways from the curtain centre (fig **9**).

9 Baste the lining and curtain fabric together at the top edge. Trim the lining at the sides to make it even with the edges of the curtain. Turn under the lining side edges for 2 cm ($\frac{3}{4}$ in) and press; turn under the hem edge for 4 cm ($1\frac{1}{2}$ in) and press, leaving a 2 cm ($\frac{3}{4}$ in) margin of fabric all round the curtain. Slipstitch

the lining to the turned-in edges of the curtain and along the hem. The stitches shouldn't come through to the right side of the curtain.

10 Turn down the top edges of the curtain the required amount and attach the heading tape (see unlined curtains, steps 8 to 11).

INTERLINED CURTAINS WITH HANDMADE TRIPLE PINCH PLEAT HEADING

For extra insulation and a sumptuous finish, add an interlining between the curtain fabric and the lining. This type of curtain always looks best with a handmade heading. A *cartridge pleat heading* can also be made by following the instructions below.

You will need
Fabric
Lining
Interlining
Matching thread
Buckram stiffening (the width of your heading)
Steel pin hooks or sew-on hooks (One hook for each pleat plus one for each edge)
Tailor's chalk
Curtain weights (optional)

Making up
1 Measure for the curtains and cut out curtain and lining widths (*see page 95*). The lining should be cut to the same width as the curtain but 8 cm ($3\frac{1}{4}$ in) less in length. Cut the interlining 10 cm (4 in) narrower and shorter than the curtain.

2 Stitch together the curtain and then the lining widths, matching any pattern (see unlined curtains, step 2).

3 To join widths of interlining, butt or slightly overlap the long edges and herringbone stitch (*see page 139*) together (fig **10**). You can also join widths with a machine zigzag stitch, but take care not to stretch the interlining when you do this.

4 Lay the curtain out flat, wrong side up and mark up for lockstitching (see curtains with locked-in lining, step 6). Place the interlining over the curtain fabric, matching top edges, the curtain's side turnings and hem showing evenly all round. Lockstitch to the fabric as for lined curtains.

5 Baste the interlining to the fabric around the edges. Turn in the curtain sides 5 cm (2 in) and turn up hem edge 10 cm (4 in), folding mitred corners (*see page 141*). Slipstitch (*see page 140*) the edges of the mitre together. Curtain weights should be added at this stage if desired (see unlined curtains, step 6).

6 Leaving the depth of the buckram stiffening plus 10 cm (4 in) unstitched at the top of the curtain side edges, herringbone stitch down the side edges and along the hem. Make sure that the turnings are being stitched to the curtain fabric and not just the interlining.

7 Place the lining right side uppermost and matching central lockstitch line to the central point of the lining. Interlock the lining to the interlining as before, following the rows of stitching on the interlining as a guide if visible. Finish the stitching just above the hem. Fold back the lining from the curtain top.

8 Turn under the lining along the sides and base as for lined curtains, step 9, and slipstitch, leaving the heading allowance unstitched.

9 At the top of the curtain, turn the curtain fabric only to the wrong side by 3 cm ($1\frac{1}{4}$ in) and press. Trim the interlining to the foldline.

10 Slip the buckram underneath and below the curtain fabric turning so that its top edge matches the trimmed interlining foldline edge. Smooth the interlining over the buckram. Fold the curtain fabric over the interlining, mitring the corners (*see page 141*). Baste firmly in place through all thicknesses (except the lining) along the edges of the buckram, making sure this does not slip from under the top turning (fig **11a** and **b**)).

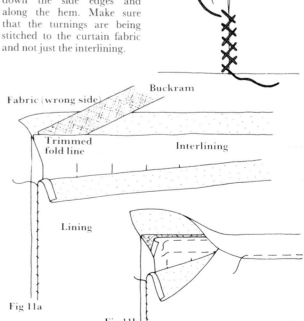

Fig 10

Buckram
Fabric (wrong side)
Trimmed fold line
Interlining
Lining
Fig 11a
Fig 11b

Fig 12

11 Turn in the top raw edge of the lining and slipstitch to the curtain 1 cm ($\frac{3}{8}$ in) below the top edge. Slipstitch the unstitched sections at the sides to close.

12 Next calculate the size and spacing of the pleats. You should have allowed two and a half times the track width in fabric for a triple pleat heading; this gives 10–15 cm (4–6 in) for each pleat, depending on the spaces between. See page 99 for notes on positioning pleats at outer and overlap edges of curtains. A width of 10 cm (4 in) makes a good fat cartridge pleat.

13 Decide approximately what width of spacing would look best on your curtains when they are made up. Fig **12** gives 15 cm (6 in) as an example. Next subtract half a flat section at each end, or the width of any overlap or return, from the *finished* width of the curtain (half the track length if you are dealing with a pair). Divide this figure by your proposed spacing width. The answer is the number of pleats that will fit across the curtain. The exact spacing width can then be found by dividing the finished curtain width (less end/overlap/return allowances) by the number of pleats less one.

14 To find out the width of each pleat, subtract the width measurement of the *finished* curtain from the width of the *flat* curtain and divide the answer by the proposed number of pleats.

15 Using a ruler or set or L-square, mark vertical lines to show the positions of the pleats on the wrong side of the curtain top.

16 Bring the two lines marking the first pleat together to form a single large pleat on the right side of the curtain. Pin, then baste down the pleat line to the lower edge of the stiffening, being careful to sew in a straight line. Repeat for each pleat. Machine or back stitch each pleat down the basting line through all thicknesses.

17 *Triple pleats only.* Working from the right side of the curtain, divide each pleat in three by folding concertina fashion. Just above the lower edge of the stiffening, backstitch several times through the base of each set of pleats to hold them in place. At the top edge of the curtain catch the pleats together at the back (fig **13**).

18 *Cartridge pleats only.* Working from the right side of the curtain, flatten each pleat gently and catch against the main fabric with a few handstitches placed each side of the pleat base just behind the fold. Pad the base of the pleat with cotton wool (batting) to give a softly rounded appearance.

19 Stab in pin hooks at the back of each set of pleats at the required depth, or sew on curtain hooks.

CASED HEADINGS

Curtains and valances can be hung by threading a pole, rod or length of wire through a channel sewn in the top of the curtain (*see page 94*)

Fig 13

known as a casing. This method is particularly suitable for hanging curtains which won't be drawn and ones that hang in a recess or against a window.

QUICK CASING FOR LIGHTWEIGHT KITCHEN/BATHROOM CURTAIN

Making up

1 Allowing 12 cm (5 in) for the heading (this gives a 4 cm/1$\frac{1}{2}$ in frill), make up an unlined curtain following the instructions on page 96, steps 1 to 6. It should have a finished width of 1$\frac{1}{2}$ times the rod/wire length.

2 Turn 6 cm (2$\frac{1}{2}$ in) to the wrong side at the top of the curtain and press. Fold over 6 cm (2$\frac{1}{2}$ in) again. Stitch along the lower edge of the turning close to the fold. Then stitch another row 2.5 cm (1 in) above this first line of stitching. This forms the casing. If the curtain support is greater than 12 mm ($\frac{1}{2}$ in) in diameter, casing calculations have to be more detailed (see below).

FIXED CURTAINS WITH FABRIC-COVERED POLE

You will need

Fabric
Heading tape
Matching thread

Making up

1 Follow the instructions for making unlined curtains, steps 1 to 6, allowing for a finished width of 1$\frac{1}{2}$ times the length of the pole. Measure the curtain length from underneath the pole, adding a casing allowance of the pole circumference measurement plus 4 cm

Fig 14

(1$\frac{1}{2}$ in) for ease, plus a further 11 cm (4$\frac{1}{2}$ in) for the ruffle.

2 When you have reached heading tape attachment stage, make the casing as follows. Fold over the curtain top by *half* the pole circumference plus 8 cm (3$\frac{1}{4}$ in). Press under the raw edges of the turning by 12 mm ($\frac{1}{2}$ in). Stitch across the curtain through all thicknesses close to the folded hem edge.

3 Stitch across the turning again, half the casing allowance plus 2 cm ($\frac{3}{4}$ in) above the first row of stitching to form the channel for the pole (fig **14**). *See page 139* for instructions on covering the pole.

FIXED CURTAINS WITH CONTRAST-BOUND HEADING

You will need

Fabric
Contrast fabric for bound heading
Matching thread

Making up

1 Follow the instructions for making up unlined curtains, steps 1 to 6. Allow a finished width of 1$\frac{1}{2}$ times the length of the pole. To the curtain length (measured from under the pole) add a casing allowance of *half* the pole circumference measurement plus 1 cm ($\frac{3}{8}$ in) for ease plus a further 7.5 cm (3 in).

2 Cut a strip of contrast fabric that measures the width of the ungathered finished curtain plus 4 cm (1$\frac{1}{2}$ in) by a depth of half the pole circumference plus 1 cm ($\frac{3}{8}$ in) for ease, plus a further 10.5 cm (4$\frac{1}{4}$ in).

3 When heading tape attachment stage has been reached, make the casing. Turn in 1 cm ($\frac{3}{8}$ in) twice at the ends of the contrast strip to make double hems. Slipstitch. With right sides together, raw edges even, stitch the contrast strip to the curtain top, taking a 1.5 cm ($\frac{5}{8}$ in) seam allowance.

4 Fold the contrast strip over the seam allowance to the wrong side of the curtain, leaving a 1.5 cm ($\frac{5}{8}$ in) margin of binding on the right side (fig **15**). Press.

Fig 15

Fig 16

5 Turn under 1.5 cm ($\frac{5}{8}$ in) along the raw edge of the strip and press. Stitch across the curtain, close to the lower fold.

6 Stitch across the curtain again half the pole circumference plus 1 cm ($\frac{3}{8}$ in) above the first row of stitching to make the casing for the pole. Slipstitch (*see page 140*) the edges of the casing together above the pole to neaten if desired.

COMBINED CURTAIN AND VALANCE

The valance shown in this bathroom is fed onto a pole in exactly the same way as a cased heading, but since it has a lower, bound ruffle, the making up method is different from that employed for a lined, cased heading previously described.

Here the lining extends below the pole and is wrapped around the bottom edge of the valance to form the binding. The lining therefore doubles as the contrast chintz.

You will need
Fabric
Contrast lining fabric
Matching thread

Making up
1 To calculate the measurements, measure the width of the pole to be used, and multiply by 1$\frac{1}{2}$, adding 2.5 cm (1 in) at each end for seam allowances to make a total of 5 cm (2 in). (The curtains, when finished and in their flat state, are attached behind the flat valance, beginning at each outer edge. They are also calculated as being 1$\frac{1}{2}$ times the width of the pole, although they are of course fixed, and will not be drawn. See step 11 below.)

2 Calculate the depth of the valance required. In the example featured here a full depth of 30 cm (12 in) has been allowed, exclusive of seam allowances, and is made up as follows of 7.5 cm (3 in) for the top ruffle, 7.5 cm (3 in) for the pole (calculated as 12 cm (5 in) in circumference plus 2.5 cm (1 in) ease allowance—a total of 15 cm (6 in); see Cased Headings), and a larger, 15 cm (6 in) ruffle below the pole.

The contrast lining fabric will therefore amount to a depth of 30 cm (12 in) plus binding and seam allowances (1.5 cm ($\frac{5}{8}$ in) × 2, plus 1.5 cm ($\frac{5}{8}$ in) × 2 = 6 cm (2$\frac{1}{2}$ in), making a total of 36 cm (14$\frac{1}{4}$ in)). See fig **16**.

3 Cut two straight grain lengths of fabric, one of print and one of contrast lining fabric, following your measurements for each strip, and taking account of the position of any print you may wish to feature.

4 Place fabric against contrast lining, right sides together and matching raw edges at the top only. Pin along the length of the valance at the top, basting if necessary, then stitch from one side to the other, 1.5 cm ($\frac{5}{8}$ in) in from raw edges. Press seam allowances open.

5 Repeat step 4 for the remaining long raw edges of the valance, to form a tube. Turn.

6 With right side of valance uppermost, fold back a binding allowance of 1.5 cm ($\frac{5}{8}$ in) at the top of the valance to the wrong side, and press all along the top edge to set. Flattening the valance tube on the ironing

board, right side uppermost, repeat this operation to form the lower bound edge of the valance.

7 At each short end of the valance, turn in 2.5 cm (1 in) to the inside of the tube, pin, baste from top to bottom and press.

8 Keeping the valance right side uppermost, measure down 7.5 cm (3 in) from the top folded edge of the binding, and mark all along the length of the valance with a line of pins or basting. Stitch along this line from end to end to form the first casing line. Measure a further 7.5 cm (3 in) down from this stitching line, and marking with pins, stitch a second line all along the length of the valance.

9 At each short end of valance, slipstitch from the top to the first casing stitch line, and from the bottom to the second casing stitch line.

10 Unpick basting stitches at each end of the casing channel, and press to finish.

To attach the valance to the curtains

11 The curtains, which are lined but not stiffened or interlined, are measured in the normal way described in the section on curtains with locked-in lining (*see page 97*), from just under the pole. Calculate 1$\frac{1}{2}$ times the width of the pole for the curtains, so that they match the valance, plus all extra seam allowances and lining details as referred to in that section.

The curtains should be fixed to the valance at exactly

the same spot as that from which they were measured i.e. from just underneath the pole, and they should therefore be attached just below the second casing stitch line. Since they are fixed and do not need to be closed, you will find that they take about half the length of the pole in total, while the valance takes up the remaining half-length, situated in the middle of the pole.

12 Set curtains flat, laying the valance over their tops so that the top of each curtain comes parallel and just under, the casing's lower stitch line, and each curtain is positioned so that its outer edge comes level with the valance's outer edge. See fig **17**. Pin, baste and stitch from each outer edge of the valance and through the curtain thickness to the inner edge of each curtain. (If the curtains seem heavy, make a double row of stitching 1 cm ($\frac{3}{8}$ in) down from the first line, to strengthen.) Press to finish.

CURVED VALANCE WITH RUFFLED, PIPED EDGE

The valance shown in this kitchen is really a short curtain, but since the technique of making it up comes closer to a combination of valance and cased heading, it has been included in this section.

PLEASE NOTE that here the pole has been calculated as being 10 cm (4 in) in diameter.

You will see from fig **18** below that the fabric and lining for the main section of the valance are of the same length. The double, bound ruffle is made up first of all,

Fig 17

Curtain

Fig 18

Cross-section

then set between lining and fabric like a sandwich filling together with the piping. The last part of the making up procedure is to set the casing stitches for the pole.

You will need
Fabric
Contrast fabric for binding and
  piping
Pre-shrunk piping cord
Lining
Cardboard
String
Pattern paper
Matching thread

Cutting the pattern for the valance

1. To calculate the width of the valance, multiply by $1\frac{1}{2}$ times the width of the pole, plus 2.5 cm (1 in) at each end for seam allowance, or a total of 5 cm (2 in).

2. To decide on the depth and shaping of the hemline you should make a template in cardboard or heavyweight brown paper, half the width of the pole, and deeper than the deepest shaped point of the valance. Divide the template into three equal sections, and mark in the vertical dividing lines from top to bottom. The valance shown here was a total depth beneath the pole of 38 cm (15 in), so mark in this measurement at the outer side of the template, and draw a line across the template 15 cm (6 in) down from the top. Make a small hole in each top corner of the template, then attach it to the pole with string so that its top is set directly under the pole. See fig **19**.

3. You will notice from the picture of the valance featured here that the ruffle dips in the section nearest to the centre of the window by roughly 5 cm (2 in) further than its position at the middle section, dropping sharply to a point in the centre of the third section nearest to the outer edge of the pole, to a depth of 38 cm (15 in). See fig **20**. Mark this curving line in on your template, then cut along this line so that you can check the depth of the valance with ruffle, against the light of the window. Adjust if necessary.

4. Remove the template. Because the ruffle ac-

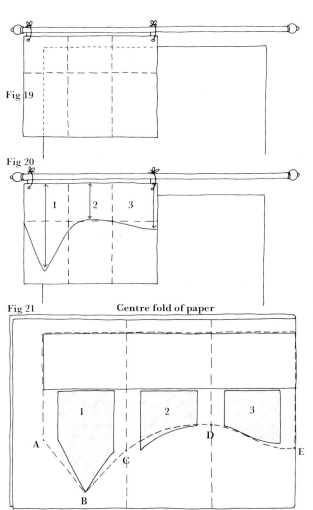

Fig 19

Fig 20

Fig 21   **Centre fold of paper**

Valance shape *minus* seam allowances

counts for the bottom 7.5 cm (3 in), draw a line this amount up from the bottom curved line and trim off. This template now forms the basis of the valance pattern, for pole to piping measurement.

5. Make a pattern of this half-shape by firstly folding a large sheet of pattern paper in half lengthwise, then marking it with a rectangle which measures 15 cm (6 in) deep (that is, to the bottom of the pole position), by the total width of the valance minus side seam allowances, and divided by half. (Decorator's lining paper is useful here because of its length.) Mark this rectangle into three equal vertical sections, continuing the lines downwards to the bottom of the paper.

6. Cut through the template at each vertical line to divide it into three parts, marking each part 1, 2 and 3. See fig **20**. Set

each of these marked sections squarely in the centre of each section on the paper pattern, lining the top of each section up with the under-pole position marked on the paper. Pin or weight template sections firmly so they will not move, then mark in points A, B, C, D and E as marked on fig **21**, and draw a new line on the pattern paper joining A to E, to form the curve required.

7. Remove the template sections. Add seam allowances of 1.5 cm ($\frac{5}{8}$ in) to the curved bottom and to the top of the pattern, and 2.5 cm (1 in) at the outside edge of the pattern. Mark the central fold position on your pattern, and cut it out.

8. To calculate the ruffle, measure the bottom of the curved valance seamline, minus seam allowances, and double for the finished width of the ruffle. Double this measurement again for the

length of fabric needed for the ruffle and add seam allowances of 1.5 cm ($\frac{5}{8}$ in). Calculating a depth of 7.5 cm (3 in), cut a strip of fabric, allowing for joins if necessary, of the above measurements. For the lining, multiply the length above by a depth of 10.5 cm ($4\frac{1}{4}$ in) and cut this out, again allowing for joins and seam allowances as above.

9. For the binding at the top of the valance cut a strip of contrast fabric the complete width of the valance plus its seam allowances at each end (see step 1), by 6 cm ($2\frac{1}{2}$ in) deep.

10. For piping, cut strips of contrast fabric to measure the same length as in step 9, but 3 cm ($1\frac{1}{4}$ in) wide only. These must be cut on the bias. Join bias strips and piping (*see page 141*).

11. Lastly, cut out the valance and lining as one, using the valance pattern and laying one piece of fabric over the other, and allowing for joins where necessary (don't forget 3 cm ($1\frac{1}{4}$ in) total seam allowances for each join). Remember to allow extra fabric for print matching, if necessary.

Making up

12. Firstly, make up the ruffle. Set lower long edge of fabric and contrast lining of ruffle right sides together, matching raw edges, and pin. Stitch along complete length of ruffle, from side to side, 1.5 cm ($\frac{5}{8}$ in) in from raw edges. Press seam allowances open, then fold contrast lining over to wrong side of fabric so that remaining raw edges of fabric and contrast lining come together, with their right sides outside. Press the fold formed, which will then also form the bound edge of the ruffle.

Fold in short ends of ruffle strip to inside at seam allowance points, 1.5 cm ($\frac{5}{8}$ in) in from the edge, and slipstitch (*see page 140*) to close. Run two lines of gathering stitches along complete length of remaining raw edges of ruffle, 1.5 cm ($\frac{5}{8}$ in) and 1 cm ($\frac{3}{8}$ in) in from edges respectively, breaking gathering stitches at equal intervals to make gathering-up easier.

Gather up ruffle to match measurement of lower curved edge of valance, and stitch along the central point of these two gathering lines from end to end, to set ruffle.

13. To make up piping, take a length of pre-shrunk piping cord equal to the joined, contrast bias strip and wrap the length of the bias around the cord, right side of bias outside and matching raw edges. Stitch along the length of the wrapped cord, close to its edge, using the piping or zipper foot on your machine. Trim seam allowances to 1.5 cm ($\frac{5}{8}$ in), see fig 22.

14. Taking up valance fabric and lining, press 2.5 cm (1 in) to the wrong side at each short end of the valance. Set aside valance lining, and laying valance fabric right side uppermost, set piping along its lower curved edge, right sides together and matching raw edges, curving the piping off at each side foldback point, 1.5 cm ($\frac{5}{8}$ in) up from the raw edge. See figs 23a) and b). Pin, baste, and stitch from end to end, stitching through piping at each folded-in edge of valance fabric as shown in fig 23b). Slash through piping seam allowance at pointed corners to ease.

15. Set right side of ruffle i.e. with its bound edge facing downwards against the valance, against right side of valance fabric and piping, with its raw edges matching those of the valance and piping, and its outside slipstitched edges matching the pressed in edges of the valance. Stitch from end to end, 1.5 cm ($\frac{5}{8}$ in) in from matching raw edges. See fig 24. Slash through seam allowances to stitching line at valance corner to ease. Trim seam allowances of ruffle to 1 cm ($\frac{3}{8}$ in) to eliminate any unnecessary bulk.

16. Set curved edge of valance lining against curved, piped and ruffled edge of valance fabric, right sides together and matching raw edges, so that piping and ruffle form a sandwich filling between lining and valance fabric. See fig 25. Pin into posi-

Fig 22

Fig 23a

Fabric (right side)

Fabric (right side)

Fig 23b

Fig 24

Fig 25

Fig 26

tion, matching folded-in sides of valance, baste, then stitch from side to side, through all thicknesses and 1.5 cm ($\frac{5}{8}$ in) in from raw edges. Trim lining fabric seam allowance to 1 cm ($\frac{3}{8}$ in) and clip curves.

17. Turn valance so that lining fabric folds to the back and the ruffle and piping are now visible at the curved lower edge of the valance. Press very carefully. See fig 26.

18. To prepare the valance for its final top ruffle binding, set top raw edges of both lining and valance fabric together and baste from one side to the other. Set one long edge of the binding against the valance fabric, right sides together and matching raw edges, turning in 2.5 cm (1 in) seam allowance at each end. Pin, then stitch from side to side. Press seam allowances open. Fold back 1.5 cm ($\frac{5}{8}$ in) at the remaining raw, long edge of the binding to the wrong side and press. Set this folded edge to the wrong side of the valance, so that the fold lies directly on top of the stitching line just made. Slipstitch along the length of the binding to attach to the lining. The ruffle binding will then be automatically formed at the top of the valance. Press flat carefully to set.

19. To form valance casing, set the valance right side uppermost, flat in front of you. Measuring down from the top of the binding to a depth of 7.5 cm (3 in), mark a line along the length of the valance parallel with the top, with pins, then mark a further parallel line 6 cm ($2\frac{1}{2}$ in) below this first line. Stitch along both pinned lines from end to end of the valance and through the lining, to form the casing for the pole. Slipstitch down each side of the valance, from the top to the first line of casing stitching, and from the second line of casing stitching to the bias point. Your valance is now complete.

SWAGS AND TAILS (JABOTS) FOR A BAY WINDOW

These look best against long windows in a room with a high ceiling. The ones shown on page 59 feature a central stripe in the print and the swags are cut on the lengthways grain so that this stripe will fall correctly. Both swags and tails (jabots) are lined. They are attached to a pelmet (cornice) board fixed to the wall. See fig 27.

You will need

Fabric for the swags, small and large tails (jabots), small and large tail (jabot) linings
Lining for the swags and small tails (jabots)
A weighted cord or chain
Pattern paper
Staple gun
Tailor's chalk

Cutting the pattern for the swag

1. Measure the width of the pelmet (cornice).

2. Decide how deep your swag should drape in the middle. As a guide it should be about one sixth of the curtain length.

3. Take a length of heavy cord or a chain and fix at one side of the pelmet (cornice) at the depth you would like the sides of the swag to finish. Let the cord drop in a gentle curve and fix at the other side of the pelmet (cornice). The length of this curve will equal the bottom edge of the swag.

4. Make a paper pattern for the swag as follows. Draw a rectangle measuring the width of the pelmet (cornice) by double the swag centre depth. Add 5 cm (2 in) to the top of the rectangle to allow for foldback over the pelmet (cornice) shelf. Mark the corners of this rectangle A, B, C and D. To achieve the curve at the bottom of the swag, subtract the C-D measurement from the chain length measurement, and add half this amount at each side of the square base, extending it to E and F. Join the outer points A and E, B and F (fig 28). Add a seam allowance of 1.5 cm ($\frac{5}{8}$ in) to the sides and base edge and cut out the pattern.

Making up

5. Cut out the number of swags you need plus the lining sections, making allowances for any print to be featured.

Fig 29

Fig 27

Fig 28

Fig 30

Fig 31

Fig 32

Fig 33

6 With right sides together and raw edges even, stitch each swag piece to each lining section, leaving the top edge of the swag open. Trim the corners and turn to the right side. Press, then matching the top raw edges, stitch across to hold.

7 Divide the swag into evenly spaced pleats at each side, drawing it up to the required depth and ending the pleating 5 cm (2 in) from the top (fig **29**). The pleats should face upwards. Baste each pleat in place. Pin each swag against the side of a table to check that the pleat falls evenly and smoothly. Sew each pleat in place by hand. Repeat for the other two swags, attach central swag to two side swags with loose hand stitches and set aside.

Small central tails (jabots)

8 Draw a rectangle 40.5 cm (16 in) across by 56 cm (22 in) deep, marking corners A, B, C and D. Draw a line from top to bottom, through the centre of the rectangle. Mark a point G, 15 cm (6 in) up from the bottom of this line, and join CGD in a curved line. On line AB, mark in points 12.5 cm (5 in) from each side, marking them E and F. Join EC and FD.

9 Add 1 cm ($\frac{3}{8}$ in) seam allowances all round ECGD and F and 5 cm (2 in) along EF, and cut out along this line. See fig **30**.

To make up

10 Cut out four fabric pieces from the pattern, matching prints if necessary. Mark two pieces and make up as linings.

11 With right sides together and matching raw edges, join a lining to a fab-ric piece and stitch around curved bottom line CD, 1 cm ($\frac{3}{8}$ in) in from raw edges. Clip seam allowance curves all along this line, turn and press. See fig **31**.

12 Baste diagonal sides of lining and fabric wrong sides together, raw edges matching, then folding in half lengthways, right sides together, stitch from top to bottom, 1 cm ($\frac{3}{8}$ in) in from raw edges. See figs **32** and **33**. Neaten seam allowance, turning up lower pointed end to conceal with a few handstitches.

Cutting the pattern for the large side tails (jabots)

13 Decide on the depth of the tail (jabot) at the side and inner edges. As a guide the side edge is equal to twice the depth of the finished swag and the inner edge is equal to the finished depth. However this depends on the effect you want to create and the proportions of the window or the curtains beneath.

14 To calculate tail width, add the width of the pelmet (cornice) return (the side of the pelmet) to the desired width of the folded part of the tail (jabot). This should cover the pleated edges of the swag by about 23 cm (9 in), but this varies according to taste and the width of the pelmet (cornice).

15 On a large sheet of pattern paper draw fig **34** to the scale indicated, marking in the pleat fold and placement lines and the width of the pelmet (cornice) return. Add 5 cm (2 in) to the top to allow for foldback over the pelmet (cornice) shelf and a seam allowance of 1.5 cm ($\frac{5}{8}$ in) on the other three edges. The pattern can be pleated following the instructions in step 20 below and pinned to the pelmet (cornice) board to check the effect. Adjustments can then be made to the pattern before cutting out.

Making up

16 Cut out the tail and lining pieces, reversing the pattern to cut the second piece (otherwise you will have two right-hand tails/jabots) matching points and transferring the markings on to the right side of the lining pieces. Separate the cut-out pieces into left- and right-hand tails (jabots).

17 With right sides together and raw edges even, stitch the tail (jabot) and lining fabric pieces together down the sides and across the diagonal edge, leaving the top edge open. Trim the corners, turn and press. Baste the raw edges of each tail together across the top.

18 Next pleat each tail (jabot). Beginning at the inner edge, fold the tail (jabot) at the first foldline and bring it over to the following placement line. Pin in place. Repeat until you have three pleats. See fig **35**.

19 Baste across the pleats at the top to hold. Set against the pelmet (cornice) to check the positioning of the

Fig 34

Fig 35

A

B

Fig 36

pleats. Adjust if necessary, then take down the tail (jabot) and stitch across the top of the pleated tail (jabot) 6 mm ($\frac{1}{4}$ in) from the raw edges. Stitch across again 6 mm ($\frac{1}{4}$ in) below the previous row of stitches.

Positioning swags and tails (jabots)

20 Staple each swag in place, overlapping the pelmet (cornice) shelf by 5 cm (2 in).

21 Place a small tail (jabot) over each swag join, lining up top raw edges. Staple in place. Catch the back of each tail (jabot) loosely to the folds of the swags so they fall naturally.

22 Position each large tail (jabot) at the edges of the pelmet (cornice), clipping into the foldback allowance at the pelmet (cornice) corners if the angle is sharp. (On page 58 the returns have been angled to fit the bay.) Staple in place. See fig **36**.

SWAG AND CONTRAST-LINED TAILS (JABOTS)

The swag and tails (jabots) on page 88 are made in plain fabric to emphasize their sculpted folds. They have been constructed in exactly the same way as in the previous instructions, but the tails (jabots) have one more pleat and both swag and tails (jabots) have been finished with tape along the top edges. The lower edge of the swag is also cut curved rather than straight. The swag fabric and lining can be cut along the length of the fabric to eliminate width joins if the swag is very wide.

The curtains shown with the swag and tails (jabots) are lined with the same contrasting glazed cotton as the tails and are interlined for warmth and drape.

You will need
Fabric for the swag and two tails (jabots)
Contrasting lining for the above
Enough 2.5 cm (1 in) wide tape to neaten the top edge of the swag and finished tails (jabots)
Staple gun
Heavy cord or a chain
Pattern paper
Tailor's chalk

Cutting the pattern for the swag

1 Repeat the instructions for swags and tails (jabots) for a bay window, steps 1 to 3.

2 Make a paper pattern for the swag as follows. Draw a rectangle measuring the width of the pelmet (cornice) by double the swag centre depth. Add 5 cm (2 in) to the top of the rectangle to allow for foldback over the pelmet (cornice) shelf. Mark the corners of this rectangle A, B, C and D. Fold the pattern in half lengthways and crease. Unfold.

3 Subtract C-D from the measurement of the curve and add half this amount at each end of the rectangle base, extending it to E and F. Subtract double the side depth from the centre depth measurement. Measure this distance from the corners E, F and mark G, H. Join these points with a curved line that touches C-D at the crease. Add a seam allowance of 1.5 cm ($\frac{5}{8}$ in) to the side and base edges. Cut out the pattern.

Making up

4 Make up the swag following the previous instructions, steps 5 to 7, clipping curved edge before turning to the right side.

5 Baste the fabric and lining together at the top of the swag. Stitch a length of tape across the top to strengthen, matching the outer edge of the tape with the raw edges of the swag. Sew the tape along all edges.

6 Use a staple gun along the taped edge to fix the swag, overlapping the pelmet (cornice) shelf by 5 cm (2 in).

Cutting the pattern for tails (jabots)

7 Follow the previous instructions, steps 13 to 15. The cutting plan shown in fig **34** should be amended as follows. To accommodate the extra pleat, the depth at the side should be two and a half times the depth of the finished swag at the centre and the inner edge should be three quarters the finished depth (*see page 103*). The top edge of the tail (jabot) should measure the pelmet (cornice) return plus four times the width of the pleated section of the tail (jabot).

Making up

8 Follow the previous instructions, steps 16 to 19, making four pleats rather than three. Stitch tape across the tail (jabot) top as before.

9 Staple each tail (jabot) in place, overlapping the top of the pelmet (cornice) by 5 cm (2 in) and clipping diagonally into the corner allowance.

PELMETS (CORNICES)

A fabric pelmet (cornice) gives a decorative finish to the tops of curtains; it can change the proportions of a window, and hide an unattractive curtain track. As a general rule between one sixth and one eighth of the curtain drop is considered a suitable depth for a pelmet (cornice), but obviously this varies according to taste and individual windows.

The pelmets (cornices) in this section consist of three layers: a top fabric and lining which are each bonded to a middle layer of double-sided adhesive stiffener and slip-stitched together around the edges. They are then fixed to a shelf, the pelmet (cornice) board, over the window, using Velcro.

If widths of fabric have to be joined, place the full width of fabric in the middle of the pelmet (cornice) and narrow panels at either side. Match patterns across seams (page 139, Ladderstitch).

THE PELMET (CORNICE) BOARD

This is a length of plywood 1.5 to 2 cm ($\frac{5}{8}$ to $\frac{3}{4}$ in) thick by 10 cm (4 in) wide. Position it just above the curtain track or window frame using small metal brackets set about 30 cm (12 in) apart and placing a bracket at each end of the board (fig 1). The board should extend at least 5 cm (2 in) either side of the curtain track. It should be rounded at the outer corners to soften the line. Before fixing the board to the wall brackets, glue the hooked half of a strip of Velcro to the sides of the board (fig 2).

Pelmet width

30 cm

Curtain track

Fig 1

Return

10 cm

Board front

Fig 2

Velcro

Return

PELMET (CORNICE) WITH PIPING AND DOUBLE RUFFLE

The stiffened part of the pelmet (cornice) and ruffle shown on page 80 are of equal 10 cm (4 in) depth. This looks best over short curtains.

Fig 3

Fig 4

Centre

Centre

Wrong side

Adhesive stiffener

Backing paper

You will need
Fabric
Curtain lining sateen
Contrast fabric for piping bias strips (*see page 141*)
Pre-shrunk piping cord
Double-sided adhesive stiffener for pelmet (cornice)
Velcro

Measuring and cutting out

1 Read through the notes at the beginning of the section. Decide on the overall depth of the pelmet (cornice) and ruffle and how deep each should be. To find the finished width of the pelmet (cornice), measure the front edge of the board (fig 2) and add 20 cm (8 in) for the returns (the board ends).

2 For the pelmet (cornice), cut or make up one piece of fabric and one piece of lining to the finished width plus 3 cm ($1\frac{1}{4}$ in) by the depth plus 3 cm ($1\frac{1}{4}$ in). Cut one piece of stiffening to the finished width and depth only with no allowances for turnings.

3 Cut out enough ruffle strips, measuring twice the desired depth plus 3 cm ($1\frac{1}{4}$ in), to equal twice the width of the pelmet (cornice) when joined. Allow 1.5 cm ($\frac{5}{8}$ in) on each strip end for joins.

4 Cut out enough bias strips from the contrast fabric to cover the required amount of piping cord when joined.

Making up

5 Cover the piping cord (*see page 141*) with the contrast bias strip. With raw edges even pin the piping to the right side of the top fabric

Fig 5   Fold over

Adhesive stiffener

piece along the lower long side edge. Pull back the covering at both ends, and snip away the cord for 1.5 cm ($\frac{5}{8}$ in). This avoids bulky turnings. Baste the piping in place.

6 Make up the double ruffle (*see page 142*), breaking the gathering stitches at intervals if necessary and leaving a seam allowance of 1.5 cm ($\frac{5}{8}$ in) at the ends. Turn in the ends and slipstitch (*see page 140*) to close. With raw edges even, apply ruffle (*see page 142*) to the right side of the lower edge of the pelmet over the piping, positioning the ends of the ruffle 1.5 cm ($\frac{5}{8}$ in) in from the pelmet (cornice) ends and adjusting the gathers evenly (fig 3). Stitch in place through all thicknesses, using the zipper foot on the machine.

7 Lay the stiffening flat. At the centre carefully cut the backing paper across the width. Peel back the paper a little way on either side and, matching centres, place the wrong side of the fabric over the exposed area of adhesive, the fabric turning allowances overlapping at either side by 1.5 cm ($\frac{5}{8}$ in) (fig 4). Continue peeling back the paper while smoothing the fabric on to the adhesive, working from the

centre outwards so the fabric does not wrinkle. Set aside.

8 Fold under the edges of the lining to the wrong side by 1.5 cm ($\frac{5}{8}$ in). Press. Baste across the corners to hold. Stitch the soft half of the Velcro strip along the top of the lining so that the pelmet (cornice) will just cover the edge of the board when it is fixed in place.

9 Removing the backing paper as you work, fold the top fabric edges to the wrong side of the pelmet (cornice), smoothing them down on to the adhesive surface (fig 5) and mitring corners (see page 141). This will bring the piping and ruffle down to the lower edge.

10 Working from the centre outwards, stick the wrong side of the lining to the wrong side of the pelmet (cornice), matching edges on all sides. Slipstitch (see page 140) the lining and fabric together around the edges.

11 Matching Velcro strips, press the pelmet (cornice) in place to hang.

PIPED PELMET (CORNICE) WITH LINED CONTRAST-EDGED RUFFLE

This is a variation of the ruffled pelmet (cornice) above, but the pelmet (cornice) has shrunk to a 5 cm (2 in) band. It is piped along both long edges and the ruffle is lined with contrasting fabric that extends round the edges to form a binding. It can be gathered by hand or you can apply standard heading tape. The pelmet (cornice) can be lined with ordinary curtain sateen.

You will need
Fabric
Contrast lining for ruffle and pelmet (cornice)
Contrast fabric for piping bias strips (see page 141)
Pre-shrunk piping cord
2.5 cm (1 in) wide standard heading tape (optional)
Velcro
Double-sided adhesive stiffener for pelmet (cornice)

Measuring and cutting out
1 Read through the general notes on pelmets (cornices) at the beginning of

the section. For the pelmet (cornice) cut one piece of fabric and one piece of lining that measures 8 cm ($3\frac{1}{4}$ in) wide by the length of the board front plus returns (fig 2) plus 3 cm ($1\frac{1}{4}$ in). Cut a piece of stiffener that measures 5 cm (2 in) wide by the length of the board front plus returns (the finished dimensions of the pelmet/cornice).

2 For the ruffle cut or make up a strip of top fabric that measures the desired depth plus 1.5 cm ($\frac{5}{8}$ in) by twice the finished width of the pelmet (cornice). Match any pattern across seams (see page 139) as necessary. Cut or make up one strip of contrast lining that measures the desired ruffle depth plus 3.5 cm ($1\frac{3}{8}$ in) by twice the finished width of pelmet (cornice).

3 Cut out enough bias strips from the contrast fabric to cover the required amount of piping cord.

Making up
4 Follow step 5 of the previous instructions to apply the piping. It is attached to both long edges of the pelmet (cornice) front.

5 With raw edges even and right sides together, stitch the contrast lining and ruffle top fabric together along the long lower edge, taking a 1 cm ($\frac{3}{8}$ in) seam allowance. Press the seam open. Turn to the right side. Pin the top raw edges together and press the ruffle; the lining will form a 1 cm ($\frac{3}{8}$ in) margin on the right side lower edge.

Fig 6

Fig 7

6 Turn in the ends of the ruffle to the wrong side by 1.5 cm ($\frac{5}{8}$ in) and slipstitch (see page 140) to close (fig 6).

7 If you wish to gather the ruffle with standard heading tape, stitch it (see page 96) to the lined side of the ruffle with the top of the row of slots lying 2 cm ($\frac{3}{4}$ in) down from the raw edges

(fig 7). Otherwise gather the ruffle in the usual way (see page 142).

8 Gather the ruffle and attach to the pelmet (cornice) as in step 6 of the previous instructions, taking a 1.5 cm ($\frac{5}{8}$ in) seam allowance. Tie the cord ends in a knot if using tape. Complete as for steps 7 to 11 of the previous instructions.

TIEBACKS

MEASURING UP

To calculate where to place the tieback and how long it should be, loop a fabric tape measure around the curtain roughly two-thirds down and arrange the curtain into the curve or folds you want. The length on the tape measure gives you the finished tieback length. Mark the walls at the correct position for the tieback hook. The depth of the tieback varies. As a rough guide the tiebacks on sill-length curtains should be no more than 10 cm (4 in) deep, but sweeping floor-length curtains can take a proportionally greater depth.

Fig 1a

Fig 1b

Fig 2

RUFFLED CASING FOR METAL ARM

You will need
Fabric
Matching thread

Measuring and cutting out
1 For each casing cut one piece of fabric that measures twice the length of the arm plus 2 cm ($\frac{3}{4}$ in) for seams by double the arm width plus 4.5 cm ($1\frac{3}{4}$ in) for seams and ease.

Making up
2 With wrong sides out, fold each strip in half lengthways so the long raw edges match. Pin and stitch the long raw edges of each casing strip together to make a tube, taking a 1 cm ($\frac{3}{8}$ in) seam allowance. Press the seam open. With the folded edge uppermost, stitch across the right-hand end of one of the casings, taking the same seam allowance as before (fig 1a). Repeat the process on the other casing, with the seamed edge uppermost. (This means the seamed edge will be at the bottom on both right- and left-hand arms). Trim the corners.

3 Turn in 1 cm ($\frac{3}{8}$ in) twice at the open end of each casing. Stitch all the way round the opening to secure the turning (fig 1b). Turn to the right side and press.

4 Beginning to one side of the opening, stitch along one long edge, around the closed end and along the other long edge, working 6 mm ($\frac{1}{4}$ in) in from the edges to form the ruffling.

5 Push the casing over the metal arm, letting it gather up to fit (fig **2**). Tighten the open end with a few hand stitches so that the casing doesn't slip off the arm during use.

SMOCKED TIEBACK

The smocking has been achieved by using ready-made heading tape. Tieback depth will be determined by the depth of the heading tape you buy. You will need twice the tieback length in fabric to gather the tape (see Headings, *page 94*).

You will need
Fabric
Smocked heading tape
Two small curtain rings to hook each tieback to the wall

Measuring and cutting out
1 Read through the measuring up notes at the beginning of the Tiebacks section. Decide on the length and width of your tieback. For each tieback cut one piece of fabric to twice the desired length plus 3 cm $(1\frac{1}{4}$ in) by the width of the heading tape plus 10 cm (4 in).

2 Cut one piece of heading tape to the ungathered length of the tieback plus an allowance for turnings (*see page 96*).

Making up
3 Fold over 1.5 cm $(\frac{5}{8}$ in) to the wrong side at the ends of the tieback piece and press. Fold over 3.5 cm $(1\frac{3}{8}$ in) to the wrong side along the long edges and press.

4 Attach the tape to the wrong side of the fabric following the manufacturer's instructions. Position it so that the turned-under ends line up with the ends of the tieback and there is a 1.5 cm $(\frac{5}{8}$ in) margin of fabric along the sides.

5 Draw up the loose cords at the unknotted end of the tape until the tieback is the right length. Knot the cords but do not cut off.

6 Attach a ring centrally to each end of the tieback just to the wrong side.

BOW TIEBACK WITH CONTRAST LINING AND EDGING

This tieback is a simple length of fabric tied in a bow around the curtain. The contrast lining is cut larger than the top fabric so that it forms an edging.

You will need
Fabric
Contrast lining
A small ring to hook each tieback to the wall
Length of string or cord at least 2 metres/yards long

Measuring and cutting out
1 Read through the measuring up notes at the beginning of the Tiebacks section. Instead of a tape measure use a length of string or cord tied in a bow round the curtain to ascertain how long your bow length should be. Decide how wide it should be inclusive of the contrast edging.

2 For each tieback cut or make up one strip of top fabric measuring the finished length plus 2 cm $(\frac{3}{4}$ in) by the finished width. Cut or make up the same number of contrast lining strips, each measuring the tieback length plus 2 cm $(\frac{3}{4}$ in) by the width plus 4 cm $(1\frac{1}{2}$ in).

3 With the right side of the top fabric strip facing, mark a point on the long side edge 3 cm $(1\frac{1}{4}$ in) from the bottom right-hand corner. Repeat at the other end, measuring from the bottom left-hand corner. Cut from the top corner to these points and you will have equally angled ends (fig **3**). Repeat the process to match on the lining strip.

Making up
4 With right sides together, match the raw edges of one long side of the fabric and lining strip. Baste along this side, then stitch, taking a 1 cm $(\frac{3}{8}$ in) seam allowance. Stitch the strips together along the other long side. The lining strip will curl up slightly.

5 Turn the bow length the right side out and press so that the lining forms a 1 cm $(\frac{3}{8}$ in) margin of fabric down either side (fig **4a**) of the tieback.

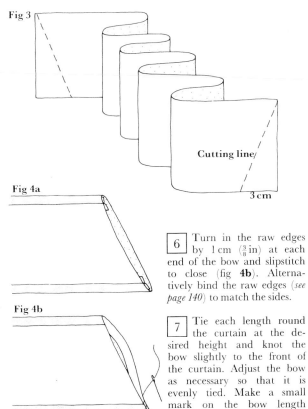

Fig 3

Cutting line

3 cm

Fig 4a

Fig 4b

6 Turn in the raw edges by 1 cm $(\frac{3}{8}$ in) at each end of the bow and slipstitch to close (fig **4b**). Alternatively bind the raw edges (*see page 140*) to match the sides.

7 Tie each length round the curtain at the desired height and knot the bow slightly to the front of the curtain. Adjust the bow as necessary so that it is evenly tied. Make a small mark on the bow length where it should be attached

to the hook at the side of the curtain. Undo the bow and attach a curtain ring to the right side of the bow length at the marked position. Place the ring over the hook and re-tie the bow round the curtain.

LINED TIEBACK WITH CORD AND CONTRAST EDGING

This tieback is threaded with decorative twisted cord which is drawn up around the curtain. The lining is cut larger than the fabric and forms a contrast edging all round. Specific measurements have been given for this tieback, but you may wish to adapt these to suit your curtains.

You will need
Fabric
Contrast lining
Length of silky twisted cord about 2 metres/yards long for each tieback
Two small curtain rings to hook each tieback to the wall

Measuring and cutting out
1 For each tieback cut one fabric strip 47 cm $(18\frac{1}{2}$ in) long by 15 cm (6 in) wide and one contrast lining strip 53 cm (21 in) by 21 cm $(8\frac{1}{2}$ in) wide.

Making up
2 With raw edges even, right sides together and the lining overlapping each end of the fabric by 3 cm $(1\frac{1}{4}$ in), stitch the fabric and lining together along each long edge, taking a 1.5 cm $(\frac{5}{8}$ in) seam allowance. The lining will curl up slightly.

3 Turn the tube right side out and press so that a 1.5 cm $(\frac{5}{8}$ in) contrast edging is formed on the front side (fig 5). Trim the seam allowances to 6 mm $(\frac{1}{4}$ in) if necessary.

4 At each end of the tube turn under the excess lining twice, folding over the fabric to form the edging (fig **6**). Slipstitch (*see page 140*) in place.

5 Mark the centre of the tieback along its length. The first buttonhole position should be marked across this line 2.5 cm (1 in) from one end, the second 6 cm $(2\frac{1}{2}$ in) from the first buttonhole and

Fig 5

Fig 6

Fig 7

47 cm

6 cm

2.5 cm 3.5 cm

the third 11.5 cm ($4\frac{1}{2}$ in) from the second buttonhole (fig **7**). Repeat from the other end.

6 Make 1.5 cm ($\frac{5}{8}$ in) buttonholes at each marked point either by machine or hand (*see page 139*) through both the fabric and contrast lining.

7 Attach the ring to the centre of each tieback as indicated. Thread the cord through the buttonholes, beginning on the right side of the tieback. Place round the curtain. Draw up and adjust to fit.

STIFFENED TIEBACK WITH CONTRAST EDGING AND ROSETTE

The lining of this tieback is wider than the top fabric and forms a contrast edging along the sides.

You will need
Fabric
Contrast lining
Pelmet (cornice) buckram or similar stiffening
Two small curtain rings to hook each tieback to the wall
Cotton wool (batting) for stuffing the rosette button

Measuring and cutting out the tieback

1 Read through the measuring up notes at the beginning of the Tiebacks section. Decide on the finished length and width of your tieback inclusive of edging.

2 For each tieback cut one piece of top fabric measuring the finished length plus 2 cm ($\frac{3}{4}$ in) by the finished width. Cut one piece of contrast lining measuring the tieback length plus 2 cm ($\frac{3}{4}$ in) by the width plus 4 cm ($1\frac{1}{2}$ in). Finally cut one piece of buckram to the finished length and width measurement minus 1 cm ($\frac{3}{8}$ in) all round.

Making up

3 Lay the buckram centrally over the wrong side of the top fabric piece, the seam allowance forming a 1 cm ($\frac{3}{8}$ in) margin around the buckram. Baste together. Herringbone stitch (*see page 139*) the edges of the buckram to catch it to the fabric. The horizontal stitches should be placed just within the fabric seam allowance (fig **8**) so they won't show on the right side when the fabric is folded over.

4 With right sides together and raw edges even, stitch the tieback front to the lining along the long edges, taking a 1 cm ($\frac{3}{8}$ in) seam allowance and leaving one end open. Be careful to sew close to but not over the edge of the buckram.

5 Turn to the right side and press, smoothing the seam allowances towards the outer edge of the tieback. The lining will form a 1 cm ($\frac{3}{8}$ in) margin along each side (fig **9**).

6 At the open ends of the tieback turn 1 cm ($\frac{3}{8}$ in) to the inside and slipstitch (*see page 140*) the folded edges together to close.

7 Hand stitch a curtain ring to the centre of each tieback end just on the wrong side.

Cutting out the rosette

8 First make up the pattern. Draw a rectangle 100 cm ($39\frac{1}{2}$ in) long by 11.5 cm ($4\frac{1}{2}$ in) wide. At one end mark a point halfway down its width. Mark another point on the long edge about 30 cm (12 in) from the top corner of the opposite end. Beginning at the bottom right hand corner, join the marks, curving the line up to the halfway point (fig **10**). Cut out the pattern.

9 Using the pattern cut out the rosette strip from the main fabric. Cut a circle of contrast fabric 6 cm ($2\frac{1}{2}$ in) in diameter.

10 Turn in the strip curved side and end twice to the wrong side by 6 mm ($\frac{1}{4}$ in) each time, and stitch (fig **11**). Press.

11 Make two rows of gathering stitches 1 cm ($\frac{3}{8}$ in) and 1.5 cm ($\frac{5}{8}$ in) from the remaining raw edge. Gather the strip until it looks suitably ruffled. Secure the threads at each end by winding them in a figure of eight round a pin.

12 Beginning at the narrow end of the strip, start winding it round and round and carefully build up the rosette (fig **12**), adjusting the gathers as necessary and pinning firmly as you work. Position the neatened end so that it won't show. Secure the rosette with a few hand stitches through its centre.

13 To make the contrasting centre, run a line of gathering stitches around the outer edge of the circle and gather up, stuffing a small wad of cotton wool (batting) into the centre as you do so, to form a soft ball (fig **13**). Secure the gathering threads by knotting them around the neck of the ball. Stitch to the centre of the rosette, tucking any raw edges out of sight.

14 Attach the completed rosette to the outside of the tieback, positioning it roughly 5 cm (2 in) from the outer end.

Fig 8

Fig 9

30 cm

Cutting line

Fig 10

Fig 11

Fig 12

Fig 13

SHAPED INTERLINED TIEBACK WITH OPTIONAL PIPING AND ROSETTE

Besides being stiffened and lined, this curved tieback has an interlining. The lining is attached by hand. The tieback is deepest at the middle and tapers gradually to the ends.

You will need
Fabric
Curtain lining sateen
Domette or bump (flannel or flannelette) for the interlining
Pelmet (cornice) buckram or similar stiffening
Pre-shrunk piping cord (if making piping)
Two small curtain rings for hooking each tieback to the wall
Pattern or graph paper
Contrast fabric and 2 cm ($\frac{3}{4}$ in) self-cover button for the optional rosette

Measuring and cutting out

1 Read the measuring up notes at the beginning of the Tiebacks section. Decide on the length and depth of your tieback. Next take a rectangle of pattern/graph paper the proposed length of the tieback by a width of at least 30 cm (12 in), and fold in half. Mark the tieback depth, A-B, on the foldline. Using the folded edge as the centre of the tieback draw the curved shape freehand (fig **14**). Cut out the pattern and hold it against the curtain to see if the proportions are right. Adjust or cut another pattern if necessary.

Half tieback length

Fig 14

Fig 15

2 For each tieback cut one piece of interlining and one piece of buckram using the pattern. Next, adding a 1.5 cm ($\frac{5}{8}$ in) seam allowance all round, cut out one piece of fabric and one of lining.

3 If you are attaching piping, cut out enough bias strips (*see page 140*) to cover the required length of piping cord when joined.

Making up

4 Lay the interlining centrally over the wrong side of the fabric so the fabric seam allowance forms an even margin around the edge. Lay the buckram over the interlining and pin in place. Herringbone stitch (*see page 139*) the buckram and interlining to the fabric as described in step 3 of the previous tieback instructions, making sure that the stitches don't go through to the front when you stitch through the buckram and interlining.

5 *For piping only.* Make up enough covered piping (*see page 141*) to go all the way round the edges of the tieback. With raw edges matching and with the piping against the right side of the top fabric (fig **15**), stitch the piping to the fabric, using the zipper foot on the machine and joining the piping (*see page 141*) at the end of a tieback.

6 Fold the fabric seam allowance (and that of the piping if applicable) over the buckram and pin. Cut notches in the inward curves to take out excess fabric. Press. Set aside.

7 Turn the lining edges to the wrong side by 1.5 cm ($\frac{5}{8}$ in) and press, cutting notches to take out the excess fabric as before. Set the lining over the wrong side of the tieback and slipstitch (*see page 140*) in place all round the edge (fig **16**).

8 Press the completed tieback and attach a ring centrally at either end just on the lining side.

Optional rosette

9 Cut one strip of contrast fabric 69 cm (27 in) long by 10 cm (4 in) wide, and one strip of self fabric 56 cm (22 in) long by 7.5 cm

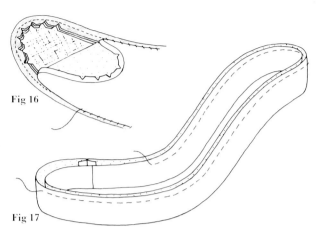

Fig 16

Fig 17

(3 in) wide. Cover the self-cover button with the contrast fabric.

10 Fold the contrast strip in half widthways and stitch the raw ends together to make a circle, taking a 1 cm ($\frac{3}{8}$ in) seam allowance.

11 Fold the circle in half lengthways, wrong sides together and matching raw edges. Stitch the raw edges together, taking a 6 mm ($\frac{1}{4}$ in) seam allowance (fig **17**). Press.

12 Make large gathering stitches around the circle 6 mm ($\frac{1}{4}$ in) from the raw edges. Draw up to a tight centre, gathers forming even folds. Secure gathering stitches.

13 Repeat steps 10 to 12 for the self fabric, set this gathered circle on top of the larger circle, matching centres. Stitch together at the centre.

14 Attach the button to the centre of the rosette. Stitch the rosette to the tieback.

BLINDS

ROMAN BLIND

Roman blinds give a tailored uncluttered finish to a window, lying flat when lowered but pulling up to form neat horizontal pleats. Made from closely woven fabric and lined, they are fixed at the top of the window to a length of wooden battening. Fine cords run up through lengths of ringed tape stitched to the back of the blind and are threaded through screw eyes driven in on the underside of the batten, which channel the cords to one side of the blind. The excess cords are then wound round a cleat fixed at the side of the window recess when the blind is raised. A wooden lath is slotted through the blind at the base to weight the edge (fig **1**).

The rings on the tapes at the back of the blind are lined up horizontally, and these form the pleats when the cords are pulled up. A distance of 10 cm (4 in) between the rows of rings would give 5 cm (2 in) deep pleats, which would be suitable for small windows. On larger windows allow between 15 and 20 cm (6 to 8 in) between rows for 7.5 cm (3 in) to 10 cm (4 in) pleats. The flap at the bottom of the blind should be half the distance between the rows of rings.

When hanging against a recessed window the blind will fit against the recess ceiling. When hanging outside a recess or against a non-recessed window, the batten will have to be positioned above the recess/window frame at the desired height. You can paint the batten or cover it with fabric to match the blind.

Fig 1

Back view of roman blind

Lath set in casing

Fig 2a

Fig 2b

Fig 2c

You will need
Fabric
Lining
Length of 50 mm by 25 mm
  (2 in by 1 in) wooden battening
  the finished width of the blind
Narrow pocketed tape
Split rings
Nylon cord
Lath, 25 mm by 5 mm (1 in by
  ¼ in)
Metal angle brackets plus
  screws (for the battening)
Cleat

Measuring and cutting out

1 Measure for the *finished* width and length of the blind. *Blind set in a recess:* Measure the width and height

of the recess (fig **2a**). *Blind set outside a recess:* Measure the width and height of the recess and extend the blind by at least 5 cm (2 in) either side. To the height measurement add whatever overlap you require at the top and bottom of the window (fig **2b**). *Blind set against a non-recessed window:* Measure the width and height from frame outer edge to outer edge. To the height add whatever overlap you require at the top of the window (fig **2c**).

2 *Top fabric.* To calculate the amount of fabric needed for each blind add 6 cm (2½ in) to the finished length measurement for the top turning and seam allowance, and add 6 cm (2½ in) to the width. *Lining.* Add 6 cm (2½ in) to the finished length measurement only; the width of the lining is the same as the finished width of the blind.

3 Cut out one piece of top fabric and one piece of lining to these dimensions for each blind.

Making up

4 Mark the centres of both fabric pieces at the top and bottom with tailor's chalk on the wrong side. Set the lining against the fabric with right sides together and raw edges even and pin, baste and stitch down the sides. Turn the right side out.

5 Pin the fabric pieces together at the marked centres at the top and bottom of the blind and, lined side upwards, press the side seams. The top fabric will form a 1.5 cm (⅝ in) margin down the sides of the blind.

6 Turn inside out again and stitch across the bottom of the blind, taking a 1.5 cm (⅝ in) seam allowance. Turn to the right side and press.

7 Lay the blind out flat with the lined side uppermost and mark the position of the lath casing by measuring up from the blind base to a distance equal to the depth of the bottom flap (see introduction above). Draw a straight line across the blind at this point and then draw a second line,

Fig 3

Lath casing

Fig 4

parallel to the first, 4 cm (1½ in) above. Stitch along these marked lines to form the lath casing. You can unpick the stitching at one seamline at a later stage to insert the lath. (fig **3**).

8 Mark vertical lines for the tapes on the wrong side of the blind with chalk or pins. These should be placed at equal distances apart about every 30 cm (12 in) with the first and last rows positioned over the side seamlines by about 12 mm (½ in) in. They should run from the lath casing to the top of the blind.

9 Cut one length of tape to the correct length, allowing for 1 cm (⅜ in) turn-under at one end. Measure off the rest against it, making sure the pockets are aligned. Position the tapes over the marked lines, turning under the raw ends at the lath casing (fig **4**). Baste down the tape centres to hold and then stitch down each side.

10 Insert split rings in each tape at equal distances apart up the blind, beginning just above the lath casing and checking that they line up horizontally (fig **1**).

11 Unstitch one of the seamlines at the side of the casing. Cut the lath to the finished curtain width minus 1 cm (⅜ in). Insert the lath and slipstitch (*see page 140*) the seam to close.

12 Measure up the finished length of the blind

from the base and mark across the top. Zigzag the fabric and lining together along the top edges to neaten. Lining up the marked line with the top edge of the battening, wrap the blind over the top of the battening and tack or staple in place. Make sure you attach the blind so it hangs straight.

13 Position a screw eye in the underside of the battening to correspond with the rows of tape. Screw brackets to the underside of the board where they are going to butt up against the window/wall.

14 Cut the cord into as many lengths as there are rows of tape. Each length should measure twice the length of the finished blind plus one width.

15 Tie a cord to each bottom ring and thread it up through the rings on the tape. Pass each cord through a screw eye and then towards the side from which you wish to operate the blind, taking the cord through each screw eye it passes (fig 1). Continue until all the cords are hanging together at the side of the blind, threaded through one screw eye. Knot together about 2.5 cm (1 in) outside screw eye. Do not cut cords.

16 Fix the battening in position. Then attach a cleat to the side of the recess, wall or window edge. Knot the cords level with the window base. Pull up the blind and wind the ends around the cleat to anchor.

Fig 5

AUSTRIAN BLINDS

These blinds work on the same principle as the Roman blind. However, they have a gathered or pencil pleated heading and need a fullness of two to two and a quarter times the batten length. They look like curtains when let down and form scallop shapes along the base edge when raised. If made slightly longer than the window and pulled up fractionally, the base edge will form scallops even when the blind completely covers the window. Austrian blinds can be lined, but beware of them looking unwieldy when drawn up. Fewer scallops drape better if making a heavier blind.

To produce the bound ruffled edge on page 8, place a standard gathered heading tape the desired depth down from the blind top, attach the tape without folding the top over, and bind the top edge. The single ruffle has also been bound.

UNLINED AUSTRIAN BLIND WITH DOUBLE RUFFLE

You will need

Fabric
Pencil pleat heading tape
Curtain hooks
Narrow pocketed tape (see Roman blind)
Thin nylon cord
Split rings
Large screw eyes for underneath of batten
Smaller screw eyes to take curtain hooks, set in the front edge of batten
Length of 50 mm by 25 mm (2 in by 1 in) battening
Cleat

Measuring and cutting out

1 See Roman blind, step 1, for instructions on measuring the window. To the length add 3.5 cm ($1\frac{3}{8}$ in) for the base hem and heading allowance. Calculate the width of the blind as explained on page 95 of Curtains, allowing 3 cm ($1\frac{1}{4}$ in) on each side for hems. Join widths if necessary to make up a fullness of two to two and a quarter times the batten length (adding too much fullness will make the swags droopy) and match any pattern across seams (*see page 139*). Join widths with French seams if they are not to be covered with lengths of tape (*see page 140*).

2 Cut strips of fabric that measure twice the depth of the ruffle (7.5 cm/3 in) plus 3 cm ($1\frac{1}{4}$ in) seam allowance by a length that equals the finished width of the blind when the strips are joined up. Allow 1.5 cm ($\frac{5}{8}$ in) for seams on each strip end.

3 Make up the ruffle complete with gathering stitches, breaking the gathering at intervals along the ruffle edge if necessary (*see page 142*). Do not pull up the gathering yet. Turn in the raw ends at each side by 1.5 cm ($\frac{5}{8}$ in) and slipstitch (*see page 140*) to close. Press.

4 At the base edge of the blind place pins 3 cm ($1\frac{1}{4}$ in) from each side edge. Divide up the base edge between these pins into the same number of sections as the ruffle edge. With raw edges even position the ruffle against the right side of the blind between the outer pins, so that the side hem allowances are left free. Matching the pins along the ruffle and blind edges, draw up the ruffle to fit. Stitch the ruffle

Fig 6

to the blind, taking a 1.5 cm ($\frac{5}{8}$ in) seam allowance. Zigzag stitch or oversew (*see page 140*) the two allowances together to neaten the edges and press upwards.

5 Press the side seams to the wrong side and baste in place.

6 Decide how many scallops you would like across the finished blind. Divide the batten length into equally sized scallops and add one to give the number of vertical rows of tape needed. For example, four scallops will need five rows of tape. The tapes are positioned at equal distances across the ungathered blind; the distance between them will be two to two and a quarter times the finished scallop width, depending on the fullness you allowed. They should run from the ruffle seamline to within 6 cm ($2\frac{1}{2}$ in) of the blind top, allowing for 1 cm ($\frac{3}{8}$ in) turn-under at the ruffle end.

7 Position the two outer rows of tape over the raw edges of the side hems (fig 5) and place the remaining lengths at equal distances in between (see step 9, Roman blind).

8 Press 2 cm ($\frac{3}{4}$ in) to the wrong side at the top of the blind. Apply heading tape (*see page 110*, step 9) 3 mm ($\frac{1}{8}$ in) down from the top edge (fig 6).

9 Insert split rings in each tape about 20 cm (8 in) apart, beginning 3 cm ($1\frac{1}{4}$ in) from the ruffle seam and ending about 15 cm (6 in) from the blind top. Make sure the levels of the rings match horizontally. Cut and attach the cords as for the Roman blind, step 15.

10 Draw up the heading tape to fit the batten. Insert a curtain hook at each end of the blind and then at 6 cm ($2\frac{1}{2}$ in) intervals in between.

11 Attach the large screw eyes to the underside of the batten to correspond with the rows of tape. Attach screw eyes along the front of the batten to correspond with the curtain hooks (fig 7).

Fig 7

Fig 8

3 Make up the ruffle complete with gathering stitches, breaking the gathering into convenient sections (*see page 142*) if necessary. Pulling back the lining, divide the top fabric bottom edge into the same number of sections on the right side. With raw edges even position the ruffle against the right side of the fabric, matching pin markers, and gather up to fit. Baste in place. With raw edges

Fig 3

Spring mechanism

Fig 4

Fig 5

12 Fix the batten in position and attach the blind by slotting a curtain hook through each of the screw eyes on the front. Thread the cords through the large screw eyes underneath as for the Roman blind, step 15.

13 Fix the cleat in position and pull the cords to raise the blind. Knot at sill level and wind the excess around the cleat.

LINED AUSTRIAN BLIND WITH RUFFLE

Besides the items needed for the unlined Austrian blind above, you will also require lining cut to the dimensions given in step 1 below.

Measuring and cutting out
1 Measure for the top fabric as described in step 1 above. Cut the fabric to the same length but allow 4.5 cm ($1\frac{3}{4}$ in) on each side for seams. Cut a piece of lining that measures the same length as this top piece, but 3 cm ($1\frac{1}{4}$ in) narrower than the blind's finished width.

Making up
2 Mark the centres of the lining as for the Roman blind, step 4. Stitch together down the sides, taking a 1.5 cm ($\frac{5}{8}$ in) seam allowance. Turn to the right side and pin the centres together. With the lined side uppermost, press the blind so that a 3 cm ($1\frac{1}{4}$ in) margin of top fabric is formed down the sides. Turn back to the wrong side again.

even stitch the lining to the top fabric across the bottom of the blind through all thicknesses, taking a 1.5 cm ($\frac{5}{8}$ in) seam allowance (fig **8**).

4 Complete the blind, following steps 6 to 13 of the unlined Austrian blind instructions, positioning the outer lengths of tape just over the side seams.

ROLLER BLIND

The fabric on the roller blinds shown in this book rolls over the front of the roller rather than from the back, because

Fig 1

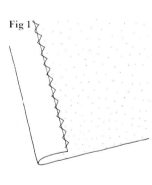

Fig 2

it is printed. If it rolled from the back you would see the unprinted side showing on the roller. The angled attic window blind on page 92 can be set at various heights because the lath at the bottom of the blind extends beyond the edges to slot into grooves cut into the window frame.

You will need
A roller blind kit (see step 1).
These usually include a wooden roller with a spring fitted at one end, two brackets a wooden lath for the bottom of the blind, tacks, cord and acorn, and a cord holder.
Mediumweight fabric
Fabric stiffener (optional)
Set or L-square (optional)

Preparing the roller and fabric
1 Decide whether you are going to hang your blind inside or outside the window recess—blinds are usually hung inside the recess. Measure the width of the recess. If you are hanging the blind outside the recess allow extra for overlap (*see page 110*).

Roller blind kits come in standard widths. Unless the blind width you need is a standard size, buy the next size up and cut the roller and lath to fit.

2 Usually two different brackets are supplied with each kit. One takes the spring end of the blind, which should go on the right if you are using a printed non-reversible fabric. Fix the brackets in place in the recess, allowing for the pin end and spring mechanism at each end of the roller. Allow a gap of 3 cm ($1\frac{1}{4}$ in) at the top to take the full roller. Measure the distance between the brackets and saw the roller to this width if necessary, making an allowance for the end cap which you still have to fit. Fit the end cap, following the kit maker's instructions.

3 If you want to stiffen your fabric this should be done before cutting to size, following the instructions provided with the stiffener.

Measuring and cutting out

4 Measure the width of the roller excluding the pin ends and deduct a further 12 mm ($\frac{1}{2}$ in) to obtain the finished blind width. Add 2 cm ($\frac{3}{4}$ in) to the width if you are not using stiffened fabric. Allow for the centring of any design you wish to feature and for extra fabric if your blind is very wide, and patterns have to be matched across seams when lengths are joined (*see page 139*).

5 Using an expandable metal ruler, measure the drop of the blind from the top of the brackets down to the sill adding 30 cm (12 in) for the bottom casing thus ensuring that the roller is still covered when the blind is fully extended.

6 Working on a flat surface, cut the fabric to size, using a set or L-square and metre/yard stick, making sure the corners are square and the ends straight (otherwise your blind will hang crooked). Use a sharp cutting knife or scalpel and a steel ruler as a guide if you are cutting stiffened fabric.

Making up

7 *Unstiffened fabric.* At each side edge turn in the edges for 1 cm ($\frac{3}{8}$ in). Pin, baste and zigzag stitch the edges in place, positioning the zigzag stitches centrally over the raw edges (fig **1**). If working with a machine that won't zigzag, work two rows of straight stitching close together down each edge. *Stiffened fabric.* There should be no need to turn in the side edges as the fabric should be fray resistant. Zigzag stitch the side edges if the fabric shows any tendency to fray. *Joining fabric widths.* Match patterns across seams (*see page 139*) overlapping the fabric in the usual way if using unstiffened fabric. There is no need to turn under a seam

allowance if joining stiffened fabric. Overlap the fabric widths so the patterns match and topstitch down both long edges to secure (fig **2**).

8 At the base turn under 4 cm (1$\frac{1}{2}$ in) twice to make a double hem (turn the hem over once only if using stiffened fabric). Stitch across the hem close to the folded inner edge and across one end to make a casing for the lath. Trim the lath to fit the casing minus 12 mm ($\frac{1}{2}$ in). Insert the lath and stitch across the open end of the casing (fig **3**).

9 Next make up the cord pull. Thread one end of the cord through the holder and knot, then thread the opposite end through the acorn. Screw the cord holder centrally to the lath on the right side of the blind. (You can screw it to the back if you wish to hide the holder.)

10 Lay the blind fabric flat *wrong* side upwards. Lay the roller on the fabric at the top with the spring mechanism to the *left* (fig **4**). Lift the edge of the fabric over on to the roller lining it up with one of the horizontal guidelines on it. Stick the edge of the fabric temporarily in place with tape and hammer tacks through the fabric into the roller at 2 cm ($\frac{3}{4}$ in) intervals, with one at each end (fig **5**).

11 Roll the fabric up tightly around the roller and fit it in the brackets. Pull the blind down to its full extent. When you give a gentle tug the blind should roll up correctly. If it doesn't do so, or the tension is sluggish remove the extended blind from the brackets and rewind by hand. Put the blind back in the brackets, extend again and give it a tug to make it roll up. The blind should now be at the correct tension.

LOOSE COVERS

SCROLL-ARMED SOFA WITH PIPING AND KICK-PLEATED SKIRT

The sofa on page 10 has been covered in striped fabric. If you close one eye and squint, the strongest stripe—the red one—will leap forward. When using boldly patterned fabric, you should feature the part that is the most eyecatching. For example, position a prominent motif at the centre of a piece of furniture and work outwards, as has been done with the red stripe on the sofa cover. Large floral motifs should be centred on cushions; each scroll should be a mirror image of the other. Stripes should match across the inside and outside arm joins and run down the chair back, seat, front and skirt in continuous matching lines as on page 10.

You may find that you have to join widths of fabric to make up the seat front, inside and outside back. In this case, centre one full width of fabric and attach narrow panels at either side. Patterned fabric should be carefully matched across seams (*see page 139*).

The sofa skirt has six inverted pleats, one at each corner, centre back and front. The opening of the cover is placed at the back right-hand corner (looking at the sofa from the back) and begins

just below the scroll. The sofa on page 10 has a fixed cover, but a snugly fitting loose cover can be achieved by securing the bottom edges of the cover under the sofa. This is done by tightening a cord threaded through a casing, which can be released when you wish to remove the cover.

Measuring the sofa

1 Remove any cushions and draw a diagram of your sofa from the back and front as shown (figs **1** and **2**). Make a list of the sections to be covered and label each one. Then measure each section lengthways and widthways at the widest point, making length measurements to the floor as indicated in figs **1** and **2**.

2 Write down these measurements against your list and indicate on the drawing which way the lengthways grain should run (as a general rule towards the floor).

3 Add 15 cm (6 in) tuck-in allowance to the lower edge of the inside back (A), inside arm (C) and to the sides and back of the seat (B). Add a tie-under allowance of 15 cm (6 in) minus the distance I–J (fig 1) to the lower edge of the outside back (G), and the seat front (F). To the outside arms (D), add this allowance (15 cm/6 in minus I–J) plus the width measurement of the arm front (E) across the base. Add 5 cm

Fig 1

Fig 2

(2 in) to all the remaining edges for pin-fitting adjustment, with the exception of the hem edges on the arm fronts and backs.

4 Decide on the finished depth of the skirt. In these instructions 15 cm (6 in) has been allowed, but it may be that a different depth would look best on your sofa. If you are unsure, cut a piece of stiff card to the proposed depth and prop it up in front of the sofa. Stand well back and see if the proportions look right (fig 3). Having made any adjustments, the same piece of card can be used with tailor's chalk to mark a line around the bottom of the chair so the skirt can be positioned accurately (see step 29).

5 To calculate the overall width of the skirt, measure round the outside of the chair at the bottom and add 20 cm (8 in) for each pleat, plus a further 10 cm (4 in) for adjustment/seam allowances at each end of the skirt. Add 5 cm (2 in) to the skirt depth for seam allowance and hem.

If you are using fabric with a pattern that has to be matched vertically as on page 10 or one which would show up seamlines, calculate fabric widths so seams are hidden in the pleats.

6 Measure the cushions in the same way as for rectangular box edged cushion with zip and piping (see page 119). If the cushions have a down filling and can be pushed through a narrow opening, there is no need to extend the zip around the corners of each cover, and it can be positioned along one of the back edges. This means you require only one piece of fabric for the back gusset (boxing strip), the same length and width as the front.

Estimating the fabric

7 Draw the pattern pieces on graph paper to the correct scale following your measurements. Label the pieces and mark the direction of the lengthways grain. You will have to allow roughly 5/6 fabric widths to make up the skirt. Don't forget to add on seam allowances of 1.5 cm ($\frac{5}{8}$ in) for the joins. Cut out the pieces.

Fig 3

Fig 4

8 Keeping the scale the same, draw a long rectangle to the width of your chosen fabric. For plain fabric arrange the pieces as closely as possible, keeping the grain line of the pieces parallel with the graph paper 'selvedges'. If you are using patterned fabric mark in the length of the pattern repeat or where the main design motifs fall, and position the pieces accordingly.

9 Measure the length of the plan and convert it to full scale to find out the amount of fabric you need. Use waste areas of fabric for the piping strips or add extra to the total amount (see page 113 for fabric estimate). Fig 4 indicates where the piping should run. Allow extra piping for joins and tucking into seams (about 38 cm/15 in).

You will need
Fabric
Contrasting fabric (optional) for piping bias strips (see page 141). (Make sure it is the same type as the main fabric because a different weight material could cause puckering when the cover is washed or dry cleaned.)
Pre-shrunk piping cord
Zips (zippers) for the cushions
Large hooks and eyes
Piece of strong cord long enough to go round the widest part of the sofa with plenty over for tying
Sharp pair of scissors
Upholstery pins and skewers (T-pins)
Tailor's chalk
Metre/yard stick
Expandable metal ruler
Stiff piece of card 13.5 cm ($5\frac{3}{8}$ in) by 30 cm (12 in)

Making up

10 Lay the fabric out smoothly, having ironed out any deep creases. Using a set or L-square and ruler, mark out all the basic rectangles in tailor's chalk according to your plan. Follow the lengthways grain carefully, keeping sides straight and corners square. As you cut out, label each piece on the wrong side with chalk and indicate which end is the top.

11 Next mark down the centre of all the sofa sections with tailor's chalk (fig 5). Repeat, to mark a central line down the wrong side of the corresponding fabric sections.

12 Start by pinning the outside back in position. Place the fabric rectangle *right side out* out over the sofa back, matching centres. Smoothing the fabric out from the centre, secure in position with pins or upholstery skewers (T-pins) pushed in along the top edge of the sofa (fig 6). (All fabric pieces should be placed on sofa right side out and pinned with wrong sides together.)

13 Repeat this sequence with the inside front, placing the tuck-in allowance at the base. Pin the outside and inside back sections together at the top and sides, making small pleats if necessary at curved corners to take in fullness (fig 7). Make sure that you push the pins well home so they do not spring out when the cover is lifted off, and avoid catching them in the chair fabric, or the cover will be difficult to remove. Chalk in the seamline and remove the skewers (T-pins) and/or pins from the sofa. Trim round the seam as neatly as possible, leaving an even seam allowance of about 2 cm ($\frac{3}{4}$ in).

14 Set the inside arm in place, positioning the tuck-in allowance at the base. Pin to the inside back including to the tuck-in allowance, which should be folded over the seat. If necessary, allow for tuck-in at the inside arm corners, between the arm and the sofa back (fig 8).

15 Position the outside arm and pin it to the inside arm just underneath the scroll. Trim seams to 2 cm ($\frac{3}{4}$ in) and chalk in seam allowances.

16 Next position the arm fronts. Hold the material in place with upholstery skewers (T-pins). If you are using patterned fabric, move the sections around until the two arms are matching. Pin each piece to the inside and outside arms, taking the seams to the floor. This pinning should be as tight and accurate as possible. Trim the seams to 2 cm ($\frac{3}{4}$ in) and clip curves to ease.

17 Position the arm backs in the same way. Mark

the top of the back opening 7.5 cm (3 in) below the inside/outside arm join.

18 Matching the centres, smooth the seat piece in position, tuck-ins to the sides and back.

19 Pin the tuck-in allowances together at the inside back and sides of the sofa, taking a 1.5 cm ($\frac{5}{8}$ in) seam allowance (fig **9**). Fit the tuck-in carefully at the back corners and front side edges. You may find you don't need much tuck-in here as some sofa seats are fixed at these positions. You will then have to taper the tuck-in to fit.

20 Position the seat front piece against the sofa

and pin to the seat piece and arm front. If the sofa isn't fixed at the front edges pin the seat front piece to the tuck-in allowance as well as the arm front and seat (fig **10**).

21 Check all the seamlines are chalked in, and the cover fits evenly and snugly. Then trim all the excess fabric at the seams to 1.5 cm ($\frac{5}{8}$ in). Take out the pins/skewers (T-pins) you have used for positioning the cover pieces. Remove the cover carefully from the sofa, taking out only as many pins from the seams as necessary.

22 If you haven't yet done so, make up the covered piping (*see page 141*). The piped seams on the cover are

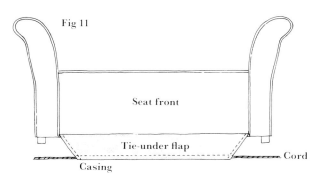

Fig 11

Seat front

Tie-under flap

Casing

Cord

indicated in fig **4**, but you can pipe any seam that outlines the sofa.

23 Removing a few pins from the cover at a time, reverse all the seams (so that the right sides of the fabric are together), repinning and inserting the piping where appropriate as you go along. Leave the back opening unpinned and the piping dangling. It will be attached when you make a facing for the opening. The back piping begins at the skirt edge, goes across the sofa back, and down to skirt height again. Begin the arm back piping in the outside back/arm back seamline. To avoid bulky seams pull back the covering from the piping end for 1.5 cm ($\frac{5}{8}$ in) and cut away the cord. The flat covering is then stitched into the seam.

24 Baste the cover together firmly. Turn to the right side and check that the seams reveal an even amount of piping.

25 Stitch all the seams that do not have piping.

Then change to a zipper foot on the machine and stitch round the fronts and backs of both arms, and then round the sofa back.

26 Next make up the tie-under flaps (fig **11**). Starting with the right front corner (looking at the sofa from the front), measure how far back the leg extends (fig **12a**). Then measure from the top of the arm front to the sofa base edge and add 1 cm ($\frac{3}{8}$ in) (fig **12b**). Mark this depth in tailor's chalk across the base of the *cover* arm front and then along the outside arm up to where the leg extends (point Y). Using a set or L-square or a large book, line up point Y with the outside arm tie-under edge and mark point Z 5 cm (2 in) further along. Rule a diagonal line in tailor's chalk from point Y to point Z. At the right-hand corner of the seat front tie-under flap measure 5 cm (2 in) to the left (point W). Rule a diagonal line from point W to point X on the arm front/seat front seam. Cut along the chalked line from W to Z. Turn under

Fig 5

Chalk

Fig 6

Fig 7

Fig 9

Clip curves

Fig 10

Fig 10

Clip curves

Arm front   Seat front

Fig 8

Inside back

Inside arm

Tuck-in allowances

the cut edge by 1 cm ($\frac{3}{8}$ in) and stitch. Repeat at each corner to produce angled flaps and hemmed arm fronts and backs.

27 Turn under top edge of each flap by 12 mm ($\frac{1}{2}$ in) then 2.5 cm (1 in) and stitch close to hem edge to make a casing for the cord (fig **12c**). Make another row of stitches just above previous row to strengthen.

28 Thread cord through the casing and fit the cover over the sofa. Pull the flaps under the sofa, but don't tighten the cord as you will have to remove the cover to attach the skirt. (Don't cut off excess cord when you do finally tighten it; tuck ends under one of the flaps.)

29 Using the card, mark skirt line around the sofa with chalk (fig **2**). It should be skirt depth minus 1.5 cm ($\frac{5}{8}$ in) from the floor.

30 Join the strips to make up the complete skirt width. Turn under 1 cm ($\frac{3}{8}$ in) and then 2.5 cm (1 in) along the base edge. Hem in place by hand or machine. Press.

31 To form the pleats, start at the opening edge, lining up the end of the skirt, right side out, with the raw edge of the opening and matching the skirt seamline

against the line chalked on the sofa. The skirt edge will be lower than the base edge of the opening. Fold half an inverted pleat at the corner (fig **13a**). Pin the skirt along sofa back. At each corner form an inverted pleat (fig **13b**). At the last corner, the opening edge, fold back half a pleat as before. Cut back any excess fabric to the opening edge seam allowance.

32 Remove the skirt from the cover, being careful to keep the pleats pinned in place. Baste across the top of each pleat to hold and press.

33 Raw edges even, baste and stitch piping to the skirt on right side (fig **14**).

34 With right sides together and skirt upside down, pin the skirt to the cover along stitching line of the piping; raw edges should line up with the chalk line marked round the cover (fig **15**).

35 Remove the cover from the sofa and baste and stitch the skirt in place, using the zipper foot, to enclose the piping in the seam. Oversew raw edges and press.

36 To face the back opening, cut a strip of self-fabric the length of the opening plus 2 cm ($\frac{3}{4}$ in) by 13 cm ($5\frac{1}{4}$ in) wide. Turn under 1 cm

($\frac{3}{8}$ in) at one end and stitch across the hem. Fold in half lengthways with wrong sides together and press. Press under 1.5 cm ($\frac{5}{8}$ in) along the long raw edges of the strip and encase the seam allowance of the outside arm and the skirt (fig **16**), placing the strip 1 cm ($\frac{3}{8}$ in) above the top of the opening. Stitch along seamline, leaving the top 1 cm ($\frac{3}{8}$ in) unattached.

37 Cut another strip the length of the opening plus 2 cm ($\frac{3}{8}$ in) by 7.5 cm (3 in) wide. Hem the bottom edge as before. Press and machine under 1 cm ($\frac{3}{8}$ in) down one long edge.

38 With raw edges even, baste the loose piping to the right side of the arm back piece and the skirt along the opening, bending back the cord into the seam allowance at the bottom and cutting it away as explained in step 23.

39 Right sides together and raw edges even, stitch the strip to the opening, leaving 1 cm ($\frac{3}{8}$ in) excess at the top.

Fig 13a — Back arm / Outside back / Outside arm

Fig 13b

10 cm / 5 cm / 5 cm / Skirt

Turn the strip to the inside of the opening (fig **17**). Press.

40 Hand sew the two strips together across the top and finish off the raw edges. Attach the hooks to the piped section of the opening and eyes to the other (fig **18**).

41 Make up the cushion covers (*see page 119*).

Fig 14

Fig 15

Fig 16

Fig 17 — Skirt / Arm back

Fig 18

Skirt (wrong side) / Corner pleat / Chalk line / Tie-under flap

Fig 12a

Fig 12b

Outside arm

Arm front

Sofa arm height

Tie-under flap

Tie-under flap

X Y Z

W

Fig 12c

Tie-under Tie-under

CUSHIONS

Cushions are the simplest way of providing finishing touches to sofas, beds, and chairs. They add comfort and colour and can be made in any shape or size. They can even be used as seating units.

The cushions in this section have been set out in their basic forms to which 'extras' can be added, such as covered piping, single or double ruffles, ruffles with contrast edgings. There are many different ways to close a cushion cover; slipstitching is the easiest. Alternatives are zips (zippers), Velcro, press fasteners (snaps), ties, buttons with holes and loops. The cushion cover is sewn to fit over a cushion pad. You should never put loose fillings straight into a cushion cover. The cushion pad can either be bought or made up if you want an unusual shape or size. Make sure the fabric used for the pad cover is compatible with the filling. Feather fillings require a covering of feather-proof cambric. (See page 120 for cushion pad instructions.) For a plump cushion, leave out the cushion cover seam allowances. Bold symmetrical patterns on fabric should be suitably placed on the cushion. A large floral design is usually centred for example. If you find it difficult to calculate how much patterned fabric you will need to make your cushion(s), make a pattern to the correct size and position it over the fabric before buying, to ascertain exactly how much you need.

KNIFE-EDGED CUSHION COVERS

These can have a side or back opening. The back opening in these instructions is closed with a zip (zipper), but other methods can be used according to preference. The side opening in the following types of cover is either zipped or slipstitched closed. Slipstitching is the simplest and most unobtrusive way of closing a cover, but the opening will have to be restitched every time the cover is cleaned and the seam won't withstand a great deal of strain.

Fig 1

	Front	Back
Cushion 1		
Cushion 2		
Cushion 3		

SQUARE OR RECTANGULAR CUSHION COVER WITH SIDE OPENING

You will need

Cushion pad

Fabric, including an allowance for ruffles (*see page 142*) and/or piping (*see page 141*) if required

Zip (zipper) (optional) the same size as the cushion opening (see step 9)

Pattern paper or metre/yard stick and tailor's chalk

Fabric tape measure

Fig 2

Measuring and cutting out

1 Using the fabric tape measure, measure the pad from seam to seam across its centre in both directions (fig **1**). Add 1.5 cm ($\frac{5}{8}$ in) seam allowance all round.

2 For each cushion you will need two pieces of fabric cut to the required size. If you are making several cushions, calculate how many cover pieces will fit into the fabric width and draw a cutting plan (fig **2**). To estimate the amount of fabric needed add up the measurements of the marked pieces down the length. For example, to make three 38 cm (15 in) square cushions you would need 82 cm ($32\frac{1}{2}$ in) of 137 cm (54 in) wide fabric.

3 Next make a paper pattern for each cover piece if desired.

4 Lay the fabric out flat and position the pattern pieces or, using the metre/yard stick as a guide, mark out the cover squares or rectangles in tailor's chalk following the straight grain of the fabric.

Making up

5 *Hand-sewn side opening.* Cut two pieces of fabric for each cushion, allowing 1.5 cm ($\frac{5}{8}$ in) for seams all round.

6 Attach ruffles and/or piping at this stage. *For a single or double ruffle* work gathering stitches along half the ruffle length and then cut the gathering threads. Make gathering stitches along the remaining length. With raw edges even and the right side of the ruffle against the right side of one of the main cover pieces, gently pull the gathering threads along half the ruffle length until this exactly fits two sides of the cover. Fit the remaining half of the ruffle in the same way. Baste ruffle in place 1 cm ($\frac{3}{8}$ in) from the cover edge (fig **3**). Clip corner.

After it has been made up a *pleated ruffle* should be basted to a cover piece with raw edges even, right sides together. *Piping* should be attached in the same way. If it is to be used with a ruffle, it should be applied first and the ruffle basted in place on top (fig **4**). Corners should be clipped to ease.

7 Place the fabric pieces with right sides together and stitch round three sides. On the unstitched side sew in 5 cm (2 in) from both ends, leaving the centre of the seam open. Trim down the seam allowance to 1 cm

($\frac{3}{8}$ in), cutting across the corners (fig **5**). Neaten the raw edges with machine zigzagging or oversew by hand. Turn the cover to the right side and press carefully, making sure the corners are fully pulled through by using a pin, very gently, to ease them out.

8 Insert the cushion pad. Turn in the opening edges in line with the remainder of the seam and slipstitch (*see page 140*) to close.

9 *Zip (zipper) fastened side opening.* Follow steps 5 and 6 above. With the opening edges of the two cushion pieces even and right sides together, stitch in for 5 cm (2 in) from each end of the seam. Baste along the rest of the seam; this forms the opening. Press the seam open. Set in the zip (zipper) (*see page 141*) and open it. Follow the instructions for

Fig 3

Cover (**right side**)

Ruffle (**wrong side**)

Fig 4

Cover (**right side**)

Piping

Fig 5

Fig 6a

Cutting line

Fig 6b

B   C

Seam allowance

Fig 6c

inserting a zip (zipper) in a piped seam if you have applied piping.

10 With right sides together, stitch round the remaining unstitched edges of the cover and finish as in step 7. Insert the cushion pad.

SQUARE OR RECTANGULAR CUSHION WITH BACK ZIP (ZIPPER) OPENING

If the cover fabric is very thick and difficult to work, a zip set in the back of the cushion is easier to sew.

You will need
Cushion pad
Fabric, including an allowance for a ruffle (*see page 142*) and/or piping (*see page 141*) if desired
Zip (zipper), the length of the widest side of the cushion less 10 cm (4 in)
Pattern paper

Measuring and cutting out
1 Calculate how much fabric you will need, following steps 1 and 2 of the square or rectangular cover with side opening.

2 Cut out two pattern pieces to equal the cushion pad measurements (fig **1**) plus

seam allowances of 1.5 cm ($\frac{5}{8}$ in) all round.

3 Set one pattern piece, marked A, aside, then draw a line across the other piece 6 cm ($2\frac{1}{2}$ in) in from one side. Cut along this line (fig **6a**). Mark pieces B and C.

4 Lay all the pattern pieces on the fabric following the straight grain, adding a 1.5 cm ($\frac{5}{8}$ in) seam allowance to the newly cut edges of B and C (fig **6b**). Cut out.

Making up
5 With right sides together and raw edges even, stitch B and C together for 5 cm (2 in) in from each end. Baste the remainder of the seam. Press the seam open and insert the zip (zipper) (*see page 141*) (fig **6c**).

Fig 7

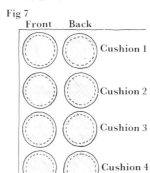

Front   Back

Cushion 1

Cushion 2

Cushion 3

Cushion 4

Fig 8

Fig 9

Gathering threads

Fig 10

6 Attach ruffle and/or piping to the cover top at this stage if desired (see step 6 for square or rectangular cover with side opening).

7 Open the zip (zipper). With right sides together and raw edges even, stitch the cover pieces together. Finish as for square or rectangular cushion with side opening, step 7. Turn to the right side. Insert the cushion pad.

ROUND CUSHION COVER WITH HAND-SEWN SIDE OPENING

You will need
Cushion pad
Fabric, to include an allowance for ruffles (*see page 142*) and/or piping (*see page 141*) if desired
Pattern paper
Length of string and pencil
Fabric tape measure

Measuring and cutting out
1 Using a fabric tape measure, measure the diameter of your cushion pad and add 3 cm ($1\frac{1}{4}$ in) for seam allowances. This gives the diameter of each cover piece. If you are making several covers, work out how many pieces will fit into the fabric width and draw a cutting plan (fig **7**). Add up the measurements of the cover pieces down the length of the fabric to find the amount you require. For example, to make covers for four 30 cm (12 in) diameter cushions you would need 66 cm (26 in) of 137 cm (54 in) wide fabric.

2 Take a square of pattern paper slightly larger than the cover diameter. Fold it into quarters. Attach a length of string to the lower end of a pencil and cut this off to equal half the diameter of the cover. (For a plump cushion subtract 1.5 cm/$\frac{5}{8}$ in seam allowance.)

3 Lay the paper on a board and pin the loose end of string to the point of the folded corner with a thumb tack or drawing pin. Draw an arc from one side of the folded paper to the other. Cut along the marked line and unfold your pattern (fig **8**).

4 Using the pattern, cut two cover circles from

the fabric.

Making up
5 Make up the optional ruffle and/or piping. *For a single or double ruffle* work gathering stitches along half the ruffle length and then cut the gathering threads. Make gathering stitches along the remaining ruffle length. Fold one of the cover circles in half and mark the halfway point at the raw edges. Open out again. With raw edges even and the right side of the ruffle against the right side of the cover, position each break in the gathering at the marked points. Gently pull up the gathering threads so that the ruffle fits evenly round the cover. Baste the ruffle in place 1 cm ($\frac{3}{8}$ in) from the cover edge (fig **9**).

After it has been made up a *pleated ruffle* should be basted to a cover piece with raw edges even, right sides together. *Piping* should be attached in the same way. If it is to be used with a ruffle, it should be applied first and the ruffle basted in place on top.

6 With right sides together and raw edges even, stitch round the circles, leaving a gap of roughly one third of the circumference through which to turn. Trim the seam allowance to 1 cm ($\frac{3}{8}$ in) if the fabric is bulky, then notch all round the seam allowance (except for the opening) to ease (fig **10**).

7 Turn the cover to the right side and add the cushion pad. Turn in the opening edges in line with the remainder of the seam and slipstitch (*see page 140*) to close.

ROUND CUSHION COVER WITH BACK ZIP (ZIPPER) OPENING

You will need
Cushion pad
Fabric, to include an allowance for ruffle (*see page 142*) and/or piping (*see page 141*) if desired
Zip (zipper), the length of the line drawn one third of the way down your cushion (see step 2) less 10 cm (4 in)
Pattern paper
Length of string and pencil

Measuring and cutting out

1 Measure and cut out the pattern pieces as in steps 1 to 4 above. Set one piece aside, marked A.

2 Taking the other pattern piece, draw a line across it roughly one third down (fig **11**). Cut along this line and mark the pieces B and C.

3 Cut out all the cover pieces, adding a 1.5 cm ($\frac{5}{8}$ in) seam allowance to the newly cut edges of the B and C pieces (see fig **12**). Remember to feature any large pattern on the front of the cover.

4 With raw edges even and the right sides of B and C together stitch along the seam for 5 cm (2 in) in from each end (fig **13**). Baste the remainder of the seam and set in the zip (zipper) (*see page 141*) (fig **14**).

Fig 11

Cutting line

Fig 12

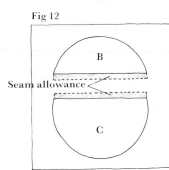

B

Seam allowance

C

Fig 13

Fig 14

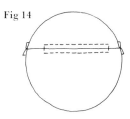

5 Make up and attach optional ruffle and / or piping, following step 5 for the round cushion cover with hand-sewn side opening.

6 Open the zip (zipper). Continue as for the round cover with hand-sewn side opening, steps 6 and 7, omitting the side opening.

HEART-SHAPED COVER WITH DOUBLE RUFFLE AND PIPING

You will need
Fabric and filling to make up a cushion pad (*see page 117*)
Cover, ruffle and piping fabric
Zip (zipper) (*see step 5*)
Pre-shrunk piping cord
Pattern paper

Cutting out the pattern

1 Cut a rectangle of pattern paper slightly larger than your intended cushion pad, say 38 cm (15 in) across by 35 cm (14 in) down. Fold the paper in half lengthways and draw half a heart, taking the fold as the central point and using a plate or bowl to help draw the curve if necessary. Cut round the shape while still folded in half, then open out. Mark this pattern piece A (fig **15**).

2 Draw round A on another piece of pattern paper and cut out duplicate piece B.

3 Take pattern piece B and rule a straight line across it at its widest point (fig **16**). Cut along the line, to make two pattern pieces.

4 Cut out the cover front using pattern A. Cut the back pieces using the two pattern B sections, adding a seam allowance of 1.5 cm ($\frac{5}{8}$ in) to the newly cut back opening edges (see fig **17**).

Making up

5 With right sides of the B sections together and raw edges even, stitch 5 cm (2 in) in from each end along the back opening seam. Baste the remainder of the seam to close. Press the seam open and set in the zip (zipper) (*see page 141*).

6 Cut out enough bias strips (*see page 140*) to cover the required length of

Fig 15

19 cm

35 cm

A

Fig 16

Cutting line

Fig 17

Seam allowance

piping cord (see step 8) when joined.

7 For the ruffle cut a strip of fabric 13 cm ($5\frac{1}{4}$ in) wide by twice the length of the outer edge measurement of the heart.

8 Make up the cushion pad as explained on page 120, taking a 1.5 cm ($\frac{5}{8}$ in) seam allowance. Make up enough covered piping to go round the heart plus 3 cm ($1\frac{1}{4}$ in) seam allowance. Make up the ruffle as explained on page 142, dividing the gathering stitches into two sections.

9 With raw edges even, baste the piping to the heart front, joining the ends (*see page 141*) wherever seems most unobtrusive.

10 Now attach the ruffle. With raw edges even, position the breaks in the gathering threads at the point of the heart and the dip and pull up each ruffle section so that it gathers evenly around the heart. Baste 1 cm ($\frac{3}{8}$ in) from heart edge.

11 Open the zip (zipper). Continue as for the round cushion cover with hand-sewn opening, steps 6 and 7, omitting the side opening.

BOX EDGED CUSHION COVERS

Adding a gusset (boxing strip) to a cushion cover produces a deeper three-dimensional shape, which gives a more tailored finish to the cushion and allows for a more solid filling. The gusset (boxing strip) itself is the strip of fabric that is inserted between the top and bottom pieces of the cover. It can be pleated, made in a contrasting or decorative fabric. Piping can be inserted in seams between the gusset (boxing strip) and top and bottom pieces.

The cushion covers that follow have a zip (zipper) set in the gusset (boxing strip). If you are making more than one cushion it may be helpful to draw up a cutting plan as in fig **2** page 117 (square and rectangular covers) and fig **7** page 118 (round cushions), allowing for the gusset (boxing) strips. Read through the introduction to Cushions for other basic information.

SQUARE OR RECTANGULAR BOX EDGED COVER WITH PIPING

If you are making a cover for an inflexible cushion pad, such as a thick piece of foam or a sprung cushion, the zip should extend around the cover corners. This means the back gusset (boxing strip) will extend round the corners as well (fig **18a**). If the cushion pad is flexible the zip (zipper) can be set into a back-width gusset (boxing strip) (fig **18b**).

You will need
Cushion pad
Zip (zipper) 10 cm (4 in) shorter or 10 cm (4 in) longer than the cushion back (see above)
Fabric
Contrast fabric (optional) for piping bias strips (*see page 140*)
Pre-shrunk piping cord
Pattern paper (optional)

Measuring for the cover

1 For the top and bottom piece of the cushion cover measure the top and bottom surfaces of the pad in

Fig 18a

Fig 18b

Fig 19

Fig 20

Half gusset
(boxing)
depth

Fig 21

both directions and add 1.5 cm ($\frac{5}{8}$ in) for seam allowances all round (fig **19**).

2 For the gusset (boxing) pieces, measure the length and depth of the sides and front of the pad and add 1.5 cm ($\frac{5}{8}$ in) seam allowance all round. Measure the length of the back gusset (boxing strip) and add 3 cm ($1\frac{1}{4}$ in) for seams. As this strip will be cut in half lengthways so the zip (zipper) can be inserted, add 6 cm ($2\frac{1}{2}$ in) to the depth of this piece (fig **20**).

For a cover with a rigid filling measure the length and depth of the cushion back and add 18.5 cm ($7\frac{1}{4}$ in) to the length and 6 cm ($2\frac{1}{2}$ in) to the depth for the zip (zipper) and side seam allowances. Measure the length and width of the cushion sides and subtract 7.5 cm (3 in) from the length. Add 1.5 cm ($\frac{5}{8}$ in) seam allowance all round. Measure the length and width of the cushion at the front and add 1.5 cm ($\frac{5}{8}$ in) for the seam allowance all the way round.

3 Cut out pattern pieces to these measurements if desired.

4 Cut out enough bias strips (*see page 140*) to cover sufficient piping to go round the cushion twice plus an allowance for joins.

5 Lay the fabric out flat and position the pattern pieces or, using the metre/yard stick as a guide, mark out the cover squares or rectangles in tailor's chalk following the straight grain of the fabric. For each cushion cover, cut out one top piece, one bottom piece and four gusset (boxing) pieces—one front, one back and two sides.

Making up

6 Cut the back gusset (boxing strip) in half lengthways. Place the two halves right sides together. On an ordinary back-width gusset (boxing strip), stitch in from each end for 2 cm (2 in) along the seam allowance. Baste along the remainder of the seam. Press open and insert the zip (zipper) (*see page 141*). If the gusset (boxing strip) is to extend round the cushion corners stitch in from each end for 4 cm ($1\frac{1}{2}$ in) along the seam allowance and repeat the process just described (fig **21**).

7 Right sides together, raw edges even, stitch gusset (boxing) strips together into a ring. Press seams open.

8 Make up enough covered piping (*see page 141*) to go round each cushion twice, allowing for joins.

9 Beginning at the back of each cushion, with raw edges even, pin piping around the cushion top and then the bottom, joining the ends neatly (*see page 141*). Clip the corners to ease

10 Matching seams to corners and with right sides facing, stitch the gusset (boxing) strip to one of the main cover pieces, using the zipper foot on the machine. Trim diagonally across the seam allowances at the corners to reduce bulk. Open the zip (zipper) and then attach the remaining main piece in the same way.

11 Press the seam allowances towards gusset (boxing strip), trimming to 1 cm ($\frac{3}{8}$ in). Insert cushion pad.

ROUND BOX EDGED CUSHION WITH PIPING

You will need
Fabric
Cushion pad
Zip (zipper) (see step 2)
Contrasting fabric for piping bias strips
Pre-shrunk piping cord

Measuring for the cover

1 Measure the diameter of the cushion pad and add 3 cm ($1\frac{1}{4}$ in). This gives the diameter of the top and bottom of the cushion cover.

2 Measure the depth and the circumference of the

Fig 22

Fig 23

Piping   Tie

pad. Cut one gusset (boxing) piece to measure half the circumference plus 3 cm ($1\frac{1}{4}$ in) by the depth plus 3 cm ($1\frac{1}{4}$ in). Cut a second strip for the zipped section to measure half the circumference plus 3 cm ($1\frac{1}{4}$ in) by the depth plus 6 cm ($2\frac{1}{2}$ in). The zip (zipper) should measure about 4 cm ($1\frac{1}{2}$ in) less than half the cushion circumference. If you won't be able to squash the cushion pad through this opening, make the zipped section of the gusset (boxing strip) longer and adjust the front section to fit.

3 Cut sufficient contrast bias strips (*see page 140*) to cover enough piping to go round the cushion twice plus an allowance for joins.

Making up

4 Insert the zip (zipper) in the back gusset (boxing) strip (*see page 141*).

5 Join the strips into a ring. Press seams (fig **22**).

6 Make up the piping and attach to the right side of the top and bottom cover pieces, raw edges even.

7 Attach the gusset (boxing strip) to the main cover pieces as in steps 10 and 11 of the previous instructions. Clip into the seam allowances all the way round the cover to ease the fabric (fig **23**). Press all seams towards the gusset (boxing strip). Turn the cover to the right side and insert the pad.

SHAPING CUSHIONS TO FIT THE CHAIR SEAT

Many wooden or cane chairs have an irregularly shaped seat, sometimes with jutting struts or arms. The cushion pad can be cut from foam or made up to fit (*see page 120*). To shape it accurately you need to make a paper pattern of the seat.

Cutting out the pattern

1 Measure the width and depth of the chair seat and cut a piece of paper slightly larger. Lay the paper on the chair and pencil around the edges to make an exact outline of the seat.

2 If you are making a cushion for a sofa or armchair back remember that it will sit on top of a seat cushion, so lay your pattern piece over the sofa/chair back with the seat cushion(s) in place.

3 The pattern pieces can now be used to make the cushion pads and to cut out the cushion cover. For box edged cushions with curved sections cut to fit round the arms of a chair, insert the zip (zipper) into the widest part of the bottom piece of the chair cover so it won't show (see square or rectangular cushion cover with back fastening).

MAKING A CUSHION PAD

You will need
Foam chips, feathers or feathers and down, according to preference and type of cushion being made
Ticking (for foam chips)
Down-proof cambric (for feathers)
Strong thread
Pattern paper

Making up

1 Cut a pattern in the intended shape and size of your cushion.

2 Cut out the fabric pieces required, adding a 1.5 cm ($\frac{5}{8}$ in) seam allowance all round, and omitting openings for back and gusset (boxing strip) zips (zippers) and trimmings.

3 Make up the cushion pad case in the same way you would the cushion cover, leaving a gap in one seam through which to stuff the case. Stitch around the case twice, one row just above the other, for strength.

4 Clip across corners diagonally and clip curves. Turn to the right side.

5 Fill the case firmly. Slipstitch (*see page 140*) the opening edges together in line with the remainder of the seam to close.

ATTACHING THE CUSHION TO THE CHAIR WITH TIES

When placed on upright wooden or cane chairs, such as those found in dining rooms and kitchens, cushions need to be firmly attached and the simplest solution is to tie them to the chair back struts.

You will need
Two pieces of fabric 61 cm (24 in) by 5 cm (2 in) to match or contrast with the cushion cover

Fig 24

Fig 25

Fig 26

Making up
1 Fold each strip in half lengthways, right sides together and matching raw edges. Stitch across one end and along the length of each tie 1 cm ($\frac{3}{8}$ in) from the raw edge. Trim the stitched corner (fig **24**) and turn the ties right side out, using the blunt end of a pencil to facilitate turning. Press the ties. Turn in the raw edges at the unstitched ends and slipstitch (*see page 140*) to close.

Attaching the ties to knife-edged covers
2 Before you have sewn the cover pieces together but after attaching any ruffle and/or piping, set one of the cover pieces on the chair and mark on the seam allowance the positions of the two (outer) struts.

3 Fold each tie in half and place at a strut position on the right side of the cover with the folded edge even with the cover back edge (fig **25**). Baste to hold.

4 Complete the cushion cover as explained in the individual instructions.

Attaching ties to a box edged cover
5 Make up the cover as explained in the individual instructions.

6 Fold the ties in half and position them so that they align with the two (outer) struts when the completed cushion is on the chair. Stitch in place (fig **26**).

BUTTONED LOUNGER CUSHION

The lounger is backed with towelling and can be filled with foam or polyester wadding (batting). It measures 60 cm (24 in) wide by 190 cm ($74\frac{3}{4}$ in) long and is divided into a back cushion section of 68 cm ($26\frac{3}{4}$ in) and a seating section of 122 cm (48 in). To

avoid fabric wastage, you could either make two loungers from 137 cm (54 in) fabric or use the remainder of the fabric width to make matching cushions. Alternatively you may wish to make up a lounger to your own size specifications. The lounger is attached to the seat at the sides with ties.

You will need
Cushion pad cut to the finished size of the lounger, using 5 cm (2 in) thick foam or two thicknesses of 8 oz polyester wadding (batting, extra loft) (see step 5 for details)
Top fabric
Towelling (terrycloth)
24 self-cover buttons 2.5 cm (1 in) in diameter
Large embroidery needle
Cotton twine

Measuring and cutting out
1 To the desired width and length of the lounger add 8 cm ($3\frac{1}{4}$ in) for depth and seam allowances. Cut one piece of top fabric and one piece of towelling (terrycloth) to these dimensions, making sure the top and bottom ends are at right angles to the selvedge and the long edges run parallel to it. You can make a paper pattern from pieces of newspaper pinned together if necessary.

2 On the right side of each cover piece, mark across the dividing line (fig **27**) between the back and seating lengths with tailor's chalk. This will be 72 cm ($28\frac{3}{8}$ in) down from the top edge if you are using the size specifications above.

Making up
3 Set the two fabric pieces right sides together, raw edges even and stitch all round, taking a 1.5 cm ($\frac{5}{8}$ in) seam allowance and leaving an opening at the foot of the

Fig 27

Fig 28

Stitching line

Dividing line

2.5 cm

cushion about 46 cm (18 in) wide through which to push the cushion pad.

4 To make the corners of the cover, stitch evenly across each corner through both thickness of fabric (fig **28**); the length of the stitching should measure 5 cm (2 in). Trim the corners and turn the cover to the right side.

5 Cut the cushion pad in two pieces, one to fit the back section (68 cm/$26\frac{3}{4}$ in) and the other to fit the seat (122 cm/48 in). Two layers of polyester wadding (batting) are used to obtain the correct thickness. These should be stitched together loosely with diagonal rows of basting before inserting into the cover.

6 Insert the cushion back foam or wadding (batting) into the top part of the cover and then pin and baste across the marked line, matching the marking on each side of the cover. Stitch from side to side through all thicknesses. Insert the remaining larger piece of foam into the lower part of the cover. Turn in the bottom edges in line with the remainder of the seam and slipstitch (*see page 140*) to close.

7 Cover 12 buttons with the top fabric and the other 12 with the towelling (terrycloth). Mark their positions at equal intervals on both sides of the lounger. Fig **29** gives the spacing for a 60 cm (24 in) by 190 cm ($74\frac{3}{4}$ in) lounger.

8 Thread the embroidery needle with a length of twine. Holding on to the loose end of twine, push the needle through the cover from the base to the top side at the first button position. Thread on a button and return to the base. Pull the needle clear of the fabric and thread on another button. Tie the twine ends with a slip knot (*see page 142*). Pull the twine ends until both buttons sink into the cover and tie off around the shank of the button. Trim the ends of twine and push them under the button. Repeat until all the buttons have been attached.

9 Make up the ties as shown in the previous

Fig 29   24 cm apart   Fig 30

20 cm apart

Fig 31

Fig 32

instructions, then stitch by hand to each side of the lounger at the dividing line between the back and the seat.

BUNK COVER

The rectangular box cushions in the yacht cabin on page 37 have been covered with vinyl coated fabric because it is both waterproof and strong. The seat back has a dual purpose: it sits in a frame hinged to the wall at the cushion top and can be raised at the bottom edge to make a bunk. The bunk is suspended from the ceiling by heavy ropes attached to the front of the frame which are then knotted through metal rings bolted into the ceiling. The cushion is held in the frame by means of eyeleted flaps set into the base seamline of the cushion. These flaps are lashed together with rope (fig **30**).

To make the cushion your machine will have to be capable of stitching six thicknesses of vinyl coated fabric together. You can test your machine on a small wad of fabric. If it can't stitch through all the thicknesses, hire an industrial machine for the day or take the fabric pieces to your local upholsterer to be sewn together—he can also set in the eyelets at the same time.

You will need
Fabric for the cushion
Fabric for the flaps
Velcro
Strong thread
Large eyelets
Rope

Measuring and cutting out
1 Cut out the fabric pieces needed to make up a rectangular box edged cushion (*see page 119*) with piping. The dimensions of the cushion will be determined by the size of the frame.

2 You will need to cut eight flaps, three for each side and one for each end. Fig **31** shows their relative sizes. Each flap has a finished depth of 15 cm (6 in). Allow 1.5 cm ($\frac{5}{8}$ in) all round for seams when cutting out. A gap of 7.5 cm (3 in) has been allowed for the suspending ropes and hinges. The outer side flaps and end flaps are positioned 2.5 cm (1 in) from the corners. Cut two pieces of fabric for each flap.

Making up
3 Taking a pair of flap pieces lay one over the other right sides together and raw edges even. Stitch around the three outer edges of the flap, taking a 1.5 cm ($\frac{5}{8}$ in) seam allowance, leaving the side that will be attached to the cushion unstitched. Trim corners and turn. On the right side of the flap topstitch round the three stitched sides 1 cm ($\frac{3}{8}$ in) from the edges and stitch across the open edge to close. Repeat for all the other flap pairs.

4 Apply eyelets to each flap, following the maker's instructions, placing them about 15 cm (6 in) apart at least 2.5 cm (1 in) in from the edges of each flap.

5 With raw edges matching set each flap in position against the right side of the cushion cover bottom piece. Stitch across the flaps twice very close together 1 cm ($\frac{3}{8}$ in) and 1.5 cm ($\frac{5}{8}$ in) in from the edges (fig **32**).

6 Follow the rectangular box edged cushion instructions to make up the cushion, double-stitching all seams for strength and inserting Velcro instead of a zip (zipper).

7 Turn the cover to the right side and place the cushion pad inside. Close the Velcro. Set the cushion in the frame and wrap the flaps around it. Thread the rope through the eyelets and criss-cross the cushion base and fasten securely. The cushion is now lashed to the frame.

TABLECLOTHS

ROUND TABLECLOTHS

The following instructions are for reference, to be used when making up individual tablecloths.

Measuring and cutting out

1 First measure the diameter of the table A to B (fig **1**). Now measure to point C from the table edge for the finished drop of the cloth. Double this measurement and add it to A-B to obtain the finished diameter of the cloth. (For the vinyl coated tablecloth, sit in a chair at the table and measure the drop (B–C) to finish at thigh height.) To the finished diameter add a further 3 cm ($1\frac{1}{4}$ in) seam/hem allowance.

2 For your tablecloth you will need an amount of fabric that equals the total diameter measurement in width and length. You may find that this measurement is wider than your chosen fabric width. In this case, widths have to be joined to make up the cloth (see vinyl coated cloth, following). However, these are never joined at the tablecloth centre. Half widths are joined at the sides to

a full width of fabric positioned down the centre of the cloth. If you need to make up your cloth in this way, your fabric requirement will double in length. Remember to add a seam allowance of 1.5 cm ($\frac{5}{8}$ in) to each edge to be joined. If your tablecloth needs wider than half-width panels at each side, you will require a total fabric length of three times the cloth diameter. To match a pattern across seams add the length of one pattern repeat to the total fabric amount for each extra full width required for the side panels.

3 To make up the fabric width needed, divide the fabric into two (three if you are attaching full widths) equal lengths. For *half-width* side panels fold one section in half lengthways and cut along the fold. The remaining uncut section will form the central panel (fig **2**).

4 With right sides together and long edges even, join the tablecloth panels with flat fell seams (*see page 140*), positioning the full width of fabric in the centre. In the case of the vinyl coated tablecloth it is unnecessary to neaten the seams in this way, since the fabric does not fray or have to stand up to frequent washing. Stitch simple seams and press the allowances open, using a pressing cloth between the iron and coated fabric.

5 Fold your piece of fabric in quarters, wrong side out, and press, matching the outer edges and any seams. (Do not press folded vinyl edges.)

6 Divide the total diameter measurement arrived at in step 1 in half, to obtain the radius of the circle you are going to cut. Firmly tie a length of string longer than the radius length to the bottom of a pencil or fabric marker pen, then pin the string with a tack or drawing pin to the folded point of the fabric (fig **3**) so that the string length equals the radius when it is held taut and the pencil upright. Draw an arc across the folded fabric from edge to edge, keeping the string taut. Cut along this line through all thicknesses and open out the cloth.

ROUND VINYL COATED TABLECLOTH

As it is not a good idea to stab a drawing pin or tack through vinyl coated fabric as instructed in step 6 of *measuring and cutting out*, a paper pattern is cut for this tablecloth.

You will need
Fabric
Pattern paper
Pencil and length of string
Tailor's chalk

Making up

1 Follow steps 1 to 5 above, omitting the pressing stage in step 5.

2 To make the pattern, cut a rectangle of paper the same size as the folded cloth. Put weights on the cloth so that it lies flat and measure the edges carefully with an expandable metal rule. Mark the folded point of the fabric on the pattern.

3 Mark the pattern paper with an arc as in step 6 above. Cut along arc line.

4 Place the pattern over the fabric and weight it down, matching the folds of fabric with the pattern edges. Draw around the arc with chalk. Remove the pattern, replace the weights and cut along the arc line through the four thicknesses of fabric.

5 Unfold the cloth. Turn under 1.5 cm ($\frac{5}{8}$ in) to the wrong side all round. Stitch round 6 mm ($\frac{1}{4}$ in) from folded edge.

ROUND TABLECLOTH WITH BOUND EDGE

You will need
Fabric, following the measurements given in steps 1 and 2, but minus 3 cm ($1\frac{1}{4}$ in) seam/hem allowance added to the diameter in step 1.
Contrast bias binding (*see page 140*) 5.5 cm ($2\frac{1}{4}$ in) wide by the cloth circumference plus 5 cm (2 in)

Making up

1 Follow steps 1 to 6 of *measuring and cutting out*.

2 Make up the bias binding strip (*see page 140*). Press in 1 cm ($\frac{3}{8}$ in) to the wrong side along one long edge.

3 Set the unfolded edge of the strip against the edge of the cloth, right sides together. Fold the end of the strip 1.5 cm ($\frac{5}{8}$ in) to the wrong side (fig **4**). Pin the bias strip all round the cloth, taking a 1.5 cm ($\frac{5}{8}$ in) seam allowance. Overlap the turned-under end by about 4 cm ($1\frac{1}{2}$ in). Baste and stitch in place (fig **5**).

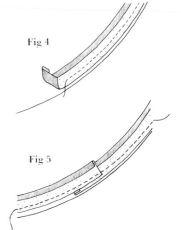

Fig 4

Fig 5

4 Clip the seam at intervals round the edge to ease.

5 Fold the bias strip over the seam allowances to the wrong side of the cloth. Slipstitch (*see page 140*) the folded edge over the previous line of stitching. Press.

Fig 1

A ————→ B

C

C

Fig 2

Drop

Edge of table

Fig 3

ROUND TABLECLOTH WITH BOUND AND HEADED RUFFLE

You will need

Fabric for the main cloth and single ruffle

Two contrast binding strips, each 4 cm (1½ in) wide by the length of the ruffle plus a seam allowance of 3 cm (1¼ in). These can be cut on the straight grain, but use bias binding (*see page 140*) if preferred

Making up

1 Subtracting 9 cm (3½ in) from the finished drop measurement, measure and cut out the main part of the tablecloth as described in steps 1 to 6 of measuring and cutting out at the beginning of the section (*page 123*).

2 For the ruffle, cut out enough 10 cm (4 in) wide strips to go twice round the cloth circumference when joined, allowing 1.5 cm (⅝ in) for seams at each strip end.

3 With right sides together and end edges even, join the strips into a ring with flat fell seams (*see page 140*). Press.

4 Bind both long raw edges of the ruffle exactly as for the circular tablecloth with bound edge, steps 2 to 5, taking a 1 cm (⅜ in) seam allowance. Press the bound edges.

5 Divide the ruffle into quarters, marking the dividing point of each quarter with two pins set close together. Run two lines of gathering stitches around the ruffle 1.5 cm (⅝ in) and 4 cm (1½ in) from the top bound edge, breaking the stitching lines at each set of pin markers. Set aside.

6 Turn 6 mm (¼ in) to the wrong side around the

tablecloth edge and stitch. Turn 1 cm (⅜ in) to the wrong side again and stitch close to the inner folded edge. Press.

7 Divide the edge of the tablecloth into quarters and mark with two pins as for the ruffle.

8 Matching pins, the wrong side of the ruffle against the right side of the cloth and the lower row of ruffle gathering stitches even with the cloth edge, draw up each ruffle quarter to fit the corresponding section of the tablecloth. Pin and baste in place just above or along the rows of gathering.

9 Work a row of topstitching 2 cm (¾ in) and then 3 cm (1¼ in) below the ruffle top edge (fig **6**). This stitching should not overlap the gathering / basting stitches, which should now be removed.

ROUND FITTED TABLECLOTH WITH GATHERED SKIRT, PIPING AND DOUBLE RUFFLE

You will need

Fabric

Pattern paper

Tailor's chalk

Pre-shrunk piping cord

Measuring and cutting out

1 Lay a piece of pattern paper over the table top and mark round the edge in tailor's chalk. Add 1.5 cm (⅝ in) all round for seams and cut out the pattern. Use it to cut out the fabric for the table top.

2 Calculate the circumference of the table (multiply the diameter by 3.14). Double this measurement to obtain the width of the gathered skirt. Measure from the table edge to the floor or just above to obtain the drop. Subtract the desired depth of the finished ruffle from this measurement and then add 5 cm (2 in) for seams. Cut out the amount of fabric rectangles needed to make up the gathered skirt width, allowing for pattern matching across seams if necessary.

3 Cut strips of fabric to measure twice the desired depth of the ruffle plus

3 cm (1¼ in) by a finished width of twice the width of the skirt. Add 1.5 cm (⅝ in) to each strip end to allow for joins.

4 For the piping, cut enough bias strips (*see page 140*) to equal the width of the skirt when stitched together, plus an allowance for joining the ends.

Making up

5 Make up the piping (*see page 141*).

6 With right sides together and raw ends even, join the strips into a circle. Fold in half wrong sides together and top raw edges even; pin and press. Divide into sections as in step 5 of the previous instructions, running the rows of gathering stitches just above and below the seamline.

7 With right sides together and raw edges even, join the sides of the skirt rectangles together to make a circle. Attach the piping to the lower edge of the skirt, joining the ends neatly (*see page 141*).

8 Fold the skirt into four equal sections along its lower edge, marking each dividing point with two pins set close together as before. With right sides together and matching raw edges and pin markers, gather up the ruffle to fit the corresponding sections of the skirt. Stitch in place.

Fig 7

Remove the lower line of gathering stitches. Neaten seam allowances and press upwards (fig **7**).

9 Fold over 3.5 cm (1⅜ in) to the wrong side at the top of the skirt and press into position all round. Divide into four sections and run gathering stitches along the skirt top as before, making the lines of stitching 6 mm (¼ in) and 12 mm (½ in) down from the top fold.

10 Divide the circumference of the top piece in four with pins. With right sides uppermost and the fold of the skirt lined up with the top section seam allowance, gather up the skirt to fit the corresponding top sections. Pin and baste in place along the gathering stitches. Then topstitch just above each line of gathering stitches to set the skirt firmly in place. Remove the gathering/basting stitches (fig **8**).

11 Turn the tablecloth to the wrong side and neaten the raw edges at the top. Press.

SIMPLE RECTANGULAR TABLECLOTH

Measuring and cutting out

1 Measure across the table top both ways, from A to B and C to D (fig **9**). Now measure the drop you require, C to E, and add double this measurement plus 15 cm (6 in) for the hem to both A–B and C–D (fig **10**).

Making up

2 If the width of the rectangle amounts to more than the width of your fabric,

Fig 8

Fig 9

Fig 10

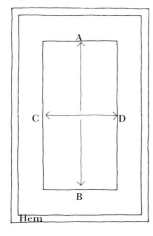

Hem

then widths have to be joined to make up the complete cloth, using flat fell seams (*see page 140*). See steps 2 to 4 of measuring and cutting for round tablecloths at the beginning of the section for details on calculating the amount of fabric you require and making up the basic cloth.

Turning up the hem

3 When you have cut out and/or made up your cloth, press 3 cm (1¼ in) to the wrong side along all edges. Turn in 3 cm (1¼ in) again and press to make a double hem.

4 Mitre the corners (*see page 141*). Baste the hem in place along the inner folded edge. With the right side of the cloth facing upwards, topstitch along the hem just inside the basting stitches. Press, and remove basting.

BEDCOVERINGS

LINED BEDSPREAD

You will need
Fabric
Lining
Tailor's chalk
Dinner plate

Measuring and cutting out

1 Measure the width, A–B, and length, C–D, of the bed with all the usual bedclothes and pillows in place. Allow for any tuck-under at the front and back edges of the pillows and add this allowance on to the length (fig **1a**).

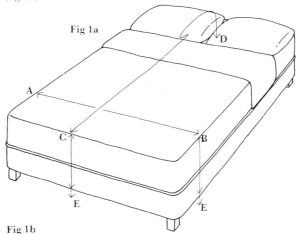

Fig 1a

Fig 1b

Half width | Full width | Half width

2 Measure the depth of the overhang at the sides, B–E. A bedspread usually reaches the floor, but if it is to be combined with a valance (dust ruffle), the bedspread should finish just below the valance (dust ruffle) top. Add the E–F measurement to C–D and double this amount to B–E. Then add a seam allowance of 1.5 cm (⅝ in) to all edges to obtain the total length and width measurements of the bedspread.

3 To cover anything but a very narrow bed, widths of fabric have to be joined down the long edges to make up the bed width. Joins on the cover should be set to either side of a central strip that runs the length of the bed (fig **1b**). Allow 1.5 cm (⅝ in) for seams. If possible, seams should be positioned at

the edges of the bed. Add the depth of one pattern repeat to the total amount required if matching patterns across seams (*see page 95, step 8*).

4 Cut out the required number of fabric and lining pieces to the correct size: one centre panel and two side sections in both fabric and lining if you are joining panels of fabric to make up the total bedspread width.

Making up

5 Make up the fabric and lining pieces if necessary. With right sides together and raw edges even, attach one side section to either side of the central panel. Press the seam allowances open.

6 Set the fabric over the lining with right sides together, matching raw edges and seams. Pin along edges.

7 Next round off the bottom edges of the bedspread if you wish. Position a dinner plate with its edges level with the raw edges of the fabric and lining (fig **2**). Draw round the plate with tailor's chalk and repeat at the other corner. Cut along the curved line.

8 Stitch all round the bedspread, taking a 1.5 cm (⅝ in) seam allowance and leaving a central gap of about 60 cm (24 in) at the top edge of the bedspread through which to turn (fig **2**). Trim the top corners and clip the curves at 1.5 cm (⅝ in) intervals. Turn and press.

9 Turn in opening edges in line with remainder of the seam and slipstitch (*see page 140*) to close.

FITTED AND PIPED BEDSPREAD WITH PILLOW GUSSETS AND KICK PLEATS

You will need
Fabric
Contrast fabric for the piping bias strips (*see page 140*)
Pre-shrunk piping cord
Pattern paper

Measuring and cutting out

1 Measure for this bedspread with the normal bedclothes and pillows in place. First measure the

Fig 2

Clip curve

Plate

width, A–B, and the length C–D. Measure the overhang C–E, and the length of the sides, F–G. Measure from H to I, beginning at the back edge of the bed and finishing 10 cm (4 in) beyond the front edge of the pillow (fig **3**). Finally measure the depth of the pillows, H–J.

2 Cut one piece of fabric for the bed top to the correct width and length, adding a 5 cm (2 in) hem allowance at the top end and 1.5 cm ($\frac{5}{8}$ in) to the three remaining edges for seams. You will not be able to cover the top of a made-up standard double bed with one width of 137 cm (54 in) wide fabric. In this case, position a panel of fabric down the centre of the cover with narrower panels set to either side (fig **3**). Extra fabric should be allowed for matching patterns across seams (*see page 95*, step 8).

3 Add twice the side measurement F–G to the width A–B. Cut enough skirt strips to equal this distance when joined, adding 10 cm (4 in) for side hems, 40.5 cm (16 in) for each pleat, and 1.5 cm ($\frac{5}{8}$ in) seam allowance for each end to be joined. The strip width should equal E–F plus 6.5 cm ($2\frac{5}{8}$ in). Allow extra fabric for pattern matching across seams if necessary.

4 Make a wedge-shaped paper pattern to the pillow gusset measurements, adding a seam allowance of 1.5 cm ($\frac{5}{8}$ in) all round. Cut two gusset pieces.

5 Cut enough contrast bias strips (*see page 140*) to cover the required length of piping cord when joined.

Making up

6 Make up (*see page 141*) enough covered piping to fit around the bed and gusset.

7 Round off the top outer corner of each gusset wedge. The rim of a small glass gives the right amount of curve. With raw edges even, pin the piping to the right side of the fabric along the top of each gusset around the curve and along the inner edge to the inner point. Push back the covering for 1.5 cm ($\frac{5}{8}$ in) at each end and cut away the cord, thus avoiding bulk in the seams. Baste.

8 With right sides together and raw edges even, stitch the pillow gussets to the top section of the bedspread, easing the fabric to fit and leaving 5 cm (2 in) free at the central section top edge for the hem (fig **4**).

9 Round off the bottom corners of the top section in the same way as for

the gussets. Pin the piping to the right side of the top section along the edges, starting at the back edge of one pillow gusset and continuing round to the back edge of the other. Trim away the cord for 1.5 cm ($\frac{5}{8}$ in) as in step 7 at each gusset back edge. Baste.

10 Join the skirt strips. Turn 2.5 cm (1 in) to the wrong side twice to make double hems along the side edges and base, folding mitred corners (*see page 141*). Hem by hand or machine in place.

11 With right sides together and raw edges even, lining up the skirt side with the gusset back seam allowance, begin pinning and basting the skirt to the top section over the piping cord. Fold an inverted pleat (fig **5**) at each corner at the bed base end. Stitch. Neaten seams (*see page 117*) and clip curves.

12 Turn under 2.5 cm (1 in) twice at the top of the bedspread to make a double hem. Hem by hand or machine in place.

13 Press the pleats and hems to finish.

LINED FITTED BEDSPREAD WITH PILLOW GUSSETS AND SCALLOPED EDGE

This bedspread is used with a valance (dust ruffle), the scalloped edge overlapping the valance (dust ruffle) top. The skirt has corner seams and each side section consists of two widths of fabric that have been joined to make up the length of the bed (about 200 cm/6 feet). Cut one full width and one half width strip for each side from 137 cm (54 in) wide fabric and trim to fit. The join should be positioned nearest the bed foot. Patterns should match across seams and line up around the bed if a fabric with a bold design has been used such as the one on page 55. Add the depth of three vertical pattern repeats to the total fabric amount to allow for this. (*See page 95 step 8.*)

If your fabric is not wide enough for you to cut the bedspread end in one piece, you can wrap the side pieces around the corners. In this

case position the side joins nearest the top of the bed so you can match the pattern across the seams at the end of the bed.

You will need
Fabric
Lining
Length of card from which to cut template

Measuring and cutting out

1 Measure the bed as in step 1 of the previous instructions. Follow steps 2 and 4 to cut out the top section and gusset pieces from both the fabric and lining, but allow 20 cm (8 in) at the top edge of the bed top section instead of 5 cm (2 in).

2 From the fabric cut the widths to make up each side section, following the notes given above. When joined, each side section should measure G–H plus 5 cm (2 in) for the side hem and 1.5 cm ($\frac{5}{8}$ in) for the corner seam. The depth should equal E–F plus 6.5 cm ($2\frac{5}{8}$ in). Cut one end section that measures A–B plus 3 cm ($1\frac{1}{4}$ in) by E–F plus 6.5 cm ($2\frac{5}{8}$ in). Repeat to cut out the lining pieces.

Making up

3 Taking the fabric pieces first, attach the pillow gussets to the top section as in step 8 of the previous instructions. Repeat to make up the lining pieces.

Join the skirt fabric pieces in the right order to make a continuous length, matching patterns across seams and taking a 1.5 cm ($\frac{5}{8}$ in) seam allowance. Repeat to join the skirt lining pieces. Press all seams open.

4 With right sides together lay the skirt fabric length over the lining, matching raw edges and seams. Baste together along the length about 10 cm (4 in) up from the bottom edge, keeping the bottom raw edges even.

5 Make a template for the scallops out of card First divide each side of the bedspread into equal sized scallops. Decide on the approximate width of the scallop and then divide the finished width of the bed-

Fig 3

Fig 4

5 cm free for hem

Clip curve

Piping

Fig 5

20 cm

10 cm   10 cm

Fig 6

Basting line

Card template.

Fig 7

Slipstitch

Basting line

Tuck-in flap

Lining (right side)

Fig 8

spread by this amount. Juggle with the width measurement until you end up with a round number. (It is more important to fit a round number of scallops into the width than it is the length.)

6 Make a card template for the scallops. Take a convenient length of card (eg four times the scallop length) a little wider than the proposed depth of your scallop and divide it into evenly sized shapes, drawing round a plate as a guide. Cut round the scallops.

7 Lining up the deepest part of the scallop curves with the skirt base edge, draw round template, working out from corner seams to mark scallops along entire base edge. Make sure a round number of scallops fits into bedspread width (fig 6).

8 Baste round the scallops just inside the marked line to hold. Stitch round the scallops, taking a 1.5 cm ($\frac{5}{8}$ in) hem allowance. Trim the seam allowances to 1 cm ($\frac{3}{8}$ in). Clip into the seam allowances at the points of the scallops to ease, and along the curved edges.

9 Join the fabric and lining lengths at both ends, taking a 1.5 cm ($\frac{5}{8}$ in) seam allowance. Turn to the right side and press. With raw edges even, pin the fabric and lining together along the top to hold.

10 With right sides together and raw edges even, baste the lined skirt to the fabric top section, matching side edges and corners to the appropriate seamlines. Stitch. Press the seam allowances upwards.

11 With right sides together and raw edges even, join the lining to the top section along the three edges of the 20 cm (8 in) top flap, taking a 1.5 cm ($\frac{5}{8}$ in) seam allowance.

12 Turn the lining to the wrong side of the bedspread, matching seams. Baste the lining in position along the bedspread top about 5 cm (2 in) in from the sides (fig 7). At each side stitch around the curved edge of the gusset through all thicknesses about 3 mm ($\frac{1}{8}$ in) from the seam. Turn under 1.5 cm ($\frac{5}{8}$ in) along the lining raw edges and slipstitch (*see page 140*) to the skirt along the seamline, enclosing the raw edges of the top section and skirt.

PATCHWORK BEDSPREAD WITH DIAGONAL QUILTING

This bedspread is much simpler to make than it looks. The most time-consuming element is the quilting. The patchwork is quilted by stitching it to a layer of wadding (batting) backed with muslin; its edges wrap round to the underside of the wadding layer which is lined. Allowance must be made for shrinkage when quilting as the rows of

stitches draw the fabric into the wadding (batting). A rough guide when using 4 oz wadding (medium loft batting) is to allow 2.5 cm (1 in) for shrinkage for every 30 cm (12 in) of fabric/wadding (batting)/lining, and it is better to err on the generous side. The finished patchwork squares in these instructions measure 8 cm by 8 cm ($3\frac{1}{4}$ in by $3\frac{1}{4}$ in).

You will need

Cotton lawn (percale) or equivalent lightweight fabric in five different prints
Lining
4 oz washable synthetic wadding (medium loft batting or polyester fiberfill quilt batt)
Lightweight muslin for backing
Matching or contrast thread for quilting
Metre/yard stick
Tailor's chalk

Measuring and cutting out

1 Measure for the bedspread as explained in lined bedspread steps 1 and 2, omitting the seam allowances.

2 Calculate how many 8 cm by 8 cm ($3\frac{1}{4}$ in by $3\frac{1}{4}$ in) squares will be needed to make up the bedspread. Add on two extra rows (more if you are making a very large bedspread) of patches at each side to allow for turn-under and shrinkage. Divide this amount by five to find out how many squares in each print you need. Next add on a seam allowance of 1 cm ($\frac{3}{8}$ in) all round the square for joins, giving a cutting dimension of 10 cm by 10 cm (4 in by 4 in). You will be able to fit 9 squares across 90 cm (36 in) wide fabric. Calculate how many rows of squares you need in each print

and multiply by 10 cm (4 in) to obtain the length of fabric required. Skip step 3 if using a quilt batt.

3 If necessary, cut enough widths of wadding (batting) to make up the total finished width of the patchwork when joined minus 1 row of squares at each side. (Wadding (batting) is usually 90 cm/36 in wide.) The length of each wadding (batting) width should measure the total finished length of the patchwork minus 1 row of squares at each end. The long edges are butted together and secured with herringbone stitches (see step 6), so there is no need to include a seam allowance for joins.

4 Cut the muslin to the same dimensions as the wadding (batting) lengths. The lining should be cut when you have completed the quilting.

Making up

5 Begin joining the squares into long strips measuring the length of the bedspread. Attach the squares in random order to give the quilt this effect when it is made up. Make up enough strips to obtain the bedspread width when joined together. Press the seams open and attach the strip lengths to each other down the long edges until you have built up the bedspread width. Try not to put two of the same print squares together. Press the seams (fig 8). Skip step 6 if using a quilt batt.

6 Butt the long edges of the wadding (batting) lengths against each other.

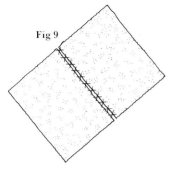

Fig 9

Herringbone stitch (see page 139) together across the gap down the back and front of the wadding (batting) to join, taking largish stitches (fig **9**).

7 Lay the patchwork out flat with the right side uppermost. Using the metre/yard stick and tailor's chalk mark a diagonal line from corner to corner. Working out from the centre, continue marking parallel diagonal lines 2.5 cm (1 in) apart until you have covered the bedspread. Draw a diagonal line to join the remaining corners and mark across the bedspread in the same way to form a diagonal grid.

8 Set the wadding (batting) centrally against the wrong side of the patchwork and lay the muslin over the top. Pin together, starting in the middle and working outwards. Baste across and down the bedspread at 15 cm (6 in) intervals, then baste diagonally across at the same intervals.

9 Make up a small sandwich of fabric, wadding (batting) and muslin backing. Using this as a test piece, stitch a few rows of quilting to check the tension of your machine and ascertain the most suitable stitch length.

10 Machine stitch along the diagonal lines through all layers to quilt the patchwork.

11 Turn the unstitched border of squares to the back of the bedspread, folding mitred corners (see page 141). Pin and then herringbone stitch loosely to the wadding (batting) and backing to secure.

12 Next cut out the lining. This should equal the square/rectangle of wadding (batting) and backing showing on the underside of the bed-

spread plus an allowance of 5 cm (2 in) all round. Join lengths of fabric if necessary to make up the overall width (see lined bedspread, step 3), taking a 1.5 cm ($\frac{5}{8}$ in) seam allowance. Press under the edges of the lining by 2.5 cm (1 in) all round.

13 With the bedspread laid out flat, the back uppermost, mark parallel lines down the unlined wadding (batting) backing section about 30 cm (12 in) apart, beginning at the bedspread centre and working outwards. Place the lining centrally over this unlined area and lockstitch (see page 140) it in place down the marked rows (see page 98, step 7), working from the centre outwards and beginning and ending the stitching 2.5 cm (1 in) from the patchwork edges.

14 Slipstitch (see page 140) the lining to the patchwork all round the edges.

PATCHWORK BEDSPREAD

This patchwork bedspread has a double border and is made up of 25 cm by 5 cm (10 in by 2 in) rectangles (finished dimensions) randomly arranged in sets of five different prints that are stitched together to form a 25 cm by 25 cm (10 in by 10 in) square. The outer border is 15 cm (6 in) wide and the inner 7.5 cm (3 in) wide. The bedspread can be quilted, following the previous instructions (see step 13 below for details). As there are very few lines of quilting stitches no allowance need be made for shrinkage. The bedspread is lined.

You will need
Cotton lawn (percale) in five
   different prints
Lining
For optional quilting: 4 oz
   washable synthetic wadding
   (medium loft batting or
   polyester fiberfill quilt batt)
Lightweight muslin backing,
   matching or contrasting
   thread for quilting

Measuring and cutting out
1 Measure for the bedspread as explained in steps 1 and 2 of the lined bedspread instructions (see page 125), omitting to add the seam allowance.

2 Subtract twice the total width of the two borders from the bedspread length and width dimensions to obtain the dimensions of the patchwork section. Calculate how many 25 cm by 25 cm (10 in by 10 in) squares will fit into this section. As you are unlikely to obtain a round number, you can either round up or down to make the bedspread slightly larger or smaller or change the rectangle or border size to fit.

3 Add 1 cm ($\frac{3}{8}$ in) seam allowance all round the rectangle dimensions to give a cutting dimension of 27 cm by 7 cm ($10\frac{3}{4}$ in by $2\frac{3}{4}$ in). Calculate how many rectangles will fit lengthways across your chosen fabric width. Divide the total rectangle amount required in one print by this number to find the number of rows of rectangles you need and multiply this by the rectangle width to get the total amount of fabric needed. (For example: 144 squares means you need 144 rectangles in one of the five prints. Three 27 cm by 7 cm ($10\frac{3}{4}$ in by $2\frac{3}{4}$ in) rectangles fit lengthways into a width of 90 cm (36 in) fabric. 14 divided by 3 equals 48 rows. 48 times 7 cm ($2\frac{3}{4}$ in) equals 336 cm/132 in). Cut the required amount of rectangles to the correct size.

4 For the inner border panel cut two strips of 9.5 cm ($3\frac{3}{4}$ in) wide fabric measuring the length of the inner patchwork section plus 19 cm ($7\frac{1}{2}$ in) and mark them A. Cut another two 9.5 cm ($3\frac{3}{4}$ in) wide strips measuring the width of the bedspread plus 19 cm ($7\frac{1}{2}$ in) and mark them B. For the outer border panel cut two strips of 17 cm ($6\frac{3}{4}$ in) wide fabric measuring the length of one of an A strip plus 34 cm ($13\frac{1}{2}$ in). In the same fabric cut another two 17 cm ($6\frac{3}{4}$ in) wide strips measuring the length of a B strip plus 34 cm ($13\frac{1}{2}$ in).

5 Cut the lining to the finished bedspread dimensions plus 1 cm ($\frac{3}{8}$ in) seam allowance all round.

6 If you are quilting the bedspread cut the wadding (batting) and backing to

the finished dimensions of the bedspread leaving off the seam allowance. (See steps 3 and 6 of the previous instructions if you need to join widths of wadding (batting) to gain the full width of the bedspread.)

Making up
7 With right sides together and raw edges even, randomly attach the fabric rectangles along the long edges to form sets of five, taking a 1 cm ($\frac{3}{8}$ in) seam allowance.

8 Make up these five-rectangle squares into a strip measuring the desired length of the patchwork section, placing the squares so that the rectangles alternate horizontally and vertically (fig **10**).

9 Continue making strips until you have enough to make up the width of the patchwork section. Be careful to begin each strip with the rectangles placed in the opposite direction to those at the beginning of the previous strip, so that the sets of rectangles will alternate vertically and horizontally across the bedspread as well as down the length. Press the seams open. Join the strips together down the long edges, taking a 1 cm ($\frac{3}{8}$ in) seam allowance. Press. Set the patchwork section aside.

10 Next join the inner border strips at the corners to make a square/rectangle. At each end of each strip fold up the short raw edge to the opposite long raw edge and press (fig **11**). Unfold and cut along the crease line.

11 Take the strips and place the angled edges together, raw edges even, right sides facing. (Make sure you place them in the appropriate order if you are stitching a rectangle.) Stitch across the ends, leaving 1 cm ($\frac{3}{8}$ in) unstitched at the inner and outer corner (fig **12**). Repeat this process with the outer border strips, leaving 1 cm ($\frac{3}{8}$ in) unstitched at the inner corners only.

12 With raw edges even and right sides together join the inner border to the

Fig 10

Fig 11

90°

Fold line

45°

Fig 12

RUFFLED VALANCE (DUST RUFFLE)

A cheap lining fabric is used for the section concealed under the mattress.

You will need
Fabric for valance (dust ruffle)
Lining fabric for bed top section

Measuring and cutting out

[1] Measure the bed without the bedding or mattress in place. For the top section measure the width A–B and the length C–D of the bed top adding 1.5 cm ($\frac{5}{8}$ in) seam allowance to the bottom and sides of the section and 2.5 cm (1 in) for turn-under at the top (fig 13). Cut one piece of lining fabric to these measurements. See lined bedspread instructions, step 3 if your bed top

outer border, taking a 1 cm ($\frac{3}{8}$ in) seam allowance. Next attach the complete border to the patchwork section. Press seam allowances open.

[13] At this stage quilt the bedspread if desired (see steps 8 to 9 of the previous instructions). Instead of sewing diagonal lines of quilting stitches, machine slightly to one side of the main vertical and horizontal seamlines joining the squares to form a 25 cm by 25 cm (10 in by 10 in) grid.

[14] Stitch round the outer edge of the patchwork section. Stitch to one side of the inner/outer border seam along all sides. Stitch along all edges of outer border 2 cm ($\frac{3}{4}$ in) from raw edges.

[15] With right sides together and raw edges even, attach the lining to the bedspread top following steps 8 and 9 of the lined bedspread instructions. If you have quilted the bedspread make sure there is no wadding (batting) included in the seam.

is wider than the width of your fabric.

[2] To calculate the finished length of the valance (dust ruffle) multiply the bed length measurement C–D by four and add twice the width A–B. Cut enough strips of fabric, measuring the depth plus 3.5 cm ($1\frac{3}{8}$ in), to equal the finished width when joined, allowing 1.5 cm ($\frac{5}{8}$ in) for seams. Allow extra fabric to match patterns across seams if necessary (*see page 95, step 8*).

Making up

[3] Make up the top section if necessary. Curve the corners using the rim of a small glass as a guide. At the top of the section press 6 mm ($\frac{1}{4}$ in) to the wrong side. Turn under 2 cm ($\frac{3}{4}$ in) again and stitch across close to the inner folded edge of the fabric.

[4] Join the valance (dust ruffle) strips and press the seams open. At each end of the valance (dust ruffle) turn under the same hem as at the top of the lining section. At the base edge turn 1 cm ($\frac{3}{8}$ in) to the wrong side twice to make a double hem. Press. Hem by hand or machine in place close to the inner folded edge.

[5] Measure twice C–D from each end of the valance (dust ruffle) and mark these distances on the valance (dust ruffle) seam allowance with two pins set close together. Divide each of the resultant three sections in half and mark on the seam allowance with two pins.

[6] Next mark the sides and bottom of the top lining section halfway along the edges.

[7] Gather the valance (dust ruffle) between each set

of pin markers, sewing two lines of gathering stitches 6 mm ($\frac{1}{4}$ in) apart either side of the seamline (*see page 140*).

[8] With right sides together, raw ends even, and matching corresponding pins, pin the valance (dust ruffle) to the top section at the pin dividers and gather up the fabric evenly in between. Baste to hold. Stitch all round the valance (dust ruffle), taking a 1.5 cm ($\frac{5}{8}$ in) seam allowance.

[9] Neaten the seam allowances (*see page 117*) and press away from top section.

SPLIT VALANCE (DUST RUFFLE) WITH CONTRAST-BORDERED TOP

This valance (dust ruffle) is a suitable compromise when the outer edges of the section that goes under the mattress would be on view but you don't want to waste expensive fabric covering the whole bed top. The border is 15 cm (6 in) wide.

You will need
Fabric for valance (dust ruffle)
Contrast fabric (optional) for top section border
Lining fabric for top section

Measuring and cutting out

[1] Measure for the top section as in step 1 of the previous instructions. Deduct 15 cm (6 in) from the length measurement and 30 cm (12 in) from the width. Add 1.5 cm seam allowance to the side and bottom edges and 2 cm ($\frac{3}{4}$ in) to the top (fig **14a**).

[2] Cut two 18 cm ($7\frac{1}{4}$ in) wide border strips that measure C–D plus 5 cm (2 in) and 1.5 cm ($\frac{5}{8}$ in) seam allowance. Cut one 18 cm ($7\frac{1}{4}$ in) wide border strip that measures the width A–B plus 3 cm ($1\frac{1}{4}$ in).

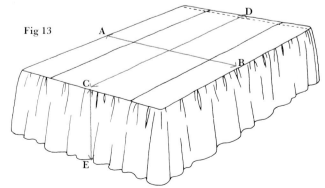

Fig 13 A D B C E

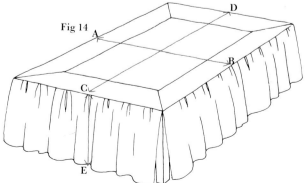

Fig 14 A D B C E

3 For each valance (dust ruffle) side width cut enough fabric strips, measuring a width of C–E plus 3.5 cm ($1\frac{3}{8}$ in), to equal twice C–D when joined. Allow 1.5 cm ($\frac{5}{8}$ in) at each strip end for joins. Cut enough same width strips to equal A–B when joined.

Making up

4 Join the three border strips as in steps 9 and 10 of patchwork bedspread instructions, taking 1.5 cm ($\frac{5}{8}$ in) seam allowance, leaving 1.5 cm ($\frac{5}{8}$ in) unstitched at bottom inner corners.

5 Right sides together, raw edges even, join border to centre section. Turn 1 cm ($\frac{3}{8}$ in) to the wrong side twice at top of the centre section to make a double hem. Stitch across the top close to inner folded edge.

6 Join strips to make up side and bed end sections of the valance (dust ruffle). Turn under 1 cm ($\frac{3}{8}$ in) twice to make double hems at the ends of each valance (dust ruffle) section. Press. Hem by hand or machine stitch. Turn under 1 cm ($\frac{3}{8}$ in) twice along base of each section. Press and stitch.

7 Divide each valance (dust ruffle) section in half and mark on the seam allowance with two pins set close together. Gather and attach the valance as in steps 6 to 9 of the previous instructions, matching the splits in the valance (dust ruffle) with the top section corners.

8 At the corner splits slip-stitch (*see page 140*) the edges together for 1.5 cm ($\frac{5}{8}$ in) down from the valance (dust ruffle) top to neaten.

FITTED QUILTED BEDSPREAD WITH CONTRAST PIPING
(single bed size)

This bedspread overlaps the top of the valance (dust ruffle). The pattern has been picked out with quilting stitches.

You will need

Fabric
Lining for top section
Contrast fabric for piping bias strips (*see page 140*)

Pre-shrunk piping cord
4 oz washable synthetic wadding (medium loft batting or polyester fiberfill quilt batt)
Lightweight muslin backing for wadding (batting)
Matching or contrasting thread for quilting

Measuring and cutting out

1 Measure the length and width of the bed with its normal bedding in place (fig **15**). To the length measurement C–D add 20 cm (8 in) for tuck-in at the top of the bed plus 1.5 cm ($\frac{5}{8}$ in) seam allowance and 20 cm (8 in) to allow for shrinkage while quilting (see the introduction of patchwork bedspread with diagonal quilting). To width add 3 cm ($1\frac{1}{4}$ in) for seams plus 15 cm (6 in) shrinkage allowance.

2 Read through paragraph one of the introduction to the lined fitted bedspread with scalloped edge instructions. You may wish to cut the side sections on the length of the fabric. Whichever way you choose to cut the fabric, the side sections should measure the depth C–E plus 12 cm (5 in) hem, seam and quilting shrinkage allowance by the length C–D plus 25 cm (10 in) side hem, seam and shrinkage allowance. Cut one end piece to measure the depth C–E plus 15 cm (6 in) by the width A–B plus 23 cm (9 in) seam and shrinkage allowance.

3 Cut the one piece of wadding (batting) and one piece of backing to the dimensions of the bed top piece. You may have to join lengths of wadding (batting) to gain the width of the bedspread top. See page 127 step 3 for details. Cut the wadding (batting) and backing side and end sections to the same dimensions as the fabric sections.

4 Cut the lining to the dimensions of the bed top section minus 15 cm (6 in) on the width and 20 cm (8 in) on the length.

5 For each pleat cut a rectangle of fabric measuring 44 cm ($17\frac{1}{4}$ in) wide by C–E plus 6.5 cm ($2\frac{5}{8}$ in) long.

6 Cut enough contrast bias strips to cover the piping cord when joined.

Making up

7 To attach the backing and wadding (batting) to each fabric piece follow steps 8 and 9 of the patchwork quilt with diagonal quilting.

8 Decide on the areas of the print you wish to feature, then beginning with a side skirt section stitch around the flowers, leaves and stalks, starting at the centre of the piece of fabric and working outwards. At the end of a section of pattern leave enough thread to be pulled through to the inside and tied off invisibly. Repeat to quilt each section.

9 When the quilting has been completed remove the basting and cut each piece to the correct size, following the measurements given above MINUS the shrinkage allowances. Curve

Fig 16

Unquilted pleat section

Fig 15

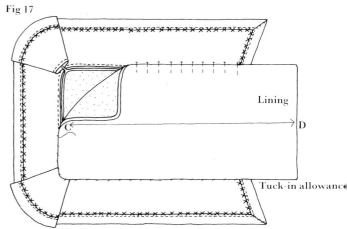

A

C

D

B

E

Fig 17

the bottom corners of the top section using the rim of a small glass to give a neat outline. Next trim the wadding (batting) from the hem and seam allowances.

10 With right sides together and raw edges even, join one kick pleat section to a side section at the bottom end, and to the end piece at the other side, taking a 1.5 cm ($\frac{5}{8}$ in) seam allowance. Repeat, to join the other pleat section. Press the seam allowances flat on to each main section.

11 Neaten (*see page 117*) the side and base edges of the skirt/pleat strip and then turn under a 5 cm (2 in) hem, mitring the outer corners (*see page 141*). Herringbone stitch (*see page 139*) the side and base hem to the wadding (batting) all round the bedspread to secure.

12 Bring each pleat seam-line so that it meets in the middle of the pleat allowance, forming a 10 cm (4 in) fold at either side (fig **16**). Pin, then baste across the pleat to hold. Press.

Lining

D

C

Tuck-in allowance

[13] Make up enough covered piping (*see page 141*) to go round the bed as indicated in fig **15**. With raw edges even baste it to the right side of the top section around three edges.

[14] With raw edges even and right sides together attach the lining to the edges of the tuck-in allowance. Clip across the corners and turn the lining to the inside. Press.

[15] With raw edges even and right sides together pin and baste the skirt to the top section, positioning a pleat at each bottom corner. Stitch, using the zipper foot on the machine. Press the seam allowances upwards and clip the corner curves.

[16] Turn under 1.5 cm ($\frac{5}{8}$ in) along the edges of the lining and slipstitch (*see page 140*) it to the skirt/top section seamline to secure (fig **17**). Press.

LINED BEDSPREAD WITH QUILTED DRAGON PANELS

This bedspread makes very creative use of Opium from the East India collection, available in 137 cm (54 in) width. The finished length of the bedspread is 265 cm (104 in) and the width 233 cm (91$\frac{1}{2}$ in). It is made of two separate halves joined together down the centre of the bedspread and bound at top and bottom to finish (fig **18**).

You will need

Fabric equal to twice the quilt length plus 53 cm (21 in) for quilting shrinkage (see introduction to patchwork bedspread with diagonal quilting), 6 cm (2$\frac{1}{2}$ in) for seams, and a pattern repeat allowance (see page 95, step 8) plus 80 cm (31$\frac{1}{2}$ in) for top and bottom binding. The stripes and border from this section are pieced together for the correct binding length, and main panels used for matching cushions.

Lining fabric to the same length as the fabric minus the pattern repeat allowance and binding allowance. (Here Suki from the East India Collection has been used.)

4 oz washable synthetic wadding (medium loft batting or polyester fiberfill quilt batt)

Measuring and cutting out

[1] Cut out the top fabric, firstly dividing it into two equal lengths, then closely following figs **18** and **19**, showing the cutting lines along the stripes. Set aside the central border strip not needed now, since this will form the backing strip for the top and bottom binding.

Making up

[2] Taking one cut length, set each cut stripe section, all right sides uppermost, against its neighbour as shown in figs **18** and **19**, folding seam allowances of between 0.5 cm ($\frac{1}{4}$ in) and 1 cm ($\frac{3}{8}$ in) to the inside, and pin and baste into position. Edgestitch from top to bottom (fig **20**,) down each join.

[3] Repeat step 2 for the other cut length of top fabric, then matching up the print repeat of each dragon with the stitched half-cover, trim away superfluous fabric to create two equal halves of the cover. Do not trim away selvedges, since these will form valuable seam allowances at a later stage.

[4] Cut the wadding (batting) into two equal lengths and set behind each top half of the bedspread, which should now measure a width of 119 cm (46$\frac{3}{4}$ in) inclusive of seam allowances at centre and selvedge. Match up the outside edges of both wadding (batting) and top fabric, allowing it to extend beyond the fabric at the centre of each half cover. This extension will be lapped and joined later on. Pin temporarily into position, working from the centre outwards, then set one lining length behind the wadding (batting), wrong side to wadding (batting), so that the wadding (batting) forms a sandwich centre between the two layers of fabric. Match outside edges of wadding (batting) and lining fabric, and leave inner, central side untrimmed.

[5] Now pin, then baste into position at 10 cm (4 in) intervals, across and down each half cover, starting in the centre and working outwards until the whole length of each piece is set lightly into position. Then baste each half cover dia-

Fig 18

Fig 19

Turn and attach raw edge to selvedge

Fig 20   Half cover

gonally at the same intervals. (This is time-consuming, but if it is not done as described, the danger of fabric moving during stitching process increases; the cover will be lumpy and uneven, and the pattern will not match.)

[6] To quilt, firstly stitch a small leftover sample of the thicknesses together to check tension and a medium stitch length. Now begin with one half cover by firstly stitching down each side of the 6-stripe panels, along the edge of each outer stripe, working from the centre, first down and then up, to each

raw edge, and through all thicknesses. Do not stitch the outer stripe on each side of the half cover. Repeat for the other half cover.

[7] For the dragon panels, follow the print lines of each dragon, beginning with the central one, and starting at his head, stitch around his flames, teeth, front foot and claws and continue down the body, stitching around each important part of the print. Complete the stitching up his back and around the feet and claws, to finish where you began. Pull threads to the lining side and neaten. Repeat

Edgestitch

Lining

Basting line

Fig 21

for each dragon, then stitch around outside of each cloud, neatening ends.

8 Repeat for the other half cover, then remove all basting stitches.

9 To join the two halves of the quilt, lay them right sides uppermost, flat in front of you, then fold under a seam allowance at the centre of the left half cover of both top and lining fabric edges to the wrong side. Trim the wadding (batting) in the middle of the left half cover to come even with the folded edges, then wrapping the top fabric over the wadding's (batting's) raw edge, baste each fold into position from top to bottom. Make sure the fold line of the top fabric is basted so that it will exactly follow the stripe pattern of two sets of three stripes each, with a small gap in the middle, when joined to the other side. Leave right half cover unfolded.

10 On the right half cover, trim the wadding (batting) to the same width as the unfolded edges, then baste top and lining fabric and wadding (batting), together. Turning back the basted edges of the left half cover out of the way, insert the right half cover's basted edge into the left half cover's centre, setting the folded edges of the left half cover over and under the right half cover, to enclose it. Now with stripe pattern in place on top of the cover, pin, then baste the two halves together, enclosing raw edges and basting into position close to the folded edges and through all thicknesses, making sure both

folded edges are included in the basting line. Edgestitch from top to bottom. See fig 21.

11 At each side of the joined bedspread, fold under the top to the wrong side along the outside edge of the stripe panel, then trim the wadding (batting) to the same width as the folded line. Unfold the top fabric and refold, wrapping over the wadding's (batting's) raw edge and baste into position. Fold under lining fabric equal to the fold of the top fabric, then baste both fabrics together. Edgestitch from top to bottom, and repeat for the other side.

12 To 'top and tail' the bedspread with the striped binding, cut widths of stripe from the 80 cm (31⅜ in) length of fabric set aside, allowing 1 cm (⅜ in) seam allowances on each side. Join these strips, matching stripes, right sides together, to equal two lengths of the width of the bedspread, plus seam allowances of 3 cm (1¼ in). Cut similar strips from the left-over central border of top fabric. Press seam allowances open.

13 Join one stripe to one border strip, right sides together along one long edge, and stitch from end to end, taking a 1 cm (⅜ in) seam allowance. Press seam allowances open, then fold under 1 cm (⅜ in) at remaining raw edges of the binding strip thus formed, to the wrong side, and wrap over the raw edge of the top of the cover, stripe to topside, border print to lining underside, so that raw edges are enclosed and butt up to the seamline joining the two sections of binding together. Baste into position along the edges of the folds, including underneath folded edge in the basting line, and tucking under seam allowances at each end, to the inside. Edgestitch all the way along, through all thicknesses and round short ends to close. Repeat for bottom of quilt to finish.

MISCELLANEOUS

GATHERED TENTED CEILING

This tented ceiling is not what it seems. It has been gathered to the centre top of a mirrored wall, rather than to the middle of a room, but the reflection of the half ceiling in the mirror gives the illusion of a complete ceiling and a room that is twice the size. The following instructions are for a complete tented ceiling as it is unlikely that most people will have the requisite mirrored wall to make the half version effective. A fabric fullness of two and a half times the total length of the walls was allowed to tent the ceiling on page 70, but one and a half times the wall length will still produce a very attractive result. A vast amount of fabric is required—in the example photographed the room, which is about 3½ metres (12 ft) square, took over 33 metres (36 yards) of fabric.

You will need
Fabric
Four 2 cm by 4 cm (¾ in by 1½ in) wooden battens the length of each wall
Four 12 mm by 3 cm (½ in by 1¼ in) wooden battens the same length as above
Three 3 cm by 6 mm (1¼ in by ¼ in) wooden fillets the same length as above
20 cm (8 in) square wooden ceiling block 2.5 cm (1 in) deep
Screws (including fine screws and ceiling screws), plastic wall plugs, and panel pins
Staple gun
Fabric glue
15.5 cm (6¼ in) diameter heavy cardboard circle
Someone to help you attach the tent

Measuring, cutting out and fixing the wall battens

1 Locate the centre of the ceiling, making sure there is a joist there and checking the position of the wiring. Attach the wooden block centrally to the ceiling at this point. Drill holes across the centre of the block about 5 cm (2 in) apart, then mark and drill corresponding holes in the joist. Insert wall plugs and screw the batten into place.

2 If your room is square measure the length of one of the walls from corner to corner, and the distance from the corner to centre of the wooden block (fig 1). If your room is rectangular, measure the length of one long and one short wall as well as the distance from the corner to the centre of the wooden block.

3 *For a square room* multiply the wall length by the fabric fullness you require; here 2½ times the length. Divide by the width of your chosen fabric and round up to the nearest width. Multiply this number by the length of the DIAGONAL to find the total amount of fabric you need to cover one wall section of the ceiling and by four to obtain the grand total. *For a rectangular room* repeat these calculations for one short and one long wall, add the two together and multiply by two to obtain the grand total. For each width of fabric required add 15 cm (6 in) to the total length for batten turn-under allowances. If matching patterns, allow 1 pattern repeat measurement per width, minus the first width, adding this calculation to the total.

4 Cut the number of fabric lengths required. Each length should measure the length of the diagonal plus 15 cm (6 in), and separate the number needed for each wall section into four piles.

5 Attach the four thicker battens to the walls with their top edges about 1.5 cm (⅝ in) from the ceiling, mitring their corners to fit. Drill holes at equal, 30 cm (12 in) intervals along the wall, insert wall plugs, mark off and drill corresponding holes along the centre of the battens, then screw them into place.

Making up

6 Beginning with one pile of fabric widths, join them together down the long edges to make one giant width, taking 1.5 cm (⅝ in) seam allowances. Repeat for

—132—

each pile of fabric widths until you have four giant widths of fabric. Leaving the selvedge free for overlap at either side, run two rows of largish gathering stitches along the wall top edge of each fabric section, about 2 cm ($\frac{3}{4}$ in) and 3 cm ($1\frac{1}{4}$ in) from the edge, breaking the gathering at convenient intervals, with one of the breaks positioned at the centre of the section.

7 Take one fabric section and gather it up to fit the wall roughly. Next set the fabric against the batten, matching the marked centre point to the centre of the batten length. The right side of the fabric should be set against the batten and the raw edges lined up with the batten top. Set each outer edge of the section tight into the corner and staple, first folding the selvedge to the wrong side. Be careful not to staple too close to the lower edge of the batten or the wood will split. Working from the wall centre outwards continue stapling the

Fig 1

Length
Diagonal — Ceiling block

Fig 2

Staple

Wrong side of fabric

fabric to the batten, adjusting the gathers evenly (fig **2**).

8 Repeat on the other walls. All four walls should now have a section of gathered fabric dangling down from the batten, wrong sides facing, ready to be attached to the wooden block at the centre of the ceiling.

9 To secure each fabric section firmly, attach the thinner battens to the first battens over the fabric, lining up base edges and mitring corners (fig **3**). Use finer screws to secure these battens, positioning them at 15 cm (6 in) intervals.

10 With your helper standing by to hold the fabric, begin attaching one fabric section to the centre block, folding even pleats and pulling the fabric so that it is taut but not too tightly stretched as shown in the photograph on page 70. Staple the pleats into position as you work, flat against the wooden block, trimming the excess fabric and working to within 2.5 cm

(1 in) of the centre of the block and not further outwards from this point than 6 cm/2$\frac{1}{2}$ in (fig **4**). Repeat, to attach the other fabric sections to the wooden block. Make sure there is no gap visible along the diagonal edges where the fabric sections meet.

11 From the trimmed fabric cut a circle 20 cm (8 in) in diameter. Cover the circular piece of card, overlapping the edges evenly and clipping the seam allowances. Stick it to the underside of the cardboard with glue (fig **5**). Baste round the edges if possible.

12 While this is drying, make up the choux (the ruffled rose-shaped object set in the middle of the tented ceiling). From the trimmed fabric cut a circle four times the diameter of the glued smaller fabric circle. Run two lines of gathering stitches around the outside of the circle and draw up the gathers tightly, stitching them flat by hand to secure. The circle of fabric formed will now be twice the diameter you require.

13 Gather and tuck the fabric into ruffled ridges by stabbing the needle and thread through the fabric both vertically and sideways at intervals. The choux should look artfully ruffled rather than mangled when finished, so don't overdo the stabbing.

14 Position the covered cardboard piece against the ceiling block, centrally over the stapled edges of the fabric. Attach with panel pins. Stitch the finished choux to the fabric circle or staple unobtrusively in place.

15 Check the length of the fillets along the underside of the battens, mitring the corners to fit. Cover each fillet with a strip of fabric, wrapping it round the fillet to the back, and overlapping edges (fig **6**). Glue or staple to secure the fabric.

16 Secure each covered fillet in position, flat against the underneath of the battening, butting it up

Fig 3
Cut-away diagram to show layers

Fig 4

Staples

Fig 5

Fig 6

against the wall, so that no wood can be seen. Secure with panel pins evenly spaced along the underside of each fillet.

GATHERED FABRIC WALLS

The fabric covering the angled wall on page 72 has a casing at the top and bottom through which wooden poles are slotted. The third pole, which holds the fabric against the wall angle, has been slotted through a channel stitched halfway down to the back of the fabric. Since the fabric is unlined, two and a half times the width of the wall has been allowed for fullness (see Headings, page 94). If you are using a boldly patterned fabric you may wish to match patterns across seams, even though the covering is very gathered. Extra fabric should therefore be allowed for this. *See page 95, step 8 for details.*

You will need

Fabric

Three (two if you are covering an ordinary wall) wooden poles the length of the wall

Brackets to hold the poles

Heavy cord

Measuring and cutting out

1 Fix the poles in position, making sure they can be removed again when attaching the wall covering.

2 Using the cord, measure from just underneath the top pole to the top of the centre pole. Depending on the slant of the wall add a small amount of drape. Note this measurement. Now measure from just beneath the centre pole to just above the bottom one and add this distance to the previous measurement.

3 To the overall length add the pole circumference measurement plus 9 cm ($3\frac{1}{2}$ in) for each casing (at the top and bottom). If you are making a covering for an angled wall add half the pole circumference plus 12 mm ($\frac{1}{2}$ in) to the length. Multiply the number of fabric widths required to cover the wall to find the amount of fabric you need.

4 Cut the required number of widths to the required length.

5 Cut strips of fabric for the centre pole channel that will measure the finished width of the wall covering when joined plus 3 cm ($1\frac{1}{4}$ in). Each strip should measure a width of half the pole circumference plus 4.5 cm ($1\frac{3}{4}$ in).

Making up

6 With right sides together and edges even, join the wall-covering widths, taking a 1.5 cm ($\frac{5}{8}$ in) seam allowance. Press seams open.

7 At each outer edge of the covering turn under 6 mm ($\frac{1}{4}$ in) to the wrong side and press. Turn under a further 1.5 cm ($\frac{5}{8}$ in). Press. Stitch from top to bottom, close to the inner folded edge.

8 At the top of the covering fold over half the pole circumference plus 4.5 cm ($1\frac{3}{4}$ in) to the wrong side.

Press. Turn under 1.5 cm ($\frac{5}{8}$ in) along the long raw edge of the fabric. Press. Stitch across the covering close to the inner folded edge.

9 Measure half the pole circumference plus 12 mm ($\frac{1}{2}$ in) up from this stitching line and stitch across the covering again at this level to form a casing for the pole. Repeat to make a casing for the bottom pole.

10 Make up the channel strip and press open seams. Fold under 1.5 cm ($\frac{5}{8}$ in) along all the edges of the channel strip and press. Stitch across the end to hold.

11 Next lay the covering flat, wrong side uppermost, and measuring from just beneath the lower stitching line of the top casing, mark the top of the centre pole, as previously noted at the side of the covering. Chalk a straight line across the covering at this level to mark the position for the channel top.

12 Lining up the top edge of the channel strip with the chalk line, pin the strip flat to the covering back along both long edges. Stitch in place close to folded edges.

13 Thread each of the poles, adjusting the gathering, and hang the covering in place.

QUILTED MOSES BASKET (BASSINET) WITH MATCHING COVERLET

This pretty covered basket has quilted sides, an unpadded base over which the mattress is set, a deep ruffle at the sides with openings for the handles, and an elasticized rim strip to hold the cover in place.

You will need

Cotton lawn (percale) (Tana lawn can be bought ready quilted to save time)

2 oz washable synthetic wadding (low loft batting)

Lightweight muslin backing

5 cm (2 in) wide broderie anglaise (eyelet edging)

2.5 cm (1 in) wide ribbon

6 mm ($\frac{1}{4}$ in) wide elastic, the length of the rim circumference minus 20 cm (8 in)

Pattern paper

Measuring and cutting out

1 Note the measurements of the following (fig **7**): the circumference of the rim, A–C–A; the circumference of the base, B–D–B; the depth of the basket, H–I; the depth of the ruffle plus broderie anglaise (eyelet edging), A–E; the distance between each outer handle edge, F–G.

2 Set a large sheet of paper against the base of the basket. Mark carefully around the edges, then remove the paper and add 1.5 cm ($\frac{5}{8}$ in) seam allowance all round. Cut out the pattern and mark it 'base'.

3 To make a pattern for the quilted sides of the basket on a large sheet of paper, draw a straight line equalling the distance A–C (half the rim circumference). Draw a second line equalling the measurement B–D at the distance A–B below the first. A–C should overshoot B–D equally on each side. Join these lines at the side. Add seam and quilting shrinkage allowance of 3 cm ($1\frac{1}{4}$ in) at the top and bottom and 5 cm (2 in) at each slanted end. Cut out this pattern and mark it 'sides, cut two'.

4 For the ruffle length double A–C and allow a width of A–E plus 2.5 cm (1 in) for seams minus the depth of the broderie anglaise (eyelet edging). Cut a pattern to these measurements and mark it 'half ruffle, cut 2'.

5 For the rim strip cut a pattern that measures A–C plus 3 cm ($1\frac{1}{4}$ in) for seams plus a width of 10 cm (4 in) and mark it 'rim strip, cut 2'.

6 Lastly cut a rectangle of paper 10 cm (4 in) wide by the distance F–G plus 3 cm ($1\frac{1}{4}$ in). Mark it 'handle strip, cut 2'.

7 Cut out all the basket sections from the top fabric (fig **8**). Cut two side sections to the same dimensions as the fabric pieces from the wadding (batting) and backing.

Making up

8 Lay the wadding (batting) over the wrong side of each fabric side section, and

Fig 7

then lay the muslin on top. Beginning at the centre baste the layers together horizontally and vertically at 7.5 cm (3 in) intervals. Next mark the side sections with diagonal quilting lines spaced 2.5 cm (1 in) apart and quilt. (See patchwork bedspread with diagonal quilting, steps 8 and 9.)

9 Trim the quilted side sections to the measurements taken in step 1, allowing 1.5 cm ($\frac{5}{8}$ in) all round for seams. With right sides together and raw edges even, join the side sections together down the short edges. Press the seam allowances open. On the right side of the quilting stitch parallel to the seamline 6 mm ($\frac{1}{4}$ in) to either side to flatten the wadding (batting).

10 With right sides together and raw edges even, join the basket base to the completed side sections, taking a 1.5 cm ($\frac{5}{8}$ in) seam allowance. Clip curves. Oversew (*see page 140*) the seam allowances to neaten (fig **9**).

11 Join the two ruffle strips with French seams (*see page 140*). With right sides together and raw edges even, attach broderie anglaise (eyelet edging) to the lower edge of the ruffle, taking a 6 mm ($\frac{1}{4}$ in) seam allowance. Press the seam allowances upwards and then topstitch along the edge of the fabric, catching in the seam allowances, to set the broderie anglaise (eyelet edging) flat.

12 On the top edge of the ruffle run two rows of gathering stitches either side of the seamline, 6 mm ($\frac{1}{4}$ in) apart.

13 Mark the outside position of the basket handles on the quilted sides with pins, allowing an extra 1.5 cm ($\frac{5}{8}$ in) for ease at each side.

Fig 8

Rim strip · Rim strip · Rim strip · Handle · Handle · Base · Side · Side · Ruffle · Ruffle

Suggested layout for 90 cm (35 in) wide fabric

Fig 9

Oversewing

14 With right sides together and raw edges even, position the ruffle against the quilted section of the basket and gather up to fit. Stitch between the pin markers, but do not attach the ruffle to the handle gap section, F–G.

15 Fold under 6 mm ($\frac{1}{4}$ in) along two short sides and one long side of the handle strips. Stitch all round. With right sides together, set the remaining raw edge of each strip against the raw edge of the quilting at the handle position, making sure all the pin markers overlap evenly at each side. Insert a ribbon length in the seam at the centre of the handle section, short raw edge against the quilting edge. Stitch along the length of each handle position through the strip and quilting, taking a 1.5 cm ($\frac{5}{8}$ in) seam allowance.

16 Turn the strip to the wrong side of the quilting, and then stitch close to the seam on the right side to flatten. Carefully neaten the unstitched side edges. Stitch firmly across each lower corner to secure.

17 With raw edges even and right sides together join the ends of the two rim strips to make a circle. Turn under 6 mm ($\frac{1}{4}$ in) to the wrong side along one long edge and press. Set a piece of elastic twice the length of A–C minus 20 cm (8 in), against this turning and zigzag in position evenly (fig **10**), working on half a rim at a time and pulling the elastic gently to ease along the folded edge. Butt the two ends of the elastic neatly together and zigzag firmly across to join (fig **11**).

18 With the right side of the rim strip to the wrong side of the ruffle, stitch

the rim strip to the ruffle only, just below the first line of stitching. Stitch from outer handle to outer handle, stopping the stitching at the handle opening, F–G.

19 To neaten the handle opening raw edges clip the seam allowance of the rim strip and gathering to just within the stitching line *at the edges of the opening*, then turn both through the gap *to the right side of the rim strip and wrong side of gathering*. Stitch along the seamline, inserting the other length of ribbon in the middle. Neaten the seam allowances together. On the right side of the ruffle stitch close to the edge from side to side of the handle opening, and across ribbon, to finish. See fig **12**.

Fig 10

Side quilting (wrong side) · Rim strip (wrong side) · Ruffle · Elastic

Fig 11

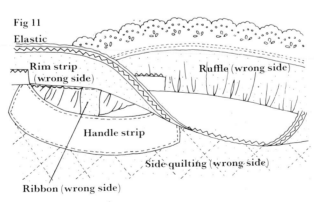

Elastic · Rim strip (wrong side) · Ruffle (wrong side) · Handle strip · Side quilting (wrong side) · Ribbon (wrong side)

Fig 12

Handle opening

QUILTED COVERLET

You will need
Fabric
2 oz washable synthetic wadding (low loft batting or polyester fiberfill quilt batt)
Lightweight muslin backing for wadding (batting)
Lining
5 cm (2 in) wide broderie anglaise (eyelet edging)

Making up
1 Take the pattern of the base of the Moses basket (bassinet) left (see step 2) and fold down 10 cm (4 in) evenly at the top of the pattern, pinning down the flap. This gives you the shape of the coverlet. Using this pattern, cut one piece of top fabric, wadding (batting) and backing, adding 2.5 cm (1 in) all round for quilting shrinkage. Cut one piece of lining to the pattern dimensions only.

2 Lay the wadding (batting) over the wrong side of the fabric and place the backing on top of it. Baste the layers together vertically and horizontally at 7.5 cm (3 in) intervals. Mark up with diagonal quilting lines set 2.5 cm (1 in) apart and quilt (see patchwork bedspread with diagonal quilting, steps 8 and 9). Trim cover to pattern dimensions if necessary.

3 Mark a line across the quilt 8 cm ($3\frac{1}{4}$ in) down from the top edge of the quilt. Cut a piece of broderie anglaise (eyelet edging) to fit across the width and neaten (*see page 140*) the raw edge.

4 With right sides together, place the neatened edge against the line marked on the quilt (the scalloped edge will face upwards). Stitch close to the neatened edge. Stitch again 6 mm ($\frac{1}{4}$ in) from the first stitching line. Press the broderie anglaise (eyelet edging) downwards. Stitch across the ends of the broderie anglaise (eyelet edging) 6 mm ($\frac{1}{4}$ in) from the coverlet edges.

5 With right sides together and raw edges matching, pin the lining to the quilt. Stitch all round, leaving a 15 cm (6 in) opening at the bottom of the quilt through which to turn. Trim the corners, clip curves and turn the coverlet to the right side. Turn in the opening edges in line with the remainder of the seam and slipstitch (*see page 140*) to close (fig **13**).

BASKET WITH QUILTED LINING

This basket is approximately 46 cm (18 in) in diameter at the rim and tapers towards the base. Shrinkage allowance for 2 oz wadding (batting) is about 12 mm ($\frac{1}{2}$ in) for every 30 cm (12 in) of fabric quilted. If your basket is much smaller or larger you can adjust the shrinkage allowance accordingly.

You will need
Fabric
2 oz washable synthetic wadding (low loft batting)
Lightweight muslin backing
2 metres/2$\frac{1}{4}$ yards 2.5 cm (1 in) wide ribbon
Broderie anglaise (eyelet edging)
Pattern paper

Measuring and cutting out

1 To make base pattern, set a piece of paper against the base of the basket and draw round. Add 3.5 cm (1$\frac{3}{8}$ in) all round for quilting shrinkage and seam allowance. Cut out.

2 To make side pattern, measure round the rim, divide this measurement in two and add 6 cm (2$\frac{1}{2}$ in) quilting and seam allowance. Draw a rectangle to equal this measurement in length, times the depth of the basket plus 5 cm (2 in) shrinkage and seam allowance. Cut out half pattern.

3 Cut out two side sections each in the fabric, wadding (batting) and backing. Cut out base fabric, wadding (batting) and backing.

4 Cut one piece of broderie anglaise (eyelet edging) that measures twice the circumference of the rim.

Making up

5 Lay a piece of wadding (batting) over the wrong side of one side section piece and place a piece of backing on top of it. Baste the layers together diagonally and vertically at 7.5 cm (3 in) intervals. Mark up with diagonal quilting lines spaced 2.5 cm (1 in) apart and quilt (see patchwork bedspread with diagonal quilting, steps 8 to 9).

6 With right sides together and raw edges even join the ends of the quilted side sections together, taking a 1.5 cm ($\frac{5}{8}$ in) seam allowance. Press the seam open.

7 At the lower edge of the joined side sections sew two lines of gathering stitches either side of the seamline 6 mm ($\frac{1}{4}$ in) apart. With right sides together and raw edges even, set the joined section piece against the base and draw up the gathering to fit. Stitch all round, taking a 1.5 cm ($\frac{5}{8}$ in) seam allowance. Oversew (*see page 140*) the seam allowances together to neaten. Press.

8 Neaten (*see page 140*) the top raw edges of the joined side sections. Trim the depth of the basket lining if necessary so that the raw edges come fractionally below the basket rim. Fold 1.5 cm ($\frac{5}{8}$ in) to the wrong side and baste.

9 Join the ends of the broderie anglaise (eyelet edging) strip to make a circle. Sew one line of gathering stitches 6 mm ($\frac{1}{4}$ in) from the edge. Set the strip against the

back of the basket lining folded edge, adjusting the gathering to fit. Baste, taking a 1 cm ($\frac{3}{8}$ in) seam allowance, attaching two pieces of ribbon, one over the other, at each handle position on the basket, right sides to the outside (fig **14**). On the right side of the basket lining stitch around the top, 6 mm ($\frac{1}{4}$ in) and 1 cm ($\frac{3}{8}$ in) down from the edge.

10 Place the lining in the basket and tie the ribbons to the handles to finish or slot them through the sides of the basket and tie in a bow.

FABRIC COVERED DIRECTOR'S CHAIR

An existing canvas cover can be overlaid with a more exciting fabric, which used by itself wouldn't be able to stand up to the strain imposed on the seat and back of this type of chair. The chair on page 46 has a seat which is attached to plastic rods that are slotted into a groove cut into each side of the seat frame. The chair back is attached in the same way. It is not difficult to dismantle this chair in order to attach a new cover. If your chair is put together in a different fashion you should still be able to remove the seat and back frames. You can then cover the seat and back fabric sections in the same way that they were made. You should only attempt this treatment if the existing cover is in reasonably good condition and isn't too badly stretched.

You will need
Mediumweight cotton fabric

Measuring and cutting out
1 Unslot the chair seat and unpick the stitching forming the rod channel at each side of the canvas. Mea-

sure the width of the seat fabric from raw edge to raw edge. Next measure the seat from front to back and add 15 cm (6 in) all round for hems. Cut a piece of fabric to these dimensions. Repeat for the chair back.

Making up

2 Trim away the hem allowance at the back and front of the canvas seat to remove bulk. Lay the canvas right side down on top of the wrong side of the seat fabric and pin together at intervals across the surface, making sure that the two fabrics are flat.

3 Wrap the fabric over the canvas at the front and back edges, folding a double hem. Pin in position. At each side of the seat at the back and front, trim away 3 cm (1$\frac{1}{4}$ in) of the hem allowance as shown in fig **15**. Stitch across the seat along the back and front edges close to the inner folded edge of the hem.

4 Fold back the sides of the seat over the canvas along the original foldlines and stitch from front to back at the required distance from each fold to make a snug casing for the rod (fig **16**). Slot the rods through the seat sides and replace in the grooves.

5 Repeat this covering procedure for the chair back, marking the position of each side screw on the outer edge of the fabric. When you replace the chair back, pierce the fabric carefully and screw the back into position.

FABRIC COVERED DECKCHAIR

The covering of the existing deckchair canvas with a different fabric employs the same method as is used to cover the director's chair above.

You will need
Mediumweight cotton fabric
Tacks

Measuring and cutting out
1 Pull out the tacks that hold the canvas in place at each end of the deckchair frame, using a chisel and

Fig 13

Fig 14

Wrong side

Fig 15

Fig 16

Fig 17

Fig 18

hammer, gently levering the chisel head between tack head and canvas. Take the length and width measurements of the canvas, adding 7.5 cm (3 in) hem allowance to each long side. Cut one piece of fabric to these dimensions.

Making up

2 Trim away the hem allowance down the long sides of the deckchair if there is any, to reduce bulk. Lay the canvas face downwards centrally on top of the wrong side of the fabric. Turn in a double hem allowance down each long side. Pin. Stitch close to the inner folded edge down both sides of the cover.

3 Remove the wooden bars from the top and bottom of the deckchair. Place the top bar on the canvas and fold over the fabric along the original foldline, folding under a seam allowance at the raw edge to neaten as before (fig 17). Hammer a tack into the centre of the bar through the cover to secure in place. Keeping the cover at right angles to the bar with the foldline running evenly along it, hammer tacks home at 5 cm (2 in) intervals along the length of the bar.

4 Repeat step 3 for the bottom of the cover, which is usually rolled on to a round piece of wood. Replace the wooden bars.

SMOCKED STOOL COVER

You will need
Fabric
Cushion pad for the stool top
Smocked heading tape of the desired depth
Tape for ties

Measuring and cutting out

1 Attach the cushion pad to each stool leg with tapes which have been stitched on to the side of the cushion at the points nearest the legs of the stool.

2 Measure the diameter of the cushion pad, A–B, its circumference B–B, and the length from the top of the pad to the ground C–D (fig 18). Cut a pattern for the top of the pad following the instructions given for the round cushion cover on page 118, step 2, adding a seam allowance of 2.5 cm (1 in) all round.

3 To calculate the width required for the skirt multiply the circumference of the cushion pad by two (or whatever multiple is required by the maker of the heading tape, as fullness requirements can vary) and add 3 cm (1¼ in) for seams. You will need a length of heading tape equal to this width plus an allowance for neatening the ends.

4 To calculate the length take the measurement C–D and add 2.5 cm (1 in) for the top seam allowance and 5 cm (2 in) for a double hem at the base.

5 The skirt will probably be wider than your fabric width. Cut two sections of the required length that will make up the width when joined down the long edges. Allow extra fabric for matching patterns across seams (*see page 95, step 8*).

Making up

6 Right sides together, raw edges even, join skirt sections down the length to make a circle, taking a 1.5 cm (⅝ in) seam allowance. Press seams open. Turn 2.5 cm (1 in) to the wrong side at top edge and press.

7 Attach the smocked heading tape following the maker's instructions and the explanations on page 94, setting the tape 3 mm (⅛ in) from the top foldline.

8 Pull up the skirt to the required circumference, knotting the tape cords but not cutting them.

9 Place the cushion top section inside the skirt, the right side of the top against the wrong side of the skirt, the top raw edges even with the folded edge of the skirt. Pin all round, adjusting gathers if necessary, then baste. Stitch along skirt top following top line of stitching on the heading tape. The cover forms a 'hat' shape.

10 Set the cover over the stool and check the length. Remove. Turn 2.5 cm (1 in) to the wrong side twice at the base edge to make a double hem. Press. Hem by hand or machine stitch close to the inner folded edge.

DROP-IN CHAIR SEAT COVER WITH DOUBLE PIPING AND BOX EDGED SIDES

You will need
Fabric for the seat top, sides and bias strips
Heavyweight fabric for lining the underneath of the chair seat
Pre-shrunk piping cord
Tacks
Wadding (batting) (optional)

Measuring and cutting out

1 Measure across the seat top both ways (fig 19); this means the part of the seat that is visible when it is dropped in place in the chair frame. Cut a piece of fabric to these dimensions plus 2 cm (¾ in) all round.

2 Remove the seat from the chair. Carefully remove the existing tacks holding the bottom lining and cover in place, using a chisel held parallel with the frame and positioned just under the head of each tack. Tap the chisel sharply with a hammer, levering with the chisel to push up the tack head, then pull out with pliers. Discard the used tacks.

3 There should be a calico (muslin) covering on the top of the chair seat. If there is a layer of wadding (batting) above it, remove this and replace with fresh wadding (batting) cut to the same size.

4 Cut out enough bias strips (*see page 140*) for the covered piping to go twice round the chair seat when joined.

5 For the chair seat sides cut one piece of fabric that measures 20 cm (8 in) wide by the length of the four sides plus 10 cm (4 in).

6 Measure the underneath of the chair seat from frame edge to frame edge and cut one piece of fabric to these dimensions plus 1 cm (⅜ in) all round.

Fig 19

Making up

7 Make up two strips of covered piping (*see page 141*) each long enough to go round the chair cover, 2 cm ($\frac{3}{4}$ in) in from the edge. Pin and baste the first length of piping to the edges of the cover piece, lining up the piping stitching line with the cover seamline. Begin and end the piping at the back of the cover, making a neat join (*see page 141*). Using the zipper foot on your machine stitch all round. Clip the piping seam allowance at the corners to ease. Attach the second length of piping directly over the first, stitching along the first stitching line (fig **20**).

8 Fold 2.5 cm (1 in) to the wrong side at one end of the side strip. Beginning midway along the back edge, with right side of the strip against the piping, pin the strip all the way round the cover along the piping stitching lines taking a 1.5 cm ($\frac{5}{8}$ in) seam allowance

Fig 20

Fig 21

Fig 22

Fig 23

(fig **21**). Overlap the folded portion of the strip by 2.5 cm (1 in) when you reach the starting point at the back. Trim the excess fabric at the strip end.

9 Clip the corners of the strip seam allowance to ease. Trim the seam allowances of the piping to 1 cm ($\frac{3}{8}$ in) and 12 mm ($\frac{1}{2}$ in) respectively to grade the seam allowance thicknesses. Press all the allowances towards the side strip.

10 Turn the cover to the right side and set upside down in front of you. If there is any, set the new wadding (batting) in place furry side down, followed by the existing pad and its frame, again upside down, inside the box shaped cover.

11 Keeping the piping level with the seat top edge, wrap the back section of fabric over the frame base and attach it temporarily with tacks set half way into the wood, starting at the centre and working outwards, placing tacks at about 2.5 cm (1 in) intervals. Lift the front of the frame so that it rests on its back edge and pull the fabric tautly into position over the front edge. Tack as before, checking the piping is lying level with the top edge. Repeat this operation on the remaining sides.

12 Pull up the fabric hard over each corner and tack it temporarily in place (fig **22**). Repeat this procedure for the other three corners. At each corner, fold the excess fabric towards the centre of each side of the frame and tack flat to neaten.

13 Check the top of the cover to make sure that the fabric lies evenly taut. Lift tacks a few at a time and reposition if you are not satisfied, then hammer the tacks home all round the frame.

14 Set the lining fabric against the seat base. Turning under 2 cm ($\frac{3}{4}$ in) along all edges, tack close to the fold at intervals of 2.5 cm (1 in), making sure the fabric is pulled taut and that it covers the first set of tacks (fig **23**).

RE-COVERING WOODEN HEADBOARDS AND FOOTBOARDS

You will need
Fabric
Gimp or flat braid for edging, as old measurements plus 20 cm (8 in)
Matching gimp pins (small headed tacks)
Round headed pins
Tacks
Clear adhesive
Pattern paper

Measuring and cutting out

1 Remove the existing gimp or braid carefully and make a note of each length. Remove the fabric from each side of the two boards following the previous instructions, step 2. Mark each piece 'front head', 'back head' and so on. Lay each section flat on the floor and calculate the amount of fabric needed. Add seam allowances of 2 cm ($\frac{3}{4}$ in) all round. If the fabric panels are wider than the width of your fabric, position a width of fabric at the centre of the bed with narrow strips set to each side. Allow extra fabric for matching patterns across seams (*see page 95, step 8*).

2 Using the old fabric pieces as your pattern, lay each piece with the right side uppermost on the right side of the fabric, the edges folded in along the original foldlines. Pin flat in position. Cut round each piece, adding 2 cm ($\frac{3}{4}$ in) seam allowance all round. Unpin the new front headboard piece and mark a chalk line down the centre on the wrong side. Mark a corresponding chalk line on the headboard.

3 Set the headboard fabric right side uppermost against the bed headboard, matching chalk lines. Pin from top to bottom of the chalk line to attach, the fabric overlapping the surround evenly. Place a tack half way in at the top and bottom, just inside the line to which the old covering extended. Then, smoothing the fabric taut, set it in position all the way round, placing tacks temporarily half way into the wood at 2.5 cm (1 in) intervals (fig **24**).

4 Remove the pins and adjust the fabric if need be, removing tacks a few at a time and re-smoothing until you are satisfied. Hammer each tack into the wooden surround, being very careful not to harm the wood.

5 Trim the fabric all the way round to the outside edges of the tack heads. Place a new length of gimp or flat braid over the tacked raw edges of the covering, butting it up to the show-wood line so that no raw edges or tacks can be seen. Set it in position using a small amount of clear adhesive, matching gimp pins or small headed tacks if you prefer. Do not use much adhesive or it will discolour the trimming. Fold the trimming into a mitre at each corner and secure it with a gimp pin (tack). Tuck under the end to the wrong side and secure with a gimp pin to finish.

6 Repeat this operation for the front footboard of the bed, then repeat for the backs of the boards, omitting the pinning stage unless the boards are padded.

Fig 24

NAPKINS

The napkins on page 45 are 60 cm (24 in) square, which means you can cut two from a 67 cm (26½ in) length of 137 cm (54 in) wide fabric.

You will need
Fabric
Matching or contrasting thread for topstitching

Making up

1 Cut out the number of napkins required, adding a hem allowance of 3 cm (1¼ in) all round.

2 Fold 1.5 cm (⅝ in) to the wrong side twice along the edge of each napkin, mitring the corners (*see page 141*). Press. Slipstitch (*see page 140*) across the mitre.

3 Stitch around each napkin to finish, close to the inner folded edge (fig **25**).

POLE END COVER

This pole end cover consists of two circles of fabric, one print and one lining, which are stitched together and gathered up over a pole end so that it blends in with the curtains.

You will need
Fabric
Lining
Length of string
Pencil
Pattern paper

Measuring and cutting out

1 Measure from the centre top of the pole end to the neck and add 5 cm (2 in) ruffle/seam allowance. This measurement is the radius of the fabric circles you are going to cut out.

2 Fold a piece of paper wider and longer than twice the radius, in half. Tie the length of string to the

Fig 25

pencil and cut it so that it equals the radius. Pin the string into the fold of the paper halfway down its length. Holding the pencil upright, draw a half circle from folded edge to folded edge. Cut round the pencil outline and unfold the pattern.

Making up

3 Using the pattern, cut out one piece of fabric and one piece of lining. Set one over the other, right sides together. Stitch all round, taking a 1 cm (⅜ in) seam allowance and leaving a gap of 10 cm (4 in) through which to turn. Clip curve.

4 Turn and press. Turn in the opening edges in line with the remainder of the seam and slipstitch (*see page 140*) to close. Run two lines of gathering stitches around the edge of the circle 4 cm (1½ in) and 3 cm (1¼ in) in from the edge (fig **26**).

5 Pull up the gathers slightly then set over the pole end. Draw up the gathers tightly and wrap the threads around the pole and tie to secure.

POLE COVER

You will need
Fabric
Matching thread

Measuring and cutting out

1 Cut 1 piece of fabric (joined if necessary) to equal twice the length of the pole plus 5 cm (2 in) for seams, by the circumference of the pole plus 4.5 cm (1¾ in) for seam allowances and ease, plus 10 cm (4 in) for double ruffle at top and bottom.

Making up

2 Follow steps 2 to 5 of ruffled casing for metal arm (*see page 106*), leaving both short ends of the tube open and neatening as in step 3. Allow double ruffles of 2.5 cm (1 in) at top and bottom of the tube.

Fig 26

SEWING TECHNIQUES

TEN USEFUL STITCHES

BASTING/TACKING (fig 1)

Fig 1

A long running stitch, basting can be worked quickly by machine or by hand and holds two or more pieces of fabric in position ready for final stitching. Begin hand basting with a knot so that stitches are easy to remove. Simply cut off the knot and pull the thread through the fabric from the other end.

BUTTONHOLE STITCH (fig 2)

Fig 2

This is used for neatening buttonholes and for stitching hooks and eyes and press fasteners firmly in place. Insert the needle upward through the fabric at the desired distance from the edge and twist the working thread around the point. Pull the needle through, bringing the knot you have formed to the edge.

HEMMING STITCH (fig 3)

Fig 3

This is used to attach a folded hem edge to flat fabric. Fasten the working thread inside the hem, then make small even slanting stitches through the fabric and hem in one movement. Pick up only one or two threads of fabric with each stitch.

HERRINGBONE (CATCH) STITCH (fig 4)

Fig 4

This is used to hold single hems firmly in place. Work from left to right with the folded hem edge facing towards you. Fasten the working thread and bring it up through the hem near the edge. Move about 6 mm (¼ in) diagonally to the right across the hem edge and take a small stitch from right to left just above the hem edge. Stitch across the hem edge 6 mm (¼ in) diagonally to the right and take a small stitch diagonally to the left. Bring the thread diagonally to the right again and take another small stitch to the left just above the hem edge. Continue along the hem.

This stitch is used to join wadding (batting) edges together. The stitches can be large and loose, catching only one or two fabric threads.

LADDERSTITCH (fig 5)

Fig 5

When joining patterned fabric the pattern must be matched across seams by tacking the fabric pieces together from the right side.

Press under the seam allowance along one fabric edge and place over the flat seam allowance of the other so that the pattern matches exactly. Pin.

Insert needle into the folded edge between the two layers of fabric and bring it out again 2 cm (¾ in) along the fold. Take a small stitch directly across the join and take another 2 cm (¾ in) down the fabric along the seamline. Take a small stitch directly across into the fold again and take another 2 cm ($\frac{3}{4}$ in) stitch. Repeat along the seam, forming ladder-like stitches.

When the seam is completed the two pieces of fabric can be folded with right sides together ready for stitching.

LOCKSTITCH (fig 6)

Fig 6

Used in curtain making to hold lining and interlining loosely against the wrong side of the curtain fabric. Fold the lining / interlining back against the pins (see Curtains, page 98). Stitch from top to bottom. Take a stitch through the folded edge and curtain fabric at right angles to the folded edge, picking up only one or two threads of fabric with each stitch. Make the next stitch about 5 cm (2 in) to the right, taking the thread over the needle to produce a loop.

OVERSEWING (fig 7)

Fig 7

This is also called overcasting and is used to neaten raw edges. Working from left to right take thread diagonally over the fabric edge, making small even stitches and bringing the needle through the fabric about 3 mm ($\frac{1}{8}$ in) from the edge.

PRICKSTITCH (fig 8)

Fig 8

Also called stabstitch, this makes a unobtrusive stitching line. Bring the needle through to the upper side of the fabric. Insert the needle just behind where the thread came out, then take a stitch about 6 mm ($\frac{1}{4}$ in) in front of that point. Bring the needle through to the upper side and repeat.

RUNNING (GATHERING) STITCH (fig 9)

Fig 9

This stitch is used mainly for gathering. Secure the thread, then make small evenly spaced stitches along the fabric. Finish with another backstitch. When used for gathering work two rows either side of the seamline 6 mm ($\frac{1}{4}$ in) apart, leaving the threads dangling at one end. To gather, pull on the threads gently and slide the fabric along. Secure the threads by twisting in a figure eight around a pin.

SLIPSTITCH (fig 10)

Used to attach a folded edge to a flat edge as in hemming or to join two folded edges together.

Fig 10a

Hemming: (fig **10a**) working from right to left with the inner folded hem edge towards you, take a tiny stitch into the main fabric close to the folded edge. Without pulling the thread through, slip the needle into the folded edge as close as possible to the first stitch and bring it out about 6 mm ($\frac{1}{4}$ in) to the left. Pull the thread through and take another small stitch in the main fabric.

Joining folded edges: (fig **10b**)

Fig 10b

fasten the thread inside one folded edge and then cross over the opening into the opposite fold. Make a stitch about 6 mm ($\frac{1}{4}$ in) long and pull the needle through the other fold again. Repeat, working backwards and forwards across the gap and inserting the needle slightly to the inside of the fold. The stitches will be invisible.

TWO USEFUL SEAMS

FLAT FELL SEAM (fig 11)

This seam is very strong and used on furnishings frequently

Fig 11

washed, such as tablecloths.

Place the two fabric pieces with right sides together and matching raw edges and stitch as for a plain seam. Press the seam allowances to one side and then trim the underneath allowance to 6 mm ($\frac{1}{4}$ in). Wrap the top seam allowance over the trimmed one to enclose its raw edge, folding 6 mm ($\frac{1}{4}$ in) under. Press flat and stitch along the folded edge.

FRENCH SEAM (fig 12)

Fig 12

Another self-neatening seam used mainly on lightweight fabrics, it can only be used on straight grain fabric edges.

Join the two fabric pieces with wrong sides together, matching raw edges, taking a 6 mm ($\frac{1}{4}$ in) seam allowance. Refold the fabric with right sides together and stitch the seam again 1 cm ($\frac{3}{8}$ in) from the first stitching line to enclose the raw edges. Press.

BIAS STRIPS AND PIPING

BIAS STRIPS

These are used for covering piping cord and for binding raw edges smoothly.

1. Find the bias of your fabric and fold over the selvedge so that it lies parallel to the weft (the cross threads of the fabric). Cut along the fold and use this edge for cutting bias strips (fig **13**).

2. Mark the strips in tailor's chalk parallel to the bias edge, using a ruler made from card to the desired strip width. If cutting strips for covering piping cord, cut them to give a 1.5 cm ($\frac{5}{8}$ in) seam allowance when wrapped around the cord. Double the seam allowance of 1.5 cm ($\frac{5}{8}$ in) and add the circumference of the cord.

Fig 13

Fig 14

3. To join bias strips match the ends as shown (fig **14**), right sides together. Stitch across the join, taking a 6 mm ($\frac{1}{4}$ in) seam allowance. Press the seam open.

PIPING

Piping is a strip of bias cut fabric inserted into the seams of furnishings to give them a tailored and professional finish. It also strengthens seams. It can either be flat or corded. In corded piping the bias strip is folded in half around a length of piping cord. This can be bought in various thicknesses ranging from 00 to 6. Number 3 is the most commonly used. The cord should always be shrunk before it is used, otherwise the finished piping could pucker badly when the home furnishing is washed.

If a length of piping goes all the way round an object the ends must be joined. Allow an extra 5 cm (2 in) for the join. The cord can also be joined by unravelling each end, cutting each strand of cord in a different place and intertwining them (fig **15**). The ends are then whipped around with sewing thread

Fig 15

Fig 16

Fig 17

Fig 18

and stitched through with the same thread (fig **16**).

1 To cover piping cord, fold the bias strip around the cord right side out, raw edges matching. Pin and stitch close to the cord, using the zipper foot (fig **17**).

2 To join covered piping, unpick the last 2.5 cm (1 in) at one end. Turn under 12 mm ($\frac{1}{2}$ in) of the fabric to conceal the raw edge. Cut off the last 2.5 cm (1 in) of the cord. Insert the other end of the covered piping so the cord ends meet and the other raw edge is enclosed (fig **18**). Stitch across the join along seamline.

MITRED CORNER

FOLDING A MITRE, SINGLE HEM

1 Turn under the two sides for the desired amount and press. Mark each raw edge where the turnings intersect with a pin (fig **19**).

2 Unfold the turnings and press in the corner at an angle from pin to pin (fig **20**).

3 Refold the turnings so that the corner folds

Fig 19

Fig 20

into a neat mitre and slipstitch its edges together. Press.

Fig 21

Fig 22

FOLDING A MITRE, DOUBLE HEM

1 Turn under the sides once and press. Double the turning along one side and mark where it falls on the other side edge with a pin (fig **21**). Unfold the turning to single width again.

2 Double the turning along the other side and mark where it falls on the other side edge with a pin (fig **22**). Unfold to single width.

3 Press in the corner at an angle from pin to pin as in fig **20** above but with single width hems folded in. Double the turnings and the corner will fold into a neat mitre. Slipstitch its edges together.

TRIMMING A MITRED CORNER

1 Follow steps 1 and 2 of folding a mitred corner in a single hem. Then trim the corner to within 6 mm ($\frac{1}{4}$ in) of the diagonal fold. Turn in 6 mm ($\frac{1}{4}$ in) across the corner.

2 If you want neatened hem edges, fold them under by 6 mm ($\frac{1}{4}$ in) and press. Fold in the hem along the original foldlines to make a mitred corner. Slipstitch its edges together. Hem by hand or stitch along the inner folded edges to secure.

FASTENINGS

CENTRED ZIP (ZIPPER)

1 Measure the length of the zip (zipper) and mark its length on the seamline. Stitch a simple seam to its

Fig 23

Fig 24

base point and then reverse to secure the stitching. Change the stitch length on the machine to a long one and baste the opening. Reverse the stitching at the top of the opening and continue stitching the seam with a normal length stitch. Press the seam open.

2 Place the zip (zipper) face down over the seam allowances with the teeth centred exactly over the seamline. Pin and baste in position through all layers 6 mm ($\frac{1}{4}$ in) to either side of the teeth (fig **23**).

3 Turn to the right side. Using the zipper foot, topstitch the zip (zipper) in place just inside the basting lines, pivoting at the corners (fig **24**). Alternatively, hand stitch, using prickstitch.

Fig 25

Fig 26

PIPED SEAM ZIP (ZIPPER)

1 Pipe one edge of seam. Do not close opening.

2 Open the zip (zipper) and place right side downwards on the piped seam, teeth against piping stitching line. Baste. Stitch close to the teeth, using zipper foot (fig **25**).

3 Turn back seam allowance to wrong side so piping lies at opening edge. Close the zip (zipper). Press under seam allowance at the other side of the opening. Bring folded edge over the zip (zipper) to meet piping. Baste seam. Stitch 6 mm ($\frac{1}{4}$ in) from folded edge and across zip ends to piping edge (fig **26**).

Fig 27

VELCRO

This fastener consists of two strips of material, one covered in loops and the other with small hooks which cling together when pressed. It is available in various widths and colour. Make sure you choose the right weight for the job. You will have to allow greater seam allowances if you are applying Velcro wider than 1 cm ($\frac{3}{8}$ in).

Fig 28

1 Pin and baste the tape in place down the long edges either side of the opening. Stitch, using a zipper foot on the machine (fig **27**).

SLIP KNOT

1 Hold the two twine ends in one hand. Put the right end over the left and bring it back over the left end again. Pull the right end up through the loop that has formed. Pull to tighten (fig **28**).

RUFFLES

The fullness of a ruffle can vary between one and a half to three times the length of the edge to which it is to be attached, depending on the fabric weight and the desired effect.

SINGLE RUFFLE

1 Decide on the finished depth of the ruffle. Add a

Fig 29

Fig 30

1.5 cm ($\frac{5}{8}$ in) seam allowance and a double hem allowance of 1 cm to 2 cm ($\frac{3}{8}$ in to $\frac{3}{4}$ in).

2 Join the ends of the ruffle strips together with flat fell seams to make a continuous or longer length. If the ruffle is not continuous make a double turning of 6 mm ($\frac{1}{4}$ in) at each end and stitch.

3 Turn up a double hem along the lower edge of the ruffle and stitch.

4 Gather up the raw edge to required size. For long ruffles divide the ruffle and the edge to which it is to be attached into an equal number of sections. Work two rows of gathering stitches in each ruffle section. With right sides together, raw edges even and matching section dividing points, gather up the ruffle to fit the main fabric edge. Pin, baste and stitch together. Neaten the seam with machine zigzagging and press upwards.

Fig 31

A | B **A | B** **A | B** **A | B**

5 The ruffle edge can also be bound with contrasting bias strips before gathering. Either turn in the long edge of the bias strip to neaten and fold it over the ruffle edge and topstitch in place (fig **29**) or seam it to the edge with right sides together, raw edges even. Turn it over the edge and hem in place on the wrong side. You do not need a hem allowance if you are binding a ruffle.

DOUBLE RUFFLE

1 Cut double the required depth plus twice the top seam allowance. Join the ends together with plain seams.

2 Fold the ruffle in half, matching raw edges and wrong sides, and gather the top edges in the same way as for a single ruffle (fig **30**).

KNIFE PLEAT RUFFLE

This is a variation on a double ruffle and is usually applied to cushions or curtain edgings.

1 Decide on an appropriate pleat width. Next divide the edge to which the pleats are to be attached by the width of pleat; this will give you the number of pleats for the edge. Multiply this number by three to get the

Fig 32

width of fabric needed for making up the pleated section and add allowances for seams and side hems, if any.

2 Cut out and make up the complete pleat strip in the same way as for a double ruffle.

3 Mark the positioning lines for each pleat on the fabric edge. Mark the pleat line A first, and then measure twice the pleat width from this line and mark the placement line B. Leave a pleat width gap and return to the beginning of the sequence, repeating until the end of the section is reached.

4 To pleat up, fold the fabric on the first pleat line and bring it to the next placement line. Pin. Repeat until all the fabric has been pleated (fig **31**). Baste along the top of the pleats and stitch in place as needed. If you are attaching a pleated ruffle to a cushion you will find it necessary to make slightly smaller pleats at each corner with the base of each pleat overlapping (fig **32**).

INDEX

Algonquin Hotel, New York, 73

Arts and Crafts Movement, The, 6, 20, 42, 78

Ascot Box, 70, 72

Austrian blinds, *see* Blinds

Baker, Olive, 6

Baskets
  Moses, quilted, with matching coverlet, 86, *87*, 134–6
  with quilted lining, 86, 87, 136

Basting, 139

Bathroom, (Bucks), 33–4
  London house, 84

Bauhaus (print), 78, *78*, 82, 83

Bay window, swags and tails, *59*, 60, 102

Bedcovers, *see* Bedspreads and Valances

Bedroom
  attic, London, 92
  boy's, 82–3
  Chinese style, 90–91
  Farmhouse, 16, 62, 64
  Sweet Pea print, 26, 28

Bedspreads, 125–132
  fitted and piped, with pillow gusset and kick pleats, 55, 56, 125–6
  fitted, quilted, with contrast piping, *73*, 74, 130–131
  lined, 18, *18*, 26, 68, 125
  fitted, with pillow gussets and scalloped edge, 28, 126–7
  with quilted dragon panels, 91, *91*, 131–2
  patchwork, 30, 64, 128–9
  with diagonal quilting, 31, 127–8

Bias strips, 140

Bladon (print), 34, *34*, 70, 72

Blinds, 109–113
  Austrian, lined, with ruffle, 9, *9*, 10, 112
  unlined, with double ruffle, *23*, 24, *24*, 55, *55*, 56, *56*, 111–2
  roller, 84, 92, 112–3
  Roman, 34, 52, 83, *83*, 109–111

Briarwood (print), 28

Bungalow, Mesnil-le-Roi, 20–21

Burnham (print), 52

Butterfield, Lindsay, P, 7

Buttonhole, 139

Capriccio (print), 9, *10*, 23, 24, 46, 72

Ceiling, tented, gathered, 72, 132–3

Chelsea Arts Club, 51, 55
  Bedroom, 55–6
  Club room, 51–52

founders, 51

Churchill, Sir Winston, 76

Clandon (print), 76, 77

Clementina (print), 38

Collections, fabric
  Chesham
    Bauhaus, 78, *78*, 82, 83
    Ianthe, 42, *42*
    Kasak, 82, 83, 84, *85*
    Lodden, 21
    Melrose, 80, 81, *81*
    Tambourine, 49
    Zebak, *51*, 52, *52*, 66, 67, 68, *68*
  Chesham II
    Clandon, 76, *76*, 77
    Clementina, 38
    Hedgerow, 24, 48, *49*
    Hermia, 64
    Melbury, 60
    Petronella, 62, 74, *75*
    Salazar, *36*, 38
    Scherzo, 68
    Trent, 10
  Cotton
    Briarwood, 28
    Hera, 42
    Honeysuckle, 21
    Penelope, 12
    Sweet Pea, 26, *26*, 28, *28*, 55, *55*
    Terrace, 74
    Willow, 56, 92, *92*
  East India, 9, 90
    Bladon, 34, *34*, 70, 72
    Capriccio, 9, 10, *10*, 23, 24, *24*, 46, 70, 72
    Keswick, 18
    Madison, 9, 10, *10*
    Mariana, 34
    Opium, 30, 31, 80, 90, 91
    Santana, 14, 44, 46
    Suki, *58*, 59, *59*, 60, 80, 90, 91
    Tana lawns, 26, 30, 31, 62, *62*, 86
    Classic, 86, 87
    Mayfair, 70, 72, *72*
  Union
    Burnham, 52

Collier, Susan, 7

Cornices, *see* Pelmets

Covers, bed, *see* Bedspreads and Valances

Covers, cushion, *see* Cushions

Covers, seat
  chair seat, drop-in, with double piping and boxed sides, 42, 137–8
  deck chair, fabric covered, 48, 49, *49*, 136–7
  director's chair, fabric covered, 46, *47*, 136
  sofa, scroll armed, loose, with piping and kick pleated skirt, 10, 113–6
  stool, smocked, 77, 137

Curtains, 94–104
  cased headings, 99

combined curtain and valance, 34, *34*, 100

curved valance and ruffled piped edge, 100–102

cutting out, 95–6

fixed, *55*, 56, 99
  with contrast bound heading, 99–100

headings, 94

interlined, with triple pinch pleat headings, 60, 88, *89*, 98–9

jabots, *see* Swags and Tails

linings and stiffenings, 95

measuring for, 95

quick casing for lightweight kitchen/bathroom curtain, 99

ruffled, with sewn-in lining and contrast piping, 14, 74, 97

stiffenings and linings, 95

swag and contrast lined tails (jabots), 88, 104

swags and tails (jabots) for bay window, 60, 102–4

track poles and accessories, 94–5

unlined, 96–7

with cartridge pleat heading, *9*, 10, 18, 21, 52, 64, 74, 96

with locked-in lining, 10, 18, 21, 52, 64, 72, 74, 77, 81, 97–8

with pinch pleat heading, 64, 81, 96

with smocked heading, 77, 96

with triple pinch pleat heading, 72, 96

Cushions, 117–122
  attaching to chair with ties, 121
  box edged, covers, 119–120
    vinyl coated, 36
  bunk cover, 38, 122
  buttoned lounger, 48, 49, 121–2
  heart-shaped, with double ruffle and piping, 91, 119
  knife edged covers, 117
  pad, 120–121
  rectangular, box edged, cover, with piping, 21, 38, 52, 119–120
  boxed edged, with piping, 52, 119
  cover, with side opening, 117–8
  round, box edged, cover with piping, 10, 81, 119, 120, 141
  cover, with back zip opening, 118–9
  cover, with double ruffle, 10, 142
  cover, with hand sewn

side opening, 118, 142
  with contrast piping, 81, 120, 141
  shaping, to fit chair seat, 120–121
  square, cover, 79, 117
  cover, with double ruffle, 10, 117, 142
  cover, with piping, 72, 83, 117, 142
  cover, with side opening, 117–8
  patchwork, 64, 128
  with knife-pleated ruffle, 28, 118, 142
  with piping, 68, 72, 117, 142

Cuzner, Bernard, 6

Deck chair, fabric covered, 48, 49, *49*, 136

De Morgan, William, 7

Delaunay, Sonia, 7, 82

Designers, 6, 7, 9, 20, 25, 66, 78

Director's chair, fabric covered, 46, *47*, 136

Doran, J M, 7

Dorrell, William Haynes, 62

Dresser, Dr Christopher, 6, 40

East India Collection, *see* Collections

East India House, 6, 9

Edwardian house, London, 9–10

Farmhouse, Morecambe Bay, 12–15
  Sevenoaks, 30–32

Fastenings, 141

Footboards, recovering, 26, 28, 136

Freud, Clement, MP, 70

Gathering stitch, 140

Goad, Valerie, 26, 30

Haward, David, 58

Haward, Sidney, 7, 26, 55, 58, *64*

Headboards, recovering, 26, 28, 138

Hedgerow (print), 24, 48, *49*

Hemming, 139

Hera (print), 42

Hermia (print), 64

Honeysuckle (print), 21

Hoshi (Edwardian schooner), 36, 38, *38*

Hotel, Ashford, Kent conservatory, 44, 46
  garden, 48–9

House, Eaton Terrace, 88
  Strawberry Hill, 58, 60

Ianthe (print), 42, *42*

Kasak (print), 82, 83, 84, *85*
Kempston, James and Ingrid, 44
Keswick (print), 18
King, Jessie, 6
Kitchen, terraced cottage, London, 78
town house, London, 23–4
Knox, Archibald, 6

Ladderstitch, 139–140
Laflin, John, 7, 9, 25, 66
Liberty, Arthur, 6, 20
Liberty Guild, 42
Littler, Edmund, 6
Lockstitch, 140
Lodden (print), 21
Loose covers, *see* Covers and Cushions

MacCaw, Sandy, 23
Madison (print), 9, 10, *10, 17*, 18
Manor house, Kent, 17–18
Mariana (print), 34
Mawson, Sidney, 7
Melbury (print), 60
Melrose (print), 80, *81*
Miles, Frank, 7
Mitred corner, 141
Morris, William, 6, 10, 20, 28, 40, *41*, 42, 56
Moses basket (bassinet), 87, *87*, 134–6

Napkins, 44, 46, 139
Napper, Harry, 7
Nevill, Bernard, 7

Office, farmhouse, 80
Opium (print), 31, 90, 91
Oversewing, 140

Paterson, Edgar, 7
Paul, William, 7
Pauwels, Madame, 20, 21
Pearson, John, 6
Peduzzi, Richard, 7
Pelmets (cornices), 105–6
cornice board, 105
piped, with lined contrast-edged ruffle, 14, 74, 106
with piping and double ruffle, 81, 105–6
Penelope (print), 12, 14, *14*

Petronella (print), 62, 74, *75*
Piping, 141
Pole, cover, 55, 56, 139
end cover, 139
Prickstitch, 140
Prints
Bauhaus, 78, *78*, 82, 83
Bladon, 34, *34*, 70, 72
Briarwood, 28
Burnham, 52
Capriccio, 9, *10, 23*, 24, *24*, 46, 70, 72
Clandon, 76, *76*, 77
Clementina, 38
Hedgerow, 24, 48, *49*
Hera, 42
Hermia, 64
Honeysuckle, 21
Grey chintz, 88
Ianthe, 42, *42*
Kasak, 82, 83, 84, *85*
Keswick, 18
Lodden, 21
Madison, 9, 10, *10*, 17, 18, *18*
Mariana, 34
Mayfair, 72
Melbury, 60
Melrose, 80, 81, *81*
Morris, William, 20, *21, 41*, 42, 56
Opium, 31, 80, 90, 91
Penelope, 12, 14, *14*
Petronella, 62, *62*, 74, *75*
Salazar, *36*, 38
Santana, 14, 44, 46
Scherzo, 63, 68
Suki, 58, *58*, 59, *59*, 60, 80, 90, 91
Sweet Pea, 26, *26*, 28, *28*, 55, *55*
Tambourine, 49
Tana lawns, 26, 30, *31*, 62, *62*, 70, 72, *72*, 86, 87
Terrace, 74
Trent, 10
Willow, 56, 92, *92*
Zebak, 51, *51*, 52, *52*, 66, *67*, 68, *68*
Prints, Liberty, history of, 6–7

Rosette trimmed tieback, 10
Ruffle, dust, *see* Valance
Ruffles, 142

Running stitch, 140

Salazar (print), *36*, 38
Santana (print), 14, 44, 46
Scherzo (print), 68
Scott, Jane, 17
Scott, Jerry, 17
Seams, 140
Seat covers, *see* Covers, seat
Sewing techniques
basting/tacking, 139
bias strips, 140
buttonhole, 139
fastenings, zip, 141
gathering stitch, 140
hemming, 139
ladderstitch, 139–140
lockstitch, 140
mitred corner, 141
folding, double hem, 141
single hem, 141
trimming, 141
oversewing, 140
piping, 141
prickstitch, 140
ruffles, double, 142
knife pleat, 142
single, 142
running (gathering) stitch, 140
seams, flat fell, 140
French, 140
slip knot, 142
slipstitch, 140
tacking/basting, 139
velcro, 142
zip fastening, 141
Silver, Arthur, 42
Silver, Harry, 7
Silver, Rex, 7
Smocked stool cover, 77, 137
tieback, 77, 107
Stewart-Liberty, Catherine, 9, 10
Stewart-Liberty, Liz, 33, 34
Stewart-Liberty, Oliver, 9
Stölzl, Gunta, 78
Stool cover, smocked, 77, 137
Studio, 66, 68
Suki (print), 58, 59, 60, 90, 91
Swags and tails, for bay window, 59, 60, 102
Sweet Pea (print), 26, *26*, 28,

28, 55, *55*
Sykes, Victoria, 26

Tablecloths, rectangular, 21, 124–5
round, fitted, with gathered skirt piping and double ruffle, 10, 124
with bound and headed ruffle, 14, 124
with bound edge, 44, 46, 123
vinyl coated, 79, 123
Tacking/basting, 139
Tambourine (print), 49
Tana lawns, *see* Collections
Tee, Susanna, 76
Terrace (print), 74
Tiebacks, bow, with contrast lining and edging, 10, 107
lined, with cord and contrast edging, 34, *34*, 107–8
measuring up, 106
ruffled, casing metal arm, 55, 56, 106–7
shaped, interlined with optional piping and rosette, *51*, 52, 60, 109
smocked, 77, 107
stiffened, with edging and rosette, 10, *10*, 108
Trent (print), 10

Valances (dust ruffle)
combined with curtain, 34, *34*, 100
curved, with ruffled piped edge, 24, 100
ruffled, 74, 129
split, with contrast bordered top, 18, 26, 28, 129–130
Velcro, 142
Victorian house, East Grinstead, 40–42
Voysey, C F A, 7

Walls, fabric, gathered, 72, 133–4
Webb, Philip, 40, *41*
Wilcock, Arthur, 7
Willshaw, Arthur, 7
Wilson, Peter, 44, 48
Winterbottom, Dudley and Mirjana, 51

ACKNOWLEDGEMENTS

The author and publishers would like to thank the following people for their help in the preparation of this book:
Algonquin Hotel, New York; Clement Freud; Valerie Goad; David Haward; Fred and Sarah Hohler; Island Cruising Club; James and Ingrid Kempston; Elina Labourdette; Paul Müller; The National Trust; Geoffrey Phillips, Liberty of London, New York; Mrs Raeburn; Mr and Mrs Rennoldson; Amanda Rowe; Paul Ruddock; Jerry and Jane Scott; Sue Scott; Catherine Stewart-Liberty; Liz Stewart-Liberty; Victoria Sykes; Bridget Watker; Dudley and Mirjana Winterbottom.
Photograph on page 21 by Pascal Hinous/Agence Top.
The furniture featured on page 41 is not on permanent display at Standen, but was chosen to suit the period of the house.
The studio on page 67 was designed by Christine McCarron, Kaufmann Ford McCarron Ltd, 94 Belsize Lane, London NW3.
Photograph on page 79 supplied with kind permission by Ideal Home.

THEDA SKOCPOL

States & Social Revolutions

A COMPARATIVE ANALYSIS OF FRANCE, RUSSIA, & CHINA

CAMBRIDGE UNIVERSITY PRESS

STATES AND SOCIAL REVOLUTIONS

States and Social Revolutions

A COMPARATIVE ANALYSIS
OF FRANCE, RUSSIA, AND CHINA

THEDA SKOCPOL
Harvard University

CAMBRIDGE UNIVERSITY PRESS

CAMBRIDGE
LONDON   NEW YORK   MELBOURNE

Published by the Syndics of the Cambridge University Press
The Pitt Building, Trumpington Street, Cambridge CB2 1RP
Bentley House, 200 Euston Road, London NW1 2DB
32 East 57th Street, New York, NY 10022, USA
296 Beaconsfield Parade, Middle Park, Melbourne 3206, Australia

First published 1979

Printed in the United States of America
Typeset by Huron Valley Graphics, Ann Arbor, Michigan
Printed and bound by Vail-Ballou Press, Inc., Binghamton, New York

Library of Congress Cataloging in Publication Data

Skocpol, Theda.

States and social revolutions.

Bibliography: p.

Includes index.

1. Revolutions–Case studies. 2. Revolutions–France–History.
3. Revolutions–Russia–History. 4. Revolutions–China–History.   I. Title.
HM283.S56   301.6'333   78–14314
ISBN 0 521 22439 X in hard covers
ISBN 0 521 29499 1 as a paperback

for Bill

Contents

List of Tables and Maps   ix

Preface   xi

Introduction

1. Explaining Social Revolutions: Alternatives to Existing Theories   3
        A Structural Perspective   14
        International and World-historical Contexts   19
        The Potential Autonomy of the State   24
        A Comparative Historical Method   33
        Why France, Russia, and China?   40

Part I *Causes of Social Revolutions in France, Russia, and China*

2. Old-Regime States in Crisis   47
        Old-Regime France: The Contradictions of
          Bourbon Absolutism   51
        Manchu China: From the Celestial Empire to the Fall
          of the Imperial System   67
        Imperial Russia: An Underdeveloped Great Power   81
        Japan and Prussia as Contrasts   99

3. Agrarian Structures and Peasant Insurrections   112
        Peasants Against Seigneurs in the French Revolution   118
        The Revolution of the *Obshchinas:* Peasant Radicalism
          in Russia   128
        Two Counterpoints: The Absence of Peasant Revolts
          in the English and German Revolutions   140
        Peasant Incapacity and Gentry Vulnerability in China   147

Contents

Part II *Outcomes of Social Revolutions in France, Russia, and China*

4. What Changed and How: A Focus on State Building   161
    Political Leaderships   164
    The Role of Revolutionary Ideologies   168

5. The Birth of a "Modern State Edifice" in France   174
    A Bourgeois Revolution?   174
    The Effects of the Social-Revolutionary Crisis of 1789   181
    War, the Jacobins, and Napoleon   185
    The New Regime   196

6. The Emergence of a Dictatorial Party-State in Russia   206
    The Effects of the Social-Revolutionary Crisis of 1917   207
    The Bolshevik Struggle to Rule   212
    The Stalinist "Revolution from Above"   220
    The New Regime   225

7. The Rise of a Mass-Mobilizing Party-State in China   236
    The Social-Revolutionary Situation after 1911   237
    The Rise and Decline of the Urban-Based Kuomintang   242
    The Communists and the Peasants   252
    The New Regime   263

Conclusion   284

Notes   294

Bibliography   351

Index   391

Tables and Maps

Tables

1. Causes of Social Revolutions in France,
    Russia, and China   155
2. Outcomes of Social Revolutions in France,
    Russia and China   282

Maps

1. Major Administrative Divisions of Old-Regime France   53
2. The Main Regions of European Russia   131
3. The Departments of France   180
4. Railroads and Major Industrial Areas of
    European Russia   212
5. The Provinces of China   245
6. Railroads and Major Industrial Areas of China   248

Preface

[handwritten notes in margin]

SOME BOOKS PRESENT fresh evidence; others make arguments that urge the reader to see old problems in a new light. This work is decidedly of the latter sort. It offers a frame of reference for analyzing social-revolutionary transformations in modern world history. And it uses comparative history to work out an explanation of the causes and outcomes of the French Revolution of 1787–1800, the Russian Revolution of 1917–1921, and the Chinese Revolution of 1911–1949. Developed through critical reflection on assumptions and types of explanation common to most received theories of revolution, the principles of analysis sketched in the first chapter of the book are meant to reorient our sense of what is characteristic of – and problematic about – revolutions as they actually have occurred historically. Then the remainder of the book attempts to make the program of Chapter 1, calling for new kinds of explanatory arguments, come alive in application. In Part I, the roots of revolutionary crises and conflicts in France, Russia, and China are traced through analyses of the state and class structures and the international situations of the Bourbon, Tsarist, and Imperial Old Regimes. Particular emphasis is placed upon the ways in which the old-regime states came into crisis, and upon the emergence of peasant insurrections during the revolutionary interregnums. Then, in Part II, the Revolutions themselves are traced from the original outbreaks through to the consolidation of relatively stable and distinctively structured New Regimes: the Napoleonic in France, the Stalinist in Russia, and the characteristically Sino-Communist (after the mid-1950s) in China. Here special attention is paid to the state-building efforts of revolutionary leaderships, and to the structures and activities of new state organizations within the revolutionized societies. In their broad sweep from Old to New Regimes, the French, Russian, and Chinese Revolutions are treated as three comparable instances of a single, coherent social-revolutionary pattern. As a result, both the similarities and the individual features of these Revolutions are highlighted and explained in ways somewhat different from previous theoretical or historical discussions.

Books grow in unique ways out of the experiences of their authors, and this one is no exception. The ideas for it germinated during my time as a graduate student at Harvard University in the early 1970s. This was— however faint the echoes now—a vivid period of political engagement for many students, myself included. The United States was brutally at war against the Vietnamese Revolution, while at home movements calling for racial justice and for an immediate end to the foreign military involvement challenged the capacities for good and evil of our national political system. The times certainly stimulated my interest in understanding revolutionary change. And it was during these years that my commitment to democratic-socialist ideals matured. Yet it would be a mistake to imply that *States and Social Revolutions* sprang immediately from day-to-day political preoccupations. It didn't. Instead it developed in the relative "ivory tower" quiet of the library and the study. As a graduate student, I pursued studies in macrosociological theory and in comparative social and political history. Puzzles kept emerging at the interface of these sets of studies. My attempts to formulate answers to problematic issues, and then to follow answers through to their conclusions, led me, through many stages of formulation, to the arguments and analyses now embodied here.

There was, for one thing, my early intellectual confrontation with the case of South Africa. The history of that unhappy land struck me as an obvious refutation of Parsonian structure–functionalist explanations of societal order and change, and as an insuperable challenge to commonplace and comforting predictions that mass discontent would lead to revolution against the blatantly oppressive *apartheid* regime. Liberal justice, it seemed, did not inevitably triumph. Marxist class analysis impressed me as much more useful than structure–functionalism or relative deprivation theory for understanding the situation of the nonwhites in South Africa and deciphering the long-term tendencies of socioeconomic change. But, working strictly in terms of class analysis, it was difficult to conceptualize, let alone adequately explain, the structure of the South African state and the political role of the Afrikaners. Yet these seemed to be the keys to why no social revolution had occurred—or likely soon would—in South Africa.

Another formative experience was a lengthy, in-depth exploration of the historical origins of the Chinese Revolution. To structure my program of study, I compared and sought to explain the relative successes and failures of the Taiping Rebellion, the Kuomintang Nationalist movement, and the Chinese Communist Party, looking at all three movements in the historically changing overall context of Chinese society. Deeply fascinated by late

against structu-fun.
Marxism not enough

Imperial and modern China, I came away from this research profoundly skeptical about the applicability (to China, and perhaps to other agrarian states as well) of received social-scientific categorizations such as "traditional" or "feudal." I also became convinced that the causes of revolutions could only be understood by looking at the specific interrelations of class and state structures and the complex interplay over time of domestic and international developments.

If most other students of comparative revolutions have moved, so to speak, from the West to the East—interpreting the Russian Revolution in terms of the French, or the Chinese in terms of the Russian—my intellectual journey has been the other way around the globe. After first investigating China, I next learned about France as part of a general program of studies on the comparative political development of Western Europe. Although I realized that France was "supposed" to be like England, her absolutist Old Regime seemed in many ways similar to Imperial China. I also deciphered basic similarities in the French and Chinese revolutionary processes, both of which were launched by landed upper class revolts against absolutist monarchs, and both of which involved peasant revolts and culminated in more centralized and bureaucratic New Regimes. Finally, I came to interpret old-regime and revolutionary Russia in the same analytic terms that I had worked out for China and France. And the emphases on agrarian structures and state building seemed a fruitful way to understand the fate of this "proletarian" revolution after 1917, through 1921 and the early 1930s.

There was yet another peculiarity worth noting about my induction into systematic research on revolutions. Unlike most sociologists who work in this area, I learned a good deal about the histories of actual revolutions *before* I read very extensively in the social-scientific literature that purports to explain revolutions theoretically. When I did survey this literature, I quickly became frustrated with it. The revolutionary process itself was envisaged in ways that corresponded very poorly to the histories I knew. And the causal explanations offered seemed either irrelevant or just plain wrong, given what I had learned about the similarities and differences of countries that had, versus those that had not, experienced revolutions. Before long, I decided (to my own satisfaction, at least) what the fundamental trouble was: Social-scientific theories derived their explanations of revolution from models of how political protest and change were ideally supposed to occur in liberal-democratic or capitalist societies. Thus non-Marxist theories tended to envisage revolutions as particularly radical and ideological variants of the typical social reform movement, and Marxists saw them as class actions spearheaded by the bourgeoisie or the proletariat. No wonder, I said to myself, that these theories offer so little insight

xiii

into the causes and accomplishments of revolutions in predominantly agrarian countries with absolutist–monarchical states and peasant-based social orders.

From this mélange of intellectual experiences, a possible project, destined to culminate in this book, presented itself to me: Use comparisons among the French, Russian, and Chinese Revolutions, and some contrasts of these cases to other countries, to clarify my critique of the inadequacies of existing theories of revolution, and to develop an alternative theoretical approach and explanatory hypotheses. Although I rejected the assumptions and substantive arguments of the theories of revolution I knew, I still had the urge to clarify the general logic that I sensed was at work across the diversely situated major revolutions I had studied. Comparative historical analysis seemed an ideal way to proceed.

To my good fortune, the three Revolutions that I wanted to include in my comparative analysis had been extensively researched by historians and area specialists. A large existing literature may be a bane for the specialist who hopes to make a new contribution based upon previously undiscovered or underexploited primary evidence. But for the comparative sociologist this is the ideal situation. Inevitably, broadly conceived comparative historical projects draw their evidence almost entirely from "secondary sources" – that is, from research monographs and syntheses already published in book or journal-article form by the relevant historical or culture-area specialists. The comparative historian's task – and potential distinctive scholarly contribution – lies not in revealing new data about particular aspects of the large time periods and diverse places surveyed in the comparative study, but rather in establishing the interest and prima facie validity of an overall argument about causal regularities across the various historical cases. The comparativist has neither the time nor (all of) the appropriate skills to do the primary research that necessarily constitutes, in large amounts, the foundation upon which comparative studies are built. Instead, the comparativist must concentrate upon searching out and systematically surveying specialists' publications that deal with the issues defined as important by theoretical considerations and by the logic of comparative analysis. If, as is often the case, the points debated by specialists about a particular historical epoch or event are not exactly the ones that seem most important from a comparative perspective, then the comparative analyst must be prepared to adapt the evidence presented in the works of the specialists to analytic purposes somewhat tangential to those they originally envisaged. And the comparativist must be as systematic as possible in searching out information on the same topics from case to case, even though the specialists are likely to emphasize varying topics in their research and polemics from one country to the next. Plainly, the work of the comparativist only becomes possible *after* a large primary literature has been built up by specialists. Only then can the comparativist hope to find at least some material relevant to each topic that must be investigated according to the dictates of the comparative, explanatory argument that he or she is attempting to develop.

As the Bibliography for this book is meant to indicate, I have been able to draw extensively upon rich literatures about France, Russia, and China. Each literature has great depth and scope, and each includes many books and articles originally published in (or translated into) English and French, the two languages that I read most easily. With occasional exceptions attributable to the thinness of interest about particular topics in one historical literature or another, the challenges I have faced have not been due to difficulties of finding basic information. Rather they have been challenges of surveying huge historical literatures and appropriately weighing and using the contributions of specialists, in order to develop a coherent comparative historical argument. How well I have met these challenges is for readers (including historians and area specialists) to judge for themselves. For myself, I shall be satisfied if this book serves in some small measure to provoke debate and inspire further investigations, both among people interested in one particular revolution or another and among people concerned to understand modern revolutions in general, their past causes and accomplishments and their future prospects. Comparative history grows out of the interplay of theory and history, and it should in turn contribute to the further enrichment of each.

Working and reworking the argument of this book over the last few years has often felt like an unending lonely struggle with a giant jig-saw puzzle. But, in actuality, many people have lent a hand, helping me to see better the overall design and pointing out where particular pieces fit, or do not.

My most fundamental scholarly debt is to Barrington Moore, Jr. It was my reading of his *Social Origins of Dictatorship and Democracy* while I was still an undergraduate at Michigan State University that introduced me to the magnificent scope of comparative history and taught me that agrarian structures and conflicts offer important keys to the patterns of modern politics. Moreover, the graduate seminars I took from Moore at Harvard were the crucibles within which my capacities to do comparative analysis were forged, even as I was allowed the space to develop my own interpretations. Moore set rigorous tasks and reacted with telling criticisms. And student fellowship in the seminars provided a supportive and intellectually lively atmosphere. In fact, two friends among fellow students in Moore's seminars, Mounira Charrad and John Mollenkopf, have given me encouragement and advice through all stages of this project on comparative revolutions.

Another crucial, longstanding influence has been Ellen Kay Trimberger. I first became aware of her kindred work on "revolutions from above" in

Japan and Turkey in 1970. And, ever since, Kay's ideas, comments, and friendship have helped me enormously to develop my analysis of France, Russia and China.

Like many first books, this one had an earlier incarnation as a doctoral dissertation. That phase of the project was certainly the most painful, because I undertook too much in too short a time. Nevertheless, in retrospect it was worth it, for a "big" thesis, however imperfect, offers more potential for the subsequent development of a publishable book than a more polished narrow dissertation. For encouraging me to undertake the nearly impossible, I owe thanks to Daniel Bell, who also made detailed and provocative comments on the thesis draft. The dissertation was formally advised by the good and admirable George Caspar Homans, who gave careful feedback and exerted unremitting pressure for me to finish quickly. The remaining member of my thesis committee, Seymour Martin Lipset, made astute suggestions from beginning to end and was kind enough not to hold it against me when the thesis took longer to complete than I had originally planned. Financial support during my final years of Ph.D. work came from a Danforth Graduate Fellowship, which leaves its holders free to pursue research topics of their own choosing.

After the dissertation was completed, Charles Tilly generously offered encouragement and recommendations for the major revisions that lay ahead. Colleagues and students at Harvard, where I teach, helped in innumerable ways to facilitate and stimulate my progress on the book. And once the revisions were partially done, many others helped speed the book to completion. Walter Lippincott, Jr., of Cambridge University Press, arranged for early reviews of the manuscript; these resulted not only in a contract for publication but also in very useful advice on the introduction from John Dunn and Eric Wolf. Peter Evans also made suggestions that helped with the revisions of the first chapter. Mary Fulbrook provided research assistance for revisions of Chapter 3, and her work was paid for by a small grant from the Harvard Graduate Society. I likewise benefited from the Sociology Department's Fund for Junior Faculty Research.

Several friends heroically took the time to make written comments on the entire book draft. These special helpers were: Susan Eckstein, Harriet Friedmann, Walter Goldfrank, Peter Gourevitch, Richard Kraus, Joel Migdal, and Jonathan Zeitlin. In addition, Perry Anderson, Reinhard Bendix, Victoria Bonnell, Shmuel Eisenstadt, Terence Hopkins, Lynn Hunt, Barrington Moore, Jr., Victor Nee, Magali Sarfatti-Larson, Ann Swidler, and Immanuel Wallerstein all made comments on related published articles of mine, comments which substantially influenced subsequent work on the book. Needless to say, whereas the abovementioned people are responsible for much of what may be good about this work, none is to be held accountable for its shortcomings.

Preface

Mrs. Nellie Miller, Louisa Amos, and Lynn McKay did wonderfully speedy and accurate work in typing the final manuscript. Mrs. Miller deserves thanks above all, for she did most of the typing in every stage of revision. I was fortunate indeed to be able to rely upon her perfectionism and intelligence.

Finally, of course, I lovingly acknowledge the help of my husband, Bill Skocpol, to whom this book is dedicated. His comments on all parts of the text through many revisions, his willingness to help with practical chores such as the typing of early thesis versions and the checking of quotes at the end, and his patience in the face of my emotional ups-and-downs throughout the entire process—all of these contributions are embodied in every part of *States and Social Revolutions*. Bill is an experimental physicist, but without his willing aid this work of comparative historical sociology could not have developed to completion.

xvii

Introduction

1 Explaining Social Revolutions: Alternatives to Existing Theories

> *Revolutions are the locomotives of history.*   Karl Marx

> *Controversy over different views of "methodology" and "theory" is properly carried on in close and continuous relation with substantive problems . . . . The character of these problems limits and suggests the methods and conceptions that are used and how they are used.*   C. Wright Mills

SOCIAL REVOLUTIONS have been rare but momentous occurrences in modern world history. From France in the 1790s to Vietnam in the mid-twentieth century, these revolutions have transformed state organizations, class structures, and dominant ideologies. They have given birth to nations whose power and autonomy markedly surpassed their own prerevolutionary pasts and outstripped other countries in similar circumstances. Revolutionary France became suddenly a conquering power in Continental Europe, and the Russian Revolution generated an industrial and military superpower. The Mexican Revolution gave its homeland the political strength to become one of the most industrialized of postcolonial nations and the country in Latin America least prone to military coups. Since World War II, the culmination of a revolutionary process long underway has reunited and transformed a shattered China. And new social revolutions have enabled decolonizing and neocolonial countries such as Vietnam and Cuba to break the chains of extreme dependency.

Nor have social revolutions had only national significance. In some cases social revolutions have given rise to models and ideals of enormous international impact and appeal—especially where the transformed societies have been large and geopolitically important, actual or potential Great Powers. The patriotic armies of revolutionary France mastered much of Europe. Even before the conquests and long after military defeat, the French revolutionary ideals of "Liberty, Equality, and Fraternity" fired imaginations in quest of social and national liberation: The effects reached from Geneva to Santo Domingo, from Ireland to Latin America and India, and influenced subsequent revolutionary theorists from Babeuf to Marx and Lenin, to anticolonialists of the twentieth century. The Russian Revo-

3

lution astounded the capitalist West and whetted the ambitions of the emerging nations by demonstrating that revolutionary state power could, within the space of two generations, transform a backward agrarian country into the second-ranked industrial and military power in the world. What the Russian Revolution was for the first half of the twentieth century, the Chinese has been for the second half. By showing that a Leninist party can lead a peasant majority in economic and military struggles, it "... has brought a great power into being which proclaims itself the revolutionary and developmental model for the poor countries of the world."[1] "The Yenan Way" and "The Countryside Against the City" have offered fresh ideals and models and renewed hopes for revolutionary nationalists in the mid-twentieth century. Moreover, as Elbaki Hermassi has emphasized, major revolutions affect not only those abroad who would like to imitate them. They also affect those in other countries who oppose revolutionary ideals but are compelled to respond to the challenges or threats posed by the enhanced national power that has been generated. "The world-historical character of revolutions means ... , " says Hermassi, that "they exert a demonstration effect beyond the boundaries of their country of origin, with a potential for triggering waves of revolution and counterrevolution both within and between societies."[2]

To be sure, social revolutions have not been the only forces for change at work in the modern era. Within the matrix of the "Great Transformation" (that is, worldwide commercialization and industrialization, and the rise of national states and expansion of the European states system to encompass the entire globe) political upheavals and socioeconomic changes have happened in every country. But within this matrix, social revolutions deserve special attention, not only because of their extraordinary significance for the histories of nations and the world but also because of their distinctive pattern of sociopolitical change.

Social revolutions are rapid, basic transformations of a society's state and class structures; and they are accompanied and in part carried through by class-based revolts from below. Social revolutions are set apart from other sorts of conflicts and transformative processes above all by the combination of two coincidences: the coincidence of societal structural change with class upheaval; and the coincidence of political with social transformation. In contrast, rebellions, even when successful, may involve the revolt of subordinate classes—but they do not eventuate in structural change.[3] Political revolutions transform state structures but not social structures, and they are not necessarily accomplished through class conflict.[4] And processes such as industrialization can transform social structures without necessarily bringing about, or resulting from, sudden political upheavals or basic political-structural changes. What is unique to social

4

revolution is that basic changes in social structure and in political structure occur together in a mutually reinforcing fashion. And these changes occur through intense sociopolitical conflicts in which class struggles play a key role.

This conception of social revolution differs from many other definitions of revolution in important respects. First, it identifies a *complex* object of explanation, of which there are relatively few historical instances. It does this rather than trying to multiply the number of cases for explanation by concentrating only upon one analytic feature (such as violence or political conflict) shared by many events of heterogeneous nature and outcome.[5] It is my firm belief that analytic oversimplification cannot lead us toward valid, complete explanations of revolutions. If our intention is to understand large-scale conflicts and changes such as those that occurred in France from 1787 to 1800, we cannot make progress by starting with objects of explanation that isolate only the aspects that such revolutionary events share with, say, riots or coups. We must look at the revolutions as wholes, in much of their complexity.

Second, this definition makes successful sociopolitical transformation—*actual change* of state and class structures—part of the specification of what is to be called a social revolution, rather than leaving change contingent in the definition of "revolution" as many other scholars do.[6] The rationale is my belief that successful social revolutions probably emerge from different macro-structural and historical contexts than do either failed social revolutions or political transformations that are not accompanied by transformations of class relations. Because I intend to focus exactly on this question in my comparative historical analysis—in which actual social revolutions will be compared to unsuccessful cases and to non-social-revolutionary transformations—my concept of social revolution necessarily highlights successful change as a basic defining feature.

How, then, are social revolutions to be explained? Where are we to turn for fruitful modes of analyzing their causes and outcomes? In my view, existing social-scientific theories of revolution are not adequate.[7] In consequence, the chief purpose of this chapter is to introduce and defend principles and methods of analysis that represent alternatives to those shared by all (or most) existing approaches. I shall argue that, in contrast to the modes of explanation used by the currently prevalent theories, social revolutions should be analyzed from a structural perspective, with special attention devoted to international contexts and to developments at home and abroad that affect the breakdown of the state organizations of old regimes and the buildup of new, revolutionary state organizations. Furthermore, I shall argue that comparative historical analysis is the most

5

appropriate way to develop explanations of revolutions that are at once historically grounded and generalizable beyond unique cases.

To facilitate the subsequent presentation of these theoretical and methodological alternatives, it should be helpful to identify major types of social-scientific theories of revolution, briefly sketching the important characteristics of each as embodied in the work of a representative writer. The kinds of theories I am about to summarize in this manner are all properly called "general" theories of revolution – that is, they are rather broadly formulated conceptual schemes and hypotheses meant to be applicable across many particular historical instances. This book itself does not represent exactly the same sort of scholarly endeavor as such general theories. Instead, like other historically grounded, comparative studies of revolutions – such as Barrington Moore, Jr.'s *Social Origins of Dictatorship and Democracy,* Eric Wolf's *Peasant Wars of the Twentieth Century,* and John Dunn's *Modern Revolutions*[8] – this book basically analyzes in depth a set of cases. Yet, also like these sister works (and perhaps even more determinedly than the latter two), this book is concerned not merely with narrating the cases one by one but primarily with understanding and explaining the generalizable logic at work in the entire set of revolutions under discussion. Plainly, the sorts of concepts and hypotheses found in general theories of revolution are potentially relevant to the explanatory task of the comparative historian; in fact, any comparative study either draws upon or reacts against the ideas put forward by social-scientific theorists of revolution from Marx to more contemporary writers. It follows, therefore, that briefly summarizing general theories, though not allowing us to explore the far richer arguments of existing comparative-historical treatments of revolutions, nevertheless does provide an economical way of identifying relevant basic theoretical issues for later commentary.

It is useful, I suggest, to think of currently important social-scientific theories of revolution as grouped into four major families, which I shall take up one by one. The most obviously relevant of these groupings is the Marxist; and the key ideas are best represented in the works of Karl Marx himself. As active proponents of this mode of social change, Marxists have been the social analysts most consistently concerned with understanding social revolutions as such. To be sure, in the tumultuous century since the death of Marx, many divergent tendencies have developed within Marxist intellectual and political traditions: Subsequent Marxist theorists of revolution range from technological determinists such as Nikolai Bukharin (in *Historical Materialism*),[9] to political strategists such as Lenin and Mao,[10] to Western Marxists such as Georg Lukács, Antonio Gramsci, and contemporary "structuralists" such as Louis Althusser.[11] Nevertheless, Marx's original approach to revolutions has remained the unquestioned, if variously interpreted, basis for all such later Marxists.

6

The basic elements of Marx's theory can be straightforwardly identified without in any way denying the fact that all of the elements are open to widely varying weights and interpretations. Marx understood revolutions not as isolated episodes of violence or conflict but as class-based movements growing out of objective structural contradictions within historically developing and inherently conflict-ridden societies. For Marx, the key to any society is its mode of production or specific combination of socioeconomic forces of production (technology and division of labor) and class relations of property ownership and surplus appropriation. The latter, the relations of production, are especially crucial:

> It is always the direct relationship of the owners of the conditions of production to the direct producers—a relation always naturally corresponding to a definite stage in the development of the methods of labour and thereby its social productivity—which reveals the innermost secret, the hidden basis of the entire social structure, and with it the political form of the relation of sovereignty and dependence, in short, the corresponding specific form of the state.[12]

The basic source of a revolutionary contradiction in society, according to Marx's most general theoretical formulation, is the emergence of a disjuncture within a mode of production between the social forces and social relations of production.

> At a certain stage of their development the material forces of production in society come into conflict with the existing relations of production, or—what is but a legal expression for the same thing—with the property relations within which they had been at work before. From forms of development of the forces of production these relations turn into their fetters. Then comes the period of social revolution.[13]

In turn, this disjuncture expresses itself in intensifying class conflicts. The generation of a nascent mode of production within the confines of an existing one—of capitalism within feudalism; of socialism within capitalism—creates a dynamic basis for the growth of the unity and consciousness of each proto-revolutionary class through on-going struggles with the existing dominant class. Thus, leading up to the European bourgeois revolutions, "the means of production and of exchange, on whose foundation the bourgeoisie built itself up, were generated in feudal society."[14]

> Each step in the development of the bourgeoisie was accompanied by a corresponding political advance of that class. An oppressed class under the sway of the feudal nobility, an armed and self-governing association in the medieval commune; here independent urban republic (as in Italy and Germany), there taxable "third estate" of the monarchy (as in France); afterwards, in the period of manufacture proper, serving either the semi-feudal or absolute monarchy as a counterpoise against the nobility, and, in fact, corner-stone of the great monarchies in gen-

7

eral—the bourgeoisie has at last, since the establishment of Modern Industry and the world market, conquered for itself, in the modern representative State, exclusive political sway.[15]

Similarly, with the establishment of capitalism the

advance of industry, whose involuntary promoter is the bourgeoisie, replaces the isolation of the labourers, due to competition, by their revolutionary combination, due to association.[16]

The proletariat goes through various stages of development. With its birth begins its struggle with the bourgeoisie. At first the contest is carried on by individual labourers, then by the workpeople of a factory, then by the operatives of one trade, in one locality . . .

Now and then the workers are victorious, but only for a time. The real fruit of their battles lies, not in the immediate result, but in the ever-expanding union of workers. This union is helped on by the improved means of communication that are created by modern industry and that place the workers of different localities in contact with one another. It was just this contact that was needed to centralise the numerous local struggles, all of them of the same character, into one national struggle between classes . . .

[The result is] more or less veiled civil war, raging within existing society, up to the point where that war breaks out into open revolution, and where the violent overthrow of the bourgeoisie lays the foundation for the sway of the proletariat.[17]

Revolution itself is accomplished through class action led by the self-conscious, rising revolutionary class (i.e., the bourgeoisie in bourgeois revolutions and the proletariat in socialist revolutions). Perhaps the revolutionary class is supported by other class allies such as the peasantry, but these allies are neither fully class-conscious nor politically organized on a national scale. Once successful, a revolution marks the transition from the previous mode of production and form of class dominance to a new mode of production, in which new social relations of production, new political and ideological forms, and, in general, the hegemony of the newly triumphant revolutionary class, create appropriate conditions for the further development of society. In short, Marx sees revolutions as emerging out of class-divided modes of production, and transforming one mode of production into another through class conflict.

The other three families of theories of revolution have taken basic shape much more recently than Marxism (though they all draw particular themes from the classical social theorists, including Tocqueville, Durkheim, and Weber, as well as Marx). Indeed, during the last two decades, theories of revolution have sprung up thick and fast in American social science. This

8

recent outgrowth has been concerned above all with understanding the roots of social instability and political violence, not infrequently for the declared purpose of helping established authorities to prevent or ameliorate these conditions at home and abroad. Whatever the intended applications, though, elaborate theories have been developed that purport either to explain revolutions as such or to subsume revolutions explicitly within some still broader class of phenomena which they claim to explain. Most of these recent theories can be identified with one or another of three major approaches: *aggregate-psychological* theories, which attempt to explain revolutions in terms of people's psychological motivations for engaging in political violence or joining oppositional movements,[18] *systems/value consensus* theories, which attempt to explain revolutions as violent responses of ideological movements to severe disequilibrium in social systems;[19] and *political-conflict* theories, which argue that conflict among governments and various organized groups contending for power must be placed at the center of attention to explain collective violence and revolutions.[20] An important and representative theoretical work has been produced within each perspective: Ted Gurr's *Why Men Rebel* within the aggregate-psychological; Chalmers Johnson's *Revolutionary Change* within the systems/value consensus; and Charles Tilly's *From Mobilization to Revolution* within the political-conflict approach.

In *Why Men Rebel*,[21] Ted Gurr aims to develop a general, psychologically based theory of the magnitude and forms of "political violence," defined as

> all collective attacks within a political community against the political regime, its actors – including competing political groups as well as incumbents – or its policies. The concept represents a set of events, a common property of which is the actual or threatened use of violence... The concept subsumes revolution... It also includes guerilla wars, coups d'état, rebellions, and riots.[22]

Gurr's theory is complex and full of interesting nuances in its full elaboration but is simple enough in essence: Political violence occurs when many people in society become angry, especially if existing cultural and practical conditions provide encouragement for aggression against political targets. And people become angry when there occurs a gap between the valued things and opportunities they feel entitled to and the things and opportunities they actually get – a condition known as "relative deprivation." Gurr offers special models to explain different major forms of political violence. He distinguishes "turmoil," "conspiracy," and "internal war" as the major forms. Revolutions are included in the internal-war category, along with large-scale terrorism, guerrilla wars, and civil wars. What sets internal wars apart from the other forms is that they are more organized than turmoil and more mass-based than conspiracy. Logically, therefore, revo-

9

lutions are explained as basically due to the occurrence in a society of widespread, intense, and multifaceted relative deprivation that touches both masses and elite aspirants.[23] For if potential leaders and followers alike are intensely frustrated, then both broad participation in, and deliberate organization of, political violence are probable, and the fundamental conditions for internal war are present.

Charles Tilly's *From Mobilization to Revolution*[24] represents, so to speak, a culminating theoretical statement for a political-conflict approach that was born in polemic opposition to frustration-aggression explanations of political violence such as Ted Gurr's. The basic counterarguments are convincing and easily specified. Political-conflict theorists argue that no matter how discontented an aggregate of people may become, they cannot engage in political action (including violence) unless they are part of at least minimally organized groups with access to some resources. Even then, governments or competing groups may successfully repress the will to engage in collective action by making the costs too high to bear. Moreover, political-conflict theorists contend, as Tilly puts it,

> that revolutions and collective violence tend to flow directly out of a population's central political processes, instead of expressing diffuse strains and discontents within the population; ... that the specific claims and counterclaims being made on the existing government by various mobilized groups are more important than the general satisfaction or discontent of those groups, and that claims for established places within the structure of power are crucial.[25]

In fact, Tilly refuses to make violence as such his object of analysis, because he maintains that incidents of collective violence are in actuality only by-products of normal processes of group competition over power and conflicting goals. Instead, the objective of analysis is "collective action," defined as "people's acting together in pursuit of common interests."[26] Tilly analyzes collective action with the aid of two general models, a "polity model" and a "mobilization model."[27] The major elements of the polity model are governments (organizations that control the principal concentrated means of coercion in a population) and groups contending for power, including both members (contenders that have routine, low-cost access to government resources), and challengers (all other contenders). The mobilization model includes variables designed to explain the pattern of collective action engaged in by given contenders. These variables refer to group interests, to degrees of organization, to amounts of resources under collective control, and to the opportunities and threats that given contenders face in their relationships to governments and other contending groups.

Revolution for Tilly is a special case of collective action in which the contenders both (or all) fight for ultimate political sovereignty over a

10

population, and in which challengers succeed at least to some degree in displacing existing power-holders.[28] Given this conception, the causes of a revolutionary situation of "multiple sovereignty" include the following. The first considerations should be any long-term societal trends that shift resources from some groups in society to others (particularly if those who gain were formerly excluded from the polity). Second, it is important to examine any medium-term occurrences, such as the proliferation of revolutionary ideologies and the increase of popular discontent, that make revolutionary contenders for sovereignty likely to emerge and large elements of the population likely to support their claims. Finally:

> The revolutionary moment arrives when previously acquiescent members of . . . [a] population find themselves confronted with strictly incompatible demands from the government and from an alternative body claiming control over the government—and obey the alternative body. They pay taxes to it, provide men for its armies, feed its functionaries, honor its symbols, give time to its service, or yield other resources, despite the prohibition of the still-existing government that they formerly obeyed. Multiple sovereignty has begun.[29]

Successful revolutions, in turn, depend not only upon the emergence of multiple sovereignty. They also probably depend upon "the formation of coalitions between members of the polity and the contenders advancing exclusive alternative claims to control over the government."[30] And they definitely depend upon the "control of substantial force by the revolutionary coalition."[31] For only if these additional conditions hold are the revolutionary challengers likely to be able to defeat and displace existing power-holders.

Whereas Ted Gurr and Charles Tilly analyze revolutions as special types of political events explicable in terms of general theories of political violence or collective action, Chalmers Johnson in *Revolutionary Change*[32] parallels Marx in analyzing revolutions from the perspective of a macrosociological theory of societal integration and change. Like the study of physiology and pathology, Johnson argues, the "analysis of revolution intermeshes with the analysis of viable, functioning societies."[33] Borrowing his sociological wisdom from the Parsonians, Johnson posits that a normal, crisis-free society should be conceived as a "value-coordinated social system," functionally adapted to the exigencies of its environment. Such a social system is an internally consistent set of institutions that express and specify core societal value-orientations in norms and roles. The value orientations have also been internalized through processes of socialization to serve as the personal moral and reality-defining standards for the vast majority of normal adult members of the society. Moreover, political authority in society must be legitimated in terms of societal values.

Revolutions are both defined and explained by Johnson on the basis of this value-coordinated social system model. Violence and change are, Johnson says, the distinctive features of revolution: "To make a revolution is to accept violence for the purpose of causing the system to change; more exactly, it is the purposive implementation of a strategy of violence in order to effect a change in social structure."[34] When they succeed, what revolutions change above all are the core value-orientations of a society. And the purposive attempt to do this takes the form of a value-oriented ideological movement that is prepared to use violence against existing authorities. Yet such a movement will not emerge in the first place unless the existing social system comes into crisis. This occurs, according to Johnson, whenever values and environment become seriously "dis-synchronized," due to either external or internal intrusions—especially of new values or technologies. Once dis-synchronization sets in, people in the society become disoriented, and hence open to conversion to the alternative values proposed by a revolutionary movement. As this happens, existing authorities lose their legitimacy and have to rely more and more upon coercion to maintain order. Yet they can do this successfully only for a while. If the authorities are smart, flexible, and skillful, they will implement reforms to "resynchronize" values and environment. But if the authorities are stubbornly "intransigent," then revolution will instead accomplish systemic change violently. This occurs as soon as some "factor contributed by fortune" comes along to undercut the authorities' necessarily tenuous and temporary ability to rely upon coercion.

> Superior force may delay the eruption of violence; nevertheless, a division of labor maintained by Cossacks is no longer a community of value-sharers, and in such a situation (e.g., South Africa today [1966]), revolution is endemic and, *ceteris paribus,* an insurrection is inevitable. This fact reveals ... the necessity of investigating a system's value structure and its problems in order to conceptualize the revolutionary situation in any meaningful way.[35]

Successful revolution finally accomplishes the resynchronization of the social system's values and environment that the incompetent or intransigent old-regime authorities were unable to accomplish. Indeed in Johnson's view, revolution rather than evolutionary change becomes possible and necessary only because the prerevolutionary authorities thus fail and lose their legitimacy. For Johnson's theory of society and social change makes value orientations and political legitimacy the key elements for explaining the emergence of revolutionary situations, the options of existing authorities, and the nature and success of revolutionary forces.

Even from such brief sketches as these, it should be readily apparent that there are enormous disagreements among the major types of social-scientific theories, not only about how to explain revolutions, but even about how to define them. In this book there is certainly no pretense of neutrality with respect to such disagreements. Quite evidently, the conception of social revolution used here draws heavily upon Marxist emphases on so-cial–structural change and class conflict. And it refuses either to abstract away from issues of structural transformation, as Gurr and Tilly do, or to make societal value reorientation the key to revolutionary social change, as Johnson does. Moreover, in my overall analysis of the causes and out-comes of social revolutions, I shall leave aside explanatory hypotheses about relative deprivation and discontent—essentially because I accept the critiques of such ideas that have been developed by political conflict theo-rists. I shall also leave aside (for reasons that will become apparent as the argument proceeds) notions of system disequilibrium, delegitimation of authority, and ideological conversion to revolutionary world-views. In-stead, for the specific purpose of understanding some of the conflicts in-volved in social revolutions, I shall rely extensively upon certain ideas adapted from the Marxist and political-conflict perspectives.

The Marxist conception of class relations as rooted in the control of productive property and the appropriation of economic surpluses from direct producers by nonproducers is, in my view, an indispensable theoreti-cal tool for identifying one sort of basic contradiction in society. Class relations are always a potential source of patterned social and political conflict, and class conflicts and changes in class relations actually do figure prominently in successful social-revolutionary transformations. For the cases to be studied in depth in this book—France, Russia, and China—class relations between peasants and landlords need especially to be analyzed. These relations were the site of underlying tensions that influenced the economic and political dynamics of the prerevolutionary Old Regimes, even during periods when overt class conflicts did not erupt. Moreover, during the French, Russian, and Chinese Revolutions, peasants *did* directly strike out at the class privileges of landlords, and these class conflicts in the countryside contributed both directly and indirectly to the overall sociopolitical transformations accomplished by the Revolutions. Plainly, therefore, it will be important to understand why and exactly how these overt class conflicts developed during the Revolutions.

For this purpose, class analysis must be supplemented by the ideas of political-conflict theorists. It is one thing to identify underlying, potential tensions rooted in objective class relations understood in a Marxist man-ner. It is another thing to understand how and when class members find themselves *able* to struggle effectively for their interests. When and how can subordinate classes fight successfully against those who exploit them? And when and how do dominant classes have the capacity for collective political action? For answering such questions, the political-conflict argu-ment that collective action is based upon group organization and access to

13

resources, often including coercive resources, is especially fruitful. Thus, in the historical case analyses of this book, I shall not only identify classes and their interests. I shall also investigate the presence or absence (and the exact forms) of the organization and resources available to members of classes for waging struggles based upon their interests.

In these specific ways, therefore, I find aspects of two of the existing theoretical approaches relevant to the project of understanding social revolutions. Nevertheless, as has already been suggested, the overriding purpose of this chapter is not to weigh the relative strengths and weaknesses of the various families of theories of revolution. It is rather to take issue with certain conceptions, assumptions, and modes of explanation that they all, despite their evident differences, in fact share.

Three major principles of analysis need to be established as alternatives to features shared by all of the currently prevalent theories of revolution. In the first place, an adequate understanding of social revolutions requires that the analyst take a nonvoluntarist, structural perspective on their causes and processes. But all existing approaches theorize on the basis of a voluntarist image of how revolutions happen. In the second place, social revolutions cannot be explained without systematic reference to *in*-*ter*national structures and world-historical developments. Existing theories, however, focus primarily or exclusively upon *intra*national conflicts and processes of modernization. In the third place, in order to explain the causes and outcomes of social revolutions, it is essential to conceive of states as administrative and coercive organizations—organizations that are potentially autonomous from (though of course conditioned by) socioeconomic interests and structures. But currently prevalent theories of revolution instead either analytically collapse state and society or they reduce political and state actions to representations of socioeconomic forces and interests.

Each of these assertions is of fundamental importance, not only as a critique of the shared shortcomings of existing theories but also as a basis for the analysis of social revolutions in this book as a whole. Each thus deserves systematic elaboration in turn.

A STRUCTURAL PERSPECTIVE

If one steps back from the clashes among the leading perspectives on revolution, what seems most striking is the sameness of the image of the overall revolutionary process that underlies and informs all four approaches. According to that shared image: First, changes in social systems or societies give rise to grievances, social disorientation, or new class or group interests and potentials for collective mobilization. Then there develops a purposive, mass-based movement—coalescing with the aid of ideol-

14

ogy and organization – that consciously undertakes to overthrow the existing government and perhaps the entire social order. Finally, the revolutionary movement fights it out with the authorities or dominant class and, if it wins, undertakes to establish its own authority and program.

Something like this model of the generic revolutionary process as a movement informed or guided by purpose is assumed by all of the theoretical perspectives we have reviewed (with such variations as the distinctive theoretical and methodological features of each perspective require). None of these perspectives ever questions the premise that, for the occurrence of a revolution, a necessary causal condition is the emergence of a deliberate effort – an effort tying together leaders and followers that is aimed at overthrowing the existing political or social order. Thus for Ted Gurr, "the primary causal sequence in political violence is first the development of discontent, second the politicization of that discontent, and finally its actualization in violent action against political objects and actors".[36] And, as indicated in the above summary of Gurr's argument, revolutions in particular are actualized only if leaders deliberately organize the expression of mass discontent. Similarly, Chalmers Johnson places emphasis upon widespread personal disorientation followed by conversion to the alternative values put forward by a revolutionary ideological movement that then clashes with the existing authorities. Tilly focuses most of his theoretical attention upon the final phase of the purposive revolutionary process – the clash of organized revolutionaries competing for sovereignty with the government. Yet he also refers to the psychological and ideological causes highlighted by the relative deprivation and systems theorists in order to explain the emergence and popular support of the revolutionary organization. Finally, it is evident that Marxism, too, generally adheres to a version of the premise that revolutions are made by purposive movements. For Marxists see the emergence, albeit through prolonged preparatory struggles, of an organized and self-conscious "class-for-itself"[37] as the necessary intermediate condition for the development of a successful revolutionary transformation out of the contradictions of a mode of production. Moreover, many of the theoretical developments within Marxism since Marx have disproportionately accentuated the most voluntarist elements inherent in Marx's original theory of revolutions. Of course this was not true of most theorists of the Second International. But a stress on voluntarism has been characteristic of Leninism and Maoism, with their emphasis on the role of the vanguard party in organizing "the will of the proletariat." And it has also been characteristic of those Western Marxists, such as Lukács and Gramsci, who argue the importance of class consciousness or hegemony for translating objective economic contradictions into actual revolutions.

It is perhaps worth noting that adherence to a purposive image of the process by which revolutions develop coaxes even theories intended to be social–structural into social–psychological explanations. For, according to the image, revolutionary crises come about only (or primarily) through the appearance of dissatisfied or disoriented people, or groups mobilizable for revolutionary goals. And the destruction and transformation of the old regime happens only because a purposive revolutionary movement has formed to accomplish that end. Consequently, analysts are inexorably encouraged to consider peoples' feelings of dissatisfaction or their consciousness of fundamentally oppositional goals and values as the central problematic issues. Tilly, for example, originally developed his theory of collective action with its emphasis on group social organization and access to resources as a clear-cut alternative to social–psychological theories of political violence. Yet because he defines revolutionary situations in terms of the *special goal* – ultimate sovereignty – for which contenders are fighting, Tilly ends up echoing Johnson's arguments about revolutionary ideological leaderships and Gurr's hypotheses about discontent as an explanation for mass support of revolutionary organizations.[38] Similarly, as neo-Marxists have come to consider class consciousness and party organization to be the key problematic issues about revolutions, they have become less and less interested in exploring questions about the objective, structural conditions for revolutions. Instead, taking for granted the adequacy of Marx's economic analysis of the objective sociohistorical conditions for revolution, they have invested innovative theoretical energy in exploring what are rightly or wrongly considered to be the more politically manipulable subjective conditions for realizing a potential revolution when the objective conditions are present.

What is wrong with the purposive image of how revolutions develop? For one thing, it strongly suggests that societal order rests, either fundamentally or proximately, upon a consensus of the majority (or of the lower classes) that their needs are being met. This image suggests that the ultimate and sufficient condition for revolution is the withdrawal of this consensual support and, conversely, that no regime could survive if the masses were consciously disgruntled. Though of course such ideas could never be completely accepted by Marxists, they can creep in by implication along with emphases on class consciousness or hegemony. Gurr and Johnson, not surprisingly, embrace these notions quite explicitly.[39] And Tilly slides into a version of them when he portrays governments and revolutionary organizations as competitors for popular support, with popular choices determining whether or not a revolutionary situation develops.[40] Yet, surely, any such consensual and voluntaristic conceptions of societal order and disruption or change are quite naive. They are belied in the most obvious fashion by the prolonged survival of such blatantly repressive and domestically illegitimate regimes as the South African.[41]

16

More important, the purposive image is very misleading about both the causes and the processes of social revolutions that have actually occurred historically. As for causes, no matter what form social revolutions conceivably might take in the future (say in an industrialized, liberal-democratic nation), the fact is that historically no successful social revolution has ever been "made" by a mass-mobilizing, avowedly revolutionary movement. As Jeremy Brecher has aptly put it: "In fact, revolutionary movements rarely begin with a revolutionary intention; this only develops in the course of the struggle itself."[42] True enough, revolutionary organizations and ideologies have helped to cement the solidarity of radical vanguards before and/or during revolutionary crises. And they have greatly facilitated the consolidation of new regimes. But in no sense did such vanguards—let alone vanguards with large, mobilized, and ideologically imbued mass followings—ever create the revolutionary crises they exploited. Instead, as we shall see in later chapters, revolutionary situations have developed due to the emergence of politico–military crises of state and class domination. And only because of the possibilities thus created have revolutionary leaderships and rebellious masses contributed to the accomplishment of revolutionary transformations. Besides, the rebellious masses have quite often acted on their own, without being directly organized or ideologically inspired by avowedly revolutionary leaders and goals. As far as the causes of historical social revolutions go, Wendell Phillips was quite correct when he once declared: "Revolutions are not made; they come."[43]

The purposive image is just as misleading about the processes and outcomes of historical revolutions as it is about their causes. For the image strongly suggests that revolutionary processes and outcomes can be understood in terms of the activity and intentions or interests of the key group(s) who launched the revolution in the first place. Thus, although Gurr does not seem to envision revolutions as much more than acts of sheer destruction, he maintains that this is straightforwardly due to the activity of the frustrated and angry masses and leaders who originally caused the revolution. For Johnson, the violent value-reorientation accomplished by revolution is the doing of the ideological movement that grew up within the old, dis-synchronized social system. And Marxists not infrequently attribute the underlying logic of revolutionary processes to the interests and actions of the historically relevant class-for-itself, either the bourgeoisie or the proletariat.

But such notions are much too simple.[44] In fact, in historical revolutions, differently situated and motivated groups have become participants in complex unfoldings of multiple conflicts. These conflicts have been powerfully shaped and limited by existing socioeconomic and international conditions. And they have proceeded in different ways depending upon how each revolutionary situation emerged in the first place. The logic of

17

these conflicts has not been controlled by any one class or group, no matter how seemingly central in the revolutionary process. And the revolutionary conflicts have invariably given rise to outcomes neither fully foreseen nor intended by—nor perfectly serving the interests of—any of the particular groups involved. It simply will not do, therefore, to try to decipher the logic of the processes or outcomes of a social revolution by adopting the perspective or following the actions of any one class or elite or organization—no matter how important its participatory role. As Eric Hobsbawm has very neatly put it, "the evident importance of the actors in the drama . . . does not mean that they are also dramatist, producer, and stage-designer." "Consequently," Hobsbawm concludes, "theories which overstress the voluntarist or subjective elements in revolution, are to be treated with caution."[45]

Any valid explanation of revolution depends upon the analyst's "rising above" the viewpoints of participants to find important regularities across given historical instances—including similar institutional and historical patterns in the situations where revolutions have occurred, and similar patterns of conflict in the processes by which they have developed. As the historian Gordon Wood points out:

> It is not that men's motives are unimportant; they indeed make events, including revolutions. But the purposes of men, especially in a revolution, are so numerous, so varied, and so contradictory that their complex interaction produces results that no one intended or could even foresee. It is this interaction and these results that recent historians are referring to when they speak so disparagingly of these "underlying determinants" and "impersonal and inexorable forces" bringing on the Revolution. Historical explanation which does not account for these "forces," which, in other words, relies simply on understanding the conscious intentions of the actors, will thus be limited.[46]

To explain social revolutions, one must find problematic, first, the emergence (not "making") of a revolutionary situation within an old regime. Then, one must be able to identify the objectively conditioned and complex intermeshing of the various actions of the diversely situated groups— an intermeshing that shapes the revolutionary process and gives rise to the new regime. One can begin to make sense of such complexity only by focusing simultaneously upon the institutionally determined situations and relations of groups within society and upon the interrelations of societies within world-historically developing international structures. To take such an impersonal and nonsubjective viewpoint—one that emphasizes patterns of relationships among groups and societies—is to work from what may in some generic sense be called a structural perspective on sociohistorical reality. Such a perspective is essential for the analysis of social revolutions.

18

brings the international system back in [handwritten annotation]

INTERNATIONAL AND WORLD-HISTORICAL CONTEXTS

If a structural perspective means a focus on relationships, this must include transnational relations as well as relations among differently situated groups within given countries. Transnational relations have contributed to the emergence of all social-revolutionary crises and have invariably helped to shape revolutionary struggles and outcomes. All modern social revolutions, in fact, must be seen as closely related in their causes and accomplishments to the internationally uneven spread of capitalist economic development and nation-state formation on a world scale. Unfortunately, existing theories of revolution have not explicitly taken this perspective. To be sure, they have suggested that revolutions are related to "modernization" – but this has entailed an almost exclusive focus on socioeconomic tendencies and conflicts *within* national societies, taken one by one in isolation.

As Reinhard Bendix has pointed out, all conceptions of modernizing processes necessarily take off from the Western European experience, because that is where the commercial–industrial and national revolutions originated.[47] However, the theoretical approaches that have been dominant until recently – structural–functional evolutionism and unilineal Marxism – have generalized too specifically from the apparent logic of English development in the eighteenth and early nineteenth centuries. Essentially, modernization has been conceived as a dynamic internal to a nation. Economic development – conceived either as innovation in technology and increasing division of labor, or as accumulation of capital and the rise of the bourgeoisie – is viewed as initiating an interrelated system of complementary changes in other spheres of social life. The assumption has typically been that every nation, perhaps stimulated by the example or influence of earlier-developing countries, would sooner or later undergo a more or less compressed version of the same fundamental kind of transformation apparently experienced by England. As Marx put it in 1867, "The country that is more developed industrially only shows, to the less developed, the image of its own future."[48] A century later, American social scientists might express uneasiness about the degree to which concrete historical patterns of national development could be expected to be exactly alike. But virtually all of them still delineated their "ideal type" concepts according to the same logic.[49]

Notions of modernization as an intranational socioeconomic dynamic harmonize nicely with conceptions of revolutions as purposive movements grounded in and facilitating societal development. Perhaps rapid and disjointed economic expansion stimulates and then frustrates mass expectations, giving rise to widespread discontent and political violence that destroys the existing government. Or else social differentiation outruns and

19

overwhelms the integration of the social system, based upon value consensus. Then, in turn, ideological movements are stimulated that overthrow the existing authorities and reorient societal values. Or possibly the gestation of a new mode of production within the womb of the old provides a base for the rise of a new class, which establishes a new mode of production through revolution. In any case, modernization gives rise to revolution through changing the temper, value commitments, or potential for collective mobilization of people or groups in society. And revolution itself creates conditions for (or at least removes obstacles to) further socioeconomic development.

But conceptions of modernization as an intranational socioeconomic process that occurs in parallel ways from country to country cannot make sense even of the original changes in Europe—much less of the subsequent transformations in the rest of the world. From the start, international relations have intersected with preexisting class and political structures to promote and shape divergent as well as similar changes in various countries. Certainly this has been true of economic developments, commercial and industrial. As capitalism has spread across the globe, transnational flows of trade and investment have affected all countries—though in uneven and often contrasting ways. England's original breakthroughs to capitalist agriculture and industry depended in part upon her strong positions within international markets from the seventeenth century onward. Subsequent national industrializations in the nineteenth century were partially—and variously—shaped by international flows of goods, migrants, and investment capital, and by the attempts of each national state to influence these flows. Moreover, as "peripheral" areas of the globe were incorporated into world economic networks centered on the more industrially advanced countries, their preexisting economic structures and class relations were often reinforced or modified in ways inimical to subsequent self-sustaining and diversified growth. Even if conditions later changed, so that industrialization got under way in some of these areas, the process inevitably proceeded in forms quite different from those characteristic of earlier national industrializations. We need not necessarily accept arguments that national economic developments are actually determined by the overall structure and market dynamics of a "world capitalist system." We can, however, certainly note that historically developing transnational economic relations have always strongly (and differentially) influenced national economic developments.[50]

Another kind of transnational structure—an international system of competing states—has also shaped the dynamic and uneven course of modern world history. Europe was the site not only of capitalist economic breakthroughs but also of a continental political structure in which no one imperial state controlled the entire territory of Europe and her overseas conquests (after 1450). Economic interchanges occurred systematically over a wider territory than any one state ever controlled. This meant, for one thing, that the increased wealth that was generated by European geographical expansion and by the development of capitalism never was simply diverted to the maintenance of a cumbersome imperial superstructure sprawling over an entire continent. Such had always been the eventual fate of riches generated in other world-economies encompassed by political empires—such as Rome and China. But the European world-economy was unique in that it developed within a system of competing states.[51] In the words of Walter Dorn:

> It is [the] very competitive character of the state system of modern Europe that distinguishes it from the political life of all previous and non-European civilizations of the world. Its essence lies in the coexistence of independent and coordinate states, whose expansionist drive provoked incessant military conflicts ... and above all the prevention of any single power from reducing the others to a state of permanent subjection.[52]

Especially as England underwent commercialization and the first national industrialization, competition within the European states system spurred modernizing developments throughout Europe.[53] Recurrent warfare within the system of states prompted European monarchs and statesmen to centralize, regiment, and technologically upgrade armies and fiscal administrations. And, from the French Revolution on, such conflicts caused them to mobilize citizen masses with patriotic appeals. Political developments, in turn, reacted to modify patterns of economic development, first through bureaucratic attempts to guide or administer industrialization from above, and ultimately also through the harnessing of mass involvement by revolutionary regimes, as in Soviet Russia.

Moreover, as Europe experienced economic breakthroughs from the sixteenth century on, the competitive dynamism of the European states system promoted the spread of European "civilization" across the entire globe. Initially, the competition of states was one condition facilitating and prompting Iberian colonial expansion into the New World. Later England, spurred by worldwide competition with France, struggled for, and ultimately achieved, formal control or de facto hegemony over virtually the whole of Europe's new colonial acquisitions and former New World holdings. Toward the end of the nineteenth century, the competition of more nearly equal European industrial powers contributed to the carving up of Africa and much of Asia into colonial territories. Eventually, in the wake of the massive economic and geopolitical shifts occasioned by World War II, these colonies would emerge as new, formally independent nations within the now global states system. By then even Japan and China, countries that had traditionally remained aloof from the West and had escaped

21

colonization, would also be fully incorporated into the states system. By preindustrial standards, Japan and China were advanced and powerful agrarian states; and both avoided ultimate or permanent subjugation in large part because Western intrusions set afoot revolutionary upheavals that culminated sooner or later in vastly enhanced powers of national defense and assertion *within* the international states system.

— Some theorists of world capitalism, including most notably Immanuel Wallerstein, attempt to explain in economically reductionist terms the structure and dynamics of this (originally European and ultimately global) international states system.[54] In order to do this, such theorists typically assume that individual nation-states are instruments used by economically dominant groups to pursue world-market oriented development at home and international economic advantages abroad. But a different perspective is adopted here, one which holds that nation-states are, more fundamentally, organizations geared to maintain control of home territories and populations and to undertake actual or potential military competition with other states in the international system. The international states system as a transnational structure of military competition was not originally created by capitalism. Throughout modern world history, it represents an analytically autonomous level of transnational reality—*interdependent* in its structure and dynamics with world capitalism, but not reducible to it.[55] The militarily relevant strengths and international advantages (or disadvantages) of states are not entirely explicable in terms of their domestic economies or international economic positions. Such factors as state administrative efficiency, political capacities for mass mobilization, and international geographical position are also relevant.[56] In addition, the will and capacity of states to undertake national economic transformations (which may also have international ramifications) are influenced by their military situations and their preexisting, militarily relevant administrative and political capacities.[57] Just as capitalist economic development has spurred transformations of states and of the international state system, so have these "acted back" upon the course and forms of capital accumulation within nations and on a world scale.

Right from the European beginnings, therefore, modernization has always meant national developments only within the contexts of historically developing transnational structures, both economic and military. The social analyst can make sense of transformations at the national level, including social revolutions, only through a kind of conceptual juggling act. As long as nation-states and their competition remain important realities, it is best (at least for analyzing phenomena that centrally involve states) to employ the state/society as the basic unit of analysis. Yet along with variables referring to patterns and processes internal to these units, transnational factors must also be taken into consideration as key contextual variables.[58] Two different sorts of transnational contexts are relevant. On the one hand, there are the *structures* of the world capitalist economy and the international states system, within which individual nations are situated in different positions. And, on the other hand, there are changes and transmissions in "world time," which affect both the overall world contexts within which revolutions occur and the particular models and options for action that can be borrowed from abroad by revolutionary leaderships.

The involvement within transnational structures of countries (actually or potentially) undergoing social revolutions is relevant in several ways. Historically, unequal or competitive transnational relations have helped to shape any given country's state and class structures, thus influencing the existing "domestic" context from which revolution emerges (or not). Furthermore, transnational relations influence the course of events during actual revolutionary conjunctures. Modern social revolutions have happened only in countries situated in disadvantaged positions within international arenas. In particular, the realities of military backwardness or political dependency have crucially affected the occurrence and course of social revolutions. Although uneven economic development always lies in the background, developments within the international states system as such—especially defeats in wars or threats of invasion and struggles over colonial controls—have directly contributed to virtually all outbreaks of revolutionary crises. For such developments have helped to undermine existing political authorities and state controls, thus opening the way for basic conflicts and structural transformations. International military balances and conflicts have, moreover, provided the "space" necessary for the completion and political consolidation of social revolutions. This is true because such balances and conflicts have divided the efforts or diverted the attention of foreign enemies interested in preventing revolutionary successes or in taking advantage of revolutionized nations during their periods of internal crisis. In the final analysis, too, the outcomes of social revolutions have always been powerfully conditioned not only by international politics but also by the world-economic constraints and opportunities faced by emergent new regimes.

As for the dimension of "world time," some aspects of "modernization" have been unique processes affecting the world as a whole.[59] With state/societies as the units of analysis, limited generalizations about similar, recurrent national developments can be formulated. But, even as this is done, attention should be paid to the effects of historical orderings and of world-historical changes. Possibilities relevant to comparing and explaining social revolutions come quickly to mind. One possibility is that actors in later revolutions may be influenced by developments in earlier ones; for example, the Chinese Communists became conscious emulators of the Bol-

23

sheviks and received, for a time, direct advice and aid from the Russian revolutionary regime. Another possibility is that crucial world-historically significant "breakthroughs" – such as the Industrial Revolution or the innovation of the Leninist form of party organization – may intervene between the occurrence of one broadly similar revolution and another. As a result new opportunities or necessities are created for the development of the latter revolution that were not open to, or pressed upon, the former, because it occurred at an earlier phase of modern world history.

A concluding point is relevant for both sorts of transnational contextual influences. In analyzing the domestic effects of transnational relations, one should never simply assume – as current theorists of revolution almost invariably seem to do – that any such effects will influence primarily the situation, wants, and ideas of "the people." This may, of course, happen (as, for example, with shifts in international trade patterns that suddenly throw the people of an entire industry out of work). But, actually, it is state rulers, necessarily oriented to acting within international arenas, who are equally or more likely to be the ones who transmit transnational influences into domestic politics. Thus the intersection of the old (governmental) regime and, later, of the emergent revolutionary regime with international arenas – and especially with the international states system – should be a most promising place to look in order to comprehend how epochal modernizing dynamics in part cause and shape revolutionary transformations.

No valid theoretical perspective on revolutions can afford to ignore the international and world-historical contexts within which revolutions occur. If, for the most part, theories of revolutions have so far tried to ignore these contexts, it has been because they have operated with inadequate intranationally focused ideas about the nature of "modernization" and its interrelations with revolutions. As a corrective, this section has briefly highlighted the transnational aspects of modernization and has suggested ways in which these aspects are relevant to analyzing revolutions – with special emphasis upon the importance of the international states system. This emphasis, in effect, foreshadows arguments to be made in the next section about the centrality of potentially autonomous state organizations in social-revolutionary transformations.

THE POTENTIAL AUTONOMY OF THE STATE

Virtually everyone who writes about social revolutions recognizes that they begin with overtly political crises – such as the financial imbroglio of the French monarchy and the calling of the Estates-General in 1787–9. It is likewise apparent to everyone that revolutions proceed through struggles in which organized political parties and factions are prominently involved.

And it is recognized that they culminate in the consolidation of new state organizations, whose power may be used not only to reinforce socioeconomic transformations that have already occurred but also to promote further changes. No one denies the reality of these political aspects of social revolutions. Nevertheless, most theorists of revolution tend to regard the political crises that launch revolutions either as incidental triggers or as little more than epiphenomenal indicators of more fundamental contradictions or strains located in the social structure of the old regime. Similarly, the political groups involved in social-revolutionary struggles are seen as representatives of social forces. And the structure and activities of the new state organizations that arise from social revolutions are treated as expressions of the interests of whatever socioeconomic or sociocultural force was deemed victorious in the revolutionary conflicts.

An assumption that always lies, if only implicitly, behind such reasoning is that political structures and struggles can somehow be reduced (at least "in the last instance") to socioeconomic forces and conflicts. The state is viewed as nothing but *an arena* in which conflicts over basic social and economic interests are fought out. What makes the state-as-political-arena special is simply that actors operating within it resort to distinctive means for waging social and economic conflicts—means such as coercion or slogans appealing to the public good. This general way of thinking about the state is, in fact, common to both liberal and Marxist varieties of social theory. Between these two broad traditions of social theory, the crucial difference of opinion is over which means the political arena distinctively embodies: fundamentally consensually based legitimate authority, or fundamentally coercive domination. And this difference parallels the different views about the bases of societal order held by each theoretical tradition.

One ideal-typical view is that the state is the arena of legitimate authority embodied in the rules of the political game and in governmental leadership and policies. These are supported by some combination of normative consensus and majority preference of the members of society. Of course this view resonates well with liberal, pluralist visions of society, which see it as being composed of freely competing groups and members socialized into a commitment to common societal values. In the theoretical literature on revolutions, one finds versions of these ideas about state and society especially in the arguments of the relative-deprivation theorist Ted Gurr and the systems theorist Chalmers Johnson. For them, what matters in explaining the outbreak of a revolution is whether the existing governmental authorities lose their legitimacy. This happens when socially discontented or disoriented masses come to feel that it is acceptable to engage in violence, or else become converted to new values wielded by revolutionary ideologues. Both Gurr and Johnson feel that governmental power and stability depend directly upon societal trends and popular support. Neither

25

believes that state coercive organizations can effectively repress (for long) discontented or disapproving majorities of people in society.[60] The state in their theories is an aspect of either utilitarian consensus (Gurr) or value consensus (Johnson) in society. The state can wield force in the name of popular consensus and legitimacy, but it is not fundamentally founded in organized coercion.

In contrast, Marxist theorists—and to a considerable degree the political-conflict theorist Charles Tilly, as well—do see the state as basically organized coercion. An important part of Tilly's polity model, recall, is a government defined as "an organization which controls the principal concentrated means of coercion within the population."[61] Similarly, Lenin, the foremost Marxist theorist of the political aspect of revolutions, declares: "A standing army and police are the chief instruments of state power. But how can it be otherwise?"[62] Neither Lenin nor (for the most part) Tilly[63] see state coercion as dependent for its effectiveness upon value consensus or popular contentment. And both are quite aware that states can repress popular forces and revolutionary movements. Not surprisingly, therefore, in accounting for revolutionary success, both Tilly and Lenin place emphasis on the breakdown of the old regime's monopoly of coercion and the buildup of armed forces by revolutionaries.

It remains true, however, that Marxists and political-conflict theorists like Tilly are as guilty as Gurr and Johnson of treating the state primarily as an arena in which social conflicts are resolved, though of course they see resolution through domination rather than voluntary consensus. For, in one way or another, both Marxists and Tilly regard the state as a system of organized coercion that invariably functions to support the superordinant position of dominant classes or groups over subordinate classes or groups.

In Tilly's collective-action theory, state and society seem to be literally collapsed. Tilly labels and discusses intergroup relations in political terms; he talks not about classes or social groups, but about "member" groups and alliances that have power in the polity, and those "challenger" groups that are excluded from it. His very definition of member groups—"any contender which has routine, low-cost access to resources controlled by the government"[64]—strongly suggests a virtually complete overlap between dominant-group power and the power of the state. The state becomes a (fundamentally coercive) instrument wielded by the "member" groups of the polity, those that have power within the population in question.

Classical Marxist theorists do not analytically collapse state and society. Marxists view societal order as founded upon class conflict and domination. State power is a specialized kind of power in society, not equivalent to or encompassing all dominant class power. Nevertheless, Marxist theorists still explain the basic function of the state in social terms: Whatever the variations in its historical forms, the state as such is seen as a feature of all class-divided modes of production; and, invariably, the one necessary and inescapable function of the state—by definition—is to contain class conflict and to undertake other policies in support of the dominance of the surplus-appropriating and property-owning class(es).[65]

Thus, neither in classical Marxism nor in Tilly's collective-action theory is the state treated as an autonomous structure—a structure with a logic and interests of its own not necessarily equivalent to, or fused with, the interests of the dominant class in society or the full set of member groups in the polity. Within the terms of these theories, it is consequently virtually impossible even to raise the possibility that fundamental conflicts of interest might arise between the existing dominant class or set of groups, on the one hand, and the state rulers on the other. Society is characterized by intergroup domination and power struggles. And the state, based upon concentrated means of coercion, fits in as a form of instrumental or objective domination and as an object of struggle, but not as an organization-for-itself.

Yet what about the more recent developments in Marxism? Lately there has certainly been a renewed interest among Marxist-oriented intellectuals in the problem of the state.[66] In critical reaction to what had become a widespread vulgarization—the notion that states were nothing but instruments manipulated consciously and directly by leaders and interest groups representing the dominant class—contemporary analysts such as Ralph Miliband,[67] Nicos Poulantzas,[68] Perry Anderson,[69] Göran Therborn,[70] and Claus Offe[71] have raised the issue of "the relative autonomy of the state" from direct control by the dominant class. Interest in this possibility has been focused especially upon capitalist societies, but also upon the absolutist phase of European feudalism. Theoretical attention has been devoted to elucidating the broad structural constraints that an existing mode of production places upon the range of possibilities for state structures and actions. And, in a more innovative vein, the argument has been developed that state rulers may have to be free of control by specific dominant-class groups and personnel if they are to be able to implement policies that serve the fundamental interest of an entire dominant class. That interest is, of course, its need to preserve the class structure and mode of production as a whole.

Recurrently as this recent debate has unfolded, certain participants—especially those most concerned with understanding how states could act against dominant-class resistance to preserve an existing mode of production—have seemed on the verge of asserting that states are potentially autonomous not only over against dominant classes but also vis-à-vis entire class structures or modes of production.[72] However, this possible line of argument has been for the most part carefully avoided.[73] Instead, some analysts, such as Claus Offe, have simply hypothesized that although state structures and policies are causally important in their own right, they objectively function because of in-built "selection mechanisms," to preserve the existing mode of production.[74] Others, especially the so-called structuralist Marxists, have replaced the discredited dominant-class instrumentalism with what might be labeled a class-struggle reductionism.[75] According to this view, state structures and functions are not simply controlled by dominant classes alone. Rather they are shaped and buffeted by the class struggle between dominant and subordinate classes—a struggle that goes on within the objective limits of the given economy and class structure as a whole. Finally, a very recent contribution to the debate has been made by Göran Therborn in a new book that focuses directly on state structures as such. Working in a related yet somewhat different vein from the class-struggle theorists, Therborn constructs and contrasts typological models of the different forms and functions of state organizations and activities in the feudal, capitalist, and socialist modes of production, respectively. He attempts for each mode to derive the state structure directly from the corresponding basic class relations. For, along with the "structuralist" theorist Nicos Poulantzas, Therborn maintains that "the state should be regarded neither as a specific institution nor as an instrument, but as a relation—a materialized concentration of the class relations of a given society."[76]

Thus the recent Marxist debate on the state stops short at the problem of the autonomy of the state, since most participants in the debate tend either to treat the state in a completely funtionalist manner, or to regard it as an aspect of class relations or struggle. It is unquestionably an advance to establish (or reestablish, since this surely was the classical Marxist position) that states are not simply created and manipulated by dominant classes. Nevertheless, it is still essential for Marxists to face more directly the questions of what states are in their own right, and how their structures vary and their activities develop in relation to socioeconomic structures. So far, virtually all Marxists continue simply to assume that state forms and activities vary in correspondence with modes of production, and that state rulers cannot possibly act against the basic interests of a dominant class. Arguments remain confined to issues of *how* states vary with, and function for, modes of production and dominant classes. The result is that still hardly anyone questions this Marxist version of the enduring sociological proclivity to absorb the state into society.

Question this enduring sociological proclivity we must, however, if we are to be well prepared to analyze social revolutions. At first glance, a social–structural determinist perspective (especially one that embodies a mode of class analysis) seems an obviously fruitful approach. This seems to be the case because social revolutions do, after all, centrally involve class struggles and result in basic social–structural transformations. Nevertheless, the historical realities of social revolutions insistently suggest the need for a more state-centered approach. As the core chapters of this book will elaborate, the political crises that have lauched social revolutions have not at all been epiphenomenal reflections of societal strains or class contradictions. Rather they have been direct expressions of contradictions centered in the structures of old-regime states. The political-conflict groups that have figured in social-revolutionary struggles have not merely represented social interests and forces. Rather they have formed as interest groups within and fought about the forms of state structures. The vanguard parties that have emerged during the radical phases of social revolutions have been uniquely responsible for building centralized armies and administrations without which revolutionary transformations could not have been consolidated. Social revolutions, moreover, have changed state structures as much or more as they have changed class relations, societal values, and social institutions. And, the effects of social revolutions upon the subsequent economic and sociopolitical development of the nations that they have transformed have been due not only to the changes in class structures, but also to the changes in state structures and functions that the revolutions accomplished. In sum, the class upheavals and socioeconomic transformations that have characterized social revolutions have been closely intertwined with the collapse of the state organizations of the old regimes and with the consolidation and functioning of the state organizations of the new regimes.

We can make sense of social-revolutionary transformations only if we take the state seriously as a macro-structure. The state properly conceived is no mere arena in which socioeconomic struggles are fought out. It is, rather, a set of administrative, policing, and military organizations headed, and more or less well coordinated by, an executive authority. Any state first and fundamentally extracts resources from society and deploys these to create and support coercive and administrative organizations.[77] Of course, these basic state organizations are built up and must operate within the context of class-divided socioeconomic relations, as well as within the context of national and international economic dynamics. Moreover, coercive and administrative organizations are only parts of overall political systems. These systems also may contain institutions through which social interests are represented in state policymaking as well as institutions through which nonstate actors are mobilized to participate in policy implementation. Nevertheless, the administrative and coercive organizations are the basis of state power as such.

Where they exist, these fundamental state organizations are at least potentially autonomous from direct dominant-class control. The extent to which they *actually* are autonomous, and to what effect, varies from case

29

to case. It is worth emphasizing that the actual extent and consequences of state autonomy can only be analyzed and explained in terms specific to particular types of sociopolitical systems and to particular sets of historical international circumstances. That is why the introduction to Chapter 2 will include a discussion of the institutional forms of state power in agrarian states such as prerevolutionary France, Russia, and China. Also, the likely lines of conflict between landed dominant classes and state rulers in such agrarian states will be indicated. There is no need to go into this discussion now. For the purposes of the argument at hand, it is enough to note that states are potentially autonomous and to explore what distinct interests they *might* pursue.

State organizations necessarily compete to some extent with the dominant class(es) in appropriating resources from the economy and society. And the objectives to which the resources, once appropriated, are devoted may very well be at variance with existing dominant-class interests. Resources may be used to strengthen the bulk and autonomy of the state itself—something necessarily threatening to the dominant class unless the greater state power is indispensably needed and actually used to support dominant-class interests. But the use of state power to support dominant-class interests is not inevitable. Indeed, attempts of state rulers merely to perform the state's "own" functions may create conflicts of interest with the dominant class. The state normally performs two basic sets of tasks: It maintains order, and it competes with other actual or potential states. As Marxists have pointed out, states usually do function to preserve existing economic and class structures, for that is normally the smoothest way to enforce order. Nevertheless, the state has its own distinct interests vis-à-vis subordinate classes. Although both the state and the dominant class(es) share a broad interest in keeping the subordinate classes in place in society and at work in the existing economy, the state's own fundamental interest in maintaining sheer physical order and political peace may lead it—especially in periods of crisis—to enforce concessions to subordinate-class demands. These concessions may be at the expense of the interests of the dominant class, but not contrary to the state's own interests in controlling the population and collecting taxes and military recruits.

Moreover, we should not forget that states also always exist in determinant geopolitical environments, in interaction with other actual or potential states. An existing economy and class structure condition and influence a given state structure and the activities of the rulers. So, too, do geopolitical environments create tasks and opportunities for states and place limits on their capacities to cope with either external or internal tasks or crises. As the German historian Otto Hintze once wrote, two phenomena above all condition "the real organization of the state. These are, first, the structure of social classes, and second, the external ordering of the states—their position

30

relative to each other, and their over-all position in the world."[78] Indeed, a state's involvement in an international network of states is a basis for potential autonomy of action over and against groups and economic arrangements within its jurisdiction—even including the dominant class and existing relations of production. For international military pressures and opportunities can prompt state rulers to attempt policies that conflict with, and even in extreme instances contradict, the fundamental interests of a dominant class. State rulers may, for example, undertake military adventures abroad that drain resources from economic development at home, or that have the immediate or ultimate effect of undermining the position of dominant socioeconomic interests. And, to give a different example, rulers may respond to foreign military competition or threats of conquest by attempting to impose fundamental socioeconomic reforms or by trying to reorient the course of national economic development through state intervention. Such programs may or may not be successfully implemented. But even if they are not carried through, the sheer attempt may create a contradictory clash of interests between the state and the existing dominant class.

The perspective on the state advanced here might appropriately be labeled "organizational" and "realist." In contrast to most (especially recent) Marxist theories, this view refuses to treat states as if they were mere analytic aspects of abstractly conceived modes of production, or even political aspects of concrete class relations and struggles. Rather it insists that states are actual organizations controlling (or attempting to control) territories and people. Thus the analyst of revolutions must explore not only class relations but also relations of states to one another and relations of states to dominant and subordinate classes. For the historical cases of social revolutions to be discussed in the core chapters of this book, the analysis of old-regime contradictions and the emergence of revolutionary crises will center especially upon the relationships of states to military competitors abroad and to dominant classes and existing socioeconomic structures at home. And the analysis of the emergence and structure of new regimes will focus especially on the relationships of state-building revolutionary movements to international circumstances and to those subordinate classes, invariably including the peasantry, who were key insurrectionary participants in the conflicts of the revolutions. The state organizations of both old and new regimes will have a more central and autonomous place in the analysis than they would in a straightforward Marxist explanation.

Yet not only does an organizational, realist perspective on the state entail differences from Marxist approaches, it also contrasts with non-Marxist approaches that treat the *legitimacy* of political authorities as an important explanatory concept. If state organizations cope with whatever tasks they already claim smoothly and efficiently, legitimacy—either in the

31

✗ adds another
clan-state
officials ?.

sense of moral approval or in the probably much more usual sense of sheer acceptance of the status quo — will probably be accorded to the state's form and rulers by most groups in society. In any event, what matters most is always the support or acquiescence not of the popular majority of society but of the politically powerful and mobilized groups, invariably including the regime's own cadres. Loss of legitimacy, especially among these crucial groups, tends to ensue with a vengeance if and when (for reasons that are always open to sociological and historical explanation) the state fails consistently to cope with existing tasks, or proves unable to cope with new tasks suddenly thrust upon it by crisis circumstances. Even after great loss of legitimacy has occurred, a state can remain quite stable — and certainly invulnerable to internal mass-based revolts — especially if its coercive organizations remain coherent and effective.[79] Consequently, the structure of those organizations, their place within the state apparatus as a whole, and their linkages to class forces and to politically mobilized groups in society are all important issues for the analyst of states in revolutionary situations, actual or potential. Such an analytic focus seems certain to prove more fruitful than any focus primarily or exclusively upon political legitimation. The ebbing of a regime's legitimacy in the eyes of its own cadres and other politically powerful groups may figure as a mediating variable in an analysis of regime breakdown. But the basic causes will be found in the structure and capacities of state organizations, as these are conditioned by developments in the economy and class structure and also by developments in the international situation.

The state, in short, is fundamentally Janus-faced, with an intrinsically dual anchorage in class-divided socioeconomic structures and an international system of states. If our aim is to understand the breakdown and building-up of state organizations in revolutions, we must look not only at the activities of social groups. We must also focus upon the points of intersection between international conditions and pressures, on the one hand, and class-structured economies and politically organized interests, on the other hand. State executives and their followers will be found maneuvering to extract resources and build administrative and coercive organizations precisely at this intersection. Here, consequently, is the place to look for the political contradictions that help launch social revolutions. Here, also, will be found the forces that shape the rebuilding of state organizations within social-revolutionary crises.

In the part of the chapter just completed, three principles of analysis shared by existing theories of revolution have been critically discussed. And alternative theoretical principles have been proposed in their stead. In fact, all of the shared tendencies for which the existing theories have been taken to task are closely interrelated: A purposive image of the causes of

32

social revolutions complements an intranational perspective on moderniza-tion. And each is most readily consistent with a socioeconomically reduc-tionist understanding of the state. Not surprisingly, therefore, the alterna-tive principles being proposed here are also mutually complementary. We shall analyze the causes and processes of social revolutions from a nonvol-untarist, structural perspective, attending to international and world-historical, as well as intranational, structures and processes. And an im-portant theoretical concomitant will be to move states—understood as potentially autonomous organizations located at the interface of class structures and international situations—to the very center of attention.

The next part discusses the method of analysis that is appropriate to the task of explaining social revolutions.

A COMPARATIVE HISTORICAL METHOD

"Social revolutions" as defined at the beginning of this work—rapid, basic transformations of a society's state and class structures, accompanied and in part carried through by class-based revolts from below—have been rela-tively rare occurrences in modern world history. Each such revolution, furthermore, has occurred in a particular way in a unique set of social-structural and international circumstances. How, then can a sociologist hope to develop historically valid explanations of social revolution as such?

The study of social revolutions in their own right has been avoided in recent American social science because scholars believe that only phenom-ena of which there are a large number of cases can be studied in a truly scientific manner. There has been a self-conscious reaction against the "natural history" approach to revolutions favored by an earlier generation of American social scientists. The "natural historians," chiefly Lyford Ed-wards, Crane Brinton, and George Pettee, examined handfuls of cases in an attempt to develop generalizations about the typical process of revolu-tion.[80] Spurning this approach as too "historical," later students of revolu-tion sought, instead, to theorize only about large numbers of cases. Thus, in the introduction to a 1964 book entitled *Internal War*, Harry Eckstein defines "a theoretical subject" as "a set of phenomena about which one can develop informative, testable generalizations that hold for all instances of the subject, and some of which apply to those instances alone,"[81] and he goes on to assert that whereas "a statement about two or three cases is certainly a generalization in the dictionary sense, a generalization in the methodological sense must usually be based on more; it ought to cover a number of cases large enough for certain rigorous testing procedures like statistical analysis to be used."[82] Many other contemporary students of revolution agree with Eckstein. Consequently, the favored strategies for

33

explaining revolutions have been premised upon subsuming them within much broader categories. These include structure–functionalist social-system categories (e.g., Chalmers Johnson) and categories such as "political violence" (e.g., Ted Gurr) or "collective action" (e.g., Charles Tilly) that refer to aspects shared by many types of political events.[83]

It is not that contemporary analysts of revolution-subsuming phenomena see their theories as irrelevant to social revolutions. They believe, of course, that their general theories should be "applied" to instances of revolution by historians or by social scientists who do analyses of single cases. In a sense, theories such as those of Johnson, Gurr, and Tilly certainly are applicable to individual cases of social revolution: One can find relative deprivation, multiple sovereignty, and system disequilibria and value-oriented ideological movements in any and all instances of social revolution. Historians or case analysts thus could, in principle, use any or all of these ideas in a discussion of a given revolution. Indeed, because the contemporary social-scientific theories are framed in such general conceptual terms, it is very difficult to tell if they ever *do not* apply to a given case. What society, for example, lacks widespread relative deprivation of one sort or another? And how do we tell a synchronized social system when we see one? Ironically, theoretical approaches that set out to avoid the pitfalls of a too-historical approach to revolutions can end up providing little more than pointers toward various factors that case analysts might want to take into account, with no valid way to favor certain explanations over others.

Marxist theory works with less general, more historically grounded categories than the recent social-scientific theories, and it offers a more elegant and complete explanation of social-revolutionary transformations as such (rather than, say, political violence in general). It is thus no accident that Marxism has been the social-scientific theory most consistently and fruitfully used by historians to elucidate various particular revolutions.[84] Yet the interaction between Marxist theory and history is incomplete because historical cases have not been used to test and modify the explanations offered by the theory. Marxist analysts have devoted themselves to highlighting the class conflicts and changes in class relations that certainly do occur during revolutions. But they have not devised ways to test whether these factors really distinguish between revolutions and other kinds of transformations or between successful and abortive revolutionary outbreaks. Perhaps especially because the factors that they consider are indeed an important part of the story, Marxists have failed to notice a crucial point: Causal variables referring to the strength and structure of old-regime states and the relations of state organizations to class structures may discriminate between cases of successful revolution and cases of failure or nonoccurrence far better than do variables referring to class

34

relations and patterns of economic development alone. Similarly, in their explanations of the outcomes of revolutions, Marxist-oriented scholars emphasize changes in class structures and even very long-run economic developments. But they virtually ignore the often much more striking and immediate transformations that occur in the structure and functions of state organizations such as armies and administrations, and in the relations between the state and social classes. Again, this has meant that they have missed identifying the distinctive political-institutional changes that set revolutions apart from nonrevolutionary patterns of national development.

A gap of one sort or another between theory and history thus plagues both Marxist scholarship and recent academic social-science theories about revolution. Historians, especially, note the existence of this gap from time to time. Some of them complain about the vagueness of recent social-scientific theories of revolution.[85] Others polemically assert the inappropriateness of Marxist concepts or explanations for whatever case they are concerned to analyze.[86] Unfortunately, disillusioned historians sometimes conclude that their discipline should avoid social-scientific theories altogether.[87] They advocate instead analyzing revolutions case by case, each in its own analytic terms, or else each in terms of the language of the actors at that time and place. In practice, no such relativist approaches are really possible, for historians must always draw, at least implicitly, upon theoretical ideas and comparative points of reference.[88] But a hiatus of communication between historians and area specialists, on the one hand, and social theorists, on the other, *is* always possible. To the extent that such a hiatus exists, as it always does to some degree, it only encourages, simultaneously, the proliferation of putatively general theories of (or about) revolution that do not actually illuminate historical revolutions and an increase of specialists' accounts of particular cases that are not self-consciously informed by more general principles of analysis and explanation. The way to counter such a split, however, is not to deplore it from a vantage point above the fray. Rather, the only effective antidote is the actual development of explanations of revolutions that illuminate truly general patterns of causes and outcomes, without either ignoring or totally abstracting away from the aspects particular to each revolution and its context.

Fortunately, a method is available to aid in the development of such explanations of revolutions, at once generalizable across cases and historically sensitive. Social revolutions as such *can* be treated as a theoretical subject; there is no inescapable requirement to formulate explanatory hypotheses only about categories with large numbers of cases. Nor need theorists content themselves only with applying general concepts to particular cases. To generalize about social revolutions, to develop explanations of their causes and outcomes, one can employ comparative historical analysis with selected slices of national historical trajectories as the units of comparison. "Comparative history" is commonly used rather loosely to refer to any and all studies in which two or more historical trajectories of nation-states, institutional complexes, or civilizations are juxtaposed. In this very broad sense, the term refers to studies with very different kinds of purposes. Some comparative histories, such as *The Rebellious Century 1830–1930* by Charles, Louise, and Richard Tilly, are meant to show that a particular general sociological model holds across different national contexts.[89] Other studies, such as Reinhard Bendix's *Nation-building and Citizenship* and Perry Anderson's *Lineages of the Absolutist State,* use comparisons primarily to bring out contrasts among nations or civilizations taken as synthetic wholes.[90] But there is still a third version of comparative history – which I am here labeling the method of comparative historical *analysis* – in which the overriding intent is to develop, test, and refine causal, explanatory hypotheses about events or structures integral to macro-units such as nation-states.

Comparative historical analysis has a long and distinguished pedigree in social science. Its logic was explicitly laid out by John Stuart Mill in his *A System of Logic*.[91] The method was applied to powerful effect by such classical social and historical analysts as Alexis de Tocqueville and Marc Bloch.[92] And it continues to be elaborated and applied by contemporary scholars, including (perhaps most notably) Barrington Moore, Jr., in *Social Origins of Dictatorship and Democracy*.[93] Comparative historical analysis is distinctively appropriate for developing explanations of macro-historical phenomena of which there are inherently only a few cases. This is in contrast to more plentiful and manipulable kinds of phenomena suitable for experimental investigations, and in contrast to other phenomena where there are the large numbers of cases required for statistical analyses. Comparative historical analysis is, in fact, the mode of multivariate analysis to which one resorts when there are too many variables and not enough cases.

Logically speaking, how does comparative historical analysis work? Basically one tries to establish valid associations of potential causes with the given phenomenon one is trying to explain. There are two main ways to proceed. First, one can try to establish that several cases having in common the phenomenon one is trying to explain also have in common a set of causal factors, although they vary in other ways that might have seemed causally relevant. This approach is what Mill called the "Method of Agreement." Second, one can contrast the cases in which the phenomenon to be explained and the hypothesized causes are present to other cases in which the phenomenon and the causes are both absent, but which are otherwise as similar as possible to the positive cases. This procedure Mill labeled the "Method of Difference." Taken alone, it is a more powerful method than the Method of Agreement alone for establishing valid causal associations

36

(provided that one can find suitable negative cases for the required contrasts). In practice, though, it is often possible, and certainly desirable, to combine these two comparative logics. This is done by using at once several positive cases along with suitable negative cases as contrasts.

That will be the approach of this book. France, Russia, and China will serve as three positive cases of successful social revolution, and I shall argue that these cases reveal similar causal patterns despite their many other differences. In addition, I shall invoke negative cases for the purpose of validating various particular parts of the causal argument. In so doing, I shall always construct contrasts that maximize the similarities of the negative case(s) to the positive case(s) in every apparently relevant respect except the causal sequence that the contrast is supposed to validate. Thus, for example, the abortive Russian Revolution of 1905 will be contrasted to the successful Revolution of 1917 in order to validate arguments about the crucial contribution to social-revolutionary success in Russia of war-related processes that led to the breakdown of state repressive capacities. Moreover, selected aspects of English, Japanese, and German history will be used in various places to strengthen arguments about the causes of revolutionary political crises and peasant revolts in France, Russia, and China. These cases are suitable as contrasts because they were comparable countries that underwent non-social-revolutionary political crises and transformations in broadly similar times and circumstances to France, Russia, and China.

At first glance, comparative historical analysis may not seem so very different from the approach of the "natural historians" Lyford Edwards, Crane Brinton, and George Pettee. They, too, analyzed and compared a few historical cases in depth. Actually, however, comparative-historical and natural-history approaches to revolutions differ both in objective and in method of analysis. Whereas the goal of comparative historical analysis is to establish causes of revolutions, the natural historians sought to describe the characteristic cycle, or sequence of stages, that should typically occur in the processes of revolutions. As Robert Park put it in his introduction to Lyford Edwards's *The Natural History of Revolutions,*

> Every social change that is capable of description in conceptual terms will have . . . its characteristic cycle. This is one of the presuppositions upon which this study is based. As a matter of scientific method, this description of the cycle seems to be the first step in the analysis of social change everywhere.[94]

Methodologically, the natural historians analyzed revolutions by trying to fit either parts of various cases (e.g., Edwards) or a few entire cases (e.g., Brinton) to metaphors that seemed to best describe their shared stages of development, hence the sequence putatively "natural" to revolutions. Brinton, for example, explicitly employed a metaphor of disease that had also been used implicitly by Edwards:

37

Introduction

> We shall regard revolutions as a kind of fever . . . In the society during the generation or so before the outbreak of revolution . . . there will be found signs of the coming disturbance . . . They are . . . [well] described as *prodromal* signs, indications to the very keen diagnostician that a disease is on its way, but not yet sufficiently developed to be the disease. Then comes a time when the full symptoms disclose themselves, and when we can say the fever of revolution has begun. This works up, not regularly but with advances and retreats, to a crisis, frequently accompanied by delerium, the rule of the most violent revolutionists, the Reign of Terror. After the crisis comes a period of convalescence, usually marked by a relapse or two. Finally the fever is over, and the patient is himself again, perhaps in some respects actually strengthened by the experience, immunized at least for a while from a similar attack, but certainly not wholly made over . . . [95]

To be sure, the natural historians also offered, at least implicitly, some theoretical hypotheses about the causes of revolution. These were primarily social–psychological, and – the significant point for our purposes – little attempt was made to use comparisons of historical cases to validate them. Instead, the theoretical hypotheses were simply applied to the analysis as a whole, and the historical materials used primarily to illustrate the metaphorical stage sequence. The resulting natural-history analyses were certainly not without value – indeed, they offer many insights into revolutionary processes and can still be read with profit today – but they were very different from a comparative historical analysis. Such an analysis uses comparisons among positive cases, and between positive and negative cases, to identify and validate causes, rather than descriptions, of revolutions. Moreover, a comparative historical analysis does not in any way assume or attempt to argue that revolutionary processes should appear descriptively similar in their concrete trajectories from case to case. For analytically similar sets of causes can be operative across cases even if the nature and timing of conflicts during the revolutions are different, and even if, for example, one case culminates in a conservative reaction, whereas another does not (at all or in the same way). In a comparative historical analysis, such differences are not obstacles to the identification of similar causes across cases of revolution. At the same time, they represent variations that can themselves be explained by comparisons of the positive historical cases among themselves.

Of course, comparative history is not without its difficulties and limitations, and several especially relevant ones deserve brief discussion. There are, in the first place, inevitable difficulties in applying the method according to its given logic. Often it is impossible to find exactly the historical cases that one needs for the logic of a certain comparison. And even when the cases are roughly appropriate, perfect controls for all potentially rele-

38

vant variables can never be achieved. Thus, strategic guesses have to be made about what causes are actually likely to be operative—that is, which ones could, or could not actually affect the object of study. The upshot is that there always are unexamined contextual features of the historical cases that interact with the causes being explicitly examined in ways the comparative historical analysis either does not reveal, or must simply assume to be irrelevant.[96]

Another set of problems stems from the fact that comparative historical analysis necessarily assumes (like any multivariate logic) that the units being compared are independent of one another. But actually, this assumption is rarely if ever fully valid for macro-phenomena such as revolutions. For, as we have already noted, these phenomena occur in unique world-historical contexts that change over time, and they happen within international structures that tie societies to one another. For much of any given comparative analysis the fiction of independent units can often be maintained. Thus, for example, I am willing to treat old-regime France, Russia, and China as basically similar and unrelated agrarian states for the purposes of exploring the causes of the French, Russian, and Chinese Revolutions. But, sooner or later in most macro-analyses, one must make allowance for the unique effects of the world setting and timing, and for interrelations among the units. Thus, I shall work into my analysis the effects of the unique world-historical contexts of the eighteenth-century French versus the twentieth-century Russian and Chinese Revolutions, and I shall take into account the fact that Russian revolutionaries actually played a role in the Chinese Revolution through the transmission of Communist party models and policies via the Comintern.

Finally, it needs to be stressed that comparative historical analysis is no substitute for theory. Indeed, it can be applied only with the indispensable aid of theoretical concepts and hypotheses. For the comparative method alone cannot define the phenomenon to be studied. It cannot select appropriate units of analysis or say which historical cases should be studied. Nor can it provide the causal hypotheses to be explored. All of these must come from the macro-sociological imagination, informed by the theoretical debates of the day, and sensitive to the patterns of evidence for sets of historical cases.

Still, comparative historical analysis does provide a valuable check, or anchor, for theoretical speculation. It encourages one to spell out the actual causal arguments suggested by grand theoretical perspectives, and to combine diverse arguments if necessary in order to remain faithful to the ultimate objective—which is, of course, the actual illumination of causal regularities across sets of historical cases. Whatever the source(s) of theoretical inspiration, comparative history succeeds only if it convincingly fulfills this goal. And when it *is* successfully employed, comparative historical analysis serves as an ideal strategy for mediating between theory and history. Provided that it is not mechanically applied, it can prompt both theoretical extensions and reformulations, on the one hand, and new ways of looking at concrete historical cases, on the other.

The preceding parts of this chapter have sketched a theoretical frame of reference and introduced a method of analysis, both of which are in principle applicable to the investigation of many possible sets of social revolutions. This book does not, of course, analyze in depth all available historical cases of social revolution. Nor does it analyze a "random" sample from the entire universe of possible cases. In fact, comparative historical analysis works best when applied to a set of a few cases that share certain basic features. Cases need to be carefully selected and the criteria for grouping them together made explicit. In the following chapters, the French, Russian, and Chinese Revolutions are to be treated together as basically similar examples of successful social-revolutionary transformations. At this point, therefore, some words are in order to justify this selection of cases.

There are some important practical reasons why these social revolutions rather than others were chosen for analysis. All of them, for one thing, happened in countries whose state and class structures had not been recently created or basically altered under colonial domination. This consideration eliminates many complexities that would need to be systematically included in any analysis of revolutions in postcolonial or neocolonial settings. Furthermore, the French, Russian, and Chinese Revolutions all broke out and—after more or less protracted processes of class and political struggle—culminated in the consolidation of revolutionary state power, long-ago enough in the past to allow a study and comparison to be made of all three as *entire* revolutionary transformations. It is possible, in other words, to trace each Revolution from the demise of the old regime through to the emergence of a distinctively structured new regime. For comparative history, Hegel's maxim indubitably holds: The owl of Minerva flies at dusk.

Stronger reasons than these, however, are needed to explain not only why France, Russia, and China have each been selected for intense study, but also why all three have been grouped together as fundamentally *similar* cases of social revolution. For, according to most existing ways of defining and grouping revolutions for comparative study, France, Russia, and China simply do not belong together—certainly not all of them in one set.[97] France was a pre-twentieth-century European revolution, typically understood as bourgeois-capitalist or liberal-democratic in nature. Depending upon one's category scheme, Russia was either an antiabsolutist revolution, or a statist–developmental revolution, or a proletarian–communist revolution. Some analysts might be willing to group it with France, others with China, but none would agree that it belongs together with both.[98] For China, especially, is not considered legitimately classifiable with France, either because the French Revolution was "bourgeois" or "liberal" and the Chinese obviously neither, or else because China should be grouped with Third World national-liberation revolutions and not with European revolutions of any sort.

But it is the premise of this work that France, Russia, and China exhibited important similarities in their Old Regimes and revolutionary processes and outcomes—similarities more than sufficient to warrant their treatment together as one pattern calling for a coherent causal explanation. All three Revolutions occurred in wealthy and politically ambitious agrarian states, none of which was ever colonially subjugated. These Old Regimes were proto-bureaucratic autocracies that suddenly had to confront more economically developed military competitors. In all three Revolutions, the externally mediated crises combined with internal structural conditions and trends to produce a conjuncture of: (1) the incapacitation of the central state machineries of the Old Regimes; (2) widespread rebellions by the lower classes, most crucially peasants; and (3) attempts by mass-mobilizing political leaderships to consolidate revolutionary state power. The revolutionary outcome in each instance was a centralized, bureaucratic, and mass-incorporating nation-state with enhanced great-power potential in the international arena. Obstacles to national social change associated with the prerevolutionary positions of the landed upper class were removed (or greatly curtailed), and new potentials for development were created by the greater state centralization and mass political incorporation of the New Regimes.

Whatever other category systems may assume, the French and Chinese Revolutions—the two "polar" cases of my trio—were not so different from one another, nor so similar (respectively) to early European, liberal revolutions and to Third World, nation-building revolutions, as their contrasting spatio-temporal and cultural settings might suggest. The French Revolution actually was in important respects strikingly different from the English Revolution of the seventeenth century, and rather similar to the Chinese and Russian Revolutions. Peasant revolts played a key role in the process of the French Revolution, and the political result was a more centralized and bureaucratic state, not a liberal-parliamentary regime. As for the Chinese Revolution, it seems remarkably shortsighted in historical terms to regard it as a new-nation–building revolution of the mid-twentieth century. China had an imperial Old Regime with a cultural and political history stretching back many hundreds of years. And the

41

Chinese Revolution as an entire process was launched in 1911 by an upper-class revolt against an absolute monarchical state, not unlike the aristocratic revolt that started the French Revolution.[99] Furthermore, the Chinese Revolution eventually gave rise to a developmentally oriented Communist regime that is certainly as much or more similar to the post-revolutionary Soviet regime as to contemporary, noncommunist Third World governments.

Given that there are, indeed, sufficient similarities to allow these three Revolutions to be grouped together for comparative historical analysis, much is to be gained by actually doing so. The similar sociopolitical features of the French, Russian, and Chinese Revolutions can be highlighted and explained in ways that would necessarily be missed by analysts determined to keep them segregated in separate type categories. Above all, there is much to be learned from the juxtaposition of these Revolutions about the causes and results of peasant participation in social revolutions. There is also much to be learned about the dynamics of the breakdown and reconstruction of state administrative and coercive organizations from old to new regimes. It is not incidental that these aspects of revolutions tend either to be played down or assumed away by many other comparative analyses. This happens because most of the alternative category schemes serve to highlight instead either bourgeois/ proletarian class configurations or patterns of legitimate political authority and the ideological self-conceptions of old and new regimes.

But we shall not only emphasize the common patterns shared by the French, Russian, and Chinese Revolutions. Given the flexibility and the historical sensitivity of the comparative method, attention can also be paid to the particular features of each of the three Revolutions. There will be no need to deny that the French Revolution had bourgeois and liberal features, that the Russian Revolution was extremely statist in its outcome, or that the Chinese Revolution had in its process elements of a national-liberation struggle. For even as we primarily look for and attempt to explain patterns common to France, Russia, and China, we can also attend to the variations that characterize pairs of cases or single cases. These can then be explained as due in part to variations on the shared causal patterns, in part to contrasts among the social structures of France, Russia, and China, and in part to differences in the world-historical timing and succession of the three great Revolutions. As a result, exactly those distinctive characteristics of the Revolutions and their world-historical setting that have prompted other scholars to segregate them into separate type categories will be cast in a new explanatory light as they are studied against the background of the patterns shared by all three Revolutions.

42

Explaining Social Revolutions

Looking Ahead

The chapters to come present a comparative historical analysis of the French, Russian, and Chinese Revolutions—an analysis conceived and executed within the frame of reference developed in this first chapter. Part I discusses the structural and historical conditions for the emergence of objective revolutionary situations in old-regime France, Russia, and China: Chapter 2 focuses upon the political crises of the absolutist states, and Chapter 3 analyzes the situation of the peasantry. In order to help validate the main lines of the argument, particular subsections of Chapters 2 and 3 briefly show that the conditions hypothesized to be crucial for producing social-revolutionary situations in France, Russia, and China were absent, or not present all together, at relevant periods in Japan, Prussia/Germany, and England. Thus the logic of comparison in Part I primarily stresses ways in which France, Russia, and China were similar. And this is underlined through contrasts to negative cases.

In Part II, on the other hand, the logic of comparison focuses entirely upon the similarities and differences among the positive cases of social revolution. For in Part II it is taken for granted that France, Russia, and China shared similarly caused revolutionary situations. The objective is to explain the revolutionary outcomes against that background. Hence this part demonstrates how the conflicts unleashed in the revolutionary crises led to social-revolutionary outcomes, with certain patterns common to all three Revolutions and others distinctive to one or two of them. Within Part II, Chapter 4 introduces the major analytic considerations to be explored for each Revolution; and Chapters 5, 6, and 7 deal with the revolutionary conflicts and outcomes of France, Russia, and China, respectively.

I Causes of Social Revolutions in France, Russia, and China

2 Old-Regime States in Crisis

For a revolution to break out it is not enough for the "lower classes to refuse" to live in the old way; it is necessary also that the "upper classes should be unable" to live in the old way.

Lenin

dependency approach

S OCIAL REVOLUTIONS in France, Russia, and China emerged from specifically political crises centered in the structures and situations of the old-regime states. The events of 1787–9 in France, of the first half of 1917 in Russia, and of 1911–16 in China not only undermined autocratic monarchical regimes but also disorganized centrally coordinated administrative and coercive controls over the potentially rebellious lower classes. The revolutionary crises developed when the old-regime states became unable to meet the challenges of evolving international situations. Monarchical authorities were subjected to new threats or to intensified competition from more economically developed powers abroad. And they were constrained or checked in their responses by the institutionalized relationships of the autocratic state organizations to the landed upper classes and the agrarian economies. Caught in cross-pressures between domestic class structures and international exigencies, the autocracies and their centralized administrations and armies broke apart, opening the way for social-revolutionary transformations spearheaded by revolts from below.

To understand the nature and causes of the political crises that launched the French, Russian, and Chinese Revolutions, we need a sense of the structures of the Old Regimes and of the conflicts to which they were prone in the times before the outbreaks of the Revolutions. We may begin with the fact that prerevolutionary France, Russia, and China were countries held together by autocratic monarchies focused upon tasks of maintaining internal order and of contending with external foes. In all three Old Regimes there were fully established *imperial states* – that is, differentiated, centrally coordinated administrative and military hierarchies functioning under the aegis of the absolute monarchies.[1] These imperial states

47

were proto-bureaucratic: *Some* offices, especially at higher levels, were functionally specialized; *some* officials or aspects of official duties were subject to explicit rules and hierarchical supervision; and the separation of state offices and duties from private property and pursuits was *partially* institutionalized (though in different particular ways) in each regime. None of these imperial states, however, was fully bureaucratic.[2] Concomitantly, none was as fully centralized or powerful within society as a modern national state would be. It is worth emphasizing in particular that the imperial states of old-regime France, Russia, and China were not in a position to control directly, let alone basically reorganize, local agrarian socioeconomic relationships. Rather they were limited to variations or extensions of the functions they had, so to speak, been built up to perform: waging war abroad; supervising society at home to maintain some semblance of general order; and appropriating socioeconomic resources through military recruitment and through taxes on land, population, or trade (but not on anything so difficult to assess as individual income).

The imperial states of Bourbon France, Romanov Russia, and Manchu China stood astride large-scale, predominantly agrarian economies in which land and (nonstate) claims to agricultural products were divided between a mass of peasant families and a landed upper class. In each Old Regime, the most important dominant (i.e., surplus appropriating) class was, fundamentally, a landed upper class. This was true even though that class might be closely tied to, and regularly rejuvenated by, commercial wealth. Market relationships were quite extensively developed in all three prerevolutionary societies,[3] and there were urban-based working classes, and classes that controlled commerce and industry. Nevertheless, most trade was locally or regionally (rather than nationally) focused, agriculture remained more economically important than commerce or industry, and capitalist relations of production did not predominate either in agriculture or in nonagricultural pursuits. Commercial and industrial upper classes were symbiotically related to the existing landed upper classes and/or very dependent upon the imperial states. The fundamental politically relevant tensions in all three Old Regimes were *not* between commercial–industrial classes and landed aristocracies. Instead, they were centered in the relationships of producing classes to the dominant classes and states, and in the relationships of the landed dominant classes to the autocratic–imperial states.

As in all agrarian states, the potential for peasant (and urban–popular) revolts was endemic in old-regime France, Russia, and China. Here this ever-present, basic tension in society need only be noted, because it will be dealt with in detail in Chapter 3. At this point, we need to focus on the relationships between imperial states and landed upper classes and on the possible conflicts to which those relationships could give rise.

In one sense, of course, the imperial states and landed upper classes of

48

prerevolutionary France, Russia, and China were simply partners in the control and exploitation of the peasantry. Whatever may have been the case historically (especially in preabsolutist France), the sheer existence of centralized administrations and armies was not being deliberately challenged by the landed classes in the times immediately before the Revolutions. The dominant classes could not defend against peasant rebellions entirely on a local basis; they had all come to depend, albeit in varying degrees, upon the centralized monarchical states to back up their class positions and prerogatives. What is more, the dominant classes had become accustomed to having opportunities for private fortune-building through state service. And, indeed, such appropriation of surpluses indirectly through state office-holding had become very important in old-regime France, Russia, and China alike.

But if, in one sense, the imperial states and the landed classes were partners in exploitation, they were also competitors in controlling the manpower of the peasantry and in appropriating surpluses from the agrarian-commercial economies. Monarchs were interested in appropriating increased resources from society and channeling them efficiently into military aggrandizement or state-sponsored and centrally controlled economic development. Thus the economic interests of the landed upper classes were in part obstacles to be overcome; for the landed classes were primarily interested either in preventing increased state appropriations or in using state offices to siphon off revenues in ways that would reinforce the domestic socioeconomic status quo.[4]

Whether, and in what forms, such objectively possible conflicts of interest between monarchs and landed upper classes gave rise to actual political conflicts in old-regime France, Russia, and China depended upon historical circumstances and upon the exact institutional forms of each autocratic–imperial state. None of these states was in any sense a parliamentary regime that afforded to dominant class representatives a routine role in state policy-making. Yet these were not fully bureaucratic states either. In various ways, dominant class members enjoyed privileged access to and use of state offices. This fact alone was certainly not enough to ensure dominant class *control* of imperial state activities. But to the extent that dominant-class members gained a capacity for self-conscious collective organization within the higher levels of the existing imperial state structures, they might be in a position to *obstruct* monarchical undertakings that ran counter to their economic interests. Such obstruction could culminate in deliberate challenges to autocratic political authority—and, at the same time, it could have the quite unintended effect of destroying the administrative and military integrity of the imperial state itself.

Ordinarily, no doubt, we would expect that monarchs of imperial states would never have attempted to pursue policies fundamentally at variance

49

with the economic interests of dominant classes possessed of such important leverage. Yet the fact is that, during the historical periods leading into the French, Russian, and Chinese Revolutions, monarchs were faced with extraordinary dilemmas. As was briefly indicated at the very beginning of this chapter, the contradictions that brought the Old Regimes to their downfall were not due to internal conditions alone. In the periods before the Revolutions, each of these regimes—Bourbon France, Romanov Russia, and Manchu China—found itself in a situation of intensifying military competition with nation-states abroad that possessed relatively much greater and more flexible power based upon economic breakthroughs to capitalist industrialization or agriculture and commerce. Success in meeting this foreign competition depended upon the ability of the monarchy suddenly to mobilize extraordinary resources from the society and to implement in the process reforms requiring structural transformations.

That agrarian states caught up historically in the international expansion of capitalism *could* defend their autonomy and implement reforms from above was not out of the question. Both Prussia and Japan—two cases that will be discussed at the end of this chapter as contrasts to France, Russia, and China—did mobilize to meet foreign competition in the nineteenth century, thus avoiding social-revolutionary transformations. In Prussia and Japan, state elites were not blocked in their efforts to meet external exigencies either by backward agrarian economies or by politically powerful landed upper classes with the interest and capacity to curb state initiatives. Instead, reforms and policies designed to mobilize and deploy increased resources could be implemented by bureaucratic officials operating in the name of traditional legitimations.

But, in late-eighteenth-century France, early-twentieth-century Russia, and mid-nineteenth through early-twentieth-century China alike, the monarchies of the Old Regimes proved unable to implement sufficiently basic reforms or to promote rapid enough economic development to meet and weather the particular intensity of military threats from abroad that each regime had to face. And revolutionary political crises emerged precisely because of the unsuccessful attempts of the Bourbon, Romanov, and Manchu regimes to cope with foreign pressures. Institutional relationships existed between the monarchs and their staffs, on the one hand, and the agrarian economies and the landed upper classes, on the other hand, that made it impossible for the imperial states to cope successfully with competition or intrusions from abroad. As a result, the Old Regimes either were dissolved through the impact of defeat in total war with more developed powers (i.e., Russia) or were deposed at home through the reaction of politically powerful landed upper classes against monarchical attempts to mobilize resources or impose reforms (i.e., France and China). Either way, the upshot was the disintegration of centralized administrative and military machineries that had theretofore provided the sole unified bulwark of social and political order. No longer reinforced by the prestige and coercive power of autocratic monarchy, the existing class relations became vulnerable to assaults from below. Social-revolutionary political crises emerged, as Lenin once so aptly put it, when it became "impossible for the ruling classes to maintain their rule in an unchanged form." There occurred a "crisis in the policy of the ruling class which cause[d] fissures through which the discontent and indignation of the oppressed classes [could] burst forth."[5]

To lay bare more exactly the intersecting forces that culminated in social-revolutionary political crises in France, Russia, and China, we must look in more detail at each case and make comparisons among them. In the remainder of this chapter I shall do this, discussing for each Old Regime the characteristics of the state, the economy, and the dominant class. I shall also examine the historically specific processes through which international dynamics interacted with the old-regime sociopolitical structures to produce the revolutionary crises. At the end of this chapter, the arguments set forth for France, Russia, and China will be further specified and validated through a brief discussion of contrasts with the causes and consequences of political crises in Prussia and Japan—two other similar countries that weathered the impacts from more developed countries abroad without undergoing social revolutions. Primarily, though, we shall examine the Old Regimes that did give rise to social-revolutionary crises, beginning with Bourbon France, and moving next to late Imperial, Manchu China (according to an order that is both analytically convenient and chronologically exact, given that the Chinese Old Regime met its demise in 1911). After China, we shall proceed to Russia under the Romanov tsars, as it developed from the mid-1800s to the outbreak of the momentous revolutionary events of 1917.

OLD-REGIME FRANCE: THE CONTRADICTIONS OF BOURBON ABSOLUTISM

Explanations of the French Revolution have long played upon one, or a synthesis, of two basic themes: the rise of the bourgeoisie and the emergence of an Enlightenment critique of arbitrary, traditional authority.[6] The Revolution has thus been attributed to causes immanent to the evolution of French society and culture. To be sure, the international setting has not been neglected. It has often been evoked precisely to demonstrate that commercial growth and the diffusion of Enlightenment ideals, though phenomena of European and Atlantic scope, were nevertheless peculiarly intense in prerevolutionary France—especially in comparison with other illiberal monarchies of the day.[7]

51

What has been done much more rarely, however, is to highlight the pervasive military competition of European states, and to focus from that perspective upon the paradoxical situation of old-regime France.[8] In a dynamic international setting increasingly dominated by commercializing England, here was a country that devolved – despite a half century of vigorous economic expansion – from near-dominance in Europe to the humiliations of martial defeats and royal bankruptcy. The explanation of why this happened renders comprehensible the specific political crisis that launched the French Revolution. Furthermore, the causal patterns invoked prove comparable to those at work in the launching of the other great Revolutions.

The State

We begin our analysis of old-regime France by locating historically the consolidation of a unified imperial state administration. Absolute monarchy, long in the making in fact and royal fancy, became the dominant reality for France only during the reign of Louis XIV (1643–1715).[9] The Fronde of 1648–53 marked the last time that sections of the territorial nobility took up arms against centralizing royalty. It also constituted "the last attempt before the Revolution to promulgate a charter limiting royal absolutism, and its failure assured the triumph of the doctine... "[10] France was henceforth governed under the royal administration. Thirty-some removable *intendants* represented the king's authority in the provinces. Relegating the once all-powerful hereditary noble governors to marginal roles, the *intendants* assumed responsibilities for direct tax collections, royal justice, economic regulation, and the maintenance of internal order. The affairs of the towns were brought under the supervision of the *intendants,* and the leading municipal offices were recurrently held for ransom by the Crown.[11] The greatest of the old nobility were drawn into the orbit of the new Court at Versailles – the ultimate symbol of triumphant absolutism – unparalleled in its splendor and replete with sinecures and intrigue.

Absolutism triumphed under Louis XIV, yet the state structure of old-regime France remained extraordinarily complex and, so to speak, multiply layered. Although the authority of the absolutist administration was supreme, its distinctive structures – royal councils and the intendancies – did not actually supplant such decentralized medieval institutions as seigneurial domains and courts, municipal corporations, and the provincial estates (representative assemblies) located in outlying provinces called *pays d'état.* Nor did the absolutist structures completely replace earlier monarchical administrative arrangements such as the *parlements* (judicial corporations, to be described more fully below), previously important offices and jurisdictions, and the practice (called "venality of office") of

52

selling positions within the royal administration to wealthy men who subsequently owned, and could sell or bequeath their offices. For, extraordinary though his accomplishments were, Louis XIV continued a long-established French royal tradition of imposing new controls "over" established arrangements without actually abolishing them. Hence triumphant autocracy tended to freeze, indeed guarantee, the very sociopolitical institutional forms—seigneurial, corporate, provincial—whose original functions it replaced or superseded.

Map 1. *Major administrative divisions of old-regime France, 1789.*
Source: M. J. Sydenham, *The French Revolution* (New York: Capricorn Books, 1966), p. 40.

53

Along with the maintenance of unity and order at home, military aggrandizement became the unabashed purpose of Bourbon absolutism. Having traversed over a century of civil wars and fended off Hapsburg imperialism, the French monarchy was geared to bid for supremacy within the European system of states.[12] Success would demand capacity to contend with two sorts of enemies at once: other land-based monarchies on the Continent and the increasingly prosperous commercial–naval powers, the Netherlands and England. Initially the prospects seemed promising enough. France was united, territorially compact, populous, and – once political order was restored – potentially prosperous. Under the Marquis de Louvois France developed the first year-round standing royal army in Europe. And Jean Baptiste Colbert created a navy, instituted mercantilist policies to guide and foster the expansion of industry, trade, and colonization, and reformed royal finances in ways that increased the revenues available for wars.[13]

During the reign of Louis XIV, France's initial military successes – in the War of Devolution (1667–8) and in the Dutch War (1672–8) – stimulated the formation of an alliance of powers pledged to stop its expansion. As a result, the French subsequently suffered serious setbacks in the War of the League of Augsburg (1688–97) and the War of the Spanish Succession (1701–14). Between 1715 and 1789, moreover, France proved not only unable to dominate Europe but even unable to hold its own as the unquestionably first-ranked power. Of course, coalitions of enemy states still allied against France. But equally serious difficulties arose from the limitations placed upon royal capacities (though never ambitions!) by the imperfections of the absolutist system completed under Louis XIV and by the nature of the French economy and class structure. Comparisons to England are especially relevant, for it was England that was, in this period, moving to overtake France in the race for European (and, as it turned out, worldwide capitalist) hegemony.

The Economy

In the seventeenth century and throughout the eighteenth, France remained a predominantly agricultural society, her economy encumbered by a complex web of proprietary interests that precluded any rapid breakthrough to capitalist agriculture or to industrialism. On the eve of the Revolution, after over fifty years of economic growth, peasants still accounted for as much as 85 percent of the national population of about twenty-six million[14]; and agricultural output constituted at least 60 percent of gross national production.[15] Commerce and some (premechanized) industries were unquestionably expanding in eighteenth-century France (although much of this growth was centered in the hinterlands of Atlantic ports that

54

were destined to suffer badly during the Revolution). Yet however much commerce and nascent industries were growing, they remained symbiotically tied to—and limited by—the social and political structures of agrarian—imperial France.[16]

At this stage in world history, the progress of industry necessarily rested mainly upon prosperity in agriculture. But French agriculture, though advanced by Continental standards, was "backward" relative both to English agriculture and to French commerce and industry.[17] Whether owned by the peasants or rented out by landlords, the land was divided into small holdings. Much farming was on the three-field strip system, in which individual holdings were splintered and scattered, and one-third of the cultivable lands, as well as certain common lands, were left fallow each year. Due to the size of France and the paucity of cheap internal transport for bulk goods, regional specialization in agriculture was slow to develop. In England and Holland during the sixteenth through the eighteenth centuries a revolution in agricultural productivity—which featured cultivation of root and forage crops, building up of livestock herds, and increased fertilization of lands that no longer needed to be left fallow—made great headway. But similar transformations achieved only limited progress in France.

The introduction of the new agricultural techniques depended upon the abolition of many communal customs and seigneurial rights to allow the consolidation and unified management of substantial holdings. But in France there existed a precarious balance of rights between a large smallholding peasantry, which owned outright approximately one-third of the land, and a landed upper class, which also had considerable property in land and possessed surviving seigneurial rights that could be commercially exploited. Thus, neither group was placed in a situation in which revolutionizing agricultural production was simultaneously to its interest and within its capacity. Innovation was also discouraged by the heavy burden and irrational modes of collection of royal taxes, which fell mainly on the peasantry. Finally, there was another, more ironical, reason why structural change in the agrarian economy was impeded. Due to over forty years of good weather, internal order, and population growth, gross agricultural production expanded enormously within largely traditional structural bounds during the mid-eighteenth century (1730–70). This growth, accompanied by rising prices and rents, brought prosperity for landowners large and small and thus probably helped to confine the perceived need for fundamental structural changes to the few governmental officials and progressive landlords who were most acutely aware of the English contrast.

French agriculture, in turn, restrained the development of French industry. Both its structure and the distribution of its benefits retarded the emergence of a steadily expanding mass market for goods. This was especially true of those of middle quality, the ones most amenable to machine production. At the end of the sixteenth century, French industry was probably ahead of English. But then from roughly 1630 to 1730, French agriculture, trade, and industry suffered repeated setbacks from wars, plague, and famines. Meanwhile the English economy grew rather steadily, and the first stages of the revolution in agrarian relations of production and technique were consummated. During the eighteenth century *both* English and French economic growth, including the expansion of foreign trade, were rapid and roughly equivalent. But England had been well ahead in per capita terms before the century began, and her agricultural revolution deepened even as production grew during the eighteenth century. Thus the stage was set for the English Industrial Revolution after 1760. General economic expansion was undoubtedly one factor underlying England's breakthrough, but the French economy in the eighteenth century experienced comparable rates of growth. In addition to her greater size and consequent difficulties of internal transportation, what clearly differentiated France was her agrarian economy. Even in prosperity the French agrarian economy provided much less of a potential mass market for industrial goods than the English, because there were proportionately fewer people with middle incomes. Nor could the traditional structure of agrarian production sustain prolonged growth. Unless checked by the ravages of war, population growth inexorably followed increases in productivity and soon outran them, producing skyrocketing prices and famine. Just such a crisis produced an industrial recession after 1770 – even as English industry was adopting the new machine technologies. "The agricultural base of the French economy once more revealed, in the 1770s and 1780s, its inability to sustain prolonged growth. In 1600–30, in 1660–90, in 1730–70 – time after time bursts of expansion came to an end in slackening demand as purses were emptied on ever-dearer food."[18]

The Dominant Class

By the eighteenth century a distinctive dominant class had emerged in France. It was no longer "feudal" in the political or juridical sense. But it was not "capitalist" either – not in the sense of "entrepreneurial" and not in the Marxist sense of a class that appropriates surplus through wage labor and market rents and reinvests to expand capitalist relations of production and industrialization. Yet there was a basically unified dominant class – one that appropriated surplus directly and indirectly primarily from peasant agriculture.[19] This surplus appropriation occured through a mélange of rents and dues enforced in part by landlord-dominated judicial institutions, and through the redistribution of revenues collected under the aegis of the monarchical state. In fact, if the term "feudal" is used in one possible Marxist manner to indicate a particular class relation of surplus appropriation (i.e., appropriation by a landed class through coercive institutional means),[20] then one may say that the dominant class of prerevolutionary France was to a significant degree feudal. But it is more important to arrive at a clear sense of what were—and were not—the characteristics and institutional bases of this dominant class.

Certainly eighteenth-century France was not a society actually stratified by estate (i.e., church, nobility, Third Estate). As François Furet indicates, social formations and ideals encouraged by the simultaneous (and symbiotic) growth of state administration and commercialization had led to the supersession of the late medieval system of orders:

> In truth, the French monarchy had for centuries played an active part in dislocating the society of estates, and it continued to do this more than ever during the eighteenth century. Tied to the development of commercial production, hostile to local powers, promoter of national unity, the state was—along with money, at the same time as money, and even more than money—the decisive source of social mobility. Progressively the state had undermined, encroached upon, and destroyed the vertical solidarity of the estates, especially the nobility. This had occurred both socially and culturally: socially, insofar as the state had constituted, most notably through its offices, another nobility than that of the feudal epoch. By the eighteenth century, the new groups made up the majority of the nobility. Culturally, the state had offered to the ruling groups of the kingdom, assembled henceforth under its aegis, another system of values than that of personal honor: the fatherland and the State. In short, by becoming the pole of attraction for wealth, because it was the distributor of social promotion, the monarchical state, even as it conserved the heritage of the estate society, created a parallel and contradictory social structure: an elite, a governing class.[21]

Wealth and office holding, not simply estate membership, were the keys to success in *ancien régime* France.[22] Noble fortunes varied enormously. The poorer nobles were excluded from Parisian high society and comfortable stylish living in the provincial cities, and they had great difficulty in purchasing the most desirable offices in the army or civil administration. On the other hand, commoners who gained great wealth through overseas commerce or royal finance, or who advanced by purchasing successive state offices, could readily gain access both to noble status and privileges, and to high society. In fact, many of the most prominent and prosperous noble families of the eighteenth century seem to have been ennobled only three or four generations previously.

The distinction between the First (ecclesiastical) and Second (noble) Estates, on the one hand, and the Third Estate, on the other, was by the eighteenth century more a fluid zone of transition than a barrier—at least from the perspective of the dominant groups. Estate was indeed a true barrier at the middle levels of the social order based largely on wealth and office holding. Yet the social tensions thus engendered – which were to set poor nobles and nonnoble members of the educated Third Estate at once against each other and against the wealthy privileged – were not fully released until during the Revolution. They did not create the Revolutionary crisis.[23]

Nor did any class contradiction – based upon a clash of incompatible modes of production cutting through the dominant strata – create the Revolutionary crisis. As the excellent research of George Taylor has demonstrated,[24] over 80 percent of the private wealth of the Old Regime was "proprietary" wealth:

> There was in the economy of the old regime a distinct configuration of wealth, noncapitalist in function, that may be called "proprietary." It embodied investments in land, urban property, venal office, and annuities. The returns it yielded were modest, ranging between 1 and 5 percent, but they were fairly constant and varied little from year to year. They were realized not by entrepreneurial effort . . . but by mere ownership and the passage of calendar intervals.[25]

In the agrarian economy, proprietary wealth took the forms both of (a) land exploited indirectly through rents from tenants who held or used pieces of "domains, farms, *métairies,* meadows, fields, stands of timber," etc.; and of (b) the "seigneury, consisting of dues, monopolies, and rights surviving from the [feudal] fief . . . , an order of property superimposed on property in fee simple."[26] Ownership of urban land and buildings was yet another source of rental incomes. And then there were venal offices and *rentes,* whose features are well described by Taylor:

> In the proprietary scale of preference, the passion for property in office was nearly as strong as that for property in land. A venal office was a long-term investment. Usually it brought a low but stable return, and, as long as the owner regularly paid the *droit annuel . . . ,* he could, under restrictions applicable to each office, sell it to a buyer, bequeath it to an heir, or even rent it out to someone . . . Generally speaking, an investment in office was an investment in standing. What made it desirable was the status, the respectability that it conferred.[27]

> In addition . . . proprietary wealth was invested in *rentes.* In the broadest sense, a *rente* was an annual revenue that one received for having transferred something of value to someone else . . . A *rente perpetuelle* was an annuity of indefinite duration, terminated only when the debtor chose, on his own initiative, to refund the principal and thereby free himself from paying the *rente* . . . Its proper domain was that of accommodations within and between families and investments in annuities sold by municipalities, provincial estates, and the royal treasury.[28]

Even the most well-to-do members of the Third Estate based their fortunes upon mixtures of *rentes,* venal offices, real estate, and seigneurial rights. Taylor argues emphatically that "there was, between most of the nobility and the proprietary sector of the middle classes, a continuity of investment forms that made them, economically, a single group. In the relations of production they played a common role."[29] Only those (mostly nonnobles) engaged in overseas commerce and those (mostly ennobled) involved in royal high finance possessed more fluid and risky forms of circulating wealth. Yet for these groups, too, proprietary wealth was ultimately more attractive. Most successful merchants or financiers transferred their fortunes to proprietary assets; likewise they typically transferred their efforts, or those of their offspring, to the corresponding socially more appropriate pursuits.

"Proprietary wealth," then, was the property basis of the dominant class. Yet an important thing to notice about proprietary wealth is how dependent it was in its various forms upon the peculiar state structure of old-regime France. Both the absolutist and the archaic aspects of the "multiply layered" state structure provided crucial supports for the socioeconomic position of the dominant class. French peasants still mostly adhered to premarket conceptions of social and economic order and would engage in riot or rebellion if their communal ideals of justice were flagrantly violated.[30] Thus, since landlords no longer controlled significant means of coercion at local levels, they depended upon the absolutist administration as their protector of last resort. At the same time, the various seigneurial, corporate, and provincial institutions that were preserved under the umbrella of absolutism also had great socioeconomic significance for the dominant class. In general, these did not set the bourgeoisie (or the upper Third Estate) against the nobility, because wealthy persons of all estates owned seigneurial rights, held venal offices, and belonged to privileged corporations of one sort or another.[31] Rather these institutions expressed and reinforced the advantages of the richer propertied against the poorer in prerevolutionary France. For, whatever their different particular social or political purposes, one thing that all of these rights and bodies had in common was that they entailed state-enforced tax advantages and opportunities for income. Along with property claims on the land, such exemptions and opportunities were a major basis of the wealth of the dominant class as a whole.

This situation of dependence on the state naturally produced a dominant class with vested interest in both the older institutional forms, such as seigneurial rights and proprietary offices, and the new absolutist functions, mainly those related to the state's capacity to promote the military success and to tax the economic expansion of the country (insofar as the tax revenues came from the nonprivileged). Such a dominant class would rise or fall with France as a commercial, but noncapitalist, agrarian-imperial power. The Revolutionary crisis emerged only when this France proved not viable, given developments in the existing international situation and conflicts of interest between the monarchy and the dominant class with its many footholds within the state structure.

Wars and the Fiscal Dilemma

As events of the eighteenth century unfolded, it became more and more apparent that the French monarchy could not fulfill its raison d'être. The victories in war necessary for the vindication of French honor on the international scene, not to mention the protection of seaborne commerce, were beyond its grasp. France fought at sea and on land in the two general wars of the mid-eighteenth century—the War of the Austrian Succession (1740–8), and the Seven Years' War (1756–63). In each conflict, the country's resources were strained to the utmost and its vital colonial trade was disrupted by the British navy. In return, no gains were made; instead, France lost to Britain large chunks of its empire in North America and India.[32]

A major difficulty for France was strategic. As a commercial power located on an island, England could concentrate virtually all of its resources on naval power—which, in turn, could be employed to protect and expand the colonial trade from whence came tax revenues for military ventures. No large standing army at home was necessary, and limited financial subsidies could be used to aid or incite allies on the Continent against France. France, however, suffered the penalties of "amphibious geography." France was, or aimed to be, "at once the greatest land power and a great maritime power . . . Partly continental, partly maritime, she could not like Great Britain [or Prussia and Austria], throw all her energies in one direction or the other; willy-nilly she had to attempt to do both."[33] France could only hope to defeat what was increasingly its main enemy, Britain, if it remained out of any simultaneous general war on the Continent and concentrated its resources on naval warfare. "This was, however, an interest which the French could not pursue except by abandoning their claims, if not to dominate, at least to exercise a determining voice in Europe . . . [But] the great achievements of Louis XIV in his early days set the standard for future generations."[34]

An even more fundamental difficulty for France was the inadequacy of the state's financial resources. Partly because of the lower level of per capita national wealth in France compared to England, and partly because the system of taxation was riddled with the exemptions or deductions of countless privileged elites—including officers, tax farmers, trading and industrial groups, as well as churchmen and the nobility[35] – the French Crown found it difficult to raise revenues sufficient to sustain protracted and repeated general warfare, especially against enemy coalitions that included England. Rather than give up its martial ambitions, the Bourbon monarchy simply borrowed at high rates of interest from private financiers – and even more regularly from the monarchy's own office holders. Like the *rentes perpe-tuelles* that the state sold to private buyers, venal offices were a form of long-term finance in which the principal need "never" be repaid.[36] In addition, the Crown continuously took short-term loans at interest from its countless financial agents (for there was no unified treasury), simply by ordering them to make payments in advance or in excess of the tax revenues they collected by virtue of their venal offices.[37]

In contrast to the French monarchy, the English government could raise loans in an emergency quickly and at low rates of interest. For the English government could work through the Bank of England – a public institution whose existence and operations depended upon England's unique degree of commercial prosperity and upon the confidence created in upper-class minds by the Parliament's careful controls over and guarantees of governmental debts. In consequence, C.B.A. Behrens tells us "though it would seem . . . that the British government's [tax] revenues in peace, even towards the end of the eighteenth century, cannot have been more than about half those of France, British expenditure, in the last stages of the two greatest wars of the century seems likely to have exceeded that of the French."[38]

As repeated wars and defeats worsened the French monarchy's financial plight, a succession of ministers of finance attempted to reform the tax system by abolishing most exemptions of privileged groups and equalizing the burden across provinces and localities. Since direct income taxes were beyond the administrative capacities of all eighteenth-century governments, existing direct taxes on agriculture and indirect taxes on articles of consumption would necessarily have continued in force, probably at higher rates for all, because the Crown needed, in the final analysis, more revenues.[39] Naturally all social groups resisted such reforms. Yet the resistance that mattered most came from those wealthy, privileged groups that were simultaneously socially prominent and strategically ensconced within the state machinery.

The most avid resisters of the Crown's attempts to squeeze out more revenues were unquestionably the *parlements*. Nominally simply part of the royal administration, these judicial corporations, situated in Paris and in leading provincial cities, were primarily courts of appeal for all civil and criminal cases. In addition, however, they had several characteristics that combined to make them the key locus of upper-class leverage against royal power. For one thing, the magistrates owned their offices and therefore could not readily be removed. Moreover, as corporate bodies, the *parlements* controlled access to their own ranks. Second, the magistrates were invariably wealthy, mostly in forms associated with tax exemptions. According to Franklin Ford, "their fortunes included not only their offices, in themselves representing large investments, but also a formidable accumulation of securities, urban property, and rural seigneuries."[40] Besides, the magistrates played a key role in protecting seigneurial property in particular. For as courts of appeal for disputes about seigneurial rights, the *parlements* defended this "bizarre form of property" held by noble and bourgeois alike. "Indeed," writes Alfred Cobban, "without the juridical backing of the parlements the whole system of seigneurial rights might have collapsed, for the royal officials had no interest in the maintenance of a system which removed income from those who were taxable [i.e., peasants] into the hands of those who could not be taxed."[41]

Third, by virtue of their varied fortunes, styles of life, and residence in major urban centers (including the important regional centers), the magistrates were remarkably "well connected." They intermarried and interacted with old-line ("sword") nobles and with those who lived off seigneurial properties, as well as with families newly rich (and recently ennobled) through commerce and finance.[42] Equally, they "kept up contact with other officeholders who had not graduated to the nobility ... [and] maintained ties with a socially less prestigious group, namely the lawyers."[43]

Finally, the *parlements* possessed, by tradition, the right to "remonstrate against" royal edicts that they considered in violation of the customary practices of the realm. In practical terms, this meant that they could delay the implementation of royal policies they disliked, in the process arousing public (mostly upper class) debate about them. The effect was often to cause the king to lose confidence in the ministers responsible for the attempted implementation of the objectionable policies.[44]

Repeatedly during the eighteenth century, the *parlements* opposed ministerial attempts at tax reform. Resistance was a generally popular cause and, besides, proposed reforms would end the privileges of wealthy proprietary groups like themselves and the seigneurs, rentiers, and other office holders to whom they were connected. Around mid-century, the *parlements* even began to assert the right to give quasi-legislative approval to royal policies as representatives of the French people against the Crown. Finally in 1787–8, the *parlements* "opened the door to revolution" by rallying upper-class and popular support once again against ministerial proposals for reforms, and by voicing the demand for the convening of the Estates-General.[45]

Ironically, the beginning of the revolutionary political crisis came in the

wake of the one eighteenth-century war in which France was unequivocally victorious. Having avoided entanglements on the Continent, France
stymied the British Navy in the War for American Independence. Still, "the
price to be paid for American Independence was a French revolution."[46]
For to finance the war to deprive England of its American colonies, royal
treasurers (between roughly 1774 and 1788) finally exhausted their capacity to raise new loans, even as they sharply increased royal expenditures
and indebtedness to astronomical heights. Expenditures jumped over two
and one-half times between 1770 and 1788,[47] while by the latter year
"debt service charges alone consum[ed] over 50 percent of annual expenditures."[48] The burden of financing the American War came before treasurers had managed to control the indebtedness from the previous (Seven
Years') general war. Taxes "were surcharged for the last time in 1780 and
1781; within the terms of the existing system of privilege-corroded fiscal-
ity, the economy could bear no more."[49] Then, too, as we have already
noted, after 1770 France slid into a cyclical general economic recession—a
circumstance that reduced tax receipts and investment funds and spurred
bankruptcies among the state's financial agents.[50]

Still, as J. F. Bosher wisely reminds us: "Most Bourbon kings had survived debt and bankruptcy; the financial difficulties in the later years of
Louis XIII, Louis XIV and Louis XV were probably as bad as those on the
eve of the French revolution."[51] "Why," he asks, "did the financial
troubles of Louis XVI develop into a major crisis?" Why did they launch a
revolution? Bosher replies that developments in eighteenth-century French
society had closed off an old escape mechanism:

> Every other financial crisis in the Bourbon monarchy had culminated
> in a Chamber of Justice [an extraordinary judicial proceeding], direct-
> ing public attention towards the accountants, tax farmers, and other
> financiers [all venal officers of the monarchy from whom it habitually
> borrowed in anticipation of tax revenues] . . . as profiteers and there-
> fore responsible for the trouble . . . Chambers of Justice had provided
> a convenient legal means for cancelling debts to the financiers and
> forcibly recovering large sums from them. On the occasion of these
> Chambers the Crown had taken advantage of the financiers' momen-
> tary weakness to make reforms in the financial institutions . . .
>
> But during the eighteenth century the Farmers General, Receivers Gen-
> eral, Treasurers General, Payers of the rentes and other high accoun-
> tants had become noble in such large numbers, and merged with the
> ruling classes to such an extent, that the Crown was in no position to
> establish a Chamber of Justice against them. The long series of Cham-
> bers of Justice came to an end in 1717 . . . Those Finance Ministers
> who attempted anything in the nature of an attack on the financiers,

63

especially Terray, Turgot and Necker, suffered political defeat and were obliged to retire. It was in these circumstances that the financial trouble ripened into a major crisis.[52]

In short, when its unquenchable penchant for war carried the eighteenth-century Bourbon monarchy into an acute financial crisis, it faced a socially consolidated dominant class. This class was dependent upon the absolutist state and implicated in its international mission. Yet it was also economically interested in minimizing royal taxation of its wealth and capable of exerting political leverage against the absolutist monarchy through its institutional footholds within the state apparatus.

The Revolutionary Political Crisis

In 1787, news of the monarchy's financial peril precipitated a general crisis of confidence within the dominant class.[53] In an attempt to preempt the *parlements,* Finance Minister Charles Alexandre de Calonne summoned an Assembly of Notables (representatives of the dominant class from all three orders) and laid before them an analysis of the financial predicaments and sweeping proposals for legal and tax reforms. Key proposals called for a new tax on all lands regardless of ownership by nobles or nonnobles and for the establishment of district assemblies representing all landowners regardless of status. Not surprisingly, the Notables rejected these ideas; Calonne fell and was replaced by Loménie de Brienne, who sent edicts embodying a modified version of the same ideas to the *parlements.* The *Parlement* of Paris refused to register Brienne's decrees, and, with widespread support, demanded the summoning of the long-defunct Estates-General. No longer confident that absolutism could solve the problems of state, and fearful for its privileges, the dominant class wanted a representative body to advise the king and give consent to any new taxes.

At first the king refused and proceeded to override the *parlements.* But resistance spread, especially in the provinces. Provincial *parlements,* provincial estates in the outlying *pays d'état,* and extraordinary bodies created by nobles and/or the upper Third Estate raised a hue and cry against "despotism" and for the Estates-General. Popular demonstrations, especially by the retainers of the *parlements,* championed the *privilégiés* against the Crown. And not all *intendants,* military governors, and army officers could be counted upon to suppress resistance.[54]

The reluctance of many army officers to suppress resistance with any vigor was a spur along with the continuing financial crisis to the ultimate royal capitulation in summoning the Estates-General. And the reluctance of the officers helped to trigger spreading administrative chaos and military breakdown. Recruited from various privileged social backgrounds— rich noble, rich nonnoble, and poor country noble—the officers had a variety of long-standing grievances. Some were directed against other officers, and others, significantly, were shared against the Crown, which could never satisfy all groups.[55] But it is likely that the decisive explanation for the behavior of the officers lies in the fact that virtually all of them were privileged, socially and/or economically. Hence many identified during 1787–8 with the *parlements*. In her classic book, *Armies and the Art of Revolution*, Katherine Chorley concludes from comparative historical studies that, in preindustrial societies, army officers generally identify with and act to protect the interests of the privileged strata from which they are recruited.[56] During its opening phases until, and even after, the king had capitulated and agreed to convene the Estates-General, the French Revolution pitted all strata, led by the wealthy privileged, against the Crown. The army officers' predictable reluctance to repress resistance during that period exacerbated the crisis of governmental authority, which in turn unleashed political and social divisions that finally made a subsequent resort to simple repression impossible either for the king or for the conservative factions of the dominant class.

For, as everyone knows, the summoning of the Estates-General served not to solve the royal financial crisis but to launch the Revolution. The facts of this launching are surely not in doubt, but there remain questions of interpretation. Many historians of the French Revolution argue that the calling of the Estates-General led to Revolution because it propelled the capitalist bourgeoisie, or else the upper Third Estate, onto the national political stage.[57] This happened as quarrels broke out over whether to operate the Estates in the traditional way, with voting by order, or in a more unified manner with voting by head. Certainly this quarrel was of decisive importance. Yet there is much to suggest that its significance was not that it pitted one class or estate against another. It was rather that the quarrel deepened the paralysis and led to the dissolution of the administrative system of the Old Regime – and thus left the dominant class vulnerable to the truly social-revolutionary implications of revolts from below.

In 1788 and early 1789, the French dominant class was virtually united in wanting a less absolutist, more representative national government. But not at all agreed about what principles should determine exactly who was represented and with what institutionalized power.[58] The summoning of the Estates-General inevitably brought to the fore those questions over which the dominant class was potentially most divided. For the Estates-General was not an established representative institution already functioning to mediate diverse interests within the dominant class. Rather the Estates had to be constituted from scratch, drawing representatives from the welter of communities, groups, and corporate bodies that comprised French society in 1789. With the "customary" guidelines having last been applied in 1614, the very process of constituting the Estates-General unleashed countless conflicts of interest and principles. This was especially true among the wealthy, privileged strata who were complexly divided by estate memberships, degrees of nobility, types of property, regional ties, affiliations to towns or to country, occupational interests, and so forth.

Moreover, insofar as broad groupings took sides in early 1789 in the quarrel over voting by order versus voting by head, those who opposed the traditional constitution and favored a unified National Assembly (which would have individually voting representatives from all three orders) included not only the representatives of the Third Estate but also a hefty minority of the nobility – with a disproportionate number of nobles who were acclimated by birth and/or regular residence to urban life and culture.[59] In fact, some of the key leaders of the "revolutionary bourgeoisie/ Third Estate" were aristocrats.[60] This should not seem surprising. For what was actually at stake in the earliest phase of the Revolution was not the class or social-estate structure – only popular revolts would put these in jeopardy – but the structure of government. And a representative system that would stress wealth, education, and broad public prestige undoubtedly made most sense of all precisely to *noblemen* with urban backgrounds and cosmopolitan connections. Thus they were understandably more divided from the parochial, rural nobles determined to revive a feudal political constitution than from Third Estate representatives who were almost invariably from cities and towns.

But, then, it did not require class contradictions or divisions purely along estate lines to launch the Revolution; the multifaceted political quarrels within the ruling class were quite enough. For these conflicts at first paralyzed and then dismantled the old-regime administrative system – which, after all, had never been based upon anything more than the routine performance of diverse corporate governing bodies and venal officers under the coordination of king, ministers, and *intendants*. With these groups and individuals squabbling among themselves in 1788 and 1789 about how representative bodies should be constituted, and what grievances should be voiced to the king, the doors were swung open for the expression of popular discontents. Leaders from the dominant class actually encouraged increasing popular participation by appealing to urban popular groups for support in their struggles for "liberty," variously defined. First the *parlements* and then the supporters of the National Assembly played this game.

By the summer of 1789, the result was the "Municipal Revolution," a nation-wide wave of political revolutions in cities and towns throughout France, including of course the celebrated "fall of the Bastille in Paris."[61] In the context of the simultaneous political and economic crises of 1788– 9,[62] crowds of artisans, shopkeepers, journeymen, and laborers roamed the cities searching for arms and grain and demanding both bread and liberty.[63] Alert leaders of the liberal revolution, supporters of the National Assembly, formed new municipal governments, displacing officials appointed by or loyal to the royal administration, and recruited the more respectable popular protesters into urban militias. In turn, the militias both served as a counterweight to the royal army and helped to guard urban order and property. Thus, by the early summer of 1789, the quarrels within the dominant class over forms of representation culminated in a victory for the Parisian National Assembly and its various liberal, urban supporters throughout France. And a concomitant of this victory was the sudden devolution of control over the means of administration and coercion from the normally centralized royal administration into the decentralized possession of the various cities and towns, mostly controlled by the supporters of the National Assembly.

Of course the Municipal Revolution proved to be just the beginning of a revolutionary process in France that would soon deepen from antiabsolutist constitutional reforms into more fundamental social and political transformations. For the struggles of the lower classes — and above all those of the peasants, whom no one within the dominant class invited into the fray — would prove to have dynamics and logics all of their own. And without the royal administration, the rural nobility, especially, would have no defenses against revolts from below. But these are matters to be explored in the chapters to come; for now, we shall leave France and move on to analyze the emergence of a revolutionary political crisis in late Imperial China.

MANCHU CHINA: FROM THE CELESTIAL EMPIRE TO THE FALL OF THE IMPERIAL SYSTEM

From the clash and clamor of the European states system, to which Bourbon France was long acclimated before it met its revolutionary nemesis, we move to an alternative, distant, self-contained world with a single hegemonic center. China, before the nineteenth century, was the focus of a rich civilization that stretched back more than two millennia — a civilization embodied in a sociopolitical structure with an over six-hundred-year history of nearly continuous cohesion. The problems of external defense for this imperial state sitting astride a vast agrarian country had been mainly those of warding off or mastering competing peoples on the Asian land frontiers, while intrusions by sea were either ignored or brushed aside by force. The rulers of traditional China became increasingly successful at these endeavors over the centuries. Alien groups might seize the command posts of dynastic rule, but the Chinese Imperial system continued to operate.[64] Indeed, the Ch'ing Dynasty (1644–1911) of the alien Manchus, a sinicized tribal people from southern Manchuria, witnessed the apogee, as well as the ultimate collapse, of that remarkable system.

By the end of the Ch'ien-lung Emperor's reign (1736–96), the boundaries of the Chinese empire extended farther than ever before or since:
west to the Ili region and the boundaries of Russian Turkestan, southwest to the Himalayas and the border states of India. Tibet was pacified and controlled; Annam was in vassalage, and the rest of Southeast
Asia was sending royal tribute; and Korea was once again part of the
Chinese sphere of influence.[65]

For the celestial Empire, peace and order, economic expansion, and
cultural elaboration prevailed – until the nineteenth century. Then an ag-
gressive, expanding, industrializing Europe forced China out of her splendid autonomy into a world of competing nation-states and imperialist
intrusions. But before we discuss the why and the wherefore of the revolutionary consequences that ensued, let us examine the logic of the Old
Regime in its own right. For, just as in the case of Bourbon France, it was
a combination of unusual external pressures with particular internal structures and developments that brought the Chinese Old Regime into revolutionary political crisis.

The sociopolitical structure of late Imperial China can best be comprehended as the interpenetration of two "worlds": (1) an agrarian economy
and society of villages involved in locally focused marketing networks; and
(2) an Imperial state administration that recruited and deployed educated
individuals certified by an elaborate examination system. Each of these
spheres can be introduced separately for analytic purposes, although it is
important to keep in mind from the outset that neither operated in isolation from the other. Indeed their interpenetration created and maintained a
remarkable dominant class – the Chinese gentry.

The Agrarian Economy and Society

In late Imperial times Chinese agriculture was in no sense "feudal" – for
there were no seigneurs with juridical rights to dues or to serf labor as in
precapitalist Europe. Nor did Chinese agriculture feature large, owner-
cultivated estates. Instead, land was owned, rented, and bought and sold
almost invariably in small units. The vast majority of Chinese, at least 80
percent, were peasant agriculturalists, living in villages of several hundred
families, each of which farmed plots of land that the family owned, or
rented, or both.[66]

To be sure, economic inequality in China was to a significant degree
expressed in the differential ownership of land.[67] Countrywide, approximately 40 percent of the farmland was rented out by landlords. About 30
percent of farm families were pure tenants, and another 20 percent rented
part of their land, leaving 50 percent as owners of plots of widely varying
sizes. But regional variations were considerable: In most of the central and

southern parts of China, tenancy rates were higher, while in most of the north and northwest, they were much lower. There were also intraregional variations among localities. In general, the renting out of land could be profitable only in regions where transport, mostly by water, allowed the marketing of grain outside of the exact local areas where it was grown. In North China (where the main crops were wheat and millet) transportation was in general more difficult, not to mention the fact that productivity was much lower than in the rice-growing heartlands of South and Central China.

Agrarian China was, in fact, significantly commercialized, even though the country as a whole was not basically integrated by market relations. Difficulties of transportation meant that trade was bottom heavy and fragmented into thousands of local markets, with most sales of agricultural products contained within "limited region[s] a few tens of miles in diameter."[68] "Long-distance trade mainly carried luxury goods to China's gentry class or necessities to China's cities."[69] Only 7 to 8 percent of all agricultural output entered into it. But local and intraregional commerce was quite important. For, while peasants raised most of their own food, they still depended upon the periodic markets of what William Skinner has labeled the "standard market town" to sell between one-fifth and two-fifths of their produce for money to pay taxes, or to purchase handicraft products and entertainment and religious services. "Insofar as the Chinese peasant can be said to live in a self-contained world, that world is not the village but the standard marketing community,"[70] including twelve to eighteen villages. Similarly, wealthy families often resided in market towns,[71] the operations of which supplied them with luxury commodities and provided opportunities for very profitable investments in handicraft enterprises or, above all, in pawnbroking and usurious moneylending. Such investments provided crucial supplements to the lower returns that wealthy families got from land rentals alone; and they represented an important mechanism of surplus appropriation in late Imperial China.[72]

The State

Wealthy families typically aspired to participate, through state service, in a cosmopolitan and universal realm of Chinese life not experienced by the peasant masses. Given the localized and fragmented character of China's enormous agrarian economy, only the Imperial state—which was focused upon a succession of native or foreign dynasties able to win and hold their position through military prowess—united China into one society. The dynasty was the kingpin of a centralized, autocratic, and semibureaucratic administrative structure staffed (under the Ch'ing) by approximately forty-thousand officials:[73]

The Emperor ruled, an absolute and legally unlimited monarch, with various of the Imperial clan clustered around him. Directly below him in the administrative hierarchy came the Grand Council and the Grand Secretariat, and below these came six (eventually increased to twelve) departments or boards roughly comparable to ministries. Under the central government came the provincial administrations headed in each case by a Governor-General (Viceroy), and/or a Governor. In addition to these officials, the Ch'ing dynasty established in eleven provinces the post of Tartar-General, who ranked "with, but before," the Viceroy.

Each province was divided into smaller units designated as *tao* or circuits over which an intendant presided. Each *tao* was made up of *fu* (overseen by a prefect), and the *fu,* in turn, were subdivided into departments (under departmental magistrates) and *hsien* (under magistrates). These officials secured their appointments from above, all commissions being issued by the Emperor.[74]

Officials were appointed from the ranks of literati degree-holders, who together with their families comprised less than 2 percent of the total population. Most literati passed government-sponsored examinations on the Confucian classics, although a minority purchased degrees and positions.[75] Aspirants to official positions could come from virtually any social background in Imperial China, and indeed persons from poor families did occasionally gain even the highest positions.[76] Yet all had to attain through their own resources, or those of sponsors, the security and leisure to cultivate the scholarly "status-manner" and to devote themselves to (the often literally lifelong) "examination life" of the Confucian literati.[77] And connection to family fortunes that included landed wealth was the only sure and appropriate way to ensure the requisite security and leisure.

Imperial officials were appointed from the exclusive ranks of upper literati — those (approximately 14 percent of all literati) who had passed the provincial or metropolitan (national) examinations, or who had purchased official titles in addition to degrees.[78] Upper literati were either officials, retired officials, or potential officials. Through their examination experiences most had gained extralocal contacts and orientations. Once appointed to offices, upper literati were subject to a set of rules designed — even at the expense of administrative rationality — both to attenuate their strong ties to home and family and to forge them into an elite corps that would take the Imperial state's point of view toward local communities. To be sure, the Chinese state never tried to remove officials permanently from their home localities; regular periods of retirement at home were built into official careers, and ties to families left behind and to local

wealth and social position remained important for even the most successful officials. But the Imperial state did attempt to enforce the loyalty of
active officials. In accordance with a "rule of avoidance," literati appointed as governors, magistrates, and so forth, had to supervise provinces
other than those in which they were born and raised. They were not
allowed to employ family members or marry local women without official
permission. In order to prevent the development of permanent cliques
within their ranks, or fixed alliances between them and the local elites of
the areas they administered, officials were frequently transferred and
scrambled in different mixes. Finally, duplicate jurisdictions and functions
were deliberately built into the provincial administrative structures, so that
the Court might have overlapping lines of surveillance and command.[79]

The lower literati – those who had passed only the basic-level (prefec-
tural) examinations (or who had purchased the basic-level degree) – were
not normally appointed to the relatively scarce Imperial offices. Yet, along
with wealthy men who adopted the Confucian manner, they typically
possessed important prestige and power in their local communities.[80] For
the Imperial administration never reached as far as the individual village or
standard market town. The basic-level official, the county *(hsien)* magistrate, was responsible for an area containing up to 200,000 persons.[81]
Needless to say, he could administer such an area only through cooperation with local people.[82] One device used by all magistrates was to employ
many low-status clerks and assistants, who were remunerated partly by
payments from the magistrate himself and partly by bribes squeezed from
the local people. In addition, resident literati and wealthy Confucian landlords typically collaborated with the magistrate, whom they could approach as a status equal. In return for lighter rates for themselves and their
friends, these local dominants might help the magistrate collect the land
tax. Even more important, the magistrate typically encouraged or allowed
local literati and wealthy men to organize community services – such as
irrigation projects, religious or clan affairs, educational efforts, or local
militias – in return for fees in payment collected from the local peasantry.
Such fees constituted an important source of income especially for the
lower literati. And, of course, the Imperial administration also backed the
rights of landlords and creditors to collect rents and payments.

The Gentry

Thus, not unlike the dominant class in prerevolutionary France, the dominant gentry class of Imperial China was simultaneously based upon office
holding and the ownership of surplus land and liquid wealth. Wealth, lent
or rented with state backing to working peasants, supported the cultiva-

tion of the Confucian status-manner. The Imperial state sanctioned Confucian learning through the examination system and took a minority of its devotees as its officials. Official incomes, as well as fees collected for organizing and managing local community affairs, provided greater returns than those attainable through mere land ownership.[83] Ultimately the wealth thus garnered was partially reinvested in landlordism and usury, thus completing the cycle of interdependence between the Imperial state and the agrarian society based upon fragmented and stratified private ownership and localized commerce.

Much controversy has surrounded the question of who "the gentry" really were in prerevolutionary China. Some argue that they were those *individuals* who held official positions and/or Confucian degrees, thus identifying the gentry strictly with what I have labeled the literati.[84] Others argue that the gentry were basically *wealthy families*, especially landlords.[85] Insofar as more than a purely semantic controversy is involved here, scholars are differing, at least implicitly, in their conceptions of the essential structure of the Old Regime. Was it fundamentally an Imperial state with a unique Confucian culture and educational system? Or was it fundamentally a class-stratified agrarian society? My view is that old-regime China was an inextricable amalgam of both of these. The dominant agrarian class depended upon the administrative/military backing of, and employment opportunities within, the Imperial state. And ruling dynasties depended upon local class dominants to extend controls over and appropriate resources from the huge, unwieldy agrarian expanse that was China. From this perspective it makes sense to argue that the core of the gentry were landlord families with degree holding official members presently in their ranks. Others who lacked all of this constellation of gentry attributes—such as wealthy families without degree-holder members, or poor literati or officials—should also be considered as marginal members of the dominant class. For they shared the distinctive Confucian culture or the sources of wealth of the core gentry, and thus partook of aspects of its power.[86] The gentry's existence and survival as the dominant class depended upon the aspirations and ability of such "marginal" members to attain whatever of the entire constellation of core class attributes they lacked. Indeed, for hundreds of years before the end of the nineteenth century, the Chinese agrarian economy flourished, thus allowing families to attain the wealth to sustain aspirants for degrees and official positions. And the Imperial state structure survived the coming and going of dynasties, thus providing backing for local dominant classes and extraordinary income opportunities for officials. During all of this time, the Chinese gentry, despite the rise and fall of individuals and families, flourished as a class based at the intersections of the Imperial state and the agrarian economy.

72

Foreign Intrusions and Domestic Rebellions

Yet the Chinese Empire did decline and collapse, opening the way to the revolutionary destruction of the gentry, and we must discover how and why this occurred. Essentially, China came under extraordinary pressures from imperialist industrial nations abroad. This happened even as long-gestating internal developments were unbalancing the system from within precisely in ways that made it unlikely that Imperial authorities would, or could, respond effectively to the foreign threat.

During the nineteenth century China was subjected to intensifying foreign pressures of an unprecedented kind.[87] Before the middle of the eighteenth century, European traders had been treated as bearers of tribute comparable to other actual or symbolic vassals of China. Then, between the mid-1700s and the mid-1800s, a limited two-way trade between Chinese and foreign merchants had been rigorously regulated, supervised, and taxed by Imperial authorities through what was known as the "Canton system." But beginning in the early nineteenth century, Britain could back the aspirations of its citizens for expanded "free trade" in all of China with the military organization and technology born of industrialization. After inflicting decisive naval defeats on Chinese forces in the Opium War of 1839–42, Britain achieved expanded trading rights. Other Western nations soon joined in the quest to "open" China. Free-trade concessions, limitations on tariffs, extraterritorial jurisdiction in proliferating treaty ports, legal immunities for Christian missionaries in the interior—all were forced step by step, in treaties following repeated foreign invasions, upon a country profoundly reluctant to bother with the West and its ways. Toward the end of the century, imperialist intrusions took an even uglier turn as the worldwide quest of competing industrial nations for colonies supplanted Britain's "imperialism of free trade." Initially, former tributary areas of the Chinese empire—including Indochina, areas of Inner Asia, and Korea—were taken over by France, Russia, and Japan. And ultimately the competing powers proceeded to carve out large "spheres of influence," using "loans, railways, leased areas, reduced land tariffs, and rights of local jurisdiction, of police power, and of mining exploitation."[88] China's sheer existence as a sovereign country was profoundly threatened.

Only the central authorities of the Imperial state could have launched economic and military projects that might have allowed China to deflect the ever-deepening incursions on her sovereignty.[89] However, in late traditional China the realities of the state's situation militated against the success of any central initiatives. Already by the late eighteenth century, the Ch'ing dynasty was beginning to be undermined—ironically, by the effects of the peace, prosperity, and political equilibrium that had prevailed when the dynasty was at its height.

73

For one thing, population growth was running up against the limitations of the agrarian economy. Within an unchanging institutional framework, the traditional Chinese economy expanded more or less steadily for over five-hundred years from the fourteenth century – above all during periods of peace and political stability.[90] Due to the opening up of new lands to cultivation and the more labor-intensive application of traditional technical inputs, per capita grain production was able to keep up with population growth, which averaged 0.4 percent per year, as the numbers of Chinese expanded from sixty-five to eighty million in 1400 to around four hundred million by the mid-nineteenth century. Commerce and handicraft industries also kept pace, and may even have experienced some real growth. These were spectacular achievements. As long as there were new lands to open up, China's traditional methods were able to prevent reduced per capita food consumption (on the average). Yet by the nineteenth century, available new lands were running out. The traditional economy was reaching the limits of its possible expansion without creating the conditions for any spontaneous emergence of industrialism.[91] As a consequence, rural disorder became more likely, especially in areas where production or trade was disrupted for any reason.

Then, too, the Imperial authorities were becoming weaker financially and administratively. Financially, the problem was with the land tax. Ever since 1712, provincial quotas for the land tax (the most important source of Imperial revenue until the late nineteenth century) had been fixed "in perpetuity."[92] Originally, under the high Ch'ing, this nourished the equilibrium of a nominally centralized empire that survived through the delicate interplay and counterbalance of local and regional vested interest. But, over time, Peking was deprived of the fruits of increases in productivity in the agrarian economy. "The statutory receipts recorded by the Peking government did not change significantly between 1712 and the third quarter of the nineteenth century."[93] Meanwhile local and provincial revenues increased disproportionately, as informal collections and fees were increased to take up the slack left by Peking's static demands.

Closely related to Peking's financial stasis was the weakening grip of the civil adminstration over the country. For, as the economy and the population grew, the Imperial bureaucracy did not keep pace, leaving the basic-level district magistrates in charge of supervising ever-larger local populations.[94] As a result, the magistrates had to lean more and more heavily on local agents and informal leaders. And these extracted their rewards in the form of burgeoning unofficial fees and cuts from the tax revenues, all squeezed from an ever more overburdened and land-hungry peasantry.

Not surprisingly, therefore, the Ch'ing was confronted from the end of the eighteenth century with peasant-based rebellions.[95] First, there was the White Lotus Rebellion of 1795–1804. Then, after a few decades of simmering internal disorders, there came three massive and well-organized revolts: the Taiping Rebellion of 1850–64, the Nien Rebellion of 1853–68, and Moslem separatist revolts in the northwest from the 1850s to the 1870s. Rebellions such as these had broken out periodically in Chinese history. Often, they indicated the decline of one dynasty and the advent of its replacement – due to such cyclical phenomena as official corruption, military inefficiency, and growing agrarian inequalities. Such traditional causes were also at work undermining the Ch'ing after 1800, but this time they were aggravated and complicated by the effects of the long-term economic and population trends discussed above. Moreover, rebellion was spurred by the side effects of the Western imperialist intrusions. Thus, the greatest and most avowedly revolutionary of the mid-nineteenth-century revolts was the Taiping, a rebellion that originated in the midst of south-eastern economic disorders seriously exacerbated by the aftermath of the Opium War. Its anti-Confucian ideology was inspired in part by Christian missionary propaganda.[96]

Of course the nineteenth-century rebellions had an enormous impact upon the Chinese Imperial state. Peking's resources were drained in combatting the rebellions, and tax receipts declined because of the terrible economic and population losses caused by the massive civil warfare. Moreover, the overt challenges to its sovereignty distracted the Ch'ing's full attention from the growing external threats. The Ch'ing dynasty nevertheless weathered the rebellions and emerged apparently "restored" to full health.[97] However, the Manchu rulers survived only at the cost of internal institutional modifications and power redistributions that left them more unable than ever to cope adequately with the challenges from abroad. And these institutional and power shifts ultimately made the dynasty and the Imperial system susceptible to overthrow from within by the dominant gentry class.

Indeed, for the purpose of explaining the downfall of the Old Regime, the most important legacy of the rebellions was the manner in which they were put down. The Ch'ing dynasty was unable to contain or put down the rebellions with its own Imperial standing armies. These had grown corrupt and inefficient after many decades of peace in the eighteenth century; moreover, they were hampered by the weaknesses of the Imperial finances and administration. As the Imperial armies proved inadequate, the task of dealing with the rebellions fell instead to local gentry-led self-defense associations, and then to regional armies led by native gentry cliques with access to village resources and recruits over wide areas.[98] By simultaneously cutting the rebels off from potential peasant recruits and defeating their armies in pitched battles, the gentry-led armies finally restored order for the Ch'ing. Yet, because of the gentry's role in putting down rebellion, the dynasty had to grant formal approval to governmental practices that ran counter to long-established policies for controlling officials and maintaining the position of the Imperial administration vis-à-vis the local gentry. Rights to collect new taxes, to retain larger portions of established taxes, and to maintain order devolved upon provincial and local officials who were often exempted from the "avoidance" rules of residence and rotation. Even after the rebellions were vanquished, the regional gentry cliques that had triumphed over them retained most of the administrative and military control of their own home areas.[99]

One decisive result of this tilting of the balance of power toward provincial and local gentry was an exacerbated financial weakness for Peking. After the middle of the nineteenth century, new indirect taxes rendered the traditional land tax less significant; but the Imperial authorities did not benefit on balance. An Imperial Maritime Customs establishment was created and run by foreign interests in order to regularize the collection of duties on foreign trade. The duties themselves were unfairly fixed by treaties imposed on China, yet the revenues collected were mostly channeled to Peking. Another tax, the *likin* impost on the production, transit, and/or sale of commodities, produced much greater revenue. But of this only about 20 percent was remitted to Peking. The rest remained with the local and provincial authorities, who collected the taxes and retained most of them. During the final years of the Ch'ing, total government revenues in China, according to scholarly estimates, tapped only about 7.5 percent of the gross national product. And the Peking government was receiving only about 40 percent of that amount, or roughly 3 percent of the GNP.[100] Simultaneously, whatever revenues Peking collected became increasingly committed to paying the indemnities imposed by the victors of the Sino-Japanese and Boxer Wars, and to servicing foreign loans (originally contracted to pay for war costs, indemnities, and limited railroad construction).

Greater resources were controlled by provincial and local authorities, and by the dominant class generally. But "from the point of view of possible economic development as opposed to maintenance of an ongoing economic equilibrium these . . . resources were almost completely neutralized."[101] Much local and provincial revenue went directly into the pockets of tax collectors and officials; the rest was distributed in ways that also reinforced the gentry-dominated order. Within that order, enterprises were created only for short-term windfall profits, and military power was suspect if it threatened to get out of control of gentry interests.

Precious little revenue, then, was available to the late Imperial Chinese authorities either to invest in modern transport and industrialization or to finance social and political reforms in ways that might strengthen central controls. Along with the novelty of the external threat and the pressing nature of internal problems in the mid-nineteenth century, this lack of real opportunity for Peking to take the initiative probably accounts for the fact that Imperial officials were slow even to admit the need for fundamental changes. Indeed, the first to experiment with modern industrial and military technologies were officials affiliated with regional power groupings.[102] But these experiments were too limited in scope and too uncoordinated to succeed in preparing China to fend off the foreign powers.[103] That task could have been undertaken with any prospect of success only under strong central direction.

Reforms and the "Revolution of 1911"

The seriousness of China's predicament was at last driven home by China's humiliating defeat in an 1895–6 war with Japan—another Oriental society, which had, since the 1860s, rapidly synthesized certain of her own traditional forms with Western industrial and military achievements. Even though certain Chinese provincial leaders had experimented with Western-style weapons and arsenals, the Sino-Japanese War was lost to a state that Imperial China had always, more or less successfully, treated as her vassal! The defeat jolted many Chinese to the conclusion that only major structural reforms introduced by central authorities could save China from permanent international humiliation, or even colonial domination. The general imperialist scramble for spheres of influence after 1895 further reinforced this conclusion. An initial attempt by mandarin reformers to have the Imperial authorities initiate changes was defeated after "the one hundred days" of 1898 by the conservative coup d'état led by the empress dowager. But within a few years after the Boxer debacle of 1899–1901, the Manchus were at last unequivocally set on the reforming course. And the upper classes in general were becoming nationalistic supporters of reforms.[104]

Between 1901 and 1911, a variety of reforms was decreed at a dazzling pace: The Confucian examination system was modified, and then abolished in 1905; modern schools purveying specialized Western-style learning for a new governmental elite were established in the localities and provinces and in Peking. University students were granted scholarships to study abroad (at first mostly in Japan). Military academies were established to train a modern officer corps. Specialized ministries for internal affairs, war, education, foreign affairs, and commerce were established in Peking, ostensibly to supervise and coordinate the programs of provincial bureaus. A true national budgeting system was instituted. Finally, the Ch'ing government undertook from 1908 to create representative assemblies, through which it hoped to mobilize the gentry in an advisory role to support the Imperial government. Local assemblies were established immediately in 1908, elections for provincial assemblies were scheduled for 1909, and a national assembly was to be elected in 1910 to plan for a parliament to be established in 1917.[105]

But "reform destroyed the reforming government."[106] For the new measures further undermined the already tenuous central power and exacerbated tensions between the gentry and the Manchu autocracy. Undertaken against the background of the developments during and after the rebellions, the reform measures only served to strengthen regional forces against the center. Modern-educated students and military officers developed radical nationalist views that synthesized provincial loyalties with hostility to the "alien" Manchu dynasty.[107] New Army officers and weaponry were absorbed into the framework of the regionally based armies surviving from the time of the rebellions; moreover, professionally trained officers had only the most tenuous loyalties to the Manchus and to the Imperial system.[108] Attempts to create new administrative structures in the provinces to counterbalance the powers of the entrenched governors were aborted as the new officials and functions were absorbed into the preexisting native cliques.[109] And most fateful of all, the newly established representative assemblies were rapidly transformed by groups of local and provincial gentry and merchants into formal platforms from which to advocate a "Constitutionalist" program of liberal, politically decentralizing reforms.[110]

As E. P. Young has pointed out, "the politicization of the gentry is perhaps the outstanding feature of [Chinese history in] the early twentieth century."[111] Unlike European nobilities, the Chinese gentry had never possessed corporate organization to represent its class interests within the state. Only individual participation had been allowed, and the protection of group interests had depended upon interpersonal connections reaching into the Imperial bureaucracy. But all of this changed after 1900. As the national crisis deepened, gentry-organized local study groups began publicly to petition the central authorities. Then the gentry gained formal class representation through the newly created local and provincial representative assemblies, which were elected on a very limited franchise that favored literati and the wealthy. Aroused to imperialist threats and impatient with the Manchu response, the gentry became nationalist in sentiment. Even more portentous, "Constitutionalism," apparently associated with the power of foreign nations, came to be seen by the gentry as an ideal program for combining their provincially and locally focused class interests with national independence and progress. Although the Ch'ing intended that the representative assemblies should remain advisory, their dominant-class members and constituents envisaged the creation of a constitutional, parliamentary monarchy, with considerable autonomy for local and provincial government controlled by the gentry. By 1910 many organized gentry groups were prepared ideologically and organizationally to assert their decentralizing program against the Manchus. When elected national assemblymen met that year in Peking—ostensibly to plan for gradual, future changes—they instead demanded the immediate creation of parliamentary government. Predictably, the Manchu authorities refused, and the frustrated gentry representatives returned to their native provinces, where many were soon to play key roles in overthrowing the dynasty.

What directly precipitated the "Revolution of 1911" was still another attempt at reform by the central government—one that, significantly enough, directly threatened the financial interests of provincial gentry groupings. In order to guarantee coordinated planning and control over a slowly developing national railroad system, Peking decided in 1911 to buy out all railroad projects from provincial groups that had invested in them. In response

> a "railway protection" movement sprang up, particularly in Szechwan [a Western province], with mass meetings and anguished petitions to Peking, all in vain. The Szechwan movement intensified. Shops and schools were closed. Tax payments were stopped. Peasant support was mobilized. In September the government moved troops, shot down demonstrators, and seized the gentry leaders. Typically, these men were degree-holders of means, with landlord-merchant backgrounds, who had studied in Japan, were now prominent in the provincial assembly, and had invested heavily in railway projects. Their antiforeign slogan, "Szechwan for the Szechwanese," represented the interest of the provincial ruling class, which had now become violently antidynastic. [112]

"The Szechwan uprising . . . sparked widespread disturbances that often had no connection with the railway issue."[113] To quell the disturbances in Szechwan, troops were brought in from the outside, including some from the Wuhan area where the next act of the drama occurred on October 10. When an anti-Manchu plot by certain military officers was discovered on October 9, some New Army units in Wuchang revolted to save the officers from retribution. The Manchu governor took fright and fled, and a brigade commander was coopted to lead the local revolution.[114] The Wuchang Rising proved a contagious example. Within the next few weeks, "the lead in declaring the independence of one province after another was taken by two principal elements: the military governors who commanded the New Army forces and the gentry-official-merchant leaders of the provincial assemblies."[115]

In the wake of the 1911 uprisings, Constitutionalist gentry and merchants, former officials, New Army officers, and youthful radicals affiliated with Sun Yat-sen's (small and generally ineffective) Revolutionary Alliance all jockeyed among themselves to define a new national political system and to replace the Manchu rulers. For, although many favored political decentralization, everyone ostensibly wanted to strengthen, not weaken, Chinese national unity. At first, a republic was declared; then the military general Yuan Shih-kai attempted to restore the Imperial system with himself as emperor. But within five years it became apparent that the real accomplishment of "the Revolution of 1911" had been simply to deliver the coup de grace to the Imperial administrative and political institutions that had already been eroded from within by the usurpations of provincial officials, military officers, and nonofficial gentry. It also became apparent that no alternative national political system could immediately emerge to replace the shattered Imperial system.[116] For the dominant-class groups that had temporarily coalesced to overthrow the Manchus were inherently divided in their loyalties and were not politically agreed about what form of institutions should replace absolute monarchy. The one persistent tendency during and after 1911 was for provincial and local gentry to assert civilian control, allying themselves with military governors. Within a few years, however, power came to rest primarily in the regionally based "modernized" military machines; and "warlord" rivalries ensued as the armies and their commanders competed for territories and material resources. Until 1949, these conditions would never be more than imperfectly and temporarily overcome. They condemned China to incessant turmoil. Yet, as we shall see in the chapters to come, they likewise provided openings for efforts to consolidate revolutionary–national power on the basis of lower-class support and mobilization.

Similarities between France and China

At this point it is worth pausing to reflect upon the striking parallels we have seen in the genesis of the revolutionary crises in Bourbon France and late Imperial China. Despite the fact that these two countries were far apart culturally and geopolitically, and although the collapse of their Old Regimes occurred in very different particular times and circumstances, still there were similar structural patterns in the Old Regimes and similar causal processes at work in their downfall.

In both *ancien régime* France and late Imperial China, relatively prosperous landed–commercial upper classes gained collective political leverage within and against the administrative machineries of monarchical autocracies. In eighteenth-century France, an increasingly socially solidary proprietary upper class, its wealth swollen by inflating rents and appropriations backed by the monarchical state, could express its political aspirations through the *parlements* and other corporate bodies entwined with the autocratic royal administration. In late-traditional China, the gentry augmented and guaranteed its rentier prosperity by achieving, in the wake of the mid-nineteenth-century rebellions, de facto control over large sectors of the Imperial administration. It then attained collective representation in the assemblies established in 1908–10 by the reforming Manchus. Likewise, the revolutionary crises emerged in both France and China

80

because the Old Regimes came under unwonted pressures from more developed nations abroad, and because those pressures led to internal political conflicts between the autocratic authorities and the dominant classes. Escalating international competition and humiliations particularly symbolized by unexpected defeats in wars (such as the Seven Years' War and the Sino-Japanese War) inspired autocratic authorities to attempt reforms that they believed would facilitate the mobilization and coordination of national resources to meet the external exigencies. However, landed–commercial upper classes stood to lose wealth and power if central authorities succeeded in their rationalizing reforms. And not incidentally, the French *privilégiés* and the Chinese gentry were attracted by the association between parliamentarism and national power in more modern foreign competitors; they hoped to preserve their own class interests and further national wellbeing at the same time.

In the end, autocratic attempts at modernizing reforms from above in France and China – specifically, tax reform in France and railroad reorganization in China – triggered the concerted political resistance of well-organized dominant class forces. In turn, because these forces possessed leverage within the formally centralized machineries of the monarchical states, their resistance disorganized those machineries. Autocratic authority was abolished. And as dominant class groups based in various institutional and geographical locations (e.g., *parlements,* provinces, representative bodies, and municipalities in France; and provinces, armies, and assemblies in China) competed in endeavors to define new political arrangements, the monarchical administrations and armies were broken irretrievably apart. Hence the successful opposition of the dominant classes to autocratic reforms inadvertently opened the door to deepening revolutions in France and China alike.

IMPERIAL RUSSIA:
AN UNDERDEVELOPED GREAT POWER

In Bourbon France and Manchu China revolutionary crises occurred during times of formal peace as autocratic attempts at reforms and resource-mobilization were resisted by politically powerful dominant classes. By contrast, in Tsarist Russia revolutionary crises developed only under the direct impact of defeats in war. Before meeting its demise, the Russian Imperial state weathered intensified competition from more-developed nations in the European state system and, indeed, instituted a series of far-reaching modernizing reforms. Thus the analysis of prerevolutionary Russia must take account of specific differences from, as well as overall similarities to, the patterns we have noted for old-regime France and China.

81

Causes of Social Revolutions

The Imperial State and the Serf Economy

Once an Oriental despotism competing for survival and suzerainty on the vast Eurasian plain, Russia was by the nineteenth century one of the dominant powers of the European states system. It was known and feared as the "Gendarme of Europe," nemesis of revolutionary hopes in central Europe. Certainly Imperial Russia was a more militarized and bureaucratized autocracy than either Bourbon France or late Imperial China.[117] Imperial Russia was born during the remarkable reign of Peter the Great (1682–1725). Exploiting the rudiments of the personal autocracy consolidated in medieval Muscovy by Ivan the Terrible, Peter suddenly imposed upon his people the latest European techniques of land and naval warfare and of "rational" administrative domination. Ironically, these methods could quickly produce more efficient state power in Russia than anywhere in the West, for Muscovy was free of the sociopolitical encumbrances of Western-style feudal legacies. Peter "mated methods borrowed from the West with ... the tradition of a despotic Eastern regime. The explosive mixture thus created ... sent the power of Russia soaring upward."[118] Above all, huge new standing armies were created. These were staffed by serfs and nobles forcibly recruited to lifelong service, armed with weapons supplied by state-initiated mines and manufactories, and financed by heavy direct and indirect taxes, including bread taxes on every adult male peasant. The taxes, in turn, were collected by an emergent civil service staffed by full-time officials. Once the new Russian armies triumphed over the formidable forces of Sweden in the Great Northern War of 1700–21, Russia was established as a multi-ethnic empire and as a Great Power in the European states system. No matter that her agrarian economy was and remained relatively backward overall; Peter's reforms and the practices of his successors created and used bureaucratic state power to counterbalance the deficit. Besides, Russia's massive military machine was technologically modern, and so it remained until the military repercussions of the nineteenth-century industrialization of Western Europe were realized.[119]

As for the socioeconomic basis upon which the Imperial state was built and maintained, throughout her tenure as a dominant power in Europe Russia remained a serf-based agrarian society. By the middle of the nineteenth century only about 8 to 10 percent of the Empire's population of about sixty million was living in cities.[120] In the vast countryside, millions of serf–peasants, tied to their own villages and to estates belonging to nobles or to the state, labored mainly to grow grain crops. Two systems of landlord/serf relations prevailed, often combined in one estate or intermixed in one locale, but also to a certain extent regionally differentiated. In the fertile black-soil provinces, serfs performed *barshchina,* or labor services on the lord's *demesne* for one-half or more of each week. In the

82

less fertile provinces, *obrok* quit-rents were more common, as they allowed the lords to share in the serfs' nonagricultural incomes from handicrafts or industrial labor.[121]

If part of the soil was infertile, the climate was invariably rigorous and unpredictable, and production organization and techniques were primitive. Agricultural technique was based upon the three-field system, scattered strip fields, communal tillage, few and scrawny work animals, and light tools. "Low yields and frequent crop failures were the not unexpected results of these many shortcomings."[122] In fact, "estimates . . . for the first half of the nineteenth century show that yields were just about the same as they had been in the preceding country, and indeed as far back as the sixteenth century and probably even earlier."[123]

Nevertheless, this was not a stagnant economy. True, techniques and yields-per-unit of land remained largely unchanged—except in certain newly settled areas in the south and southwest, where capitalist agriculture developed on estates employing wage laborers. Yet agricultural production kept pace through extensive growth as Russia's population nearly quadrupled between 1719 and 1858 (growing from roughly sixteen to sixty million).[124] Although over two-million square miles were annexed to the Empire, most of the population growth came from natural increase in the older areas of the realm. Plowlands were expanded in the black-earth provinces, and peasants in the non-black-earth areas supplemented their incomes through handicrafts production or employment in trade and industry.[125] Thus, while agriculture experienced extensive growth, handicraft and workshop industries proliferated throughout the eighteenth and into the nineteenth century. And commercial development occurred at both local and interregional levels.[126] Despite all of this, however, before the building of a rail network in the last third of the nineteenth century, transportation difficulties remained an insurmountable obstacle to any fundamental breakthrough to industrialization in a country so vast.[127]

The Crimean Debacle and Reforms from Above

But industrialization *was* transforming the economies of Western Europe during the early nineteenth century, and its effects soon put Imperial Russia on the defensive in the vital international arenas of war and diplomacy. Given her geopolitical situation, a basic Russian interest was control of access to the Black Sea.[128] Not surprisingly, therefore, the chain of events that carried Imperial Russia from dominance in Europe after the revolutions of 1848 to disintegration and revolution in 1917 began with the Empire's ignominious defeat in the limited Crimean War of 1854–5. In this conflict over naval control of the Black Sea and influence in the waning Ottoman Empire, Russia faced France and England without the support of its former Austrian ally. Ultimately the war became focused on a siege of the Russian fort at Sevastopol in the Crimea. The Russian Black Sea fleet, consisting of "sailing vessels that were no match for the steam-driven warships of the powerful allied squadrons"[129] had to be scuttled at the entrance to the Bay of Sevastopol. Then, after months of a dogged defense by the forces on the spot, Sevastopol itself fell to the Anglo-France-Ottoman expeditionary force of seventy thousand. The peace settlement rolled back Russian influence in the Near East and deprived the country of its naval presence in the Black Sea:

> Russia's position in Europe was changed ... In 1815 Russia appeared the strongest single power on the Continent ... After 1848 she seemed far to have outdistanced the other land Powers: Russian primacy had turned into Russia domination. The Crimean War reduced Russia to one among several Great Powers ... As long as a Tsar ruled in St. Petersburg, Russia never regained the eminence of 1815.[130]

Yet defeat for Russia in the Crimean War had even more important effects upon internal politics, for it highlighted the inadequacies of the Imperial system resting on serf-based, preindustrial society. In the words of Alexander Gerschenkron:

> The Crimean War imparted a severe blow to the serene image of Russia's strength. It revealed Russian inferiority in many crucial respects. The Russian men-of-war were no match for the English and French navies, and their conversion into submarine reefs was the only use to which they could be effectively put; the primitive Russian rifle was primarily accountable for the loss of the crucial battle of Alma; the supplies of men and ammunition to the besieged Sebastopol were hindered by the poverty of the transportation system. In the minds of the emperor and the higher bureaucracy, the course of the war and its outcome left the feeling that once more the country had been allowed to lag too far behind the advanced nations of the West. Some degree of modernization ... was indispensable for regaining a strong military position.[131]

As before in Russian history, the sense of military backwardness spurred a series of reforms spearheaded from above by Imperial officials backed by the tsar. The conscious aim was to reshape – "liberalize" – Russian society just enough so that it might better support the Great Power mission of the state, yet not so much as to cause any politically dangerous instability. The first round of reforms, formulated and implemented during the generation after the Crimean War, included the establishment of a modern judicial system, the introduction of universal military service and the extension of professional officer training, and the creation of *zemstvo* representative assemblies and municipal *dumas* with very carefully circumscribed powers of local self-government.[132] But the most important reform of all was the

Emancipation of millions of Russian serfs, a process initiated, according to the first in a series of tsarist decrees, in 1861.

As with the other reforms enacted by Alexander II in the immediate wake of the Crimean debacle, the intent of the Emancipation was more to liberate social energies in a manner consistent with the stability and military effectiveness of the Imperial state rather than directly to promote economic development.[133] For one thing, juridical equality for the peasantry was prerequisite for the establishment of a modern army of "citizen" conscripts. Moreover, there was a very real fear of serf revolts, whose incidence had increased during and after the Crimean War. Tsar Alexander declared that it was "better to abolish serfdom from above than to wait until it will begin to abolish itself from below."[134] Thus he overrode the clear opposition of the majority of noble estate owners and required them to accept the legal emancipation of the serfs. The landowners were also required to assign to the peasants the legal ownership of substantial portions of the agricultural land that most nobles tended to regard as completely their own property.

Here let us pause to place these Russian events of the 1850s and 1860s in comparative perspective. From such a perspective it seems thoroughly unsurprising that the humiliating effects of military defeat at the hands of more economically developed nations precipitated a crisis for the Russian Imperial state and prodded it to institute modernizing reforms. What does seem surprising, however, is that these reforms—including especially the Emancipation, which directly violated the established economic interests of the landed nobility—were *successfully implemented* by the Imperial authorities. To be sure, opposition was voiced by dominant-class interests, both to the content of the post-Crimean reforms and to the autocratic and bureaucratic modes of their formulation and implementation.[135] But, whereas dominant class opposition to monarchical reform efforts actually succeeded in deposing autocracy and dissolving the Imperial state systems in France in 1787–9 and China in 1911, no such thing happened in mid-nineteenth-century Russia. To understand why not, we must look at the situation of the Russian landed nobility.

The Weakness of the Landed Nobility

Sandwiched between the mildly commercialized serf economy and the Imperial state was the Russian landed nobility. Like the French proprietary upper class and the Chinese gentry, this Russian dominant class appropriated surpluses both directly from the peasantry and indirectly through remuneration for services to the state. But in sharp contrast to the French and Chinese dominant classes, the Russian landed nobility was economically weak and politically dependent vis-à-vis Imperial authorities.

85

Even before Peter the Great, the status of the Russian nobility and the intergenerational continuity of the wealth of individual families had been virtually completely dependent upon service to the tsars.[136] Serfdom in Russia was consolidated not by commercializing landlords (as in much of Eastern Europe after 1400) but rather under the impetus of centralizing tsars determined to extract from the people sufficient resources to support military forces for defense and expansion in threatening geopolitical environments.[137] Traditionally footloose Russian peasants had to be tied to the land if they were to be kept at work producing taxable surpluses; concomitantly, the tsars needed military officers and officials to man the state organizations required for external warfare and internal social control. Over a period of centuries the lands of independent nobles and princes were expropriated and passed out as rewards for official careers to a new class of service nobles. As this happened, the tsars took pains to ensure that no new groupings of independent landed aristocrats could arise. Service nobles were given rights to serf "souls" and to landed estates. Yet typically, their possessions were not concentrated in one locality or even one province, but were scattered over different regions of the empire. Under these conditions, local and regional solidarity among nobles could hardly develop.

Peter the Great carried this state of affairs to its logical extreme: He made lifelong military or civil service careers mandatory for every adult male noble. Compelled to permanent service, shunted about at central commands from assignment to assignment and from region to region, the nobles became an aggregate completely dependent upon the state. Solidary ties to provinces and home estates were further weakened. "Consciously or vicariously, they assimilated the militaristic, bureaucratic, and global point of view that dominated Russian public life."[138] Service became "the basic normative framework for individual and social relationships, and ... service rank became the only recognized form of noble status."[139]

During the eighteenth century Russian nobles were finally released from lifelong state service, and their private-property rights were fully and officially confirmed. The new freedom to retire from service posts led to some regeneration of social and cultural life in the provinces. Nevertheless, the situation of the nobles did not change much.[140] Now increasingly oriented to Western European upper-class life styles, the Russian nobles still gravitated toward state employments as the one sure site of opportunities to reside in the cities and to earn salaries and rewards to supplement the very meager incomes that most obtained from the serf estates, which were subdivided in each generation. Even if the nobles had been culturally prepared to plunge into agricultural management, the Russian agrarian economy provided (throughout most of the country) little incentive for such an alternative way of life. What is more, Russian serf-owners had little to invest in agriculture (or any other economic ventures), because they were quite poor by European standards. Approximately four-fifths of them (83 percent in 1777; 84 percent in 1834; 78 percent in 1858) owned fewer than one-hundred (adult male serf) "souls" – the minimum deemed necessary to support a cultivated life-style.[141] And in the struggle to maintain a suitable standard of living, the serf owners had not only flocked into state employments but had also sunk themselves into ever-worsening indebtedness – partly to private financiers, but mainly to the state. Thus, by 1860, 66 percent of all serfs were "mortgaged" by their noble owners to special state credit institutions.[142]

Ironically, though, as the serf-owning nobility continued to depend upon the Imperial state, the autocracy became less dependent upon the landed nobility. Peter the Great had opened a clear path of upward mobility into noble statuses for literate commoners who served the civil bureaucracy.[143] Inexorably, the recuitment of nonnobles from ecclesiastical and urban families produced a stratum of service nobles divorced from the land, even while burgeoning numbers of families of educated nonnoble government workers supplied ever more bureaucratic aspirants. In consequence, a recent quantitative study concludes that

> by the end of the eighteenth century the civil bureaucracy in the central agencies, and by the 1850s in the provinces also, was an essentially self-perpetuating group. Recruits came from a nobility that was in large measure divorced from the land, and from among the sons of nonnoble government workers (military, civil, and ecclesiastical).[144]

University education and willingness to commit oneself to a lifelong career were the keys to success in state service. Landed wealth seems to have mattered only insofar as it facilitated these, and it was by no means the only way.

> Lack of serfs was not a barrier to bureaucratic success in the mid-nineteenth century. Of the total noble group [of officials studied] nearly 50 percent had no serfs at all in their families . . . It is particularly important that the serfless nobles were by no means confined to the lower ranks. Even at the top over 40 percent of the nobles serving had no serfs at all in their family.[145]

The upshot of the foregoing conditions taken together was that Russian nobles had little independent class- or estate-based political power. Nobles in the provinces were, if they stayed there long, poor, restless, and deferential to state officials. Their corporate institutions performed only social and cultural functions. Meanwhile, in the state service, old-line nobles competed for vital career advancement with the ennobled and the aspirants to service nobility. Promotions came through royal approval or rigid adherence to commands and routines. Collective policy initiatives or protests were neither encouraged nor facilitated. In contrast to *ancien régime* France,

there were no well-established representative bodies, quasi-political corporations, or venal offices to afford leverage to the dominant class within the
Imperial state structure. In this respect Russia was more like Imperial China
(before 1908). Yet even when the Chinese Imperial system was at its height,
the gentry had enjoyed much more political power and independence at
local levels than did the Russian nobility. And nothing comparable to the
growth in China after 1840 of local and provincial gentry power occurred at
any point in old-regime Russia. Whether landlords, or officials, or both (and
this overlapping category was shrinking), nobles in Imperial Russia enjoyed
little autonomous, collective political power. They depended instead upon
their individual relations with the centralized machinery of the state, and
upon the generalized commitment of the autocracy to the stability of the
existing status order.

Against this background we can complete our analysis of the Emancipation of the serfs. Clearly, the weakness of the Russian landed nobility
explains why this class was unable to prevent the Emancipation, much less
to bring down the autocratic–imperial political system in the name of an
aristocratic or liberal "constitutionalist" program. Had the Russian landed
nobility possessed economic strength and political–administrative leverage
vis-à-vis the Imperial state at all comparable to the strength and leverage
of the French and Chinese dominant classes, then quite possibly a revolutionary political crisis might have emerged in Russia in the 1860s. Instead,
the tsarist autocracy actually succeeded in pushing through the reforms
that it undertook in the aftermath of the humiliating Crimean defeat—
including the reforms that ran significantly counter to the economic interests and social prerogatives of the serf-owning nobility.[146]

Nevertheless, it would be a mistake to conclude that, because the Russian landed nobility could not effectively take the political offensive
against reforming autocracy, it therefore had no effect upon the contours
of the Emancipation settlement. Actually the landed nobility did end up
exerting considerable influence, specifically in the process of policy implementation. This happened because of the landed nobility's sheer existence as the serf-owning dominant class, and because of the inherent limitations placed upon the effective power of the Imperial state, given its
existing institutional relationship to the rural class structure.

As we have already noted, the autocracy's prime goal in liberating the
serfs was to stabilize Imperial rule. Consequently, the tsar and his officials
decided not only to grant personal, legal "freedom" to the peasants but
also to assign them the ownership of considerable amounts of the lands
they worked.[147] To leave the ex-serfs without property, it was felt, would
guarantee rebellions and the equally abhorred disorders of sudden and
massive proletarianization. But who would decide how much (and which)
lands to give to the ex-serfs? Policy-implementation mechanisms had to be

arrived at for apportioning properties between nobles and peasants locality by locality and estate by estate. Because, historically, Imperial jurisdiction stopped just outside the doors of the noble-owned serf estates—with the nobles or their agents left responsible for maintaining order and collecting taxes—only the nobles and their agents possessed the detailed knowledge of the structure and workings of the serf economy that was essential for the implementation of the Emancipation in many localities. Inevitably, therefore, committees of nobles were entrusted by the Imperial authorities with working out the exact apportionment of lands to their ex-serfs.[148] Naturally, this arrangement ensured that the nobles would be able to maximize their own interests within the bounds of the overall Emancipation decrees. And this they did. In fertile regions, the peasants were left with minimal lands, whereas in the less fertile zones they were forced to pay redemption on maximal holdings. Moreover, everywhere the peasants tended to be cut off from access to crucial resources such as water or grazing lands or woods, which they subsequently had to rent from their former masters.

Implemented thus within the confines of the existing agrarian class relations, the Emancipation reforms could not—and did not—clear the way for the sudden modernization of Russian agriculture.[149] For the peasants were left with insufficient lands subject to crushing redemption payments, which had to be paid to the government over many decades. And the nobles were hardly spurred to invest in the modernization of agriculture, because they were left with legal possession of about 40 percent of the land and with access to cheap labor, whereas most of their financial-redemption windfall (paid to the nobles by the state) went to pay off previously accumulated indebtedness (mostly to the state itself). What the Emancipation unquestionably did accomplish was to give the Imperial state a more direct and exclusive role in controlling the peasantry and appropriating revenues from agriculture. The landed nobility was shoved aside by the tsarist regime. But, although significantly weakened by the Emancipation and its aftereffects, the landlords were left in place as the dominant class in a largely stagnant agrarian economy. Consequently, that economy could serve as a drag on subsequent Imperial efforts to promote economic development. And the landed nobles remained as a potential target for peasant revolts.

Finally, it should be noted that the Russian nonofficial nobility, including those who still were landlords, remained quite politically impotent vis-à-vis the autocracy after the 1860s. This was true despite the formation, as part of the reforms of the decade, of *zemstvos*—local and provincial representative bodies to which nobles enjoyed disproportionate electoral access. At best the *zemstvos* established a foothold in local social and cultural affairs through the provision on a very restricted fiscal basis of educational, welfare, and advisory–economic services. But this service sector controlled by elected governing bodies grew up alongside, not within, the hierarchy of societal political power. For the Imperial authorities retained a monopoly of administration and coercion and continued to tax away most of the agricultural surplus; and the *zemstvos* were tolerated by the Imperial bureaucracy only to the extent that they did not challenge central controls and policy-making prerogatives.[150]

The contrast to what happened when upper-class–dominated representative assemblies were established in China (1908–10) is interesting and enlightening. There the gentry already had great de facto administrative and military influence, whereas the Imperial authorities were financially weak and lacked effective central controls. Thus the new assemblies served to give collective political expression to the power already enjoyed by the dominant class in China. But in old-regime Russia, the autocracy was in such a strong position that it could effectively create the thoroughly circumscribed representative organs that the Manchus had intended, but failed, to establish in China. The Russian *zemstvos* (and municipal *dumas*) did not become politically threatening to the autocracy until 1905, when the state temporarily faltered during a losing war. Until then (and again after 1906), the Imperial state retained the power and initiative to squeeze and significantly remake Russian society, even to the further detriment of the interests of the nobility.

State-Guided Industrialization

After the post-Crimean modernizing reforms, the next major initiative of the Russian state was a remarkable effort to spur industrialization from above–but this did not come until after some initial experiments with laissez-faire capitalist policies. During the 1860s and 1870s, Russia was opened wide to foreign trade and investments on the theory that it could acquire modern industrial and transportation materials and techniques from abroad in exchange for stepped-up agricultural exports.[151] Railroad mileage was steadily, if slowly, expanded, largely through the efforts of private entrepreneurs, foreign and domestic. But the steel used was made with imported materials, so that "Russian mining and metallurgy got little encouragement."[152] Meanwhile agricultural productivity stagnated, while international prices for grain dropped, and Russia's foreign indebtedness and needs for imports grew. War (i.e., the Russo-Turkish War of 1877–8) and military preparations (i.e., the Bulgarian Crisis of 1886) continued to gobble up government revenues. At the same time, the peasant taxpayers' ability to pay was strained to the utmost, leading to widespread famines in 1891.[153] Clearly, the glory of the Russian state required yet another strategy.

That came in the 1890s under a minister of finance, Sergei Witte, who firmly believed that "the political strength of the great powers which are called to fulfill great historical tasks in the world" rested directly upon relative industrial power. "International competition does not wait," Witte warned Tsar Nicholas II in 1900:

> If we do not take energetic and decisive measures so that in the course of the next decades our industry will be able to satisfy the needs of Russia and of the Asiatic countries which are—or should be—under our influence, then . . . it is possible that the slow growth of our industries will endanger the fulfillment of the great political tasks of the monarchy. Our economic backwardness may lead to political and cultural backwardness as well.[154]

Witte proposed a crash governmental program to promote national industrialization. His "System" of policies, implemented fully during his tenure as minister of finance from 1892 to 1903, involved heavy government expenditures for railroad building and operation; subsidies and supporting services for private industrialists; high protective tariffs for Russian industries (especially for the heavy industries and mines whose products were purchased for railroad building and military modernization); increased exports; stable currency; and encouragement of foreign investments. Government expenditures to spur industrialization were paid for with stepped-up regressive indirect taxes on articles of mass consumption, and by foreign loans (which had to be dependably repaid).[155]

In absolute terms, this venture in rapid state-guided capitalist development was brilliantly successful.[156] During the 1890s Russian industrial growth averaged 8 percent per year. Railroad mileage grew from a very substantial base by 40 percent between 1892 and 1902; the interior communications of European Russia were greatly intensified and the link to Siberia completed. Stimulated in turn, Russian heavy industries—mining, iron and steel, and petroleum—mushroomed, built with huge plants and the latest European technology. Light industries also expanded, though less spectacularly, for of course industrialization was not based upon mass-market demand. Concurrently, Witte managed to more than double government tax receipts and to stabilize the currency by introducing the gold standard. Agricultural "surpluses" were squeezed from the peasants and marketed abroad to finance purchases of foreign technology and to maintain the balance of payments. All of this, finally, set the stage for continued rapid industrial growth (averaging 6 percent per year) between 1906 and 1913, when, in the wake of the Russo-Japanese War of 1904–5, the state was in a weaker position for taking the investment initiative.

Nevertheless, by virtue of both its achievements and its limitations, rapid industrialization in turn-of-the-century Russia set the stage for two revolutions—one ultimately a failure in 1905, the other a success in 1917.

91

Partly it did this by creating new classes and exacerbating social tensions. The overall picture is well sketched by Arthur Mendel:

> Besides dangerously concentrating a proletariat, a professional class, and a rebellious student body in the centers of political power, industrialization infuriated both these new forces and the traditional rural classes. It radically displaced the intensely status-conscious gentry and oppressed the peasantry through forced exports, monopoly prices, and regressive taxation that ultimately paid the bill of modernization. It furthered in all segments of society the painful collapse of old roles, values, motivations, and expectations... It left no money to ameliorate the deplorable urban conditions into which the already distressed and disoriented peasantry flocked in quickly disillusioned hope of something better.[157]

Specifically, as future events would demonstrate, the most important domestic change during the last decades of the Old Regime was the rapid formation of an industrial proletariat.[158] Numerically small within the total Russian population, this class was nevertheless disproportionately concentrated both in large-scale industrial enterprises and in major industrial centers, including, fatefully enough, the capital cities of European Russia—St. Petersburg and Moscow. The new proletarians were suddenly, recently, and often incompletely separated from the peasant villages. At the very first, perhaps, the newness of their exposure to the urban–industrial environment made it difficult for recent recruits to protest—though the ex-peasants may also have carried native-village traditions of collective solidarity and resistance into the factories. In any event, before long, cohorts of industrial workers gained experience and a sense of identity in the industrial world. And the conditions they faced—economic privation, lack of social services, and (nearly continuous) tsarist prohibitions against legal labor unions—certainly provided reasons enough for the industrial workers to become, as they did after 1890, increasingly prone to strike and receptive to the antiautocratic and anticapitalist ideas of radical political parties. Rapid industrialization thus created a formidable popular force capable of opposing both the Imperial state and the capitalist captains of industry whose activities the state so fervently encouraged.

Equally if not even more important, however, were the international implications of Russian industrialization. For one thing, the processes of financing rapid industrialization tied the Russian state and economy more closely to Western Europe. To supplement the weak capacities of the native bourgeoisie, foreign private investors were officially encouraged to invest in industries behind the tariff wall. Foreign capital invested in (mostly heavy-industrial) firms in Russia grew from 215 million rubles in 1890 to 911 million in 1900, to over 2 billion by 1914.[159] "In 1900 there were 269 foreign companies in Russia of which only 16 had existed before

92

1888. French and Belgian capital was mostly in the southern metallurgical industry and mines, British in petroleum, and German in chemicals and electrical engineering."[160] At the same time, to pay for imports of industrial equipment and to maintain the balance of international payments upon which depended currency stability and investor confidence, Russia relied upon agricultural exports, mostly to England and Germany.[161] And to help finance government investments in industry (which exceeded even the massive foreign investments), the tsarist regime depended upon loans brokered in Germany, England, and, above all, France.[162] The amounts involved were very great:

> The national debt . . . [grew] almost in step with the rising national income . . . By 1913 . . . Russia stood second among the nations of the world in absolute amount of national debt. In amount of payments per year on service of the debt, however, Russia was first . . . The amount of Russian debt held abroad slightly exceeded the amount held at home.[163]

So closely, therefore, was the Russian economy tied to European finance that when, in 1899–1900, the Western money markets contracted, Russian industry, which had grown so rapidly in the 1890s, plunged into a crisis deeper and more prolonged than the recession that concurrently struck Western European industry.[164] This setback "aggravated the discontent throughout society in the five years or so preceding the Revolution of 1905."[165]

Was late Imperial Russia, then, a semicolony of Western Europe? A case can be made for this view. After all, she imported Western technology and surplus capital in return for primary exports and interest payments. At the same time, native consumption was squeezed to maintain the trade balance and the gold standard. Moreover, Russian political alliances came to favor her main creditors, France and England. On the other hand, in per capita terms, Russian foreign indebtedness was less than that of Sweden or the United States.[166] And investigators have failed to find that foreign firms or investors sought control in addition to profits, or that government officials in either Russia or Western Europe regarded the tsarist state as dependent by virtue of her economic ties.[167] In any case, those ties extended to Germany as well.

Rather, it makes more sense to assume that Russia continued to operate as a competing Great Power in the European states system. Russian alliances leading into World War I can be explained perfectly well on that basis. During much of the nineteenth century, Russia was loosely allied with Prussia and Austria-Hungary, and diplomacy could be relied upon to protect Russian interests. Then came the unification and rapid industrialization of Imperial Germany – an occurrence that unsettled European diplomacy and threatened Russia (and especially its interest in the Balkans, as Germany gradually slid into an Austrian alliance). It was, therefore, well within the logic of the European "balance of power" that Russia was "pushed . . . toward a Western alliance which put the security of her Western frontiers on a military rather than a political footing."[168]

But this is not all meant to imply that late Imperial Russian economic development was not fraught with serious international political implications – just that the most important effects had to do with Russian *capacities* to meet international military competition. For despite the impressive record of industrial expansion after 1880, especially in heavy industry, Russian economic development left the country still very far behind other nations with which it had to deal diplomatically and, potentially, militarily. By the eve of World War I, for instance, real income per capita in Russia was still only one-third that of the United Kingdom and the United States.[169] Even more telling is the fact that, although Russia's average rate of growth in terms of real income per capita was between 1860 and 1913 about equal to the European-wide average, it nevertheless fell considerably below the 2½ percent rate in the United States, the 2 percent rate in Germany, and the 3 percent rate for Japan (1878–1912).[170] Clearly Russia "failed to catch up economically with the western world and even fell farther behind its leaders."[171]

The decisive problem was the low level of real growth in agriculture – which remained the preponderant sector of the Russian economy. Even the extraordinary and disproportionate expansion of heavy industry after 1890 could not make up for the backwardness of Russian agriculture. Thus Witte's program of forced industrialization failed to achieve the strategic objective of international parity that had motivated the tsar to back it in the first place, even as it reinforced social tendencies at home hostile to continued absolutist rule.[172]

The Impact of Wars

By the turn of the twentieth century, then, the stage was set for a revolutionary crisis precisely because Imperial Russia remained "a Great Power set, as part of its harsh destiny, into the crosscurrents of European and global power politics" even as its economic development lagged.[173] Born and tempered in warfare, insulated from, and supreme against, the forces of society, the Russian state could only succumb through massive defeat in total war. Thus World War I was to be a necessary cause – as well as the occasion – of the revolutionary crisis that brought Imperial Russia to its demise.

To see exactly why, it is most instructive to contrast February 1917 with the failed Russian Revolution of 1905. Trotsky once called 1905 a "dress rehearsal" for 1917. Indeed virtually the same social and political forces took part in both dramas. And yet the plots were very different. Isaac

Deutscher is really closer to the truth when he suggests that in 1917 the revolution "started again from the points at which it had come to a standstill in 1905. . . . The 'constitutionalist' phase of the revolution had actually been played out before 1917."[174]

The 1905 "Revolution" resembled that of 1917 in that it came in the midst of a losing war. Thinking to combine semicolonial acquisitions in the Far East with the diversion of internal unrest in what Minister of the Interior Viacheslav von Plehve supposed would be a "victorious little war," the tsarist regime went to war with Japan in 1904. But as the Imperial army and navy reeled from defeat to defeat, a revolutionary movement encompassing all classes of society gathered momentum at home. Representing landowners, professionals, and bourgeois, the All-Russian Zemstvo Congress demanded (in November 1904) civil liberties, legal equality for all classes and nationalities, and a national, representative, legislative assembly – in effect, a liberal constitutional monarchy. A mounting wave of industrial strikes voiced economic demands and supported the political movement against autocracy. Naval units rose in the famous Potemkin Mutiny of June 1905. The climax came in October 1905 with a rail strike, which turned into a general political strike. In the face of all this – seemingly a very Western-style social revolution indeed – the tsar retreated: Civil liberties and a legislative Duma based on a wide franchise were granted in the October Manifesto.[175]

Yet the Revolution of 1905 was rolled back and defeated by 1907. Why? The reason was starkly simple. With short-term defeat apparent and revolution threatening, the regime quickly concluded the war with Japan. The Peace of Portsmouth was signed in September 1905, leaving the Imperial army in Manchuria in a position to be redisciplined and then selectively reintroduced into turbulent European Russia.[176] Clearly the Revolution of 1905, and the labor and agrarian unrest that continued into 1906, went as far as they did not only because war aggravated social tensions and because defeats disillusioned the upper classes but also because during 1905 "European Russia was largely denuded of troops."[177] But that was a temporary condition that tsardom could readily correct given the limited and peripheral nature of the Russo-Japanese conflict. Thus as the troops came home to crush strikes and agrarian revolts and arrest troublesome political leaders, Nicholas II rolled back his constitutional concessions one by one, until absolutism was, in substance, fully restored. For him the Revolution of 1905 became a "passing squall."[178]

World War I created a very different situation. This conflict engulfed the whole of the European states system. Russia could neither remain aloof nor withdraw at will once the war was underway. "The Russian decision to mobilize in 1914 was a direct response to Austria's military action against Serbia and to the threat to Russian territory which Germany's support of Austria posed."[179] Once France and Britain had entered the war, they depended upon the cooperation of their ally. Imperial Russia was condemned to a protracted confrontation with formidable Germany.

The inexorable consequences for the Imperial regime were military defeats and economic and administrative chaos. These in turn gave rise to the revolutionary crisis. Objective conditions allowed no other outcome. From 1914 to 1917 Russia mobilized fifteen-million men for its armies, but the country lacked the economic infrastructure to support their efforts against Germany. (Substantial victories were gained only against Austro-Hungarian and Turkish forces.)

At the beginning of the war Russian infantry divisions had only half as many light artillery batteries as German divisions. The discrepancy of heavy batteries was worse: The Russian army had 60, to 381 for the Germans. As for ammunition, the annual output of state factories was 600,000 rounds, whereas the annual requirement during the war quickly became seventy times that. Private industries were ill-equipped to convert to munitions production, and did so only very slowly. As early as the fifth month of the war the army was acutely short of munitions; many front-line soldiers went into battle without rifles. Only by 1917 was Russia producing enough weapons— though failing to keep up with technological innovations by the enemy.[180]

By then, however, Russian armies had suffered repeated massive defeats at the hands of the Germans. Millions of men had been killed, wounded, or taken prisoner, and a large proportion of the original professional officer corps had been wiped out. The officers could be replaced only by educated civilian reservists and promotions from the ranks. Fatefully, no longer was the tsarist army a professional organization segregated from society and led by staunch conservatives.[181]

Another fetter for Russia was the transportation system. Given the lack of good roads and the insufficiency of inland waterways, railroads were the key factor. But however fast and considerable the expansion of the Russian rail system since 1860 had been, by 1914 the density of the German system (miles of railroads to square miles of territory) was over ten times that of the Russian. In addition, the Russian rolling stock was technologically obsolete. Lacking air brakes, for example, freight cars had to move very slowly.[182] This meant that support services (supplies and evacuations) for the armies on the fronts were hampered. It also meant that, in the rear, industrial production was curtailed and that the cities— swollen by increased numbers of military recruits, workers in war industries, and personnel for auxiliary services—were deprived of vital transportation services. "Hardest hit by the inadequacy of the railroad system were the large cities, where shortages of food, fuel, and raw materials became acute in the winter of 1916–17."[183]

The Revolutionary Political Crisis of 1917

How did these conditions translate themselves into the revolutionary crisis? As the magnitude of Russian defeats (beginning from the spring of 1915) became apparent, the dominant strata steadily lost confidence in the tsar and autocracy. And as the strains imposed by the endless war persisted, the lower classes, suffering terribly, became war-weary and rebellious. Finally these social discontents—given new potency due to the breakdown under wartime conditions of the usual barriers between state organizations and social groups—crystallized in the cities of Russia to give political expression to the near-universal repudiation of the autocratic regime.

At the beginning of the war all politically articulate groups (except the Bolsheviks and a few Mensheviks) pledged "enthusiastic" support for the defense of "the Homeland." As the difficulties of the war effort surfaced, the initial response of the privileged strata was to create committees and to extend existing representative and local organizations to provide maximum support for the army and administration. In August 1914, provincial *zemstvos* joined together to form the All-Russian Union of Zemstvos for the Relief of Sick and Wounded Soldiers, and the municipalities united to create the All-Russian Union of Towns. Receiving financial resources from the government, these organizations helped military authorities to maintain military hospitals and hospital trains and to supply the army with food and clothing. They also aided in the evacuation of refugees, participated along with war-industries committees in the drive to mobilize private industries for war production, and did what they could to meet civilian needs. By 1915, close relations, institutionalized in special councils, had been established among the heads of these voluntary/representative organizations, Duma members, and the ministers and bureaucrats of the autocracy.[184]

The main significance of this *rapprochement* between the state and privileged society turned out to be political. For although some headway was made in meeting the immediate needs of the army for supplies and services, even this fusion of bureaucracy and voluntary organizations could not overcome the basic difficulties. Defeats at the front and "the creeping disorganization of economic life on the home front" continued.[185] Partly in response to these realities, and partly in response to the peculiar behavior of Tsar Nicholas in the crisis (for, while continuing to assert his absolute authority, he narrowed his contacts to his German wife, to the bizarre Rasputin, and to a court clique of formerly pro-German arch-conservatives), a reformist political program was formulated by the majority of the Duma, supported by the *zemstvos,* towns, and committees. In August 1915 it was demanded of the tsar that he appoint only ministers enjoying "public confidence" and the support of legislative institutions, and that he implement liberal measures of conciliation toward national minorities and trade unions. Perhaps because they had been brought by the war into ever closer working relations with the "constitutional liberals," many ministers, state bureaucrats, and army officers supported these very moderate demands. But Nicholas would not sacrifice the autocratic principle: and so upper- and middle-class civilian and official disgust with him grew. Public criticism flourished especially because it could be couched in nationalistic terms, deploring the mismanagement of the war effort for which the tsar and his coterie were held responsible as convenient scapegoats. Still more ominous for Nicholas, talk of a possible coup d'état spread within the officer corps, swollen with recently promoted or recruited members.

Yet—fearful of popular explosions, and perhaps realizing that they could not in fact handle the wartime difficulties any better with the tsar gone—the privileged strata held back. They never acted decisively to change the regime. When the tsar prorogued Dumas, they obeyed. Instead, in February 1917, when bad weather exacerbated delays in the supply of food to the city, the workers and soldiers of Petrograd toppled the moribund autocracy from below. Indeed:

> The collapse of the Romanov autocracy in March 1917 was one of the most leaderless, spontaneous, anonymous revolutions of all time . . . No one, even among the revolutionary leaders, realized that the strikes and bread riots which broke out in Petrograd on March 8 would culminate in the mutiny of the garrison and the overthrow of the government four days later.[186]

To be sure, the insurgents of Petrograd benefited from the initial acquiescence of the privileged strata and the supreme army command at the front in the abolition of tsardom.[187] Yet links were forming between workers and the army rank and file that would soon nullify any attempted upper-class resistance. For the garrisons of the cities in the rear—including the crucial Petrograd garrison—were swollen with recent recruits apprehensive about going to the front and directly familiar with the circumstances of the civilian workers suffering from skyrocketing prices and shortages of basic necessities.[188] Thus, when an industrial shutdown and demonstrations on International Women's Day coincided in Petrograd to produce swelling protests generously leavened with calls for the overthrow of the autocracy, it was not too difficult for fraternizing demonstrators to convince police and army units not to fire upon them. Once the initial rebellion was underway, it spread irrepressibly from military unit to military unit, from factory workers to railway men, from the capital of Petrograd to Moscow and to the provincial cities.[189]

Suddenly the tsarist autocracy was gone, and the state rapidly disintegrated. After February, organized political forces in the capital and other cities, working through and around the new "Provisional Government," maneuvered to define and control the organs of a unified, liberal-democratic national government to replace the defunct autocracy. But in the immediate wake of the tsar's abdication, the rebellious military garrisons became virtually impossible to coordinate from above. And the Imperial administration soon became incapacitated and disorganized as soviets and other popular political organs competed with *dumas, zemstvos,* and the Provisional Government for authority over its various agencies and functions. Party rivalries in the cities only served to deepen and politicize the spreading chaos, which was also aggravated by the inexorably on-going war.[190]

Meanwhile, revolts from below were gathering force – in the cities, at the fronts, and in the vast countryside. And without the protection of the Imperial administration and armies upon which they had always been so thoroughly dependent, the urban privileged strata and the landed nobility would be nakedly vulnerable to assaults from below. The result, as we shall see in Chapters 3 and 6, was to be the most rapid and spontaneous overthrow of an established regime and dominant classes in the annals of modern revolutions.

Now that Bourbon France, Manchu China, and Romanov Russia have been analyzed in some detail, we can tentatively conclude that revolutionary political crises emerged in all three Old Regimes because agrarian structures impinged upon autocratic and proto-bureaucratic state organizations in ways that blocked or fettered monarchical initiatives in coping with escalating international military competition in a world undergoing uneven transformation by capitalism. In France and China, prosperous and politically powerful landed upper classes blocked even the initial progress of modernizing reforms. In Russia, a weak landed nobility could not block reforms from above. Yet the agrarian economy and class structure served as brakes upon state-guided industrialization, thus making it impossible for tsarist Russia to catch up economically and militarily with Imperial Germany, her chief potential enemy in the European states system. In all three cases, moreover, the ultimate effect of the impediments to state-sponsored reforms was the downfall of monarchical autocracy and the disintegration of the centralized administrative and military organizations of the state. Revolts from below might emerge and spread without the dominant classes having recourse to the accustomed backing of the autocratic–imperial states. Social revolutions were at hand.

JAPAN AND PRUSSIA AS CONTRASTS

The arguments presented here about the distinctive causes of revolutionary political crises in France, Russia, and China must stand or fall primarily according to how well they make sense of these three historical cases. Yet, in terms of the logic of comparative historical analysis, we can be more certain of the adequacy of these arguments if it can be demonstrated that the causes highlighted for France, Russia, and China also differentiate their patterns of societal development and crises from broadly similar patterns and crises in comparable countries that did not experience social-revolutionary transformations. For this purpose, comparisons to some of the conditions accompanying the Japanese Meiji Restoration of 1868–73 and the Prussian Reform Movement of 1807–15 are most enlightening. By asking why these political crises were not proto-social-revolutionary, rather preludes to effective structural reforms instituted from above, we can further validate by contrast the arguments about the distinctive causes of the social-revolutionary political crises. Comparisons of Prussia and Japan to France and China are especially appropriate, and these will be stressed in the following discussion. At the end of each section, though, relevant comparisons to Russia will also be made.

The Japanese Meiji Restoration

The Meiji Restoration of 1868–73 was a sudden and fundamental reorganization of the Japanese polity. A set of regionally based aristocratic governments constituting the *baku-han* system under the hegemony of the Tokugawa Shogunate was transformed into a bureaucratic and fully centralized national state focused on the Meiji Emperor.[191] The Restoration set the stage for fundamental modernizing reforms administered from above by the Meiji oligarchs in the 1870s and 1880s—reforms that, in turn, rendered possible Japan's rapid industrialization and ascent into the ranks of major modern military powers.

Like the revolutionary political crises of Bourbon France and (especially) Manchu China, the crisis leading to the Meiji Restoration was triggered by foreign military pressures. After the arrival of Admiral Perry in 1853, there were recurrent intrusions by industrializing Western powers upon Tokugawa Japan's political sovereignty, forcing her to open ports to foreign emissaries and traders. Coming as they did at a time when the Tokugawa shogunal administration had become weakened relative to many *han* (provincial domains) administered by *daimyo* lords nominally vassals of the shogun in Edo, the foreign intrusions set off not only antiforeign movements but also struggles within Japan's political elite. The results, however, were in sharp contrast to political developments in the wake of internationally induced crises in France and China. Tokugawa Japan had a far less centralized structure of government than either Bourbon France or late Imperial China, so that there were seemingly ideal conditions for the success of would-be anticentralist movements. Nevertheless, the actual scenario of the Japanese Meiji Restoration

100

was *not* (as in France and China) one of resistance against monarchical attempts at rationalizing reforms. Instead, noble leaders who came primarily from outlying and less privileged *han* carried through in 1868 a coup d'état at the center, replacing the Tokugawa Shogun with the emperor as head of state. They then used the military power of their native *han* along with the resources and prestige of the new central government to push through, step by step, a series of fundamental social and administrative changes. Aristocratic statuses and privileges were abolished, to make all citizens formally equal. And previously decentralized and fragmented administrative jurisdictions were superseded by a unified, centralized, and highly bureaucratic national government, which subsequently undertook further reforms from above, including state-promoted industrialization.

Why could the Japanese Meiji Restoration happen as it did? A key part of the explanation lies in the *absence* of a politically powerful landed upper class in Tokugawa Japan. We have noted that in old-regime France and China, economically prosperous landed upper classes had gained collective footholds within imperfectly bureaucratized imperial state organizations— footholds that they used to drain potential state revenues away from central control, and from which they could prevent the implementation of modernizing reforms that hurt their class interests. In Tokugawa Japan, too, there were landlords—families roughly comparable to landed gentry and rich peasants in China, in that they were economically prosperous and dominant in local villages and market towns.[192] However, along with merchants, these landlords were excluded from extralocal levels of military and administrative power. For historically in Tokugawa Japan, there had developed a virtually complete bifurcation between private economic wealth and the administrative power of the shogun, the *daimyo,* and their numerous agents of the *samurai* caste. Wealth holders such as landlords and merchants were forbidden to bear arms and could hold governmental posts only at local levels, within their communities and under the strict supervision of *samurai* administrators.[193] Concomitantly, the Tokugawa regime, though imperfectly centralized, had achieved an extraordinarily high level of bureaucratic rationalization for a preindustrial and aristocratic regime. Within virtually all of the *han* domains, *samurai* agents of the lords had been, since the sixteenth century, separated from direct, personal ownership of lands and supervision of peasant communities and had been gathered together within urban garrisons and administrative centers. Excluded thus from control of the land, the *samurai* were rendered dependent upon stipend salaries paid through central treasuries. Gradually but inexorably they found themselves transformed from rude warriors into formally educated, and often specialized, officials, subject to tight and increasingly impersonal and meritocratic discipline in their assigned duties as administrators for the domains of the shogun and the *daimyo.*[194]

101

This remarkable bifurcation between landed–commercial wealth and bureaucratic political power that was built into the Tokugawa system helps to explain why the changes of the Meiji Restoration happened as they did in response to Western pressures on Japan. The men who led the Restoration were *samurai*.[195] Their access to administrative and military power in the "outer" *han* of Choshu and Satsuma provided them with independent resources to use against the Tokugawa Shogun. Yet because they were not landlords or closely tied to them, nothing prevented these men from pursuing national salvation for Japan through programs of political centralization. "Not being of a landed aristocracy, their ambitions could be met by success only in government service."[196] And the same was true for many other members of the Tokugawa governing stratum, who either participated in the Meiji movement or acquiesced in its reforms in return for appointment to the new state offices that replaced those that were abolished.

It was also important that the struggles of the Restoration crisis could proceed within the ranks of the existing bureaucratic governing stratum, without at any point involving landed upper classes who possessed political power to resist state centralization. Such a politically powerful landed upper class simply did not exist in Tokugawa Japan. Thus, its resistance could not undermine autocratic political authority, challenge the existing state functions, and disorganize state controls over the lower strata, as the resistance of landed classes did in France and China. Rather in Japan, the political and administrative strata remained agreed on the continuation of routine fiscal and policing functions throughout the Restoration crisis.[197] Changes in the overall structure of the political regime were accomplished bit by bit by the Meiji reformers, working through the established structures and personnel. "While the shogunate and the *han* were abolished, it nevertheless proved possible to utilize many of the old channels of authority and much of the existing machinery of administration, and thus to satisfy modern needs with small incremental changes."[198]

Classes and groups formerly excluded from politics thus gained no new opportunities to intervene during the Restoration, which has been aptly described as a "revolution from above."[199] Most crucially, although localized "peasant riots," common enough prior to the mid-nineteenth century, continued to occur—and even became more frequent during and after the Restoration—no nationwide peasant rebellion contributed to the Meiji transformations. As Hugh Borton points out.

> the Meiji Restoration developed independently of the peasants. The Restoration was directed against the danger of foreign pressure threatening the semicolonization of Japan and against the Tokugawa regime because of its inability to govern effectively. It was brought about by a coup d'etat within the Imperial Palace and the farmers found them-

selves victims of changes engineered and perpetrated by members of the ruling class of warriors . . . The power to rule had shifted from one group of leading warriors (the Tokugawa) to the Emperor and the group of Western Clans which supported him. There was no overthrow of the ruling warrior class, no rise of the peasants to power and no radical change in their conditions.[200]

Non-*samurai* became involved in the Restoration only through carefully controlled military mobilizations. Moreover, when violent clashes did break out, they tended to happen after the fact of the changes they attempted to resist, and they involved rather small disaffected sections of the Tokugawa political elite. From the start the military forces loyal to the emperor had the technological edge, and they grew steadily stronger after 1868.[201]

The Meiji Restoration—as a centralizing and nationalizing political revolution without landed upper-class obstruction and without class-based revolts from below—proved *possible* as a response to imperialist pressures on Japan precisely because the Tokugawa regime had already become so bureaucratized despite its imperfect centralization. Once foreign threats made state centralization mandatory for Japan's sovereign survival, sections of the Tokugawa governing elite could quickly accomplish a political transformation from within and above. And they could do this without destroying existing administrative arrangements or disturbing controls over the lower strata—exactly what the more complexly intertwined monarchical staffs and politically powerful landed classes in Bourbon France and Manchu China could not do.

Finally, what about the comparison of Japan to Tsarist Russia? In both Japan and Russia from the 1860s, autocratic political authorities managed, unlike those of Bourbon France and late Imperial China, to ride out internationally induced crises and to implement modernizing reforms from above. Significantly, though, the economic changes that transpired after the Restoration, propelled or encouraged by the Meiji regime, were much more successful in meeting the exigencies of Japan's international situation than the tsarist post-Crimean reforms and programs of state-guided industrialization were in meeting the exigencies of Russia's situation. A complete analysis of all of the reasons for Japan's rapid development after 1880 is beyond the scope of this discussion; nevertheless, it is interesting to note that Japan enjoyed advantages corresponding to disadvantages that have previously been emphasized for Russia.

For one thing, early-industrializing Japan was not fettered by a lagging agricultural sector. Structured very much as it had been in Tokugawa times before the Meiji Restoration, the Japanese agricultural sector was able, as the Russian was not, to increase its productivity very markedly between 1870 and 1920. To explain this fully, we would have to delve into the different production possibilities and requirements of riziculture

103

versus bread-grain agriculture. For the fact is that Japanese agricultural development in both Tokugawa and Meiji times occurred without "modernized" inputs, through the more labor-intensive application and spread of traditional technologies. Population growth had not caught up with productivity increases in Tokugawa Japan, as it had in late Imperial China, and there was room for more growth along the same lines for a time after 1870.[202] As a result, Japanese agriculture not only provided exports (as did Russian agriculture, under unremitting pressure from the state) but also contributed investment resources (channeled through the state), food and manpower, and support for small-scale industries, to the first stages of Japanese industrialization. In large part because of its ability to rely upon such contributions from agriculture (and, indeed, from the traditional economic sector generally) the Meiji regime was able to avoid, as the tsarist regime could not, heavy reliance upon foreign investments and borrowing in its efforts to promote infrastructural and heavy-industrial development through state investments.[203]

Moreover, Japan enjoyed another advantage. After the successful consolidation of an autonomous national state in the Meiji Restoration, early-industrializing Japan did not face nearly so frustrating or threatening an international military environment as Tsarist Russia. Around the turn of the century, Japan fought two limited wars, one against China and the other against Russia. And as the victor in both conflicts, she avoided disruptions of defeat such as those that faced the tsarist authorities in 1905–6. Yet, of course, the key difference is that early-industrializing Japan was not fully involved in the European states system and, consequently, was never subjected to the terrible blows of any such prolonged and total modern war as World War I. Thus both sets of differences between Meiji Japan and post-Emancipation Tsarist Russia point to the lesser involvement of early-industrializing Japan in international relations that might have undermined her autonomy and stability. The early industrialization of Tsarist Russia, in contrast, only pulled her ever more deeply into such involvements, leading to the dissolution of the Imperial state in World War I.

The Prussian Reform Movement

Compared to the political transformations wrought in the Meiji Restoration, those involved in the Prussian Reform Movement of 1807–14 were slight indeed. The overall structure of Hohenzollern absolute monarchy remained essentially unchanged; the only significant modification "was the replacement of capricious royal rule by a more impersonal system of bureaucratic absolutism . . ."[204] That is, the direct, personal, and dictatorial monopoly by the king over all policy initiatives and supervision of admin-

104

istrative and military affairs was replaced by a more flexible and professional system of de facto rule by "the legally regulated collective autocracy of the bureaucratic aristocracy, headed by a small elite of ministers and ministerial councilors responsible to their conscience and to . . . strong 'prime ministers' . . ."[205] The occasion for this political modification was the advent of a succession of reforming ministers appointed and given unusually free rein by the Prussian king after his armies incurred disastrous defeats at the hands of Napoleon at Jena and Auerstadt in 1806. The reforming ministers, as they strengthened their own official positions within the absolute monarchy, simultaneously introduced a series of socioeconomic and military reforms designed to revitalize the Prussian system: the abolition of status (*Stände*) monopolies on access to occupations and rights to own landed estates; the elimination of the personal disabilities of serfdom; and the institution of universal military conscription.[206]

Several things are remarkable about the Prussian Reform Movement: first, that the Prussian state survived to implement it at all; second, that the struggles involved remained entirely factional political intrigues within the governing class, "the internal affair of the upper ten thousand,"[207] without involving the lower strata except as objects of manipulation; third, that resistance by landed nobles was limited and in considerable part overridden; and fourth, that merely a limited set of changes served so thoroughly to revitalize the Prussian state as to enable it to help defeat Napoleon after 1814, and thereafter to go on to take the lead in the unification of an industrializing Germany.

In 1806, the defeat of the Prussians and other German forces by Napoleon's *grande armée* led to the occupation of many German territories (including for a time parts of East Prussia), to the formal loss of Prussian territories west of the Elbe, and to the imposition by France of crushing indemnities. Yet the Hohenzollern autocratic regime did not collapse, as did the Romanov regime in 1917 Russia. Both the battles and defeats were sudden, and quickly resolved, and considerations of the post-1806 power balance between France and Russia dictated that Prussia east of the Elbe should be left at peace and nominally independent.[208] Thus the international pressures on Prussia in 1806, though great, were not as massive and unremitting as those on Russia during World War I.

Once again, as with the Meiji Restoration, the immediately significant comparison is with France and China. Why could Prussian bureaucrats initiate reforms leading to only limited resistance, whereas comparable attempts by the Bourbon ministers in 1787–8 and the Manchus in 1905–11 precipitated revolutionary political crises? The answer is not quite so simple as in the case of Japan, because Prussia did have a landed upper class, the Junkers, many of whose members were officials in the army and civil administration.

In fact it was precisely from some Junker landlords that there arose resistance to many reforms, and even political counterinitiatives calling — reminiscent of the French nobility in 1787–8 – for the establishment of representative estates to share governing with the monarch. But the effectiveness of Junker resistance was limited (like that of the Russian nobility against the post-Crimean reforms) to modifying the implementation of decrees freeing the serfs. Readily overridden or ignored by the reforming ministers were any complaints against the removal of status restrictions on estate ownership and occupations, as well as reactionary demands for reinstitution of *Ständestaat* government (monarchy checked by decentralized noble assemblies).[209] Clearly the French privileged strata had much more leverage against the Bourbon monarchy, as did the Chinese gentry against the Manchus in 1911. What, then, made Prussia different, even though it too was a regime based on a political alliance between a landed upper class and a royal autocracy?

"The uniqueness, the extraordinary strength . . . [of] Prussia lay in the fusion of the economic and military power of its nobility with the order, system and efficiency of its bureaucracy."[210] Here was an agrarian state in which the landed nobility retained complete political control at local levels, yet participated only as an aggregate of manipulable and disciplined individuals in the royal military and administrative machineries that knit provinces together into the kingdom. In the French and Chinese systems, wealthy upper-class individuals *and groups* were allowed to infiltrate the middle and upper reaches of royal administrations; and they gained formally recognized rights to impede centrally coordinated administrative functions. But this could not and did not happen in Prussia, "the classic country of monarchical autocracy."[211]

The old saying that Prussia was not a country with an army, but an army with a country, suggests the reason why. From the mid-seventeenth through the eighteenth century, a succession of Hohenzollern kings, intent upon making their dynasty a recognized power in European politics, forged an extraordinarily disciplined and efficient administrative machine. This machine was meant solely to unify and exploit financially a diverse collection of dynastically inherited and noncontiguous territories, including primarily relatively poor ones east of the Elbe River.[212] The first crucial steps were taken by the Great Elector Frederick William of Brandenburg in the 1650s and '60s, when he built up a standing army and used it to clip the powers of the noble-dominated representative estates that had previously administered the disparate Hohenzollern territories and controlled financial grants to kings. The successors of the Great Elector went on to develop an administration modeled on military principles of organization, which was designed to squeeze out every possible penny "to support the army of a first-rate power on the resources of a third-rate state . . ."[213]

106

In the Prussian administration, unlike the French, the number of officials
was kept to a minimum, and no significant offices were for sale. Taxes
were not "farmed out" to independent enterprisers but collected by officials who were held strictly accountable under a surprisingly modern system of annual budgetary controls. Officials were not allowed to exercise
personal judgment or initiative but were kept under tight, multiple, and
continuously documented controls by peers and superiors, with lines of
information and initiative converging only on the king himself.[214] Although the Prussian bureaucracy employed mainly nobles from landed
upper-class backgrounds, there were no corporate groups such as the
French *parlements* ensconced in the Prussian administration, and officials
had no property in office. Indeed, they did not even possess security in
office: At the slightest suspicion of an official's corruption or disobedience,
the king could, and often did, dismiss, imprison, and even execute the
person in question. "The bureaucrat was the galley slave of the state . . .
The entire bureaucratic mechanism was based on the assumption that no
official could be trusted any further than the keen eyes of his superiors
could reach."[215]

Then too, by 1740, the "Prussian crown had stripped its nobility of the
last remnants of political power in the provinces"[216] – something that
neither the French Bourbons nor the Manchus in China accomplished with
their privileged upper classes. This was possible in Prussia not only because the Hohenzollerns could coerce the Junkers but also because the
Junkers, as a class of landlords owning commercial estates worked by
serfs, had characteristics and needs that complemented the Hohenzollern
military hegemony. Left politically sovereign on their estates and in the
rural counties, the Junkers could keep the peasants in place, producing to
pay taxes, and available for military conscription. In turn, since the
Junkers had such absolute local control, they lost little by surrendering
provincial and kingdom-wide leadership, and they gained in compensation
some protection from the marauding armies of neighboring Great Powers.
Even more important, since the agrarian economy of eighteenth century
Prussia was not prosperous, the Junkers gained opportunities for the employment of family members in the king's service.[217] This system of alliance between the state and the landed upper class was somewhat similar to
the Chinese system at its prime; however, the Chinese state was much less
centralized and militaristic, and Chinese society was more prone to peasant-based rebellions. And, of course, it was precisely the internal and
external military failures of the Manchus that opened the way to encroachments by the gentry on the provincial levels of state power after 1840. As
for the comparison to France, the contrasts are obvious: The French monarchy succeeded in edging aside the seigneurs at the local levels of power.
It did this, however, only to suffer from the infiltration of diverse but

increasingly allied groupings of holders of proprietary wealth at the middle and upper levels of the royal administration – thus losing potential bureau cratic initiative versus dominant-class social and economic interests. This was not the difficulty to which the Prussian monarchy was prone.

The Prussian system succeeded during the reign of Frederick the Great (1740–86) in providing the wherewithal for military victories in the Seven Years' War that turned Prussia suddenly into a Great Power.[218] Through the end of the eighteenth century, the bureaucracy continued to generate taxes very efficiently. But once Prussian territories had expanded and the decisive coordination and leadership of Frederick the Great was gone, the Prussian administration and officer corps became predictably lumbering and inflexible overall – the natural penalty of encouraging blind official obedience to rules at the expense of initiative. When forced suddenly to confront the speed and flexibility of Napoleon's plebiscitary dictatorship, the Hohenzollern autocratic machineries proved inadequate.

Yet they retained the potential for speedy recovery once threatened from without.[219] Professional administrators such as Karl von Stein and Karl August von Hardenberg, and military reformers such as Gerhard von Scharnhorst and August Neithardt von Gneisenau could step to the fore, push aside the debilitated personal controls of Hohenzollern despotism, and use the still existing and functioning state organizations to implement limited measures to make the economy and society more flexible supports for military autocracy. Noble titles and prerogatives were not abolished but were rendered legally accessible to born commoners who could afford to purchase the landed estates or obtain the education and patronage necessary for promotions in the bureaucracy or officer corps. Serfs were given their personal freedom. And universal military conscription was begun, a measure that allowed the Prussian armies to expand suddenly and to benefit from the increased enthusiasm of citizens newly benefited by the reforms or aroused to hostility by several years of French intervention and financial exactions. All of these reforms *could* be implemented from above relatively smoothly because the Prussian state was already so very strong within society, and because the Junkers – whose established economic and status interests were somewhat contradicted by the reforms – were nevertheless in no institutional position to block concerted policy initiatives by the state.

Thus comparisons with Bourbon France and late Imperial China clarify why the Prussian state was able successfully to implement immediately adequate modernizing reforms in 1807–14. But a final point about the Prussian reforms needs to be made through a comparison to the Russian Emancipation of the serfs. As we have seen, the Russian Emancipation was implemented within the confines of the preexisting agrarian class structure. And that structure condemned Russian agriculture to very slow rates of growth (without breakthrough to modern techniques) after 1870. Now, it happens that the liberation of the serfs in Prussia after 1807 also occurred as a series of juridical reforms and property adjustments implemented in ways that reinforced the preexisting class relations between landlords and peasants. Yet the Prussian abolition of serfdom helped to facilitate the modernization and increasing prosperity of Prussian agriculture during the first two-thirds of the nineteenth century.[220] How do we explain this important difference between the effects of the tsarist post-Crimean reforms and the Prussian reforms after 1806?

The answer lies in differences, both before and after the abolition of serfdom, between the agrarian relations of production of the two countries. In Russia, the actual processes of agrarian production were mostly controlled by serf (and later peasant-smallholder) communities, with landlords functioning mainly as appropriators of surplus through dues and labor services, or through rents. But in Prussia, agricultural production, both under serfdom and afterwards, was centered on large, commercially oriented estates owned and run by the lords or their agents. In Prussia as in Russia, when serfdom was abolished, the landlords influenced the process in ways that ensured as far as possible the maintenance of their accustomed economic hegemony in new forms. Prussian peasants were forced to cede to the large, Junker-owned estates one-third to two-thirds of the holdings they had worked for themselves under serfdom, in order to gain property title to the lands that remained. This meant that the vast majority were left with inadequate land to support themselves, thus ensuring that they would continue to work on the Junker estates, henceforth as wage laborers.

Thus, once the Prussian reforms had both abolished serfdom and opened the market for noble estates to all well-to-do investors, Prussian landlords—owners of large, consolidated domains under unified management—could begin to adopt innovative techniques that required "free" wage labor. They were able to respond to new market opportunities to sell grain both within greater Germany and abroad. The resulting agrarian prosperity (which lasted until about 1870) helped to support the successful bid of the Prussian state to become the core of a unified, rapidly industrializing, and internationally powerful, Imperial Germany.[221] In contrast, as we have seen, the sluggishness of Russian agriculture after the Emancipation fettered tsarist attempts to adapt Imperial Russia to the exigencies of the modernizing European states system.

Summing Up

Our brief examination of the conditions underlying the political crises of the Meiji Restoration and the Prussian Reform Movement has tended to

contrast the central arguments of this chapter about the
utionary political crises in France, Russia, and China. Bour-
ohenzollern Prussia, Tokugawa Japan, Manchu China, and
ia – all became subject to military pressures from more eco-
oped nations abroad, and all experienced in response soci-
ses. Yet only France, Russia, and China were plunged into
the upheavals of social revolution, whereas Prussia and Japan, relatively
speaking, adapted speedily and smoothly to international exigencies
through reforms instituted from above by autocratic political authorities.
The different fates of these agrarian monarchical regimes faced with the
challenges of adapting to the exigencies of international uneven development can be explained in large part by looking at the ways in which
agrarian relations of production and landed dominant classes impinged
upon state organizations – although it is also important to assess the sever-
ity of the pressures from abroad with which each regime had to cope.

In Russia, the revolutionary crisis of autocratic rule and dominant-class
privilege was due to the overwhelming stress of World War I upon an
early-industrializing economy fettered by a backward agrarian sector. The
Imperial regime was strong enough to override dominant class interests
and enforce modernizing reforms after the shock of defeat in the Crimean
War, but it was not able to reorganize agrarian class relations that were
inimical to modern economic development or rapid increases in productivity. Even extraordinary successes of state-propelled industrialization were
not enough to allow Tsarist Russia to make up her economic lag behind
the West, and she remained entangled within the European states system
as it careened toward World War I. By contrast, neither Japan nor Prussia
was as agriculturally backward or as internationally pressed during early
industrialization as Tsarist Russia.

Both Bourbon France and Manchu China had fairly prosperous agrarian
economies and experienced foreign pressures no greater than those experienced by Tokugawa Japan and Hohenzollern Prussia. Another pattern is
the differentiating cause here: specifically, the presence or absence of a
landed upper class with institutionalized political leverage at extralocal
levels, leverage in relation to fiscal and military/policing functions centrally
organized by royal administrations. If such politically organized and administratively entrenched landed classes were present, as they were in
France and China, then the reactions of these classes against autocratic
attempts to institute modernizing reforms deposed the monarchies and
precipitated breakdowns of administrative and military organizations. This
meant that externally induced political crises developed into potential social-revolutionary situations. But if, as in Japan and Prussia, politically
powerful landed classes were absent, so that the old-regime states were
more highly bureaucratic, then foreign-induced crises could be resolved

110

through political struggles confined, broadly speaking, within the established governing elite and administrative arrangements. And this precluded the possibility for social revolution from below.

Social revolutions in France, Russia, and China were launched, it has been argued in this chapter, by crises centered in the structures and situations of the states of the Old Regimes. Still, the actual occurrence of social revolutions in these three countries depended not only upon the emergence of revolutionary political crises but also upon the conduciveness of the agrarian sociopolitical structures of the Old Regimes to peasant revolts. To go on with the analysis from here, therefore, we must reexamine the prerevolutionary societies from the opposite perspective, no longer from the top down with emphasis on the state, the dominant class, and the international context, but now from the bottom up with emphasis on the structural situation of the peasants in the agrarian economy and in local political and class relations. This is the task of Chapter 3.

3 Agrarian Structures and Peasant Insurrections

> *When non-peasant social forces clash, when rulers are divided or foreign powers attack, the peasantry's attitude and action may well prove decisive. Whether this potential is realized is mainly dependent upon the peasants' ability to act in unison, with or without formal organization.*
>
> Teodor Shanin

MASSIVE AS THEY WERE, societal political crises alone were not enough to create social-revolutionary situations in France, Russia, and China. Administrative and military breakdowns of the autocracies inaugurated social-revolutionary transformations – rather than, say, interregnums of intraelite squabbling leading to the break-up of the existing polity or the reconstitution of a similar regime on a more or less liberal basis. This result was due to the fact that widespread peasant revolts coincided with, indeed took advantage of, the hiatus of governmental supervision and sanctions. In Barrington Moore's vivid phrase, "the peasants . . . provided the dynamite to bring down the old building."[1] Their revolts destroyed the old agrarian class relations and undermined the political and military supports for liberalism or counterrevolution. They opened the way for marginal political elites, perhaps supported by urban popular movements, to consolidate the Revolutions on the basis of centralized and mass-incorporating state organizations.

Peasant revolts have in truth attracted less attention from historians and social theorists than have urban lower-class actions in revolutions – even for the predominantly agrarian societies with which we are concerned here. This is understandable. Urban workers, whether preindustrial or industrial, have often played highly visible parts in (failed as well as successful) revolutions. And their aims and achievements have been linked to those of self-consciously revolutionary leaderships. Hence insurrectionary urban workers seem like true revolutionaries compared to peasants who merely "rebel" in the countryside, far from the centers of national-political consciousness and decision.

Nevertheless, peasant revolts have been the crucial insurrectionary ingre-

112

dient in virtually all actual (i.e., successful) social revolutions to date,[2] and certainly in the French, Russian, and Chinese Revolutions. This is not really surprising, given that social revolutions have occurred in agrarian countries where peasants are the major producing class. Without peasant revolts, urban radicalism in predominantly agrarian countries has not in the end been able to accomplish social-revolutionary transformations. The cases of the English and German (1848) Revolutions (to be discussed below) help to demonstrate this assertion. Both of these contrast cases had vigorous urban – popular revolutionary movements. Yet they failed as social revolutions in part for want of peasant insurrections against landed upper classes.

This does not mean that revolts of urban workers made no difference in the Revolutions at hand, especially the French and Russian. The actions of French *sans culottes* and Russian industrial workers helped to shape the revolutionary conflicts and outcomes distinctive to France and Russia. As we saw in Chapter 2, the revolts of urban workers constituted intervening moments in the processes by which the French and Russian Old Regimes were undermined (although the fundamental causes were the international pressures and dominant class/state contradictions discussed in depth). Moreover, as we shall see in Part II, urban revolts contributed crucially to the political struggles through which new, urban-based revolutionary regimes were built up in France and Russia. But here, in this chapter, our concern is with causes of social revolutions in France, Russia, and China alike. Peasant revolts against landlords were a necessary ingredient in all three Revolutions, whereas successful revolts by urban workers were not. Thus, for the explanatory purpose at hand, attention to the conditions for and against peasant insurrections is far more important than a focus, however more customary, upon the urban revolts.

How, then, shall the peasant contribution to the great Revolutions be explained? To begin, it is necessary to identify those aspects of peasant participation in the revolutionary drama that led to its social-revolutionary impact. The peasant revolts of the French, Russian, and Chinese Revolutions were remarkable in that they became at once widespread and directed particularly against landlords. Their revolutionary impact depended upon these two facets. Because they spread across wide areas of France, Russia, and China, the peasant revolts achieved an impact transcending the localities to which peasant organizations remained confined. By striking especially against the property and powers of dominant-class landlords, the revolts weakened mainstays of the socioeconomic and political orders of the old regimes. Together the extensiveness and antilandlord focus of the revolutionary peasant revolts created decisive constraints at the societal level on the range of sociopolitical options available to elites contending for national power.

113

Here was something really new in the histories of France, Russia, and China. Historically there had been in these countries massive revolts of marginal regions against the exactions or representatives of the central monarchies. In China, such revolts ended up (if they did not begin) under the leadership of gentry, so that actual and potential antilandlord actions were ultimately suppressed or diverted.[3] In France, some regional revolts were led throughout by nobles. Others started that way and then gave rise to peasant revolts against their lords, thus facilitating repression by the monarchy in which peasants also lost out.[4] In Russia, traditional peasant-based rebellions involved a larger component of direct attacks on land-lords. But this was true only because border-dwelling Cossacks, rather than landlords with regional political and military leverage, provided the military impetus and shield for any large-scale uprisings.[5] On their own in traditional times—without the aid of regional revolts—peasants in all three countries certainly engaged in localized and sporadic violent resistance against landlords. But peasants had never achieved a successful, wide-spread, direct assault on the property or claims of landlords.

However, a widespread direct assault on landlords is exactly what ulti-mately *did* come about in the French, Russian, and Chinese social revolu-tions. Thus we are looking for an explanation of a pattern of peasant behavior that transcended spotty and localized unrest, and that accom-plished something very different from previous peasant-based rebellions. Our explanatory hypotheses give short shrift to the factors typically made central in other approaches, such as revolutionary ideology, the simple presence of exploitation, or the acuteness of relative deprivation.

We need not dwell upon explanations that attribute "peasant revolu-tion" to peasants' arousal by new goals, values, or system-transcending ideologies. It can hardly be overemphasized that peasant goals in the French, Russian, and Chinese Revolutions were *not* intrinsically different from previous peasant aims in rebellions or riots. Peasants participated in these Revolutions without being converted to radical visions of a desired new national society, and without becoming a nationally organized class-for-themselves. Instead they struggled for concrete goals—typically involv-ing access to more land, or freedom from claims on their surpluses. Such goals were entirely understandable in terms of the existing local economic and political circumstances in which peasants found themselves. In France and Russia, peasants mobilized for action through traditional village com-munity organizations. In China, peasants first participated as traditional "social bandits" and then finally were directly (re)organized by the Chi-nese Communist Party. Even then, however, Chinese peasants acted for concrete, immediate goals,[6] not unlike those they had attempted to achieve in historical riots and rebellions.

As for the possibility that peasants become revolutionary in reaction

114

against exploitation,[7] this approach tries to turn a constant feature of the peasant condition into an explanatory variable. By definition, peasants are invariably subjected to nonreciprocal claims on their production. Peasants are primary agricultural cultivators who must, because of political and cultural marginality and relative socioeconomic immobility, bear the burden of varying combinations of taxes, rents, corvée, usurious interest rates, and discriminatory prices.[8] Peasants always have grounds for rebellion against landlords, state agents, and merchants who exploit them. What is at issue is not so much the objective potential for revolts on grounds of justifiable grievances. It is rather the degree to which grievances that are always at least implicitly present can be collectively perceived and acted upon.

The short-term subjective exacerbation of specific grievances—the factor that is emphasized by relative-deprivation theorists—may well play a precipitating role, accounting for the timing of particular rebellious acts. Yet it is important to remember that relative deprivation is an aggregate-psychological state for which it is almost impossible to find genuine direct historical evidence. Strictly speaking, peasants in many localities would have had to have been interviewed individually at the outbreak of, and recurrently during, the three Revolutions. But this kind of evidence, or even the more usual indirect measures of relative deprivation,[9] still cannot address the question of how and why something—and specifically what—can be done about felt grievances by an aggregate of individuals. The really important question is what transforms the peasantry, if only at local levels, into a collective force capable of striking out against its oppressors.

As Eric Wolf has pointed out, "ultimately, the decisive factor in making a peasant rebellion possible lies in the relation of the peasantry to the field of power which surrounds it. A rebellion cannot start from a situation of complete impotence . . . "[10] If they are to act upon, rather than silently suffer, their omnipresent grievances, peasants must have "internal leverage"—some organized capacity for collective action against their exploitative superiors. In my view, the extent to which peasants have had such internal leverage, particularly during historical political crises of agrarian states, is explained by structural and situational conditions that affect: (1) the degrees and kinds of solidarity of peasant communities; (2) the degrees of peasant autonomy from direct day-to-day supervision and control by landlords and their agents; and (3) the relaxation of state coercive sanctions against peasants revolts. The first two factors—peasant solidarity and autonomy—have to be investigated through analysis of the agrarian structures of prerevolutionary old regimes. Class structure and local political structure both matter, and something can be said here about why each is important and how each should be investigated.

In examining class relations in the countryside, it is never enough merely to identify different strata of property holders, abstracting away from

115

institutional contexts. This widely employed approach[11] can be misleading about the power base of a landed upper class, underestimating it in instances where such a class (e.g., the Chinese gentry) supplements its income from sheer landownership with other complementary forms of surplus appropriation. Similarly, many analysts have been misled about possible degrees of solidarity among peasants when they have noted only facts about individual property-holding and economic differentiation between richer and poorer peasants. They have neglected to examine kinship and community institutions with collective economic functions that may tie richer and poorer relatively closer together than their individual property interests might suggest.[12]

Rather, to investigate a class structure means to look for the *historically specific institutional arrangements* by which two analytically basic kinds of social relationships are simultaneously established: on the one hand, relations of direct producers "to one another, to their tools and to the land in the immediate process of production," and on the other hand, relations "by which an unpaid-for part of the product is extracted from the direct producers by a class of non-producers."[13] Peasant solidarity and autonomy may (or may not) be built into agrarian class structures depending upon the exact institutional form that these relationships take.

Certain tentative findings do seem to have emerged from previous studies sensitive to the effects of institutionalized class relations on peasant insurrectionary capacity.[14] Agricultural regimes featuring large estates worked by serfs or landless laborers tend to be inimical to spontaneous, self-organized peasant rebellions. This is true not simply because the serfs and laborers are poor, but because they are divided from each other and subject to close and constant supervision and discipline by landlords or their managers. Rentier agrarian systems, where smallholder peasant families possess and work the land on their own, are notoriously more susceptible to peasant revolts[15]—in particular, I would argue, where socioeconomically based community relations tie the individual families together in opposition to landlords. As we shall see, class relations in France and Russia fit this rentier/community pattern.

However, even if large-estate agriculture is not present, an agrarian order may still be immune to autonomous peasant revolts if landlords directly control administrative and military sanctioning machineries (such as militias and poor relief agencies) at local levels. This points to the necessity of going beyond class analysis alone if we are adequately to comprehend the conditions for and against peasant revolts. We must analyze the political structures of agrarian orders, looking especially at the nature of local government and its relationship to central political authorities, monarchs and their agents. Do peasants, bureaucrats, or landlords control local political decision-making? Do landlords serve as, or instead

116

of, local agents of the monarchical state? Apparently, those agrarian orders most vulnerable to sudden and autonomous peasant revolts were those that not only had class relations favorable to peasant solidarity and autonomy. These vulnerable agrarian orders also had sanctioning machineries that were centrally and bureaucratically controlled, even as peasant communities enjoyed considerable local political autonomy.

Finally, though, it needs to be stressed that an exclusive focus on the structural situation of peasants in local class and political structures is not sufficient to explain either the simple occurrence or the specific patterns of the widespread, antilandlord revolts that occurred in the French, Russian, and Chinese Revolutions. For in all three Revolutions, the revolutionary political crisis of the autocratic state—itself occasioned by national and international developments quite independent of the peasantry—was also a crucial cause. This political factor interacted with the structurally given insurrectionary potential of the peasantry to produce the full-blown social-revolutionary situation that neither cause alone could have produced. It was the breakdown of the concerted repressive capacity of a previously unified and centralized state that finally created conditions directly or ultimately favorable to *widespread* and *irreversible* peasant revolts against landlords. If similar agrarian class and local political structures had not previously given rise to the same pattern of peasant revolts, it was because the missing ingredient was a world-historical development in the affairs of the dominant class. As soon as—and only when—that class, under international pressure in a modernizing world, had backed itself into a revolutionary political crisis, did the peasantry become able to achieve long-implicit insurrectionary goals. The conjunctural result was social revolution.[16]

Nor does a conjunctural analysis of peasant revolts in social revolutions properly stop with the discussion of the causes of the peasant revolts themselves. In addition, the immediate achievements of peasant revolts have potent "feedback" effects upon the course of national politics within the unfolding revolutionary crises. Such effects provide indispensable keys to shared and varied patterns of social-revolutionary dynamics and outcomes. Yet on this score, the reader must wait until Part II. The chapter at hand necessarily takes for granted that peasant revolts are consequential for the course of social revolutions and seeks to understand the structural and situational conditions that explain their occurrence.

Arguments about these conditions have been previewed, but they need to be spelled out in detail for each case of social revolution and for appropriate contrast cases (where successful social revolutions did not occur). Let us therefore turn to the cases. We shall begin with France, proceed next to Russia, and then examine seventeenth-century England and Germany in 1848–50 as contrasts. Finally, we shall discuss, against the background of all of the previous case analyses, the special issues raised by China.

117

PEASANTS AGAINST SEIGNEURS
IN THE FRENCH REVOLUTION

One of the most celebrated dates of the French Revolution is August 4, 1789. On the evening of that famous day members of the Constituent Assembly vied with one another to denounce and renounce "feudal" structures of French society and politics. Seigneurial dues, the venality of judicial offices, tax immunities, hunting rights, court pensions, seigneurial justice—all were surrendered "as one speaker after another renounced his own—or his neighbour's—privileges."[17] Symbolically, the changes that would earn the Revolution the right to be labeled a *social* revolution—one that went beyond political changes to transform society—were launched that night. Yet the liberal nobles and Third Estate representatives assembled at Versailles would never have initiated this session of sweeping reforms had not a spreading agrarian revolt against the seigneurial system forced their reluctant hand. Shocked and surprised by intensifying peasant resistance to the payment of dues and tithes and by mounting violence against *chateaux* and individuals, the men of property and privilege sitting at Versailles hastily decided to make unplanned concessions. Without the peasant revolution—which the greatest historian of the Revolution, Georges Lefebvre, has labeled "spontaneous" and "autonomous"—"one can be sure that the Constituent Assembly would not have struck such serious blows against the feudal regime . . . "[18] The Revolution might never have developed beyond constitutional reforms.[19]

Structural Conditions

The potential for the peasant revolts that erupted in 1789 was inherent in an agrarian social structure peculiar to France (and to the western parts of a disunited Germany) within eighteenth-century Europe. Not that the oppression of the French peasantry was the worst—though real grievances surely existed. Rather the socioeconomic and political conditions influencing the ability of peasants to react against seigneurial exploitation were comparatively very favorable in France.

In contrast to the serfs of Eastern Europe and to the increasingly dispossessed agricultural lower strata of England, the French peasantry virtually owned a substantial portion of the land of France. At least one-third of the land—and an even higher proportion of the cultivable soil—was held by millions of peasant farmers in small pieces that could be managed, bought and sold, and passed to heirs, subject only to various seigneurial claims. In addition, because very few large landlowners directly cultivated their own holdings, roughly another two-fifths of the land was rented to peasant

118

tenants and sharecroppers in mostly small pieces. Peasants therefore controlled the use of most of the land involved in agricultural production.[20]

Yet they did so only subject to heavy rental claims on what they produced. The "ground rent – royal, seigneurial, tithe and proprietorial – ...
[was] the driving force of the realm and of its social system. Rent-payers
[were] the ruled, receivers of rent and their agents the rulers."[21] The
tithe – collected in kind at harvest time – averaged about 8 percent and
went largely to wealthy bishops, canons, and lay lords outside the local
parishes. Seigneurial dues (which went to bourgeois landowners and religious houses as well as to nobles) varied enormously by region and locality; in general, they were heavy in Brittany and eastern France and light in
the areas south of the Loire (where, however, tithes were heavier). Taxes –
from which noble landowners were largely exempt – took between 5 and
10 percent of gross production in the *pays d'élection,* but less in the *pays
d'état.* Proprietorial rents were often the heaviest drain: In areas of the
south and west where *métayage* (sharecropping) predominated, the sharecroppers had to yield half the harvest to the landlords; otherwise rents
claimed at least a fifth of the harvest. Overall, the various rental claims on
the peasants' production took between one-fifth and three-fifths of their
gross income (that which remained after at least one-fifth of the harvest
was held back for seed, and the subsistence of laborers and costs of production and maintenance were met), with important variations across regions and time. Normally the rental claims were burdensome; in times of
crises of production or marketing they loomed as an almost insupportable
drain on the margin of livelihood or subsistence.

Peasant well-being depended upon the extent to which a family possessed
land subject to minimal rental claims plus the means, including tools and
livestock, necessary to work the land. But in all areas of eighteenth-century
France, those who could live securely on their own holdings, or on substantial rented farms, were a small proportion of the peasantry.[22] True, each
community might have one or two rich *coqs de village* who perhaps acted as
agents for the seigneurs, or, failing that, at least some substantial *laboureurs*
(independent middle-peasant owners), but the majority were poor and insecure. Either as tenants they had to pay heavy rents to work small pieces of
land for subsistence, or else they owned nothing but a house and garden and
had to find supplementary income through agricultural day-labor, industrial putting-out employment, or seasonal migration to find work away
from home. At the very bottom of the socioeconomic scale were vagrants
who lacked even the minimal holdings that would give them a home and
community. As population rose faster than the rate of economic growth
could provide new employment, the numbers of such impoverished vaga-
bonds – those who lived by a combination of beggary, occasional employment, and brigandage – grew at the end of the Old Regime. And many

119

settled families were never far from the fate of the wanderers. Rising prices for land and grain could not help them, for their prospect – and problem – was merely to hold on to enough land and employment to pay rental claims and eke out a subsistence.

Settled French peasants under the Old Regime did not, however, face the struggle for survival merely as an aggregate. They were not yet, as Marx would aptly write in the mid-1800s, like so many potatoes in a sack. True, economic differentiation within the ranks of the peasantry was far advanced, and "agrarian individualism" had gained solid footholds in the countryside.[23] Nevertheless, the peasant community, shaped through centuries of struggle for economic security and administrative autonomy, was still a reality. The fundamental basis of the community was economic. The center of the setup was the *terroir,* that is, "the sum of all the types of land cultivated or exploited by a group of men either centered on a big village or around several hamlets or else dispersed over a patchwork of scattered holdings."[24] The peasant community was vested in "collective ownership and use of . . . communal goods" or "collective constraints upon private property for the benefits of the inhabitants as a group . . . "[25] In the *pays de bocage* of Normandy and Brittany, where farmsteads were dispersed, peasant communities possessed common lands, including woods, which had to be administered for the collectivity and defended against the counterclaims and encroachments of outsiders. In the north and east, peasant villages held fewer common lands, but cultivation itself was hedged by communal rules about rotation of crops, fixing of harvest dates, rights to pasture on the fallow, regulations on enclosure, and so forth. These customs, too, not only had to be applied to community members but also upheld against outsiders. In most places, the seigneurs – whose domain lands with attached peasant tenures overlapped the peasant communities – were the key competitors for agrarian rights. At stake were such important rights as access to woods or pasture, or prerogatives to decide how lands would be cultivated. And it was above all in struggles against the seigneurs over such matters that the peasant communities, despite internal tensions, maintained a certain residuum of cohesion and self-consciousness.

By the eighteenth century, moreover, peasant communities enjoyed a substantial degree of self-government. The penetration by the royal administration into the localities and gradually edged aside the seigneur, leaving him merely the "first subject of the parish." He, or his agents if he was an absentee (as was often the case), did retain the control of seigneurial justice; yet this was a right with much economic but little political significance. Otherwise the peasants, with the aid of the local priest, handled their own local affairs – responsible to the *intendant* through his subdelegate. *Terroirs* frequently coincided with parishes, so that the assembly of the heads of households of the community typically met after mass on

Sundays to handle a wide range of community affairs, such as "sale, purchase, exchange or leasing of communal property; the maintenance of the church, of public buildings, roads, and bridges; the election of communal syndics, of the schoolmaster, the communal shepherd, the hayward, the collectors of tithes, the assessors and collectors of the *taille*."[26]

Although it was true that the village assemblies were more often than not informally dominated by the well-to-do peasants, still they potentially functioned as vital arenas for the discussion of local affairs by all family heads; and their decisions controlled key aspects of village life.[27]

The Impact of the Political Crisis of 1789

But how exactly did these structural conditions help to bring about the demise of the Old Regime in the countryside? To find the answer we must look to the trends and events of the revolutionary period. We shall begin with some economic trends that helped to ignite popular disturbances in 1788–9, and then focus upon the combination of agrarian structural conditions and national political events that ensured that the popular uprisings of 1789 would have a revolutionary aspect.

The formidable economic historian Ernest Labrousse has established, through painstaking research on price and wage trends, that a crisis in the French economy precipitated popular uprisings at the end of the Old Regime.[28] From about 1733 to 1770 the French economy was in the upswing of a cycle that was part of a nearly century-long phase of economic expansion. Agricultural and industrial productivity, colonial and domestic commerce, all were expanding. Prices and rents were rising faster than wages, so the growth benefited entrepreneurs and larger landowners disproportionately. Nevertheless, many poorer people could manage so long as the expansion continued. After 1770, however, a "period of economic distress, a period of contraction, set in . . . [and] by the end of 1778 at the latest, it was an accomplished fact. Prices were everywhere in full decline."[29] Agrarian incomes fell and industry languished; unemployment rose.

> The old problem of mouths and the food to fill them, already aggravated during the first two thirds of the century by the decline in the mortality rate, entered an acute stage and for a time became much more explicit as the conflict . . . between a revolutionary increase in population and an economy in a state of contraction became most strikingly apparent.[30]

By the mid 1780s the economy was beginning to recover. Then in 1788 there came a "serious accident of a kind that happened periodically."[31] The grain harvest failed. Rural incomes fell (as there was too little to sell even though prices were high), and agricultural unemployment increased. Markets for industrial products contracted, and so more laborers were thrown out of work. Meanwhile bread prices shot up (1789–90), and the millions of poorer peasants and urban artisans and laborers who had to buy all or part of their food suddenly faced acute want.

Popular response to rising bread prices in 1789 followed well-established forms.[32] Recurrently in the eighteenth century, whenever bread prices rose suddenly, the rural and urban poor responded with bread riots. Peasant communities seized grain being transported for sale outside their communities and instead sold it for a "just price" to local consumers. Urban consumers responded to shortages and high prices by seizing bakers' stocks and handling them in a similar way. Off and on, the royal government attempted to promote national free trade in grain, but the people still believed in fixed prices and guaranteed local supplies for everyone. Not long before the Revolution, in 1775, massive bread riots (the *"querre de farines"*) forced the Crown to abandon innovative policies and restore order through a combination of supplying grain to the needy and repressing demonstrations. Much of what happened in 1789 was a replay of this recurrent form of popular unrest.

In 1789, however, the results were extraordinary. In part this was because urban bread riots coincided with quarrels among the privileged elites over formulas for political representation to produce the Municipal Revolution.[33] Even more, it was because events developed into full-fledged social revolution in the countryside. During the spring, well before the Municipal Revolution, peasants began to go beyond bread riots to attack the seigneurial system. "The first wave of rural uprisings was ... aimed mainly at tithes, feudal rights, and the men who received them ... "[34] Very often the target was the feudal records of the local seigneur, but there were also seizures of "hoarded" grain stores. Even these early outbreaks were widespread, occurring in Anjou, Dauphiné, the Paris region, Picardy, Hainault, and the Midi. With the coming of summer, unrest intensified and spread over most of the country, partly through the awesome agency of "the Great Fear."[35] This was a collective panic inspired by the belief that "brigands" would attack the ripening grain crop. The belief grew that an "aristocratic plot" to starve the people was afoot; and the peasants organized themselves to meet the nebulous threat. Hostility fused with the hopes for change that had been aroused by the convening of the Estates-General, to intensify the revolt against the upper classes:

> Now that the States-General were assembled but slow in responding to ... expectations of liberty, the great mass of the peasantry reached a simple, spontaneous decision. The harvest was over. They would stop paying the tithe-gatherers, the seigneurs, and even the royal tax-collectors. Angry minorities assailed charter rooms and châteaux with pitchforks and firebrands. The majority adopted the safer and more effective course of passive resistance, and refused to pay up.[36]

122

Thus the supports were pulled out from under the Old Regime in the countryside, and the urban-based political reformers were faced with an uninvited crisis of property and order that they would have preferred to avoid.

Why did the peasants rebel starting in 1789 – and why did they in general revolt against the seigneurial system first and foremost? The causes consisted in the interaction of existing socioeconomic and political structures with political events in 1789 that reinforced the existing capacities, and created new opportunities, for collective antiseigneurial revolts.

Of enormous significance were the processes set in motion by the king's decision of January 29, 1789, to convene the Estates-General. Deputies for the Third Estate were to be elected in the *bailliages* by delegates of urban and rural communities. In each rural community, every man twenty-five or older who paid any amount of taxes was eligible to participate in a meeting that both elected representatives to the *bailliage* assembly and drew up a *cahier de doléances* expressing local grievances. Extraordinary as it may seem, every peasant community was invited by order of the king to ruminate collectively upon its troubles. The result surely was, on the whole, to heighten possibilities for the peasants to rebel, especially against seigneurs and nonlocal recipients of the tithes. Not that the *cahiers* explicitly singled out these targets; instead the *cahiers* were mostly filled with limited and highly varied local complaints.[37] Moreover, any more general demands for change contained in them cannot simply be attributed to the peasantry, because the assemblies were often led or influenced by priests, bourgeois, and local representatives of the seigneurs.[38] But more significant than the content of the *cahiers* was the process by which they were drawn up. That process raised hopes for change and brought peasants together in community settings where antiseigneural struggles, especially, had historically been a shared enterprise.

The strengthening of collective consciousness and organization associated with the drawing up of the *cahiers* better prepared the peasants to act for the insurrectionary ends of 1789. Some revolts, in fact, occurred in the immediate wake of the local assemblies. Apparently, this was because in certain instances peasants believed that the mere act of expressing grievances in the *cahiers* meant that particular payments or practices were henceforth abolished. Lefebvre reports the laments of royal officials on this point:

> "What is really tiresome," wrote Desmé de Dubuisson, lieutenant-general of Saumur *bailliage* during the elections, "is that these assemblies that have been summoned have generally believed themselves invested with some sovereign authority and that when they came to an end, the peasants went home with the ideas that henceforward they were free from tithes, hunting prohibitions and the payment of feudal dues" . . .

123

> And at the other end of the kingdom, the *sub-délégué* for Ploërmel uttered a cry of alarm on 4 July 1789: " . . . All the peasants around here and in my area generally are preparing to refuse their quota of sheaves to the tithe-collectors and say quite openly that there will be no collection without bloodshed on the senseless grounds that as the request for the abolition of these tithes was included in the *cahiers* . . . such an abolition has now come into effect."[39]

And, even if they did not occur until long after the *cahiers* had been drawn up, revolts typically emerged from the same settings in which such community meetings had always normally been held:

> So often did the same type of [anti-seigneurial] revolt break out in exactly the same way right up to 1792. Things would begin to stir on a Sunday: throughout the whole period, this day, like feast days in honour of local saints and *baladoires,* was always a most critical day; the peasants would go to mass, then having nothing else to do, would drift along to the local café: there was nothing like this for starting a riot.[40]

Another major condition facilitating the spread of revolts from 1789 was the disorganization and division of the upper strata, including those in charge of police and army. Especially after the Municipal Revolution in July, the propertied classes were in a poor position to repress the rural disturbances. Many *intendants* had been chased from their posts. Urban militias had seized arms and ammunition. Desertions from the army were increasing. Moreover, the peasant soldiers were as usual allowed to go home for the summer to help with the harvest, and they carried along news of the political events in the towns.[41]

Perhaps even more decisive was the fact that the supporters of the National Assembly were in a quandary: If (as many would have preferred) they used militias or called upon the royal army to protect property rights in the countryside, they would play into the hands of autocratic reaction. This was a chance that most were unprepared to take.[42] Only in a few localities did urban forces act against the peasants. Overall, the repressive forces were uncoordinated and not decisively deployed, thus encouraging the peasant revolts and resistance to spread across the country.

Finally, urban forces were vociferously attacking what they labeled "the aristocratic reaction." This probably encouraged peasants to focus on exploitative practices that they particularly associated with nobles—that is, seigneurial dues, tax exemptions, and tithes (most of which did *not* go to the curés for local church expenses). Through the *bailliage* assemblies, peasant delegates came into regular contact with urban leaders. And, ultimately, the Constituent Assembly's reform decrees would make it easier for the peasants to focus continuing effective resistance right through 1793 on tithes and feudal dues, rather than upon regular rents and taxes.

All of these factors specific to the political crisis of 1789 help to account

124

for the fact that there were *widespread* revolts of peasant communities especially against the seigneurial system commencing in the spring of 1789. To be sure, these conjunctural factors alone could not have been effective had it not been for the broad conduciveness of French rural structures to antiseigneurial peasant revolts. To varying degrees in different places, but more or less everywhere, seigneurs and tithe collectors for privileged absentee recipients vexed peasants who possessed considerable property, community autonomy, and antiseigneurial solidarity. There was, in short, a preexisting potential for antiseigneurial revolts. And the events of 1789 enhanced peasant solidarity and consciousness and weakened dominant-class (and particularly seigneurial) defenses in exactly the ways that could release that potential.

Regional variations in combinations of community structures, landholding patterns, forms of rent extraction, and eighteenth-century socioeconomic trends were apparently not very important in determining the general shape and incidence of peasant revolts in 1789 (however, much they may have had to do with which particular grievances were emphasized and which specific targets were attacked by individual peasant communities). What happened after 1788 was spurred by a *national* political crisis into which peasants everywhere – those with potential as well as actual grievances – were drawn through almost simultaneous, kingdom-wide events such as the drawing up of the *cahiers* and the Municipal Revolution. The peasant rebellion was indeed autonomous and spontaneous – but only within this national context. Peasant actions in 1789 thus cannot be understood merely as extensions of "subterranean" struggles carried on in localities throughout the eighteenth century. The French social historian Emmanuel Le Roy Ladurie has drawn upon detailed studies of rural social relations to show that there were marked regional variations in the form, extent, and intensity of peasant struggles during the (major-rebellion-free) period from 1675 to 1788.[43] "Antiseigneurial" struggles were important only in the north and northeast, where modernizing landlords were using "feudal" mechanisms to expand commercial farming against the resistance of peasant communities. In central, southern, and western regions, landlords were less powerful and less dynamic; and peasant struggles were mild and not notably antiseigneurial. Yet, as Le Roy Ladurie himself notes, in 1789, even peasant communities in Basse-Auvergne and Brittany, which had been quite passive between 1675 and 1788, readily joined in the antiseigneural revolts of 1789. And peasants in Languedoc merged their long-standing resistance to tithes into the general revolutionary ferment.

What these facts suggest is that, for the specific purpose of explaining the peasant revolution that began in 1789, one must assign greater weight to both (1) the broadly similar structural features characterizing agrarian social relations across all of France and (2) the national political dynamics

125

of 1789, than to the local and regional variations on the overall themes. It would be nice to be able to correlate detailed information on social–structural patterns and the exact processes of political mobilization for each locality and region. But until that is possible we should–and can–continue to make generalizations about the Revolution as a whole. For it was, by nature, quite other than simply an aggregation of local or regional events and processes. As Charles Tilly has very aptly put it, "a revolution is a state of a whole society, not of each segment of society."[44]

The Limits of the French Peasant Revolution

Although a full discussion of the outcomes of the French Revolution in the countryside depends upon an analysis (to be made in Chapter 5) of how urban politics and the consolidation of revolutionized state power intersected with the agrarian situation, nevertheless one final issue needs to be discussed in this chapter. We have already seen that, before the Revolution, straightforward proprietorial rents were probably the heaviest charge on the peasantry as a whole. They were surely more of a drain overall than seigneurial dues and tithes. Moreover it was noted that during the eighteenth century in France, rising population had promoted acute land hunger among the majority of peasants, who either owned or rented no land at all or else not enough to support their families by agricultural production alone. Yet it is a clear-cut fact about the French Revolution that, despite the crucial contribution of peasant revolts to its success, there was very little redistribution of land ownership as such. Only about 10 percent of the land, confiscated from the Church and from some emigrés, changed hands in the Revolution. And no more than half of that went to peasants.[45] Besides, recipients of confiscated lands had to purchase them from revolutionary governments hard-pressed for resources, and this requirement effectively barred the poorer peasants from acquiring new lands. An obvious question about the agrarian component of the French Revolution is why the rebellious peasantry, given that a majority were land hungry, stopped short of actually seizing the lands owned by seigneurs, the Church, and others, including rentier townsmen?

The answer lies in the intrinsic limits of village community solidarity.[46] As we have seen, the French peasantry was internally differentiated with respect to individual ownership of land, livestock, and equipment. Even more important, community customs, although they might limit the uses to which individuals' property could be put, did *not* involve any infringements on individual ownership, such as rules against private sales or periodic redistributions of individually owned plots. Instead community customs united groups of individual cultivators against outsiders whose rights and claims affected them all. Thus customary practices and universal self-

126

interest alike united entire villages against tithes, seigneurial dues and noble tax exemptions, and seigneurial claims on designated common lands. But any attacks on individual land-ownership would have threatened many rich- and middle-peasant smallholders, the very people who were the leaders of local communities. Furthermore, such attacks would have necessitated collective peasant action for entirely nontraditional goals.

The peasant revolution stopped well short of any such radical, antiproperty revolts. When it came to dues and tithes, collective resistance by peasant communities to paying them – or to buying them out as the Assembly first decreed in 1789 – was persistent. Because it was so unequivocal and persistent, this resistance was ultimately and permanently rewarded with success when these claims were abolished without compensation in 1793. Overall, the peasantry was relieved of a drain of about 10 percent on its income (although, again, the benefits went disproportionately to the better-off landowners). Especially as the Revolution wore on, peasant communities also frequently resisted the claims of the revolutionary authorities for taxes and manpower. But this form of traditional resistance was doomed to defeat insofar as it dared to emerge, because (as we shall see) the Revolution only strengthened centralized administration in France. As for the remaining seemingly 'logical" target for peasant revolt – larger private landholdings as such – no real movement for radical equalization developed. There were many (indeed a majority of) poorer peasants consciously in need. Nevertheless, the agrarian social patterns that facilitated and shaped the initial collective revolts against seigneurialism simultaneously blocked their extension against landed property in general.

Indeed, a most ironic result of the French peasant revolution was that its very success tended to undermine the residual community solidarity that had made the revolution possible in the first place. For the seigneur – the traditional local antagonist against whom the peasant community had been forged and united – was removed, institutionally speaking, from the scene. And the legal changes of the Revolution strengthened private property, thus facilitating the break-up of communal controls in agriculture. To be sure, many collective customs long survived the Revolution, and there were communally based peasant disturbances in France through the middle of the nineteenth century.[47] Nevertheless, the agrarian revolution of 1789–93 left French peasants more internally divided in their economic interests, and with less capacity for united action against nonpeasants. "What happened," writes R. R. Palmer, "was that during the Revolution the peasant bloc, the communal village, agrarian solidarity, were broken. Never again could there be a universal agrarian upheaval as in 1789."[48]

The agrarian revolts of the French Revolution, in sum, were the accomplishment of richer and poorer peasants alike. But the results were inordi-

127

nately to the benefit of those peasants who were already economically secure and well established as leaders in local politics.

THE REVOLUTION OF THE OBSHCHINAS: PEASANT RADICALISM IN RUSSIA

Turning from revolutionary France to Russia, one sees that similar factors – rentier agriculture, peasant community structures, and the breakdown of the repressive apparatus – explain the origins and nature of peasant revolts. Indeed the logic of events in Russia is more starkly apparent, for the picture is painted in bolder hues.

Serfdom was historically consolidated as the basis of the Russian autocracy "not in the absence of opposition, but in spite of it."[49] Fettered to estate lands, communities of peasants were held collectively responsible for payments and labor obligations to service-nobles who possessed nearly exclusive jurisdiction over them (unless they belonged directly to the tsar). With the establishment of the Imperial regime, heavy taxes and provision of military recruits were added to the obligations of the serf communities. Peasant resistance took the form of either flight to the open steppes or sporadic local outbursts. Occasionally these conflicts exploded into murderous assaults (especially on the nobles), when allies from the towns and the border Cossacks could be found. But by the end of the eighteenth century the Russian state had pacified the steppe frontiers and coopted the Cossacks as an Imperial gendarmarie. The Pugachev Rebellion of 1773–5 was the last massive revolt before 1905. Faced with a unified repressive apparatus, and without any countervailing military force, the peasants could express no more than sporadic, localized resistance – always more or less quickly and ruthlessly crushed.[50]

As we saw in Chapter 2, the "Emancipation" of the serfs in 1861 came at the initiative of the tsar and his bureaucrats, and its purpose was to enhance the social stability and political vitality of the Imperial system. How ironic, then, that the Emancipation itself set the stage for the agrarian revolution that uprooted the prerevolutionary social order in 1917. For the actual effect of this reform was to reinforce those structural patterns that rendered the Russian rural order prone to rebellion, without stimulating the economic development and social transformation of the bulk of the countryside that might have undercut the potential for rebellion.

Agrarian Conditions after the Emancipation

The Emancipation was initiated at the insistence of the Imperial authorities, but the details of its implementation were left to the nobles of the various regions. Partly because of the landlords' intervention and partly

128

because of the claims of the state after the 1860s, the peasants were liberated with more obligations to meet than they had experienced under serfdom.[51] In the infertile northern forest provinces, nobles ceded extra lands to peasants in return for inflated redemption payments that the ex-serfs could pay only by turning increasingly to seasonal industrial employments. In the black soil and southern steppe provinces, landlords "cut off" more than one-fifth of the lands formerly worked by the serfs so that the peasants would be forced to rent or work the landlords' soil. Former state serfs and those tied to Polish landlords enjoyed better terms in their settlements. But ex-domestic serfs were left landless. Furthermore, all allotment holders were to remain tied to the land for forty-nine years in order to pay off what the state advanced to the nobles in compensation for the loss of their serfs. As a whole, liberation from serfdom had little but bitterly ironic consequences for the peasants. Although the Emancipation alloted the peasants over one-half of the land, it left them economically worse-off. They still yearned for liberation from exploitative obligations and for access to the remaining lands of the nobles, which the peasants believed should be theirs to own and work for themselves.

Even more important than the economic consequences of the Emancipation was its institutional basis. For ownership of the lands allotted to the ex-serfs was assigned according to traditional patterns, which meant that collective ownership through the *obshchina* remained the predominant form of land tenure in European Russia.[52] The *obshchina* was a village commune that controlled property in land and distributed access to it among individual households. These often consisted of patriarchical extended families, each of which managed cultivation and reaped the fruits on an individual basis. Each household, depending upon its size, putatively had an equal right to an allotment of plowland and access to meadows, common pastures, and forests. Periodically the community's land was "repartitioned" in order to reaffirm the principle of equal access in the face of changing family composition.

Historically, the *obshchina* had been reinforced by the nobility and the state, because it provided a useful mechanism for the collective guarantee of peasant obligations and for assuring the maintenance (at subsistence levels) of the maximum number of serf "souls."[53] The Emancipation continued this tradition in a new way, for the state would act as intermediary in the process of redemption only if all of the households in a community jointly assumed responsibility for subsequent repayments over the forty-nine year period.[54] Once this was agreed, it became virtually impossible for an individual peasant to break his ties to the *obshchina*. To do so, he had to pay off his entire portion of redemption or find someone to buy him out. Moreover, individualist agricultural practices were discouraged; for any consolidation of holdings, or escape from the rhythm of collectively enforced three-field cultivation, required the assent of two-thirds of the village assembly. Finally, the communes themselves had to have government permission to sell off allotment lands. The effect, inescapably, was to keep the bulk of the peasants on the land, at work in the old ways.

To be sure, there were important regional variations in the development of Russian agriculture and relations of production in the last decades of the nineteenth century, for the Emancipation reinforced preexisting trends that furthered the commercialization of agriculture around the edges of European Russian while the core remained untransformed.[55] In the Baltic provinces an early emancipation in 1817 had freed serfs without land allotments and denied them the right to migrate; thus landlords enjoying access to Western grain markets were able to develop large-scale capitalist estates worked by wage laborers. In the western Ukraine, peasants rented allotment lands to previously established capitalist grower–processors of sugar beets and sought work, along with seasonal migrants, in these "factories in the fields." In the southeastern regions, railway construction allowed many former Imperial serfs, who had been freed with relatively generous allotments, to turn to commercial smallholder farming. Similarly, after 1890, with the construction of the Trans-Siberian railroad, new settlement in Siberia was promoted by the state. And those petty nobles and wealthier peasants who could take advantage of this opportunity founded small capitalist farms without regard to traditional forms of community or cultivation. Finally, in the northern forested provinces (of the Lakes, Central Industrial, and Northern regions), where agriculture could not be commercially profitable except near big cities, nobles avidly sold off their remaining lands after the 1860s. In the same areas, peasant communities saddled with extensive allotment lands accelerated the pre-Emancipation tendency of sending seasonal migrants to industrial jobs in the cities. This trend particularly intensified with the growth of factories after 1880. And, when the Stolypin reforms of 1906 allowed peasants to break their communal ties, many northern peasant–workers took advantage of this opportunity to migrate permanently to urban areas.

Yet the massive core of agricultural Russia—comprising the many provinces of the Central Black Earth and the adjacent steppes of the middle Volga region—remained largely uncommercialized, with traditional relations of production surviving in modified form.[56] This was the area where the Emancipation had left "cut-off" lands in the hands of the nobles, and where the controls of the *obshchina* over peasant property and cultivation were strongest and almost universally present. Some poorer nobles sold their lands. (Indeed, by 1905, Russian peasants in general had increased their share of ownership to nearly two-thirds of all farmlands.).[57] Yet many landlords held on by renting out pieces of their estate lands in return for labor dues or shares of the crop.

Map 2. *The main regions of European Russia. Source:* Hugh Seton-Watson, *The Russian Empire 1801–1917* (New York: Oxford University Press, 1967), p. 770.

> Since the peasants were tied to the soil and increasingly land hungry the noble could easily rent out his estate in small plots for extraordinarily high rates and live from the proceeds. Rentier relations were easily substituted for the traditional [noble–serf] relation of subsistence agriculture. This enabled the noble to draw an income from the estate lands while leaving the bulk of the responsibility for managing cultivation and providing the implements and livestock to the peasants.[58]

The renters were frequently whole peasant communities. Otherwise the leased lands appear to have gone primarily to peasant families (tied to communities) who simply needed more soil to work for subsistence. Especially in the core provinces, land purchases and rentals did not generate a strong rich-peasant stratum. Rather such purchases and rentals "served as a prop to subsistence cultivation among those elements of the peasantry which still retained the minimal requisite capital to till the land."[59]

On the eve of the 1917 Revolution, fully one-half to two-thirds of the peasant households in Russia were still essentially subsistence producers.[60] These were concentrated in the central regions of rentier agriculture and included a mixture of allotment holders and tenants who coexisted within the traditional *obshchina* framework. Theirs was a continuous struggle for survival in the face of deepening poverty brought about by the coincidence of stagnant technology, poor market opportunities, and rising population – all in addition to the heavy exactions imposed upon peasant incomes by the landlords and the state.

Although the Emancipation and its aftermath made economic survival even more problematic for its members, paradoxically, the peasant community was freed in most respects from political control by the nobility and its estate managers. The peasants were given rights of self-government under the supervision of bureaucratic agents of the Imperial State.[61] The *mir*, or village assembly of all household heads, became the center of formal political authority. In addition to its basic economic functions of allocating land and regulating the crop cycle, the *mir* now had responsibilities for the enforcement of community obligations for taxes and redemption payments as well as the regulation of the passport system governing movements of peasants from the village. The elected elder, traditionally an informal leader of the collectively self-governed *mir*, was made responsible to and removable by land captains and police, the official overseers of village affairs. In this sense, the peasant conduct of village affairs was modified by bureaucratic intrusions. Still, the overall effect of the post-Emancipation measures was to increase the peasants' collective handling of their own local political affairs and thus to render the villages more autonomous and solidary against outsiders.

How could there have been a set of conditions more conducive to agrarian revolution? A nobility in economic and political decline maintained,

132

nevertheless, a foothold in the countryside – tied to the peasants by baldly exploitative and functionless rentier relations. Meanwhile, the collective institutions and political independence of the peasant communities had been strengthened, while the peasants were burdened with heavier outside demands to be met with unchanged methods of production. Indeed, as the taxes necessitated by Witte's industrialization programs coincided with the general agricultural crisis to render the peasants' situation desperate, local disturbances occurred more frequently after 1890, even in the face of sure repression.[62] All that was necessary to ensure a general conflagration was the failure of coercive controls. That happened temporarily in 1905, and again – this time irreversibly – in 1917. Both times the occasion was war and defeat for the Imperial military.

The Impact of the Political Crises of 1905 and 1917

The Revolution of 1905 began in the cities but soon spread to the countryside. With the army bogged down in the futile war with Japan and the government preoccupied with urban unrest, peasants joined the fray beginning in the spring of 1905.[63] For a time the peasants were free from effective repression. As Gerschenkron points out:

> The government had long developed a simple technique for dealing with peasant violence or resistance. An army detachment would be sent into the riotous village, dispersing the crowds, if necessary by the use of firearms, arresting the ringleaders, staging mass whippings, and then departing with peace and order re-established. Those methods were efficient enough as long as riots were few and far apart. When they became a nearly ubiquitous mass phenomenon, with large segments of the government forces deflected by the war in the Far East, and, when in addition peasant rebellion coincided with a widespread strike movement in transportation, communications, and manufacturing, the revolution was at hand.[64]

Following its own rhythm punctuated by the seasons, the peasant movement reached a peak in the autumn of 1905, then tapered off, only to revive substantially in the spring and summer of 1906. During the last half of 1906, however, the government – having reintroduced the army into European Russia after hastily concluding the Russo-Japanese War in the fall of 1905 – was able, bit by bit, to suppress violently the peasant rebellion.

Peasant actions during the abortive Revolution of 1905 followed patterns that render certain possible explanations more plausible than others. Data concerning what happened come from a questionnaire sent out in 1907 by the Imperial Free Economic Society to correspondents in forty-seven out of fifty provinces of European Russia. Analyses of this information have been made by G. T. Robinson, in his *Rural Russia Under the*

133

Old Regime, and by Maureen Perrie, in an article entitled "The Russian Peasant Movement of 1905–1907."[65]

The immediate peasant objectives in the Revolution of 1905 were overwhelmingly economic, not political. Their quarrel was with the landlords, and conflicts with police and other governmental representatives came mainly as a by-product of these conflicts with the landlords. According to Perrie:

> The forms assumed by the movement against the landowners were determined primarily by the system of land-tenure and agrarian relationships in each given locality. The movement was strongest in those areas, such as the Central Black Earth, the Volga, and the Ukraine, where the exploitation of the peasant renters by the gentry landowners was greatest, or where the severest hardships had been caused by the transition from renting to large-scale capitalist farming. Here the predominant form of the movement was the attack on the landowner's estate. This often involved the destruction of the manor house and outbuildings, to ensure the "master" would never return, and the seizure of the estate lands and property by the peasants. In some areas, such as those in the west, where the estates were worked by an agricultural proletariat, strikes for better wages and conditions were common.[66]

Respondents to the 1907 questionnaire downplayed the effects of agitation by revolutionary parties on the peasants, but they emphasized that local leadership frequently fell to peasants with extralocal contacts and experiences as town laborers or army recruits. However, Robinson points out that

> the practice of going away temporarily to the towns for wage-work was much more widespread, and this particular kind of opportunity for mass contact with urban ideas was therefore more general, in the villages north of the forest-*step* boundary than in those to the southward, whereas the economic situation of the peasants was in general more difficult in the *guberniias* lying in a broad band along and below this boundary; and ... with exceptions ... it was not to the north of this boundary, but to the south of it that the most serious agrarian disturbances of this revolutionary period took place.[67]

Furthermore, Robinson argues that it was "probably not a matter of pure coincidence that among the twenty *guberniias* [provinces] in which the landlords suffered the heaviest losses during the disturbances of the Autumn of 1905, sixteen show a predominance of repartitional tenure over hereditary holding by individual peasant households."[68] Finally, Perrie maintains that "in most cases, the peasants participated in the movement as an entire village or commune... ,"[69] and that, in the name of the traditional "labor principle" of equal access to the land by all families that worked it, the peasant communities frequently attacked rich peasants with separate individual farms as well as the estates of the nobility.[70]

134

From all of this it makes sense to conclude that the deepest impulses of the agrarian revolts in 1905–7 came from the impoverished peasant *obshchinas* of the core provinces of European Russia. The basic "reason" for revolt was economic hardship, and a temporary opportunity was provided by the Russo-Japanese War. Quite traditional ideas and forms of community solidarity shaped the struggle: "The organizational basis of the peasant revolution was, so to speak, 'ready made' in the villages."[71]

Certainly this was the conclusion reached by the tsarist authorities. Having squeaked by the Revolution of 1905, the tsarist regime abandoned its policy of shoring up the peasant commune. It undertook in the so-called Stolypin reforms to promote the break-up of repartitional lands into private holdings and to facilitate land sales by poorer peasants and purchases by richer ones. Between 1905 and 1917, these measures, in tandem with general economic developments, helped somewhat to alleviate agrarian stagnation, promote permanent migration to urban industrial areas, and increase economic differentiation and individualism in the countryside. Still, by 1917–although the proportion of peasant households officially holding allotments under hereditary as opposed to communal tenure had increased from less than one-fourth to more than one-half–only one-tenth of all peasant families had, since 1905, been resettled on consolidated individual holdings.[72] One must also consider that "after a separation of title alone, the old land-linkage was still preserved in many of its aspects, and that even a physical consolidation failed in many cases to cut the last tie of common property." Thus one cannot but agree with Robinson that "a great deal still survived of the old collective interests and the old apparatus for collective action . . . "[73] Even where the new measures were most successful in promoting permanent migration by the poor or separation by the rich peasants, they may simply have reinforced the radical solidarity and control over the village assemblies of the middle peasants who remained behind. Moreover, the Stolypin reforms had "little impact on the central provinces where the peasant problem was most acute."[74]

Not surprisingly, therefore, the agrarian revolution of 1917 closely resembled that of 1905 in its forms and rhythm.[75] In the wake of the February Revolution against tsardom in the cities, the peasant movement against the local estates commenced in the spring with encroachments upon landlords' properties and the withholding of rent or labor services. Then the conflict gradually accelerated and deepened into direct, violent attacks on manors and seizures of estate lands to be redistributed among the peasants. The climax was reached by the autumn of 1917 and was officially sanctioned after the Bolsheviks came to national-urban power in October. As in 1905, peasant actions were most violent and radical in "the block of provinces south and southeast of Moscow which made up the Central Agricultural and Middle Volga Regions,"[76] where rentier landlords and repartitional

135

communes prevailed. To be sure, landlords elsewhere were, sooner or later, also driven out—either through less violent direct actions by peasants and agricultural laborers, or through the administrative extension of revolutionary policies, or both. But the peasant movement in the core provinces set the pace and tone of the agrarian revolution.

The really important difference between 1917 and 1905 lay in what happened with the army. Whereas in 1906 a basically intact Imperial army could be used to crush rural revolts, during the summer and fall of 1917 the bloated army that had been mobilized to fight a total European war disintegrated. The decisive defeat of the June offensive into Austria was what finally turned the front-line troops defeatist.[77] After that, the dissolution of the army and the deepening of agrarian revolt became intertwined. Former soldiers returned to the villages to join in, and often lead, the land seizures. The Provisional Government had no reliable troops to suppress the spontaneous and violent movement against property, which it never could accept and endorse. And the peasants became increasingly emboldened as they sensed that no official force could be brought against them, and as the social power of their collective solidarity was reinforced by the arms of the ex-soldiers. "Apart from resentment at the Government's ineffective attempts at repression and from the natural momentum with the passing of time, the upswelling of the peasant movement in the autumn of 1917 is explained by the arrival of more and more soldiers, demobilized and 'self-demobilized,' in the villages."[78] Above all, the soldiers' arrival, and the collapse of official repression that it implied, sealed the success of the peasants revolution in 1917, in contrast to its costly defeat in 1906–7.

The Leveling Outcome in Russia

What the Russian peasants wanted most out of the Revolution and what they immediately achieved was possession of the land and the available means for working it.[79] Virtually everywhere the landed estates of the nobility were seized or requisitioned, and their arable land, woods and water, livestock, buildings and tools were divided up by the peasants. In many (though by no means all) cases the proprietor himself or herself was violently attacked and the estate buildings burned in order to ensure the irrevocability of the land transfer: "One man explained in quaint language what this aim was: 'the *muzhiki* [peasants] are destroying the squire's nests so that the little bird will never be able to return'—the 'bird' here being a euphemism for large-scale landed property in general."[80] In addition to the landed estates, the peasants, especially in the core provinces, seized the farms of the *khutors*, peasants who had consolidated individual properties and separated them from the *obshchina* (perhaps in response to the Stolypin reforms). Similarly, they pressured peasants who had enclosed individual farms within the villages to once again submit to the collective disciplines of repartition and coordinated cultivation.

In the aggregate, the Russian peasantry gained possession of the land and resources formerly held by the landlords and they freed themselves from rental obligations to the former estate owners. Of course there were losses as well as gains, because much of the land seized had formerly been rented out to peasants and because possibilities for wage labor disappeared with the estates. One contemporary statistical estimate showed an average increase in land held by the peasants of about three to five acres per household.[81] But there were enormous variations across provinces and even localities – because the increase in peasant lands depended upon the exact location of the noble and tsarist properties that were taken. Moreover, not all of the lands gained were equally useful. And not all were actually cultivated even if they were useful, because their new owners often lacked the necessary tools or seeds. Overall, many peasant households failed to gain much from the land revolution.[82]

Of more interest and significance than aggregate results were the distributional effects within the peasantry. By 1919, virtually all agriculture in Russia had become the activity of peasant smallholders. For, as Chamberlin has pointed out, the "general result of the wholesale peasant land seizure of 1917 was a sweeping levelling in peasant agriculture."[83] Richer peasant households were proportionately fewer and possessed on the average less land and fewer cows and horses. Households formerly of middling wealth seem to have held their own or gained a bit. And certainly the middling ranks were proportionately swelled by the agrarian revolution. For the big gainers were previously land-poor peasants, who especially benefited from the division of the estates. Likewise many (though not all) landless agricultural laborers and others without land who returned to the villages during the crisis were allotted modest holdings.[84]

Plainly, the accomplishments of the Russian peasant revolution of 1917 contrast in important ways with the accomplishments of the French peasant revolution of 1789. In France, seigneurial claims and controls were abolished by the rebellious peasants. But private property, including both larger estates and rich peasant farms, was respected and not attacked. And within the French peasantry the big winners were those rich and middle peasants who already owned their own land (and other means of production). In Russia, however, the peasant revolution not only abolished rental claims of landlords but also seized and redistributed most private landed properties. This worked to the inordinate benefit of the less well-to-do and land-poor peasants. Still it is true that the processes of the French and Russian peasant revolutions were similar in many ways. And both the similarities and the differences can, analytically speaking, be explained in comparable terms.

137

For one thing, in Russia as in France, the peasant village assembly, relatively autonomous as it was from outside control, provided the organizational basis for spontaneous and autonomous revolts. As Teodor Shanin says of the peasant rebellion in Russia: "Its organization was remarkable. Village assemblies decided how to divide the non-peasant property in each locality. Then action was taken, all households being compelled to participate in order to ensure success—and equal responsibility in the event of possible subsequent reprisals."[85] Higher authorities, try as they might to control or channel the local peasant revolts, had little success.[86] Land committees, set up by the Provisional Government as part of a bureaucracy to moderate the land revolution, were infiltrated from below and redirected to the peasants' own goals of land appropriation and local autonomy. Similar things happened to Socialist-Revolutionary Party organs and Bolshevik-inspired soviets during 1917–18. As a result, no one (the Bolsheviks after October included) could preserve the economic integrity of large estates. And the nature and extent of property redistributions were determined at village, district, or, at most, county levels, depending upon the extent of grass-roots cooperation among neighboring villages. The ironic result could be that peasants in some parts of provinces or counties got far more land to divide up than others, with higher authorities unable to promote wider redistribution. Yet it all makes sense when one realizes that the land revolution was above all autonomously controlled by the local village assemblies themselves.

Another comparison with France points to a difference between the two peasant revolutions. In both cases locally controlled peasant revolts were influenced by the specific nature of the society-wide political crises within the context of which they occurred. In France, the revolutionary crisis was primarily an internal political development. Although the royal administration and army were eventually weakened enough to become ineffective against the peasants, there was nothing similar to the sudden breakup of the huge armies that had been mobilized to fight World War I in Russia. Not only was that breakup essential to the success of the Russian peasant revolution, it also influenced the rapidity and the shape of the peasant accomplishments. For much of the intravillage politics of rural Russia in 1917 took the form of younger men, with guns and ideas brought home from their wartime military experience, challenging the authority and caution of the older traditional leaders of the *mir*, who were also often heads of patriarchal extended families. The result was almost certainly to push the land revolution to its conclusion sooner and more violently. Furthermore, part of the explanation for the leveling down of richer peasant households that occurred during 1917–18 is that formerly extended families were tending to break up during the crisis, leaving more households overall with smaller average size and wealth.[87] Some of this surely occurred as a by-product of the self-assertion of the younger men. This, in turn, can be attributed to the fact that Russia's revolutionary political crisis came in the midst, and because of, national defeat in a massive, modern war. By contrast, in France the revolutionary political crisis first impinged upon the villages when the king called for elections to the Estates-General. Radicalizing as this was, we can imagine that the village assemblies for the occasion were convened and led, not (as in Russia) by militant "Young Turks," but by the usual (older as well as richer) community influentials.

Finally, we come to the common analytic factor that makes sense of the major difference between the two peasant revolutions: Just as the socioeconomic basis of the French peasant community explained the accomplishments and limits of the peasant revolution in France, so did the qualitatively different basis of the *obshchina* provide the key to the content of the peasant victory in Russia. French peasant communities, based as they were simply upon the coordination of the agricultural cycle and the management of residual common lands, supported the antiseigneurial revolts of 1789. But then they disintegrated in the face of the conflicting interests of richer and poorer peasants over private property rights. In contrast, the Russian *obshchina*, though it recognized and made possible landholding and cultivation by individual peasant households, did not legitimate private landed property as such. Rather "all land belonged to God," and the peasant community as a whole strove to gain access to as much as possible and then distribute it roughly equally to households (according either to their number of adult male laborers, or their number of "eaters," or some combination of these criteria). Furthermore, all land allocations were only temporary, until the next periodic repartition, when individual households would gain or lose strips of land according to their relative size. Obviously peasant communities with this sort of socioeconomic basis did nothing to enforce respect for private property (especially not that of exploiting landlords) among Russian peasants. Moreover, the repartitional aspect of the *obshchina* gave enormous leverage to advocates of equalitarianism within the Russian village.

In Russia during 1917, the pace of the peasant revolution was set where the *obshchina* was strongest. And even in areas where communal tenure or repartition had fallen into disuse, these practices were frequently revived for the revolutionary occasion. Contemporary observers wrote that the "land commune, coming alive with quite exceptional force, was undoubtedly the basic ideological kernel of the social mechanism which in fact carried out the agrarian revolution within the peasantry itself."[88] Understandably so, since the *obshchina* was the best and most familiar instrument at hand for the peasants to strike out effectively against their landlord antagonists. And it was the collective interest of the *obshchina* in expanding its landholdings, as well as its traditional deemphasis of private property rights, that rendered the Russian peasant revolution so all-encompassing and leveling in its accomplishments.

TWO COUNTERPOINTS: THE ABSENCE OF PEASANT REVOLTS IN THE ENGLISH AND GERMAN REVOLUTIONS

The agrarian upheavals that contributed indispensably to the French and Russian social revolutions could happen because both Old Regimes were in similar ways structurally prone to peasant revolts against landlords. Given that revolutionary political crises had deposed the absolute monarchs and disorganized centralized administrations and armies, agrarian class relations and local political arrangements in France and Russia afforded peasant communities sufficient solidarity and autonomy to strike out against the property and privileges of landlords. Conditions so conducive to peasant revolts were by no means present in all countries. And their absence could account for why a successful social revolution could not occur, even given a societal political crisis. Again, as in our examination of the causes of revolutionary political crises in Chapter 2, we can help to confirm the appropriateness of the hypotheses set forth for positive cases of social revolution by making contrasts to cases in which successful social revolutions did not occur. The English Revolution of the seventeenth century and the German Revolution of 1848–50 are two such cases. Though their respective characteristics and outcomes were quite different—the English Revolution was a successful *political* revolution, whereas the German Revolution was a *failed* social revolution—both were prevented from becoming successful social-revolutionary transformations. This was true in large part because the agrarian class and political structures of the English and German (East of the Elbe) old regimes gave predominant power to landlords and not to peasant communities. The national political capacities and interests of the English and the East Elbian landed upper classes were not the same; hence the differences between the Revolutions as wholes. But, for our purposes here, the significant point is that, in contrast to France and Russia, English and German landlords could not be successfully challenged from below, even during revolutionary political crises. To see why in a bit more detail, let us look briefly at each case in turn.

The English Parliamentary Revolution

The key events of the English Revolution span half of the seventeenth century, from the calling of the Long Parliament in 1640 through the "Glorious Revolution" of 1688–9, though most of the relevant action

140

took place between 1640 and 1660.[89] In many ways the dynamics of the English Revolution resembled those of the French. Charles I, facing a war-induced financial crisis, convened an upper-class-dominated parliament. This parliament quickly went on the offensive against his policies and demanded institutional changes to limit royal powers. Parliament benefited from popular demonstrations (especially by journeymen, artisans, and other petty propertied people)[90] and from a municipal revolution in London.[91] This upheaval gave it some of the administrative and military resources it needed to forestall an attempted royal coup and later to field forces against the royalists in the Civil War. Successive crises split and polarized the original revolutionary supporters. And before it was ultimately reversed in the 1650s and '60s, the radicalization of the Revolution culminated in the arrest and execution of the king, the declaration of a republic, the popular assertion of democratic political and social demands, and the emergency establishment of a centralized political and military dictatorship. All of these were very similar indeed to the developments that would mark the trajectory of the French Revolution 150 years later.

Partly because of such similarities and partly because both Revolutions happened in countries that became capitalist, liberal democracies, the English and the French Revolutions are often similarly labeled "bourgeois revolutions." Whatever the appropiateness of this label for either Revolution,[92] it should not blind us to the very important differences between them. Though the English Revolution was certainly a successful revolution, it was not a *social* revolution like the French. It was accomplished not through class struggle but through a civil war between segments of the dominant landed class (with each side drawing allies and supporters from all of the other classes and strata). And whereas the French Revolution markedly transformed class and social structures, the English Revolution did not. Instead it revolutionized the political structure of England. It abolished the right (and institutional capacity) of the king to intervene in local political, economic, and religious affairs, and, in general, forced him to rule only with the confidence and legislative support of Parliament.[93] Henceforth Parliament was by law regularly convened, and it became the central arena of British national politics, securely and solely controlled by the dominant class until the nineteenth century. To be sure, this political revolution functioned to further capitalist socioeconomic development in England. Yet it did so not because it suddenly placed a new class in power, but because it reinforced and sealed the direct political control of a dominant class that already had many (well interspersed and socially integrated) members engaged in capitalist agriculture and commerce.

Indeed, if we want to understand the English Revolution, we must look to the class that launched it, led it throughout, and ultimately benefited from it. That class, though it had merchant components, was fundamen-

141

tally a landed upper class, consisting of a small elite stratum of juridical aristocrats and a large majority of landed gentry (who were socially regarded as gentlemen, though not legally ennobled). In sharp contrast to the aristocrats, seigneurs, and other *privilégiés* in France after 1789, this English landed upper class was not in any way (structurally) displaced by the Revolution. True, there were challenges to its hegemony especially from the Levellers, popular democrats somewhat similar to (though much less important than) the *sans culottes* of the French Revolution.[94] But what was missing in England—something that would have constituted both a direct assault on the base of power of the dominant class and an opening for urban radicals—were widespread peasant revolts against landlords. And it is not difficult to understand why such revolts were missing when we examine the agrarian class and local political structures that existed in England at the time.

By the seventeenth century, the English peasantry, though by no means as marginal as it would eventually become, had lost the battle to retain control over the approximately one-half of the agricultural land that it had held subject to the lords in medieval times.[95] There was a certain tragic irony here. Like the French peasantry, the English peasantry had won its freedom from serfdom during the fourteenth and fifteenth centuries, but unlike the French, the English ex-serfs were not finally able to achieve secure tenure in their customary holdings. At first, they seemed to be doing better in this respect than the French, because they escaped seigneurial dues and began to establish clear freehold claims to their tenements. But English landlords succeeded in expanding their own domains and in keeping many peasants as "copyholders," which meant that their holdings could be sold or inherited only subject to the payment of fines to the lord. And, as economic historian Robert Brenner writes, "in the end entry fines often appear to have provided the landlords with the lever they needed to dispose of customary peasant tenants."[96] The way was left open for landlords to engross and enclose large holdings to rent out (capitalist-style) to leasehold tenants, a development that was greatly encouraged by expanding market opportunities for wool and grain producers from the sixteenth century on. The upshot was that by the seventeenth century, the English landlords seem to have owned at least two-thirds of the land, which (unlike the French) they were not merely renting to peasants in small plots but often leasing to commercial tenants.[97]

Similarly, during the entire period (from the sixteenth century on), the peasant community was in many places being polarized from within by, on the one hand, the rise of prosperous commerically oriented yeomen farmers (some becoming tenants of great landlords and others rich freeholders) and, on the other hand, the decline into poverty or insecurity of husbandmen with inadequate land.[98] These became increasingly dependent

142

upon servants' work or (where available) wage labor. Unlike the situation in France, where of course some such economic differentiation also occurred, rich and poor could not unite against seigneurial dues and controls that affected all peasant landholders, for these did not exist in England.

As if such socioeconomic impediments were not enough, local political arrangements in seventeenth-century England were even more unfavorable to widespread and concerted peasant actions against landlords; and these affected peasants everywhere, even in the many places where enclosing landlords did not hold sway. There were no peasant-run village assemblies partially subject to a royal bureaucracy and partially shielded from landlord dominance by that same bureaucracy. For the kings (or queens) of England had no paid bureaucracy or standing armies that penetrated (even nominally) into the localities. Instead, from the time of Henry VIII, they ruled (if at all) through unpaid appointees from among the county landed gentry.[99] Landed gentlemen served as lords' lieutenants, deputy lieutenants, justices of the peace, and sheriffs. And yeomen closely allied to them often served in important subordinate offices such as that of constable.[100] Parish clergy, far from being as in France potential allies or protectors of the peasants, were appointed by and loyal to the landlords. These county landed establishments, as they may very appropriately be labeled, controlled all important political and judicial affairs. They dispensed justice, ran the militia, enforced the poor laws, and did whatever implementing of royal decisions they were inclined to do. Peasants as a whole had no unity or autonomy in the face of these county establishments. For the yeomen were in effect coopted as subordinate officials, and the laborers and servants were typically strongly tied to their landlord masters. Even when local disorders such as resistence to enclosures could be mustered, sanctioning instruments of cooptation and repression were close at hand for threatened landlords.

Indeed, it was from its bastions of county-level political power that the English landed upper class came together through its elected representatives to Parliament in 1640–1 to challenge the would-be absolutist Charles I in the name of upper-class liberty. And throughout the Civil War, even as national political quarrels divided the "natural rulers," county-level political machineries continued to operate. Mostly these machineries remained under the leadership of whichever landed families were tied to the ascendant faction; and, at the same time, kinship and social relations still functioned to tie the local landed classes together.[101] Only at the radical height of the Revolution did the county committees that governed in each locality sometimes fall under the leadership of people not from the dominant class, such as yeomen. Yet even yeomen, much as they might sympathize with Leveller ideas about political democracy for all economically independent citizens, were not interested in leading (or allowing) a peasant revolt against landlords.

143

Besides, the radical phase of the Revolution, with its dual threat (from the viewpoint of the landed upper class) of political centralization and social leveling, soon passed. The landed upper class compromised its way back into a restored monarchy, though this time one that had to respect the ultimate control by the county rulers and their Parliament over military forces, taxation, church affairs, and economic regulation. When another Stuart monarch started to forget in the 1680s, he was quickly reminded (and replaced), this time with very little fuss. Meanwhile, the preindustrial English lower classes remained on the defensive politically and economically as the country moved toward capitalist industrialization. They—especially the peasantry—had not possessed the collective strength to challenge successfully the landed upper class, even when it quarreled with the monarchy and within its own ranks during the English Revolution. Consequently, that Revolution remained an upper-class–dominated political revolution, rather than developing into a social revolution from below.

Now we move through two-hundred years of history to look briefly at another revolution, this time an aborted social revolution, where the absence of peasant revolts against an entrenched landed class also made a difference.

The Failed German Revolution of 1848–50

The German Revolution of 1848–50 was really a series of revolts centered primarily in the urban capitals of the various separate monarchies and principalities that comprised the loosely integrated Germanic Confederation. These were but a subset of a rash of similar revolts that swept through all of Europe. Yet they culminated in a concerted attempt to establish through the work of the Frankfurt Parliament a unified, liberal-democratic German nation, with the former Prussian king as an elected constitutional monarch.[102]

The social and political program worked out by the German liberals assembled at Frankfurt—liberal civil rights for all citizens; representative government; and removal of social and political obstacles to national unification and economic freedom—was not much different from that enacted in 1789–90 by the constitutional monarchists of the French Revolution. Nor should this seem surprising, because Germany in 1848 was not much more economically or politically developed than France in 1789. And the social composition of the Frankfurt Parliament (mostly lawyers in and outside of government employ) was very similar to the composition of the French revolutionary Assemblies.[103]

There were also important similarities between the dynamics of the German Revolution and those of the French. In both cases, liberal politicians rose to official power when monarchs were put on the defensive by

144

popular uprisings, especially those of urban artisans, shopkeepers, and journeymen disgruntled by harsh economic conditions in recessions. It is often stressed in accounts of the German Revolution that the goals of such popular rebels – lower food prices; higher wages; political guarantees of guild organization and/or employment – were irrelevant to the political objectives of the liberal politicians and antithetical to the dominant laissez-faire liberal economic ideas of the time. Indeed, this is typically cited as a major explanation for the failure of the German Revolution.[104] But, of course, during the French Revolution, popular and "bourgeois liberal" goals were equally at odds,[105] and yet that Revolution succeeded.

What really set the German Revolution apart from the French, and accounted crucially for the failure of 1848–50, was the ability of the Prussian king, after a year of revolutionary politics, to put a decisive stop to the whole affair. He was able to ignore the laboriously constructed Frankfurt Constitution, disband the Parliament, and crush any resistance throughout Germany by force. We can easily imagine that, by 1790 in France, Louis XVI would have dearly loved to have been able to do the same. But he could not. What accounts for the difference?

Part of the answer lies in the contrasting behavior of the French dominant class in 1787–8 and the Prussian Junkers in 1848. We have already noted that the French privileged strata, in launching the French Revolution, rendered the royal armies unreliable as instruments for suppressing the initial popular demonstrations and set in motion processes inside and outside the army that facilitated the eventual breakdown of military discipline. In contrast, the German Revolution was not launched by noble revolts against monarchs. Rather it was triggered by news of the suddenly successful Parisian revolution against Louis Philippe, an event that emboldened urban rioters in German capitals and rendered German monarchs nervous about their ability to remain in power without making political concessions to liberals. Specifically, in Prussia, "revolutionary events" all over Europe combined with news of Metternich's fall in Austria and with the eruption of violence in Berlin between soldiers and popular protestors to inaugurate dramatic changes. The rather timid Frederick William IV, acting against the vehement advice of his military advisors, withdrew his army from Berlin, authorized the creation of an urban militia, and turned ministerial powers over to liberals.

Thus the Prussian monarchy (like many other German monarchies) was perhaps not quite so weakened when the liberals took over as was the Bourbon monarchy in France by 1789. However, a potentially social-revolutionary situation had emerged just as surely in Prussia in the spring of 1848 as in France by the early summer of 1789. In both cases the monarchy was on the defensive in the face of a municipal revolution, and its military monopoly and authority were weakened. When Louis XVI sent his troops away from Paris after July 14, 1789, he too, or some of his supporters, must have hoped that they could be used if necessary later on. But Louis XVI's initial hesitancies evolved into a rout for him, and for the monarchy and the nobility, whereas the equally indecisive and timid Frederick William IV proved able to change his mind a year later.

Surely an important part of the explanation for the contrasting evolution of events lies in the failure of popular, particularly peasant, revolts to promote the dissolution of the Prussian armies in 1848–9. In contrast, by 1790, after a year and a half of urban and rural popular revolts throughout all of France, the French royal armies had suffered mass desertions and politicization leading to breakdowns of discipline, as well as the loss of thousands of noble officers spurred to emigrate in substantial part because of the popular revolts.[106] (Besides, if the comparison to Russia in 1917 is considered, we may note that there peasant revolts accelerated the dissolution of standing armies even though the revolutionary political crisis was not originally launched by dominant class actions against the monarchy.)

Not that peasant revolts were entirely absent in Germany in 1848. In fact there *were* intense antiseigneurial revolts – apparently similar in objectives, forms, and results to the peasant revolts of the French Revolution – in the small states of southwestern Germany and moderately widespread ones of the same kind in central Germany (Saxony and Hanover). But East of the Elbe, except for some outbreaks in Schleswig-Holstein and Silesia, no major peasant insurrections developed. However restive they may have been, the peasants of the Junker heartlands, recruiting grounds for the officers and men of the formidable Prussian armies, did not revolt.[107] Indeed, the differential incidence of peasant revolts in Germany in 1848 corresponds to the contrast between features of agrarian sociopolitical structure in the regions of Germany west versus east of the River Elbe along the very lines that our general hypotheses about conditions for peasant revolts would predict.

Generally speaking, agrarian structures west of the Elbe in Germany resembled those of France. Land was divided up into small, scattered units to a large extent owned or rented by individual peasants, but with patterns of land use still subject to significant community controls. Peasants had become free in their persons and possessed secure rights to own and transfer lands. And the feudal prerogatives of the lords survived primarily in the form of rents, fees, and dues, and weak rights to influence the use and transfer of the former seigneurial lands. Local political jurisdiction had mostly passed to the agents of monarchs anxious to afford the communities of peasant taxpayers independence and protection from encroachments by the nontaxpaying nobility.[108]

In stark contrast, east of the Elbe the Junker landlords were in a much stronger position than their western noble cousins. As David Landes writes:

> Noble estates *(Rittergüter)* tended to be large and the demesne was farmed as a commercial enterprise; the bulk of the lord's income came from the sale of cash crops, primarily cereals, both within Germany and abroad. Even peasant homesteads often stood apart and were not subject to the communal servitudes of the open-field system.[109]

Throughout the eighteenth century, the Junker estates were worked by serf laborers subject to virtually unlimited claims on their persons and labor time. The claims were readily enforced because the Junkers were not only estate lords but also the local agents of the Prussian state. Like the English gentry, the Junker landlords controlled justice and military units for their own purposes. After the Reform Movement, many serfs received personal "freedom," but the continuation of the Junkers' monopoly on local administrative sovereignty, and the paucity and precariousness of peasant landholdings in the east, combined to guarantee that many ex-serfs would remain as laborers on the *Rittergüter*.[110] Certainly the abolition of serfdom put the peasants east of the Elbe in no better position to revolt collectively against their oppression in the nineteenth century than they had been in the fifteenth through eighteenth centuries. Thus their relative quiescence in 1848, while their already much better-off counterparts in the west were revolting against the remnants of seigneurial authority, is hardly surprising.

Yet the consequences for Germany were momentous. Not only did the class power of the Junkers remain intact, so did the military capacity for counterrevolutionary reversal of gains already achieved in 1848. If there had been widespread and continuing peasant revolts in Prussia in 1848, then, given that the Prussian army was recruited almost exclusively in the rural districts, its officer corps would have been disrupted and its rank and file "would have been susceptible to revolutionary propaganda. As it was the Prussian army remained a reliable instrument in the hands of the King."[111] And Frederick William used it in 1849–50 to destroy the liberal and social revolution throughout Germany. The close alliance of the Junker nobility and the bureaucratic Prussian monarchy remained intact and ascendant, soon to unify Germany on an authoritarian basis.

PEASANT INCAPACITY AND GENTRY VULNERABILITY IN CHINA

Finally, it is time to turn to the complexities of the third positive case of social revolution. The Chinese Revolution is, by common consent, the most obviously peasant-based social revolution of the trio featured in this book. Surprising as it may seem, though, the agrarian class and local political structures of old-regime China, despite some similarities to France

147

and Russia, resembled those of England and Prussia in key respects. By analyzing the Chinese agrarian structures in comparative perspective, we shall put ourselves in a position to understand the distinctive rhythms and patterns of China's revolutionary interregnum between 1911 and 1949. A peasant revolution against landlords did ultimately occur in China as in France and Russia, but the peasants of China lacked the kind of structurally preexisting solidarity and autonomy that allowed the agrarian revolutions in France and Russia to emerge quickly and relatively spontaneously in reaction to the breakdown of the central governments of the Old Regimes. In contrast, the Chinese agrarian revolution was more protracted. And it required for its consummation the establishment through military conquest of secure "base areas," within which collective organization and freedom from direct landlord control could be created for the peasants.

Structural Conditions

As in eighteenth-century France and post-Emancipation Tsarist Russia, agrarian life in China was significantly shaped by rentier relations between peasants and landlords, although the extent of inequality of landholding in particular was least in China. About 40 percent of the land overall was rented – relatively much more in the south, and less in the north. Between 20 and 30 percent of all peasant families rented all of the land they tilled, and many of the remainder rented pieces to supplement their own small holdings. Landlords who did not work or live in the villages (though they often lived in local towns) owned about three-quarters of the rented-out land. This means that they possessed about 30 percent of the land overall, and such lands brought them rents of up to 50 percent of the crop.[112] From these facts about landholding alone we might conclude that Chinese landlords were considerably weaker and that Chinese peasants were considerably stronger than their respective French and Russian counterparts.

But this was not the case, either economically or sociopolitically. It is important to remember that the Chinese gentry appropriated surpluses not only through land rents. They also realized earnings through usurious interest rates on loans to peasant producers, sharing in Imperial taxes and local surtaxes, and claiming fees for organizing and directing local organizations and services (such as clans, Confucian societies, irrigation projects, schools, and militias).[113] Imperial taxes were similarly a source of income for the French and Russian dominant classes, but usury and the various local fees and taxes were forms of surplus appropriation much more distinctive to the Chinese gentry. In turn, these reflected and depended upon the fact that, in sharp contrast to French seigneurs and Russian estate owners, the Chinese gentry had a preponderant organizational position within local communities. Theirs was a position somewhat analogous, especially in its political consequences for the peasantry, to the local hegemony of the English landed class and the Prussian Junkers. Chinese peasants did not have their own village communities set in opposition to the landlords. And, although they were smallholders like the French and Russian peasants (and owned more land to boot), Chinese peasants, like their hapless English and Prussian counterparts, lacked ties among themselves that might have supported communal-class solidarity against the gentry. Instead, the Chinese gentry dominated local rural communities in ways that simultaneously enhanced their economic position (from what it would be through landholding alone) and kept an internally fragmented peasantry under firm sociopolitical control.

To fully understand this situation in its particular Chinese form, we must note that the basic unit of community in traditional China was *not* the individual village (i.e., cluster of peasant residences and/or individual holdings) but the marketing community composed of a cluster of villages. As G. W. Skinner writes:

> What might be called the basic ground plan of Chinese society was essentially cellular. Apart from certain remote and sparsely settled areas, the landscape of rural China was occupied by cellular systems of roughly hexagonal shape. The nucleus of each cell was one of approximately 45,000 market towns (as of the mid-nineteenth century), and its cytoplasm may be seen in the first instance as the trading area of the town's market. The body of the cell—which is to say the immediately dependent area of the town—typically included fifteen to twenty-five villages, usually but not necessarily nucleated.[114]

Though they resided and worked in individual villages, the marketing community was the significant local world of the peasants. There they regularly bought and sold at the periodic markets, obtained craftsmen's services, secured loans, participated in religious rites, and found marriage partners.

The local gentry, not the peasants, directly or indirectly provided the leadership for organized social activities within the market community and represented the locality at its interfaces with the larger society. Clans (where they flourished) and many kinds of peasant-recruiting associations—which were everywhere organized for religious, educational, welfare, or economic purposes—all tended to be based within marketing communities and managed by gentry. Especially in wealthier, more internally stratified localities, gentry organized and controlled militias and other organizations that functioned, in effect, as channels of popular control and poor relief. Ironically, this meant that the relatively wealthiest gentry, in areas with the highest tenancy rates, were perhaps least susceptible to local class-based peasant revolts against their privileges. But the same sort of thing occurred throughout China: The gentry, by creating and leading local organizations, coopted peasants, thereby enhancing local bargaining

149

power in relation to imperial officials and deflecting potential unrest from themselves.[115]

Whereas associational, clientage, and extended quasi-kinship ties thus cut across class distinctions between peasants and gentry landlords in traditional China, peasants in the villages were largely isolated from and in competition with one another. As Fei Hsiao-tung put it: "As far as the peasants are concerned, social organization stops at the loosely organized neighborhood. In the traditional structure, peasants live in small cells, which are the families, without strong ties between the cells."[116] Except where gentry-run organizations played a role (say, in building and maintaining irrigation works), agricultural production was managed by individual, basically nuclear families.[117] These families had to possess or rent their own land and possess or buy their own equipment and (if needed) supplementary labor. Families were constantly maneuvering to acquire more than their neighbors in a system where factors of production could be bought and sold, and where the very poor could lose out altogether. There were no common lands for the peasants themselves to manage; if clans or associations owned lands, they were managed by gentry or their associates. And peasants rarely cooperated to perform agricultural tasks except on a commercial–contractual basis. In short, unless Chinese peasants came together organizationally under gentry aegis, they tended to remain in competitive isolation.

Patterns of Agrarian Unrest

Given these characteristics of local communities, it should hardly seem surprising that, in late Imperial times, agrarian unrest rarely took the form of concerted attacks by peasants against landlords within their communities. From time to time individual landlords were attacked by peasants who protested the hoarding of grain in periods of dearth or the collusion of gentry in corrupt tax-collections. But the more prevalent and better organized forms of agrarian rebellion involved attacks upon the official agents of the Imperial state. These ranged from frequent riots at the office-compounds (*yamens*) of county magistrates, held to protest taxes or demand famine relief, to occasional massive rebellions that erected counteradministrations encompassing entire regions and sometimes succeeded in toppling, and replacing, ruling dynasties.[118]

Certainly both riots and rebellions always depended upon peasant participation. And their declared goals always made reference to peasant grievances—especially against "evil practices" such as official corruption, hoarding of grain, and prices and rents perceived as unusually exorbitant. Then, too, non-Confucian secret societies that sought to recruit poor peasants frequently elaborated millenarian ideologies featuring utopian dreams of political justice and equality of access to land.[119] The Taiping ideology, as a kind of extreme case, envisaged a social world without gentry, and with both economic and male-female equality within agrarian communities.[120]

In terms of organization, though, all of the more sustained forms of peasant-based revolt were sooner or later led or infiltrated by nonpeasants. Locally and regionally based secret societies with heterodox religious or political purposes often provided the organizational basis for revolts. Yet they were frequently led by merchants or would-be literati who had failed the Imperial exams—that is, by individuals on the margins of (and aspiring to join) the gentry.[121] Riots against taxes or officials were very often led by local gentry themselves.[122] Furthermore, when any rebellion grew to significant proportions, it usually attracted orthodox Confucian gentry into positions of active support and leadership, and hence eventual influence over the movement's goals and practices. Historically, even peasant bandit leaders who successfully led rebellions that made them emperors came to rely upon the gentry to govern the country. For the gentry alone had the connections and interests that bridged the gaps between administrative towns and the vast settled countryside. At the height of its power in the mid-nineteenth century, the Taiping Rebellion was showing similar tendencies, although it was not so successful at winning gentry supporters—a failing that may help to explain its ultimate defeat.[123] Throughout Imperial Chinese history, peasant grievances fueled revolts—but especially the successful rebellions simply revitalized the existing system. For peasants lacked the local community-based autonomy to render their resistance even potentially revolutionary.

Does all of this mean that the Chinese gentry were as invulnerable to widespread peasant revolts as the English and Prussian landed upper classes? In many respects they were in a comparably strong position because of their similar local hegemony over the peasantry. Yet there were important ways in which their situation was less secure. For one thing, whereas the seventeenth-century English and nineteenth-century Prussian landlords were masters of agrarian sectors that (albeit in different ways) were making successful transitions to capitalist production, the Chinese gentry were the dominant class in a significantly commercialized but developmentally stymied agrarian economy. Furthermore, the Chinese gentry were sitting atop, not yeomen farmers and/or agricultural laborers, but a mass of peasant smallholders, most of whom would stand to gain if gentry lands were redistributed and their surplus appropriations abolished. In these strictly economic respects, therefore, the situation of the Chinese gentry was like that of the French seigneurs and the Russian estate owners.

Besides, although the local sociopolitical predominance of the Chinese gentry resembled that of the English and Prussian landlords, their relationship to the central political power, the monarchy, was not the same as either. On the one hand, in contrast to the Prussian Junkers, the Chinese gentry (especially from the mid-nineteenth century on) found themselves increasingly at odds with the monarchy and its bureaucratic agents. And, as we saw in Chapter 2, the locally and provincially ensconced gentry played an active role in bringing down the dynasty and dismantling the Imperial state in 1911 and immediately after. But, on the other hand, unlike the English landed upper class, the Chinese gentry was historically *dependent upon* a centralized, significantly bureaucratic imperial state. There was no national parliament to knit together dominant-class representatives from all of the various marketing communities. No such simple conjunction of local and national power had developed historically in a country so vast as China, with its several levels of administration intervening between Peking and each locality. Instead the locally rooted Chinese gentry was knit together on regional and country-wide bases only through participation in and cooperation with the Confucian Imperial bureaucracy. Likewise, only the unified administrative and coercive power of the Imperial state could provide certain backing over the long run for the dominant-class position of the gentry. The irony is that although the Chinese gentry had, during the period leading into 1911, both the capacity and the interests to undermine the Imperial state, once that had happened they were vulnerable as a class to any extralocally organized political force that might become determined to attack their position in the agrarian order.

Nor would such an antilandlord force be unable to recruit peasant supporters for a struggle against the landlord gentry. True, settled, working peasants would be hard to reach at first. But there was a *component* of the long-run cycle of dynastic decline, rebellion, and renewal that involved greater peasant insurrectionary autonomy than processes in or involving settled communities. During periods of central administrative weakness and economic deflation and catastrophe in Chinese history—phenomena that tended to happen together—"social banditry"[124] invariably blossomed. Precisely because Chinese agrarian relations were significantly commercialized, peasants were often not cushioned against economic dislocations by any village communal ties. During periods of economic decline, poorer peasants, especially in communities without well-to-do local elites to employ them, would lose property, livelihood, and even family, and be forced to migrate to avoid starvation. Impoverished migrants often gathered as bandits or smugglers operating out of "border areas" at the edges of the empire or at the intersections of provincial boundaries, places where they were beyond the reach of the local gentry and of the Imperial state when it was not at its very strongest. To survive or prosper the bandits attacked settled communities and, whenever possible, especially their richer members, because attacking the rich maximized the bandits' income and also improved chances of escaping capture by the authorities.

152

In such social banditry, therefore, class struggle was expressed, even if only indirectly and, historically speaking, always ephemerally.

The nineteenth century and the first half of the twentieth century constituted a period of dynastic decline and political interregnum in China. Economic difficulties, peasant impoverishment, spreading social banditry, and violent conflicts among local militias, bandit groups, and warlord and/or "ideological" armies, characterized the entire time span and peaked during the mid-nineteenth century and during the 1920s and 1930s. As we have seen, this period of central government decline was complicated in novel ways by Western and Japanese imperialist intrusions. Yet although imperialism fundamentally dislocated and revolutionized dominant-class and national politics, it did not fundamentally alter the economic and political situation of the vast majority of peasants and rural communities.[125] Except near the treaty ports, major navigable waterways, and the sparse railroad network (built after the 1880s), the traditional standard marketing networks, agents, and patterns of exchanges were not displaced by modern economic development. Peasants continued to work the land with traditional techniques, raising mainly grain crops for subsistence and to sell for money to pay rents and taxes (unless payments were claimed in kind). Insofar as life became more difficult for peasants in a given locality or region—or perhaps even overall (the evidence is not conclusive)—the reason was not that modern economic forces were fundamentally altering agrarian relations of production. It was rather that political disorders were endemic and brought in their train economic dislocations and confiscatory "taxes" and that recurrent catastrophies, such as floods or droughts, resulted in greater suffering when no stable government existed to facilitate relief and rehabilitation. Peasants got by if they could; if not, they rioted, starved, migrated, or joined an army or bandit gang. The grievances of the ever-increasing numbers who were displaced in the early twentieth century were acute, but no different and no more pressing than they had recurrently been, especially throughout recent Chinese history. Nor had any basic structural changes fundamentally altered the terms by which the peasants themselves could strike out at the causes of their troubles.[126]

Instead, as we shall see in Chapter 7, a new kind of national political leadership, the Chinese Communist Party, operating in the context of political–military fragmentation, ultimately found it necessary to attempt to fuse its efforts with the forces of peasant-based social banditry in order to build a Red army capable of taking and holding regions to administer. Then, under the umbrella of protection afforded by Communist military and administrative controls, local politics was finally reorganized in a fashion that afforded Chinese peasants the collective leverage against landlords that they had historically lacked. Once this occurred—as it did in North China in the 1940s—peasants revolted violently against the remnants of the gentry and destroyed its class and power positions. Thus, the peasant contribution to the Chinese Revolution resembled much more a mobilized response to a revolutionary elite's initiatives than did the peasant contributions in France and Russia. The reasons for this mass-mobilizing aspect had little to do with revolutionary ideology and everything to do with the "peculiarities" (as seen from a European perspective) of the Chinese agrarian sociopolitical structure. That structure did not afford settled Chinese peasants institutional autonomy and solidarity against landlords. But it did, in periods of political–economic crisis, generate marginal poor-peasant outcasts whose activities exacerbated the crisis, and whose existence provided potential support for oppositional elite-led rebellions – including, in the twentieth-century context, a revolutionary movement. Thus the activities of the Chinese Communists after 1927, and their ultimate triumph in 1949, depended directly upon both the insurrectionary potentials and the blocks to autonomous peasant revolts built into the existing Chinese agrarian order.[127]

But the details of the story of how the Chinese Communists, originally an urban-based and -oriented party, ended up in the countryside, and how first bandits and other displaced peasants and then settled peasant cultivators contributed to the success of a Communist consolidation of the Revolution in China, must remain to be told in Chapter 7. For, uniquely in the Chinese case, peasant revolution and the consolidation of national power by a revolutionary elite were so intertwined as to be virtually indistinguishable.

Summing Up

Chapters 2 and 3 have presented a comparative-historical analysis of the causes of social revolutions in France, Russia, and China. I have argued that (1) state organizations susceptible to administrative and military collapse when subjected to intensified pressures from more developed countries abroad and (2) agrarian sociopolitical structures that facilitated widespread peasant revolts against landlords were, taken together, the sufficient distinctive causes of social-revolutionary situations commencing in France, 1789, Russia, 1917, and China, 1911. Table 1 summarizes the causal arguments that have been developed at length for France, Russia, and China, as well as those made somewhat more briefly for Prussia/Germany, Japan, and England as contrast cases.

Yet "social revolutions" are so labeled only because societal crises have culminated in the emergence of new sociopolitical arrangements. Thus our analysis cannot stop with causes. It must proceed to show what changed in the French, Russian, and Chinese Revolutions and why those changes logically emerged from the social-revolutionary situations whose origins we have already traced. These are the tasks undertaken in Part II.

Table 1. *Causes of Social Revolutions in F*

A. Conditions For Political Crises

Table 1. *(contin*

B. Conditions

	Monarchy/ Dominant Class		
France	Landed–commer dominant class ha leverage within semibureaucratic absolue monarchy.	c agri	
Russia	Highly bureaucratic absolutist state; landed nobility has little political power.	Extensive growth; little devel- opment in core regions.	
China	Landed–commercial dominant class has leverage within semi- bureaucratic absolutist state.	No developmental breakthrough; near limits of growth, given population and available land.	Strong. Defeats imperialist

Contrasts

Prussia/ Germany	Highly bureaucratic absolutist state; landed nobility has little extralocal political leverage.	Transition to capitalist agriculture.	1806 – Strong 1848 – Mild
Japan	Highly bureaucratic (though not fully centralized) state. No true landed upper class.	Productivity increasing within traditional structures.	Strong; Imperialist intrusions.
England	No bureaucratic state. Landed class dominates politics.	Transition to capitalist agriculture.	Mild

155

	Agrarian Class Structures	Local Politics
	Peasant smallholders own 30-40% of land; work 80%+ in small plots. Individual property established, but peasant community opposes *Fukd* seigneurs, who collect dues.	Villages relatively autonomous under supervision of royal officials.
ssia	Peasants own 60%+ and rent more; control process of production on small plots; pay rents and redemption payments. Strong community based upon collective ownership.	Villages sovereign under control of tsarist bureaucracy.
China	Peasants own 50%+ and work virtually all land in small plots. Pay rents to gentry. No peasant community.	Gentry landlords, usurers, and literati dominant local organizational life; cooperate with Imperial officials.

Contrasts

Prussia/ Germany	West of Elbe: resembles France. East of Elbe: large estates worked by laborers and peasants with tiny holdings, and no strong communities.	Junker landlords are local agents of bureaucratic state; dominate local administration and policing.
Japan	Communities dominated by rich peasants.	Strong bureaucratic controls over local communities.
England	Landed class owns 70%+. Peasantry polarizing between yeomen farmers and agricultural laborers. No strong peasant community.	Landlords are local agents of monarchy; dominate administration and policing.

Table 1. (*continued*)

C. Societal Transformations

	Results of A plus B
France	1787–9: Breakdown of absolutist state; and widespread peasant revolts against seigneurial claims.
Russia	1860s–90s: Bureaucratic reforms from above. 1905: Unsuccessful revolutionary outbreak. 1917: Dissolution of state; widespread peasant revolts against all private landed property.
China	1911: Breakdown of Imperial state; spreading agrarian disorder, but no autonomous revolts by peasants against landlords.
Contrasts Prussia/ Germany	1807–14: Bureaucratic reforms from above. 1848: Failed social revolution; bureaucratic monarchy stays in power.
Japan	Political revolution centralizes state; followed by bureaucratic reforms from above.
England	Political revolution establishes parliamentary predominance within nonbureaucratic monarchy.

no social revolution?

157

II Outcomes of Social Revolutions in France, Russia, and China

4 What Changed and How: A Focus on State Building

Every great revolution has destroyed the State apparatus which it found. After much vacillation and experimentation, every revolution has set another apparatus in its place, in most cases of quite a different character from the one destroyed; for the changes in the state order which a revolution produces are no less important than the changes in the social order.

Franz Borkenau

SOCIAL-REVOLUTIONARY CRISES in France, Russia, and China set in motion political and class struggles that culminated in fundamental and enduring structural transformations. Important patterns of change were common to all three Revolutions. Peasant revolts against landlords transformed agrarian class relations. Autocratic and protobureaucratic monarchies gave way to bureaucratic and mass-incorporating national states. The prerevolutionary landed upper classes were no longer exclusively privileged in society and politics. They lost their special roles in controlling the peasants and shares of the agrarian surpluses through local and regional quasi-political institutions.[1] Under the Old Regimes, the privileges and the institutional power bases of the landed upper classes had been impediments to full state bureaucratization and to direct mass political incorporation. These impediments were removed by the political conflicts and class upheavals of the revolutionary interregnums. At the same time, emergent political leaderships were challenged by disunity and counterrevolutionary attempts at home, and by military invasions from abroad, to build new state organizations to consolidate the Revolutions. Success in meeting the challenges of political consolidation was possible in large part because revolutionary leaderships could mobilize lower-class groups formerly excluded from national politics, either urban workers or the peasantry. Thus, in all three Revolutions, landed upper classes (at least) lost out to the benefit of lower-class groups on the one hand and new state cadres on the other. In each New Regime, there was much greater popular incorporation into the state-run affairs of the nation. And the new state organizations forged during the Revolutions were more centralized and rationalized than those of the Old Regime. Hence they were more potent

161

within society and more powerful and autonomous over and against competitors within the international states system.

Yet, of course there were also important variations in the outcomes of the French, Russian, and Chinese Revolutions, which need to be understood along with the patterns common to the outcomes of all three Revolutions. The results of the French Revolution, to begin, contrasted to those in Soviet Russia and Communist China in ways suggested by the usual labeling of the French outcomes as "bourgeois." The Russian and Chinese Revolutions gave rise to party-led state organizations that asserted control over the entire national economies of the two countries and (in one way or another) mobilized the populace to propel further national economic development. In France, however, no such results occurred. Instead, the French Revolution culminated in a professional–bureaucratic state that coexisted symbiotically with, and indeed guaranteed the full emergence of, national markets and capitalist private property. Democratic popular mobilization was (after 1793) either suppressed or channeled into military recruitment and routinized, symbolic political pursuits. And despite the massive presence in society of the French state as a uniform and centralized administrative framework, further national economic development and social differentiation remained primarily market-guided and outside the direct control of the government.

In contrast to France, Soviet Russia and Communist China resembled each other as development-oriented party-states. But otherwise they differed in key respects, with the Russian regime exhibiting some important similarities to France. For like the French Revolution, the Russian Revolution gave rise to a professionalized and hierarchical state oriented to the firm administrative supervision of social groups. This applied in particular to the domination of the peasant majority in society in the name of urban interests.

There were, of course, differences between France and Russia: Aside from the greater direction of the economy and national development exercised by the Soviet state, the state administration in Russia, though privileged and dominant in relation to the rest of society, was itself subjected (along with the populace at large) to manipulation and coercion by the top leaders of the Communist Party and their police agents. The Soviet regime, in short, became an amalgam of, on the one hand, dictatorial and coercive political controls (supplied by or in the name of the Party) with, on the other hand, professionalized bureaucratic administration along formal hierarchical lines not too different from those of capitalist systems. Indeed, as we shall see, formal hierarchies of command and control and inequalities of rank and reward were in important respects extraordinarily extreme in Soviet society after 1928.

In China, the Revolution generated a state that was, to be sure, highly

162

centralized and in basic ways thoroughly bureaucratic. But it was also oriented to fostering broad and penetrating popular mobilization. Party or army organizations served not only as means of control over the state administration and the society, as in France and Russia, but also as agents of popular mobilization – especially to further national economic development. The contrast to France and Russia has been most striking with respect to the mobilization of peasants for rural development. As a corollary, the Chinese New Regime (compared to the French or Russian) has been less amenable, though by no means immune, to professionalism and a stress on formal rules and unitary hierarchies of routinized command.[2] Furthermore, the Chinese Communists have uniquely made recurrent attempts to reduce or prevent the unchecked growth of inequalities of rank and reward in state and society.

The tasks for Part II as a whole are suggested by the discussion so far: The outcomes of the Revolutions need to be characterized more fully. And the actual conflicts of the revolutionary interregnums must be analyzed and compared in order to explain how the broadly similar and individually distinct outcomes emerged from the original social-revolutionary crises. These tasks are straightforward enough; what requires more discussion is the approach that will be used to accomplish them. The analysis of the processes and outcomes of the Revolutions will focus upon the struggles surrounding the creation of new state organizations within the social-revolutionary situations. The characteristics of those states in relation to the socioeconomic orders of the New Regimes will also be examined. Each Revolution will be followed from the original crisis of the Old Regime through to the crystallization of the distinctive sociopolitical patterns of the New Regime. And the thread that we shall follow throughout will be the emergence and consolidation of new state organizations and the deployment of state power in the revolutionized societies. Why does this approach make sense, and what does it entail? The balance of this introductory chapter seeks to answer these questions.

One reason for a focus on state building is almost definitional: "A complete revolution," writes Samuel P. Huntington, "involves . . . the creation and institutionalization of a new political order."[3] It is the position of this book that social-revolutionary outcomes were, so to speak, on the agenda in French, Russian, and Chinese history once the Old Regimes had broken down. Nevertheless, it is of course true that the Revolutions were fully consummated only once new state organizations – administrations and armies, coordinated by executives who governed in the name of revolutionary symbols – were built up amidst the conflicts of the revolutionary situations. In all three revolutionary situations, political leaderships and regimes – the Jacobin and then the Napoleonic in France, the Bolshevik in Russia, and the Communist in China – emerged to reestablish national

163

order, to consolidate the socioeconomic transformations wrought by the class upheavals from below, and to enhance each country's power and autonomy over and against international competitors. Had this not happened, we would not speak of the French, Russian, and Chinese Revolutions as "successful" (i.e., complete) social revolutions. At most, they would be considered abortive cases, like Germany in 1848 and Russia in 1905.

Beyond definitional considerations, the reasons for a focus on state building are suggested by Franz Borkenau's assertions that "the changes in the state order which a revolution produces are no less important than the changes in the social order."[4] Social revolutions do, of course, accomplish major changes of class relations; and they affect basic areas of social and cultural life such as the family, religion, and education. Equally if not more striking, however, are the changes that social revolutions make in the structure and function of states, in the political and administrative processes by which government leaders relate to groups in society, and in the tasks that states can successfully undertake at home and abroad. Nor are such changes in the "state order" at all mere by-products of the changes in the social order. Indeed, to a significant degree, it is the other way around: The changes in state structures that occur during social revolutions typically both consolidate, and themselves entail, socioeconomic changes. Thus in Russia and China, the Communist Party-states not only sanctioned attacks from below on the existing dominant classes (as did the French revolutionaries). They also completed and extended the overthrow of those classes as the Party-states stepped in to take up many of the economic functions formerly performed by private property owners. Analogously in France, the strengthening of private property and the national market economy were in large part due to changes wrought by the Revolution in the structure of the French state. An emphasis on state building is warranted, therefore, because of the clear importance not only of political consolidation but also of state structures in determining revolutionary outcomes.

POLITICAL LEADERSHIPS

Having established that state building may be a fruitful thread to follow in analyzing social revolutions, it remains to clarify what such an emphasis entails. One thing it means is that the political leaderships involved in revolutions must be regarded as actors struggling to assert and make good their claims to state sovereignty. This may sound obvious, but it is not the usual way in which political leaderships in revolutions are analyzed. Typically, such leaderships are treated as representatives of classes or social groups, struggling to realize economic or status interests, and/or as actors attempting to implement a certain ideological vision of the ideal social

164

order. Congruent with such ways of looking at political leaders, their individual backgrounds are often searched for evidence of origins within, or connections to, the classes or groups they are said to represent. And if the appropriate origins or connections are manifestly missing, then emphasis is placed upon showing how their ideological orientations and activities resonate with the relevant social interests. What tends to be missed in all of this is that which political leaderships in revolutionary crises are above all *doing* – claiming and struggling to maintain state power. During revolutionary interregnums, political leaderships rise and fall according to how successful they are in creating and using political arrangements within the crisis circumstances that they face. Struggles over the most fundamental issues of politics and state forms go on until relatively stable new state organizations have been consolidated; thereafter political struggles continue about how to use state power in its broadly established form.

To regard political leaderships in revolutions as would-be state builders means to take their activities more seriously than their social backgrounds. Nevertheless it is true and of some interest that the backgrounds and "career" orientations of those political leaderships that were ultimately successful in consolidating new state organizations in the three Revolutions are at least congruent with a view of these leaderships primarily as state builders rather than as representatives of classes. For in France, Russia, and China alike, the relevant political leaderships precipitated out of the ranks of relatively highly educated groups oriented to state activities or employments. And the leaders arose especially from among those who were somewhat marginal to the established dominant classes and governing elites under the Old Regimes.

Through much of its course, the French Revolution was led by groups operating in and through a series of nationally elected assemblies – the National/Constituent Assembly of 1789–91 the Legislative Assembly of 1791–2, and the Convention of 1792–4. All of these bodies were predominantly populated by administrative and professional men from the Third Estate. The most important leaders of the early phases of the Revolution, from 1788 through 1790, are best described as "notables," that is, nobles or wealthy and privileged members of the Third Estate. Yet of the members of the National/Constituent Assembly from the Third Estate, fully 43 percent were venal office holders, mostly from the provinces and localities, and another 30 percent were lawyers or other professional men.[5] The subsequent Legislative Assembly was even more heavily dominated by local-level officials and politicians.[6] And the Convention drew 25 percent of its membership from office holders and a hefty 44 percent from lawyers and other professionals.[7] Moreover, as the Revolution entered its most radical phase in 1792–4, the actual national leadership was taken over by Montagnard Jacobins. They were (especially as contrasted to the more

165

moderate Girondin faction within the Convention) disproportionately likely to come from administrative–professional rather than commercial families and to hail from small or medium-sized provincial administrative towns, rather than from the cosmopolitan, privileged, and wealthy regional capitals or commercial seaports.[8] Eventually, to be sure (as we shall see later in more detail), the most radical leaders of the French Revolution fell from state power, which was ultimately usurped by Napoleon and his administrative and military agents. These people, however, included many former Jacobins. They also included former functionaries of the Old Regime, especially middle-level civil and military officers from both petty noble and nonprivileged Third Estate backgrounds[9] – that is, other formerly marginal elites who also achieved career mobility through the state during, and as a result of, the Revolution.

The leaders of the French Revolution were "marginal" because they tended to come from lesser, provincial urban centers and/or from the lower levels of the former royal administration. The revolutionary leaderships in Russia and China, however, included some people who were marginal by virtue of social origins and others who, although they came from privileged social backgrounds, had been converted to radical politics during the course of modern secondary or university education. The Bolsheviks of Russia and the Communists of China recruited people from all strata, including the working class and the peasantry. But in both parties, most of those in top and intermediate-level positions of leadership came either from dominant-class backgrounds or from families on the margins of the privileged classes (e.g., especially urban middle-class families in Russia, and especially rich peasant families in China).[10] Moreover, both revolutionary leaderships included very high proportions of people who had received formal secondary and (domestic or foreign) university educations.[11] Traditionally in Tsarist Russia and Imperial China, education was the route into state service. And when modern schools and universities were established in the two societies, they were intended to provide officials for the state. (In post-1900 China, large numbers of young people were also sent to foreign universities for the same purpose.) But modernized forms of higher education also became a route by which some students in each cohort, regardless of their disproportionately privileged backgrounds, became converted to critical perspectives calling for the fundamental transformation of the Old Regime.[12] As a result, many were inducted not into state service but into the career of the "professional revolutionary," ready to turn from political organizing and propaganda to efforts at revolutionary state-building whenever opportunities might arise.

The original leaders of the Chinese Communist Party were not too different in background and career trajectories from those of the Kuomintang Nationalist Party, and the Bolshevik leaders in Russia also shared

166

many social characteristics with the rival Menshevik leaders.[13] But it is interesting to note that, in both countries, the ultimately successful (communist) revolutionary leaderships possessed from the start (and gained increasingly over time) general ethnic and regional profiles that were closer than those of their rivals to the background characteristics traditionally associated with elite political status in the old, imperial regimes. Thus, the Bolsheviks in Russia were more disproportionately and homogeneously Great Russians from the core provinces of the empire than were the Mensheviks, who were more likely to come from minority regions and nationalities.[14] And, in China, the Communists came more frequently from Central (and finally also North) China, and more often from interior areas, than the Kuomintang leaders, who were heavily recruited from South China and the most Westernized coastal areas in general.[15] Note that these patterns for Russia and China resemble the contrast between the Montagnards and the Girondins of the Convention in France: The Montagnards tended to come from the administrative centers that had formed the base of the absolutist monarchy, whereas the Girondins were heavily recruited from commercial port cities, that had historically existed in some dissociation from, and tension with, the monarchical state.[16]

Two sets of considerations help to account for the fact that political leaderships in all of our social revolutions came specifically from the ranks of educated marginal elites oriented to state employments and activities. In the first place, Bourbon France, Manchu China, and Tsarist Russia all were "statist" societies. Even before the world-historical era of capitalist development, official employments in these societies constituted both an important route for social mobility and a means for validating traditional status and supplementing landed fortunes. All such agrarian states as France (after the consolidation of royal absolutism),[17] Tsarist Russia, and Imperial China (as well as Prussia/Germany and Japan) more or less continuously generated surpluses of aspirants for participation in state employments. And some such people were always potentially available for rebel or revolutionary political activities in crisis circumstances.

In the second place, with the advent of capitalist economic development in the world, state activities acquired an import greater than ever in those agrarian states that were forced to adapt to the effects of economic development abroad. As we have seen, the inescapable effects of such development initially impinged upon the state's sphere in the form of sharply and suddenly stepped-up military competition or threats from more developed foreign nations. Concomitantly, the cultural effects of development abroad first impinged upon the relatively highly educated in agrarian bureaucracies – that is, upon those who were mostly either employed by the state or else connected or oriented to its activities. It was thus understandable that, as agrarian states confronted the problems raised by development abroad,

167

virtually all politically aware groups, from conservative reformers to radicals and revolutionaries, viewed *the state* as the likely tool for implementing changes at home to enhance national standing in the international context. This is obvious for Russia and China. Consider, as well, the fascination of educated officials and laymen in prerevolutionary France with British economic and political models, and the widespread calls for implementation of reforms by the monarchy. Edward Fox has pointed to the irony of the fact that during the eighteenth century in France,

> in the middle of what has been described as the "democratic revolution," an entire generation of gifted social critics and publicists should all but unanimously demand the royal imposition of their various programs of reform. In the theoretical and polemical literature of the time, the "absolute" monarchy was criticized for its failure to exercise arbitrary power. To Frenchmen of the *ancien régime,* it was the monarchy that represented what was modern and progressive; and political "liberties" that appeared anachronistic . . . For virtually all the inhabitants of continental France, fiscal and judicial reforms were far more urgent issues than the development of political liberty; and the monarchy was the obvious agency for their implementation. Only the king's failure to live up to their expectations drove his subjects to intervene. [18]

In France, as in Russia and China, civicly aware critics of the Old Regime, including, of course, the administrative–professional groups from whom the future revolutionary leaders would come, were oriented to the need and possibility for changes in and through the state.

In sum, the backgrounds of the revolutionary leaderships that came to the fore during the French, Russian, and Chinese Revolutions are congruent with the perspective advanced here that these were *state-building* leaderships. They were people who created administrative and military organizations and political institutions to take the place of the prerevolutionary monarchies. Nevertheless, knowing the general background characteristics of the revolutionary leaderships hardly tells us *why* the Revolutions had the (shared and varied) outcomes they did. Why did revolutionary leaderships end up creating the specific kinds of centralized, bureaucratic state structures (with varying relations to social groups and varying functions within society) that they did?

THE ROLE OF REVOLUTIONARY IDEOLOGIES

To answer this question a particular explanatory tack is often taken by those students of revolution who *do* take revolutionary leaderships seriously as politicians. More often than not, such investigators argue or imply that the *ideologies* (such as "Jacobinism" and "Marxism–Leninism") to which revolutionary leaderships are committed provide the key to the

168

nature of revolutionary outcomes. They believe, too, that ideologies reveal the practical strategies that the revolutionary leaders follow as they act to bring the outcomes about.[19] Analyses of revolutionary processes and outcomes that stress the ideological orientations of revolutionary vanguards are typically premised upon a certain notion. According to this view: although the contradictions and inherent conflicts of the old regime may bring about a societal crisis in which revolutionary transformations are *possible,* nevertheless the actual carrying through of revolutionary changes – and especially what particular kinds of changes are carried through – depends upon the intentions of determined, organized revolutionary vanguards. If this is true, then it seems to follow that explanations for revolutionary outcomes must refer primarily to the ideological visions of the revolutionary leaderships. For how else can one account for the realization of particular possibilities rather than others within the open-ended societal crisis? This line of reasoning has a certain plausibility. Let us therefore examine the role of revolutionary ideologies.

Certainly it does seem that revolutionary ideologies such as Jacobinism and Marxism–Leninism functioned to sustain the cohesion of political leaderships attempting to build and consolidate state power under social-revolutionary conditions.[20] Likewise, commitment to these ideologies helped the revolutionary politicians to struggle in appropriate ways. Here a brief look at the Meiji reformers of Japan can point toward what I mean by contrast. The Meiji radicals could struggle for state power in a very different ideological and organizational style than the Jacobins, the Bolsheviks, and the Chinese Communists. The Meiji radicals came together and sustained group cohesion through particularistic connections within and between existing *han* governments (since most of the leaders of the Restoration came from Satsuma and Choshu, two "outer" provinces). They attained state power and effected far-reaching changes through factional infighting and manipulation of established institutional mechanisms. And they could justify innovative and universalistic actions to themselves and to other elites through references to a previously deemphasized yet traditionally available legitimating symbol, "the emperor." Certain traditional institutions, connections, and symbols could be used thus by the Meiji radical reformers because of the unique flexibilities and potentials for quick adaptations to modern conditions of the Tokugawa regime from which they emerged.[21] These were characteristics that, as we have seen in Chapter 2, the Bourbon, Manchu, and Romanov regimes lacked. Within social-revolutionary situations in France, Russia, and China, *new* ideologies and organizations had to serve functions for revolutionary leaderships similar to those served for the leaders of the Meiji Restoration by the emperor symbol, the *han* ties, and the potentials for factional manipulations within established political arrangements.

169

Revolutionary ideologies such as Jacobinism and Marxism–Leninism could help political elites committed to them to struggle for, build, and hold state power within social-revolutionary situations for several reasons. First, these were (in their historical and national contexts) universalistic creeds that could allow and encourage people from very diverse particularistic backgrounds to work together as fellow citizens or comrades. This was important in France, Russia, and China because the Revolutions were not consolidated through takeovers by formerly existing sectional elites as in Japan. Moreover, the only preexisting society-wide political legitimations were the monarchical symbols that became discredited within the social-revolutionary situations. Revolutionary ideologies then came to the fore to justify the rebuilding and the exercise of state power.

Second, these ideologies enjoined the revolutionary elites to proselytize and mobilize the masses for political struggles and activities. And this orientation, even if it did not lead to many real conversions, nevertheless gave Jacobins, Bolsheviks, and Chinese Communists access to crucial additional resources for politico–military struggles against counterrevolutionaries whose ideal and material interests made them less willing to call upon, or benefit from, mass initiatives. Third, Jacobinism and Marxism–Leninism were both secular "totalitarian" outlooks that provided justification for the actors who believed in them to employ unlimited means to achieve ultimate political ends on earth—ends such as "the enactment of the General Will" and progress toward the "classless society." And, as Egon Bittner has suggested, if totalitarian ideologies are to be sustained as exclusive faiths within groups, certain kinds of organizational mechanisms may very well need to be established. These would include mechanisms such as controls to encourage the undivided commitment of cadres to the group and hierarchical lines of authority focused on extraordinary symbols and leaders.[22] However unappealing such mechanisms may be from the perspective of liberal political theory, the fact is that they are likely to give to armed minorities formidable advantages in unlimited political struggles of the sort that mark revolutionary civil wars.

Thus revolutionary ideologies and people committed to them were undoubtedly necessary ingredients in the great social revolutions under investigation here. Nevertheless it cannot be argued in addition that the cognitive content of the ideologies in any sense provides a predictive key to either the outcomes of the Revolutions or the activities of the revolutionaries who built the state organizations that consolidated the Revolutions. Any line of reasoning that treats revolutionary ideologies as blueprints for revolutionaries' activities and for revolutionary outcomes cannot sustain scrutiny in the light of historical evidence about how Jacobinism and Marxism–Leninism actually did develop and function within the unfolding social-revolutionary situations in France, Russia, and China.[23] Jacobin

170

ideologues shared in the rule of revolutionary France for only about one year, and the "Reign of Virtue" failed completely to take hold. The Jacobins accomplished instead more mundane tasks—of state building and revolutionary defense—indispensable to the success of the Revolution that devoured them.[24] In Russia, the Bolsheviks were pummeled by the exigencies of the attempt to take and hold state power in the name of Marxist socialism in an agrarian country shattered by defeat in total war. They found themselves forced to undertake tasks and measures that directly contradicted their ideology. In the end, triumphant Stalinism twisted and upended virtually every Marxist ideal and rudely contradicted Lenin's vision in 1917 of destroying bureaucracies and standing armies.[25] In China, the Communists set out in proper Marxist–Leninist fashion to take power through proletarian risings in the cities. Not until well *after* these were crushed and new and viable peasant-oriented movements had taken root in military base areas in the countryside did "Maoist" doctrine develop to sanctify and codify what had been done. Thereafter epicycles were always added to the basic model whenever necessary to justify practical detours on the road to national power.[26]

In short, ideologically oriented leaderships in revolutionary crises have been greatly limited by existing structural conditions and severely buffeted by the rapidly changing currents of revolutions. Thus they have typically ended up accomplishing very different tasks and furthering the consolidation of quite different kinds of new regimes from those they originally (and perhaps ever) ideologically intended. This should not seem surprising once we realize and reflect upon a straightforward truth: Revolutionary crises are *not* total breakpoints in history that suddenly make anything at all possible if only it is envisaged by willful revolutionaries! There are several reasons why this is so. For one thing, revolutionary crises have particular forms, and create specific concatenations of possibilities and impossibilities, according to how these crises are originally generated in given old regimes under given circumstances. Furthermore, although a revolutionary crisis does entail institutional breakdowns and class conflicts that quickly change the parameters of what is possible in the given society, many conditions—especially socioeconomic conditions—always "carry over" from the old regime. These, too, create specific possibilities and impossibilities within which revolutionaries must operate as they try to consolidate the new regime. And so do the given world-historical and international contexts within which the entire revolutionary transformation occurs.

The Analysis to Come

Now all of the defining features of the explanatory approach to be followed in the rest of Part II can fall into place. We shall follow the thread of state building through from the original revolutionary crises to the crystallization of the basic revolutionary outcomes. And we shall take revolutionary leaderships seriously as politicians struggling to consolidate and use state power. But we shall *not* seek to decipher or explain the revolutionary developments from the perspective of ideological world views or programs. Instead, we shall direct our attention to how the forms of the revolutionary crises and the legacies of the Old Regimes shaped and limited the efforts and achievements of the state-building revolutionary leaderships. Several sets of circumstances impinging upon the state-building efforts will be brought into each case analysis and will constitute the analytic basis for comparisons among the Revolutions.

Above all, close attention will be paid to the particular features of each social-revolutionary crisis, thus referring back to much that has already been established about each Revolution in Part I. This analytic emphasis has two aspects. In the first place, the specific way in which each Old Regime broke down politically (as analyzed in Chapter 2) had important consequences. It determined the initial patterns of political conflict during the revolutionary interregnum and influenced the possibilities (or impossibilities) for temporary stabilization of liberal political regimes. It also helped to determine the kind of administrative and military tasks that had to be faced by mass-mobilizing leaderships as they emerged within the revolutionary situations.

In the second place, much depended upon the timing and nature of peasant revolts or agrarian disorder within the revolutionary crises, matters explicable in terms of the agrarian sociopolitical structures discussed in Chapter 3. Where peasant revolts occurred suddenly and autonomously, as they did in France and Russia, they had immediate, uncontrolled effects upon the course of national–urban political struggles. In China, peasant revolts against landlords were delayed until peasants of necessity were politically mobilized into the process of revolutionary state-building. It was thereby ensured that Chinese peasants were uniquely influential in shaping the New Regime. Yet even though revolutionary state-builders in France and Russia politically mobilized urban workers rather than peasants, they, too, had to come to terms with the peasantry and with the revolutionized agrarian orders. And to see how they did this is to understand much about the course and outcomes of each Revolution.

Old-regime socioeconomic legacies will also figure in the case analyses, especially for the purpose of explaining variations among the Revolutions. Attention will be paid to the particular kinds of urban-centered commercial, industrial, and transportation structures carried over from the Old Regimes. Were there modern industries or not, and if so, what kind and where were they located? The answers help to explain the kinds of urban-based social classes and class conflicts that figured in each revolutionary drama, the possible bases and limits of urban support for revolutionary state-builders, and the opportunities (open or not) for using revolutionary state power, once consolidated, to promote national industrialization (of one sort or another) under state control.

Finally, we shall, of course, consider the influences of world-historical circumstances and international relations upon the emergent revolutionary regimes. The world-historical timing and sequence of the Revolutions affected the models of political-party organization and of ways for using state power that were available to the successive revolutionary leaderships. Moreover, in France, Russia, and China alike, both military invasions from abroad during the revolutionary interregnums and international military situations after the initial consolidation of state power powerfully affected the development of the Revolutions. The particular kinds of international influences varied from France to Russia to China, but such realities were important in shaping the revolutionary outcomes in all three cases.

In the remainder of Part II, some arguments are going to be developed to explain *shared patterns* across all three Revolutions, and others to explain *key variations* among the Revolutions against the background of the shared patterns. Thus I shall try to demonstrate that the emergence of more centralized, mass-incorporating, and bureaucratic states in France, Russia, and China alike is explicable in terms of broadly similar exigencies, challenges, and opportunities. These were created for revolutionary state-builders by the original conjunctures in all three cases of old-regime breakdown and widespread peasant unrest. At the same time, I shall use comparisons among the three cases to specify how the particular features of each revolutionary conjuncture in the given world-historical setting, along with the specific conditions carried over from the Old Regime, served to shape the struggles and the outcomes distinctive to each Revolution.

Chapter 5 examines the process and outcomes of the French Revolution from 1789 to the consolidation of the Napoleonic regime. Chapter 6 deals with Russia from 1917 through the triumph of Stalinism in the 1930s. And Chapter 7 analyzes developments in China from the aftermath of 1911 through 1949 to the 1960s.

173

5 The Birth of a "Modern State Edifice" in France

> *The centralized State power, with its ubiquitous organs of standing army, police, bureaucracy, clergy, and judicature – organs wrought after the plan of a systematic and hierarchic division of labour – originates from the days of absolute monarchy . . . Still, its development remained clogged by all manner of mediaeval rubbish, seignorial rights, local privileges, municipal and guild monopolies and provincial constitutions. The gigantic broom of the French Revolution . . . swept away all of these relics of bygone times, thus clearing simultaneously the social soil of its last hindrances to the superstructure of the modern State edifice raised under the First Empire, itself the offspring of the coalition wars of old semi-feudal Europe against modern France.*
> Karl Marx

THE COURSE OF the French Revolution was shaped by the consequences of a social-revolutionary crisis in which liberal stabilization proved impossible, and by the emergence through mass mobilization of centralized and bureaucratic state organizations. As in Russia and China, such state organizations served to consolidate the Revolution in the context of civil and international warfare. Our examination of the dynamics and outcomes of the French Revolution will emphasize these fundamental developments. As a prelude to this analysis, though, let me first enter into the ongoing historiographical debate about how the French Revolution as a whole should be characterized.

A BOURGEOIS REVOLUTION?

What fundamentally changed and how in the French Revolution – these are subjects of much controversy among contemporary historians. Telling criticisms have been leveled against the until-recently dominant "social interpretation" – a view of largely Marxist inspiration, which holds that the Revolution was led by the bourgeoisie to displace feudalism and the aristocracy and to establish capitalism instead.[1] No counterinterpretation of comparable scope and power has yet achieved widespread acceptance.[2] This is true in part, perhaps, because debates over possible reinterpretations have remained largely within the socioeconomic terms of the established frame of reference. As Marxist notions about the centrality of the bourgeoisie and the transition from a feudal to a capitalist mode of production have been opened to question, the most vociferous debates about what to put in their place have merely tinkered with parts of the original argument, leaving its substantive focus and structure intact. New groups, other than the bourgeoisie, with economic interests corresponding to the not-so-capitalist economic outcomes of the Revolution have been sought out.[3] Or else a more indirect and cautious way to restate a faint echo of the Marxist argument in social but not economic terms has been stressed.[4] The upshot has been the placing of interpretive emphasis upon very partial aspects of the revolutionary outcomes. Thus any links between the historical rise of capitalism and capitalists and the actual political events and struggles of the French Revolution have been rendered more and more tenuous, even though some intrinsic ultimate connection is still supposed to exist—and indeed to "explain" the Revolution overall.

Meanwhile, changes wrought by the French Revolution in the structure and functioning of the French state have been largely ignored by contemporary interpreters trying to discern the overall meaning of the Revolution.[5] Yet hints have appeared, here and there in interpretive essays and syntheses, and even more clearly in the findings of empirical studies on developments in the army and administration during the Revolution. These indicate that the overall logic of the conflicts and outcomes of the Revolution may lie primarily in sociopolitical and juridical transformations—that is, bureaucratization, democratization, and the emergence of a politico-legal framework favorable to capitalism—wrought through a confluence of political struggles for state power and peasant struggles against seigneurial rights, rather than in a basic transformation of the socioeconomic structure effected by the class action of a capitalist bourgeoisie.[6] To be sure, the differences involved here are matters of emphasis and perspective, but such differences can be very consequential, especially if they prompt us to try to explain the processes and outcomes of the Revolution in new ways.

The Revolution and Economic Development

Proponents of the view that the French Revolution was a "bourgeois revolution" can point to evidence that seems to support their position. Certainly, the political elites that emerged did not take direct control of the economy to spur national industrialization; instead, the Revolution strengthened classes based on private property ownership. Regional, estate, and guild barriers to the formation of a national market were eliminated. And, in time, France did undergo capitalist industrialization.

175

However there are equally important facts that contradict any economically grounded version of the "bourgeois revolution" thesis. Before the Revolution, French industry was overwhelmingly small scale and non-mechanized; and commercial and financial wealth coexisted nonantagonistically, indeed symbiotically, with the more settled and prestigious "proprietary" forms of wealth (land, venal office, annuities). During the Revolution, political leadership came primarily from the ranks of professionals (especially lawyers), office holders, and intellectuals. The men who dominated France after the Revolution were not industrialists or capitalist entrepreneurs but primarily bureaucrats, soldiers, and owners of real estate.[7] And the economically relevant reforms enacted during the Revolution were either spurred by revolts from below or else were the culmination of " ... the century old movement for the abolition of the internal customs ... [a movement] led throughout, and ultimately brought to success, not by the representatives of commercial and industrial interests, but by reforming officials" of the French state.[8]

More telling, the Revolution almost certainly hindered capitalist industrialization in France as much as it facilitated it. Immediate roadblocks to development might be expected to accompany any period of revolutionary turmoil. Thus:

> the series of upheavals and wars that began with the French Revolution and ended with Waterloo ... brought with them capital destruction and losses of manpower; political instability and a widespread social anxiety; the decimation of the wealthier entrepreneurial groups; all manner of interruptions to trade; violent inflations and alterations of currency.[9]

One disruption was especially important. Before the Revolution, many of France's nascent industries had been nourished by a wide-ranging and expanding overseas trade.[10] But this trade collapsed as a result of the Revolution and the ensuing wars, so that, although " ... from 1716 to 1789 the foreign trade of France quadrupled ... , " it did not again attain its prerevolutionary levels until well after 1815.[11]

The Revolution hindered French economic development in even more fundamental ways as well. The socioeconomic structure that emerged from the revolutionary upheavals featured a nonindustrial bourgeoisie and a securely entrenched peasantry.[12] To be sure, the postrevolutionary bourgeoisie was wealthy, ambitious, and enjoyed unalloyed rights of private property ownership. However,

> the base of the ... bourgeoisie was not in industry, but rather in trade, the professions and the land. The new men who thrust themselves forward as a result of the opportunities created by social upheaval ... did not see in industrial investment and production the main avenue

176

for taking advantage of the new-won freedoms. Fortunes could be built up far more quickly in speculation in land and commodities. They might later find their way into industry, but only as and when opportunities presented themselves.[13]

Yet (especially compared to the situation in England) opportunities for industrial investments emerged only gradually in nineteenth-century France. The postrevolutionary economy remained predominantly agrarian, and the peasants continued to work the land in virtually unchanged fashion. The Revolution strengthened rural smallholders through the abolition of seigneurial privileges and transfers of some land and through the legal reinforcement of partible inheritance. And as Alexander Gerschenkron has pointed out:

> There can be no doubt that the French family farm deserves a place of distinction in the array of hindrances and handicaps placed in the path of French economic development.
>
> First of all, the French farms proved a very inadequate source of labor supply to the cities. The French farmer clung to his land ... At the same time, ... the desire to purchase additional land always seemed to rank highest in determining the economic decisions of the French Peasantry. Thus its proverbial thrift meant abstention from buying additional consumers' goods; yet little of the savings was used for the acquisition of capital goods such as machinery and fertilizers ... As a result, the French peasantry not only failed to aid industrial development by providing it with cheap and disciplined labor ... ; it also failed to act as a large and growing market for industrial products.[14]

After 1814, French industry found itself far behind British industry and turned to the strengthened French state "to perpetuate in France a hothouse atmosphere in which antiquated and inefficient enterprises were maintained at high cost, while new plants and enterprises lacked both the sting of competition and unobstructed connection with foreign countries for the importation of capital goods and know-how."[15] More beneficial contributions by France's strengthened state to the facilitation of capitalist industrialization had to await the advent of the railroad age. Even then, French economic development merely seems to have picked up not far beyond where it left off in 1789 and to have proceeded steadily in a socioeconomic environment not, overall, much more or less favorable to growth than that of the Old Regime. As a case for which economic historians have been unable to agree on any period as the time of "industrial takeoff," France provides poor material indeed for substantiating the notion of a bourgeois revolution that supposedly suddenly breaks fetters on capitalist development.[16]

Political Accomplishments

Nor is it sufficient simply to transfer the classic bourgeois-revolution thesis from a primarily socioeconomic to a more strictly political level of analysis, arguing that the French Revolution was the triumph of bourgeois liberalism accomplished through political struggles fueled by class conflicts and led by the bourgeoisie.[17] The political struggles of the French Revolution were not in any meaningful sense led by a capitalist bourgeoisie or its representatives. Key changes wrought by the Revolution in the political structure of France strengthened executive–administrative dominance within government rather than parliamentary–representative arrangements. And the possibilities for authoritarian rule were furthered at the expense of civil liberties. Perhaps most important of all, any analyst trying to make sense of the conditions that influenced the political struggles and accomplishments of the Revolution must pay special attention to the effects of French involvement from 1792 to 1814 in major European wars. For state building in revolutionary France was more powerfully and directly shaped by the exigencies of waging wars and coping with their domestic political repercussions than by the class interests of conflicting social groups.

A bird's-eye view of what the French Revolution did most strikingly accomplish is – interestingly enough – nowhere better expressed than in the passage quoted as the keynote for this chapter, taken from Karl Marx's pamphlet on "The Civil War in France."[18] This remarkable passage puts the "medieval rubbish" of the Old Regime in correct perspective by suggesting that it was closely intertwined with the state apparatus of the monarchy. Superimposed upon the increasingly fluid and modern socioeconomic structure of prerevolutionary France (as we saw in Chapter 2) was a cumbrous collection of institutionalized and politically guaranteed local, provincial, occupational, and estate rights and corporate bodies. Some of these had forms or labels inherited from medieval times, but all of them had long since been functionally transformed through the expansion of absolute monarchy and the spread of commercialization. What the social and political upheavals of the Revolution certainly succeeded in doing was eliminating this "medieval rubbish," which had both depended upon the monarchical state for its continued existence and, simultaneously, limited the efficient functioning of royal absolutism. Seigneurial privileges and rights were swept away, leaving an agrarian economy dominated by medium and small landholders with exclusive private rights to their lands. The Nation – composed of citizens stripped of estate and corporate distinctions and officially equal before the laws of the land – replaced hereditary, divinely sanctioned monarchy as the symbolic source of legitimate political sovereignty. As Map 3 shows, uniform, rationally ordered political jurisdictions – featuring 80–90 "departments" (themselves encompassing districts and communes) – replaced the hodgepodge of "35 provinces, 33 fiscal *généralités* . . . , 175 *grands bailliages,* 13 *parlements,* 38 *gouvernements militaires,* and 142 dioceses" of the Old Regime.[19] Nationwide systems of law, taxation, and customs replaced the regional variations and local barriers of prerevolutionary times. In the army and state administration, fully bureaucratic principles for recruiting, rewarding, and supervising officials replaced the practices of venal office-holding, farming out of governmental functions, and special recognition of noble status and of corporate privileges that had so compromised the unity and effectiveness of the monarchical state. The central government expanded in size and functions. And the new national polity became more "democratic," not only in the sense that the nation of civil equals replaced monarchy and aristocracy as the source of legitimacy but also in the sense that the state reached farther, and more even-handedly, into society. In so doing, it attempted to distribute services and opportunities without formal regard for social background and demanded more of everyone, more active involvement in state functions, and more resources of money, time, and manpower to carry out national objectives.

In sum, the French Revolution was "bourgeois" only in the specific sense that it consolidated and simplified the complex variety of prerevolutionary property rights into the single individualistic and exclusive form of modern private property. And it was "capitalist" only in the specific sense that it cleared away all manner of corporate and provincial barriers to the expansion of a competitive, national market economy in France. Of course these were very important changes. They represent the elimination of quasi-feudal forms of surplus appropriation and the establishment instead of promising juridical conditions – though not ideal socioeconomic conditions – for capitalist appropriation and for the capitalist industrialization of France.[20] But we should not forget that these transformations were only a part of the story. They were in a sense simply complements to the more striking and far-reaching transformations in the French state and national polity. These political changes, in turn, were not simply or primarily "liberal" in nature, nor were they straightforwardly determined by bourgeois activity or class interest. Rather they were the result of complex crisscrossings of popular revolts and the efforts at administrative–military consolidation of a succession of political leaderships. By virtue of both its outcomes and its processes, the French Revolution – as the remainder of this part will attempt to demonstrate – was as much or more a bureaucratic, mass-incorporating and state-strengthening revolution as it was (in any sense) a bourgeois revolution.

Map 3. The departments of France (excluding Corsica), 1790 and after. Note: Paris became the Department of the Seine; Rhône-et-Loire was divided into two departments, Rhône and Loire. As a result of the first annexations, Mont-Blanc (i.e., Savoie and Haute-Savoie) came from Savoy; Alpes-Maritimes from Nice and Monaco; Mont-Terrible (i.e., Territory-de-Belfort) from the district of Porentruy; and Vaucluse from Avignon and the Comtat-Venaissin. By 1799, there were 90 departments in all. *Source:* M. J. Sydenham, *The French Revolution* (New York: Capricorn Books, 1966), p. 70.

180

A "Modern State Edifice" in France

If the French Revolution was chiefly the transformation of an absolute monarchy encumbered by "medieval rubbish" into a centralized, bureaucratic, and mass-incorporating national state, then how and why did this happen? The political outcome of the French Revolution, fully consolidated under Napoleon, was not that preferred by the economically dominant groups in France. Although they never could agree on the institutional specifics, what most wealthy, propertied Frenchmen probably wanted out of the Revolution was something like the English parliamentary system. This was a system with local governments and a national assembly (or assemblies) dominated by representatives of educated, well-to-do people, and with the national representative body enjoying powers to initiate legislation and exert financial controls on the executive. But this liberal sort of political outcome is not what emerged from the social-revolutionary process in France, any more than in Russia or China. Right from the start, from 1789 on, the social-revolutionary crisis—marked by the incapacitation of a monarchical administration upon which the dominant class had depended, in combination with uncontrollable peasant revolts—contained the seeds of breakdown for attempts to consolidate the Revolution in liberal forms. To see how and why this was true, it is useful to contrast briefly the French sociopolitical structure and revolutionary trajectory with those of England during her seventeenth-century parliamentary Revolution.

Dominant-Class Political Capacities

From the beginning, the French dominant class had less capacity than the English to make a liberal political revolution against the monarchy. The English Parliament was a functioning national assembly during the century before the English Revolution, and it brought together prosperous notables representing both urban and rural areas. (Indeed many county cliques of landed gentry had simply absorbed the rights to represent the urban corporations of their areas in the House of Commons.) Moreover, the representatives in Parliament had well-established ties to local governments that controlled most of the means of administration and coercion in the country.[21] When the English dominant class set out to clip the powers of the monarchy, therefore, it acted to assert and defend the powers of an already-existing national representative assembly. And when quarrels broke out over control of armed forces, followed by the Civil War, the dominant class factions supporting Parliament could use their connections to local governments (London and many counties) to

181

mobilize military and financial resources at least equal to those available to the king and his supporters.

In France things were very different. The dominant class was internally divided from the start over what kind of representative institutions it wanted vis-à-vis the king. The Estates-General was really nothing more than a historical precedent; and preexisting politically relevant privileges would be at stake if provincial estates, *parlements,* and voting by order were sacrificed for the alternative of a unified national assembly. By the late spring of 1789 the liberal notables of the Third Estate and the aristocracy had won the battle for the National Assembly. Yet, unlike the English Parliament, this newborn French body enjoyed no established ties to strong local governments. Instead, its survival in the face of royal opposition was only secured through the spontaneous, nationwide Municipal Revolution of the summer of 1789.

Although the National (renamed Constituent) Assembly obviously benefited from the Municipal Revolution, it did not in any sense direct this movement. And afterwards it could do little more than constitutionally sanction the decentralizing results. It was true that the new municipal committees were strongly oriented to national politics and anxious to support the Revolution.[22] Yet, administratively speaking, the result of the Municipal Revolution was not only to disorganize the royal government but also to forestall the emergence of an effective revolutionary government. "The fundamental fact," wrote Alfred Cobban, paraphrasing an earlier historian, "is that before 1789 ... there was not a single truly elected assembly in the country, but only government officials; in 1790 there was no longer a single official, but only elected bodies."[23] So great was the distrust of any centralized executive power in the early phases of the Revolution, that no workable system was created to replace the monarchical one. Instead the localities were confirmed as virtually autonomous authorities, though without adequate arrangements for them to raise revenues.[24] Simultaneously, the national government found it increasingly difficult to implement policies on a coordinated basis, or even to raise adequate revenues through taxation. To govern the country, the members of the Assembly had to rely upon their own ability to persuade local authorities to follow national directives.

English parliamentary leaders faced similar difficulties during the Civil War. But at least they could deal with well-established and familiar local authorities, masters of local governments with proven powers of social control. French local authorities after 1789 were brand new and without adequate means to perform their assumed functions. As soon as departments had been created in 1790 as an important level of government "above" the municipalities, the two sets of local authorities, each tending to represent different kinds of interests, often found themselves at odds with one another. And changing national leaderships or competing national factions courted first one level of local authorities, then the other.[25] Through all of this, furthermore, the political integration of rural areas was potentially weak – and subject to breakdown when and where peasant and urban interests became contradictory. For the most active local authorities in the newly emerging national system were strictly town based. Overall, then, the revolutionary liberal government that emerged in France in 1789–90 was more tenuously based than the English parliamentary government. This was hardly surprising, given the origins of the French liberal regime. It had only been able to form in the first place by virtue of the decentralizing disorganization of the royal administration upon which the prerevolutionary dominant class had depended.

The Impact of Peasant Revolts

To make matters worse, the French liberal revolutionaries immediately and persistently faced more dire threats than the English parliamentarians – threats both of uncontrollable revolts from below, and of deepening dominant-class polarization over fundamental social and political issues. Here peasant revolts become important. For the reasons spelled out in Chapter 3, widespread peasant revolts against dominant-class landlords never developed in the English Revolution. The English upper class was left free to quarrel over political forms (about which they were potentially much more unified than the French anyway) without facing a social-revolutionary challenge from below. But peasant revolts, directed especially against holders of seigneurial rights within the French dominant class, did emerge in France in the spring and summer of 1789. And their consequences for the French Revolution were very substantial. Most basically, of course, the direct accomplishment of the peasant revolts was an attack on the existing class structure, the elimination of one existing mode of surplus appropriation and control over agricultural property and production. Of equal, if not more, importance were the "feedback" effects of the peasant revolts on the course of national revolutionary politics. Because of their impact upon the actions of the Constituent Assembly (directly in August 1789 and indirectly after that), the peasant revolts spurred the abolition not only of seigneurialism but of many other old-regime institutions as well. They facilitated the emergence of the uniform, rational administrative and legal system that has characterized modern France since 1790. But at the same time, the peasant revolts and their national political repercussions promoted increasing political polarization within the dominant class. Thus the peasants helped to ensure that the institutionalization of a liberal, constitutional-monarchist regime would be a mirage ever fading as the moderate revolutionary leaders reached out for it.

183

The snowballing rural unrest of the summer of 1789 presented the newborn Constituent Assembly with stark choices and created a crisis mentality among the members. In contrast to the urban popular unrest of July, the peasant revolts could not be managed or coopted by any constituted authorities. Nor could they be systematically repressed without regenerating the absolutist administration that had so recently been disassembled and partially replaced in the cities and towns. Some of the more militant deputies in the Assembly saw the crisis situation as an opportunity to speed up and guarantee the elimination of many particularistic privileges that compromised national unity and the ideal of juridical equality for all citizens. So on the famous night of August the fourth seigneurial rights were "abolished" (actually made commutable through monetary payments). In addition, a succession of special privileges, property rights, and tax immunities—of towns, provinces, court nobles, provincial nobles, venal officers, and the Church—were surrendered in a partially engineered, partially spontaneous outburst of renunciations. Compensation was voted for economically significant losses (such as seigneurial rights, venal offices, and reduced ecclesiastical tithes). Nevertheless a lot of "medieval rubbish" was swept away very quickly.[26]

Privileges of the Third Estate elites as well as nobles and churchmen were sacrificed. Yet for many conservatives who had already been forced to accede reluctantly to the establishment of the National/Constituent Assembly, these socioeconomic losses so quickly superimposed upon the loss of political privileges were too much to accept. In addition, within months, the Assembly was forced to confiscate Church lands in order to rescue the still deteriorating national finances; for new state obligations to venal officeholders and the Church had been incurred as a result of the August reforms. Rural unrest continued to simmer and recurrently boil over, as the peasants refused to pay redemption for seigneurial dues while still withholding the dues themselves. Occasionally the peasants struck out violently at seigneurs or their manors.[27] And discipline in the army continued to deteriorate as rank-and-filers, here, deserted in large numbers and, there, refused to obey or rebelled against the mostly noble officers.[28] Nobles, especially, became ever more disproportionately vulnerable to attacks and losses. For the means of administration and coercion were now largely in the hands of municipal authorities. Thus the nobles—and especially the rural nobles— were without direct control over or access to any administrative or military means to protect their interests and position. Thus, in steadily increasing numbers from the fall of 1789 on, many rural nobles, as well as other conservatives who abhorred popular disorders and national political developments, emigrated from France.[29] They often went to join the counterrevolutionary army being formed by the king's brother Artois, who was appealing to other European monarchs to intervene militarily in France.

Meanwhile at home, the king and other reluctant conservatives never ceased to demonstrate distaste for the Revolution and refused to cooperate wholeheartedly with moderate leaders, who kept trying to consolidate a nationally unified constitutional monarchy. The king and his friends had no administrative or military means at their disposal to reverse the Revolution. Yet their noncooperation, especially in the context of the growing counterrevolutionary rhetoric from the emigrés abroad, was enough to reinforce radical – and ultimately republican and democratic – political tendencies within the Assembly and among those who followed its proceedings across France and in Paris.

Thus from August 1789 onward a dynamic of polarization was set up that inexorably strengthened the extreme of full-scale aristocratic–monarchical revival on the one hand. On the other hand, there was intensified distrust of the king and fear of counterrevolution, leading ultimately to radical republicanism. As we shall soon see, the tensions increasingly immobilized and finally (under wartime conditions) tore apart the tenuously united liberal revolutionary government of 1789–92. In turn, this would provide openings for urban mass mobilization by radical political elites, men who were marginal to the old landed–commercial dominant class and primarily oriented to self- and national advancement through state-building activities. Comparable openings for urban popular radicals and state-building elites never emerged in the English Revolution. There the center of gravity – and the leadership of the revolutionary New Model Army – remained with landed gentlemen from a dominant class securely politically based in parliament and local governments. No such nexus of political power was available to the French dominant class. Once the revolutionary crisis of 1789 had emerged, therefore, not only did owners of seigneurial rights have to cope with peasant revolts in the uncontrollable countryside. Equally fateful was the fact that the liberal sectors of the dominant class also proved unable to replace absolute monarchy with any solidly based parliamentary-style government that would be capable of reuniting the propertied strata and securing their rule against potential bureaucratic and popular political threats.

WAR, THE JACOBINS, AND NAPOLEON

Ultimately it was the French declaration of war on Austria in April 1792 – involving the nation in the first of a series of international conflicts that were to embroil Europe until 1815 – that delivered the coup de grace to the liberal phase of 1789–91. This act set in motion the processes of governmental centralization and popular political mobilization that were to culminate first in the Montagnard Terror of 1793–4, and then in the Napole-

185

onic dictatorship. As Marcel Reinhard once succinctly put it, "La guerre révolutionna la Révolution."[30] The pressures upon the French revolutionary leaders after 1791 to mobilize for wars on the Continent, even as they fought counterrevolutionaries at home, must be reckoned as a set of conditions comparable in importance to the effects of the social-revolutionary conjuncture of 1789 in determining the centralizing nature of the outcomes of the French Revolution. Again France contrasts to England, for the English revolutionaries did not face invasions from major military powers.

How could we conclude, as have one set of interpreters, that war was a historical accident that "blew the Revolution off course"?[31] To believe this is to suppose that the Revolution could have proceeded, let alone broken out, in a France somehow suddenly and miraculously ripped out of the context of the European states system in which it had always been embedded. Neither the domestic actors in the French revolutionary dramas nor the foreign spectators, kings and peoples, ever succumbed to such an illusion. Underlying the initial outbreak of war (between France and Austria) in 1792 and the recurrent outbreaks on ever wider scales thereafter were simply the long-established tensions and balance-of-power dynamics of the European states system—now interacting with the uncertainties and sudden changes of the unfolding Revolution.[32] Within revolutionary France conflicting groups were repeatedly tempted (like Court cliques under the Old Regime) to use for factional purposes preparations for wars, and the anticipated or actual consequences of successful campaigns. Similarly, the other powers of Europe discovered in both the initial debasement of monarchical France, and then in the threatening results of the renewed strength of Republican and Napoleonic France, reasons aplenty to fight again and again. Ultimately the French Revolution gave direct rise to a militant system that attempted, as Louis XIV had dreamed, to master the entire Continent. It failed because both France and the other Continental land monarchies were outflanked by, on the one hand, the burgeoning commercial–industrial power of Britain and, on the other, by the unconquerable vastness of Imperial Russia.[33] With that failure the unique impetuses of the revolutionary legacy were spent, without having achieved international supremacy for France. Nevertheless, under the aegis of mobilization for war and military intervention in unstable internal politics, a centralized bureaucratic state had been constructed, to be bequeathed to a consolidated French nation. Thus warfare was far from extrinsic to the development and fate of the French Revolution; rather it was central and constitutive, just as one would expect from knowing the nature and dilemmas of the Old Regime from which the Revolution sprang.

186

Popular Discontents and Mobilization for Revolutionary Dictatorship

When the Brissotins engineered France into declaring war against Austria in April 1792, they supposed that the effort would unify a patriotic and revolutionary nation and propel it to easy victories. But, in fact, internal political polarization was only exacerbated. The armies performed poorly, debilitated by the emigration or disaffection of many officers, and by the insubordination or lack of training of rank-and-file soldiers. The ensuing French military defeats, in turn, raised the hopes and fears of reactionaries and radicals at home. At the same time, war ineluctably brought inflation as the value of the *assignat* plummeted. While radical politicians spread republican slogans, the worsening political and military crises and the rising cost of basic foodstuffs aroused the discontent of the masses of urban *menu peuple*.

Who were these urban *menu peuple,* and what was the basis of their role in the revolutionary process? They were not a class in any modern (especially capitalist) sense, for their loosely defined ranks included: property owners such as shopkeepers, master artisans, and small merchants; proto-wage workers, such as journeymen and hired hands; and minor salaried or professional people.[34] If such people had anything socioeconomic in common, it was that they worked for a living, acquired or held property (if at all) only in close conjunction with their work, and shared a mutual resentment of the rich and privileged (including bourgeois) who "lived nobly." Likewise, the *menu peuple* shared a concern about the price and sheer availability of basic necessities. For as nonprivileged urban dwellers in a historical period when the supplying of cities with bread and other goods was recurrently problematic due to the vagaries of weather, difficult transportation, and "imperfect" markets, they could never be certain of affording or getting enough to take care of their families. Certainly, as the researches of George Rudé have demonstrated, the basic anxiety of the *menu peuple* about affordable necessities underlay popular political participation at virtually all of the decisive turning points (*journées*) of the Revolution from 1788–9 until 1795.[35]

Yet there was another factor at work: selective and steadily deepening political awareness.[36] For the *menu peuple* at each point in the Revolution threw their support to those political elites who seemed the surest supporters at first (1788–9), of "liberty" and, then (1791–), also of "equality" – equality in political rights and the right to livelihood. And as the threat of armed counterrevolution grew, the politically active *menu peuple,* above all in Paris, became the self-consciously republican, antiaristocratic, and moralistically equalitarian *sans culottes.* They demanded that the distinction be-

187

tween "active" and "passive" citizens enshrined in the original 1790 Constitution be abolished. And they organized their own political and military participation in neighborhood sections (in Paris), in urban communes, in committees of surveillance, and in *armées révolutionnaires* (armed bands of self-appointed defenders of the Revolution, which also increasingly took it upon themselves to procure basic supplies for the towns and cities).[37]

By the end of 1792, due in large part to the active intervention of the *sans culottes* in key political demonstrations and armed actions, not only the Brissotins, but the monarchy and the Legislative Assembly as well, were swept away in favor of a liberal-democratic Republic. Initially, though, the structure of national government remained as administratively noncentralized as before, supposedly coordinated by the elected Convention while it was at work drafting a new constitution. As might be expected, this was not adequate to the crisis circumstances of the day. Events soon overwhelmed the Convention and tore apart at the seams the decentralized form of government carried over from the liberal antimonarchical revolution. Notwithstanding some fortunate early victories by the armies of the Republic, by early 1793 foreign enemies were pressing in anew upon France. Simultaneously there were internal revolts. Spurred by the threat of conscription to the national army, the peasants of the Vendée rose against the revolutionary government in March. And as events in Paris (such as the purging of the Girondins from the Convention in late May) outran political developments in the provinces and threw ever more disaffected politicians into opposition, numerous local rebellions based upon departmental or municipal governments broke out to challenge the authority of Paris. By early summer over one-third of the departments of France were involved in such counterrevolutionary or "federalist" revolts, in some cases providing favorable opportunities for foreign military intervention.

What emerged to meet the crisis of defending the Revolution from its armed enemies at home and abroad was a dictatorial and arbitrary system of government. The leaders were dedicated minorities of Montagnard Jacobins, who mobilized, manipulated, and channeled the spontaneous discontents and fervor of the *sans culottes*.[38] In Paris, Robespierre and other Montagnard deputies in the Convention established themselves in the Committee of Public Safety and Committee of General Security and maintained links to spokesmen for the *sans culottes* of the Paris Commune. Working through "representatives on mission" and "national agents" dispatched from the Convention, through local district committees of surveillance, and through the network of Jacobin clubs throughout France, the Committees imposed steadily tighter central coordination on the nation's politics. "Elections were suspended, and the renewal of [local] administrative councils was turned over to the national 'representatives' with the help of the popular societies . . . To the extreme decentralization

of the Constituent Assembly, there now succeeded the strongest centralization that France had yet known."[39] Draconian and summary judicial measures, known as the Terror, were adopted to imprison and execute enemies
of the Revolution. Urged upon the Montagnard government by its popular
supporters, these measures struck nobles, refractory priests, and rich bourgeois most frequently (in relation to their proportion of the total population). But in absolute numbers many more peasants and urban poor were
affected, most of them from rebellious areas. The overall patterns of exe-
cutions in the Terror conclusively suggest that its primary function was not
class war but political defense, that in the words of Donald Greer it was
"employed to crush rebellion and to quell opposition to the Revolution,
the Republic, or the Mountain . . . "[40] Without such measures it is difficult
to imagine how any semblance of centralized government could have so
suddenly emerged. Even with the Terror (indeed in part because of its
violent arbitrariness), the system that did emerge was at first not at all
routinized. Instead it featured representatives on mission and local bodies
doing widely various, even contradictory, things in different places, all in
the name of defending the Revolution (and the Montagnards).[41] Only
gradually were more standardized controls instituted.

The chief purpose and most enduring achievement of the Montagnard
dictatorship was to expand, envigorate, and supply the national armies of
France. One of the first measures adopted (in August 1793) by the Committee of Public Safety was the famous *levée en masse,* which proclaimed:

> All Frenchmen are in permanent requisition for army service. The
> young men will go to fight; the married men will forge arms and carry
> supplies; the women will make tents and uniforms and will serve in the
> hospitals; the children will shred the old clothes; the old men will be
> taken to the public squares to excite the courage of the combatants,
> the hatred of royalty and the unity of the Republic.[42]

The armies of France expanded enormously, and the members of the Committee on Public Safety, above all Lazare Carnot, "the organizer of victory,"
busied themselves with selecting and advising new generals for the armies,
propagandizing the troops, and bending all of the government's powers to
the enormous problems of supplying the armies. For as it promoted mass
military mobilization, the Montagnard government also requisitioned and
purchased food and other supplies for the armies and cities, organized the
manufacture of armaments, and regulated prices for basic commodities and
labor. The "regulation of the economy was soon as extensive as the bureaucracy of the day and the power of coercion could make it."[43] This was not
only because, as many interpreters of the Revolution stress, the Montagnards were under constant pressure from the *sans culottes* to relieve popular
economic distress. It was also because only through such tight controls
could the revolutionary armies be supplied with food and materials.

189

Yet an important point about the revolutionary dictatorship's military achievement should be made. The Montagnards did not start from scratch. Nor did they scrap the regular armies and simply replace them with armed volunteers, organized into self-governing units as the early revolutionary militias had been. As the recent researches of S. F. Scott have demonstrated,[44] the line armies of France, though weakened considerably by unusually high rates of rank and file desertion in 1789 and 1790, and unsettled by the massive emigration of noble officers from 1789 through 1792, nevertheless were organizationally quite intact in 1793 when the Montagnards took over. Line army units had, moreover, already recovered to normal rank-and-file strength by 1791–2, and the officer corps had been replenished by promotions of pre-1789 enlisted men (who constituted more than half of the officers by early 1792). During 1793–4, the Montagnards amalgamated volunteer units and newly mobilized citizen soldiers with the existing line units of the standing armies. Simultaneously, politically loyal and victorious officers were promoted from within by representatives on mission from the Committee of Public Safety. To be sure, the armies were vastly expanded and infused with new patriotic élan; and (as will be discussed later) certain new kinds of battle tactics became possible with highly motivated citizen troops. But these troops were–for all their political awareness and involvement–incorporated into the framework of line armies that had not completely dissolved in 1789–92. Despite transformations, these had survived to serve as a basis for revolutionary statebuilding in the context of Continental land warfare.

The Fall of the Montagnards

Under the dictatorial rule of the Committee of Public Safety the armies of revolutionary France turned from demoralization and defeats to frequent victories. By early 1794, they had mastered every major internal and external military threat to the Republic. From then on, however, dissatisfaction grew among former supporters of the Montagnard dictatorship. And by the summer of 1794 Robespierre and his key lieutenants were dispatched to the guillotine as the Convention revoked its support for the Committee dictatorship.

There were both political and economic precipitants to the Dictatorship's downfall. To consider the economic difficulties first, the Montagnard attempt to control prices and wages had, in actuality, been virtually impossible to administer in such a decentralized preindustrial economy.[45] The emergency needs of the state had been met, but social groups were left disgruntled. In the urban centers, shopkeepers, merchants, and small employers complained of too-low prices and too-high wages. And the poorer members of the *sans culottes* complained above all when the Montagnards tried to lower the wage maximum in the spring of 1794, a time when reasonably priced bread was still hard to come by.

Meanwhile, property-owning peasants in the countryside were increasingly reluctant to produce or sell in return for artificially low prices, or in the face of forcible requisitions by government agents and armed bands of urban revolutionaries. The irony is that these peasants were the same ones who had been most advantaged by the agrarian changes of the Revolution. They had benefited most not only from the peasantry's collective struggle from below against seigneurial claims and tithes but also from the legal decrees by which radicals in the Convention sought to court peasant support during the military crisis of the Revolution. Montagnards were willing to sanction the peasants' victory of 1789–92 by eliminating the (unenforceable) laws calling for peasants to compensate owners of the old seigneurial rights. The Montagnards also made some efforts to allow peasants to purchase in small units lands confiscated from the Church and emigré nobles. Yet, like all other political leaderships during the French Revolution, they consistently aimed to reinforce the legal rights of individual property owners. In fact, this was the only sensible political strategy for the Montagnards to follow, given that their "party" enjoyed no extensive organizational basis in the countryside, and given that French poor peasants had no collective organizations of their own through which to press programs for land redistribution (or for legal protection of those particular collective rights carried over from feudal times that guarded their interests). Politically, the best that the Montagnards could hope to do was to attach as many peasant smallholders as possible to the revolutionary cause by legally sanctioning the gains already made, and by allowing as many individuals as possible to purchase national lands. Simultaneously, however, this had the effect of reinforcing the hold over the agrarian economy of the very same peasant proprietors whose interests would necessarily be aggrieved by the emergency price controls and forcible grain requisitions of the Montagnard dictatorship in 1793–4.

In addition, the Montagnards were facing political contradictions, again the logical result of their own policies.[46] Perhaps sensing their insecure position, the Montagnards actually intensified the official Terror after the decisive military victories were won. And they used it not only to punish defeated counterrevolutionaries but also to strike out at factions to the immediate right (Dantonists) and left (Hebertists) of the leadership of the Dictatorship. This served to make moderates in the Convention uneasy, rousing them to look for ways to revoke their mandate to the Committees. And it severed the Committees' strongest leadership ties to the popular movement in Paris. The loss of the Hebertist link to the left was especially serious because, by the spring of 1794, the *sans culottes* were no longer the spontaneous revolutionary force they had been when their interventions

191

originally brought the Montagnards to power. Ironically, one of the prime accomplishments of the Dictatorship had been to tame and routinize the popular movement. Popular assemblies and bodies that had once been direct democracies were either discouraged from meeting or were coopted as subordinate organs of the Dictatorship, with their leaders in many cases becoming paid government officials. The all-out war effort, moreover, had depleted the ranks and fervor of the original *sans culottes,* as many went to the fronts, and as the energies of those left behind were channeled into routine support work. Add to all of this the growing economically motivated disgruntlement of the *sans culottes* with the Montagnard government, and it is not difficult to understand why Robespierre could be toppled in Thermidor without effective resistance from below.

Some combination of these economic and political contradictions is usually invoked by historians as sufficient to explain why the Montagnard dictatorship was curtailed and the radicalization of the French Revolution ended in 1794. Indeed, the aforementioned contradictions *were* sufficient, but only because they operated in the sociopolitical and world-historical context of late-eighteenth-century France. As we shall see in the next major part of this chapter, very similar difficulties pressed in upon the Bolsheviks in 1921 in the immediate wake of their Civil War victories. Had the Bolsheviks fallen from power, historians could easily attribute their fall to the worker and peasant discontent and to the economic contradictions of the "war communist" command economy – both of which conditions were acutely apparent in 1921. However, the Bolsheviks managed to execute economic policy changes (including concessions to market-oriented interests and peasant smallholders) and remain in national political power. Why could they do it, and not the Montagnards in 1794? As the "party of the proletariat," operating in a twentieth-century society that already had large-scale, modern industries, the Bolsheviks enjoyed two advantages: They possessed both an ideological self-justification and a realistic organizational basis for a political mission that could sustain their movement in state power beyond the military defense of the Revolution. The Bolsheviks could "fall back" on state-controlled industries and could devote themselves after 1921 to devising ways to use state power to expand those industries and the numbers of factory workers employed in them. By contrast, the Montagnards in France, even if they had been consistently willing to conceive of themselves as the "party of the *sans culottes,*" did not have objectively available to them any expansionist economic mission to sustain them in state power beyond the military victories of 1793–4. The *sans culottes* themselves were an inextricable mixture of market-oriented small property owners and nonpropertied people who had an interest in resisting current trends of economic development. More important, a French economy consisting almost entirely of small-scale agricultural and commercial units (and some nonmechanized industrial enterprises) simply could not be directed from above by a political party. There were no "commanding heights" for the state to manage; and even foreign models of large-scale industry were entirely lacking at that point in world history.

In revolutionary France, therefore, the potential practical contributions of the Jacobin radicals to French national power and development ended when the dire counterrevolutionary military threats were overcome. At that point little remained for them to do but to continue violent punitive measures against ever more vaguely defined counterrevolutionaries, and to attempt to enforce the cultural forms of the Republic of Virtue, complete with the "Cult of the Supreme Being" to replace Catholicism.[47] The political cohesiveness of the Montagnards decreased as their potential opponents in the country and the Convention grew bolder. Even the "twelve who ruled" on the Committee of Public Safety did not stick together or act with decisiveness of purpose from the spring of 1794 — a real contrast to the way the Bolshevik leaders would act in 1921.

The Search for Stability

After the fall of Robespierre, the Thermidorian Convention quickly dismantled the judicial apparatus of the Terror and the centralized controls of the emergency revolutionary government. Suffering the effects of rising prices and the sudden loosening of economic restraints, the Parisian *menu peuple* rose again in the spring of 1795.[48] But without radical political elites willing and able to channel their support, the urban *menu peuple* could no longer be the arbiters of the Revolution. Indeed, this time their initiative was brutally suppressed and their leadership eliminated, as the Convention called in the army against them. By the end of 1795, a regime called the Directory (because it featured five executive directors) was installed under a new republican constitution. This constitution was designed both to preserve moderate politicians of the Convention in power (by law, two-thirds of them had to be elected or appointed to the Directory's councils) and to give wealthier citizens considerable local administrative and national legislative power. Once again an attempt was being made to consolidate the Revolution in liberal form. But the liberal-republican Directory was to be no more successful than the pre-1792 constitutional monarchy, for it was plagued with similar problems and inadequacies.

The Directory did not dismantle everything inherited from its predecessors; it retained most civil servants and expanded the central administrative bureaus. "The central bureaucracy was thus given a renewed stability, which paved the way for the vital role it was to play in the new state moulded by Napoleon and bequeathed by him to later generations."[49]

193

Nevertheless, executive authority was weak. Nominally there were agents of the Directors charged with supervising local departmental authorities, but they were usually influential men of their communities appointed through the patronage of local representatives in the legislative councils. Faced with overwhelming problems of economic crises (especially in 1795–7), continuing foreign wars and financial crises, and outbreaks of White Terror and resistance to anti-Catholic policies, the Directors found themselves without effective legitimate means to influence the composition or policies of either the national legislative councils or the local governments. "[T]he central government proved incapable of enforcing its own decrees. It could not persuade electors to vote. It could not force recalcitrant authorities to levy the forced loan [a device to alleviate the government's financial crisis], pursue refractory priests, or answer government questionnaires. It could not prevent them from condoning massive desertion."[50] The Directory's difficulties reflected not only its inefficient institutional structure but also its weak social support.[51] Though its structure and policies were meant to (and did) benefit the property-holding strata, these did not wholeheartedly support the Directory in return. Partly this was because the Directory, despite its anti-Jacobin policies, was still far too radical in its personnel and its antiroyalist and antichurch policies for many propertied elements. Partly, too, it was because the dominant economic groups in France were by 1795 more politically fractionated than ever, with royalists opposing republicans and each camp divided within its own ranks. In the wake of the popular mobilizations of 1793–4, with their threats to rights of property and to social hierarchies, the French propertied strata were even less capable than they had been before 1793 of compromising about and operating within a set of decentralized, liberal political institutions. The Directory represented an attempt by republican politicians of the Thermidorian Convention to retain and liberalize state power with property holders' support. But it was an unsuccessful attempt, both because of its institutional inadequacies and because the propertied would not – and probably could not – cooperate politically.

Lacking either broad social support or administrative means for authoritarian rule – and of course unwilling to resort to mass political mobilization – the precariously based Directory turned to the armies of France to shore up its rule, not only through direct repression of armed rebels but also through repeated purges of the elected legislative councils. Meanwhile the national armies were evolving into highly professionalized and organizationally self-contained bodies: One-time revolutionary volunteers were "increasingly indifferent to domestic political squabbles, and increasingly aware of the special skills and interests of the soldier's trade."[52] And the officers, once dependent upon civilian governments for advancement to the higher ranks, were now being coopted from within by

194

the generals. "By the end of the Directory, the fastest way to achieve promotion was to join the clientele of an influential general."[53] Thus, even as government leaders came to rely routinely upon the armies, their leaders were becoming less subject to civilian political control.

Predictably enough, it was not long before an adventurous general (invited to intervene by some of the Directors in 1799) proved willing to exploit the indispensability and prestige of the army to seize power in a coup d'état. Napoleon Bonaparte used his base in the army to establish himself (step by step) first as de facto dictator, then as First Consul for life, and finally as full-fledged dynastic emperor.

Much more important, though, were the institutional developments under Napoleon. By legally confirming the status quo of the social and economic accomplishments of the Revolution and by reintroducing administrative centralization, Napoleon managed to put end to the violent civil conflicts of the revolutionary period. His approach worked so well especially because, to assemble his regime, Napoleon borrowed personnel without prejudice from politically flexible survivors of all previous regimes. As Godechot puts it:

> This gigantic administrative reorganization, involving state appointment to a large number of well paid posts, gave Bonaparte the opening for a work of reconciliation. The Directory owed its fall partly to the narrowness of its political foundations. Bonaparte, well aware of that fact, looked for allies on the Right as well as on the Left, and his most successful method of winning sympathy was to appoint men from all sections of the political world to the new posts which were opening . . . [A]mong the prefects: in the first batch were 15 *constituants,* 16 *legislateurs,* 19 *conventionnels* and 26 former members of the Directory's Councils. Some had been terrorists, others belonged to the nobility.[54]

To make his eclectic system work, Napoleon judiciously dispensed with nonroutinized mass mobilizations and with all manifestations of ideological commitment. Wielding instead the symbols, rituals, and propaganda of a highly generalized French nationalism, Bonaparte decorated his essentially authoritarian–bureaucratic regime with a hodgepodge of symbolic concessions to the inherited factions: plebiscitary and patriotic rituals for the radicals; consultative councils with restricted electoral bases for the liberals; and a Concordat with the Catholic Church for conservatives.[55]

After a breather in 1802–3, the price of Napoleon's internal settlement was continuing French participation in general European wars. Napoleon marshalled French enthusiasms and resources more efficiently than ever before for foreign military adventures, which remade much of the face of Europe. Nevertheless, Napoleon's project of conquering the entire Continent was ultimately doomed to failure. French conquests soon stimulated nationalist reactions in the other countries of Europe, so that Europe's long-standing patterns of state competition and power balance triumphed again in new political forms. Moreover, Napoleon's inland-oriented "Continental" system could not at that point in world history hope to best England's commercial–industrial empire based on sea power.[56]

Yet no matter how much strain his military exploits put on French resources, Napoleon never lost his grip at home while they were at all successful. Given the only purposes to which the enhanced state power generated by the Revolution *could* have been (at that point in world history) directly and immediately applied – that is, to stabilization at home and to the attempt to establish French hegemony in Europe through military conquests – Napoleon's political "solution" to the power struggles of the Revolution indeed made more sense than the Jacobins' extravagant dream of the Republic of Virtue. Napoleon was only removed from power by foreign interventions after military collapse. Even then, his basic institutional accomplishments remained behind, because subsequent regimes could afford neither to reverse the revolutionary settlement nor to dispense with the administrative power bequeathed to them by Bonaparte.

THE NEW REGIME

What kind of sociopolitical system did Napoleon's military dictatorship consolidate? To understand the basic and enduring features of the outcomes of the French Revolution, we need to retrace our steps. This time, though, it is important to pull back a bit from the dynamics of the Revolution in order to review systematically the most striking changes wrought by the revolutionary struggles in the structure of the French state and its functioning within society.

Changes in the Army

Nowhere were the bureaucratic and "democratic" accomplishments of the Revolution better exemplified than in the army. With respect to two lines of military development in Europe – professionalization of the officer corps and the emergence of a national army – the French Revolution represented a true watershed.[57]

Under the Old Regime, the officer corps constituted an inflated set of honorific as well as functional positions. The highest offices were virtually monopolized by men with noble status and connections at the royal court and with the wealth to pay for commissions and promotions. Officers' duties, conceived as prestigious "service" in the feudal tradition, were not paid for as if they constituted a full-time occupation. Moreover, to afford the expenses of display associated with the status, most officers had to combine their military pursuits with remunerative activities on the side.[58]

196

The Revolution basically changed the organization and functioning of the officer corps.[59] The abolition of nobility and establishment of equality of opportunity formally opened access to officer posts to citizens from all social backgrounds. The number of officer positions was restricted as honorific functions gave way to the strictly utilitarian. For the same reason, the technologically advanced artillery was raised from the last-ranking to the first-ranking branch of service.[60] Venality of commissions and promotions was abolished, and military officers were provided with salaries adequate to allow them to become full-time, career specialists. Finally, promotions, which came unusually frequently in the midst of the internal strife and wars of the revolutionary period, were made on the basis of education, skill, and, above all else, military experience, including service in the ranks (though, of course, political connections always mattered, especially for promotions to the highest positions).

These organizational changes, together with the social and political upheavals of the Revolution, ensured an influx of men of nonnoble (especially urban, educated middle class) backgrounds into an officer corps that had been over 90 percent noble before 1789. Nevertheless, many men of noble background survived and even prospered unusually under the new system. In fact, nothing better confirms the fact that the changes wrought by the Revolution were as much organizational as purely or primarily social than the remarkable career success in the army of the revolutionary period of many poor, provincial nobles. Such individuals could not have expected to compete successfully with wealthy, court-connected nobles under the Old Regime.[61] Napoleon Bonaparte himself provides a striking example of provincial-noble mobility during the Revolution. Born the son of a minor Corsican nobleman, he attended a provincial military academy under the Old Regime and was commissioned a lieutenant. The Revolution remarkably enhanced what could only have been a dead-end career. Connections to the Jacobins enabled Bonaparte to be placed in command of the artillery in the battle to subdue rebellious Toulon, and after the victory over the royalists there Napoleon was promoted to brigadier general. Thermidor brought temporary setbacks, but before long, after helping to suppress royalist demonstrations against the regime in 1795, Napoleon rose in the service of the Directory to become commander-in-chief, first of the Army of the Interior and then of expeditionary forces in Italy. Such were the possibilities for army men of talent and guile during the Revolution, even for many of politically disadvantageous noble background.

The Revolution brought changes for the rank-and-file infantry as well. Before 1789, enlistment was "voluntary" but did not attract those with decent civilian livelihoods. Discipline was crude and arbitrary, and the pay and upkeep were low and undependable. The standing army, numbering about two-hundred thousand, was not large relative to France's population of twenty-five million; Prussia, for example, enlisted a much higher proportion of her subjects. And one-sixth of the French army consisted of foreigners.[62] With the Revolution came increasing mass military involvement in forms celebrated as patriotic. It began with the establishment, and then gradual expansion to include poorer citizens, of the urban National Guards, and reached a peak in the celebrated *levée en masse* of 1793. The French armies swelled to 770,000 by 1794.[63] With the continuation of wars, the Directory passed in 1798 a Law of Conscription, which set the framework for a permanent national standing army: "Every Frenchman is a soldier and owes himself to the defense of the Fatherland," the law declared.[64] Napoleon put organizational teeth into this law and used it to raise ever-increasing numbers of soldiers. "In the ten years from 1804 to 1813 he drafted 2,400,000 men . . . "[65] His campaigns spent men liberally, for he extended systems of fighting and maneuver inherited from the fierce battles of 1792–4. In these campaigns civilly treated and politically propagandized citizen soldiers were hurled against enemy armies in huge, loosely supervised masses and were urged to live off the land and to attack and pursue the enemy until his armies were destroyed. In sum, as Gordon Craig writes:

> The destruction of the old régime and the granting of fundamental rights to all citizens had an immediate effect upon the constitution of the French army. They made possible the creation of a truly national army, and one which, because its rank and file was composed of citizens devoted to the national cause, was freed from the rigid limitations of eighteenth-century warfare. It was no longer necessary for the French to concentrate their forces in close array upon the battlefield, forbidding independent manoeuvre lest it lead to mass desertion. The French *tirailleurs* advanced in extended order, fighting, firing, and taking cover as individuals, and the army gained immeasurably in tactical elasticity in consequence. Troops could, moreover, be trusted to forage for themselves, and it was now possible to divorce French units from the cumbersome supply trains and the dependence on magazines which restricted the mobility of the old model armies. This liberation from the tyranny of logistics, combined with the new tactics and the perfected divisional organization, introduced a completely new kind of warfare to Europe—the type of lightning war of which Napoleon showed himself the master in the Italian campaign of 1800.[66]

Changes in the Civil State

Analogous to the changes wrought in the military sphere, the French Revolution brought about in the civil state a "conjunction of democratic government with bureaucratic administration," variations of which have ever after

198

marked the political system of France.[67] The first and most basic thing to be noted is the sheer growth in size of the French administrative machinery during the Revolution. One scholarly authority, Clive H. Church, has been reported as estimating that during the Revolution "the size of the bureaucracy may have risen from 50,000 to nearly a quarter of a million; the staff of the central ministries, for example, increased from 420 in 1788 to over 5,000 by 1796."[68] Indeed, according to Richard Cobb, perhaps as many as 150,000 new bureaucrats were appointed during the Terror alone. Cobb quips that the Revolution created *"La France fonctionnaire."*[69]

Obviously this seems appropriate given the numerical expansion alone; it seems all the more so once we comprehend the social and organizational implications of the bureaucratizing changes wrought by the Revolution. These implications have been brilliantly documented for the realm of state finances by J. F. Bosher. His book, *French Finances, 1770–1795,* is tellingly subtitled "From Business to Bureaucracy," to convey that "in the realm of government finance, the French Revolution seems to have brought to an end an era of private capitalism and inaugurated an age of public administration."[70] For "something happened that was more fundamental than the victory of one social class over another. This was the invention of an administrative weapon for social and political domination."[71]

Under the Old Regime there was no unified royal treasury and no central budgetary accounting or control over governmental revenues and expenditures. Instead the management of state finances was in the hands of venal officers—at once noblemen and profit-seeking businessmen—such as the farmers general, receivers general, treasurers general, payers of the *rentes,* and other high accountants. These

> higher offices had become the private property of accountants and were fast becoming the patrimony of noble families. Accountable only to the Chambers of Accounts, these high financial figures were not part of an administrative hierarchy and not subject to ministerial inspection or command. Most of their income did not come from salaries but from profits on their activities as the Crown's bankers, collecting and spending revenues, lending the government more and more money, and engaging in their own business activities. Loosely organized in professional corps or *compagnies* with committees to review their corporate interests, the financiers exercised a profitable monopoly over the collecting and spending of royal revenues and over the short-term credit business in the system.[72]

What elements of true bureaucracy there were under the Old Regime were confined to the scattered *bureaux,* consisting of groups of clerks working for the independent higher officers or for the bureau heads of the royal ministries. As salaried employees these "might be thought of as having bureaucratic status, except that they were more like the domestic servants

199

of the men they served,"[73] for they assisted their masters in personal business as well as in the management of royal finances, and they were hired and fired at will.

Fundamental changes came with the Revolution, for the "National Assembly, in large majority, did not like the financial system precisely because it was in the hands of profit-seeking capitalists—they used that word—"[74] and it sought to establish national management of public finances instead.

> The National Assembly planned to guard the public finances by bureaucratic organization. With a vision of mechanical efficiency and articulation, ... the revolutionary planners hoped to prevent corruption, putting their faith in the virtues of organization to offset the vices of individual men. This hope was at the very heart of the financial revolution. Instead of several hundred separate caisses (funds) in the hands of independent, profit-seeking accountants and tax farmers, France was to have a consolidated central fund in a bureaucratic Treasury composed only of salaried officials performing their duties according to a rational plan of functions. The Treasury grew and grew over the revolutionary years, absorbing the other caisses one after another. The assembly demanded lists of employees, salaries and operating expenses, and arranged for full annual accounts such as the monarchy never had.[75]

The social concomitant of these measures for the state's officialdom was change from a system of entrepreneurial independence and personal hierarchy of precedence and patronage to one of administrative hierarchy based upon impersonal but firm supervision of officials by their superiors. Henceforth, moreover, state officials were expected to engage in the execution of specifically defined public duties distinct from private business. The positions and emoluments of the venal and aristocratic financial agents were abolished. Bureau heads, once independent and well-paid aspirants for the noble higher offices, were reduced to mere *fonctionnaires* with lowered salaries not far above their subordinates. And their clerks were turned into regularly paid civil servants, freed from "personal dependence on their masters, who became merely their superiors."[76] What emerged was a ladder of salaried civil servants all paid by one central authority and subject to central supervision and control.

As for the mode of executive control that enveloped the increasingly bureaucratized staffs of the state administration, the Revolution (as we have seen) passed through a succession of phases. A single legitimating theme ran through all of the phases: an identification of executive functions with the implementation of the nation's or the people's will. Not incidentally, even Bonaparte accomplished his work under the guise of a national-democratic dictatorship. Four times Napoleon, who styled himself the "first representative of the nation," had his rule endorsed by national plebiscites.[77] Nevertheless, Napoleon's institutional achievements were anything but democratic (or liberal).[78] Essentially he added to the reorganized bureaus and staffs inherited from the revolutionary assemblies and from the Directory a system of centrally appointed general administrative and judicial officials. At the apex of the system, was the Council of State, a body of experts appointed by Napoleon and vested with wide de facto powers. Government ministers did not form a cabinet, but instead reported individually to the Council (and to Napoleon). New laws were regularly formulated and deliberated in the legislative section of the Council, and its other working sections (on war, navy, interior, and finance) supervised relevant parts of the state bureaucracy. Below this technocratic apex stretched a hierarchy of appointed judges and administrative officials, reaching down to subprefects and mayors. The crucial link in the hierarchy was the departmental prefect, comparable to the *intendant* of the Old Regime, yet more controllable—and also more powerful, because his jurisdiction was smaller and unencumbered with privileged corporate bodies.

Of course France has had many political regimes since Napoleon's dictatorship—indeed, Bonaparte himself lasted only until 1814, when he was followed by, first, restored Bourbon monarchs, then a "bourgeois" monarchy, a Second Republic, a Second Empire, a Third Republic, and so on into the twentieth century. Most of these regimes involved more significant attempts (than Napoleon I's) to institute (more or less democratic) liberal-parliamentary political controls. Yet as Herbert Leuthy cogently points out, an observer who concentrates only on the recurrently changing constitutional forms will miss understanding the real basis and enduring power of French government.

> If one looks at a constitutional handbook one will find no mention of, or at most a casual footnote devoted to, any of the great institutions on which the permanence of the state depends . . . No mention is made of the Ministries which remain after the Minister of a day has departed. No mention is made of the Council of State which, because of its jurisdiction over the administrative machine, rules supreme over the instruments of state power, is indispensable to an executive incapable of carrying out its will without it, interprets according to its own code the true content of laws passed by Parliament or quietly buries them, and as the universal advisor of Governments usually gets its own way even in the formulation of Government policy, because it has authority and permanence, and the Government has not. No mention is made of the general staff of the financial administration, which is able to modify and interpret the budget passed by Parliament as autocratically as the Council of State is able to modify and interpret its laws, and by its control over state revenue and expenditure is able to

> exercise a decisive influence over the life and death of Govern-
> ments ... Not one of these institutions is derived "from the people."
> They represent the state apparatus of the absolute monarchy, perfected
> and brought to its logical conclusion under the First Empire. When the
> crowned heads fell, the real sovereignty was transferred to this appara-
> tus. But it works in the background, unobtrusively, anonymously, re-
> mote from all publicity and almost in secret ... It is not so much a
> state within a state as the real state behind the facade of the demo-
> cratic state.[79]

Crystallizing this "real state" in the process of ending and consolidating
the Revolution was not only Napoleon's most important task, it was also a
remarkably enduring achievement.

The State in Society

The revolutionized French state had a stronger grip on more functions
than the old-regime monarchy. University and secondary education were
brought under government control to form a highly selective, centralized,
and elitist system from which state administrators and experts could be
recruited.[80] Napoleon's settlement with the Catholic Church made some
concessions (including granting Church control over most primary education). But the Church, with much of its property gone and its priests now
paid by the state, was no longer the independent corporate power that it
had been under the Old Regime. Equally striking was the change in state
financial administration: With taxes now collected by permanent state
appointees not by venal entrepreneurs or elected local authorities, revenues
could be relied upon and the cooperation of bankers obtained to create a
Bank of France, which "rendered considerable service to the state by advancing funds in the form of banknotes."[81] It is true that French public
finances were never fully stabilized under Napoleon's regime. But, in decisive contrast to the Old Regime, the new state could ride out financial
crisis. Napoleon could confiscate funds from financiers and ignore the
protests of dominant economic groups, whereas the monarchical state had
been torn asunder by financial crisis in 1787–9.[82] The state now had the
potential edge even over its most powerful citizens.

Moreover, the revolutionized French state impinged more directly than
ever before on the lives of all citizens, whether they wanted it or not. In the
words of William McNeill:

> What the French revolutionaries did was to sweep away obstacles to
> manipulation of men and resources by a single national command
> center. Peculiar local practices and immunities were systematically sup-
> pressed ... After revolutionary legislation had been codified and ap-
> plied throughout France, individual citizens confronted the august em-

202

bodiment of the Nation, as it were, fact to face, without the protecting integument of corporate identities and roles . . . In actual fact, what a citizen confronted was an agent of the central government—whether representative-on-mission, prefect, tax collector, or recruiting sergeant—who, in the name of the People, demanded goods and services on a far more massive scale than royal agents had ever been able to command.[83]

The effect of this extended reach of the state could be especially jolting for rural communities. Based on their studies of the relations of peasant communities in Brittany to the pre- and postrevolutionary governments, Le Goff and Sutherland concluded that the "Revolution came as an unprecedented and often unwelcome intrusion into the lives of many . . . people. After 1790, the demands the central government made on citizens for attention, activity and loyalty went far beyond the claims of the ramshackle administration of the old regime."[84] Before the Revolution, as long as taxes were paid and major rebellions did not develop, the Breton peasants were left to settle their own disputes, police themselves, and themselves tend to whatever community concerns they and their priest cared to define. Priests and royal government often cooperated informally to channel information "up" and official concerns "down" the state-community ladder. With the Revolution, the local priests were first bypassed by the authority of the departments, districts, and communes, and then officially turned into public employees. Local people were supposed to give more resources and attention to supravillage levels of government run by town-based and urban-minded officials. At the radical height of the Revolution, moreover, many peasants were subject to outright coercion from revolutionary supporters determined to acquire supplies of grain, enforce military conscription, and implement measures to punish refractory priests and suppress Catholic rituals.

In parts of France, including especially Brittany and other areas of the west, the post-1789 changes helped to stimulate peasant resistance to revolutionary authorities, ranging from local actions to guerrilla warfare and participation in large-scale regional revolts. Available studies on the socioeconomic bases of peasant reactions to the Revolution suggest that they were likely to be more amenable to the revolutionary changes in areas where established market relations tied together propertied peasants and local townsmen. Peasants were likely to be less amenable—hence inclined to resist, if possible—in areas where market relations were newly penetrating or where noncommercially oriented peasants were active but unsuccessful competitors with townsmen for lands sold during the Revolution.[85] In the end, though, all overt resistance was suppressed because, due to developments we have already traced, the "Revolution shifted the initiative from the community to the government and at the same time gave government a power to coerce which its counterpart in the old regime had never possessed."[86]

The Napoleonic settlement did, however, back off from the sorts of coercive economic policies and extreme anti-Catholic measures that had turned entire peasant communities and rural regions against the Revolution. Instead, the newly consolidated administrative state, while claiming taxes and conscripts more firmly than ever before, sought an accomodation with property owners in each locality. Well-to-do landowners, including richer peasants, rentier townsmen, and often former nobles, were elected through a limited franchise to cooperate in local government with centrally appointed executive and judicial officials.[87] One result—which politically paralleled the desolidarizing consequences of the successful anti-seigneurial revolts—was to undermine the remnants of village-based solidarity between richer and poorer peasants. This process occurred as oligarchies of richer peasants were officially set apart from, and above, their poorer neighbors and became more closely linked to propertied townsmen and to the centralized state administration. Perhaps more striking still was the cost for village political autonomy. This is well summarized by Thomas Sheppard, who traced the "village" of Lourmarin in Provence through the Revolution. During the eighteenth century, he writes,

> if the village council did not initiate any major programs, neither was it completely submissive to outside authority. It was Lourmarin's political vitality, relatively broad participation in village affairs, and its continuing concern for all its inhabitants, that were hallmarks of the *ancien regime* in Lourmarin. This vitality and excitement were gone after the Revolution and Lourmarin became in the nineteenth century . . . a mere cog in the administrative machinery of the central government. The municipal council discussed only those matters referred to it, made very few decisions itself, and functioned primarily to administer laws and orders channelled to it by the prefect. Bureaucracy and centralization had come to Lourmarin, but the village paid heavily for such modernization.[88]

Yet although French peasants—as indeed all Frenchmen—had to contend after the Revolution with a more powerful and intrusive state, this state was obviously not as all-encompassing or dynamic a presence in the society and economy as the Communist Party-states of revolutionary Russia and China would be. The overall outcome of the French Revolution can be characterized as the symbiotic coexistence of a centralized, professional-bureaucratic state with a society dominated by some moderately large and many medium and small owners of private property. In this French New Regime, the state was not oriented to promoting further social-structural transformations. It was geared instead to maintaining itself and guaranteeing the social order based upon professional or bureaucratic status and upon private property and market relations. Moreover, just as the strengthened state could now operate on a more autonomous basis, so were private wealth-holders now (at least marginally) more likely to pursue their economic interests on the market rather than by purchasing state offices or directly using politico–juridical mechanisms to appropriate surpluses.

Thus, despite the fact that they had not caused the Revolution, or been suddenly furthered by it, capitalist relations of production could expand gradually but steadily in the relatively favorable legal and administrative framework crystallized by the Revolution. By a century after 1789, France was becoming an industrial capitalist nation. Yet, even in capitalist industrialization, France has continued to be marked by social and institutional pecularities: Through generations of modern economic development, large numbers of French peasants have clung to the land as tenants or small-holders; and the French national state has always been a major force in economic life, making and breaking opportunities for private investors and profoundly shaping the regional and sectoral contours of industrial development. Not only conditions broadly favorable to capitalist development, therefore, but also sociopolitical patterns that have made France relatively distinctive among capitalist industrial nations, are traceable to the major accomplishments of the French Revolution. Indeed, the Revolution is best understood as a "gigantic broom" that swept away the "medieval rubbish" of seigneurialism and particularistic privilege–freeing the peasantry, private wealth-holders, and the state alike from the encumbrances of the Old Regime.

6 The Emergence of a Dictatorial Party-State in Russia

The great achievement of the Bolsheviks was not in making the revolution, but in slowing it down and diverting it into Communist channels . . . The astonishing feat of the Bolsheviks was their success in checking the elemental drive of the Russian masses towards a chaotic utopia.   Paul Avrich

NO MODERN SOCIAL REVOLUTION has been as thorough-going as the Russian. In a matter of months during 1917–18 massive revolts by industrial workers, peasants, and soldiers undercut the landed and capitalist classes and sealed the dissolution of the state machineries of the tsarist regime. The organized revolutionaries who claimed leadership within the revolutionary crisis were, moreover, dedicated to socialist ideals of equality and proletarian democracy. Yet the Russian Revolution soon gave rise to a highly centralized and bureaucratic party-state, which eventually became committed to propelling rapid national industrialization by command and terror. To understand why and how these outcomes developed, we shall analyze the possibilities, imperatives, and impossibilities created for conflicting forces by the Russian revolutionary situation after March, 1917. As in the French Revolution, two basic processes arising out of the revolutionary situation intersected to shape the outcomes of the Revolution. These were popular (especially peasant) revolts and the struggles of urban-based political leaderships to build new state organizations. But the Russian revolutionary crisis deepened much more rapidly and chaotically than the French. And revolutionary state-builders in Russia faced more demanding tasks–at first of sheer revolutionary defense, and then of state-propelled industrialization–under far more threatening domestic and international conditions. The result was a Russian New Regime broadly similar to the French in its political centralization and urban-bureaucratic basis, yet also qualitatively different from the French New Regime in its dynamic orientation toward national industrialization under Party-state control.

206

A Dictatorial Party-State in Russia

Let us analyze the course of the Russian Revolution, beginning with the implications of the revolutionary conjuncture of 1917.

THE EFFECTS OF THE SOCIAL-REVOLUTIONARY CRISIS OF 1917

In the historiography of the Russian Revolution a vast preponderance of effort has been devoted to arguing—with a tone of either praise or blame— why the Bolsheviks were able to destroy (or overcome) the liberal "February" phase of the Revolution. From a comparative perspective, this debate seems misdirected. We saw that even in the French Revolution, liberal political arrangements did not prevail. True, such arrangements did survive for several years. In the French Revolution liberalism was a genuine phase. But in Russia there never was any viable liberal regime to be overcome by anyone. The reasons follow from the divergent origins of the two revolutionary crises. The French revolutionary crisis of 1789 was brought about through the initiatives against the monarchy of broadly based internal political forces. After monarchical absolutism had been stymied in France, there were national and local revolutionary bodies led by liberals that enjoyed genuine popular support because they had been established through processes that mobilized unprecedentedly widespread political participation.[1] In sharp contrast to France in 1789, the Russian Revolution broke out only because—and when—the tsarist state was destroyed by the impact of prolonged involvement and repeated defeats in World War I. The *dumas* and *zemstvos* had been too timid to launch the Revolution in the first place; and the Provisional Government after February was not based on any sort of national suffrage or popular political participation. In addition, whereas the French National Assembly enjoyed the luxury of peacetime conditions from 1789 to 1791, the fledgling Russian authorities had to try to direct military efforts and cope with the consequences of wartime overexertion and defeats. Not surprisingly, given that the Russian Revolution developed from the start in this fashion, chaos and fundamental conflicts were immediate potentials, soon to be fully realized to the detriment of even temporary liberal stabilization.

Dilemmas for the Provisional Government

Between February and October, 1917, attempts were made by leaders of political parties and tendencies, ranging from constitutional-monarchist to moderate socialist, to stabilize the Russian Revolution in liberal-democratic form. Appointed by a committee of former Duma members, the Provisional Government declared itself the head of government and trustee for the Revolution until a Constituent Assembly could be elected to

207

create a new constitution. Simultaneously, there sprang up in Petrograd and throughout the country soviets, councils of deputies elected and periodically reelected by groups of industrial workers, soldiers, and (occasionally) peasants. The soviets claimed the right to oversee the activities of the Provisional Government and of the upper-class—dominated district and provincial *zemstvos* and municipal *dumas* with which the Provisional Government soon became formally affiliated. Thus the suddenly deposed tsarist autocracy was replaced by a pair of networks of councils.[2] One network, centered on the initial leadership of the Provisional Government, represented mostly privileged Russians, landowners, bourgeois, professionals. The other, centered on the Petrograd Soviet, represented (mainly through the intelligentsia of the socialist parties) those heretofore completely excluded from national politics. At first, the Provisional Government, wherein resided the formal authority to govern Russia, was led exclusively by nonsocialist politicians; after April, it became a coalition that included Menshevik and Socialist Revolutionary leaders also responsible to the soviets. But whether a coalition or not, the Provisional Government always relied upon the Petrograd Soviet for support and help in executing any policy that involved the cooperation of workers or soldiers. Those whose cooperation was most essential included the all-important workers who ran the railroad and telegraph systems and the soldiers who garrisoned the capital and other key urban centers.

If the liberal goals initially shared by nearly all politically conscious Russians,[3] jubilant at the overthrow of the autocracy, were to be realized, then the Provisional Government and the Soviets together had to generate and administer solutions to the grievous problems of a war-weary land and people. But this proved quite impossible. As the problems themselves became more and more overwhelming, it very quickly became apparent that the capacity of the nascent liberal system to deal with them was even less than that of the old autocracy.

The very difficulties that had set the stage for the February Revolution continued and grew worse afterwards. The railroad system, for example, still could not handle the simultaneous demands of supplying the fronts, evacuating the wounded, transporting food to the cities, and providing raw materials for industries. After February, moreover, there were railway workers' strikes and an upsurge of local and syndicalist initiatives directly or indirectly affecting railroad properties and functions. All of these activities caused added difficulties for any authorities attempting to use the vital railroads to run the country.[4]

Nor did the war stop. Until after the Bolshevik takeover, no Russian government was willing to abandon completely the country's role in the war. Liberal leaders, who valued Russia's alliance with the Western powers, had grown disgusted with the tsar in large part precisely because

208

he seemed to be running the war ineptly. Now that they were in charge they hoped to revitalize the war effort through revolutionary nationalist appeals and to win victories that would both secure the Western alliance and stabilize a bourgeois–liberal sociopolitical order at home. Moderate socialists were less enthusiastic about the war, and they forced the liberals to renounce publicly all imperialist war aims inherited from the old regime. Yet they were not willing to abandon what they, with considerable justice, perceived as defensive warfare against the Central Powers. Moreover, whatever the attitudes of the Provisional Government leaders, the Russian government by 1917 was bankrupt in a situation where the economy was collapsing due to the strains of total war and the prolonged absence of normal foreign trade. And the Western Allies of Russia were willing to provide financial support for the new regime only if she remained at war.

As the successive leaderships of the Provisional Government tried to keep the war as well as the country going, the masses of Russians grew more and more disillusioned about the February Revolution. Acting through their own grass-roots collective arrangements, they began to take matters increasingly into their own hands at the expense of the existing dominant classes.[5] We have already noted that, throughout the vast Russian heartlands, peasant communes encroached upon gentry rights, and then began to seize their lands.[6] Meanwhile, popular revolts also occurred in the cities and at the fronts. Workers' factory committees initially made wage and hours demands and then began to supervise management, to initiate efforts to procure supplies to keep factories running, and, ultimately in some cases, to take over completely the running of entire enterprises.[7] Soldiers' committees formed at first to secure civil rights for soldiers and to enforce humane standards of discipline upon the officers. Gradually many of these committees in practice usurped the right to veto all command decisions, especially those that might have political consequences or might involve the threat of death in battles at the front.[8] The soviets, periodically reelected by the grass-roots groups, tended after moderate time lags to reflect and sanction the goings-on below. At the same time, they moved to involve themselves ever more directly in administrative matters originally left to the Provisional Government, the *zemstvos,* and the *dumas.*[9]

The Provisional Government completely lacked the authority or power to halt the attacks on privileged groups and the evolution toward anarchy. Right after the February Revolution, much of the former Imperial administration, including the police, dissolved. Attempts made to build anew through the *zemstvos* and *dumas* faced enormous problems of coordination of these diverse local and regional bodies.[10] Even more important, these liberal representative organs lacked real authority with the masses of peasant and proletarian Russians who had previously been excluded from them and subjected directly to autocratic controls. Now that they were suddenly free, the peasants, workers, and soldiers revitalized or formed their own grass-roots collectivities. And these were much more suited for channeling direct popular political action than for ensuring the subordination of the people to the liberal government—especially in a time of crisis when that government could not and would not respond to the basic needs and wishes of the ordinary people.[11]

Nor could the Provisional Government fall back on force. The war-swollen army was the only conceivable means of official coercion, but it became steadily more unreliable.[12] At no point could raw, overwhelmingly peasant recruits be used to suppress the agrarian revolts. As for the situation in the cities, beginning immediately after the February Revolution, garrison troops in Petrograd, Moscow, and other major centers shared the attitudes of the urban workers. They could be ordered about only with the approval of the soviets, ever wary of imagined or real counterrevolutionary threats. For a time the front-line troops were more willing than the garrison troops to follow the Provisional Government. But by July, an attempted Russian offensive into Austria had been defeated, the peasant revolution was gathering steam at the soldiers' homes in the countryside, and the officers began to be suspected of counterrevolutionary tendencies (soon confirmed by General Lavr Kornilov's attempted coup). Reacting to these developments, the troops at the fronts, too, became virtually uncontrollable and the armies began to disintegrate through widespread desertions.

In sum, then, the dominant strata and the Provisional Government were steadily undetermined by popular revolts, which inexorably spread and deepened after February, and which finally alienated even the nominal political support of many of the soviets for the policy initiatives and administrative efforts of the official Petrograd leaders. Because it was unwilling and unable to abandon the war and to sanction or stop the agrarian revolts, the Provisional Government could not escape having its flimsy political bases swept away, as social conflicts deepened and disorder spread in the cities, at the fronts, and in the countryside.

Limited Bases for National Political Order

Indeed, if we look beneath the surface political formalities to the underlying social-revolutionary dynamics, it becomes apparent that from the summer of 1917 on the real dilemma of the Russian Revolution was not who should govern. It was rather whether anyone *could* govern, whether national order could be reestablished at all. Certainly, the bases—social and organizational—upon which order could be reestablished were very limited. With the administrative and military infrastructure of the Old Regime

210

shattered, no simple monarchical restoration or military coup d'état was possible. (Thus Kornilov's attempted coup in September 1917 barely got off the ground and was readily stymied by railroad workers, Red Guards, and soldiers loyal to the soviets.)[13] Instead, the only real hope for regenerating national order lay with the various political parties contending to mobilize popular followings as they became disgruntled with the Provisional Government.

Of the potential popular followings, the peasantry, despite the fact that it was the vast majority, was the least likely source of disciplined popular support for a new national order. To see why, we need only recall that, by virtue of the widespread existence of the *obshchina,* the peasants were able during 1917 to coordinate autonomously their own local revolts against landlords, rich farmers, and remnants of the Imperial bureaucracy. The peasants did not have to rely upon direct support or leadership from urban revolutionary forces. And once the nonpeasant lands and resources were seized and redistributed among the peasant smallholders within the village communities, the peasants wanted mostly to be left alone to govern their own affairs locally and to engage in their partially subsistence-oriented mode of agricultural production. The peasants' main concerns about national politics were the strictly negative and defensive ones of seeking to prevent the coming to power of any government that might restore the landlords and/or exploit them through taxation and conscription.

Any new national political order would necessarily be built from the towns and cities outward. Within the urban sector the most organizable popular revolutionary base was the industrial working class. To be sure, the garrison soldiers were a constant source of revolutionary ferment throughout 1917 because of their determination not to be sent to the war fronts. Yet as they revolted, the military units dissolved into indiscipline and desertion, and therefore could not serve even as an initial basis for reconstructing a new order.[14] Industrial workers, too, engaged in revolts that undermined existing patterns of authority in the factories and existing political arrangements in the cities. Still industrial workers depended for their very livelihood upon somehow keeping factories in operation, and upon the existence of at least minimally reliable economic flows between consumers and producers, town and countryside. Thus, as the chaos spread, they had a growing interest in cooperating with any organized revolutionary force that would work to overcome it.

Because prerevolutionary Russia had undergone rapid and extensive industrial development, there were significant concentrations of factories and industrial workers throughout European Russia, including important concentrations in the capitals of St. Petersburg (Petrograd after 1914) and Moscow and in other administrative and garrison towns, all linked together by the railroad and telegraph networks.[15] Russian industries and

211

railroads had not been advanced enough to allow the Old Regime to compete militarily with Imperial Germany, but they were sufficiently developed to give the edge in a civil war situation to any internal competitor that gained control of the core of the country. If an urban-based political party could mobilize industrial workers and use their support to establish administrative and military organizations in the place of those through which the tsarist autocracy had ruled, then some semblance of national government might be restored to revolutionary Russia. This, of course, was to be the achievement of the Bolsheviks.

THE BOLSHEVIK STRUGGLE TO RULE

Amidst the deepening chaos in Russia during the spring and summer of 1917, only the Bolshevik Party, originally the tiniest and most extreme of the socialist parties, maneuvered successfully to develop increased tactical effectiveness and to gain strategically located popular support. The Provisional Government and the moderate socialists had kept the war going, temporized about approving peasant land seizures, and struggled against

Map 4. Railroads and major industrial areas of European Russia, to 1917. *Source:* Hugh Seton-Watson, *The Russian Empire, 1801–1917* (New York: Oxford University Press, 1967), pp. 780–2.

the breakdown of discipline in the army and the spread of workers' control in industry. Meanwhile, the Bolsheviks remained entirely in opposition and, through constant critical propaganda directed at industrial workers and at garrison and front-line troops, rode along with the wave of spontaneous popular rebellions, calling for peace, land, bread, workers' control, and "all power to the soviets."[16] These tactics brought a flood of new members into the Bolshevik Party and led the Bolsheviks to win elected majorities in one soviet after another from midsummer on into the autumn.[17] Above all, the Bolsheviks gained the edge over competing parties in the towns and army units of the regions surrounding Petrograd, including Moscow, the Urals, and the northern stretches of the military front lines. In contrast, the Mensheviks retained the greatest relative strength in the peripheral areas of the Caucasus and Georgia, whereas the Socialist Revolutionaries were the strongest in the provincial cities and towns of the most heavily agricultural provinces and along the western and southwestern fronts.[18] Moreover, although the Bolshevik Party was far from a doctrinally unified monolith in 1917, it did retain relatively more organizational coherence than the other socialist parties, even as it remained much more closely in touch with popular sentiments in the urban centers.[19]

The Party Claims Exclusive Sovereignty

"October" in the Russian Revolution was but the moment when the Provisional Government, whose power and authority had been completely undermined by popular revolts, was finally officially pushed aside through the Bolshevik bid for state sovereignty. This bid was placed merely by picking up the few tiny pieces that were left of the shattered potential for state power in Russia. The Bolsheviks organized in the capital a military coup, made through the Petrograd garrison under the authority of the Military Revolutionary Committee of the Petrograd Soviet, and made in the name of the Soviets of workers', peasants', and soldiers' deputies.[20] Because of the positions they had already attained in the soviets of northeastern Russia, and because there were no accessible and intact military units loyal to groups willing to oppose their coup, the Bolsheviks faced no immediate military opposition that could not be overcome in brief struggles.[21] But it was one thing to claim state power and another thing to maintain and exercise it. To make good their claim to sovereignty would take the Bolsheviks years of work at building state organizations and parlaying the available resources of party loyalty, urban popular support, and remnants of old-regime expertise into a centralized government capable of controlling and defending a revolutionized Russia.

Right from the start the Bolsheviks faced political opposition to their attempt to rule alone. Especially the other socialist parties, but also some soviets and workers' unions, called instead for a coalition socialist government through the soviets. Moreover, long-scheduled elections based on universal suffrage for the national Constituent Assembly were held soon after the Bolshevik coup. And when the delegates assembled in November and December, the Bolsheviks found themselves only a large minority, well behind the Socialist Revolutionaries, who had been elected by masses of peasant votes. There was still much apparent support in the country for a liberal-democratic government to be set up through the Constituent Assembly, bypassing the soviets and nullifying the Bolshevik coup.

Hardly surprisingly, though not until after considerable intraparty bickering, the Bolsheviks were persuaded by Lenin not to surrender the fruits of their coup. The Party, presenting itself as the leader and representative of the proletariat, undertook to preserve and extend its rule and thereby consolidate and defend the Russian Revolution. The Constituent Assembly was disbanded with the aid of small detachments of Red Guards, and a variety of manipulative and coercive tactics were used to reduce and ultimately remove the influence of the Mensheviks and the Socialist Revolutionaries in the soviets. A new government was set up, ostensibly based upon a pyramid of soviets with elections from the bottom up. But in practice the affairs of the soviets became increasingly dominated by executive committees, which were "elected" through Party influence or intervention and were responsible for implementing administrative decisions originating from the Party-dominated Council of Peoples' Commissars at the center.[22]

In all of this, of course, the Bolsheviks had to move with great care and political finesse, for at first their continued ascendancy depended solely on the combined resources of Party loyalty and strategically located popular followings. Thus, as they worked to weaken competing parties, the Bolsheviks were careful not to alienate too much popular support. Immediately after coming to power, they sanctioned the peasants' confiscation of landlords' estates, announced their intention to negotiate an end to the war, and decreed the election of officers by enlisted men and the abolition of rank distinctions in the armies. They even went along for a time with the principle of workers' control of industrial plants.[23] All of these popular movements had the advantage, from the Bolsheviks' point of view, of destroying the remnants of the property bases of the dominant classes of the Old Regime. These movements also undermined the remaining institutional bases of competing parties—such as the trade unions, where the Mensheviks remained influential for a time.

Victory Through Centralized Coercion

Thus, for a time after the October coup, the Bolsheviks continued to sanction anarchist forms of popular insurrection. However, the logic of their claim to state power, given the circumstances in which they had to struggle to maintain and further that claim, also prompted them to begin at once to rebuild administrative and military organizations and to enforce ever more centralized discipline within the Party. In the summer of 1917, Lenin, in *State and Revolution,* sketched a vision of a proletarian regime in which standing army and bureaucracy would be abolished and, instead, all of the people would govern directly through job rotation and elected and recallable representatives. But in the conditions that Russia and the Bolsheviks faced by 1918 this vision was impossible, at best a utopia for the far-distant future. With the social and economic crises deepening, and the armies now completely dissolving, the Communists were in even a worse position to administer the country than the previous regime had been. Moreover, the German military threat continued into 1918. By the time it had faded, due to Russia's negotiated surrender in March 1918 and the subsequent defeat of the Central Powers in the West, counterrevolutionary regimes based upon armies led by former tsarist officers had sprung up in Siberia and the south, and Western expeditionary forces scattered around the periphery of European and Asian Russia were initiating attempts at foreign intervention. To meet the enormous difficulties they faced, the Bolsheviks quickly turned to organized coercion—the naked *ultima ratio* of state power. And they soon turned that coercion not only against foreign and domestic counterrevolutionaries but also—in order to restore order and discipline to Russian society and government—against the mass constituents of the Revolution as well.

The Cheka, or political police, was organized immediately after the October Revolution as a special, autonomous administrative agency charged with combatting counterrevolutionary subversion by any means deemed necessary or expedient. Armed Cheka units were not subject to the control of soviet authorities or even regular Party members, but only to central Party leaders. As an official document rather gruesomely put it: "In its activity the Cheka is completely independent, carrying out searches, arrests, shootings, afterwards making a report to the Council of People's Commissars and the Soviet Central Executive Committee.[24] Of course the Cheka's most apparent activity was the summary arrest and imprisonment or execution of actual or suspected party and class enemies of the Soviet regime. But it also became an important means for enforcing general administrative control and especially for enforcing decisions associated with the attempts of the new state to manage economic activities. For as William H. Chamberlin points out:

> no government could have survived in Russia in those years without the use of terrorism . . . The national morale was completely shattered by the World War. No one, except under extreme compulsion, was willing to perform any state obligation. The older order had simply crumbled

215

away; a new order, with new habits and standards of conduct, had not yet formed; very often the only way in which a governmental representative, whether he was a Bolshevik commissar or a White officer, could get his orders obeyed was by flourishing a revolver.[25]

Thus, if the Red Army or urban centers needed supplies, Cheka units might extort them from peasant villages; or, if urban authorities wanted to enforce rationing plans, the Cheka might arrest and shoot "speculators" and confiscate their goods; or, if strategically situated transportation or administrative workers showed signs of noncooperation with the Red regime, the Cheka might arrest or execute exemplary cases.

In all such endeavors, if the Cheka was not available, or if more force was needed, Party-organized workers' committees as well as Red Army units might provide the coercive sanctions instead. The continued reliance upon grass-roots collective action, although increasingly stimulated and managed from above, signified the Communists' desire to tap popular enthusiasm and participation whenever it could be depended upon to further the consolidation of a new order. Because industrial workers were the most available and organized Communist supporters, they were usually the ones involved. As the Bolsheviks reached out into the countryside for supplies, attempts were also made to organize poor peasants against richer ones in support of the new urban-based regime.[26] However, the peasants, self-sufficient and relatively united in their communities, could not, on the whole, be integrated into the New Regime on a voluntary basis. Still, peasants constituted the vast majority of Soviet citizens, and their economic products were crucial to the survival of urban Russia. Thus the Bolsheviks could not just leave them alone with their newly extended landholdings, as the peasants themselves clearly desired. Rather, ways had to be found, involuntary if necessary, to involve the peasants in the New Regime. One of the earliest forms in which the peasant dilemma unavoidably presented itself was in the development of a Red Army to fight the Civil War.

Unlike the armies of revolutionary France in 1793, the Russian Red Army had to be created literally from scratch amidst a war-weary population no longer amenable to nationalist appeals.[27] During the summer and fall of 1917, the regular units of the old Imperial armies, and especially the ones most affected by Bolshevik propaganda, rapidly dissolved. "Nationalist" appeals to defend the country against the Germans were of little use after years of defeats and suffering in World War I. In sharp contrast indeed to the French revolutionary leaders, the Bolsheviks had to dispense with nationalist popular mobilization and accept cutbacks in the territory of the former Russian Empire.[28] The imperatives of consolidating a Revolution born out of defeat in World War I forced the leaders of the Russian state (during 1917–21 and indeed until after World War II) into a retreatist–defensive and almost entirely nonexpansionist posture.[29]

216

At first, through mid-1918, the Revolution was defended against the emerging counterrevolutionary armies by nothing more than workers' armed Guards, occasional loyal military units, and scattered partisan bands of peasants anxious to protect their homes and land seizures.[30] To the top leaders of the Communist Party, situated in the urban centers of European Russia, such a spontaneous and disunited defense seemed worthless. Unless the decentralizing trends were reversed, a counterrevolutionary triumph or else dissolution into anarchism and competing nationalisms seemed (and probably would have been) the only possible outcomes of the oncoming Civil War. For, as John Ellis points out,

> because the Bolsheviks had already seized state power and taken over many of the administrative functions of the government, they were unable to retreat to the hinterland before the White offensives without completely destroying their credibility. Having seized power they were forced to try and maintain it. To do this they had to create large armies, in the shortest space of time. Such large armies were of necessity to be composed of peasants.[31]

With Leon Trotsky as Military Commissar, backed by Lenin and the Party Central Committee, a centralized, professional, and disciplined Red Army was developed.[32] Compulsory military conscription was decreed and, although a cautious start was made among loyal industrial workers, soon the recruiters had to turn to the profoundly war-weary peasants. In the end, peasants came to constitute over four-fifths of the Red Army, which grew to over five-million men by 1921.[33] So that these mostly illiterate and very reluctant recruits might be quickly transformed into some approximation to an effective fighting force, the traditional disciplinary prerogatives of officers, including their right to order soldiers to be shot, were fully revived. A ministry of war, staffed by specialists inherited from the Old Regime, was given command control over all field operations. And as many former tsarist officers as could be induced or coerced into joining the Red Army were given leadership posts and authority commensurate with their (supposedly politically neutral) technical skills.[34] Thus, within a year, the Bolsheviks reversed many of the revolutionary–democratic measures they had once encouraged for the sake of undermining the Provisional Government, and they returned instead to professional and bureaucratic principles of military organization.

To these Trotsky added a system of centralized Party controls, rendered inescapable by the need to ensure the successful amalgamation of reluctant peasant recruits, politically unreliable tsarist officers, and irregular revolutionary fighting units all into one centralized and effective military organization. Political commissars were assigned to watch over and ensure the loyalty of "specialist" officers, and fighting units of dedicated Communists (Party members and workers) were sprinkled among the peasant units to

217

leaven the combat effectiveness of the entire army. Equally crucial, all Communists in the army were directly subjected to the discipline and disposition of a political administration, established to eliminate spontaneous and uncoordinated political initiatives by Party cells or commissars.

> In this way there grew up a fully centralized machine for all political activity in the army, . . . itself directed by . . . the Central Committee [of the Communist Party], and in turn controlling through the subordinate political departments of divisions both the commissars and all political activity with units.[35]

Between 1918 and 1921 the Red Army accomplished two basic tasks for the Communist regime. First and crucially, it defeated the counterrevolutionary military threats. The Reds fought largely according to the conventional military principles of the time and enjoyed the strategic advantages of interior lines and access to the cities and railroads of European Russia. In addition, they enjoyed the benefit of popular preference over the Whites—including the marginal preference of most peasants, without which the Russian Revolution surely would have failed to be consolidated in the Civil War. For however much peasants may have resented *both* Red and White attempts to involve them and their resources in the Civil War, they feared (especially in the core areas of Russia) that White victories would entail the return of the landlords they had expropriated.[36]

As for the second task accomplished by the Red Army: Even as the White armies were beaten in succession, the army developed into a secure basis for continued highly centralized rule by the Bolshevik-Communist Party. Masses of recruits were incorporated into its professional and Party-dominated structure. And irregular military units—such as proletarian Red Guards and peasant guerrilla bands—that had sprung up during the anarchic phases of the Revolution were displaced and absorbed by the Red Army. Ultimately, those partisan units that could not be absorbed, such as Makhno's peasant guerrillas in the Ukraine, were defeated and destroyed.[37]

State Controls in the Economy

The Civil War years also witnessed the establishment of a bureaucratic and Party-supervised civil administration and the centralization and extreme extension of state controls over the Russian economy. The development of civil state administration was analogous to that of the Red Army officer corps. Because of their scarce technical skills, former old-regime officials and staff members were retained or reemployed, nominally under the supervision of the soviets, but actually subject to control by (the proportionately few) Party cadres sprinkled among and over them.[38]

This quickly regenerated state apparatus was charged with more duties, especially of economic control and supervision, than ever before. Diverse circumstances—including the effects of peasant and working-class revolts against holders of private property, the desperate need to supply the armies and the cities in the midst of economic breakdown and civil war, and the heady visions of communist society cherished by some Bolshevik cadres—all combined to produce between 1918 and 1921 a system known as "War Communism": "in which the state aspired to the role of sole producer and sole distributer, in which labor under state direction and regimentation was compulsory, in which payments were in kind, in which both the need for and the use of money had largely disappeared."[39]

With the emergence of this system, workers' control of industry was an immediate casualty.[40] The Bolshevik leaders noted that syndicalist controls of production only furthered economic chaos. They thus moved within months after the October Revolution to nationalize many key industries and transfer controls over them to central administrative organs working in cooperation with trade unions. Once purged of Menshevik influences and safely staffed by Communist Party members, the trade unions were used to displace the workers' committees or soviets that had initially seized the factories from the bourgeois owners and managers. In turn, the unions ceded management rights to directors (often former "bourgeois" managers) appointed by the Soviet administration. With respect to the larger factories, this system proved permanent, its essentials enduring after 1921 when other features of War Communism were temporarily scrapped.

For the Communists' immediate attempt to abolish market mechanisms entirely and to direct all aspects of production and distribution by command could not outlast the desperate Civil War years. Enforced by terror, measures such as forcible seizures of peasant surpluses, rationing of all consumption goods, and the eventual attempts to militarize labor discipline, could and did aid the victories of the Red Armies. This was true at a time when, however disaffected they might become, the majority of people were unwilling to throw their support to the White armies, which were equally brutal and counterrevolutionary to boot. But under War Communism the Russian economy collapsed and contracted even more rapidly than it had during World War I.[41] Once the Whites were defeated, the newly consolidated Soviet regime soon found it necessary and expedient to retreat from the attempt to enforce total state controls over the economy. By 1921, the regime was faced at once with workers desperate for amelioration of starvation wages and long hours of enforced labor and with spreading peasant revolts against grain requisitions.[42] Consequently, while taking care to maintain their political monopoly and to tighten internal discipline within the Party, the Communist leaders retreated to a "New Economic Policy," in which market forces in peasant agriculture, as well as private initiatives in medium and small industries and retail commerce, were allowed to revive. Given the end of wars and civil conflicts, these policies facilitated by 1925 the recovery of the Russian economy and population to roughly pre–World War I levels. Still, during the recovery, large-scale industries and foreign trade remained under central Party-state controls, thus leaving the Communists (unlike the French Jacobins after 1793) with a solid organizational basis and interest in the economy.[43]

For all practical purposes, this organizational grounding of Party-state power in industry was all that was left by 1921 of the Bolsheviks' proletarian base. In the eloquent words of Gerard Chaliand: "The 'proletarian revolution' had triumphed, but the working class itself had virtually melted away."[44] Originally, to be sure, the political program of the Bolsheviks had attracted the spontaneous support of self-organized revolutionary workers. But the Civil War had either dissipated or used up the original proletarian supporters of the Bolsheviks: Some had scattered from the starving cities to rural areas; other had died in the armed defense of the Revolution; and still other had (like many *sans culottes* in France during 1793) experienced upward mobility, away from industrial employments and into official positions in the newly triumphant Party-state. New workers of mostly peasant origin eventually came to take the place of the proletariat of 1917, but they could hardly constitute a politically experienced and self-conscious base—or a democratic counterweight—to the increasingly monolithic and bureaucratized Party-state leadership. From 1921 on, the shape of the revolutionary New Regime depended upon how that leadership exercised and deployed state power in Russian society.

THE STALINIST "REVOLUTION FROM ABOVE"

The "New Economic Policy" (NEP) that prevailed right after the end of the Civil War did not prove to be the stable outcome of the Russian Revolution. By the late 1920s, the NEP system gave way to a totally collectivist and bureaucratically administered society under the direction of a dictatorial Party-state dedicated to rapid, heavy industrialization. At this point, it is important to gain some understanding of why this was the culmination of a Revolution originally made by people with libertarian and socialist hopes. We must consider, first, the inherent contradictions of the NEP and, then, the situational conditions inherited from the Old Regime and the political propensities carried over from the Civil War period. All of these factors help to explain why the Communist Party turned under Stalin's leadership to the forcible collectivization of agriculture and a crash program of heavy industrialization.

During the early 1920s the hybrid NEP system functioned well enough— the economy recovered and population grew. But by 1926 emergency difficulties signaled that basic changes would have to be made. The most serious dilemmas were posed by the fledgling Soviet regime's relationships with the peasantry, both economic and political.

220

The Peasant Contradiction

By 1926, Russian industry had largely recovered with the framework of pre–World War I capital investments. Yet, without some extraordinary infusions of capital and manpower, it was not going to produce either enough consumer goods to supply the masses of peasant producers or enough capital goods to allow the further rapid expansion of industrial productive capacities.[45] The peasants, in turn, were not going to expand agricultural production, or even surrender existing surpluses to feed the cities and supply industries, unless they could purchase manufactured goods at reasonable prices with incomes derived from sales of grain and materials. Because of the particular agrarian socioeconomic structure that existed in NEP Russia, the peasants had the aggregate capacity, so to speak, to make or break the national economy. In the wake of the peasant revolution of 1917, the larger noble and rich-peasant estates, which had produced a disproportionately large share of the marketed crops before 1914, were gone; instead, there were virtually only petty producers, including a large proportion operating at a near-subsistence level. These petty producers, whose population was rising during the 1920s, could, if they chose, hold their grain off the market. They could either hoard it in anticipation of higher prices later or use it instead for feeding family members or livestock.[46]

It is worth underlining the contrast between this agrarian result of the Russian peasant revolution and the situation that resulted from the antiseigneurial peasant revolts in France.[47] Even before the French Revolution, France was quite highly commercialized for a preindustrial agrarian country, especially in terms of the relatively high degree of involvement of many peasants in market exchanges with local towns.[48] It is true that the sociopolitical solidarity of the peasant village communities was enough to encourage collective resistance (and, in 1789, revolts) against seigneurs and other outside claimants of shares of peasant surpluses. Nevertheless, communal forms did not override or compromise the essential individualism and orientation to private ownership of the French peasant proprietors. Thus the French peasant revolution abolished seigneurial claims but did not expropriate or redistribute most privately owned lands, either those of nonpeasant landlords or those of the richer peasants. And although many communal restrictions on individual land use survived, the Revolution weakened these and furthered long-standing trends toward individualistic farming. The postrevolutionary French agrarian economy featured a mixture of medium, small, and tiny individual owners; and agricultural producers on the whole were no less, and perhaps more, oriented toward regular market participation than under the Old Regime. As a major consequence, in the wake of the Revolution the French commercial–industrial economy could continue to grow steadily, if indeed only gradually, without active state direction – and especially without active state intervention in agriculture.

But in Soviet Russia in the 1920s, the situation was very different. The Russian peasant revolution had, unlike the French, expropriated and redistributed private landed property. It had tended to equalize peasant holdings at a generally impoverished level, and it had strengthened communal controls inimical to individual entrepreneurship.[49] As a result, Russian agricultural producers were, on the whole, less market oriented than before 1917. And the much greater preponderance of peasant smallholders within the national economy posed a threat to the viability of any market-guided national economic system (let alone any plan for state-directed industrialization).

Given the agrarian socioeconomic structure that resulted from the Russian peasant revolution, the NEP was destined to face economic contradictions after it initially promoted recovery from the extreme contraction of production under War Communism. The essential problem was simple: without extremely favorable economic inducements – i.e., plentiful and cheap consumer goods beyond the productive capacity of Soviet industry and very high prices for agricultural produce, which Soviet authorities were not inclined to allow, given their vested interest in manipulating the terms of trade in favor of state-controlled industries – Russian peasants had every reason to participate less and less in the national economy. Indeed, marketings of grain remained proportionately lower throughout the 1920s than before 1914. And by 1927 the peasants were marketing so little grain as to cause a crisis situation.[50]

Nor was the Soviet regime in any position to use political-organizational means to *persuade* the peasants to surrender surpluses, much less to adopt new production practices. For the Party, the soviets, and the state administration had only the most superficial footholds within and influence upon the rural peasant communities.[51] Because the Bolsheviks had come to power through urban insurrections and conventional warfare, they had not in the process penetrated the villages or succeeded in establishing within them political leaders who were at once influential among the peasants and loyal to the Party and Soviet regime. Besides, the reliance upon market mechanisms to facilitate the recovery of agricultural production during the early 1920s only encouraged the emergence of relatively well-to-do local peasant leaders who were naturally hostile to any policy turn toward political mobilization in agriculture. Thus, at the time when the crisis of the peasantry's relationship to the national economy became acute, the Soviet regime lacked any reliable local-political means to reach, reorganize, and reorient the peasantry. Whatever local Soviet and/or Party cadres there were in the rural areas were relatively few in number. And they were either politically unreliable from the regime's point of view (e.g., because they were market-oriented, richer peasants) or else politically ineffective among their neighbors (e.g., because they were young, poor agricultural laborers "elected" or appointed to local office by higher administrative fiat).

If, however, the regime were to resort again to the crude and coercive procurement methods of War Communism, while yet leaving the peasant small holders and villages in control of agricultural production, the peasants could respond by merely planting less and hoarding more. Exactly this began to happen after 1927, as deficient grain deliveries and marketing by the peasants provoked the regime to apply administrative force, and that, in turn, contributed to shrinking harvests in 1928 and 1929.[52] Thus the NEP system—based as it was upon the uneasy coexistence of small-holding, communally autonomous, and subsistence-prone peasantry with a Party-state uneasy about market forces, anxious to expand state-directed industries, and lacking any firm political basis in the countryside—evolved into deepening crisis, with town and country set increasingly at odds.

The Commitment to Rapid Industrialization and Forced Collectivization

Crucial policy decisions had to be made—and within the Communist Party intertwined leadership and policy struggles raged over how to proceed.[53] On what became known as the "Right," Nikolai Bukharin and his allies advocated increased production of manufactured consumer goods at lowered prices, in order to induce the peasantry to raise and sell more agricultural products in exchange. On the other hand, adopting policies originally advocated by the defeated Trotskyist "Left," Josef Stalin gradually groped toward an alternative approach. This ultimately would entail huge, sustained investments in heavy industries, coupled with the administrative imposition of the collectivization of agriculture in order to force the peasantry to grow and surrender grain and to release manpower for the sudden urban-industrial expansion. Stalin's approach was the one that ultimately triumphed—in large part because of the sheer momentum of events once the Party-state and the peasantry began to clash over grain procurements. Yet it was also true that insofar as clear-cut policy alternatives were posed and debated during the mid and late 1920s, Stalin's gradually emerging approach came to be seen by much of the Soviet leadership as preferable to Bukharin's strategy. This was true chiefly because Stalin's measures (whose ultimate implications were never foreseen at the start) seemed the better way to bring the Party-state's capacities to bear upon solving Russia's economic dilemma.[54] Stalin's approach seemed more promising for two main sets of reasons.

First, it was an approach designed to lift Russia *quickly* by her bootstraps to a higher level of economic and military development. This seemed obviously important not only because socialism was assumed to be attainable only by an industrialized society, but also because by the mid 1920s the Bolsheviks had become acutely aware that socialist revolutions were not going to occur immediately in Western Europe. Their socialist Revolution would have to survive "in one country" if at all, and thus it followed that economic development would have to proceed on a nationally autonomous basis. Besides, Soviet Russia was geopolitically situated, just as Tsarist Russia had been, within the European states system, ever prone to recurrent warfare. No Russian leadership could fail to include military preparedness in any plan for national economic development; and in this respect Stalin's strategy of promoting the rapid expansion of heavy industries naturally seemed more propitious than Bukharin's approach. For Bukharin's approach, if it could have worked at all, would necessarily have condemned the country to a very gradual economic growth. The Party and the state administration would have been called upon to sit back and let market forces, consumer demand, and the expansion of light industries dictate much of the direction and pace of national economic development.[55]

Stalin, in contrast, called in speeches full of martial metaphors for a reversion to Civil War-style *activism* by the Bolshevik Party-state. This brings us to the second set of reasons for the stronger appeal of his strategy (including the ultimate offensive against the peasantry) for the existing political elite. The Party and state organizations, originally built up during the Civil War and still led primarily by men whose most vivid and rewarding revolutionary experiences had been during that period of intense struggle, were well suited and naturally inclined toward exactly the activist stance proposed by Stalin. Mobilizing urban-based Party and worker teams to go out into the politically hostile countryside to seize grain from and reorganize the peasant communities was exactly the kind of activity that had led to victories for the same men in the recent heroic past. Besides, it was not just a question of personal memories and predispositions. For (as we have already seen) the Party-state itself was structured in such a way as to make it necessary for any major attempt politically to influence the peasantry to take the form of measures imposed upon the villages from without, rather than reorganization promoted from within. Given the available political-organizational means, the real choice at hand in the crisis of the NEP probably *was* between the extremes of either leaving the peasantry alone or "attacking" it. When collectivization came between 1929 and 1935, it precisely did take the form of an attack upon the bewildered and resistant peasantry by Party-controlled task forces of urban administrative and industrial workers.[56] Not surprisingly, many such Soviet cadres were predisposed to respond to Stalin's call to return to Civil War-style expedients in order to cope actively (rather than passively "retreat" in the face of) still another crisis for the Party-directed Revolution.

Yet, of course, this time the task at hand was not winning a Civil War but propelling national economic development. The Stalinist strategy, consonant though it was with Bolshevik revolutionary experiences and organizational capacities, *could* work at all only because the Party-state built upon economic conditions continuing from the prerevolutionary era. Stalin's ultimately successful program of crash heavy industrialization[57] obviously benefited from being able to build upon the substantial existing heavy-industrial base (which, of course, was also a crucial organizational foundation of the Party's power). Bukharin's strategy would have been more promising if Soviet Russia had inherited well-developed consumer industries and a rural sector sufficiently prosperous and commercially oriented to provide strong demand for light industries. The fact that neither of these conditions was present suggests that Bukharin's approach was inherently unworkable.[58] Stalin's approach meant essentially that as the Party-state pursued further Russian economic development all the cards would be bet on expanding state-controlled heavy industries. The significance of agricultural collectivization was brutally simple: state "procurement of produce *at minimum cost*"[59] no matter what the price in terms of peasant lives and well-being or the efficiency of agricultural production. Recent research suggests that collectivization may not have allowed actual increases in surpluses appropriated from Russian agriculture as a whole.[60] But it certainly did entail and allow the rapid expansion of state-controlled activities in both the industrial and agricultural sectors. After the collectivization of agriculture, the political control of the Soviet Party-state was fully consolidated in the countryside, as it had been by 1921 in the cities. The peasantry no longer had to be propitiated with pro-market or laissez-faire policies because it could no longer withhold minimally necessary produce (especially grain) from the state procurement agencies. Once Soviet political control in the countryside was thus consolidated, state-directed heavy industrialization could pick up in Soviet Russia from where the Old Regime had left it, and it could proceed – insofar as the rulers were prepared to pay a heavy human cost – at a much more rapid pace.

THE NEW REGIME

In the years immediately after 1928, as the collectivization of agriculture was accomplished and as the Stalinist programs for crash heavy industrialization were implemented, the basic pattern of the outcomes of the Russian Revolution was crystallized. What were the important features of that pattern, and why does it make sociological sense in terms of what we have seen about the causes and dynamics of the Revolution?

Outcomes of Social Revolutions

A Strengthened State in a Revolutionized Society

Certainly the most striking feature of the New Regime was the predominance of a Party-state complex ever so much larger and more dynamically powerful within society than the tsarist regime had been. Size statistics alone tell some of the story. Comparing pre- and post-Revolution statistics on "personnel in the state administration proper and in the police and judiciary systems—exclusive of personnel in the armed forces," Alf Edeen estimates that in 1897 there were 260,000, of whom 105,000 were in the police system, whereas by 1929, when Russia's administrative territory was considerably *smaller* than in 1897, there were 390,000, of whom 142,000 were in the Soviet police apparatus.[61] Soviet statistics presented by E.H. Carr suggest even higher numbers.[62] Of course the year 1897 was twenty years before the demise of the Old Regime, so some of this expansion surely occurred before the accession of the Soviet regime (especially during World War I). Yet the trend of expansion of the numbers of state personnel during the Old Regime between the 1860s and 1890s could not account for the increase from 1897 to 1929. Moreover, Edeen's 1929 estimate does not include the increases of state employees due to the revolutionary takeover of industrial enterprises. This is not to mention the huge increases in numbers of managers, technical specialists, and party functionaries, all working in one way or another as employees of the Soviet Party-state, that accompanied state-propelled rapid industrialization from the late 1920s to the 1950s. Broadly speaking, this expansion seems to have been over five-fold, while the Soviet population grew by only about one-third during the same period.[63] Thus, the Soviet system featured huge and constantly expanding state administrative organizations. This was true both because the Soviet regime was, from 1921 onward, of intrinsically greater political weight than even the relatively politically weighty and bureaucratic tsarist state, and because the Soviet state pushed industrialization much faster and through more directly political administrative means after the middle 1920s.

Not only was the Soviet state larger, it was also capable of accomplishing more in society with less need to pay heed to social opposition than the tsarist autocracy could ever have imagined, for two basic reasons. First, the (Bolshevik) Communist Party replaced the tsar and his network of personal adherents as the agent of executive coordination for all state functions.[64] The obvious difference here is that the Party was larger in numbers of members and more ramified in its reach. It consisted of hierarchically ordered cadres subject to appointment and explicit discipline by the top Party leadership, thus allowing much more effective central coordination than the tsar could achieve. Moreover, although by the mid-1930s there was a convergence between the holding of Party membership and the holding of

226

elite administrative and technical posts, nevertheless the Soviet Communist Party continually attempted, through recurrent recruitment drives, to attract at least some members from every walk of life and sector of society.[65]

This points to the second reason why the Soviet regime was intrinsically more powerful than the tsarist government. The tsarist autocracy had rested content with leaving organized representative and social groups (e.g., *zemstvos,* the Church, *obshchinas*) isolated from, though subordinated to, executive-administrative state power. The Communists, in contrast, sought to link the executive at the center closely with the masses, integrating all people at work and where they resided directly into the Party-state system.[66] This was done through representative and mass-membership organizations, including local soviets, trade unions, cooperatives, and neighborhood groups. Such organizations involved aggregates of people in public affairs and placed them under the direction of leaders who were (de facto, if not officially) appointed by and responsive to the directives of higher authorities, especially Party leaders. Students of the Soviet Union (and other communist party-states) have labeled such organizations "transmission belts" in order to stress their role in linking executive authority to mass popular response and involvement in the implementation of state policies.[67] In addition, we should note that such organizations certainly put Soviet political leaders into (at least potentially) much more direct and continuous contact with popular moods and situations than the tsarist authorities had been.

This larger and more dynamically powerful Soviet Party-state of course established itself in a revolutionized society where the special privileges of aristocrats, tsarist officials, and capitalists had been abolished. Together, the popular revolts of 1917–21 and various decrees implemented by the Soviet government from 1918 to 1929 accomplished the complete elimination (structurally speaking) of the estate of nobles, with their various honorific and political privileges and their landed properties. The class of capitalists, too, with its private ownership and control of various industrial and commercial enterprises, met its demise in this period. One immediate social effect of the elimination of these privileged strata was the opening up of many new opportunities for social advancement to new Soviet citizens of humble class backgrounds.[68] Especially during the 1920s, Red Army and Party leaders were heavily recruited from industrial-worker and peasant backgrounds. During the 1930s, there was more of a trend to recruit Party members from incumbents of non-Party elite positions. Yet the huge new requirements for administrators and technical specialists to staff the expanding state-directed industrial sectors led to the rapid expansion of opportunities for people from all social backgrounds to achieve upward mobility either directly through industry and Party channels or through state subsidized secondary and higher education. To be sure, rates of upward social mobility in Soviet society declined after the initial bulges due to the extraordinary upheavals of the Civil War, the start of crash industrialization, and the violent purges of existing elites in the mid-1930s. Nevertheless, there was from 1921 on much more equal access to any available opportunities for education and social mobility than there had been under the Old Regime, where nobles and the wealthy had privileged legal and/or de facto access to such opportunities. In general, too, it may be said that by the mid-1930s all of the duties and rights (such as they were) of Soviet national citizenship were formally democratic, that is, equal for all citizens—something that had never been fully achieved in the political–juridical system of the Old Regime.

The Fate of Workers and Peasants

There are, however, other, less flattering points that need to be made in order to sharpen our perception of the revolutionary outcomes in Russia. We can begin by considering the situations of workers and peasants. Soviet society may have been more equalitarian and democratic than the tsarist order in the senses just indicated. Nevertheless, the post-1928 Soviet regime certainly did not enhance the general welfare or sociopolitical autonomy of urban workers and collectivized peasants—even in terms of the low standards set under the Old Regime, let alone compared to the relatively favorable conditions of the 1920s.

Before 1928, Soviet trade unions, though led by Party members amd organized under government authority, had rights to participate in enterprise management and to bargain over wages and working conditions on behalf of their worker members. After the turn to forced-draft industrialization, however, the authority of single enterprise directors, appointed by the state and supervised by the Party, became officially absolute within the factories. Trade unions no longer had any influence over the "the hiring of labor, the planning of production, the determination of wage rates, the establishment of output norms, and the fixing of hours of labor."[69] Instead the unions were "instructed to act primarily as organizers and mobilizers in the interest of plan fulfillment,"[70] so that the workers became subject to more direct and intense prodding than at any phase of modern industrialization in Russia. Soviet unions did retain jurisdiction over the administration of certain welfare benefits and social services. But, because the resources allocated to these were minimal during the initial industrial push, this function would have little impact on average worker welfare. Indeed, not only because social benefits were scanty, but especially because wages remained low while prices for necessities were high, workers' living standards deteriorated markedly in the early 1930s—to standards below the pre-1914 levels—and improved only gradually after that.[71]

228

With the advent of collectivization in the countryside, Russian peasants lost their family-run smallholdings and their collective village political autonomy.[72] Most peasants were organized into collective farms called *kolkhozes*. Here, all land except household garden plots was owned and worked collectively for the overriding purpose of delivering predetermined amounts of specified products to state procurement agencies in return for low fixed prices. This system was firmly enforced by officials, most of whom were of urban origin, and all of whom were appointed by and loyal to the Party-state. These included not only the *kolkhoz* managers themselves, but also various officials and political agents affiliated with machine–tractor stations. Set up to lease agricultural machinery to groups of *kolkhozes,* these stations also served as organs for bureaucratic surveillance and additional surplus appropriation by the state.

To finance heavy-industrial development, Russian peasants and workers alike were intensely exploited by the Soviet state: Much of the revenue invested came from the difference between low procurement prices paid for agricultural products and high retail prices paid by urban consumers for food.[73] Yet the peasant *kolkhoz* members suffered even more than urban workers. They did not enjoy the security of regular wages (however low). Instead, their remuneration was based on individually earned shares of the income left after obligations to the state (and for future production needs) were met. Thus peasant incomes fluctuated with the vagaries of harvests—so that, for example, during the early 1930s when disruptions of agricultural production in the wake of forced collectivization were worst, millions of peasants simply starved after state procurements took away their subsistence.[74] Moreover, social services in rural areas were, if they existed at all, even less adequate than in the urban industrial centers. Hardly surprisingly, Russian peasants never adapted enthusiastically to these "collective" forms of agriculture, which were not in their interest. As a direct and ironic result, most of the increases of productivity that occurred in Russian agriculture after 1928 came not in the *kolkhoz* sector but from peasants' efforts on their tiny household plots.[75] The products of these plots could be sold on open markets, where those urban dwellers fortunate enough to do so were more than willing to shop, in order to supplement what little they could obtain from government outlets.

Hierarchy and Coercion

Turning now to the overall features of the Soviet system after 1928, we may note that pronouncedly inegalitarian patterns of hierarchical control and socioeconomic rewards became established. Within the Soviet administration during the 1930s, all attempts to keep officials from becoming privileged and authoritarian were abandoned. As Alf Edeen puts it, "many

229

rules and stipulations were once again [as under the Old Regime] introduced for the purpose of gaining control over and at the same time granting authority to the powerfully expanding and differentiated administrative apparatus."[76] Elaborate ranks and sharp salary differentials were introduced to set officials off from nonofficials, and to put different ranks of officials in hierarchical order. Remarkably enough, by the 1940s, both the Soviet civil administration and the officer corps of the Red Army had institutionalized official titles, ranks, and uniforms that were just as elaborate and ostentatious—and in fact exactly parallel to—those established under the Old Regime by Peter the Great.[77]

Meanwhile, in society at large, sharply differentiated economic rewards—such as special bonuses and consumption perquisites for highly skilled or super-productive individual workers, and piece-rate wages (with norms set above average) for un- and semiskilled workers—were introduced in order to spur efforts to achieve extremely high production targets.[78] Similar differentials were instituted among peasants, sometimes flying in the face of the efforts of the *kolkhozniks* to retain egalitarian standards of reward under collectivization.[79] Moreover, the early Bolshevik principle that managers, specialists, and Party officials should not receive substantially higher pay or benefits than skilled workers was contemptuously abandoned (as "petty bourgeois egalitarianism") by Stalin. Thus, not only was managerial authority over workers and peasants greatly strengthened, but the economic managers and their technical staffs (like state administrators and army officers) were also given much higher salaries and more job-associated benefits than production workers.[80]

Finally, the Soviet regime came to rely to an extraordinary degree—compared both to the admittedly repressive tsarist autocracy and to other post-social-revolutionary regimes—upon administratively organized coercion and terror as techniques for ruling its citizens and for purging and controlling its own official cadres. Here one need only cite certain vividly known instances and facts to make the point. The collectivization of Soviet agriculture was, for instance, implemented only through the application of unlimited coercion against the reluctant peasants. And, in the process, several million richer peasants (*kulaks*), as well as poorer peasants who resisted collectivization, were totally expropriated and deported from their communities.[81] During forced industrialization, Soviet citizens at all levels of society were subjected to intense secret police surveillance and were constantly subject to possible arrest for real or imagined infractions, often followed by long, indeed indeterminate sentences to forced-labor prison camps. So huge, in fact, were these camps, that they constituted a self-contained administrative—economic empire and provided an important source of super-exploited labor that could be used by the regime to complete strategic infrastructural projects under harsh conditions (where it would have been difficult and expensive to employ free labor).[82] And, of course, general fear of arrest and imprisonment among the Soviet population only served to reinforce labor discipline and productive efforts among those who remained out of prison.

The leading groups of Soviet society were not free from surveillance and fear either. On the contrary, the "Great Purges" of the 1930s represent perhaps the most sweeping historical instance of the application of terror in peacetime by part of a society's domestic elite against other parts.[83] Stalin's drive to establish and maintain his own personal dictatorship — whatever the cost in human suffering and waste of leadership skills and experience — provides the most straightforward "explanation" for these arrests and murders of thousands of Party and non-Party leaders, including virtually all that remained of the "Old" (i.e., original) Bolsheviks. Nevertheless, the context in which Stalin's vendetta against other members of the Party-state leadership emerged and was actually carried through was one in which powerful coercive organizations had already been established to punish and goad the population at large. In the Great Purges, those organizations were turned against the Party and administrative elites most aware of (and responsible for) the costs exacted from the population in the initial stages of forced collectivization and industrialization. Thus the way was opened for upwardly mobile beneficiaries of the Stalinist system to move to the fore. The effect beyond the very short run, therefore, was probably to help stabilize many institutional features of that system.

In sum, the Soviet system that crystallized after 1928 was at once more formally equalitarian and popularly inclusive and more rank-ridden, effectively authoritarian, and coercive than the prerevolutionary absolutist and aristocratic system. Why did this peculiar concatenation of outcomes emerge from the Russian Revolution? Essentially we have already spun all of the strands of an adequate explanation and need only weave them together here in conclusion.

Because the tsarist state was so crucial as the bulwark of the social hierarchies of the Old Regime and then, in 1917, collapsed so completely and suddenly, massive popular revolts from below could arise quickly within the revolutionary political crisis. Given the communal–equalitarian orientation of most of the peasantry and the absence in the cities of securely established trade unions and democratic–parliamentary institutions to channel popular participation under liberal leadership, the popular revolts of 1917 rapidly undermined the positions of privileged groups. This ensured that the Revolution would be sweepingly equalitarian in its basic accomplishments; and, indeed, the Russian social revolution of 1917 was the most thoroughgoing and sudden the world has ever seen.

Yet the suddenness and completeness of that social revolution also meant that the politically organized revolutionaries – who sought to consolidate the Russian Revolution by building up new state organizations to fend off counterrevolutionaries and foreign invaders—were faced with terrible dilemmas. The new revolutionary state organizations had to be built up quickly and virtually from scratch, given the completeness of the dissolution of the tsarist army and administration. Moreover, the vast peasant majority was at best an indirect and unenthusiastic ally for any would-be state builders. To build up the revolutionary state organizations amidst these conditions, the Bolsheviks relied upon the expedients of impressing the services of functionaries of the Old Regime and coercing manpower and supplies from the reluctant peasantry. Not surprisingly, the resulting institutional pattern of the nascent Soviet state apparatuses featured a combination of the following: bureaucratic hierarchy, stress on the prerogatives of professional experts, and highly centralized and coercive Party controls over both the state functionaries and popular groups, especially the peasantry.

Nor did the peasant problem go away after the initial consolidation of revolutionary state power. Due to the agrarian economic effects of the peasants' revolution against large landholders and the Bolshevik Party-state's lack of any secure organizational basis in the countryside, the fledgling Soviet regime was caught very quickly in a national economic crisis. For a variety of situational reasons—including the regime's international isolation and insecurity, and the economic legacies of the prerevolutionary economy—the Party-state turned to rapid, state-propelled heavy industrialization as its way out of the crisis it faced in the 1920s. Yet this inevitably meant that the New Regime would revert to and exaggerate the basic institutional patterns of state structure and state/society relationships that had first appeared during the Civil War crisis. For now there had to be certain continuously available means at the disposal of the New Regime—centralized controls, individualized unequal incentives, *and* the omnipresent possibility of coercive sanctions. These means were needed to mobilize and manipulate both leaders and led to undertake the enormous efforts, sacrifices, and social disruption necessarily entailed by sudden industrialization with priority given to heavy industries, not consumer goods and services. There was no abstract, general "imperative of industrialization" at work here.[84] But there were imperatives of state-propelled, heavy industrialization, undertaken by a regime with a narrow and precarious political basis in a predominantly agrarian society where the peasantry was both independently organized and hostile to the regime.

Indeed, the great irony—and poignancy—of the Russian Revolution lies in the role and fate of the peasantry. For the peasants made their own thoroughgoing social revolution in 1917—and as a result became a threat to the viability of Russia as a revolutionized nation-state in a world of militarily competing nation-states. The efforts of the revolutionary state-builders to cope with this autonomous peasantry, even as they dealt with organized political competitors at home and abroad, led them bit by bit to erect a regime of monstrous proportions and consequences – especially for the peasantry. Thus the outcome of the Russian Revolution was a totally collectivist and authoritarian system in which the mass energies of all of the Russian people were finally turned – through coercion and terror if voluntary enthusiasm was not forthcoming – from the anarchic rebellions of 1917 toward active participation in centrally determined and directed efforts. At first these efforts involved the construction at reckless and breakneck speed of heavy industries. Then they turned to the defense of the Russian nation against a ruthless foe in World War II. Whatever the human costs – and they were terrible – this revolutionized system ultimately proved itself as a national state power. One need only compare the fate of Soviet Russia in World War II and after to that of Tsarist Russia in World War I to convince oneself of this.

France and Russia:
The Argument in Retrospect

At this juncture it should be helpful to step back and summarize the overall logic of the major arguments that have been developed so far in Part II about the dynamics and outcomes of the French and the Russian Revolutions. Analytically speaking, I have proceeded in an unorthodox way. The French and Russian Revolutions are usually explained primarily by reference to the socioeconomic interests and political actions of urban classes, with analysts stressing how completely different the two Revolutions were in their logic and results. Thus the French Revolution is seen as a capitalist and liberal revolution led by the bourgeoisie, whereas the Russian Revolution is viewed as an anticapitalist, communist revolution made by the industrial proletariat and the Bolshevik Party. In contrast, I have analyzed the French and Russian Revolutions in similar terms: For both I have emphasized the interplay between, on the one hand, the direct accomplishments and indirect political consequences of peasant revolts against landlords and, on the other hand, the struggles of political leaderships to build and use state organizations within the given domestic and international circumstances.

From this perspective, much more than from those of the more orthodox approaches, it becomes clear and explicable that the French and Russian Revolutions shared certain important similarities of political process and outcome. In both cases, largely spontaneous and autonomous peasant revolts functioned to make either counterrevolution or liberal stabilization impossible, yet also made it impossible for revolutionary political movements to base themselves in the countryside. And, in both cases, the pres-

233

sing need for urban-based revolutionary leaderships to build state orga-nizations powerful enough to defeat domestic counterrevolutionaries and foreign enemies meant that the Revolutions gave rise to more centralized and bureaucratic regimes. Neither of these was in any meaningful sense either liberal-parliamentary or directly democratic, although both were originally built up by tapping the unprecedented participation and enthusi-asm of urban working people (the *sans culottes* in France and the indus-trial proletariat in Russia).

Within the analytic framework that I have employed, it is also possible to understand the important differences between the French and Russian Revolutions more realistically than if one simply treats them as two differ-ent species of occurrences. Basically, I have invoked two sets of factors together to explain differences in the processes and outcomes of these Revolutions: (1) the different specific forms in each case of the same variables used to explain underlying similarities, that is, the peasant revolts and the tasks of state building within the given revolutionary crisis; and (2) the contrasting socioeconomic, world-historical, and international con-texts specific to each Revolution.

Thus I have suggested that the Russian Revolution deepened and radi-calized much more suddenly than the French because of the contrasting ways in which revolutionary political crises originally emerged in the two cases. And the Russian Revolution was consolidated through perhaps even more coercive and authoritarian expedients than the French because revo-lutionary armies had to be built completely from scratch in war-torn Rus-sia, whereas the Jacobins in France could expand preexisting standing armies.

Taken together, several other differences explain why the French Revo-lution culminated in the coexistence of a centralized, bureaucratic state with a private-propertied society and market economy, whereas the Rus-sian Revolution gave rise to a Party-state devoted to state-controlled national industrialization. In France, peasant revolts stopped short of attacking or leveling individual landed property. Domestic socioeconomic structures (both those that already existed and those resulting from the peasant revolution against seigneurialism) favored market-oriented eco-nomic development, and there were no world-historically available mod-els for state-controlled industrialization. Thus no communist-style, mass-mobilizing political party could consolidate state power. Moreover, France's strong position on the Continent favored the channeling of revo-lutionary mobilization into militarily expansionist nationalism rather than further politically directed transformations at home. In Russia, by con-trast, the peasant revolution seized and redistributed larger landed pro-perties, with the result that possibilities for market-guided national eco-nomic development were seriously impaired. There were preexisting,

234

large-scale industrial enterprises in Russia, and there were world-historically available models of state control over industries. Moreover, Russia was geopolitically situated in a profoundly vulnerable position within the European states system. For all of these reasons, the Bolsheviks were enabled and circumstantially urged, first to consolidate Party-state power on an urban-industrial base, and then to extend that power from above over the peasantry and use it to propel the rapid national industrialization of the Soviet Union.

The reader has perhaps noticed that some of the same realities that figure prominently in bourgeois/proletarian interpretations of the French and Russian Revolutions also enter in here. The difference, however, is that I have treated the urban industrial and class structures of France and Russia as contextual features – as backgrounds against which the (for me) more analytically important agrarian upheavals and political dynamics played themselves out. To be sure, I have argued that the different urban industrial and class structures profoundly influenced the revolutionary processes and outcomes. They did so, however, not because a bourgeoisie or a proletariat was the key political actor. Rather they did so because, along with the differing results of the peasant revolutions, the contrasting urban structures differently conditioned the possibilities for consolidating and using revolutionary state power in France and Russia.

235

7 The Rise of a Mass-Mobilizing Party-State in China

Revolutions are profoundly influenced by the character of ruling classes. The entrenched localism of the gentry power made it inevitable that the Chinese revolution, in contrast to the revolutions of France and Russia, would come from the outlying areas to the center rather than the reverse . . .

Franz Schurmann

LIKE THE RUSSIAN and the French Revolutions, the Chinese Revolution was launched by the breakdown of an autocratic and semibureaucratic Old Regime. And it culminated in a New Regime more centralized, mass-incorporating, and in many ways more fully rationalized and bureaucratic than the prerevolutionary Old Regime. In all three Revolutions, moreover, peasants provided the major insurrectionary force to transform old class relations. In France and Russia, social-revolutionary changes depended upon the occurrence of peasant revolts. Nevertheless, revolutionary state organizations were built up with the aid of primarily urban popular support and imposed through administrative hierarchies upon the rural areas. The postrevolutionary states in France and Russia both were (despite many differences) professional–bureaucratic regimes. In the Chinese Revolution, however, peasants ended up providing *both* the revolutionary insurrectionary force and the organized popular basis for the consolidation of revolutionary state power. And the result was a revolutionary New Regime uniquely devoted to fostering widespread participation and surprisingly resistant to routinized hierarchical domination by bureaucratic officials and professional experts.

The reasons for these differences that set the Chinese Revolution apart from the French and the Russian lie, as they did for each of the other cases, in the particular characteristics of the social-revolutionary situation and the surviving legacies of the Old Regime. After the fall of the Imperial state in China, gentry landlords remained entrenched in the rural localities, and warlords held sway at provincial and regional levels. Hence revolutionary state-builders faced formidable obstacles. Ultimately, the Chinese Revolution could be completed only when some revolutionary leaders

236

learned to tap the enormous insurrectionary, productive, and political energies of the peasant majority.

THE SOCIAL-REVOLUTIONARY SITUATION AFTER 1911

Once the facade of Imperial authority was stripped away through the overthrow of the Manchus, state power in China devolved entirely into those regional, provincial, and local centers wherein it had been accumulating for decades. In a sense this situation resembled what happened in France in 1789 and in Russia in 1917. For in all three instances the formerly centralized monarchical administrations disintegrated, and opportunities for political participation and initiatives became much more widespread as purportedly representative institutions replaced the king, tsar, or emperor. Yet China was distinctive because of the role of her regionally based military organizations after 1911.

The Warlord Context

In the French and Russian Revolutions, regionally based movements were not a factor until *after* centralized revolutionary governments had begun to emerge. During 1917 in Russia the Imperial armies – already highly professionalized and centrally controlled before 1914 – simply dissolved in the chaos of wartime defeats and anarchic revolution from below. In the early stages of the French Revolution, regional or provincial militarism was not a problem. This was true because the Old Regime had long since brought the once-independent provincial military governors under central administrative controls, and because, in 1789, the royal administration was displaced by a loose network of urban committees and militias that oscillated between national and local orientations.

But in post-1911 China – especially after the death in 1916 of President (and would-be Emperor) Yuan Shih-k'ai, who had been a key military leader under the Ch'ing and was capable of commanding the loyalty of many generals – such political control as there was on an extralocal scale centered in the coercive capacities of "warlord"-dominated regional military machines. Constitutional and parliamentary political arrangements never became at all effective.[1] Instead: "Throughout the country there existed independent military–political groupings, each of which controlled territory and exploited local resources. Each, as a system, was similar to all the others; they differed primarily in scale."[2] These regimes were "structured hierarchies usually organized for both civil administration and warfare."[3] Authority in them depended upon the loyalty of subordinates to a given warlord who, in turn, had to reward his officer-followers with money, weapons, and control over military units and territorial subbases. Because these regimes were constantly in competition with each other, their chief activities were resource extraction, military recruitment, negotiations with potential allies and foreign supporters, and, of course, violent civil warfare.[4]

The sources of warlordism have to be traced back to developments under the Old Regime and to the manner in which the Imperial system was brought down. During the final decades of the Old Regime, some scattered modern transportation facilities and industries including arsenals were developed, mostly near the coastal treaty ports, but also in certain inland cities controlled by influential provincial authorities.[5] The impact on Chinese society and the economy as a whole was very superficial.[6] But enough modern development did occur to make more destructive weapons and new potential sources of revenue available to various regional military commanders. Moreover, the adoption of modern military methods by provincial military authorities was actually encouraged by the expiring Ch'ing. For this was seen as the only feasible way to transform the regional armies that had emerged during the Taiping Rebellion into professional armies capable of defending the various parts of China against imperialist intrusions.[7] However, as we have seen, instead of becoming effective instruments of national defense, these "New Armies" joined the gentry to overthrow the Ch'ing. Then, once the dynasty was gone, and with the already partially dismantled Confucian Imperial administration in disarray, the New Armies evolved into the warlord-dominated instruments of regional rule and interregional competition that prevailed completely by 1916.

For Chinese society as a whole, the consequence of the warlord era was a vicious circle. Inherently unstable yet naturally ambitious, the various warlord regimes constantly jostled for territory, each perhaps hoping ultimately to reunite the country. In order to better pursue the struggle with its rivals, each regime milked its own base area to the fullest degree possible. Crushing tax burdens and military requisitions drove many peasants from their lands, causing the warlord armies to expand even further, as peasants joined to escape the worsening rural conditions.[8] At the same time, cities and industries were viewed by the warlords not as dynamic centers of modern economic expansion to be nursed to maturity but as sources of military resources even more inviting and accessible than the countryside.[9] In extreme cases, warlords even milked merchants out of business. Thus, society grew weaker, and warlords and their friends grew stronger and richer—yet always, curiously, within an overall "balance of weakness," so that national political reintegration escaped China.

The Survival of the Local Gentry

Meanwhile, what was happening to China's dominant socioeconomic class? How did the demise of the Imperial system and the advent of warlord rule affect the gentry? To answer, we must distinguish between the literati and officials, on the one hand, and the locally rooted landlords and managers of community organizations, on the other hand.

Certainly the Confucian elite—literati and officials—disintegrated after 1911 (indeed from 1905 on) as a structured, national administrative and cultural body.[10] Moreover, the upper literati and former civil officials did not fare very well in the political climate that followed the overthrow of the Ch'ing. Before 1911 (as we saw in Chapter 2), literati had gained control of the newly established provincial representative assemblies; and officials, including many provincial governors nominally loyal to the Ch'ing, had drifted toward allegiance to regional governing cliques. When the Revolution of 1911 came, many assemblies and provincial civil officials managed to govern for a time in league with the military officers who controlled the armed forces. But by 1915 the assemblies were defunct, and many formerly extralocally prominent gentry were left with nothing to do but fall back on leisured living or "bourgeois" economic ventures in the bigger cities. With the full advent of regional-militarist rule, and on into the period of Kuomintang–Nationalist rule after 1927, some former literati-officials managed to find positions in the regimes of the warlords. Yet under the warlords and the Nationalists civil positions were limited in numbers and their functions and perquisites circumscribed; for military organization was the primary locus of power and authority. Besides, former Ch'ing officials and literati had to compete with upwardly mobile, non-Confucian-trained "upstarts" for whatever positions there were. In sum, many or even most former Imperial officials and upper literati may have achieved personal accommodations with changing regional and national power structures, or they may have prospered through modern urban pursuits. Nevertheless, these sectors of the gentry lost their distinctive power and identity after 1911. Their fate in this sense resembled that of both the French Court and urban aristocracy and the Russian official nobility.

The impact of the demise of the Imperial state and the emergence of warlordism upon the gentry in its guise as the local dominant class was much more equivocal—and certainly very different from the implications of the fall of the monarchical regimes for the French seigneurs and the Russian landed nobles. Because the French and Russian peasants enjoyed considerable community solidarity and autonomy from noble control, they could and did revolt on their own against the seigneurs and landed nobles once the monarchical administrations and repressive controls were suddenly disorganized in 1789 and 1917. But, for reasons that we investigated in Chapter 3, the Chinese peasants were, in the normal local scheme of things, not in a structural position to revolt collectively and autonomously against the landlord gentry. Consequently, the dissolution of the Imperial

239

system around 1911 did not directly create favorable circumstances for peasant revolts against landlords in China; and the local socioeconomic base of the gentry, its landholding and leadership of community organizations, was not immediately undermined from below.

In fact, the already significant local political power of the gentry was only further enhanced by the downfall of the dynasty and the Imperial administration. Since the mid-nineteenth-century rebellions, local gentry had formally or informally usurped district magistracies and moved into subdistrict offices created by the Ch'ing in the hope of coopting their local leadership. After 1911, the local gentry merely continued their hold on these positions. In addition, they took extra advantage of their control of local taxing and policing functions to tighten their hold over and exploitation of the peasantry.[11]

Still, the demise of the Imperial state system did have disorganizing consequences for the local gentry, in at least three important ways. First, it tended to make it difficult for local community leadership groupings to achieve contact with each other. This would make it impossible for the traditional dominant class to defend itself against any large-scale rebellious or revolutionary movement without substantial help from warlord or national armies. Nothing like the gentry self-defense against the Taipings could recur.[12]

Second, the fall of the Imperial state eliminated well-institutionalized contacts between regional and national power centers and local elites. The warlord regimes that controlled various regions of China after 1911, the Kuomintang after 1927, and the Communists and the Japanese in the late 1930s and 1940s—all of these regimes attempted to extend administrative and military controls into local areas, often through cooperation with local gentry. Thus, in place of the Imperial bureaucracy (whose administrative style, policy perspectives, values, and ideology were well known to them), local gentry had to contend with a bewildering succession of military commanders, bureaucrats, parties, and "isms." Naturally, this situation bred instability in local elite circles. Whoever had the best contact with the warlord or party currently in power could enhance his local position. But once that warlord or party was displaced, new men with new connections would reap the rewards, and the old elites might lose power, property, or even their lives.

Third, the passing of the Confucian state decreased the weight of Confucian-educated elements, whether literati or cultured landlords, within the local dominant classes, even as commercialization and political instability probably increased the weight of others such as merchants, speculating landlords, and smugglers.[13] The lack of well-defined relationships between local elites and central powers, as well as the absolute increase of local dominant-class power unrestrained by outsiders with a "national perspective," led to what several writers have labeled an increase in "opportunism" among the local gentry. What this meant in practice was that the peasants were subjected to more ruthless and normatively unrestrained exploitation. The result was that peasants were increasingly prone to rebel if they should become able, or else to abandon the local communities to join bandit gangs or roving armies. These in turn threatened the security of the gentry and the remaining settled peasants.

Thus, after 1911, the national political and cultural extensions of China's locally based dominant class disintegrated along with the institutions of the Imperial state. Meanwhile, within the local rural communities, the gentry landlords and other economically dominant elements became at once more entrenched and more vulnerable. They were vulnerable especially to attacks from any extralocally organized forces that might be determined to ally with the restive peasantry rather than with the local dominant classes.

To sum up from a comparative perspective: Whereas the French and Russian Revolutions began with the complete disorganization or total collapse of monarchical states followed by the rapid undermining of the dominant classes through revolts from below, the removal of the autocracy in China in 1911 did not result so directly in social revolution. To be sure, the result was deepening political disintegration and increasing social tensions, for the Imperial–Confucian civil administrative system dissolved. Within this context, room for maneuver was available for revolutionary political movements aiming to reunite the nation and to mobilize popular support for that goal. Nevertheless, the continuing military (and administrative) power of the warlords and their local gentry allies was a potent obstacle that had to be overcome if revolutionary efforts were to succeed. Chinese revolutionaries after 1911 faced far more entrenched and militarily potent remnants of the Old Regime than did French revolutionaries after 1789 and (especially) Russian revolutionaries after 1917.

The most important implication of this special Chinese social-revolutionary situation after 1911 was that "the unification of China and re-creation of central authority could begin only from within the militarist system itself."[14] Means had to be found to surpass the normal constraints and dynamics of the naturally divisive system of warlord competition, even as would-be unifiers successfully competed within it. Here was the challenge and dilemma confronted most decisively, first, from the early 1920s on, by the Kuomintang (originally aided by the urban-based Chinese Communist Party) and, then, after 1927, by the Communists exiled to rural areas. Each of these revolutionary political movements developed the military means to acquire a secure geographical base for the establishment of a governmental administration within China, because each sooner or later tapped extraordinary resources not available to, or utilized by, its competitors. In time, these two movements pushed aside the "mere" warlords and confronted only one another as serious competitors to unify and govern China. Let us now proceed to take a close look at the reasons for the Kuomintang's initial successes and eventual failure and for the Chinese Communist Party's early defeats and ultimate success.

THE RISE AND DECLINE OF
THE URBAN-BASED KUOMINTANG

The French Revolution had the Jacobins and the Russian Revolution had the Bolsheviks. Yet the Chinese Revolution had *two* parallel revolutionary political movements that aimed at and achieved considerable success in consolidating state power within the post-1911 social-revolutionary situation. One, the Kuomintang, based itself primarily upon urban support and resources; the other, the Chinese Communist Party, based itself after 1927 primarily upon peasant support and rural resources. Certainly (as we shall see) the ultimate success of the Communists depended upon their ability to penetrate rural communities, displace the remnant gentry, and mobilize peasant participation to a degree unprecedented in (at least recent) Chinese history. But the survival and final victory of the Communists also depended upon the failure of the Kuomintang to consolidate state power on an urban basis. Thus in this section we must not only analyze the development of the Kuomintang but also seek to understand why this urban-based movement could not succeed in China—in contrast to the Bolsheviks and the Jacobins (and their bureaucratic and military successors), who *were* able to consolidate state power on urban bases in their predominantly agrarian and peasant societies. Only in this way can we see why there were in revolutionary China two major movements to consolidate state power—including a distinctive peasant-based movement that ultimately succeeded—rather than just a single urban-based movement.

That movements for political reunification *would* arise in the post-1911 situation was implicit in the orientations of all politically aware Chinese. Those still faithful to traditional ideals remembered the benefits of Imperial unity. Even warlords fought with the avowed goal of promoting reunification. But more important, increasing numbers of modern university-educated Chinese, as well as Chinese businessmen who grew in economic weight and independence during the World War I period, became converts to various Western cultural ideals and turned into vociferous advocates of Chinese national autonomy and assertion against the humiliating privileges of the imperialist powers. These modern nationalists were concentrated most of all in the great coastal cities, many of which were westernized treaty ports. These same cities were the prime sites of periodic mass anti-

242

imperialist movements in the wake of World War I, the settlement of which enraged the Chinese in that it openly snubbed their aspirations for national integrity. Against this background, it is not surprising that the original leaderships and organized popular bases of both the Kuomintang and the Chinese Communist Party came from (or by way of) these more "modernized" urban centers of early-twentieth-century China.[15]

Alliance and Break with the Communists

The Kuomintang and Communist parties emerged at about the same time and soon became allies in a nationalist, antiwarlord struggle. In July 1921, the First Congress of the Chinese Communist Party (CCP), consisting of thirteen representatives of left-leaning intellectual circles, convened in Shanghai. In late 1922, Sun Yat-sen's Kuomintang (KMT) – which was a loosely organized party primarily consisting of urban-based intellectuals and was the successor to the Teng Meng Hui revolutionary organizations of 1911 – agreed to accept aid and advice from the Soviet Union and to reorganize itself into a mass-based democratic–centralist party. Finally, by 1924, the CCP and the new KMT, both acting according to Soviet advice, agreed to unite and work together for a "nationalist, democratic revolution." CCP members were thereupon admitted to simultaneous membership and leadership roles in the reorganized KMT.

Between 1923 and 1926, the Kuomintang, including from 1924 the Communists, accomplished three important things.[16] First, it created an effective Nationalist Government within its gradually enlarging base area around Canton. Second, it developed a well-armed and well-trained centrally controlled and politically indoctrinated Nationalist Revolutionary Army and groomed it for the Northern Expedition to defeat warlordism and reunite China. And, third, it built a centrally organized, yet mass-based, antiimperialist party oriented toward social reform. The crucial ingredients in the KMT's formula for developing the strength to defeat warlord regimes were Soviet financial and military aid as well as popular mobilization and nationalist ideology – for these were resources that the warlords lacked, at least in combination.

A requisite for the KMT's consolidation of power in Kwangtung Province was the development of the National Revolutionary Army (NRA). At the Whampoa Academy, officers for the NRA were trained and politically indoctrinated by Chinese and Russian instructors. Russian financial and arms aid, channeled through central KMT authorities, facilitated control over the variety of units that made up the NRA. By 1925, Chiang Kai-shek was able to lead the army against rival militarists in Kwangtung. Their defeat allowed the Nationalist Government, with the aid of a newly established Central Bank financed through a Russian loan, to centralize and

243

rationalize provincial tax collection procedures, thus increasing its revenues and further extending its ability to recruit and control military units.

Meanwhile, Communist and "Left KMT" cadres provided the organizational élan that allowed KMT membership, between 1923 and 1926, to increase from a few thousand to over 200,000 – not counting parallel huge increases in Party-related mass-movement associations.[17] As a result of its special efforts, the CCP and its youth organization also grew substantially, especially after 1925. This early CCP saw itself as the "party of the proletariat." Thus the Party

> attempted to organize the entire proletariat into a network of industrial unions . . . linked in functional and metropolitan federations and all tied together in a national General Labour Union controlled by the Party itself. In a few years of intense work a score of young intellectuals . . . succeeded . . . in creating, or in penetrating and taking over, hundreds of unions, several large federations, and a national organization which claimed some three million members in mid-1927.[18]

For all those within the Nationalist Alliance, consolidation of the Kwangtung base was but preparation for the launching of a military expedition to reunite China. Initiated in July 1926 by the National Revolutionary Army, "the basic objectives of the Northern Expedition were first to capture the Wu-Han cities (Hankow), then to take Shanghai and Nanking, and finally to capture Peking. This plan called for the defeat of Wu P'ei-fu [Warlord of Hupei, northern Hunan, and Honan], Sun Ch'uan-fang [Warlord of Fukien, Chekiang, Kiangsu, Anhwei and Kiangsi], and Chang Tso-lin [Warlord of Manchuria, Shantung, and Chihli (Hopei)] in succession."[19] By October 1926 the Wu-Han cities had been captured in a rapid northward drive. After a period of reorganization to incorporate former enemy units that had responded to the initial Nationalist victories by converting to "the revolution," the Nationalist forces were able to take Shanghai and Nanking in the spring of 1927. But at this point further drives to the north were interrupted due to the breakup of the Nationalist Alliance.

As Wilbur has aptly put it, "as soon as the first successful burst of the Northern Expedition was over, the issues of 'how much social revolution?' and 'how much anti-imperialism?' became acute."[20] Strains always inherent in the Nationalist Alliance became contradictions. Within the KMT leadership, Communists and Left KMT leaders who shared their views envisioned the Northern Expedition as more than a campaign to unite the country; they saw it as a prelude to substantial social reform, or revolution, as well. Many of these leftist leaders had worked to mobilize mass enthusiasm among workers and peasants.[21] They had promised the masses social change and expected, in return, to use mass support and social revolution to gain the upper hand within the KMT leadership.

244

Map 5. *The provinces of China and adjacent areas, 1930. Source:* James Sheridan, *China in Disintegration* (New York: The Free Press, 1975), p. iv.

245

Right KMT leaders, on the other hand, had long distrusted both the leftists and the mass movements, for they envisaged the "revolution" as strictly a unifying and cautiously antiimperialist affair. Besides, they had no intention of being pushed aside by a Communist coup. After 1925, the mass movements grew, and enthusiasm for the Northern Expedition led to increased strikes, demonstrations, and rural unrest. As a result, Right KMT leaders had little trouble finding sympathy for their views among the bourgeoisie, the gentry, and among army officers whose landlord families were threatened by peasant associations. Attacks on foreign civilians during the early stages of the Northern Expedition also aroused the fears of the Western powers, prompting them to send armed forces to protect the lives of their nationals in the great treaty ports of Central China.

Thus by 1927 the Nationalist Alliance reached a point of critical decision. Chiang Kai-shek, as leader of the NRA and the personal focus of the entire loose coalition of armies that comprised the Alliance's military force, was in the best position to decide the issue. And so he did: Beginning with the Shanghai Coup of April 1926 and extending through a period of violent purges of Communists and mass-movement leaders throughout KMT-held territories, the Kuomintang was reoriented. It turned away from continued reliance upon Soviet aid and Communist-inspired mass mobilization. Instead, it began to rely increasingly upon the financial resources of Chinese businesses in the newly conquered cities of Central China, and to depend upon revenues from the international trade of the treaty ports and assistance (including military advice) from Western powers.[22]

How could the choice have gone differently? From its inception the Nationalist movement had been aimed primarily at military conquest. Soviet aid and advice had been accepted by Sun Yat-sen only because they seemed to offer extraordinary resources in the struggle against other military regimes. Mass mobilization, the specialty of the Communist cadres, also constituted a unique resource. As soon as striking workers or rebellious peasant associations began to get out of hand, however, it understandably seemed to the military unifiers increasingly a liability, likely only to alienate upper-class Chinese nationalists and draw foreign intervention against the KMT. Moreover, in the wake of the initial successes of the Northern Expedition, the wealth of the urban centers of central China beckoned as a welcome substitute for Soviet subsidies. And, indeed, once mobilized through the fiscal innovations of T. V. Soong, that wealth allowed Chiang Kai-shek to consummate the drive to reunite (nominally) most of the country during 1928–31. This campaign proceeded through campaigns based in classical warlord fashion upon an adroitly orchestrated combination of actual battles, diplomatic maneuvers to divide opponents, and the buying off of potential enemies with subsidies of money or arms.[23]

246

The Failure to Consolidate National Control

However, in all of this there was a long-run price to be paid, even in terms of the Nationalists' own supreme goal of unity and strength for China. For no regime based primarily on the treaty port–centered modern urban sector of China could realistically hope to consolidate centralized state power in post-1911 China. Brief comparisons to revolutionary France and Russia will help explain why.

Somewhat like the commercial port cities of eighteenth-century France, these modern Chinese cities were outwardly oriented, perched on the edges of the continental realm, and marginal to the urban-administrative hierarchy through which the Imperial authorities had ruled.[24] In the national assemblies of revolutionary France, politicians who came from or were oriented to the interests of the French commercial ports tended to be displaced as revolutionary state power was consolidated by politicians from the inland towns and cities.[25] But no such straightforward succession of urban-based revolutionary leaderships could occur in China. The rural dominant class, the gentry, remained entrenched at the bottom of the old administrative hierarchy, astride the basic-level nexus between town and country. Besides, within the context of the warlordism that prevailed after 1916, competition for national power was thoroughly militarized, and already ensconced warlords could not be quickly or easily removed from the inland areas. There could be no Montagnard Jacobins in China.

Yet why couldn't the Kuomintang (or some other urban-based party) imitate the state-building strategies of the Bolsheviks by relying upon modern industries, proletarian mobilization, and the military advantages of rail transportation? The answer is that the resources just were not there. Although China had experienced some degree of modern industrialization and railroad development before 1928, the overall degree of development was much less than in Russia before 1917. Thus in China (up to 1949, let alone 1928) the total output of modern industries never exceeded 3.5 percent of the national income, and industrial workers remained substantially fewer than 1 percent of the labor force. (Roughly comparable figures for late Tsarist Russia were 16 percent and 5 percent, respectively.)[26] Besides, Chinese industries were primarily light industries, small or medium in scale. And (as Map 6 indicates) they were mostly concentrated along the eastern coast. The rail lines (also indicated on Map 6) were few and scattered and did not at all constitute a complete primary network linking all of the major cities and towns of China. In contrast (as indicated by Map 4 in Chapter 6) Russia had before 1917 a complete primary rail network; and her modern industries were mostly large-scale heavy industries, located in many of the urban administrative centers throughout European Russia. Thus during the Russian Revolution the Bolsheviks could

mobilize strategically located proletarian support to help them build new
state organizations in the place of the urban–administrative hierarchy
through which the tsarist authorities had kept Russia united and had
dominated the countryside. But no such possibility was open to the Kuomintang (or any Chinese urban-based party). It could only hope instead to
tax the output of China's much smaller and more marginal modern commercial–industrial sector. Because of the limitations of its modern urban
base, the Kuomintang after 1927 never succeeded in breaking out of the
vicious circle of inadequate revenues and insufficient central political control that had plagued all previous militarist regimes in twentieth-century
China. Rather the Nationalist government only reproduced the old war-

Map 6. *Railroads and major industrial areas of China, to 1930.*
Sources: James Sheridan, *China in Disintegration* (New York: The
Free Press, 1975), p. iv; and Jean Chesneaux, *The Chinese Labor
Movement, 1919–1927,* trans. H. M. Wright (Stanford, Calif.: Stan-
ford University Press, 1968), pp. 423–6.

lord forms on a larger, superficially "national" scale – as a bit closer look at the post-1927 patterns will clearly reveal.

Nationalist military victories, whether by fighting or by conversion of intact enemy units, came so quickly after 1925 and on through the mid-1930s that political indoctrination and central organization and financing were not able to keep up with the growth as it occurred. It was not possible to disband or completely reorganize those warlord units that converted to the Nationalist cause. So they typically had to be left intact under the command of their original officers and allowed to maintain themselves primarily through drawing, as before, on the financial, industrial, and manpower resources of their established geographical bases. Loyalty to the center could be sustained only through subsidies of money or arms from Nanking.[27] These arrangements naturally ensured that the Nationalist Government would have neither a unified, efficient, centrally manageable national army nor administrative access to the resources of large areas of the country.

Thus, even after the anti-Communist campaigns of 1931–35 had given Nanking an extraordinary opportunity to extend central controls beyond its original base in Chekiang and Kiangsu Provinces into ten others designed as "Bandit Suppression Zones," the Kuomintang regime still "was not free . . . to make appointments without consulting provincial rulers . . . Neither was Nanking able to establish a uniform, centralized administrative system throughout the zones. Matters of provincial finance continued to remain outside central control."[28]

Moreover:

> outside the ten Bandit Suppression Provinces, the Kuomintang's authority was nominal or nonexistent. A high degree of provincialism continued to exist in Shansi, Kwangsi, Kwangtung, Yunnan, and Szechwan. Varying degrees of autonomy also existed in Kweichow and the outlying provinces in the north and northwest. Here provincial or regional militarists appointed their own officials and ran their own administrative and financial affairs with little or no concern for the wishes of the central authority.[29]

Finally, even in the provinces where it established unchallenged military and administrative control, the Nanking regime demonstrated very little capacity or inclination to reorganize village-level politics and enforce socioeconomic reforms. Below the *hsien* (county) base of the bureaucracy, the gentry still held sway.[30]

In turn, because of the superficiality of its political control of the country, the Nationalist regime between 1928 and 1936 relinquished to local and provincial rulers the claims to land taxes. Instead the regime depended entirely upon the easy-to-collect urban revenues: excise taxes on consumer necessities, tariffs on international trade, and borrowing through high-interest bonds issued by government-controlled banks.[31] But this approach to government finance was self-limiting. For, at best, these fiscal measures had a neutral impact on the nascent modern commercial and industrial sector; at worst, they restricted consumer purchasing capacity and destroyed incentives for saving or long-term productive investments. The growth of the urban economy upon which the Nationalist Government so depended was thus severely restricted, if not totally throttled.[32] Nor could the government begin to invest directly in economic development, for virtually all its revenues were eaten up by administrative, patronage, and military expenditures.

Ultimately, as the regime lost dynamism, it became drained of all political vitality and degenerated into a series of bureaucratically entrenched cliques focused through ties of personal loyalty on Chiang Kai-shek.[33] The "Generalissimo," directing the strategic Military Council, devoted most of his attention and skill to military campaigns against remaining warlords and the Communist "bandits." He also had to be concerned with the delicate processes of keeping competing political cliques and restless military subordinates either paid off with subsidies or honorific positions, or else off-balance and unable to unite against him. Civilian consultative and administrative institutions functioned only as adjuncts of the military hierarchies and were staffed according to the patronage needs of Chiang's personal followings. The Kuomintang Party ceased to recruit popular supporters and lost the decision-making and coordinating functions it had exercised during the period of Soviet tutelage. Mass organizations were either allowed to atrophy or else were used purely for purposes of enforcing the depoliticization of workers, peasants, and students.

If this Kuomintang regime had faced only domestic military challenges for two or three decades rather than only one decade, possibly it could have achieved prolonged military–political hegemony over the core of China, at the price of continued socioeconomic stagnation. Even this seems unlikely, however, if only because deepening agrarian crisis would almost certainly have provided inexhaustible supplies of peasant recruits for bandit and remnant Communist armies. But what national government in the modern era has been free from foreign pressures? In the case of Nationalist China, the regime's inability, between 1930 and 1936, to challenge Japanese encroachments, only invited the full-fledged invasion that came in 1937. Needless to say, Nanking could not meet the challenge of a large-scale war with an industrial power. This was true not only because of the strength of the enemy but also because of the internal weakness of an imperfectly unified and centralized regime unable to mobilize the potential wealth of China and unwilling to jeopardize militarist and upper-class dominance through mass political mobilization.

The forced retreat of the Nationalists away from the rich coastal cities and into the hinterland only exacerbated all of the regime's inherent weaknesses. Lacking a large modern urban sector to tax, the Nationalist Government relocated at Chungking turned to the expedients of, on the one hand, sucking taxes through local gentry intermediaries out of accessible parts of the southwestern rural economy and, on the other hand, floating loans at soaring rates of interest and issuing unbacked paper currency. The collecting of taxes exacerbated rural distress without ensuring adequate revenues or supplies, and the loans and the currency policy generated uncontrollable inflation in the cities. Government functionaries and urban dwellers generally were caught in a tightening vise of soaring prices and shortages of basic necessities. Any investment other than the purely speculative, on a short term, became completely meaningless.[34]

Nor, despite all of this suffering, were the patriotic sentiments of urban supporters of the KMT rewarded, for the war against Japan never went well. The situation portrayed by Barbara Tuchman in her book, *Stilwell and the American Experience in China,* is understandable as the fate of a militarist regime cut off from easily exploitable resources and increasingly preoccupied with sheer survival.[35] The Chungking regime's military organization during World War II was a decentralized collection of armies, all but a few controlled by area commanders who combined civil and military functions. Ostensibly decentralization was meant to preclude China's defeat by Japan in one blow. Actually it reflected and perpetuated Chiang's inability to control all forces from the center. No one commander could be ordered or persuaded to use his troops first against the Japanese unless directly attacked for fear that he would lose his base to other commanders, or that his strength would be weakened. Further, Chiang himself was reluctant to use the best-equipped units he controlled either against Japan or to assert control over quasi-independent subordinates, because he was saving them for the clash with the Communists that he felt certain would occur once the West had defeated Japan. What control Chiang did have over the various Nationalist armies depended upon the financial resources he personally commanded as government leader and, especially, his skill at maneuvering and counterbalancing units into an overall balance of weakness. The end result was the situation that so maddened General Stilwell in the 1940s: a huge, sprawling military establishment that was virtually useless for waging war, essentially because it constituted the loose political integument of Chiang's militarist regime. Very little could be disturbed lest the whole structure collapse.

Moreover, once the war ended, it did not take much or long to make Chiang's regime collapse, especially because the fortunes of a formidable competitor, the Chinese Communist Party, were enhanced by the same conditions that undermined the Nationalists. To see why, let us return chronologically to 1927 and see what happened to the Communists after they were expelled from the first Nationalist Alliance.

THE COMMUNISTS AND THE PEASANTS

The early political strength of the Chinese Communist Party was decimated in the Kuomintang purge of 1927–8. Mass movements were disbanded, and thousands of cadres were killed. To their sorrow, the purge taught the Chinese Communists "the bitter lesson that without military forces of their own, wooing of the elite, creation of a Party organisation and leadership in the peasant and labour movement came to naught in the swiftly changing currents of warlord-Kuomintang China."[36]

A Peasant-Based Red Army

The opportunities open to the surviving remnant of Communist leadership were severely limited. They faced enemies – warlords and the ascendant Kuomintang government – who could draw upon the benefits of urban productivity and foreign aid to maintain the military strength to exile the Communists from the cities of China. To be sure, fascination with the cities was to die hard with many Party leaders. For years after 1927, recurrent attempts were made to retake cities, riding to power upon mass uprisings of aroused peasants and workers and gambling on the strength of small, supposedly loyal, military units, often defectors from the Kuomintang. All such attempts proved abortive and costly in human lives. Gradually, even as some leaders continually attempted to retake cities, and as Moscow (as well as Chinese Party leaders based underground in urban centers) urged the CCP not to desert the proletariat, various groups of Communists began to grope their way toward a new strategy – peasant-based guerrilla warfare – that would help to carry the Party to victory.[37]

Precisely because this military strategy was the only one possible in the circumstances, the Chinese Communist Party after 1927 was forced to come to terms with the peasantry in a way far different from what happened in France and Russia. Peasants could not just be forcibly drafted into professionally led standing armies directed and supplied through urban centers; instead they had to be persuaded to volunteer manpower and supplies for the Red Armies. Peasants would not willingly and reliably provide such support unless the Communists seemed to be fighting in their interests and in a style that conformed to their localistic orientations. Guerrilla warfare is a decentralized mode of fighting, and therefore it was potentially suited to peasant proclivities.[38] But, in principle, nothing prevents guerrilla-type military forces from being (or developing into) scattered, disunited bands of armed men who may end up merely preying upon the populace. What made the Chinese Communist Red Army buildup from the late 1920s to the 1940s so distinctive was that it combined guerrilla tactics with political–ideological unification through Party con-

252

trol. And it evolved toward a mode of operation that entailed not only fighting battles but also cooperating with and mobilizing the peasantry.

Like the Soviet Red Army during the Russian Civil War (and the Montagnard-directed French revolutionary armies of 1793–4), the Chinese Red Army was permeated with political commissars and committees. Yet the overriding aim of the Soviet Party representatives had simply been to enforce the loyalty of a stratified, professional, primarily conscript army. The Chinese Communist cadres in the Red Army, on the other hand, placed more emphasis upon educating all members of the military to dedicated cooperation for the achievement of Party-defined purposes.[39] Though basic military discipline was never slackened, rank and reward differences between officers and men were downplayed, and universal ideological commitment was emphasized. All of this was necessary to allow effective military action in economically stringent circumstances in a situation in which rigid, centralized structures could not exist. For, as a guerrilla army, the Red Army was necessarily composed of small units capable of independent, flexible action on a decentralized basis. Yet it also had to be effectively coordinated and ready to combine for larger-scale operations when conditions allowed.

In another sharp contrast to (especially) the Soviet Red Army, the Chinese Army was trained to "unite" with the civilian peasantry.[40] Most basically this meant treating peasant lives, property, and customs with scrupulous respect. It also meant that whenever Red Army units secured occupied settled areas, they tried to become involved with the ongoing lives of the peasantry in two main ways. First, to supply themselves without burdening or violating the peasantry, army units engaged in production activities. And, second, to gain the active support of the peasantry, Red Army units promoted political education, Party activities, and militia organization in the villages with which they had sustained contact. In short, in order to become a "fish swimming in the sea of the people," the Red Army had to undertake economic and political as well as combat activities.

In the years immediately after 1927, the Red Army actually began to take shape. Guerrilla warfare was at the time the only really viable possibility open to the Communists. Fighting units could be organized in inaccessible areas where control by the Nationalists or the warlords was weak or else overlapping and divided. It was also very important that small, scattered guerrilla units could *initially* be composed of individuals or groups who were not actually settled in rural communities – which areas, of course, tended to be still under landlord gentry control, directly or indirectly. Instead, initial recruits for guerrilla warfare could come from the ranks of peasants who had been displaced into illegal activities centered in remote "border areas" – that is, places in the mountains and between provinces. Fortunately for the Chinese Communists—but not incidentally, in the light of what we have already learned about agrarian dynamics in China and the crisis conditions of the period—potential displaced peasant recruits were available in large numbers when the Chinese Communists needed them.

Information is available on two such early concentrations of Communist guerrilla forces in the late 1920s: the Communist partisans of the Shensi-Kansu-Ningsia border area (Shen-Kan-Ning)[41] and the "Fourth Red Army" led by Mao Tse-tung and Chu Teh into the Chingkang-shan Mountains of central China.[42] In both areas "revolutionary" forces (much to the horror of top Party leaders) consisted of déclassé elements, such as bandits, ex-soldiers, and smugglers. These were led by a combination of their own indigenous leaders plus Communist Party cadres, usually former intellectuals with no previous military experience. For the groups of partisans in both places simple survival as organized military units was the first pressing problem. With the exception of scattered, poor villages located in mountain strongholds, these tiny Red units do not seem to have held large territories, containing many communities, for long periods of time. Contacts with settled peasants were mostly fleeting, and often clandestine (e.g., contacts at night with friends in villages outside mountain strongholds). Like bandits, these early Red Armies had to solicit, or more often confiscate, resources from outside their strongholds in order to live. Yet these were bandits with a difference. Party members among them were constantly preaching to the troops, and to peasants in villages held for any length of time, concerning the basic principles and goals of the Communist program. Whenever possible, furthermore, the Reds tried to appeal to the poorer peasants by confiscating and redistributing the lands of the gentry and rich peasants.

Such Red social banditry was only a transitional phase, however. Obviously, the Communists themselves had much larger purposes in mind. Besides, to the extent that this early approach succeeded, it allowed the Red forces to survive and expand. And expansion brought them face to face with what would be the central dilemma in the Chinese Communists' quest for victory through rural guerrilla warfare: how to achieve direct and stable contact with the settled and productive peasants. Unless this could be done, scattered guerrilla units could hardly expand into armies capable of winning state power. In principle, the Communists could offer a variety of policies—such as tax or rent reduction, seizure and redistribution of gentry property, provision of local social services, and protection against marauding armies—that might appeal to the felt needs of the settled peasantry. But the actual implementation of such policies depended upon gaining direct access to the peasants in their communities, which meant working around and under—and ultimately displacing—the local gentry and rich peasants and their supporters. That, in turn, was an intricate political process that could only be successfully carried through by Communist cadres working right in the villages under the security of at least a minimal military–administrative shield. Yet achieving this sort of military and administrative control over territorial bases was exactly what the expanded Red Armies supported by settled peasants were needed for in the first place! The Chinese Communists would not be on the road to final victory until they partly found and partly created conditions that combined some degree of territorial security with possibilities and pressures to penetrate and reorganize local communities – thus allowing them to forge a direct link to the settled peasantry.

The early tactics of Red social banditry were applied in rural settings where enemy military forces were weak or divided (as they were during 1928–30 in central China due to conflicts between the Nationalists and warlords in the wake of the Northern Expedition). These tactics soon "began to pay off in the creation of larger inland bases and armies."[43] Thus by 1931 the Communists succeeded in establishing the "Kiangsi Soviet" administration, governing a settled population that ranged depending upon the fortunes of war from nine to thirty million. During the short life of the soviet, the Communists had their first opportunities to experiment with mass-mobilization techniques for drawing upon rural resources to support their armies.[44] But little or no success was achieved at permanently transforming village class and political structures in ways that would allow maximum mobilization of economic resources and peasant manpower by the Communists. For the administration of the soviet remained rudimentary, never reaching directly into the localities to displace local elites. And the security of the base area from military attacks was never sufficient to allow the Red Army to provide reliable protection for peasants who attacked landlords and rich peasants, and who shared in confiscated spoils given to them by Communist cadres.

Once having quelled the major centers of warlord opposition to the Nanking regime in Central China, Chiang Kai-shek, with the willing acquiescence of local and provincial authorities anxious about the Communists' social-revolutionary policies, directed his well-equipped armies against the Kiangsi Soviet. At first guerrilla tactics succeeded in holding the Nationalists at bay. But by 1935, Chiang's fifth "Encirclement and Annihilation" Campaign, designed by German military strategists, succeeded in forcing the Communists to abandon altogether the wealthier central regions of China. Only after the grueling ordeal of "The Long March"[45] did remnant Communist forces arrive in an area where they could regroup and survive – the poor, desolate, rural backwater of the Shensi-Kansu-Ningsia border region of northwest China. Here there already flourished a Red guerrilla movement that had enjoyed considerable success in appealing to

255

the impoverished peasants of the region.[46] Reinforced by the forces evacuated from central China, the Shen-Kan-Ning base soon began to expand.

The Second United Front:
Cadre Recruitment and Administrative Control

At this point, national and international political developments—which are quite understandable in terms of what we have learned about the inherent weaknesses of the Nationalist regime—intervened. These developments ensured that the Communists would have time to entrench themselves solidly in the northwest and that they would enjoy favorable circumstances to expand their movement and territorial footholds throughout much of China. For one thing, Japanese encroachments on Chinese sovereignty since 1930 were causing many politically articulate Chinese to become disillusioned about the nationalist credentials of Chiang Kai-shek's regime. Chiang remained determined to overcome internal opposition before confronting the Japanese threat; but that policy, no matter how politically understandable from Chiang's point of view, was unappealing to the educated urban public. Thus when the Communists in 1935 began to reassert their own quite valid nationalist credentials by calling for a "United Front" against Japan, the idea inspired considerable support in the cities.[47] In addition, once the Communists had ensconced themselves in the northwest, Chiang Kai-shek had to rely upon the partially autonomous warlord, Chiang Hsueh-liang, to prosecute the civil war against them. But Chiang Hsueh-liang's forces were Manchurians who had been expelled from their homeland by the Japanese, and they proved susceptible to the Communists' offer of a de facto alliance against the Japanese. Consequently, when Chiang Kai-shek came to Sian in 1936 intending to prod his warlord ally into more vigorous activity against the Reds, Chiang Hsueh-liang "arrested" the Generalissimo, releasing him only when he publicly agreed to establish an anti-Japanese United Front with the Communists.[48]

For the Communists this was a needed respite and a welcome chance to expand the appeal of their movement to educated Chinese in the context of the patriotic struggle. Upon joining the Front, the Communists placed their armies and base areas under nominal Nationalist authority. They agreed to deemphasize class struggle and instead to encourage national unity along with moderate reforms. In return, they received the usual kinds of subsidies paid by the Nationalist Government to allied regional regimes and benefited for a time from the relative absence of KMT military opposition.[49]

The Japanese invasion of China, fully unleashed in 1937, was, to be sure, a military disaster for all of the main-force military units of the new Nationalist Alliance. For none of these forces could stem or roll back the Japanese attack. Yet the conditions created by the Japanese occupation of

large areas of the country afforded the Communists, already oriented toward rural mobilization, certain new political opportunities:

> For, while the Japanese invaders were able to occupy the cities, where
> the Kuomintang had been based, they did not have the manpower to
> effectively control the countryside, where Communist guerilla bases
> multiplied rapidly during the war years. The retreat of Kuomintang
> military forces to the west in the face of invading Japanese armies, and
> the concurrent collapse of Nationalist governmental authority in much
> of China, allowed the Communists to break out of their remote sanctu-
> ary in Shensi and expand their military and political influence through
> vast areas of the countryside in northern and central China . . . The
> gradual growth of peasant-supported Communist political and military
> nuclei in many parts of China during the war years was to prove deci-
> sive when the revolutionary struggle with the Kuomintang was resumed
> with full fury in 1946 in a massive civil war.[50]

The ability of the Communists to take advantage of the same wartime
conditions that debilitated the Kuomintang depended upon their eventual
success in combining nationalist appeals to potential educated recruits
with concrete responses to the interests of the peasantry (including both
the peasantry's interest in effective defensive measures against Japanese
terror and its interest in eliminating the power of the gentry over local
economic and political life).[51] On the one hand, the ability of the Communists to identify their cause with the nationalist interest in vigorous
resistance to Japan allowed them to recruit "thousands of students and
intellectuals [who] migrated to Yenan . . . There, at the Northwest Anti-
Japanese Red Army University, many were trained . . . to become important political, administrative, and military cadres for the rapidly expanding Communist base and guerilla areas."[52] And, on the other hand, their
ultimate ability to reach directly into the villages and organize the peasants for resistance, production, and class struggle afforded the Communists access to the extraordinary resources they needed to drive the
Kuomintang off the mainland after 1946. However, the accomplishment
of these two mobilizations did not occur at once or without potential
contradictions.

Initially, between 1937 and 1940, the period of the effective United
Front, the main focus of Communist interest seems to have remained
averted from the internal affairs of the villages. To be sure, taxes were
collected along reformed lines; young men were encouraged to join the
Red Army; local defense work was carried out; and occasional outside
work teams visited the villages. But systematic mobilization of peasants
was somewhat neglected, and no large-scale redistribution of land was
attempted.[53] It is worth noting that many traditional dominant-class families and elite individuals fared quite well during the United Front. Not that

the Communist presence made no difference: Landlords, for example, often had to go through the forms of reducing rent and interest rates; and richer families officially paid taxes at higher rates of assessment than the poor. Yet there were subterfuges: Landlords might secretly threaten peasants with eviction unless "normal" rents were paid under the table; or rich families might quietly divide their lands among several sons, or temporarily "give" lands to poor clan relations, in order to escape higher tax rates. Without emphasis upon intravillage organization to enforce reforms, changes were sometimes effected more in appearance than in reality. Furthermore, during the United Front period, members of all classes were allowed, indeed encouraged, to participate in politics. Consequently, many landlords and former landlords served in the government and some became Party members.

Essentially, during the United Front the Communists acted like a newly established traditional Chinese dynasty or a partially successful rebellion—or a provincial military power under Nationalist tutelage, which they in a sense were. They devoted their efforts to building upon and consolidating control at the regional and base area levels.[54] Naturally, building up mainforce Red Army units and supporting guerrilla and militia organizations constituted a major part of this effort. In addition, there were thousands of students and intellectuals drawn to Yenan after the advent of the United Front, together with veteran higher-level Party cadres and traditional officials who remained behind (as they were encouraged to do during this period). All were put to work as administrators at the county and regional levels to develop socioeconomic policies and plans for the administration. Powerful functional departments, each at the top of a vertical hierarchy of departments extending downward from the regional level, emerged as the major centers of policymaking. These were top-heavy, oriented to policy rather than villages. Their effect was to bureaucratize Communist administration, not to mobilize the peasants for change. Local administrators, though supposedly closest to the people, were left with little to do but apply policies, if they could. By 1940 the Communists had in their northern base areas about the degree of regional administrative and military control that an effective traditional Chinese government might have had. To be sure, the Japanese presence kept them out of towns and cities and prevented access to major communication and transportation networks. Constant fighting also made for unstable base-area boundaries (though this problem became acute only after 1940, according to Mark Selden). Still, on the whole, the first three years of the United Front had proved to be a boon for the Communists, allowing them, with grudging KMT acquiescence, to consolidate firm administrative control over extensive areas and populations.

However, by 1941, the very success of the early United Front program

258

"undermined its basis: rapid [Communist] expansion precipitated sharp clashes with the Japanese and the Kuomintang."[55] The Japanese began to launch major attacks against the Communists, who "posed the dominant threat to Japanese aspirations for conquest,"[56] and the KMT tightened its blockade of Communist-held areas and cut off subsidies to the Red Army and Communist administration. Under pressure from without, the Communists were forced to place ever greater burdens on the peasantry. And unless changes were made, they would necessarily do so through an administrative apparatus remarkably similar in style to the traditional one. As Selden puts it:

> By 1941, at a time of nationwide military setbacks and blockade, increased tensions between the peasantry and the government confronted the Communists with fundamental problems concerning the adequacy of their administration in the border region. Had the traditional elite merely been replaced by a new cadre elite, leaving basic elements of rural poverty and oppression unresolved? Were local cadres capable of carrying out rural reforms and permanently superseding the traditional landlord elite as the dominant power in village life? Could the border regions' isolated villages be effectively linked with over-all policy emanating from higher levels of Party and government? Was a costly and remote bureaucracy with a monopoly on educated and experienced administrators the most effective means for governing and politicizing the border region?[57]

Mass Mobilization for Production, War, and Land Revolution

By 1942, the Chinese Communists realized the necessity of achieving a higher level of mass mobilization to support the war effort against Japan and the civil war against the Nationalists. Their pressing needs led them to develop "concrete methods for linking the military effort and rural social and economic problems in a single program of wartime mobilization penetrating to every village and every family, and involving every individual."[58] This program did not at first call for all-out class struggle against landlords and rich peasants, rather for Party cadres to work directly with villagers to improve economic production. Indeed, increased agricultural productivity was at base the key to whether the blockaded base areas could survive, to whether the people within them could be provided for and sufficient resources diverted to nonagricultural efforts such as industry, education, and the all-important military effort.

Before Party cadres could assume new mass-mobilization roles in local areas, reforms within the Party were necessary. From 1942 to 1944 a Party rectification (called *cheng-feng*) was carried out.[59] This was an intensive internal education project, utilizing techniques of group discussion and criticism. It was designed to unify and discipline the disparate elements that constituted the Party—including reformist intellectuals, holdover traditional elites, and poor, young peasants—on the basis of Maoist interpretation of Marxist–Leninist principles. Out of the *cheng-feng* campaign came, as well, a commitment by the Party to "mass line" techniques. These sanctioned a recurrent interplay between the formulation of general strategies for change and direct involvement by cadres with grass-roots political organizing and concrete local problems. "From the masses, to the masses," was Mao Tse-tung's way of summing up the mass line. "This means," Mao wrote:

> take the ideas of the masses (scattered and unsystematic ideas) and concentrate them . . . , then go to the masses and propagate and explain these ideas until the masses embrace them as their own, hold fast to them and translate them into action, and test the correctness of these ideas in such action. Then once again concentrate ideas from the masses and once again take them to the masses . . . And so on, over and over again in an endless spiral, with the ideas becoming more correct, more vital and richer each time.[60]

This presentation of the mass line undoubtedly underrepresents the degree to which the basic goals and initiatives came not from the masses but from the top leadership of the Party. Yet it does convey the extent to which the Chinese Communists forged in the crucible of the early 1940s a uniquely persuasive and participatory style of political leadership. As Mao put it in the same document just quoted: "The harder the struggle, the greater the need for communists to link their leadership closely with the demands of the broad masses, and to combine general calls closely with particular guidance."

During the same period as the Party rectification, changes were also made in border-area administrative structures.[61] Thousands of higher-level (i.e., mostly intellectual) cadres were sent to work at the county and subcounty levels. Emphasis was shifted from functional departmental work at the regional level to village-oriented mass-mobilization work at the local levels. Party influence over administrative work increased, for the Party specialized in policy coordination and mass-mobilization activities. Finally, Party cadres—especially the young, poor peasant cadres, who had dominated the previously rather do-nothing county and subdistrict administrations, but also many intellectual cadres—were encouraged to assume informal leadership in new intravillage associations concerned with production, whose creation the Party was encouraging.

Both Mark Selden and Franz Schurmann emphasize that the Cooperative Movement (launched by the CCP in 1943) was significant not only as a device for increasing agricultural productivity but also as the means by which new patterns of organization and leadership were developed within North China villages.[62] New patterns were not administratively imposed. Instead, traditional forms of labor combination were strengthened and transformed into associations led by Party cadres and peasant activists, rather than by wealthy patrons or their agents. Then these cooperatives were put to work at tasks that helped improve the peasants' livelihood as well as furthering the war effort. The Cooperative Movement was notable as the first occasion upon which the Party became actively involved at the village level in the productive activities that were the very core of peasant existence. Party involvement in production work, always previously oriented to an economy dominated by landlords and rich peasants, came during a period in which many aspects of Party and administrative work (e.g., those concerned with education, economic reforms, war mobilization) were focused upon village life. This set the stage not only for economic development in the villages but also for basic changes in village sociopolitical structure and, finally, for land revolution fueled from below.[63]

Indeed, in 1946–7, after the war with Japan had ended but just as intensive civil war with the Kuomintang was resuming, the Communists instituted a policy of radical land reform in the Liberated Areas. All landlord, institutional, and rich-peasant land was to be confiscated and redistributed to poor and middle peasants, as nearly as possible on a basis of absolute individual equality of land ownership, regardless of sex and age. Such a policy was hardly calculated to promote internal stability during a period when the Liberated Areas were undergoing all-out mobilization for civil war. And, as Schurmann points out, during periods before and after 1949 in which high economic productivity and/or maximum administrative control have been their major aims, the Chinese Communists have avoided radical "class struggle" policies.

Why, then, did this revolutionary land reform occur in the late 1940s, just as the CCP was engaged in its final military effort to come to power at the national level in China? Schurmann suggests an intriguing two-pronged answer.[64] On the one hand, the Communists' previous efforts at mass mobilization had created a new intravillage elite of young, poor peasant cadres already engaged in day-to-day conflicts with traditional local leaders over the running of all sorts of village affairs. (Also, though Schurmann fails to emphasize this point, outside intellectual cadres were involved in the villages; and they tended to support, or push for, more radical changes than might otherwise have occurred.) On the other hand, in the context of the civil war, higher-level Party leaders had reason to want, once and for all, to be rid of the traditional dominant class. For, as long as these families retained any power, they might have the will and capacity to organize internal resistance against the Communists. Besides, property confiscated from landlords and rich peasants could be allocated to poor and middle peasants, who would then be all the more motivated to support local militias and the Peoples' Liberation Army as these military organizations fought for their right to keep the new lands.[65] Schurmann's reasoning suggests both why higher-level Party leaders agreed to radical land reform and why that policy led to the eruption of a genuine revolution from below in many villages. For, once underway,

> land reform had a momentum of its own. The repeated references by the [Party's] leaders to "left excesses" indicate that they did not have full control over the actions of village cadres. Land reform is remembered by many persons who left China in the late 1940s and early 1950s as a period of terror. As the military struggle became more intense, so did the radicalism of land reform. What had begun as a program of land redistribution ended as revolutionary terror in which China's traditional rural elite was destroyed.[66]

What happened in North China between 1946 and 1949 was a unique synthesis between the military needs of the Chinese Communists and the social-revolutionary potential of the Chinese peasantry. For in the process of mobilizing peasant efforts to support the base-area administrations and armies, the Chinese Communists penetrated and reorganized the local communities. Thus the peasants as a class were provided with an organizational autonomy and solidarity that they had not enjoyed within the traditional agrarian sociopolitical structure. Once the peasants acquired these means to become (within the villages) a class for themselves, they could and did strike out against the landlords just as thoroughly as did the Russian peasants in 1917. Except, unlike the Russian peasants, the Chinese peasants rebelled against the landlords only with the aid and encouragement of local Communist cadres; and the Chinese land revolution as a whole took place under the military and administrative "umbrella" provided by the Party's control of its base areas. Thus the Chinese peasant revolution did not culminate, as did the Russian peasant revolution of 1917, in an anarchistic turning-in of the peasant villages upon themselves. Instead it strengthened the existing political alliance between the peasants and the Communists and encouraged peasants to redouble their efforts to support the Red Armies, upon whose victorious efforts they depended if they were to maintain their social-revolutionary political and property gains in the villages. In short, the Chinese Communist Party's quest for rural resources to make possible military victories against Japan, the warlords, and the Nationalists finally resulted in social revolution in the Chinese countryside. And social revolution, in turn, generated the final increments of enthusiastic peasant recruits and the directly harnessed agrarian productivity that the Red Armies needed to drive the demoralized forces of the Kuomintang from the cities and, indeed, from the entire mainland of China.

THE NEW REGIME

The establishment of the People's Republic of China was proclaimed in Peking by the victorious Communists on October 1, 1949. By the late 1950s, after several years of transition to rule in and through the urban centers, the Communists had consolidated a New Regime that embodied marked departures from China's Imperial and "Republican"/warlord pasts. In its structure and dynamics, this new Chinese Communist sociopolitical system resembled the French and Russian New Regimes in broad respects, yet also differed from each in very important ways. This section will therefore conclude Part II, as well as this chapter on the outcomes of the Chinese Revolution, by discussing these shared and distinctive patterns in the Chinese revolutionary outcomes.

A Strengthened State Bureaucracy

Like the French and Russian Revolutions, the Chinese Revolution gave rise through the class and political struggles of the revolutionary interregnum to a much larger, more powerful, and more bureaucratic new political regime. Government, responsible for administrative functions, and Party, responsible for policymaking, coordination, and supervision, constituted separate but closely intertwined organizational hierarchies stretching from Peking through multiple intermediate levels down into each village, factory, school, and neighborhood. This Party-state was, from its inception, much larger in size than the apparatus of a mere forty-thousand offices[67] that existed under the (nineteenth-century) Imperial system, and also much larger than the two-million functionaries of the Kuomintang Nationalist government at the end (in 1948).[68] Thus, by 1952, the number of Communist "state cadres," or white collar and administrative personnel in government organs and enterprises, was already 3,310,000 and by 1958 it was nearly 8 million.[69] The size of the Communist Party as such is also of interest: In 1953, there were 6.1 million Party members, with membership rising quickly, on its way to 17 million in 1961.[70] This already constituted over 1 percent of the population officially estimated at 583 million in 1953.[71] In contrast, literati holders of Confucian degrees—those who, analogous to Communist Party members, staffed the key leadership positions in the state and in local politics—constituted less than one-third of 1 percent of the population during the nineteenth century.[72]

The Communist regime, as A. Doak Barnett points out, "extended the outreach and impact of central power to an unprecedented degree":

> Traditionally in China, central power, transmitted through a well-established bureaucracy, reached the county (hsien) level with some degree of effectiveness—at least during periods when the country was

unified under a strong regime—but at subcounty levels "informal government," run by traditional elite groups such as the "gentry" and by a variety of nongovernmental social institutions tended to dominate the scene. The Communists have basically altered this situation. They have largely destroyed both the old elite groups and most of the traditional social institutions, substituting for them a new Communist Party elite and new Communist-established and -dominated mass organizations, and have extended the formal bureaucratic instruments of Party and government rule down to the village level.[73]

Likewise the new political system expanded its activities into functional areas, such as the direction of economic production and the provision of social and educational services, which before the Revolution were not part of the state's sphere.[74]

Once consolidated, the Communist New Regime was markedly more bureaucratic than the Old Regime, even though the prerevolutionary Imperial state had been in one sense unusually bureaucratic for an agrarian monarchy due to its universalistic mode of recruiting officials through the Confucian examination system. Communist leaders were recruited on the basis of new criteria that gave as much or more weight to considerations of (deprived) class background and political virtue as to educational credentials or technical expertise. Yet political criteria were, ideally, supposed to be applied in an impersonal manner. And even if the Communist system could conceivably be rated less bureaucratic than the Old Regime on the single dimension of recruitment to formal offices per se, nevertheless it was much more bureaucratic in other ways. The key changes are similar to those in France, where comparable obstacles to full bureaucratization had existed under the Old Regime. More leadership positions in society, especially at local levels, became formal, salaried offices within organizational hierarchies. Likewise, all leadership positions and their duties and prerogatives became much more impersonally defined, in two senses. First, they became offices in organizations with specific goals to attain, in contrast to the very generally defined positions with broad, mixed responsibilities that predominated in the Imperial–Confucian system. Second, they became much more truly offices *separated* from the private interests and property of their holders than the Imperial positions had been. No longer could officials legitimately pool public revenues and personal incomes, or normally combine their family (or clan or local) business and political pursuits with the accomplishment of tasks for the state or Party.

What these changes meant above all was that the locally and regionally based power blocs that had so undermined the central administrative and military authority of the Chinese Old Regime in the nineteenth century, and which had continued to exist after its demise in 1911, were dissolved with the rise of the Communist Party-state. For the existence of those pre-1949 power blocs depended both upon the fusion of political power and private property interests and upon the inability of Chinese central authorities to control the deployment and activities of government personnel and local political leaders. Although provincial political factions and problems of fully controlling local leaders have recurrently troubled China since 1949, nevertheless the establishment of the Communist Party-state essentially overcame the basic structural obstacles to centralized state power in China. Would-be regional bosses could be (and have been) transferred or sacked,[75] and central authorities could initiate and implement policies that profoundly affected local communities.

Communist China and Soviet Russia

If the Chinese New Regime shared these broad features of centralization, bureaucratism, and greater weight within society with both the French and the Russian New Regimes, nevertheless in its particular characteristics it obviously resembled the Russian New Regime much more closely than the French. In Ezra Vogel's apt phrase, the Chinese Communist regime was a "politicized bureaucracy,"[76] rather than, as in France, a rational–legal administrative state within the context of a market-guided national economy. That is, as in Soviet Russia, all governmental organizations were permeated by Party controls and subject to coordination to achieve goals set by top Party leaders for the nation as a whole. Furthermore, also as in Russia, the Chinese Party-state could implement policies in part through direct links to the populace at large. This was true because citizens were aggregated into politically coordinated "transmission belt" organizations, including representative assemblies (at all levels of government from local to national), neighborhood and work groups, mass-membership associations for youth, women, industrial workers, and so forth.[77]

Why was the Chinese New Regime so much more similar to the Russian than the French? This is a rhetorical question, to be sure, but still worth answering. After all, in my previous discussion of why a party-controlled state emerged from the Russian Revolution whereas the Jacobins fell from power in France, I stressed the importance of large-scale modern industries (which existed in Russia but not France). Such industries provided a basis for the survival and consolidation of control by a mass-mobilizing, ideologically oriented party *after* it accomplished initial tasks of rebuilding new state organizations and defending against counterrevolutionary threats. Yet, taking the pre-1949 Chinese economy as a whole, it much more closely resembled the late-eighteenth- and early-nineteenth-century French economy than the already significantly industrialized economy of late Tsarist Russia. Both the late-eighteenth-century French economy and the pre-1949 Chinese economy were overwhelmingly agrarian–commercial and dominated by small production units. That the basic forms of the Chinese revolutionary outcomes nevertheless ended up much closer to the Soviet forms than to the French only points to the important effects upon the course and outcomes of the Chinese Revolution of two sets of world-historical and international contextual factors: (1) political influence upon China from previously revolutionized Soviet Russia; and (2) enhanced possibilities in the twentieth century for state-propelled national industrialization.

First, it obviously mattered for the shape of its ultimate outcome that the Chinese Revolution deepened into a social revolution and gave rise to revolutionary political movements only *after* the Bolsheviks had triumphed in Russia. As we may recall, both the Chinese Communist Party and the Kuomintang started out under Soviet tutelage and borrowed the Leninist model of party organization. What is more, the Chinese Communist Party in its fledgling phase also imitated the proletarian-based and -oriented revolutionary strategy of the Bolsheviks. Even though this early strategy failed and the Party in the countryside eventually became cut off both from the proletariat and from direct Soviet tutelage, the Chinese Communists always retained the fundamentals of Leninist party structure and an ideological allegiance to "proletarian" revolution.[78] Party organization made it possible for them actively to mobilize peasant popular support during the 1940s, establishing a solid political basis in the countryside such as the French revolutionaries had never possessed. And after 1949, the Leninist organizational and ideological heritage readily predisposed the Chinese Communists to copy features of the Soviet regime as they asserted control over the cities and the nation as a whole.

Second, it also mattered that there were after 1949 both infrastructural possibilities and international inducements for the Chinese Communists to consolidate a Soviet-style Party-state. Here we must stress that by the mid-twentieth century, as opposed to the late eighteenth and early nineteenth century, national autonomy and power depended upon industrialization. Equally significant, state direction of large-scale modern industries, as well as state planning and mobilization for further national industrialization, were very real possibilities – especially for any regime that came to power in a country with *some* existing modern industries. In China, from the late nineteenth century, foreign capitalists and treaty port Chinese had built up some modern industries on the fringes of the country, and above all in Manchuria, which the Chinese regained after the Japanese defeat in World War II. And there was the Stalinist example of state-propelled national heavy industrialization for the Chinese Communists to try to imitate after 1949. For all of these reasons, then – because the Chinese Communist Party had started out as a proletarian-based Party under Soviet tutelage, because it had established a mass basis in the countryside after exile from the cities, because a few large-scale modern industries were available to be taken over

to form the "commanding heights" of a state-directed economy, and because the Stalinist model of rapid industrialization beckoned to be
imitated – the Chinese Communists, when they marched into the cities and
consolidated truly national political power after 1949, did *not* resign themselves to functioning as mere state administrators in a reformed agrarian
economy of peasant smallholders. Rather they moved step by step during
the 1950s: to extend Party and state management over financial, industrial,
and commercial enterprises; to bring mass organizations of urban people
(workers, students, professionals, consumers) under Party influence; to
carry through the collectivization of agriculture; and to implement plans for
state-controlled national industrialization. Moreover, the Chinese Communists operated (during the first half of the 1950s) under direct Soviet
tutelage: Technical experts and capital equipment were brought in from the
Soviet Union; and the Chinese were supposed to pay for this aid with
agricultural exports and with loyal subordination to the hegemony of the
Soviet Union in matters of foreign policy.[79]

Indeed, by the middle of the 1950s, it looked as if Communist China
would increasingly become, institutionally speaking, a carbon copy of the
Soviet Stalinist system. An unequivocally Stalinist strategy for national
economic development was embodied in China's first Five Year Plan for
1953–7, whose key objectives are succinctly summarized by Alexander
Eckstein:

> First, overriding commitment to achieving a high rate of economic
> growth more or less year by year or at least over an average of five
> years. Second, particular concentration upon industrial progress.
> Third, a heavy-industry-oriented pattern of industrialization and eco-
> nomic growth. Fourth, a high rate of saving and investment so as to
> attain the first three objectives. Fifth, industrialization at the expense
> of agriculture. Sixth, institutional transformation [i.e., collectivization]
> in agriculture and other sectors of the economy, and seventh, a bias
> toward capital-intensive methods in the choice of industrial production
> technology.[80]

In order to implement these policies, the Chinese Communists tried to
copy Soviet patterns of economic planning and control.[81] National ministries were established to plan industrial investments and supervise resource
allocations and enterprise operations. Especially in larger production units,
"one-man management" was instituted: Under this system, the factory
director was responsible for fulfilling national plan specifications. Within
the enterprise itself he exercised control over all operations through explicit, hierarchical chains of command and with the aid of precise procedur-
al rules and individualized production norms. To make these systems of
industrial planning and control work, individuated and increasingly differentiated socioeconomic rewards were encouraged. At the same time, all

267

those working within the modern, large-scale, heavy industrial system widened their privileges vis-à-vis the peasant majority and urban and rural workers in small-scale industrial or commercial units. During the 1950s, these sectors were undergoing collectivization, yet their role in the existing national economic plan could only be to produce surplus economic resources to be channeled into the privileged urban and heavy-industrial sector.

But from 1957 onward, basic Chinese Communist policies were reoriented. Even before the end of the first Five Year Plan, Chinese Communist leaders began to conclude that Soviet-style policies were inappropriate to Chinese conditions. Through hard-fought debates, a tentative new leadership consensus emerged in favor of more balanced development plans that would stress the growth of agriculture and of rural- and consumer-oriented industries.[82] By the early 1960s, moreover, the Chinese–Soviet alliance was broken. Soviet aid and technicians were withdrawn from China, and the Chinese were pursuing their own foreign-policy line, hostile to the Soviet Union, and developing their own independent nuclear capacity.

Even as these basic policy reorientations emerged, the Chinese Communist leaders also became divided over how much to rely in promoting national development upon mass political mobilization and upon complementary policies to deemphasize inequalities between urban and rural sectors, between leaders and led, and among various strata of the population. For, when the Chinese Communists first undertook to reorient their economic policies at the end of the 1950s, certain leaders, including Mao Tse-tung, pushed not only for greater emphasis on agricultural development. They also called for greater reliance upon the mobilization by Party leaders of increased popular, especially peasant, participation in development efforts – and for modifications of organizational structures and reward systems that would facilitate this approach. A first trial for such an approach was badly botched during the Great Leap Forward of 1958–60. In consequence, there emerged during the 1960s fierce struggles over policy options. Very broadly speaking, there were "Maoists," who wanted to push forward with rural-oriented and mass-mobilizing development strategies, extending them to urban industries and higher educational institutions as well. And there were "Liuists," who wanted to retrench toward an urban-oriented, educationally elitist, and bureaucratically administered development strategy, with agricultural development to be prompted through added capital investments and privileges for more efficient peasant producers. Only after intra-Party struggles had culminated in the Maoist-encouraged mass uprisings (and temporary Peoples' Liberation Army takeover) of the "Great Proletarian Cultural Revolution" of 1965–8, was the policy struggle decided for the time being primarily in favor of the Maoist line.[83]

268

Now, ten years later, many leaders formerly purged by Maoists are definitely coming back to power and modifying many of the policies introduced in the Cultural Revolution period. Nevertheless, in all of the see-sawing of leaderships and policy emphases since the late 1950s there has never been (so far) any return to direct imitation of Stalinist patterns or to close alliance with the Soviet Union. Rather the Chinese Communists have struggled over different strategies and tactics for pursuing China's own distinct revolutionary path. Nor have Chinese Communist leadership struggles followed the same trajectory as the Bolshevik struggles in the twenties: There has been in China no cataclysmic denouement like the triumph of Stalinism in Russia.[84] Instead leadership groups have been purged (dismissed from power and disgraced, but not murdered) only to reemerge later; and policy tendencies have alternated over time, with previous accomplishments being rolled back, but not completely undone in succeeding phases. Out of all of these leadership struggles and alternations of policy lines, there have emerged in China since 1957 a national-development strategy, modes of political coordination and leadership, and patterns of social stratification all quite different not only (as is obvious) from the outcomes of the French Revolution, but also from those in Russia. Let us take a closer look at these Chinese revolutionary outcomes.

A Balanced Strategy for National Development

In contrast to Stalinist Russia's extremely one-sided emphasis on rapid urbanization and heavy-industrial development, Communist China has evolved strategies of "walking on two legs." Investments in large-scale, technologically advanced industries have continued. But more emphasis has been placed upon fostering agricultural development and upon the growth of small rural and medium-scale regional industries designed to serve peasant consumers, to produce inputs (e.g., fertilizer, electricity, tools) of use to agriculture, and to process local resources and the products of agriculture.[85] Administrative means have been used to control urbanization, keeping its overall rate slower than that of economic growth and channeling most urban growth into small cities and towns rather than the largest metropolitan centers. Consequently, in the words of Jon Sigurdson:

> The migration from the rural areas—and the internal brain drain—which was very much in evidence during the 1950s, has basically been reversed . . . Since the Cultural Revolution, the countryside has been affected by two flows of reverse migration.

> First . . . a substantial number of urban middle-school students were asked to resettle more or less permanently in rural areas . . .

269

Second, in the process of setting up various infrastructure services, a very large number of professionals – teachers, administrators, doctors and other medical personnel – have gone to the countryside.[86]

Moreover, ways have been devised in Communist China not only to send educated urban people to the countryside but also to adapt modern techniques and expertise to rural needs and possibilities. Relevant measures include the improvisation of "intermediate technologies" for local industries, programs of widespread, simplified paraprofessional training such as the "barefoot doctor" program, and the creation of a national educational system that provides both primary and agriculturally oriented secondary education in the rural localities themselves.[87]

In the context of such national-development programs, collectivized peasant agriculture has become a dynamic sector in China, productive in its own right and supportive of complementary advances in local industries and social services. The Chinese Communists have *not* used collectivization and Party-state structures in the countryside simply as a means for expropriating agricultural surpluses or imposing bureaucratic controls over rural life. Since the early 1960s, the basic unit of production and accounting in Chinese agriculture has been the local "team," a unit of collective ownership, planning, and work that corresponds to a small village, or a neighborhood in a larger village, consisting of about twenty peasant households.[88] Teams are directed not by salaried state bureaucrats, but by elected local leaders who work right alongside other peasants. In turn, part-time "brigade" cadres at the village level are responsible for coordinating team plans and mobilizing manpower for industrial and infrastructural projects to benefit the whole village. Of course, team and brigade leaders are subject to influence from above. The Party reaches directly to the brigade level, and the basic unit of state administration in rural Communist China is the commune, which corresponds to the traditional marketing area. Full-time salaried officials at this level oversee the fulfillment of production plans negotiated between localities and the state, and they coordinate agricultural extension services and social services and run commune-owned industrial enterprises. Peasant producers are obligated to surrender grain to the state in the form of taxes and sales at fixed prices; and they also contribute funds for the maintenance of commune and brigade functions. Nevertheless, the remarkable thing about Chinese rural local government is its decentralization of leadership responsibilities and the leeway given to team, brigade, and commune leaders to retain and reinvest surpluses generated by local agriculture and industrial enterprises. As a result, Chinese peasants can often see direct links between politically directed and collectively based projects and the welfare of their own families and villages. Like Russian peasants after collectivization, Chinese peasants have retained and made very productive use of private family plots.

270

But because of all of the ways in which the Chinese Party-state has materially supported agriculture and used local, peasant-based organizations, collective agriculture in China – in contrast to what happened in the Soviet Union – has become economically productive and socially vital for Chinese peasants and for Chinese Communist society as a whole.[89]

There is also a contrast to be drawn to France, where peasants after the Revolution were left largely unprotected by the state to undergo the vagaries of market-guided national development. Gains went to those areas of agricultural France and privileged individuals within the peasantry that were commercially favored, while others stagnated or lost out altogether.[90] In Communist China, there have also been important differences in wealth and development, especially among different localities and regions within the countryside.[91] But at least the presence of collectives linked to, and periodically mobilized by, the Party-state has meant that virtually all peasant communities and families within the peasantry could be included in agricultural development, achieving important gains in income and welfare in the process.[92]

Political Coordination, Mass Mobilization, and Egalitarianism

If Communist China has evolved a distinctive approach to national economic development, her patterns of leadership in organizations and in society as a whole have also differed from the highly centralized and formalized hierarchies of control characteristic of the Soviet Stalinist system. Two aspects of the Chinese patterns deserve mention. First, China's strategy of "balanced" national economic development has placed a premium on coordination and responsible leadership at local and provincial as well as national levels. It has been impossible for all projects to be planned and controlled according to explicit blueprints and procedures handed down from central ministries. Instead, much responsibility for initiating and managing non-large-scale industries, social services, and agricultural development has been delegated to "lower level" local or regional leaders. Planning procedures, especially those designed to mesh economic activities in given territories, have been flexible, with the emphasis placed not on carrying out detailed orders from above, but more on adapting and coordinating local resources to meet goals specified within the framework of general national objectives.[93] Obviously, such decentralized patterns of leadership and planning have been crucial to the development of industrial–agricultural linkages.[94] It is also worth noting that even in large-scale industrial organizations, attempts to institute Soviet-style one-man management were given up after the mid-1950s in favor of various patterns of direction by committees. This occurred in part because the new

271

patterns were better suited to coordinating diverse efforts and exchanges within the enterprise and between the enterprise and its environment, whereas one-man management focuses overridingly on enforcing compliance on centrally dictated plans according to preconceived, formally specified procedures.[95]

Second, unlike the complete reversion in the Soviet Union to controls over production workers by professional experts and authoritarian managers wielding individually differentiated sanctions, there have been in China recurrent attempts to use "mass-line" styles of collective political mobilization within villages and urban institutions.[96] Political pressures from above on existing organizational leaders seem always to have been necessary in such attempts, because managers, entrenched political leaders, and technical experts have to be prodded into giving up their own privileges of rewards and authority in order to "merge with" rank and file workers. The idea is that authoritarian and highly stratified patterns of control over workers may alienate workers from fully contributing their skills and efforts, so that if these barriers can be removed by mass-line style leadership, more rapid economic and social development should result.[97] This "Maoist" leadership philosophy has by no means been continuously dominant in Chinese work settings. But from the Great Leap Forward, to mobilizations for production projects in the villages, to the management committees with workers' representatives established in many factories during and after the Cultural Revolution, it has made—and left—its mark.[98]

A very important concomitant of these patterns of leadership in Communist China has been that, compared to Russia, a much greater premium has continued to be placed on organized political leadership as such. This is true whether the leadership has been provided by the Communist Party or, as during the Cultural Revolution, by the politicized Peoples' Liberation Army (which temporarily took over the Party's role after its own organization was shattered). In Stalinist Russia, the Communist Party of the Soviet Union tended to degenerate into an elite club for leaders whose power was based on their functional positions as managers, state bureaucrats, and professional specialists.[99] This could happen because real power in Soviet society became extremely concentrated in centralized bureaucracies and "one man" organizational elites; the Party was left with little to do but supervise and ensure the unity and loyalty of the bureaucratic ruling stratum. But in Communist China, political cadres and committees have shared in functions, such as policymaking and especially the coordination of policy implementation, that were monopolized as fully as possible by central-government ministries in Soviet Russia.[100] And there have continued to be recurrent efforts at ideologically oriented mass mobilization in China, a style of leadership for which political rather than bureaucratic direction is essential. In sum, as A. Doak Barnett points out:

272

A Mass-Mobilizing Party-State in China

The crucial role of the Party in China, even by contrast with other Communist-ruled countries, is reinforced by the fact that the Party has tended to go far beyond acting as director and supervisor of other political organizations and has constantly encroached upon government administration as such . . . On many occasions and in many fields the Party has not simply supervised the running of things but has tended to step in and run them itself.[101]

Finally, the patterns of stratification that have emerged in China since the 1950s are worthy of comment. Compared not only to Stalinist Russia but also to capitalist industrial countries and to other developing countries today, Communist China is relatively egalitarian. Concerted efforts have been made to hold steady or reduce inequalities of income and status among strata of employees, betwen urban and rural workers, and between leaders and led.

Income-distribution statistics tell part of the story. According to Alexander Eckstein, urban-rural income differentials in China narrowed considerably after 1951, because agricultural purchase prices rose much more than prices for industrial products sold in rural areas and because industrial real wages increased "only marginally betwen 1957 and 1972."[102] Within the urban-industrial sector itself, Eckstein estimates that Chinese wage differentials (among skill grades of factory workers) have been similar to those in many other contemporary developed and underdeveloped countries (although I would add that they are markedly more equal than Soviet wage differentials in the 1930s). However, one must consider the entire span of wages and salaries from laborers to top managers and professionals. China—with a span to 10 to 1 (or if very extreme cases are considered, up to as much as 20 to 1)—looks much more egalitarian than Russia in 1934, where the span (comparable to the 10 to 1 figure for China) was 29 to 1, and also much more egalitarian than India (30 to 1) or the United States (up to 50 to 1) today.[103] Furthermore, Eckstein points out that income differentials are even less in real terms in China compared to the United States or India, because necessities are rationed and priced low and access to luxuries is made very difficult. Nor for the most part have elites in Communist China enjoyed special bonuses or consumption privileges comparable to those lavished on managers, party leaders, and privileged workers in Stalinist Russia.

Beyond tendencies to control or reduce income differentials, there have been attacks as well on inequalities of social prestige and authority. This was especially true in the years immediately after the Cultural Revolution, when many striking measures were instituted (or fully implemented after previous tentative beginnings).[104] Rank insignia on Red Army uniforms were abolished. "Intellectuals, office workers and Party officials [were] expected periodically to be sent down from their posts to engage in man-

273

ual labor . . . , " and factory managers, engineers, and commune officials were "required to spend regular periods of time doing manual work alongside the workers and peasants they supervised."[105] Factory committees with worker representatives were given managerial power in industrial units. Perhaps most extraordinary, direct access to higher education on the basis of competitive exams taken by middle-school graduates was suspended. Instead, all graduates were supposed to go to work in industry or agriculture, and local communities and production units were given considerable say in the final selection of university students. This was a remarkable attempt to undercut the social reproduction of university elites virtually exclusively recruited from educated, urban families and cut off from the realities of productive labor in the factories and villages.

Of course it would be a mistake to interpret any of the above as evidence that inequalities of status and authority, any more than income differentials, have ever been abolished in China. For one thing, radical measures such as those instituted during the Cultural Revolution have always been rolled back (though rarely completely abandoned) in subsequent periods. More to the point, there has never been, even during high tides of Maoist experimentation, any serious intention (on the part of powerful leaders in China) actually to abolish inequalities. Instead, as Martin Whyte argues, Chinese Communist egalitarianism is better understood as aiming at the fullest possible involvement of all people in national development by means of measures designed to "mute the consequences" of existing inequalities. "The distinctiveness of Chinese egalitarianism is to be found," says Whyte,

> not so much in its reduction or elimination of differences in income, power and educational skills, although some of this has occurred, but in its attempt to mute the consequences, in terms of matters like life styles, consumption patterns and interpersonal deference, of the inequalities that do exist. People in high positions in China are viewed as entitled to certain kinds of differential rewards and authority, but at the same time flaunting authority or engaging in conspicuous consumption is tabooed. There is thus a concerted effort to blunt the subjective impact which existing inequalities might have on the initiative and dedication of the have-nots in whose name the revolution was fought.[106]

Still, from a comparative perspective, Communist Chinese egalitarianism seems remarkable enough. This will be true even if the recurrent "Maoist" thrusts toward further equalization and deeper mass-mobilization turn out to have ended permanently after Mao Tse-tung's death. For the fact is that neither in France nor in Russia were there tendencies during the decades immediately after the consolidation of revolutionary state power toward economic or sociopolitical equalization. Thus China from the mid-1950s to the mid-1970s really stands out.

274

Reasons for China's Distinctive Outcomes

If Chinese revolutionary outcomes have been distinctive (especially as compared to the Russian Communist system) in the various ways discussed in the preceding pages, then the obvious question is: *why* has this been true? From the analytic perspective of this book, the explanation lies most fundamentally in the conditions and possibilities to which Chinese Communist leaders responded, according to their political capacities, once they had consolidated state power and national socioeconomic control by the mid-1950s. Three sets of factors were especially important: the economic legacies inherited from the Old Regime; the strategic realities of the post-World War II era; and the distinctive political capacities accumulated by the Chinese Communist Party during its rise to power, especially in relation to the peasantry. Together these make sense of why the Chinese New Regime developed as it did, especially from the late 1950s on.

First, the economic legacies of pre-1949 China help explain why the Chinese Communists abandoned Stalinist-style development plans within a very few years after they were first undertaken. That the Chinese Communists were so readily able and willing right after 1949 to pursue a Soviet-style strategy of placing emphasis on heavy industries can in large part be attributed to the fact that they had suddenly regained, although in war-damaged condition, modern industrial plants that had been in formerly enemy-occupied areas. With relatively modest investments of capital and administrative expertise, such industries could be quickly rebuilt up to and somewhat beyond pre-World War II levels.[107] But once the Communists had thus restored the industries of Manchuria and the coastal centers to their prewar levels, they began to come up against the limits of an economy very different from the one with which the Russians had to deal during the 1920s.[108] There was a well-developed heavy-industrial base only in Manchuria. In other centers, overall modern industrial development was much less, and light industries and commercial enterprises were predominant. Even more decisive, the rural economy of China had characteristics very different from those of Russian agriculture. Chinese agriculture had become, between 1400 and 1900, maximally productive within the limits of the traditional technology, social structure, and available land area. And the Chinese population had expanded steadily from 1700, until it virtually saturated the expansive capacity of the agrarian sector from roughly 1850 on.[109] Moreover, much of Chinese economic life remained, right through 1949, oriented to and dependent upon well-developed intraregional and intralocal marketing-area networks of trade and nonmechanized production.[110]

Thus, in terms of impediments, the Chinese Communists faced a situation in which even the most brutal methods of exploiting peasant agriculture for the sake of urbanized heavy-industrial development could not have worked as they did in post-1928 Russia. For the inherited modern industrial base on which the Chinese would have to build was far more restricted than that available to the Soviets, whereas the objective barriers to forcing sudden increases in agricultural production and marketing were much more formidable than they had been in Russia. There was, in fact, little alternative except to invest in agricultural development and in industries oriented to agriculture at the same time as heavy industrialization was pursued.

Besides, to consider the positive side, Chinese economic life has always been most vital in the localities and regions. Peasants were traditionally involved in economic and social relations beyond the bounds of their own villages and were accustomed to following the leadership of educated non-peasants in local organizations and projects. Flourishing systems of inter-dependence among (nonmechanized) industries and agriculture already existed in many rural areas. In short, opportunities to further—and of course "modernize"—rural economic development beckoned to be seized after 1949 if the appropriate political will and organizational means could be forged by the New Regime.

Secondly, international relations and strategic conditions also affected the development of the Communist Chinese regime. Strains were always present in the Sino-Soviet Alliance of the 1950s.[111] The Chinese Communists, after all, had come to power very much on their own, and tended to chafe under Soviet hegemony. The Soviet Union was seeking peaceful co-existence with the United States at the same time that China felt threatened by U.S. intervention in Korea and also wanted Soviet support for attempts to regain Taiwan. Furthermore, the beginnings of the reorientation of Chinese development plans away from the Soviet model created additional tensions between the two countries.

The decisive break between the Peoples' Republic and the Soviet Union came as a result of China's determination to develop her own nuclear capacity—the ultimate symbol and basis of independent, national strategic military power in the post-World War II era.[112] The interesting point here, though, is not that the Sino-Soviet Alliance broke over this issue, but that, given the peculiar nature of nuclear weapons, China *could* develop such weapons. This entailed giving up Soviet military protection while American imperialism was expanding in Asia, even as China also pursued a strategy of national economic development that was *less* exclusively oriented to heavy-industrial growth. Obviously this daring combination of initiatives was possible for the Chinese Communists around 1960 only because nuclear weapons require a relatively small economic and industrial investment compared to equipping huge land armies with sophisticated mechanized armaments and air protection. This latter had been the stra-

276

tegic imperative facing the Soviets in the 1930s and, as we have seen, it powerfully affected their choices about necessities for national economic development. But the Chinese Communists, facing a post-World War II strategic situation, could at least consider gambling on a military analogue to the economic policy of "walking on two legs." They could intensively pour some resources into developing a nuclear-deterrent capacity, and at the same time maintain a large, unmodernized Peoples' Liberation Army, whose capacity for organizing decentralized guerrilla resistance in a huge country would (hopefully) discourage any would-be invaders. Finally, once the Sino-Soviet split was complete and after the United States stopped escalating its active military presence in Asia, the Chinese Communists could take advantage of the international strategic situation in a new way – by playing one superpower, the United States, off against the other, the USSR. None of these arguments are meant to imply that anything about the post-World War II international situation positively prompted China to develop as she did after the mid-1950s. But thinking in terms of the comparison to Russia's situation in the European states system after World War I, it does seem valid to say that the Chinese faced circumstances that *allowed* them to develop differently insofar as domestic economic conditions and – especially – their Party-state's accumulated political capacities encouraged them to do so.

For, third and finally, no factor has been more important than the Party's accumulated political capacities in prompting the Chinese Communists to undertake those agriculturally oriented and relatively participatory and egalitarian approaches to national development that have been the hallmark of new-regime China. Above all, the already developed political relationship of the Chinese Communist Party to the peasantry was crucial. As the Chinese Communists in the 1950s fully consolidated Party-state power and undertook to promote national development, they enjoyed a tremendous advantage that the Bolsheviks had lacked in the 1920s – direct political ties to the peasant villages.

We should recall that the Chinese peasantry had historically been linked and subordinated to the gentry landlords within local (market) communities. Peasants had not been able to overthrow the economic and local political power of the landlords on their own; instead social revolution in the Chinese countryside came only with the aid of Red Army protection and locally present Communist leadership. Land revolution occurred in North China during the final stages of the Civil War between the Communists and the Nationalists, and then was extended into South China in the early 1950s, after the Communists had claimed national power. In both phases, the process had important political concomitants and implications. The landlords and their supporting institutions were displaced only as Communist cadres penetrated each village, organized poor and middle peasants into associations, recruited leaders for these associations from among the local peasants themselves, and then – finally – encouraged the peasants to strike out against the landlords (and rich peasants as well). The aftermath was not only the redistribution of large landholdings and other properties among the peasants; in addition, new leaders and peasant-based political institutions were established at the local level to replace the old landlord-dominated arrangements, including clans. For the Chinese Communist Party there was of course an enormous dividend in this. The situation was unlike that in Russia after the autonomous peasant revolts of 1917, when the peasant communities became more cut off from outside influences than ever, leaving the Bolsheviks with no solid base in the countryside and no good way to gain one in the future. In China, the peasant communities in the wake of land revolution were organizationally linked to the Communist Party-state. The revolutionized villages were full of old and new "middle peasant" families who had directly benefited from the land redistribution orchestrated by the Communists. And they were governed through new organizations led by local peasant cadres who were either Party members themselves or accustomed to cooperating with the Communists.

After 1949–52 such rural cadres constituted an invaluable reservoir of grass-roots support and leadership for the Communist Party-state to draw upon in the course of socialist mobilization.[113] And draw upon them it did, first for organizing in many areas "mutual aid teams" to support and supplement smallholder production, and then, from 1955 to 1958, for promoting the actual collectivization of most land ownership and agricultural production. In certain external aspects – such as the goal of facilitating political control over agricultural production and surpluses, and the pattern of an originally moderately conceived program accelerating and becoming radicalized once it was underway – the Chinese collectivization drives resembled the Soviet drives of 1928–33. Nevertheless, there were major differences in means and results. As Thomas Bernstein puts it, the Russian Communists collectivized agriculture through "command mobilization," based on heavy doses of coercion applied by urban emissaries, because the Russians lacked numerous or reliable cadres within the villages. In contrast, the Chinese Communists could proceed through "participatory mobilization," using a mixture of persuasion, group manipulation, and small doses of coercion, because leadership in their drive was provided mostly by politically reliable peasants operating in or near their own home areas.[114] And whereas Soviet collectivization caused the short-term devastation of agricultural production as well as long-term stagnation in the collective sector, the Chinese collectivization drive (in itself, leaving aside the Great Leap Forward) caused much less immediate disruption and laid the organizational basis for a productive collective sector in the future.

278

What difference did all of this make for the New Regime as a whole? The Chinese Communists were able to carry through the collectivization of agriculture relatively smoothly by activating and extending their already existing political basis in the countryside. This, in turn, made it possible for them to rely upon and actively shape agricultural growth and rural development as a part of a strategy of state-propelled national development. Thus the unique relationship originally forged between the Communists and the peasants in the course of completing and consolidating the Chinese social revolution created special possibilities afterwards for the Party-state to mobilize peasants for active involvement in socialist transformation.

Likewise, it has created persistent "pulls" toward the implementation and maintenance of relatively balanced and equalitarian policies of national development. For even if peasants potentially could be persuasively involved in national development through the political-organizational means at hand, nevertheless they would not actually respond unless real benefits were forthcoming. To activate their potential political capacities the Chinese Communists have had to do the very sorts of things they have done—encourage investments in agriculture and rural industries and social services, and raise peasants toward national standards in education, health, and consumption, while not letting the more modern urban enclaves greatly widen their advantage. Such policies, in turn, have depended for their implementation upon responsible and active local political leadership and upon recurrent collective mobilization. Without such policies and leadership patterns, peasant involvement—through persuasion—would not have been successful. With them, the whole of China has been able to move forward, slowly perhaps, and with recurrent troubles, but nevertheless with remarkable overall progress in economic development and social equality.

Thus in China, as in France and Russia, the revolutionary outcomes depended very much upon the accomplishments of the peasantry and its relationship to the state-building leadership that consolidated the Revolution. In Russia, the peasantry made its own leveling revolution on the land and then became a passive threat to the economic and political viability of the revolutionized nation. As a result, the Stalinist outcomes were ultimately shaped in large part by the efforts of the Bolsheviks forcibly to control the peasants by command and terror. In France, the peasantry made a more limited revolution against certain claims on its surpluses, lost much of its unity in the process, and finally found itself partly forced and partly induced to coexist in a national market context with an administrative-bureaucratic state, while capitalism gradually but inexorably eroded its position. Uniquely in China, though, the peasantry could not make its own revolution, and the organized revolutionaries could not come to power directly within the cities and towns. The Communists and peasants necessarily allied to complete the Revolution. In consequence special possibilities were created for the revolutionaries once in state power to use participatory mobilization in the further transformation of the economy and society, and for peasant activities and welfare to become a fundamental part of national development in China.

Summing Up

Revolutionary struggles have emerged from crises of state and class domination, and social-revolutionary outcomes have been powerfully shaped by the obstacles and opportunities offered by those crises. Likewise, social-revolutionary outcomes have been shaped and limited by the existing socioeconomic structures and international circumstances within which revolutionary leaderships have struggled to rebuild, consolidate, and use state power. Such, speaking in general terms, have been the analytic arguments set forth in Part II. Table 2 presents a summary of the overall logic and of many of the specific points made about the individual Revolutions along the way.

The arguments and comparative logic of Part II have rested squarely upon the results established in Part I. Broad similarities in the causes and outcomes of the French, Russian, and Chinese Revolutions have been attributed to the basic similarities of the social-revolutionary crises — featuring conjunctures of administrative/military disorganization and peasant insurrections — from which all three Revolutions emerged. Variations in the revolutionary conflicts and outcomes have been explained partly in terms of the specific features of each revolutionary crisis: exactly how each old-regime state broke apart; exactly what kinds of peasant revolts were facilitated by existing agrarian structures. And variations have also been explained partly by reference to the specific socioeconomic structures and international situations carried over, more or less, from each Old to New Regime.

Social revolutions accomplish major transformations, to be sure. But they effect such transformations only within the confines of historically given domestic and international situations. The class and political conflicts of social revolutions emerge, moreover, from historically specific crises of old regimes. Thus explanations of the conflicts and outcomes of social revolutions best flow, as they have in this book, from a prior understanding of the structures and situations of old regimes and from a prior analysis of the causes of social-revolutionary crises. Revolutionary changes are accomplished upon such foundations and within such circumstances.

The outcomes of social revolutions do not, of course, mark the end of all change. History has continued in France since the early 1800s, in Russia since the 1930s, and in China since the 1960s. Yet revolutionary outcomes in all three countries did set limits for future developments. And they created new obstacles and opportunities for future political struggles – both within each nation and on a global scale.

Table 2. *Outcomes of Social Revolutions in France, Russia, and China*

Effects of Social-Revolutionary Crises	Socioeconomic Legacies of the Old Regimes	International and World-Historical Circumstances
Similarities		
Liberal stabilization impossible. Dominant classes vulnerable. Popular groups available for political mobilization.	Society remains predominantly agrarian with peasants a major presence.	Nation intensively caught up in international competition during and after revolution.
France		
Liberal phases, but not stable. Organizational framework of royal line armies survives. Peasant revolts abolish seigneurialism, but do not redistribute landed property.	Agrarian-commercial economy of small and medium units; industry nonmechanized. No industrial proletariat. Petty-propertied groups dominate economy.	France involved in Continental military competition as a potentially hegemonic power. State control of national economic development not yet a world-historical possibility.
Russia		
No real liberal phase. Tsarist armies dissolve completely. Peasants drive out landlords, redistribute landed property; turn inward at village level.	Significant development of large-scale modern enterprises, mainly heavy-industrial. Strategically located proletariat.	Russia on defensive in European states system from 1917 through World War II. State-propelled industrialization is possible.
China		
Political and military disunity of warlord era. Peasants cannot revolt on own; landed gentry remain powerful in localities.	Traditional agrarian–commercial economy largely untransformed. A few, marginal, modern-industrial enclaves, mostly light-industrial.	China invaded during World War II; on defensive after WWII, though in a world dominated by United States and USSR as nuclear superpowers. State-propelled industrialization is possible.

Table 2. (*continued*)

Process of Revolutionary State-Building	Nature of New Regime
Similarities	
Politico–military mobilization of popular support in wars against domestic counterrevolutionaries and competitors, and against foreign invaders.	State larger and more centralized, bureaucratic, and mass-incorporating than under Old Regime. State more autonomous at home and abroad. Landed class privileges gone.
France	
Jacobin proto-party mobilizes urban popular forces to revitalize national army; no enduring basis in industry or among peasants. Jacobins fall after military consolidation; administrative consolidation only under Napoleonic military dictatorship.	Professional–bureaucratic state, not party-controlled; promotes domestic stability and military expansion. Private-propertied society and market-guided economy. Capitalist development facilitated, favoring richer property holders.
Russia	
Bolshevik Party mobilizes industrial proletariat; no base in countryside. Must rebuild state organizations suddenly, from scratch, with coercive means. To survive among peasants and in threatening international circumstances, regime turns to forced collectivization and crash heavy industrialization.	Party-state, hierarchical, authoritarian, and coercive. State-propelled national economic development; emphasis on heavy industry and rapid urbanization. Exaggerated inequalities of status and economic rewards.
China	
Urban-based revolutionary consolidation fails. CCP mobilizes peasants for guerrilla war and land revolution. After 1949, Party-state controls industries, but also retains and uses unique political basis in countryside.	Party-state, relatively decentralized and mass-mobilizing. State-propelled national economic development, with much emphasis on agricultural and rural development. Attempts to reduce or hold steady inequalities.

283

Conclusion

"THE BASIC QUESTION of every revolution is that of state power," Lenin wrote in the midst of the Russian Revolution of 1917.[1] Here was Lenin the revolutionary organizer speaking. As a theorist, nevertheless, Lenin followed Marx in maintaining that historical developments in class relations were the structural matrix from which revolutionary contests for state power arose, and in believing that class conflicts were the means by which questions about the forms and functions of state power would be resolved. Bourgeois revolutions had served to strengthen states as instruments of bureaucratic and coercive domination. Yet anticapitalist, socialist revolutions would pave the way for the atrophy of the state as such, because there would be no occasion for state domination over the producing classes in whose name, and by whose efforts, such revolutions would be made.[2]

The analysis of this book suggests both the truth and the limits of Lenin's vision of states and revolutions. Questions of state power *have* been basic in social-revolutionary transformations, but state power cannot be understood only as an instrument of class domination, nor can changes in state structures be explained primarily in terms of class conflicts. In France, Russia, and China, class conflicts – especially between peasants and landlords – were pivotal during the revolutionary interregnums. But both the occurrence of the revolutionary situations in the first place and the nature of the New Regimes that emerged from the revolutionary conflicts depended fundamentally upon the structures of state organizations and their partially autonomous and dynamic relationships to domestic class and political forces, as well as their positions in relation to other states abroad.

284

Conclusion

Prerevolutionary France, Russia, and China all had well-established imperial states with proven capacities to protect their own hegemony and that of the dominant classes against revolts from below. Before social revolutions could occur, the administrative and military power of these states had to break down. When this happened in France 1789, Russia 1917, and China 1911, it was *not* because of deliberate activities to that end, either on the part of avowed revolutionaries or on the part of politically powerful groups within the Old Regimes. Rather revolutionary political crises, culminating in administrative and military breakdowns, emerged because the imperial states became caught in cross-pressures between intensified military competition or intrusions from abroad and constraints imposed on monarchical responses by the existing agrarian class structures and political institutions. The old-regime states were prone to such revolutionary crises because their existing structures made it impossible for them to meet the particular international military exigencies that each had to face in the modern era.

Once the old-regime states had broken apart, fundamental political and class conflicts were set in motion, not to be resolved until new administrative and military organizations were consolidated in the place of the old. Revolts from below directly attacked the property and privileges of dominant classes, thus accomplishing changes in class relations that otherwise would not have occurred. Yet equally important were the effects of peasant and urban working class revolts on the course of national political struggles. Possibilities for counterrevolutionary restoration or liberal stabilization were undermined, and revolutionary leaderships found it possible to mobilize popular support in the process of building up new state organizations to defend against domestic competitors and foreign invaders. Compared to the imperial states of the Old Regimes, the new-regime states that emerged in France, Russia, and China alike were stronger and more autonomous within society and more powerful over against foreign competitors within the international states system. Moreover, peasants and urban workers were more directly incorporated into national politics and state-run projects after the Revolutions whose triumph they had helped to ensure. Strengthened national states were not the only accomplishments of the French, Russian, and Chinese Revolutions, but such changes in the state order were among the most striking and important revolutionary transformations.

Strengthened states — more centralized, bureaucratic, and autonomously powerful at home and abroad — emerged from all three Revolutions. This fact points to the operation of persistent influences regardless of whether the intranational conflicts of a revolution were anticapitalist, as in Russia and China, or on balance favorable to capitalist development, as in France. One such influence was the competitive dynamic of the international states

285

system. Wars and imperial intrusions were the midwives of the revolutionary crises, and the emergent revolutionary regimes consolidated state power not only amidst armed domestic conflicts but also in militarily threatening international circumstances. In France, Russia, and China alike the exigencies of revolutionary consolidation in a world of competing states helped ensure that leaderships willing and able to build up centralized coercive and administrative organizations would come to the fore during the Revolutions, and that their handiwork would create a permanent base of power for state cadres within the revolutionized social orders.

Furthermore, modern social revolutions like the French, Russian, and Chinese have invariably occurred in countries caught behind more economically developed competitor nations. Increasingly over "world time," opportunities and models have become available for using state power to promote national economic development. Especially in Russia and China, therefore, revolutionary leaderships have been able to use state power after the initial consolidation of the New Regimes to propel further socioeconomic transformations. These transformations have contributed indispensably to national survival (i.e., Russia in World War II) or to the material well-being of the people as a whole (i.e., China). Yet they surely could not have been accomplished without dynamic state intervention or without political controls over many aspects of social and economic life.

We might be tempted to conclude that, in contrast to Lenin, Max Weber is a better and more infallible guide to revolutionary outcomes. In Weber's view, revolutions function in the end to further bureaucratic domination, all the more inevitably so to the extent that they establish state controls over the economy.[3] But this perspective offers insufficient insight into the varying outcomes of the French, Russian, and Chinese Revolutions – especially with respect to their consequences for the peasantries who participated so decisively in all three revolutionary dramas, and who constituted the vast majority in society after the Revolutions as well as before. Given the ultimate fate of the Russian peasantry under Stalin, it is obviously impossible to hold that anticapitalist, communist revolutions have necessarily served peasant interests better than noncommunist social revolutions such as the French (or the Mexican). But neither will it do to assert that peasants inevitably fare worse under "totalitarian" communist revolutionary regimes. The Chinese Revolution belies this facile conclusion and challenges the received categorical opposition of "democracy" versus "totalitarianism" just as surely as the results of the Russian Revolution challenge any automatic equation of anticapitalism with socialist democracy. As a direct result of the socioeconomic and political accomplishments of the Chinese Revolution, Chinese peasants as a whole enjoy not only markedly better material conditions than before 1949. They also possess more direct control over and participation in decisions about the affairs of their locally focused lives than did either the

Russian peasantry after 1929 or the French peasantry after 1789–93. Moreover, however centralized and bureaucratic the Chinese Communist Party-state may be compared to prerevolutionary Chinese regimes, it nevertheless has afforded considerable scope for provincial and local planning and initiative. These considerations suggest, *pace* Weber, that anticapitalist, state-strengthening revolutions need not necessarily result merely in a more total form of Western-style bureaucratic domination.

To be sure, the outcomes of the Chinese Revolution must not be romanticized. The best ideals of socialist democracy are far from being realized in a context where political life is marked by group manipulation and by intolerance for many kinds of dissent. Nevertheless, it would be folly to let our received political categories blind us to the participatory qualities of the Chinese Communist polity as a whole or to the genuine gains in local community decision-making that have been achieved by and for the Chinese peasant majority as a result of the Revolution. The Chinese state has been strengthened and, at the same time, so has local-level collective democracy. This revolutionary outcome cannot be adequately comprehended by any theoretical perspective that posits a unilinear, world-historical march of bureaucratic rationalization. Rather it must be understood from a comparative perspective that gives weight to the distinctive forms of old-regime breakdown, revolutionary conflicts, and peasant mobilization in the course of revolutionary state-building that were specific to the history of the Chinese Revolution.

The French, Russian, and Chinese Revolutions, whose similarities and variations this book has explored at length and sought to explain, have not, of course, been the only social-revolutionary transformations in the modern world. Most observers would probably agree that social revolutions in roughly the sense meant here – that is, rapid, basic transformations of a society's state and class structures, accompanied and in part carried through by class-based revolts from below – have also occurred in Mexico between 1911 and the 1930s and since World War II in Yugoslavia, Vietnam, Algeria, Cuba, Bolivia, Angola, Mozambique, Guinea-Bissau, and Ethiopia. All of these share certain broad resemblances to the French, Russian, and Chinese Revolutions. They occurred in predominantly agrarian countries, and they became possible only through the administrative–military breakdown of preexisting states. Peasant revolts or mobilization for guerrilla warfare played a pivotal role in each revolutionary process. Furthermore, in every one of these cases, organized revolutionary leaderships (recruited from the ranks of previously marginal, educated elites) emerged or came to the fore during the revolutionary crisis. And these leaders acted to build new, strengthened state organizations to consolidate revolutionary changes and assert national autonomy.

Conclusion

Such broad resemblances raise the issue of the generalizability of the arguments presented in this book. Can they be applied beyond the French, Russian, and Chinese cases? In a sense, the answer is unequivocally "no": one cannot mechanically extend the specific causal arguments that have been developed for France, Russia, and China into a "general theory of revolutions" applicable to all other modern social revolutions. There are two important reasons why such a strategy would be fruitless. In the first place, the causes of revolutions (whether of individual cases, or sets of similar cases) necessarily vary according to the historical and international circumstances of the countries involved. "We do not know any universal principles of historical change," C. Wright Mills once wisely wrote, because "the mechanisms of change . . . vary with the social structure we are examining . . . Just as there is a variety of social structures, there is a variety of principles of historical change."[4] And, in the second place, patterns of revolutionary causation and outcomes are necessarily affected by world-historical changes in the fundamental structures and bases of state power as such. The likelihood and the forms of revolutions tend to change over world time, because, as Mills also noted in the same passage quoted above, "historical change *is* change of social structures, of the relations among their component parts."

The force of the first point is apparent when we consider that virtually all modern social revolutions other than the French, Russian, and Chinese have occurred in relatively small, formerly colonial countries situated in highly vulnerable and dependent positions within the world capitalist economy and the international states system. In Mexico and Vietnam, to take two possible and quite different examples, social-revolutionary crises did not emerge as a result of confrontations of historically autonomous and well-established imperial states with foreign military competitors or intruders. To understand the roots of these revolutionary crises, the analyst must trace both the historical legacies of colonialism as it specifically affected each indigenous sociopolitical structure, and the indirect repercussions for Mexico and Vietnam of economic and military power shifts within global political and economic systems. Thus in Mexico, weak national government was one of the legacies of Spanish colonialism. And both the rise and fall of the tenuously centralized and militarily feeble prerevolutionary regime of Porfirio Diaz (1870–1911) were strongly affected by shifts among the leading North Atlantic industrial powers, by flows of foreign investments into the various regions of Mexico, and by the changing political balances and foreign policy orientations of successive U.S. governments.[5] Similarly, social revolution in Vietnam emerged only after French colonialism, which had itself displaced the previously existing indigenous imperial regime, was disrupted by Japan's conquests and subsequent defeat during World War II.[6]

288

Moreover, the course and outcomes of social revolutions in dependent countries are powerfully conditioned not just by the requisites of military defense and assertion against actual and potential foreign invaders but also by direct economic and military aid from abroad. Often such aid is offered to the emerging revolutionary victors by major foreign powers anxious to influence the shape and policies of the new regimes. This is not to suggest that such revolutionized regimes simply become "clients" of great powers. Indeed, these regimes are more internationally autonomous than their pre-revolutionary predecessors, and their relationships with foreign sponsors are frequently fraught with tensions. Yet it does seem fair to say that the policies followed by revolutionary regimes in small, dependent countries have been more directly influenced by foreign sponsors and more tightly constrained by transnational economic relations than were the policies of the French, Russian, and (even) the Chinese New Regimes. An extreme case in point is Cuba. The Revolution overcame extreme dependence upon the United States and allowed Cuba to pursue more autonomous and equalitarian policies of state-directed economic development. Yet at the same time Cuba became very reliant upon Soviet economic aid and had her foreign policies tied closely to those of the USSR.[7]

Limits are thus placed on the generalizability of the specific causal patterns identified for France, Russian and China because other social revolutions have occurred (mostly more recently) in countries with significantly different political histories located in more dependent international positions. Additional, still more fundamental limits on the generalizability of the classic social-revolutionary patterns can be traced to historical transformations, relevant on an international scale, in the forms and bases of state power. Especially since the end of World War II, as dozens of new nations have emerged from colonialism in a world economically dominated by capitalism and militarily dominated by rival superpowers, modern weapons technologies and bureaucratic–professional forms of military organization have diffused to virtually every sovereign state. National authorities everywhere have wanted the symbolic trappings and coercive support of a modern military establishment. And the various leading powers have obliged by competing among themselves to recruit and supply allies or client states. One consequence has surely been to make social revolutions much less likely overall than they might otherwise have been if most new nations lacked modern militaries. In part this is because of the sheer repressive strength of modern military establishments. As Katherine Chorley declared in 1943, "no revolution will be won against a [domestic] modern army when that army is putting out its full strength against the insurrection."[8] Since then, the gap, already great, between official, state-controlled force and the coercive means that can be mustered (without foreign aid) by unofficial and popular groups has increased still more. Yet

289

this gap in itself is not the only consideration. After all, even the premodern armies of old-regime France could repress revolts from below.

More important than their sheer coercive advantage is the fact that modern, professional military establishments tend to be organizationally and socially differentiated from the dominant economic classes of the countries they "serve." In most Third World countries today, military officers are not predominantly recruited from landed or capitalist classes, but instead from the ranks of minor official families and small property owners. And military officer corps have strong but circumscribed interests centered on furthering their own corporate interests within the state apparatus, as well as preserving state authority as such.[9] As long as their own career and organizational interests are not threatened, such professional officer corps can remain aloof from political quarrels between state executives and dominant classes. Besides, whether they remain aloof or choose to intervene through coups, the coercive power of the military itself is not jeopardized by such quarrels. Thus post-World War II social revolutionary crises have *not* emerged as they did in Bourbon France and Manchu China, as a by-product of political quarrels between executives and dominant-class groups possessing organizational leverage within the state, including leverage within the military officer corps. Rather, international disruptions of colonial controls have been the most common origin of revolutionary crises. And once decolonization was completed, with modern military establishments successfully installed, then social revolutions became much less likely – although military coups of various sorts have become very frequent. But virtually all coups, even very "reformist" ones, have perpetuated existing state forms and controls, and they have usually prevented mass mobilization or revolts from below.[10]

Changing world-historical circumstances, therefore, as well as contrasting political histories and international situations, make it difficult to extend automatically to other social revolutions the specific descriptive generalizations and causal arguments of this book about the French, Russian, and Chinese Revolutions. Other revolutions require analyses in their own right, through comparisons of broadly similar cases among themselves and contrasts of countries that have experienced social revolutions to similarly situated countries that have not undergone social-revolutionary transformations. Much valuable work along these lines has already been accomplished by scholars such as Eric Wolf, John Dunn, Jeffery Paige, and Susan Eckstein;[11] and even more beckons to be undertaken. As this happens, the analytic frame of reference, the basic principles of analyses, used here to set up the comparative analysis of France, Russia, and China, should also prove fruitful for comparative analyses of the causes and outcomes of other social revolutions. The importance of systematic attention to the international and world-historical circumstances that influence revolutionary outbreaks and culminations is obvious from the foregoing brief survey of recent revolutionary patterns. And all comparative historical analysts of twentieth-century revolutions have in fact highlighted such influences.

Less obvious, perhaps, but equally pressing is the need for investigators of contemporary as well as historical revolutions to take a structural perspective, to emphasize objective relationships and conflicts among variously situated groups and nations, rather than the interests, outlooks or ideologies of particular actors in revolutions. Organized revolutionary vanguards have with time become increasingly self-conscious and vociferous about their indispensable role in "making" revolutions. It nevertheless seems to me that recent revolutionary crises, just as surely as those that launched the classic social revolutions, have come about only through inter- and intranational structural contradictions and conjunctural occurrences beyond the deliberate control of avowed revolutionaries. Nor have Third World vanguards been any more strategically prescient about the course of revolutions than were the Jacobins, Bolsheviks, and Chinese Communists. Despite the temptation to analyze revolutions "through the eyes" of ideological vanguards, therefore, the real challenge for comparative historical analysts is to decipher the structural/conjunctual causes of post- and neocolonial revolutionary crises and the socioeconomic and political conditions that have shaped the revolutionary conflicts and consolidations.

Finally, the key to successful structural analysis lies in a focus on *state organizations* and their relations both to international environments and to domestic classes and economic conditions. In peripheral countries, the possibilities for revolutionary outbreaks have crucially depended upon the continuities or disruptions of state machineries during crises of decolonization, and upon the relative coercive capacities and international vulnerabilities of neocolonial regimes. Once under way, social-revolutionary struggles have revolved around the state-building efforts of revolutionary leaderships. And revolutionary outcomes have been shaped by the domestic and international economic conditions faced by revolutionary state-builders and by the relationships of such state-builders with foreign states, opponents and supporters. Equally important have been the relations of revolutionary state-builders to class forces. Peasant cultivators have revolted spontaneously, or been directly mobilized by revolutionary parties in all peripheral social revolutions from the Mexican to the Vietnamese. Industrial proletarians have played key roles in many instances (such as the Bolivian and Mexican Revolutions). Domestic or international capitalist classes have also figured at least indirectly in each revolutionary conflict. The exact patterns of state/class relations have varied considerably and defy uniform description. But the analytically relevant point remains central: In a revolutionary situation, class forces, whether capitalist classes that retain control over strategic means of production and economic linkages, or popular classes whose revolts or military mobilization contribute to the revolutionary struggle, are bound by ties of conflict and cooperation, command and mobilization to the dynamic and partially autonomous activities of states and of state builders. Revolutionary patterns have varied from one type of regime to another, from one world-historical period to the next, and indeed from case to case. Yet a focus on the nexes of state/state, state/economy, and state/class relationships remains useful for deciphering the logic of social-revolutionary causes and outcomes, from France in the 1790s to Vietnam, Angola, and Ethiopia in the 1970s.

Karl Marx's theory of revolutions and vision of socialism have served as more or less explicit points of reference for many of the arguments of this book. So far in modern world history, social revolutions, though they have entailed elements of class conflict, have plainly not conformed to Marx's theoretical expectations or moral vision. They have occurred in agrarian countries caught behind foreign competitors, not in the most advanced capitalist industrial nations. And even those revolutions that have expropriated domestic capitalist classes in the name of socialist ideals have hardly resulted to date in the prosperous, democratic communist societies envisaged by Marx.

The lack of fit between Marx's theory of revolutions and the actual historical patterns of social revolutions suggests more insistently than many contemporary Marxian socialists may want to admit the need for rethinking some of the basics of Marx's approach. True enough, Marx's call for working-class-based socialism remains valid for advanced societies; nothing in the last hundred years of world history has undercut the compelling potential, indeed necessity, of that call. The fact remains, nevertheless, that classical Marxism failed to foresee or adequately explain the autonomous power, for good and ill, of states as administrative and coercive machineries embedded in a militarized international states system. Even if, *especially* if the working classes of the advanced societies should become politically self-conscious revolutionaries on national and international scales – something very different and more difficult to achieve than the local-level class organization that lay behind peasant revolts in France, Russia, and China – they would still have to contend with the repressive capacities of existing states and with the possible threat of new forms of state domination emerging unforeseen and unintended from actual revolutionary transformations. Peasant revolts in the great historical revolutions ended up dovetailing with the efforts and ultimate domination of state-building revolutionary leaderships. No working-class socialist revolution worthy of the name could repeat this pattern.

Let me close on a highly speculative note. If a social revolution were to transform an advanced industrial nation, it would, I can only suppose, have to take a very different form, and occur under quite different international conditions, from the great historical social revolutions. Because it seems highly unlikely that modern states could disintegrate as administrative—coercive organizations without destroying societies at the same time, a modern social revolution would probably have to flow gradually, not cataclysmically, out of a long series of "non-reformist reforms,"[12] accomplished by mass-based political movements struggling to democratize every major institution from the economy to the political parties, army, and civil bureaucracy. Yet for true democratization to become possible within any given advanced industrial country, it would surely be necessary for democratizing movements to proceed roughly simultaneously in all advanced countries, with each movement making it a key objective to achieve steady progress toward disarmament and international peace. In order to deprive authoritarian state executives of their self-perpetuating raison d'être, there would need to be a dampening of the very military rivalries that helped to trigger and shape social revolutions in the past.

In short, the causes and outcomes of the great social revolutions of the past could hardly be recapitulated in future democratic—socialist revolutions in advanced industrial societies. Still, the past does have something to teach us about the future: It suggests that in future revolutions, as in those of the past, the realm of the state is likely to be central. As Franz Neumann once put it, "the struggle for political power—i.e., the struggle for the control of the coercive organizations, for police, justice, army, bureaucracy, and foreign policy—is the agent of historical progress."[13] Only if this is well understood can people work effectively to realize Marx's vision of socialist society as "an association, in which the free development of each is the condition for the free development of all,"[14] and in which the state is transformed "from an organ dominating society into one completely subordinate to it."[15]

Notes

1. EXPLAINING SOCIAL REVOLUTIONS: ALTERNATIVES TO EXISTING THEORIES

1. Franz Schurmann, *Ideology and Organization in Communist China*, 2nd ed. (Berkeley: University of California Press, 1968), p. xxxv. Also, the previous sentence on China and Russia is paraphrased from Schurmann.

2. Elbaki Hermassi, "Toward a Comparative Study of Revolutions," *Comparative Studies in Society and History* 18:2 (April 1976): 214.

3. Good examples are the peasant-based rebellions that recurrently shook medieval Europe and Imperial China. The Chinese rebellions occasionally succeeded in toppling, and even replacing, dynasties, but did not fundamentally transform the sociopolitical structure. For more discussion and references, see Chapter 3.

4. As I understand this case, the English Revolution (1640–50 and 1688–9 taken together) is an excellent example of a political revolution. What it fundamentally accomplished was the establishment of parliamentary government through the revolt of sections of the dominant landed class against would-be absolute monarchs. This case is discussed in Chapter 3 and Chapter 5. Another good example of a political, but not social, revolution is the Japanese Meiji Restoration, which will be discussed in Chapter 2.

5. For examples of attempts to explain revolutions through strategies of analytic simplification, see the various works cited in notes 18 and 20 for this chapter. More will be said below about the ideas of two important theorists, Ted Gurr and Charles Tilly, both of whom subsume revolutions within broader analytic categories, albeit of contrasting kinds.

6. Three examples of scholars who leave (structural) change contingent are: Arthur L. Stinchcombe, "Stratification among Organizations and the Sociology of Revolution," in *Handbook of Organizations*, ed. James G. March

Revolution (Reading, Mass.: Addison-Wesley, 1978), chap. 7; and D.E.H. Russell, *Rebellion, Revolution, and Armed Force* (New York: Academic Press, 1974), chap. 4. Those who want to leave change contingent usually argue that nothing is lost by doing so, given that after one has examined the causes of all outbreaks whether or not they result in actual changes, then one can proceed to ask what *additional* causes explain the subset of outbreaks that do lead to successful changes. But to accept this sort of argument, one must be willing to assume that successful social-revolutionary transformations have no distinctive, long-term, structural causes or preconditions. One must assume that social revolutions are simply political revolutions or mass rebellions that possess some additional, short-term ingredient such as military success or the determination of ideological leaders to implement changes after grabbing power. The entire argument of this book is based upon the opposite assumption – that social revolutions do have long-term causes, and that they grow out of structural contradictions and potentials inherent in old regimes.

7. Here I make no pretense to survey the entire social-scientific literature on revolutions. Two books that provide surveys of the literature are A. S. Cohan, *Theories of Revolution: An Introduction* (New York: Halsted Press, 1975) and Mark N. Hagopian, *The Phenomenon of Revolution* (New York: Dodd, Mead, 1974). Useful critiques are to be found in: Isaac Kramnick, "Reflections on Revolution: Definition and Explanation in Recent Scholarship," *History and Theory* 11:1 (1972):26–63; Michael Freeman, "Review Article: Theories of Revolution," *British Journal of Political Science* 2:3 (July 1972):339–59; Barbara Salert, *Revolutions and Revolutionaries: Four Theories* (New York: Elsevier, 1976); Lawrence Stone, "Theories of Revolution," *World Politics* 18:2 (January 1966): 159–76; Perez Zagorin, "Theories of Revolution in Contemporary Historiography," *Political Science Quarterly* 88:1 (March 1973):23–52; and Theda Skocpol, "Explaining Revolutions: In Quest of a Social–Structural Approach," in *The Uses of Controversy in Sociology*, eds. Lewis A. Coser and Otto N. Larsen (New York: Free Press, 1976), pp. 155–75.

8. Barrington Moore, Jr., *Social Origins of Dictatorship and Democracy: Lord and Peasant in the Making of the Modern World* (Boston: Beacon Press, 1966); Eric Wolf, *Peasant Wars of the Twentieth Century* (New York: Harper & Row, 1969); and John Dunn, *Modern Revolutions: An Introduction to the Analysis of a Political Phenomenon* (Cambridge: Cambridge University Press, 1972).

9. Nikolai Bukharin, *Historical Materialism: A System of Sociology*, trans. from the 3rd Russian ed., 1921 (University of Michigan Press, 1969), esp. chap. 7.

10. See: Robert C. Tucker, ed., *The Lenin Anthology* (New York: Norton, 1975), esp. pts. 1–3; and Stuart R. Schram, ed., *The Political Thought of Mao Tse-tung*, rev. and enlarged ed. (New York: Praeger, 1969), esp. pts. 2–6. A nice exposition of the basics of Lenin's and Mao's theories of revolution is to be found in Cohan, *Theories of Revolution*, chap. 5.

11. See especially: Georg Lukács, *History and Class Consciousness*, trans. Rodney Livingstone (Cambridge: The MIT Press, 1971); Antonio Gramsci, *Selections from the Prison Notebooks*, ed. and trans. Quintin Hoare and Geoffrey Nowell Smith (New York: International Publishers, 1971); and Louis Althusser,

83. For example, Chalmers Johnson's definition of revolutionary change, framed in terms of social-systems theory with its universality of reference to all societies in all times and places, subsumes everything from revitalization movements in tribal societies to religious wars in premodern agrarian societies to revolutions in contemporary nation-states. And both Ted Gurr and Charles Tilly, notwithstanding their sharp disagreements, attempt to situate revolutions within more general theories of "political violence" and "collective action" respectively. Precisely because they want to theorize only about categories containing large numbers of events so that their models will be open to quantitative testing, both Gurr and Tilly define revolutions in terms of analytic aspects that they have in common with many other kinds of political occurrences—that is, political violence for Gurr and organized political action and displacement of sovereign power holders for Tilly—leaving aside any concern with the major structural transformations distinctive to revolutions, especially social revolutions as such.

84. "Bourgeois revolutions" such as the French and the English have been interpreted as wholes in terms of Marxist theory. For nonbourgeois revolutions, the focus is upon the role of class contradictions and conflicts in the causes and processes, but outcomes are rarely analyzed in Marxist terms.

85. See for example: Stone, "Theories of Revolution" and Zagorin, "Theories in Contemporary Historiography." (Full citations in note 7.)

86. See for example: Alfred Cobban, *The Social Interpretation of the French Revolution* (Cambridge: Cambridge University Press, 1964); and J. H. Hexter, *Reappraisals in History* (New York: Harper & Row, 1963).

87. This argument is most typically resorted to by historians such as Cobban and Hexter who are attacking the application of Marxist concepts and interpretations to particular revolutions.

88. This argument is developed in E. H. Carr, *What is History?* (New York: Vintage Books, 1961).

89. Charles, Louise, and Richard Tilly, *The Rebellious Century 1830–1930* (Cambridge: Harvard University Press, 1975).

90. Reinhard Bendix, *Nation-Building and Citizenship* (New York: Wiley, 1964). See note 69 for Anderson citation. Although Bendix's theoretical perspective is Weberian and Anderson's is Marxist, both use a similar kind of comparative approach.

91. See Ernest Nagel, ed., *John Stuart Mill's Philosophy of Scientific Method* (New York: Hafner, 1950), bk. III, chap. 8.

92. For a discussion of Tocqueville's use of the comparative method, see Neil J. Smelser, *Comparative Methods in the Social Sciences* (Englewood Cliffs, N.J.: Prentice-Hall, 1976), chap. 2. On Marc Bloch, see William H. Sewell, Jr., "Marc Bloch and the Logic of Comparative History," *History and Theory* 6:2 (1967):208–18.

93. For contemporary discussions of comparative analysis, see: Smelser, *Comparative Methods;* Arend Lijphart, "Comparative Politics and the Comparative Method," *American Political Science Review* 65:3–4 (1971):682–93; Hopkins and Wallerstein, "Comparative Study of National Societies"; and Morris Zelditch, Jr., "Intelligible Comparisons," in *Comparative Methods in So-*

ciology, ed. Ivan Vallier (Berkeley: University of California Press, 1971) pp. 267–307.

94. Edwards, *Natural History,* p. xviii.

95. Brinton, *Anatomy of Revolution,* pp. 16–17.

96. This difficulty is stressed in Adam Przeworski and Henry Teune, *The Logic of Comparative Social Inquiry* (New York: Wiley, 1970). Smelser, *Comparative Methods,* chaps. 6–7 passim, discusses ways to handle it.

97. Marxist-oriented scholars, for example, posit fundamental distinctions between "bourgeois" revolutions (such as France) and "socialist" (or at least anticapitalist) revolutions (such as Russia and China). Somewhat analogously, non-Marxist scholars often draw a sharp distinction betwen antiabsolutist, liberal-democratic revolutions, on the one hand, and collectivist, state-strengthening revolutions, on the other. Finally, it is currently becoming very common for analysts to set off from all "European revolutions" (ranging from the English to the Russian) a category of national liberation revolutions, such as have occurred since World War II in various Third World countries. This distinction is used both by Elbaki Hermassi in "Toward a Comparative Study of Revolutions," *Comparative Studies in Society and History* 18:2 (April 1976):211–35, and by Martin Malia, in "The Escalation of European Revolution: 1640, 1789, 1848, 1917," (Paper presented at the Annual Meeting of the Modern European Section of the American Historical Association, Atlanta, Georgia, December, 1975), pp. 5–9. Both Hermassi and Malia consider the Chinese Revolution to be a national liberation ("periphery" or "Third World") revolution.

98. Malia, "Escalation," treats Russia as an antiabsolutist revolution along with all other European revolutions, including the French. Hermassi, "Comparative Study," sees Russia as the prototype "developmental" revolution, in contrast both to "democratic" revolutions such as the French, and "peripheral" revolutions such as the Chinese. Barrington Moore in *Social Origins* treats Russia and China as "peasant"/communist revolutions in contrast to the bourgeois–liberal French Revolution. Moore's grouping is probably most typical, though other scholars would usually affix different labels.

99. Often scholars assume that China had two revolutions, one in 1911 and another, pitting the Chinese Communists against the Nationalists in the 1930s and '40s. However I believe that it is more fruitful to see the Chinese Revolution as one process stretching from the fall of the Old Regime in 1911 (and the failure of any new national regime to consolidate itself at that point) through the emergence and competition for sovereignty of two state-building movements, the Nationalists and Communists, with the ultimate victory of the latter partially determined by the fact that the Nationalists never really succeeded in uniting and controlling China under one government. Thus, for example, if one accepts Samuel P. Huntington's distinction in *Political Power in Changing Societies* (New Haven: Yale University Press, 1968), chap. 5, between "Western" revolutions that begin with the collapse of an old regime, and "Eastern" revolutions where a movement arises to challenge a feeble Third World government, then I am arguing that China really is more like the "Western" type. Huntington's analytic distinction is useful, but he has the cases sorted wrong, and his labels need to be changed!

303

2. OLD-REGIME STATES IN CRISIS

1. For the concept of "imperial state" as a type of state, I draw upon Frances V. Moulder, *Japan, China and the Modern World Economy* (Cambridge: Cambridge University Press, 1977), p. 45. However, in contrast to Moulder, I hold that imperial states are *partially* bureaucratic, rather than nonbureaucratic.

2. The criteria of bureaucracy employed here come, of course, from Max Weber, *Economy and Society*, ed. Guenther Roth and Claus Wittich, 3 vols. (New York: Bedminster Press, 1968), chap. 11, esp. pp. 956–63.

3. Further discussion and specific references (for this and other introductory statements) will appear in each case analysis below. For comparisons of urban networks (partially based upon marketing systems) in five premodern agrarian states, including France, Russia, and China, see Gilbert Rozman, *Urban Networks in Russia, 1750–1800, and Premodern Periodization* (Princeton, N.J.: Princeton University Press, 1976), chap. 5.

4. My analysis of the sociopolitical structures of prerevolutionary France, Russia, and China draws upon both Marxist and Weberian approaches without, however, fully accepting the theoretical proclivities of either perspective. On the Marxist side, there are especially close resemblances to Perry Anderson's conception of the absolutist state in early modern Europe in his *Lineages of the Absolutist State* (London: New Left Books, 1974), but with two important differences. First, whereas Anderson draws a sharp line between European absolutisms and non-European agrarian empires, I see important parallels of socioeconomic and political organization (including the abrogation of the political autonomy of towns) betwen late Imperial China and the agrarian absolutist states of continental Europe in the early modern era (without of course denying that the entire continental contexts of Europe and East Asia were quite different). Even more important, I cannot agree with Anderson that the particular form of state organization in question here – protobureaucratic monarchy – is fundamentally determined by the mode of production and form of surplus appropriation in society. Within "feudal" Europe, state forms changed and varied not just in tandem with the presence or absence of serfdom or other forms of control and exploitation of the peasantry by landlords.

Obviously my way of looking at the state/society relationship owes a good deal to Max Weber (see *Economy and Society*, chaps. 9–13). Yet on this side, too, there are some differences. For one thing, Weber tended to theorize about major forms of political structures in terms of the dominant kinds of ideas – tradition, charisma, rational–legal norms – through which the authority of rulers or their staffs was legitimated, whereas the focus here is much more on the material-resource base and organizational form of state power. Second, insofar as Weber was willing to theorize about societal sociopolitical structures as wholes, he tended to use categories that referred to political forms alone, in isolation from socioeconomic structures, and he analyzed political dynamics above all by examining struggles between rulers and their staffs. In contrast, my conception of the structures of prerevolutionary France, Russia, and China emphasizes the interdependence of socioeconomic and politico–military structures, and it suggests that the basic, potentially contradictory tensions in these societies were those inherent in the relationships of producing classes to dominant classes, and of each class to the state.

5. Stefan T. Possony, ed., *The Lenin Reader* (Chicago: Henry Regnery, 1966), p. 358. The quote comes from Lenin's "The Collapse of the Second International," written in 1915.

6. Useful recent reviews of French Revolution historiography are to be found in: Alfred Cobban, *Aspects of the French Revolution* (New York: Norton, 1970); François Furet, "Le Catéchisme Révolutionaire," *Annales: Economies, Sociétés, Civilisations* 26:2 (March–April 1971): 255–89; and Gerald J. Cavanaugh, "The Present State of French Revolutionary Historiography: Alfred Cobban and Beyond," *French Historical Studies* 7:4 (Fall 1972): 587–606.

7. See, for examples: Georges Lefebvre, *The French Revolution*, trans. Elizabeth Moss Evanson (New York: Columbia University Press, 1962), vol. 1; and George Rudé, *Revolutionary Europe, 1783–1815* (New York: Harper & Row, 1966).

8. A start in this direction is made by C.B.A. Behrens in *The Ancien Régime* (London: Harcourt, Brace and World, 1967).

9. General background for this and the next paragraph (and for later statements about French absolutism) was provided by: Pierre Goubert, *Louis XIV and Twenty Million Frenchmen*, trans. Anne Carter (New York: Vintage Books, 1970); Pierre Goubert, *L'Ancien Régime 2: Les Pouvoirs* (Paris: Armand Colin, 1973); W. H. Lewis, *The Splendid Century* (New York: Doubleday, Anchor Books, 1957); Menna Prestwich, "The Making of Absolute Monarchy (1559–1683)," in *France: Government and Society*, eds. J. M. Wallace-Hadrill and J. McManners (London: Methuen, 1957), pp. 105–33; and G.R.R. Treasure, *Seventeenth Century France* (London: Rivingtons, 1966).

10. Leo Gershoy, *The French Revolution and Napoleon* (1933; reprint ed., New York: Appleton-Century-Crofts, 1964), p. 6.

11. Nora Temple, "The Control and Exploitation of French Towns during the Ancien Régime," *History* 51:171 (February 1966): 16–34.

12. Ludwig Dehio, *The Precarious Balance: Four Centuries of the European Power Struggle*, trans. Charles Fullman (New York: Vintage Books, 1962), chap. 2.

13. Treasure, *Seventeenth Century France*, chaps. 19–21.

14. Behrens, *Ancien Régime*, p. 25. Behrens's estimate of the peasant proportion of the population is probably highly inclusive, counting the rural poor as well as all who owned or rented land to work.

15. Jan Marczewski, "Some Aspects of the Economic Growth of France, 1660–1958," *Economic Development and Cultural Change* 9:3 (1961), 379.

16. For a general treatment that nicely captures both the dynamism and limits of economic growth in this period, see Jan De Vries, *The Economy of Europe in an Age of Crisis, 1600–1750* (Cambridge: Cambridge University Press, 1976).

17. This paragraph and the next are based upon: Paul Bairoch, "Agriculture and the Industrial Revolution," in *The Industrial Revolution*, ed. Carlo M. Cipolla, The Fontana Economic History of Europe, (London: Collins/Fontana,

1973), vol. 3, pp. 452–506; Marc Bloch, *French Rural History,* trans. Janet Sondheimer (Berkeley: University of California Press, 1970); Ralph Davis, *The Rise of the Atlantic Economies* (Ithaca, N.Y.: Cornell University Press, 1973), chaps. 17 and 18; F. Crouzet, "England and France in the Eighteenth Century: a Comparative Analysis of Two Economic Growths," in *The Causes of the Industrial Revolution in England,* ed. R. M. Hartwell (London: Methuen, 1967), chap. 7; Behrens, *Ancien Régime,* pp. 25–46; and George V. Taylor, "Noncapitalist Wealth and the Origins of the French Revolution," *American Historical Review* 72:2 (January 1967), pp. 472–6.

18. Davis, *Atlantic Economies,* p. 313. The analysis of this paragraph relies heavily on Davis, but it also draws upon Crouzet, "England and France."

19. My arguments about the dominant class in eighteenth-century France have been in large part inspired by Pierre Goubert, *The Ancien Régime: French Society, 1600–1750,* trans. Steve Cox (New York: Harper & Row, 1974), esp. chap. 6.

20. See, for example, the discussions of feudalism by Perry Anderson in his *Passages From Antiquity to Feudalism,* and *Lineages of the Absolutist State* (London: New Left Books, 1974).

21. Furet, "Le Catéchisme Révolutionnaire," p. 272. The quoted passage has been translated from the French by me, with the gratefully acknowledged help of Jerry Karabel.

22. This paragraph and the next are based upon: J. McManners, "France," in *The European Nobility in the Eighteenth Century,* ed. Albert Goodwin (New York: Harper & Row, 1967), pp. 22–42; Behrens, *Ancien Régime,* pp. 64–84; Colin Lucas, "Nobles, Bourgeois and the Origins of the French Revolution," *Past and Present,* no. 60 (August 1973): 84–126; William Doyle, "Was There an Aristocratic Reaction in Pre-Revolutionary France?" *Past and Present,* no. 57 (November 1972): 97–122; D. D. Bien, "La Réaction Aristocratique avant 1789: l'Example de l'Armée," *Annales: Economies, Sociétés, Civilisations* 29:1 (January–February 1974): 23–48; Jean Egret, "L'Aristocratie Parlementaire Française à la Fin de l'Ancien Régime," *Révue Historique* no. 208 (July–September 1952): 1–14; Robert Forster, *The Nobility of Toulouse in the Eighteenth Century* (Baltimore: The Johns Hopkins Press, 1960); Robert Forster, "The Noble Wine Producers of the Bordelais in the Eighteenth Century," *Economic History Review,* 2nd series 14:1 (August 1961): 18–33; and Behrens, *Ancien Régime,* pp. 64–84.

23. As George V. Taylor puts it, "the struggle against . . . aristocracy was the product of a financial and political crisis that it did not create" ("Noncapitalist Wealth," p. 491).

24. George V. Taylor, "Types of Capitalism in Eighteenth-Century France," *English Historical Review* 79:312 (July 1964): 478–97; and Taylor, "Noncapitalist Wealth." See also Guy Chaussinand-Nogaret, "Capital et Structure Sociale sous l'Ancien Régime," *Annales: Economies, Sociétés, Civilisations* 25:2 (March–April 1970): 463–76.

25. Taylor, "Noncapitalist Wealth" p. 471.

26. Ibid., p. 472.

27. Ibid., pp. 477 and 478–9.

28. Ibid., pp. 479 and 481.

29. Ibid., pp. 487–88.

30. Louise Tilly, "The Food Riot as a Form of Political Conflict in France," *Journal of Interdisciplinary History* 2:1 (Summer, 1971): 23–57.

31. "Privilege" in the sense of distinctions or legal exemptions enjoyed by particular individuals and groups but not others was by no means limited to the noble and clerical estates. C.B.A. Behrens has an excellent discussion in *Ancien Régime,* pp. 46 ff. She notes that "the nobility constituted only one among many privileged groups, and had [materially] useful privileges that were less extensive than those of many bourgeois" (p. 59).

32. Walter L. Dorn, *Competition for Empire, 1740–1763* (New York: Harper & Row, 1963), esp. chaps. 6–8.

33. Ibid., p. 114.

34. Behrens, *Ancien Régime,* p. 153.

35. Betty Behrens, "Nobles, Privileges and Taxes in France at the End of the Ancien Régime," *Economic History Review,* 2nd series 15:3 (April 1963): 451–75.

36. "Among other things, it [the *rente perpetuelle*] engendered that characteristic insouciance toward debt for which the old regime was famous . . . Only when service on the long-term debt was so large as to make deficits inescapable would a controller general have to consider refunding principal, but then, of course, he would find it impossible to pay. This was precisely the quandry . . . after the American war" (Taylor, "Noncapitalist Wealth," pp. 481–2).

37. J. F. Bosher, *French Finances, 1770–1795: From Business to Bureaucracy* (Cambridge: Cambridge University Press, 1970); and George T. Matthews, *The Royal General Farms in Eighteenth Century France* (New York: Columbia University Press, 1958).

38. Behrens, *Ancien Régime,* p. 149.

39. Behrens, "Nobles, Privileges, and Taxes."

40. Franklin L. Ford, *Robe and Sword* (New York: Harper & Row, 1965), p. 248.

41. Alfred Cobban, *A History of Modern France* (Baltimore: Penguin Books, 1957), vol. 1, *Old Regime and Revolution, 1715–1799,* p. 155.

42. Ford, *Robe and Sword;* Forster, *Nobility of Toulouse;* J. H. Shennan, *The Parlement of Paris* (Ithaca, N.Y.: Cornell University Press, 1968); and Egret, "L'Aristocratie Parlementaire."

43. Georges Lefebvre, "The French Revolution in the Context of World History," in *Revolutions: A Comparative Study,* ed. Lawrence Kaplan (New York: Vintage Books, 1973), p. 164.

44. William Doyle, "The Parlements of France and the Breakdown of the Old Regime, 1771–1788," *French Historical Studies* 6:4 (Fall 1970): 415–58.

45. Shennan, *Parlement of Paris;* Ford, *Robe and Sword;* and Cobban, *History of Modern France,* vol. 1.

46. Cobban, *History of Modern France,* vol. 1, p. 122.

47. Pierre Goubert, *L'Ancien Régime, 2: Les Pouvoirs* (Paris: Armand Colin, 1973), pp. 136–7.

48. Matthews, *The Royal General Farms,* p. 258.

49. Ibid., p. 257.

50. Bosher, *French Finances,* pp. 183–96 and p. 308.

51. Ibid., p. 304.

52. Ibid., pp. 304–5.

53. This paragraph draws upon: Norman Hampson, *A Social History of the French Revolution* (Toronto: University of Toronto Press, 1963), chap. 2; and A. Goodwin, "Calonne, the Assembly of French Notables of 1787 and the Origins of the Revolte Nobiliare," *English Historical Review* 61:240 (May 1946): 202–34 and 61(241) (September 1946): 329–77.

54. Hampson, *Social History,* chap. 2; Jean Egret, "The Origins of the Revolution in Brittany (1788–1789)" and "The Pre-Revolution in Provence (1787–1789)," in *New Perspectives on the French Revolution,* ed. Jeffrey Kaplow (New York: Wiley, 1965), pp. 136–70; and Jean Egret, *La Pré-Révolution Française* (Paris: Presses Universitaires de France, 1962).

55. On the French army at the end of the Old Regime, see: Bien, "Réaction Aristocratique: l'Exemple de l'Armée"; Emile G. Léonard, "La Question Sociale dans l'Armée Francaise au XVIII Siècle," *Annales: Economies, Sociétés, Civilisations* 3:2 (April–June 1948): 135–49; Louis Hartmann, "Les Officiers de l'Armée Royale a la Veille de la Révolution," *Révue Historique* 100 (January–April 1909):241–68, and 101 (May–August 1909):38–79; P. Chalmin, "La Désintégration de l'Armée Royale en France à la Fin du XVIIIe Siècle," *Révue Historique de l'Armée* 20:1 (1964):75–90; and S. F. Scott, "The French Revolution and the Professionalization of the French Officer Corps," in *On Military Ideology,* eds. M. Janowitz and J. Van Doorn (Rotterdam University Press, 1971), pp. 18ff.

56. Katherine Chorley, *Armies and the Art of Revolution* (1943; reprint ed., Boston: Beacon Press, 1973), pp. 138–39.

57. The classic statement of this thesis is to be found in Georges Lefebvre, *The Coming of the French Revolution,* trans. R. R. Palmer (Princeton, N.J.: Princeton University Press, 1947), pt. II.

58. Certainly the various sectors of the late old-regime dominant class seem to have been much more united on the basic premise of wanting national representative arrangements for the privileged than were the various noble and official groups that participated in the Fronde of 1648–53. By the eighteenth century, the sheer existence of a unified, national French state came to be taken for granted, whereas the privileged groups that participated in the Fronde took fundamentally contradictory positions for or against the centralized state as such.

59. J. Murphy and P. Higonnet, "Les Députés de la Noblesse aux Etats Généraux de 1789," *Révue d'Histoire Moderne et Contemporaine* 20 (April–June 1973): 230–47.

60. Elizabeth L. Eisenstein, "Who Intervened in 1788? A Commentary on *The Coming of the French Revolution,*" *American Historical Review* 71:1 (October 1965): 77–103.

61. On the Municipal Revolution see especially: Lynn A. Hunt, "Committees and Communes: Local Politics and National Revolution in 1789," *Comparative Studies in Society and History* 18:3 (July 1976): 321–46; and George

Rudé, "The Fall of the Bastille," in *Paris and London in the Eighteenth Century* (New York: Viking Press, 1973), pp. 82–95.

62. The nature of the French economic crisis of 1788–9 will be discussed in Chapter 3.

63. George Rudé, *The Crowd in the French Revolution* (New York: Oxford University Press, 1959), chapters 4, 12, and 13.

64. For general background see: Mark Elvin, *The Pattern of the Chinese Past* (Stanford: Stanford University Press, 1973); and Wolfram Eberhard, *A History of China,* 3rd ed. (Berkeley: University of California Press, 1969).

65. Frederic Wakeman, Jr., "High Ch'ing: 1683–1839," in *Modern East Asia: Essays in Interpretation,* ed. James B. Crowley (New York: Harcourt, Brace and World, 1970), pp. 4–5.

66. Albert Feuerwerker, *The Chinese Economy, ca. 1870–1911,* Michigan Papers in Chinese Studies, no. 5 (Ann Arbor: Center for Chinese Studies, University of Michigan, 1969), p. 15. Actually 80 percent is probably a minimal estimate for the proportion of peasants in the pre-1911 Chinese population.

67. Background for this paragraph and the preceding one comes from: Dwight H. Perkins, *Agricultural Development in China, 1368–1968* (Chicago: Aldine, 1969); John Lossing Buck, *Chinese Farm Economy* (Chicago: University of Chicago Press, 1930); and R. H. Tawney, *Land and Labour in China* (1932; reprinted, Boston: Beacon Press, 1966).

68. Perkins, *Agricultural Development,* p. 115. The facts on trade reported in this paragraph come from chapter 6 of Perkins's book.

69. Ibid., p. 172.

70. G. William Skinner, "Marketing and Social Structure in Rural China (Part I)," *The Journal of Asian Studies* 24:1 (November 1964), p. 32.

71. Gilbert Rozman, *Urban Networks in Ch'ing China and Tokugawa Japan* (Princeton, N.J.: Princeton University Press, 1973), p. 82.

72. Perkins, *Agricultural Development,* p. 184.

73. Franz Michael, "State and Society in Nineteenth-Century China," in *Modern China,* ed. Albert Feuerwerker (Englewood Cliffs, N.J.: Prentice-Hall, 1964), p. 58.

74. Quote from Robert C. North and Ithiel de Sola Pool, "Kuomintang and Chinese Communist Elites," in *World Revolutionary Elites,* eds. Harold D. Lasswell and Daniel Lerner (Cambridge: MIT Press, 1966), p. 320.

75. Chung-li Chang, *The Chinese Gentry* (Seattle: University of Washington Press, 1955), pt. 2.

76. Ping-ti Ho, *The Ladder of Success in Imperial China* (New York: Columbia University Press, 1962).

77. Wakeman, "High Ch'ing," in *Modern East Asia,* ed. Crowley, pp. 12–15; and Chang, *The Chinese Gentry,* pt. 3.

78. Chang, *The Chinese Gentry,* pt. 1. Wealthy Chinese, like wealthy Frenchmen, could buy their way into government offices. In China, this involved purchasing Confucian degrees as well as honorific or active government posts. However, even though this "purchase system" expanded considerably in mid-nineteenth century China (when the dynasty was under stress and desperate for revenues), it never became the *dominant* mode of entry into government service, as

was the system of venality of office in absolutist France. (See Chang, *The Chinese Gentry*, pt. 2, esp. pp. 138–41).

79. Michael, "State and Society," in *Modern China*, ed. Feuerwerker, p. 66.

80. Chang, *The Chinese Gentry*, pt. 1.

81. Michael, "State and Society," in *Modern China*, ed. Feuerwerker, p. 58.

82. In addition to the citations in notes 80 and 81, see: T'ung-tsu Ch'ü, *Local Government in China Under the Ch'ing* (Cambridge: Harvard University Press, 1962), chap. 10; and Yuji Muramatsu, "A Documentary Study of Chinese Landlordism in Late Ch'ing and Early Republican Kiagnan," *Bulletin of the School of Oriental and African Studies* 29:3 (1966): 566–99.

83. Chang, *Income of the Chinese Gentry*; Michael, "State and Society," in *Modern China*, ed. Feuerwerker; and Perkins, *Agricultural Development*. Perkins notes: "Because the rate of return on land was low, most landlords made their fortunes outside of agriculture and held land as an easily marketable asset and a source of prestige" (p. 184). Office holding and commerce were the chief loci of fortune building.

84. Scholars who take basically this position include Chang Chung-li, Franz Michael, and Mary C. Wright.

85. Scholars who take basically this position include William Skinner, Philip Kuhn, Fei Hsiao-tung, and John King Fairbank.

86. Frederic Wakeman nicely conveys how marginal gentry could share the power of core gentry is his essay "High Ch'ing," in Crowley, ed., *Modern East Asia*, pp. 12–15.

87. Background for this paragraph comes from: John K. Fairbank, Edwin O. Reischauer, and Albert M. Craig, *East Asia: Tradition and Transformation* (Boston: Houghton Mifflin, 1973), chaps. 9, 16, and 19–21; and Frederic Wakeman, Jr., *The Fall of Imperial China* (New York: Free Press, 1975), chaps. 7–9. See also Frances V. Moulder, *Japan, China and the Modern World Economy* (Cambridge: Cambridge University Press, 1977), chap. 4.

88. Fairbank, Reischauer, and Craig, *East Asia*, p. 625.

89. For comparative-historical evidence on this point see: Alexander Gerschenkron, *Economic Backwardness in Historical Perspective* (Cambridge: Harvard University Press, 1962); David S. Landes, "Japan and Europe: Contrasts in Industrialization," in *The State and Economic Enterprise in Japan*, ed. William W. Lockwood (Princeton, N.J.: Princeton University Press, 1965); and Barry Supple, "The State and the Industrial Revolution, 1700–1914," in *The Industrial Revolution*, ed. Carlo M. Cipolla, The Fontana Economic History of Europe, vol. 3 (London: Collins/Fontana, 1973), pp. 301–57.

90. Perkins, *Agricultural Development*.

91. Ibid.; Elvin, *Pattern of Chinese Past*, chap. 17; and Feuerwerker, *Chinese Economy, ca. 1870–1911*, chaps. 1–3.

92. This paragraph is based upon: Yeh-chien Wang, *Land Taxation in Imperial China, 1750–1911* (Cambridge: Harvard University Press, 1973); and Feuerwerker, *Chinese Economy, ca. 1870–1911*, chap. 5.

93. Feuerwerker, *Chinese Economy, ca. 1870–1911*, p. 64.

94. Wakeman, *Fall of Imperial China*, pp. 105–6.

95. An excellent brief survey is provided by Albert Feuerwerker, *Rebellion in Nineteenth-Century China*, Michigan Papers in Chinese Studies, no. 21 (Ann Arbor: Center for Chinese Studies, University of Michigan, 1975).

96. On the Taiping Rebellion, see especially: Yu-wen Jen, *The Taiping Revolutionary Movement* (New Haven: Yale University Press, 1973); Philip A. Kuhn, *Rebellion and Its Enemies in Late Imperial China* (Cambridge: Harvard University Press, 1970); Vincent Y. C. Shih, *The Taiping Ideology: Its Sources, Interpretations, and Influences* (Seattle: University of Washington Press, 1967); and Frederic Wakeman, Jr., *Strangers at the Gate: Social Disorder in South China, 1839–1861* (Berkeley: University of California Press, 1966).

97. Mary C. Wright, *The Last Stand of Chinese Conservatism: The T'ung-Chih Restoration, 1862–1874* (Stanford: Stanford University Press, 1957).

98. Kuhn, *Rebellion and Its Enemies,* especially pts. III and IV.

99. Ibid., pt. VI.B.; Feuerwerker, *Rebellion,* chap. 5; and Stanley Spector, *Li Hung-chang and the Huai Army: A Study in Nineteenth-Century Chinese Regionalism* (Seattle: University of Washington Press, 1964).

100. These figures and this paragraph as a whole are based upon Feuerwerker, *Chinese Economy, ca. 1870–1911*, pp. 64–72.

101. Ibid., p. 63.

102. Feuerwerker, *China's Early Industrialization*, pp. 12–16; and Ralph L. Powell, *The Rise of Chinese Military Power, 1895–1912* (Princeton, N.J.: Princeton University Press, 1955), chaps. 1 and 2.

103. See, for example, John L. Rawlinson, "China's Failure to Coordinate her Modern Fleets in the Late Nineteenth Century," in *Approaches to Modern Chinese History,* eds. Albert Feuerwerker, Rhoads Murphey, and Mary C. Wright (Berkeley: University of California Press, 1967), pp. 105–32.

104. Wakeman, *Fall of Imperial China*, chap. 10.

105. Ibid.; Fairbank, Reischauer, and Craig, *East Asia*, pp. 726–37; and Mary C. Wright, ed., *China in Revolution: The First Phase, 1900–1913* (New Haven: Yale University Press, 1968), intro.

106. Wright, ed., *China in Revolution*, p. 50.

107. See, for example: Mary Backus Rankin, *Early Chinese Revolutionaries: Radical Intellectuals in Shanghai and Chekiang, 1902–1911* (Cambridge: Harvard University Press, 1971).

108. Yoshihiro Hatano, "The New Armies," in *China in Revolution,* ed. Wright, pp. 365–82; and Powell, *Rise of Military Power.*

109. John Fincher, "Political Provincialism and the National Revolution," in *China in Revolution,* ed. Wright, pp. 185–226.

110. P'eng-yüan Chang, "The Constitutionalists," in *China in Revolution,* ed. Wright, pp. 143–84.

111. Ernest P. Young, "Nationalism, Reform, and Republican Revolution: China in the Early Twentieth Century," in *Modern East Asia: Essays in Interpretation,* ed. James B. Crowley (New York: Harcourt, Brace and World, 1970), p. 166. Background for this paragraph comes from: Ibid.; Chang, "The Constitutionalists," in *China in Revolution,* ed. Wright; Chuzo Ichiko, "The Role of the Gentry: an Hypothesis," in *China in Revolution,* ed. Wright, pp. 297–318;

and Edward J. Rhoads, *China's Republican Revolution, The Case of Kwangtung, 1895–1913* (Cambridge: Harvard University Press, 1975), esp. chaps. 6–9.

112. Fairbank, Reischauer, and Craig, *East Asia,* pp. 738–9.

113. Wright, ed., *China in Revolution,* p. 50.

114. Fairbank, Reischauer, and Craig, *East Asia,* p. 748; and Vidya Prakash Dutt, "The First Week of Revolution: the Wuchang Uprising," in *China in Revolution,* ed. Wright, pp. 383–416.

115. John K. Fairbank, *The United States and China,* 3rd ed. (Cambridge: Harvard University Press, 1971), p. 192.

116. On the aftermath of 1911, see: Young, "Nationalism, Reform, and Republican Revolution," in *Modern East Asia,* ed. Crowley, pp. 171–75; Wakeman, *Fall of Imperial China,* pp. 248–55; and C. Martin Wilbur, "Military Separation and the Process of Reunification under the Nationalist Regime, 1922–1937," in *China in Crisis,* eds. Ping-ti Ho and Tang Tsou (Chicago: University of Chicago Press, 1968), vol. 1, bk. 1, pp. 203–63. The arguments of this paragraph will be further developed in Chapter 7.

117. Background on Imperial Russia comes especially from: Marc Raeff, *Imperial Russia, 1682–1825* (New York: Alfred A. Knopf, 1971), chaps. 1–3. On the entire sweep of old-regime history, see Richard Pipes, *Russia Under the Old Regime* (New York: Scribner, 1974).

118. Ludwig Dehio, *The Precarious Balance: Four Centuries of the European Power Struggle,* trans. Charles Fullman (New York: Vintage Books, 1962), p. 96.

119. Thomas Esper, "Military Self-Sufficiency and Weapons Technology in Muscovite Russia," *Slavic Review* 28:2 (June 1969), p. 208.

120. My estimate for percentage of urban population represents Jerome Blum's figure in his *Lord and Peasant in Russia: From the Ninth to the Nineteenth Century* (Princeton, N.J.: Princeton University Press, 1961), p. 326, adjusted upward to reconcile with a somewhat lower figure for total population taken from Gilbert Rozman, *Urban Networks in Russia, 1750–1800* (Princeton, N.J.: Princeton University Press), pp. 98–9. I have used Rozman's population figures because they appear to be based on more recent and careful scholarship.

121. See: Blum, *Lord and Peasant,* chap. 20; Geroid Tanquary Robinson, *Rural Russia Under the Old Regime* (1932; reprint ed., Berkeley: University of California Press, 1969), chaps. 3 and 4; and Peter I. Lyashchenko, *History of the National Economy of Russia,* trans. L. M. Herman (New York: Macmillan, 1949), chap. 17.

122. Blum, *Lord and Peasant,* p. 329.

123. Ibid., p. 330.

124. Rozman, *Urban Networks in Russia,* pp. 98–9; also see my comments in footnote 120.

125. Blum, *Lord and Peasant,* chap. 15.

126. Cyril E. Black, et al., *The Modernization of Japan and Russia* (New York: Free Press, 1975), p. 76. See also: Lyashchenko, *History of National Economy,* chaps. 15–20.

127. Alexander Baykov, "The Economic Development of Russia," *Economic History Review* 2nd series 7:2 (1954): 137–49.

128. Roderick E. McGrew, "Some Imperatives of Russian Foreign Policy," in *Russia Under the Last Tsar,* ed. Theofanis George Stavrou (Minneapolis, Minn.: University of Minnesota Press, 1969) pp. 202–29.

129. Sergei Pushkarev, *The Emergence of Modern Russia, 1801–1917,* trans. Robert H. McNeal and Tova Yedlin (New York: Holt, Rinehart and Winston, 1963), p. 121.

130. Hugh Seton-Watson, *The Russian Empire, 1801–1917* (New York: Oxford University Press, 1967), p. 331.

131. Alexander Gerschenkron, "Russian Agrarian Policies and Industrialization, 1861–1917," in *Continuity in History and Other Essays* (Cambridge: Harvard University Press, 1968), p. 143.

132. On the reforms in general, see Seton-Watson, *Russian Empire,* chap. 10. On the reforms in local government and their limitations, see S. Frederick Starr, *Decentralization and Self-Government in Russia, 1830–1870* (Princeton, N.J.: Princeton University Press, 1972), pts. III–VI.

133. See the arguments of Gerschenkron in "Agrarian Policies" in *Continuity in History.* I have relied heavily on this article.

134. Quoted from an 1856 speech by Alexander II in Lazar Volin, *A Century of Russian Agriculture* (Cambridge: Harvard University Press, 1970), p. 40.

135. Terence Emmons, *The Russian Landed Gentry and the Peasant Emancipation of 1861* (Cambridge: Cambridge University Press, 1968).

136. This paragraph is based especially upon Pipes, *Old Regime,* chaps. 2–4 and 7.

137. Blum, *Lord and Peasant,* chaps. 8–14; and Richard Hellie, *Enserfment and Military Change in Muscovy* (Chicago: University of Chicago Press, 1971).

138. Raeff, *Origins,* p. 50.

139. Ibid., p. 119.

140. My interpretation of the situation of the Imperial Russian nobility relies heavily upon Marc Raeff, *Imperial Russia,* chaps. 3–5, and *Origins of the Russian Intelligentsia: The Eighteenth-Century Nobility* (New York: Harcourt, Brace and World, 1966). Unlike other writers (Blum for example) Raeff does *not* believe that noble class power vis-à-vis autocracy expanded significantly during the eighteenth century.

141. Raeff, *Imperial Russia,* p. 96; and Blum, *Lord and Peasant,* pp. 368–9, and chap. 19 generally.

142. Blum, *Lord and Peasant,* p. 380.

143. Raeff, *Imperial Russia,* chap. 3.

144. Walter M. Pintner, "The Social Characteristics of the Early Nineteenth-Century Russian Bureaucracy," *Slavic Review* 29:3 (September 1970), p. 442.

145. Ibid., pp. 438–9.

146. In his book *The Russian Landed Gentry and the Peasant Emancipation of 1861,* Terence Emmons stresses the extent to which the gentry *did* exert collective political influence during the 1860s. But by Emmons's own account, the original impetuses, both for reforms and for encouraging gentry involvement, came from the tsarist state. And, in the end, liberal and reactionary gentry groups alike

failed to achieve any aspects of their political programs that were at variance with tsarist interests or programs. I believe that all of the evidence Emmons presents accords with the formulations I have offered here; my differences in interpretive emphasis are due to the fact that I am discussing Russia from a *comparative* perspective.

147. Gerschenkron, "Agrarian Policies," in *Continuity in History,* pp. 140–7 and 159–65.

148. Ibid., pp. 165–74.

149. On the terms of the Emancipation and its consequences, see: Ibid.; Volin, *Century,* chaps. 2–3; and Robinson, *Rural Russia,* chaps. 5–8.

150. See the citations in note 132; and Alexander Vucinich, "The State and the Local Community," in *The Transformation of Russian Society,* ed. Cyril E. Black, pp. 191–208 (Cambridge: Harvard University Press, 1960).

151. George Barr Carson, Jr., "The State and Economic Development: Russia, 1890–1939," in *The State and Economic Growth,* ed. Hugh S. J. Aitken (New York: Social Science Research Council, 1959), p. 117.

152. Seton-Watson, *Russian Empire,* p. 407; on railroads, see pp. 405–6.

153. Carson, "State and Economic Development," in *State and Economic Growth,* ed. Aitken, pp. 117–18; and Theodore H. Von Laue, *Sergei Witte and the Industrialization of Russia* (New York: Columbia University Press, 1963), chap. 1.

154. Von Laue, *Sergei Witte,* pp. 2–3.

155. Ibid., chap. 3.

156. The facts and assessments presented in this paragraph are taken from: Von Laue, *Sergei Witte,* chap. 8; Carson, "State and Economic Development," in *State and Economic Growth,* ed. Aitken, pp. 118–27; and Alexander Gerschenkron, "Problems and Patterns of Russian Economic Development," in *The Transformation of Russian Society,* ed. Cyril E. Black (Cambridge: Harvard University Press, 1960), pp. 47–61.

157. Arthur Mendel, "On Interpreting the Fate of Imperial Russia," in *Russia Under the Last Tsar,* ed. Theofanis George Stavrou (Minneapolis, Minn.: University of Minnesota Press, 1969), pp. 20–1.

158. An excellent review essay on the late Imperial Russian proletariat is Reginald Zelnik, "Russian Workers and the Revolutionary Movement," *Journal of Social History* 6 (Winter 1971–72): 214–34. Other sources on the proletariat include: Leopold Haimson, "The Problem of Social Stability in Urban Russia, 1905–1917," *Slavic Review* 23:4 (December 1964): 619–42 and 24:1 (March 1965): 1–21; Arthur P. Mendel, "Peasant and Worker on the Eve of the First World War," *Slavic Review* 24:1 (March 1965): 23–33; Gaston W. Rimlinger, "Autocracy and the Factory Order in Early Russian Industrialization," *Journal of Economic History* 20:1 (March 1960): 67–92; Theodore H. Von Laue, "Russian Labor Between Field and Factory, 1892–1903," *California Slavic Studies* 3 (1964): 33–65; and Allan K. Wildman, *The Making of a Workers' Revolution: Russian Social Democracy, 1891–1903* (Chicago: University of Chicago Press, 1967).

159. John P. Sontag, "Tsarist Debts and Tsarist Foreign Policy," *Slavic Review* 27:4 (December 1968): pp. 530–1.

160. Seton-Watson, *Russian Empire,* p. 531.

161. Ibid., p. 530.

162. Sontag, "Tsarist Debts," p. 533.

163. Carson, "State and Economic Development," in *State and Economic Growth,* ed. Aitken, pp. 130–31.

164. Lyashchenko, *History of National Economy,* pp. 647–61.

165. Mendel, "Interpreting the Fate," in *Russia Under Last Tsar,* ed. Stavrou, p. 21.

166. Sontag, "Tsarist Debts," p. 534.

167. Ibid.; and McGrew, "Some Imperatives," in *Russia Under Last Tsar,* ed. Stavrou.

168. McGrew, "Some Imperatives," in *Russia Under Last Tsar,* ed. Stavrou, p. 228.

169. Raymond W. Goldsmith, "The Economic Growth of Tsarist Russia, 1860–1913," *Economic Development and Cultural Change* 9:3 (April 1961), p. 443.

170. Ibid., pp. 474–5.

171. Ibid., p. 443.

172. Theodore H. Von Laue, "The State and the Economy," in *The Transformation of Russian Society,* ed. Cyril E. Black (Cambridge: Harvard University Press, 1960), pp. 209–23.

173. Theodore H. Von Laue, *Why Lenin?, Why Stalin?* 2nd ed. (Philadelphia: Lippincott, 1971), p. 60. Von Laue notes: "In this respect the position of Russia was unique in modern world history. No other country among those classified as backward—neither nineteenth-century Japan, nor China, nor India, not to mention the lesser ones now protected by the stalemate between the USSR and the USA—has had to bear the burden of such an extreme exposure" (p. 60, footnote).

174. Isaac Deutscher, "The Russian Revolution," in *The New Cambridge Modern History,* 2nd ed. (Cambridge: Cambridge University Press, 1968), vol. 12, p. 403.

175. My account of 1905 follows William Henry Chamberlin, *The Russian Revolution, 1917–1921,* 2 vols. (1935; paperbound reprint ed., New York: Grosset & Dunlap, 1965), vol. 1, chap. 3.

176. Katherine Chorley, *Armies and the Art of Revolution* (1943; reprint ed., Boston: Beacon Press, 1973), pp. 118–119, and chap. 6 generally.

177. Chamberlin, *Russian Revolution.* vol. 1, p. 51.

178. Von Laue, *Why Lenin?, Why Stalin?,* p. 52.

179. McGrew, "Some Imperatives," in *Russia Under Last Tsar,* ed. Stavrou, p. 218.

180. Nicholas N. Golovine, *The Russian Army in the World War* (New Haven: Yale University Press, 1931), pp. 32, 39, 126, 160.

181. Chorley, *Armies,* chap. 6.

182. Golovine, *Russian Army,* pp. 34–6.

183. Pushkarev, *Emergence of Modern Russia,* p. 393.

184. Ibid., pp. 394–403. This and the following paragraphs on the roles of the upper and middle classes in 1914–1916 are based mainly on Pushkarev's excellent and detailed account.

185. Ibid., p. 400.

186. Chamberlin, *Russian Revolution,* vol. 1, p. 73.

187. Marcel Liebman, *The Russian Revolution,* trans. Arnold J. Pomerans (New York: Vintage Books, 1972), p. 107. Liebman writes: "On February 28th . . . Tsarism was quite dead, but still the Tsar clung to his crown . . . When his hopeless situation was finally brought home to him, he ordered a number of front-line regiments into Petrograd. Unfortunately for him the army no longer obeyed his orders, and even the supreme command deserted him." However, the officers may have opposed only Nicholas, preferring to keep the monarchy with another tsar. And even if they had tried to attack the capital, it is not fully clear that rebellious railwaymen and soldiers would not have stopped them. This certainly became the situation before long.

188. Chorley, *Armies,* p. 113.

189. Chamberlin, *Russian Revolution,* vol. 1, chap. 4; and Liebman, *Russian Revolution,* chap. 4.

190. Deutscher, "Russian Revolution" in *New Cambridge Modern History,* 2nd ed., vol. 12; and Paul P. Gronsky and Nicholas J. Astrov, *The War and the Russian Government* (New Haven: Yale University Press, 1929), chaps. 4–8, and pp. 122–7.

191. For accounts of the Meiji Restoration see: W. G. Beasley, *The Modern History of Japan* (New York: Praeger, 1963), chaps. 5–8; John K. Fairbank, Edwin O. Reischauer, and Albert M. Craig, *East Asia: Tradition and Transformation* (Boston: Houghton Mifflin, 1973), chaps. 17–18; and John Whitney Hall, *Japan: From Prehistory to Modern Times* (New York: Dell, 1970), chaps. 11–13. On interpretive points, I closely follow Hall.

192. Thomas C. Smith, *The Agrarian Origins of Modern Japan* (Stanford: Stanford University Press, 1959), chap. 11; and Thomas C. Smith, "The Japanese Village in the Seventeenth Century," *Journal of Economic History* 12:1 (Winter 1952): 1–20.

193. Hall, *Japan,* chap. 10; John Whitney Hall, "The Castle Town and Japan's Modern Urbanization," *Far Eastern Quarterly* 15:1 (November 1955): 37–56; and Harumi Befu, "Village Autonomy and Articulation with the State," *Journal of Asian Studies* 25:1 (November 1965): 19–32. Both articles are reprinted in John W. Hall and Marius B. Jansen, eds., *Studies in the Institutional History of Early Modern Japan* (Princeton, N.J.: Princeton University Press, 1968).

194. See: Hall, "Castle Town"; John Whitney Hall, "Foundations of the Modern Japanese Daimyo," *Journal of Asian Studies* 20:3 (May 1961): 317–29; Thomas C. Smith, " 'Merit' as Ideology in the Tokugawa Period," in *Aspects of Social Change in Modern Japan,* ed. R. P. Dore (Princeton, N.J.: Princeton University Press, 1967), pp. 71–90; Thomas C. Smith, "Japan's Aristocratic Revolution," *The Yale Review* 50 (1960–61): 370–83; Marius B. Jansen, "Tokugawa and Modern Japan," *Japan Quarterly* 12:1 (January–March 1965): 27–38; and R. P. Dore, "Talent and the Social Order in Tokugawa Japan," *Past and Present* no. 21 (April 1962): 60–67. The Hall, Jansen, and Dore articles are reprinted in Hall and Jansen, eds., *Studies in Institutional History.*

195. Hall, *Japan,* pp. 266–8.

196. Ibid., p. 269.

197. Hall remarks: "throughout the period of political adjustment which accompanied the abandonment of the *han,* higher authority managed to remain in force so that even the collection of taxes went on uninterrupted" (*Japan,* p. 276).

198. Hall, *Japan,* p. 273.

199. See: Ellen Kay Trimberger, *Revolution From Above: Military Bureaucrats and Development in Japan, Turkey, Egypt, and Peru* (New Brunswick, N.J.: Transaction Books, 1978).

200. Hugh Borton, *Peasant Uprisings in Tokugawa Japan* (1938; reprint ed., New York: Paragon Book Reprint Corporation, 1968), intro., p. 2. Borton is here summarizing the results of research by a Japanese scholar, Aoki Koji.

201. Hall, *Japan,* pp. 279–81. See also: Roger F. Hackett, "The Military: A. Japan" in *Political Modernization in Japan and Turkey,* eds. R. E. Ward and D. A. Rustow (Princeton, N.J.: Princeton University Press, 1964), pp. 328–38.

202. Cyril E. Black et al., *The Modernization of Japan and Russia* (New York: The Free Press, 1975), pp. 81, 179–80, 184–5; and Smith, *Agrarian Origins,* pp. 208–11.

203. David S. Landes, "Japan and Europe: Contrasts in Industrialization," in *The State and Economic Enterprise in Japan,* ed. William W. Lockwood (Princeton, N.J.: Princeton University Press, 1965), pp. 96–7, 163; and Thomas C. Smith, "Pre-Modern Economic Growth: Japan and the West," *Past and Present* no. 60 (August 1973): 127–160.

204. Hans Rosenberg, *Bureaucracy, Aristocracy, and Autocracy: The Prussian Experience, 1660–1815,* paperback ed. (Boston: Beacon Press, 1966), p. 208.

205. Ibid., p. 209.

206. For accounts of the Reform Movement, see: Rosenberg, *Bureaucracy,* chap. 9; Gordon A. Craig, *The Politics of the Prussian Army, 1640–1945* (New York: Oxford University Press, 1955), chap. 2; Hajo Holborn, *A History of Modern Germany, 1648–1840* (New York: Alfred A. Knopf, 1963), chap. 13; and Walter M. Simon, *The Failure of the Prussian Reform Movement, 1807–1819* (Ithaca, N.Y.: Cornell University Press, 1955). My interpretations of controversial points usually follow Rosenberg.

207. Rosenberg, *Bureaucracy,* p. 204.

208. Holborn, *History,* pp. 382–5.

209. See Rosenberg, *Bureaucracy,* chap. 9.

210. Walter L. Dorn, "The Prussian Bureaucracy in the Eighteenth Century," *Political Science Quarterly* 46 (1931), p. 403.

211. Ibid., p. 408.

212. See: Rosenberg, *Bureaucracy,* chap. 1; F. L. Carsten, *The Origins of Prussia* (London: Oxford University Press, 1954), pt. III; A. Goodwin, "Prussia," in *The European Nobility in the Eighteenth Century,* ed. Albert Goodwin, paperback ed. (New York: Harper & Row, 1967), pp. 83–101; and Sidney B. Fay and Klaus Epstein, *The Rise of Brandenburg-Prussia to 1786* (New York: Holt, Rinehart and Winston, 1964).

213. Dorn, "Prussian Bureaucracy," 46 (1931), p. 404.

214. Dorn, "The Prussian Bureaucracy in the Eighteenth Century," *Political Science Quarterly* 46 (1931): 403–23, 47 (1932): 77–94, and 47 (1932): 259–73; and F. L. Carsten, "Prussian Despotism at its Height," *History*, new series 40 (February and June 1955): 42–67.

215. Dorn, "Prussian Bureaucracy," 47 (1932), p. 94.

216. Ibid., p. 262.

217. Rosenberg, *Bureaucracy*, chap. 1; Dorn, "Prussian Bureaucracy"; and Goodwin, "Prussia," in *European Nobility*, ed. Goodwin.

218. Walter L. Dorn, *Competition for Empire, 1740–1763* (New York: Harper & Row, 1963), passim.

219. See especially: Rosenberg, *Bureaucracy*, pp. 218–28; and Craig, *Prussian Army*, chap. 2.

220. See: Ibid.; Landes, "Japan and Europe," in *State and Enterprise*, ed. Lockwood, pp. 157–63; and Tom Kemp, *Industrialization in Nineteenth-Century Europe* (London: Longman, 1969), pp. 85–9, and chap. 4 generally.

221. Of course Prussian agriculture alone does not explain why Imperial Germany was so far ahead of Imperial Russia at the outbreak of World War I. Rather, the significant point for the argument of this chapter is that the divergent consequences of the Russian and Prussian agrarian reforms are explicable in common analytic terms.

3. AGRARIAN STRUCTURES AND PEASANT INSURRECTIONS

1. Barrington Moore, Jr., *Social Origins of Dictatorship and Democracy* (Boston: Beacon Press, 1966), p. 480.

2. Cases like Cuba and Yugoslavia are borderline. In both, peasants did provide logistic support for militarized revolutionary movements, but it is debatable whether such peasant participation constitutes a "class-based revolt from below." However, revolts of urban workers were not important either.

3. Chinese peasant rebellions are further discussed below.

4. This carefully worded sentence represents my way of dealing (for the limited purpose at hand) with the complexities of a lively debate among historians of France about seventeenth-century revolts in particular. The main protagonists are: Boris Porchnev, *Les Soulèvements Populaires en France de 1623 à 1648,* Oeuvres Etrangeres, no. 4 (Paris: Ecole Pratique des Hautes Etudes, VI Section, Centres de Recherches Historiques, 1963), versus Roland Mousnier, *Peasant Uprisings in Seventeenth-Century France, Russia, and China,* trans. Brian Pearce (New York: Harper & Row, 1970), and "Recherches sur les Soulèvements Populaires en France avant la Fronde," *Révue d'Histoire Moderne et Contemporaine* no. 5 (1958): 81–113. See also: Leon Bernard, "French Society and Popular Uprisings under Louis XIV," *French Historical Studies* 3:4 (Fall 1964): 454–74.

5. See Paul Avrich, *Russian Rebels, 1600–1800* (New York: Schocken Books, 1972).

6. A good argument that Chinese peasants acted for concrete rather than ideological goals is to be found in Joel Migdal, *Peasants, Politics, and Revolution* (Princeton, N.J.: Princeton University Press, 1974), chap. 10. I do not agree with Migdal's overall argument as a causal explanation for peasant revolution in

China specifically (for reasons partly given in note 126 below). But his analysis of the process of exchange between the Chinese Communists and the North China peasantry seems excellent to me. I make a similar argument in Chapter 7.

7. Elements of this kind of argument are to be found in Chapter 9, "Peasants and Revolution," of Moore, *Social Origins,* especially pp. 470–1.

8. See: Eric Wolf, *Peasants* (Englewood Cliffs, N.J.: Prentice-Hall, 1966), chap. 1; and Teodor Shanin, ed., *Peasants and Peasant Societies* (Baltimore, Md.: Penguin Books, 1971), p. 15, and passim.

9. Political and/or economic indices as indirect measures of relative deprivation are used, for example, in Ted Robert Gurr, "A Causal Model of Civil Strife: A Comparative Analysis Using New Indices," *American Political Science Review* 27 (1968): 1104–24; and David Snyder and Charles Tilly, "Hardship and Collective Violence in France, 1830 to 1960," *American Sociological Review* 37:5 (October 1972): 520–32. The latter study looks at indices over time in order to better approximate the logic of relative-deprivation arguments; it finds that such arguments do *not* predict patterns of collective violence over time in France.

10. Eric Wolf, *Peasant Wars of the Twentieth Century* (New York: Harper & Row, 1969), p. 290.

11. See, for two examples: Hamza Alavi, "Peasants and Revolution," in *The Socialist Register 1965* (London: The Merlin Press, 1965), pp. 241–77; and Jeffery M. Paige, *Agrarian Revolution* (New York: Free Press, 1975). Alavi is a foremost participant in a debate that has long gone on about whether "poor" or "middle" peasants are inherently more revolutionary – something which, in my view, simply cannot be decided outside of institutional, organizational, and situational contexts. Paige's carefully crafted book carries a purely economic approach even further. It tries to *derive* the social organization and the political propensities of agricultural cultivators and noncultivators alike from the property holdings and income sources of each class. In the detailed exposition of his theory, and even more in his historical case analyses, Paige actually reintroduces all of the important social–structural and political–organizational factors that are needed to make sense of agrarian politics. But his theoretical claims are – mistakenly, in my view – narrowly economic determinist.

12. The most celebrated analyst who was mistaken in this way was Lenin in his views about the Russian peasantry: He saw proletarians versus bourgeois where actually there were remarkably equalitarian peasant communities. (The argument is developed below in the section on Russia). Also, Paige in *Agrarian Revolution* argues that smallholder peasants are *inherently* inclined against common action. In truth, it all depends upon the presence or absence, and exact kind, of community properties and functions, and also upon whether peasant communities are pitted in competition for resources against landlords.

13. These phrases, summing up Marx's views on forces and relations of production, come from Robert Brenner, "Agrarian Class Structure and Economic Development in Pre-industrial Europe," *Past and Present* no. 70 (February 1976), p. 31.

14. Especially useful are: Ibid.; Arthur L. Stinchcombe, "Agricultural Enterprise and Rural Class Relations," in *Class, Status, and Power,* 2nd ed., eds. Reinhard Bendix and Seymour Martin Lipset (New York: Free Press, 1966), pp.

182–90; Wolf, *Peasant Wars;* and Moore, *Social Origins.* More eclectic, but also informative are Henry A. Landsberger, "The Role of Peasant Movements and Revolts in Development," in *Latin American Peasant Movements,* ed. Landsberger (Ithaca, N.Y.: Cornell University Press, 1969), pp. 1–61; and Landsberger, ed., *Rural Protest: Peasant Movements and Social Change* (New York: Barnes & Noble Books, 1973).

15. Stinchcombe especially emphasizes this in "Agricultural Enterprise and Agrarian Class Relations." Paige in *Agrarian Revolution* sharply disagrees, in part for the good reason that (as he argues) smallholders can be divided against one another. But Paige fails to realize that community patterns (in opposition to landlords) have overcome divisions among smallholders in some cases. See my comment in note 12 above.

16. Social-scientific analyses of revolutions almost *never,* as far as I can tell, give sufficient analytic weight to the conjunctural, unfolding interactions of originally separately determined processes. Yet both the causes and the development of revolutions probably have to be understood in this way, which of course means that analyses and explanations must be historically grounded.

17. Norman Hampson, *A Social History of the French Revolution* (Toronto: University of Toronto Press, 1963), p. 82.

18. Georges Lefebvre, "The French Revolution and the Peasants," in *The Economic Origins of the French Revolution,* ed. Ralph W. Greenlaw (Lexington, Mass.: D.C. Heath & Company, 1958), p. 76.

19. I do not mean to imply that the thrust for revolutionary, structural changes came only from the peasantry. Certainly the liberal leaders of the National Assembly had in mind basic political transformations, which would also necessarily have had social implications. But the peasants' revolt provided the primary thrust against seigneurial institutions in the countryside. It also created a crisis situation in which other social and political changes could be quickly put through, at least in principle.

20. Georges Lefebvre, "Répartition de la Propriété et de l'Exploitation Fonçières a la Fin de l'Ancien Régime," in *Etudes sur la Revolution Française* (Paris: Presses Universitaires de France, 1963), pp. 279–306; and Ernest Labrousse, "The Evolution of Peasant Society in France from the Eighteenth Century to the Present," in *French Society and Culture Since the Old Regine,* eds. E. M. Acomb and M. L. Brown, Jr. (New York: Holt, Rinehart and Winston, 1966), pp. 44–6.

21. Pierre Goubert, *The Ancien Régime: French Society, 1600–1750,* trans. Steve Cox (New York: Harper & Row, 1974), p. 102. The details in this paragraph are based on Chapter 6, "Landed Income and Ground Rentiers," especially pp. 122–34.

22. The sources for this paragraph include: Goubert, *Ancien Régime: Society,* chaps. 2, 5; Alun Davies, "The Origins of the French Peasant Revolution of 1789," *History,* new series 49:165 (February 1964): 24–41; and Georges Lefebvre, *The Great Fear of 1789,* trans. Joan White (New York: Pantheon Books, 1973) pt. I.

23. "Agrarian individualism" refers to a situation in which an individual property owner has unencumbered rights to manage a consolidated holding,

free from customary practices such as rights to common grazing or gleaning, etc. See Marc Bloch, "La Lutte pour l'Individualisme Agraire dans la France du XVIIIᵉ-Siècle," *Annales d'Histoire Economique et Sociale* 11:7 (July 1930): 329–81 and 11:8 (October 1930): 511–56.

24. Goubert, *Ancien Régime: Society,* p. 78.

25. Albert Soboul, "The French Rural Community in the Eighteenth and Nineteenth Centuries," *Past and Present* no. 10 (November 1956), p. 82. The remainder of this and the next paragraph draw heavily upon Goubert and Soboul.

26. Soboul, "Rural Community," p. 81.

27. At the end of the Old Regime, the Crown attempted to formalize local government in a way that would favor the richer inhabitants. The Edict of 1787 established in all communities of the *pays d'élection* local governing councils on which the local lord and priest were to sit *ex officio,* joined by three to nine peasants elected by secret ballot from parish assemblies that were to be limited to those who paid ten *livres* in taxes or more. Thus the functions of the general assembly of all community members were reduced. However, when, in 1789, assemblies were convened to draw up the *cahiers* and elect *bailliage* representatives, all taxpayers of age twenty-five or over were eligible to be included. Thus royal policy did not, in the last months before the Revolution, consistently undermine peasant community solidarity.

28. C. E. Labrousse, *La Crise de l'Economie Française à la Fin de l'Ancien Régime et au Début de la Révolution* (Paris: Presses Universitaires de France, 1943).

29. C. E. Labrousse, "The Crisis in the French Economy at the End of the Old Regime," in *The Economic Origins of the French Revolution,* ed. Ralph W. Greenlaw (Lexington, Mass.: Heath, 1958), p. 64. This piece is a translation of a section of the introduction of the much larger work cited in the preceding note.

30. Ibid., p. 66.

31. Ibid., pp. 66–7.

32. See: Louise A. Tilly, "The Food Riot as a Form of Political Conflict in France," *Journal of Interdisciplinary History* 2:1 (Summer 1971): 23–57; and George Rudé, "The Outbreak of the French Revolution," in *Paris and London in the Eighteenth Century* (New York: Viking Press, 1973), pp. 63–81.

33. On the Municipal Revolution, see the discussion and references at the end of the section on France in Chapter 2.

34. Goubert, *Ancien Régime: Society,* p. 14. Drawing on the works of Georges Lefebvre, Goubert (pp. 12–15) identifies three waves of peasant uprisings between 1788 and 1793.

35. See Lefebvre, *Great Fear.* This is a classic work.

36. Goubert, *Ancien Régime: Society,* p. 14.

37. See George V. Taylor, "Revolutionary and Nonrevolutionary Content in the *Cahiers* of 1789: An Interim Report," *French Historical Studies* 7:4 (Fall 1972), pp. 489–91.

38. On this point see Charles Tilly, *The Vendée,* paperback ed. (New York: Wiley, 1967), pp. 164–5, 177.

39. Lefebvre, *Great Fear,* pp. 39–40.

40. Ibid., p. 43.

41. Katherine Chorley, *Armies and the Art of Revolution* (1943; reprint ed., Boston: Beacon Press, 1973), p. 141.

42. Hampson, *Social History,* pp. 76 ff.

43. Emmanuel Le Roy Ladurie, "Révoltes et Contestations Rurales en France de 1675 à 1788," *Annales: Economies, Sociétés, Civilisations* 29:1 (January–February 1974): 6–22.

44. Tilly, *Vendée,* p. 159.

45. Hampson, *Social History,* pp. 251–5.

46. This and the next two paragraphs are based especially upon: Soboul, "Rural Community," pp. 85ff.; and Davies, "Origins of Peasant Revolution," pp. 40–1.

47. See: Soboul, "Rural Community," pp. 91–3; and Albert Soboul, "The Persistence of 'feudalism' in the Rural Society of Nineteenth-Century France," trans. Elborg Forster, in *Rural Society in France: Selections from the Annales: Economies, Sociétés, Civilisations,* eds. Robert Forster and Orest Ranum (Baltimore, Md.: Johns Hopkins University Press, 1977), pp. 50–71.

48. R. R. Palmer, "Georges Lefebvre: The Peasants and the French Revolution," *Journal of Modern History* 31:4 (1959), p. 337.

49. Geroid Tanquary Robinson, *Rural Russia Under the Old Regime* (1932; reprint ed., Berkeley: University of California Press, 1969), p. 33.

50. See Robinson, *Rural Russia,* chaps. 1–2; and Paul Avrich, *Russian Rebels, 1600–1800* (New York: Schocken Books, 1972).

51. Sources for this paragraph include especially: Lazar Volin, *A Century of Russian Agriculture* (Cambridge: Harvard University Press, 1970), chap. 2; Terence Emmons, "The Peasant and the Emancipation," in *The Peasant in Nineteenth Century Russia,* ed. Wayne S. Vucinich (Stanford: Stanford University Press, 1968), pp. 41–71; and Alexander Gerschenkron, "Russia: Agrarian Policies and Industrialization, 1861–1917," in *Continuity in History and Other Essays* (Cambridge: Harvard University Press, 1968), pp. 140–248.

52. "This type of peasant cultivation predominated throughout the empire; for the whole of European Russia approximately three-fourths of all male peasants utilized communally owned land, and about four-fifths of all the allotment land was thus controlled." Only in the Ukraine and other western areas did individual hereditary tenure prevail. Francis M. Watters, "The Peasant and the Village Commune," in *The Peasant in Nineteenth-Century Russia,* ed. Wayne S. Vucinich (Stanford: Stanford University Press, 1968), pp. 146–7.

53. Ibid., pp. 137–8; and Jerome Blum, *Lord and Peasant in Russia* (Princeton, N.J.: Princeton University Press, 1961), chap. 24.

54. Ibid., pp. 138–41, 151–7; and Robinson, *Rural Russia,* chaps. 6–7.

55. For information on regional variations I am drawing especially upon the excellent synthesis of Craig Jenkins in an as yet unpublished M.A. thesis, "Agrarian Class Structure and Peasant Revolution – Russia 1917" (Department of Sociology, State University of New York at Stony Brook, 1974), pp. 47–54. Gerschenkron, "Agrarian Policies," in *Continuity in History* presents a similar picture.

56. This paragraph is based upon: Jenkins, "Agrarian Class Structure," pp. 55–76; Volin, *Century,* chap. 3; Robinson, *Rural Russia,* chaps. 6–8; and Watters, "Peasant and Commune," in *Peasant in Russia,* ed. Vucinich, pp. 147–51.

57. Volin, *Century,* p. 70.

58. Jenkins, "Agrarian Class Structure," p. 52.

59. Ibid., p. 71.

60. This is Jenkins's considered estimate. Jenkins draws especially on the detailed research of Teodor Shanin, *The Awkward Class* (New York: Oxford University Press, 1972), pt. II. Shanin deals with the Marxist belief that economic differentiation within peasant villages was generating a class of rich, independent *kulaks.* He shows that this view was mistaken because researchers such as Lenin failed to take into consideration the effects of different sizes of peasant households. Once the variations in family landholdings that are accounted for by fluctuations in family size are taken into account, then a considerable proportion of the economic differentiation within the ranks of the peasantry is explained. Most of the rest was due, Jenkins argues, not to the growth of a *kulak* stratum, but to the utter impoverishment of those who could no longer produce their own subsistence and were forced to rent out their allotment lands and seek industrial employment.

61. Jenkins, "Agrarian Class Structures," pp. 131–2; and Alexander Vucinich, "The State and the Local Community," in *The Transformation of Russian Society,* ed. Cyril E. Black (Cambridge: Harvard University Press, 1960), pp. 191–4.

62. Volin, *Century,* chap. 3 and p. 95.

63. For a general account of the Revolution of 1905 from the "peasant perspective," see Robinson, *Rural Russia,* chaps. 9–10.

64. Gerschenkron, "Agrarian Policies," in *Continuity in History,* p. 230.

65. Robinson, *Rural Russia,* pp. 152–3; and Maureen Perrie, "The Russian Peasant Movement of 1905–1907: Its Social Composition and Revolutionary Significance," *Past and Present* no. 57 (November 1972): 123–55.

66. Perrie, "1905–1907," p. 127.

67. Robinson, *Rural Russia,* p. 155.

68. Ibid., p. 153.

69. Perrie, "1905–1907," p. 138.

70. Ibid., p. 143.

71. Jenkins, "Agrarian Class Structure," p. 158.

72. Robinson, *Rural Russia,* pp. 225–6.

73. Ibid., p. 227.

74. W. E. Mosse, "Stolypin's Villages," *Slavonic and East European Review* 43:101 (June 1965), p. 273.

75. For overviews of the peasant revolts of 1917, see: William Henry Chamberlin, *The Russian Revolution, 1917–1921,* 2 vols. (1935; reprint ed., New York: Grosset & Dunlap, 1965), vol. 1, chap. 11; and John L. H. Keep, *The Russian Revolution: A Study in Mass Mobilization* (New York: Norton, 1976), pt. III, "The Countryside in Revolt."

76. Chamberlin, *Russian Revolution,* vol. 1, p. 252.

77. On developments in the army see: Marc Ferro, "The Russian Soldier in 1917: Undisciplined, Patriotic, and Revolutionary," *Slavic Review* 30:3 (September 1971): 483–512; and Allan Wildman, "The February Revolution in the Russian Army," *Soviet Studies* 22:1 (July 1970): 3–23.

78. Chamberlin, *Russian Revolution*, vol. 1, pp. 252–3.

79. On the overall accomplishments of the peasant revolts of 1917–18, see (in addition to Chamberlin): Volin, *Century*, chap. 6; Shanin, *Awkward Class*, chap. 8; and Keep, *Russian Revolution*, chaps. 15, 16, 29, 30.

80. Keep, *Russian Revolution*, p. 213.

81. Ibid., p. 414.

82. Shanin is especially pessimistic on this score.

83. Chamberlin, *Russian Revolution*, vol. 1, p. 256.

84. Keep, *Russian Revolution*, pp. 412–13, reports 1919 Soviet statistics that present this picture of the overall distributional effects.

85. Shanin, *Awkward Class*, p. 150.

86. Keep, *Russian Revolution*, chaps. 17–19, 28, provides a valuable account of the interaction between local peasant and national political and administrative organizations.

87. See especially Shanin, *Awkward Class*, pp. 153ff.

88. Quoted in ibid., p. 151.

89. Good historical overviews are to be found in G. E. Aylmer, *The Struggle for the Constitution*, 2nd ed. (London: Blandford Press, 1968); and Christopher Hill, *The Century of Revolution, 1603–1714* (New York: Norton, 1966).

90. Although I do not agree with his interpretations, Brian Manning provides a vivid account of popular mobilization in "The Nobles, the People, and the Constitution," in *Crisis in Europe, 1560–1660* ed. Trevor Aston (New York: Doubleday [Anchor Books], 1967), pp. 261–84; and "The Outbreak of the English Civil War," in *The English Civil War and After,* ed. R. H. Parry (Berkeley: University of California Press, 1970), pp. 1–21.

91. See Valerie Pearl, *London and the Outbreak of the Puritan Revolution* (London: Oxford University Press, 1961).

92. In Chapter 5 I shall discuss the appropriateness of the "bourgeois revolution" label for the French Revolution. For the English Revolution, the label may be appropriate, provided it implies no more than a *political* revolution made by a class with significant capitalist interests. Usually, though, the term carries the added implication that a revolution is made through class struggle and transforms the class structure, and these were *not* features of the seventeenth-century English Revolution.

93. For interpretations of the English Revolution along these lines, see especially Perez Zagorin, "The Social Interpretation of the English Revolution," *Journal of Economic History* 19:3 (September 1959): 376–401; and Lawrence Stone, *The Causes of the English Revolution 1529–1642* (New York: Harper & Row, 1972).

94. The fullest account of the Levellers is H. N. Brailsford, *The Levellers and the English Revolution*, ed. Christopher Hill (Stanford: Stanford University Press, 1961).

95. The one-half approximation comes from F.M.L. Thompson, "The

Social Distribution of Landed Property in England since the Sixteenth Century," *The Economic History Review,* 2nd series 19:3 (1966), p. 513.

96. Robert Brenner, "Agrarian Class Structure and Economic Development in Pre-industrial Europe," *Past and Present* no. 70 (February 1976), p. 62. This entire paragraph is based upon Brenner's synthesis, pp. 61ff. Of course, a classic argument is R. H. Tawney, *The Agrarian Problem in the Sixteenth Century* (1912; reprint ed., New York: Harper & Row, 1967).

97. Thompson, "Social Distribution," pp. 513–17.

98. Ibid.; and Peter Laslett, *The World We Have Lost,* 2nd ed. (New York: Scribner, 1971), chaps. 2–3.

99. Background for this paragraph comes from: Aylmer, *Struggle,* pp. 20–2; Christopher Hill, *Reformation to Industrial Revolution* (Baltimore: Penguin Books, 1969), pt. 2; Ivan Roots, "The Central Government and the Local Community," in *The English Revolution 1600–1660,* ed. E. W. Ives (New York: Harper & Row, 1971), pp. 36–47; and Laslett, *World Lost,* chap. 8.

100. Mildred Campbell, *The English Yeomen Under Elizabeth and the Early Stuarts* (New Haven: Yale University Press, 1942), chap. 9.

101. See Alan Everitt, "The County Community," and D. H. Pennington, "The County Community at War," in *The English Revolution 1600–1660* ed. E. W. Ives (New York: Harper & Row, 1971), pp. 48–63 and 64–75. For a detailed study of one county, see especially Alan M. Everitt, *The Community of Kent and the Great Rebellion, 1640–60* (Bristol, England: Leicester University Press, 1966).

102. For accounts of the German Revolution of 1848–9, see: Hajo Holborn, *A History of Modern Germany, 1840–1945* (New York: Alfred A. Knopf, 1969), chaps. 2 and 3; and Theodore S. Hamerow, *Restoration, Revolution, Reaction* (Princeton, N.J.: Princeton University Press, 1958). I rely on these sources throughout this section.

103. Hamerow, *Restoration,* pp. 124–5. Compare this to Norman Hampson, *A Social History of the French Revolution* (Toronto: University of Toronto Press, 1963), pp. 60–1, 132–3.

104. This theme is central to Hamerow. See also Holborn, *History,* pp. 99–100.

105. No major historian of the French Revolution fails to emphasize this, including Albert Soboul, Georges Lefebvre, Norman Hampson, and Alfred Cobban.

106. S. F. Scott, "The Regeneration of the Line Army during the French Revolution," *Journal of Modern History* 42:3 (September 1970): 307–30; and S. F. Scott, "The French Revolution and the Professionalization of the French Officer Corps, 1789–1793," in *On Military Ideology,* eds. Morris Janowitz and Jacques Van Doorn (Rotterdam, Holland: Rotterdam University Press, 1971), pp. 18–28.

107. Hamerow, *Restoration,* pp. 101–10, and chap. 9; and Holborn, *History,* pp. 58–9.

108. David S. Landes, "Japan and Europe: Contrasts in Industrialization," in *The State and Economic Enterprise in Japan,* ed. William W. Lockwood (Princeton, N.J.: Princeton University Press, 1965), pp. 121–7; J. H. Clapham,

Economic Development of France and Germany, 1815–1914 (1936; reprint ed., Cambridge: Cambridge University Press, 1961), chap. 2; and Hamerow, *Restoration,* chap. 3.

109. Landes, "Japan and Europe," in *State and Enterprise,* ed. Lockwood, p. 121.

110. See the references in note 108.

111. Holborn, *History,* p. 100.

112. Dwight H. Perkins, *Agricultural Development in China, 1368–1968* (Chicago: Aldine, 1969), chap. 5.

113. See the discussion and references in the section on the Chinese gentry in Chapter 2.

114. G. William Skinner, "Chinese Peasants and the Closed Community: An Open and Shut Case," *Comparative Studies in Society and History* 13:3 (July 1971), p. 272. See also: Skinner, "Marketing and Social Structure in Rural China (Part I),"*Journal of Asian Studies* 24:1 (November 1964): 3–43.

115. In addition to Skinner, "Chinese Peasants" and "Marketing," see: Hsiao-tung Fei, "Peasantry and Gentry: An Interpretation of Chinese Social Structure and its Changes," *American Journal of Sociology* 52:1 (July 1946): 1–17; Maurice Freedman, *Lineage Organizations in Southeastern China* (London: University of London, 1965); Morton H. Fried, *The Fabric of Chinese Society* (New York: Praeger, 1953); and Philip A. Kuhn, *Rebellion and Its Enemies in Late Imperial China* (Cambridge: Harvard University Press, 1970).

116. Fei, "Peasantry and Gentry," p. 3.

117. Ibid.; and R. H. Tawney, *Land and Labour in China* (1932; reprint ed., Boston: Beacon Press, 1966), chaps. 2–3. The article by Ramon H. Myers on "Cooperation in Traditional Agriculture and Its Implications for Team Farming in the People's Republic of China" in *China's Modern Economy in Historical Perspective,* ed. Dwight H. Perkins (Stanford: Stanford University Press, 1975), pp. 261–78 does not, despite its title, counter the overall picture presented here. Such "cooperation" as there was among peasants in prerevolutionary China was either organized by landlords or else based on commercial–contractual exchanges among households.

118. Jean Chesneaux, *Peasant Revolts in China, 1840–1949* (New York: Norton, 1973), chap. 1; Kung-chuan Hsiao, *Rural China: Imperial Control in the Nineteenth Century* (Seattle: University of Washington Press, 1967), chaps. 9 and 10; Wolfgang Franke, *A Century of Chinese Revolution 1851–1949,* trans. Stanley Rudman (New York: Harper & Row, 1971), chap. 1; and C. K. Yang, "Some Preliminary Statistical Patterns of Mass Actions in Nineteenth-Century China," in *Conflict and Control in Late Imperial China,* eds. Frederic Wakeman, Jr. and Carolyn Grant (Berkeley: University of California Press, 1975), pp. 174–210.

119. See: Yuji Muramatsu, "Some Themes in Chinese Rebel Ideologies," in *The Confucian Persuasion* ed. Arthur F. Wright (Stanford: Stanford University Press, 1960), pp. 241–67; Vincent Y. C. Shih, "Some Chinese Rebel Ideologies," *T'oung Pao* 44 (1956): 150–226; and C. K. Yang, *Religion in Chinese Society* (Berkeley: University of California Press, 1961), chap. 9.

120. See Vincent Y. C. Shih, *The Taiping Ideology* (Seattle: University of Washington Press, 1967).

121. Chesneaux, *Peasant Revolts*, pp. 16–18. See also Jean Chesneaux, ed., *Popular Movements and Secret Societies in China, 1840–1950* (Stanford: Stanford University Press, 1972).

122. Hsiao, *Rural China*, pp. 433–53; and Yang, "Preliminary Statistical Patterns," in *Conflict and Control*, eds. Wakeman and Grant, pp. 198–204.

123. On gentry in rebellions, see: Franke, *Century*, chap. 1; Etienne Balazs, "Tradition and Revolution in China," in *Chinese Civilization and Bureaucracy*, trans. H. M. Wright (New Haven, Yale University Press, 1964); and, for an exemplary case, Romeyn Taylor, "Social Origins of the Ming Dynasty, 1351–1360," *Monumenta Serica* 22 (1963): 1–78. In *Rebellion and Its Enemies in Late Imperial China*, Philip Kuhn discusses how the inability of the Taipings to win over the gentry in large numbers compromised their chances for consolidating a new dynasty.

124. The concept of "social banditry" has been explicated by E. J. Hobsbawm in his *Primitive Rebels* (New York: Norton, 1965), chap. 2; and in an especially valuable essay called "Social Banditry," in *Rural Protest: Peasant Movements and Social Change*, ed. Henry A. Landsberger (New York: Barnes & Noble Books, 1973), pp. 142–57. In the latter piece, Hobsbawm argues that certain types of agrarian societies, China included, gave rise to a relatively permanent and self-conscious kind of social banditry that Hobsbawm calls *haidukry:* "the haiduks were always there in the mountains, . . . as a recognized nucleus of potential dissidence. Unlike the Robin Hoods, who exist as celebrated individuals or not at all, the haiduks exist as a collective entity . . . " (p. 154). "Haidukry is perhaps the closest that social banditry comes to an organized, conscious movement of potential rebellion . . . " (p. 155).

125. Albert Feuerwerker, *The Chinese Economy, 1912–1949*, Michigan Papers in Chinese Studies, no. 1 (Ann Arbor: University of Michigan, Center for Chinese Studies, 1968); Marie-Claire Bergère, "De la Chine Classique à la Chine Actuelle: Fluctuations Economiques et Révolution," *Annales: Economies, Sociétiés, Civilisations* 24:4 (July-August 1969): 860–75; G. William Skinner, "Marketing and Social Structure in Rural China (Part II)," *Journal of Asian Studies* 24:2 (February 1965): 195–228; and Rhoads Murphey, "The Treaty Ports and China's Modernization," in *The Chinese City Between Two Worlds*, eds. Mark Elvin and G. William Skinner (Stanford: Stanford University Press, 1974) pp. 17–72.

126. Comparative analysts of peasants in revolution typically make the mistake (as I see it) of interpreting the very real economic distress of twentieth-century Chinese peasants as due to the *effects of suddenly intruding Western capitalism.* Both Eric Wolf in *Peasant Wars of the Twentieth Century* (New York: Harper & Row, 1969) and Joel S. Migdal in *Peasants, Politics, and Revolution* (Princeton, N.J.: Princeton University Press, 1974) attempt in this way to assimilate Chinese experience to that of the formerly colonized Third World. What happens is that such observers mistake the long-established ("traditional") commercial openness of late Imperial Chinese villages for something new. They also mistake patterns of disorder and revolt that had long coexisted with established rural sociopolitical structures for an unprecedented breakdown of the old order in the countryside. These mistakes have been all the easier for comparativists to make

because they have, quite naturally, relied on village case studies of places in China where imperialist economic forces *did* penetrate most–for those were also the places, near to major cities and modern transportation, most likely to be studied by social scientists! But China was a huge country and, as the references in the preceding note argue, most of it was *not* transformed by imperialism (or any other force of modern economic development). Above all the places where the Communists ultimately built secure base areas were not so transformed.

127. See: Lucien Bianco, "Les Paysans et la Révolution Chine, 1919–1949," *Politique Etrangère* no. 2 (1968): 117–41; and Chesneaux, *Peasant Revolts,* chaps. 5–8. See also the discussion and references in the section on "The Communists and the Peasants" in Chapter 7.

4. WHAT CHANGED AND HOW:
A FOCUS ON STATE BUILDING

1. Such institutions included the *parlements,* provincial estates, and seigneurial courts and claims in France; the *zemstvos* and landed estates in Russia; and the local clans and associations and the subdistrict, county, and provincial governments in China.

2. My conceptualization of this aspect of the divergences in revolutionary outcomes draws heavily upon Martin King Whyte, "Bureaucracy and Modernization in China: The Maoist Critique," *American Sociological Review* 38:2 (April 1973):149–63. More will be said below in the section on China.

3. Samuel P. Huntington, *Political Order in Changing Societies* (New Haven: Yale University Press, 1968), p. 266.

4. Franz Borkenau, "State and Revolution in the Paris Commune, the Russian Revolution, and the Spanish Civil War," *Sociological Review* 29:41 (1937), p. 41.

5. Alfred Cobban, *Aspects of the French Revolution* (New York: Norton, 1970), pp. 110–11.

6. Norman Hampson, *A Social History of the French Revolution* (Toronto: University of Toronto Press, 1963), pp. 132–3.

7. Cobban, *Aspects,* p. 111.

8. Patrice L. R. Higonnet, "Montagne, Gironde et Plaine: Bourgeoisie Provinciale, Bourgeoisie Urbaine, Bourgeoisie Rurale," unpublished paper (Cambridge: Department of History, Harvard University, n.d.), pp. 14–16.

9. See: Cobban, *Aspects,* p. 111; Crane Brinton, *The Jacobins* (1930; reprint ed., New York: Russell and Russell, 1961), p. 231; and S. F. Scott, "The French Revolution and the Professionalization of the French Officer Corps," in *On Military Ideology,* eds. Morris Janowitz and Jacques Van Doorn (Rotterdam, Holland: Rotterdam University Press, 1971), pp. 28–50.

10. On the Bolsheviks, see: David Lane, *The Roots of Russian Communism* (University Park, Penn.: Pennsylvania State University Press, 1975), pp. 21–4, 32; and Jerome Davis, "A Study of One Hundred and Sixty-three Outstanding Communist Leaders," *American Sociological Society Publications,* vol. 24, *Studies in Quantitative and Cultural Sociology* (1929), p. 48. On the Chinese Communists, see: Robert C. North and Ithiel de Sola Pool, "Kuomintang and

Chinese Communist Elites," in *World Revolutionary Elites,* eds. Harold D. Lasswell and Daniel Lerner (Cambridge: MIT Press, 1966), pp. 376–9.

11. Lane, *Roots,* p. 27; Davis, "Study," pp. 48–9; North and Pool, "Elites," in *World Revolutionary Elites,* eds. Lasswell and Lerner, pp. 381–2.

12. For background on student conversions to critical perspectives and radical politics, see: George Fischer, "The Intelligentsia and Russia," in *The Transformation of Russian Society,* ed. Cyril E. Black (Cambridge: Harvard University Press, 1960), pp. 263–7; Martin Malia, "What Is the Intelligentsia?," Richard Pipes, "The Historical Evolution of the Russian Intelligentsia," and Benjamin Schwartz, "The Intelligentsia in Communist China: A Tentative Comparison," all in *The Russian Intelligentsia,* ed. Richard Pipes (New York: Columbia University Press, 1961); and John Israel, "Reflections on the Modern Chinese Student Movement," *Daedalus* (Winter 1968):229–53.

13. See: Lane, *Roots,* pp. 20–32; and North and Pool, "Elites," in *World Revolutionary Elites,* eds. Lasswell and Lerner, pp. 376–82.

14. Lane, *Roots,* pp. 32, 39–46.

15. North and Pool, "Elites," in *World Revolutionary Elites,* Lasswell and Lerner, eds., pp. 393–404.

16. Higonnet, "Montagne, Gironde, et Plaine," pp. 14–16. The tension between the commercial port cities of France and the absolute monarchy is a major theme in Edward Whiting Fox, *History in Geographic Perspective: The Other France* (New York: Norton, 1972).

17. On the generation of surplus aspirants in France during the eighteenth century (after the seventeenth-century consolidation of Bourbon absolutism) see Colin Lucas, "Nobles, Bourgeois and the Origins of the French Revolution," *Past and Present* no. 60 (August 1973):84–126.

18. Fox, *Other France,* p. 90. See also C.B.A. Behrens, *The Ancien Regime* (London: Harcourt, Brace, and World, 1967), pts. III–IV.

19. Countless historical analyses of the Russian Revolution focus mainly upon the ideology and organization of the Bolshevik Party. Franz Schurmann's *Ideology and Organization in Communist China,* 2nd ed. (Berkeley: University of California Press, 1968) does a very sophisticated job of analyzing the Chinese revolutionary outcomes in terms of Chinese Communist ideology. In French Revolution historiography some analysts have always emphasized the Enlightenment ideals of radical political elites rather than the interests of the bourgeoisie as a class. And, of course, the stress on ideological orientations is found in more general theories of revolution, such as especially the systems/value–consensus theories and the Gramscian variety of Marxist–Leninist theory.

20. On "Jacobinism" as a revolutionary movement, see Brinton, *Jacobins,* especially chaps. 2, 4, 5–7.

21 See the discussion and references in the section on Japan in Chapter 2.

22. Egon Bittner, "Radicalism and the Organization of Radical Movements," *American Sociological Review* 28 (1963):928–40.

23. Of course it almost certainly is true that general idea systems— that is, the Enlightenment, including Rousseau's philosophy; and the social-historical theories of Karl Marx—had to be historically available to the revolutionary

leaders of the French, Russian, and Chinese Revolutions. Arguably, these idea systems provided indispensable general orientations—for example, toward all-encompassing end-states for society or history, relevant for universal-democratic reference groups such as "the people" or "the proletariat." Such broad orientations could then be combined during the revolutionary crises with goals, models, and strategies and tactics more specifically suited to the concrete and changing political circumstances to which revolutionary elites had to adapt in order to succeed in building new revolutionary state organizations. From this perspective, though, the interesting questions about the influence of the relevant general-idea systems in the French, Russian, and Chinese Revolutions become questions about exactly how revolutionary leaderships adapted and specified these general-idea systems. Thus we need to inquire about the particular social and historical circumstances to which these leaders were responding as they created and transformed their revolutionary ideologies. For one particularly good study along these lines, see: Maurice Meisner, *Li Ta-chao and the Origins of Chinese Marxism* (New York: Atheneum, 1973).

24. See: M. J. Sydenham, *The French Revolution* (New York: Capricorn Books, 1966), chaps. 7–8.

25. See: Barrington Moore, Jr., *Soviet Politics—The Dilemma of Power* (New York: Harper & Row, 1965); Arthur Rosenberg, *A History of Bolshevism* (New York: Oxford University Press, 1934); and Robert Vincent Daniels, *The Conscience of the Revolution* (Cambridge: Harvard University Press, 1960).

26. See: Stuart R. Schram, *The Political Thought of Mao Tse-tung*, rev. and enlarged ed. (New York: Praeger, 1969), esp. the intro.; and Roland Lew, "Maoism and the Chinese Revolution," *The Socialist Register 1975* (London: Merlin Press, 1975):115–59.

5. THE BIRTH OF A "MODERN STATE EDIFICE" IN FRANCE

1. For a short, concise statement of an undiluted "bourgeois revolution" interpretation, see especially Albert Soboul, "Classes and Class Struggles During the French Revolution," *Science and Society* 17:5 (Summer 1953):238–57. For hard-hitting (and, by now, very well known) criticisms of this sort of interpretation, see: Alfred Cobban, *The Social Interpretation of the French Revolution* (Cambridge: Cambridge University Press, 1964); and Cobban, "The Myth of the French Revolution," in *Aspects of the French Revolution* (New York: Norton, 1970), pp. 90–111.

2. See Gerald J. Cavanaugh, "The Present State of French Revolutionary Historiography: Alfred Cobban and Beyond," *French Historical Studies* 7:4 (Fall 1972):587–606.

3. For example, Norman Hampson has aptly suggested that Alfred Cobban's conclusions point toward "a non-Marxist economic interpretation of the Revolution." Consider this passage from Cobban's *Social Interpretation*: "It was not wholly a revolution for, but largely, one against, the penetration of an embryo capitalism into French society. Considered as such, it largely achieved its ends. The peasant proprietors in the country, and the lawyers, *rentiers* and men of property

in the towns, successfully resisted the new economic trends. The latter, in particular, took control of the revolution and consolidated their regime by the dictatorship of Napoleon" (p. 172).

4. Perhaps the most important example – and culmination – of this strategy is Norman Hampson's *A Social History of the French Revolution* (Toronto: University of Toronto Press, 1963). But the trend was started by Georges Lefebvre's magisterial *The French Revolution,* 2 vols., trans. Elizabeth Moss Evanson (vol. 1) and John Hall Stewart and James Friguglietti (vol. 2) (New York: Columbia University Press, 1962, 1964).

5. Of course, one of the classical interpreters of the French Revolution, Alexis de Tocqueville, placed the state at the center of his analysis in *The Old Regime and the French Revolution,* trans. Stuart Gilbert (New York: Doubleday [Anchor Books], 1955).

6. See: Cavanaugh, "Present State," pp. 599–606; and M. J. Sydenham's *The French Revolution* (New York: Capricorn Books, 1966), in which the author has: "deliberately chosen to reassert the importance of political developments . . . particularly . . . the emergence of the new religion of nationalism and the attempt to reconcile constitutional authority with popular control of power" (p. 5). Even Albert Soboul, especially in his interpretive essay, *A Short History of the French Revolution, 1789–1799* trans. Geoffrey Symcox (Berkeley: University of California Press, 1977), invokes Tocqueville frequently and highlights developments in the state – though his basic theoretical argument of course remains that the French Revolution "marks the advent of bourgeois, capitalist society in French history" (p. 1). For relevant empirical studies, see works cited in the last section of this chapter, on "The New Regime."

7. Cobban, *Social Interpretation,* chaps. 6, 8, 12–14.

8. Ibid., p. 70.

9. David S. Landes, *The Unbound Prometheus* (Cambridge: Cambridge University Press, 1969), pp. 142–3.

10. Walter L. Dorn, *Competition for Empire, 1740–1763* (New York: Harper & Row, 1963), pp. 252–3; and F. Crouzet, "England and France in the Eighteenth Century: A Comparative Analysis of Two Economic Growths," chapter 7 of *The Causes of the Industrial Revolution in England,* ed. R. M. Hartwell (London: Methuen, 1967).

11. Henri Sée, *Economic and Social Conditions in France During the Eighteenth Century,* trans. Edwin H. Zeydel (New York: F. S. Crofts & Co., 1931), p. 154.

12. Tom Kemp, *Economic Forces in French History* (London: Dobson Books, 1971), chaps. 5–6.

13. Ibid., p. 102.

14. Alexander Gerschenkron, "Reflections on Economic Aspects of Revolutions," in *Internal War,* ed. Harry Eckstein (New York: Free Press, 1964), pp. 188–9.

15. Ibid., p. 190. See also: Landes, *Unbound Prometheus,* pp. 142–50; and Kemp, *Economic Forces,* chap. 6.

16. See: Kemp, *Economic Forces;* Jan Marczewski, "Some Aspects of the Economic Growth of France, 1660–1958," *Economic Development and Cul-*

tural Change 9:2 (1961):369–86; Jan Marczewski, "The Take-Off Hypothesis and French Experience," in *The Economics of Take-off into Sustained Growth*, ed. W.W. Rostow (New York: St. Martin's Press, 1963), pp. 119–38; Claude Fohlen, "France 1700–1914," in *The Emergence of Industrial Societies (1)*, ed. Carlo M. Cipolla, The Fontana Economic History of Europe, vol. 4 (London: Collins/Fontana, 1973) pp. 7–75; and Barry Supple, "The State and the Industrial Revolution 1700–1914," in *The Industrial Revolution*, ed. Carlo M. Cipolla, The Fontana Economic History of Europe, vol. 3 (London: Collins, 1973), esp. pp. 327–33.

17. See, for example, Soboul, *Short History*. Also relevant here is the chapter on France in Barrington Moore, Jr., *Social Origins of Dictatorship and Democracy* (Boston: Beacon Press, 1966). Moore downplays the idea that the bourgeoisie led the Revolution (even more than Soboul, who has himself always emphasized that the Revolution was actually pushed along from 1789–1794 by popular revolts). But Moore nevertheless considers the overall result and significance of the Revolution to be the elimination of obstacles to liberalism and democracy. He does not significantly explore the extent to which the Revolution also created or strengthened obstacles to these political forms.

18. Quote from Karl Marx, "The Civil War in France" (1871), reprinted in Karl Marx and Frederick Engels, *Selected Works* (New York: International Publishers, 1968), p. 289.

19. Hampson, *Social History*, pp.112–13.

20. Except that laws mandating equal inheritance by all sons of a family promoted the steady division of property, especially among the peasantry, and this represented something of a drag on capitalist development. See Kemp, *Economic Forces*, pp. 103–4.

21. See: G. E. Aylmer, *The Struggle for the Constitution*, 2nd ed. (London: Blandford Press, 1968), esp. chaps. 1–2; D. Brunton and D. H. Pennington, *Members of the Long Parliament* (London: Allen and Unwin, 1954); and Ivan Roots, "The Central Government and the Local Community" in *The English Revolution, 1600–1660*, ed. E. W. Ives (New York: Harper & Row, 1971).

22. This point is strongly emphasized by Lynn A. Hunt in "Committees and Communes: Local Politics and National Revolution in 1789," *Comparative Studies in Society and History* 19:3 (July 1976): 321–46.

23. Alfred Cobban, "Local Government during the French Revolution," in *Aspects of the French Revolution* (New York: Norton, 1970), p. 118.

24. Ibid., pp. 118–20.

25. Ibid., pp. 121ff.

26. For accounts of August 4th, see: Hampson, *Social History, pp. 78–85;* and Sydenham, *French Revolution*, pp. 51ff.

27. For a particularly vivid incident, set in the context of the continuing peasant unrest into 1791–2, see Georges Lefebvre, "The Murder of the Comte de Dampierre," in *New Perspectives on the French Revolution*, ed. Jeffrey Kaplow (New York: Wiley, 1965), pp. 277–86. See also Hampson, *Social History*, pp. 95–6.

28. On the unrest in the army in 1789–90, see: S. F. Scott, "The

Regeneration of the Line Army during the French Revolution," *Journal of Modern History* 42:3 (September 1970):307–18; and Katherine Chorley, *Armies and the Art of Revolution* (1943; reprint ed., Boston: Beacon Press, 1973), chap. 8.

29. Donald Greer, *The Incidence of the Emigration During the French Revolution* (Cambridge: Harvard University Press, 1951), pp. 21–31.

30. This quote is borrowed from the keynote of Chapter 6 of Hampson's *Social History*, p. 132.

31. François Furet and Denis Richet, *The French Revolution*, trans. Stephen Hardman (New York: Macmillan, 1970), chap. 5.

32. See Geoffrey Bruun, "The Balance of Power During the Wars, 1793–1814," in *The New Cambridge Modern History* (Cambridge: Cambridge University Press, 1965), vol. 9:250–74. Also, for one attempt by a nonhistorian to analyze European international dynamics during the French Revolution, see Kyung-won Kim, *Revolution and International System* (New York: New York University Press, 1970).

33. See Ludwig Dehio, *The Precarious Balance*, trans. Charles Fullman (New York: Vintage Books, 1962), chap. 3.

34. George Rudé, *The Crowd in the French Revolution* (New York: Oxford University Press, 1959), esp. chap. 12.

35. Ibid., esp. chap. 13.

36. This point is particularly well developed by Gwyn A. Williams, *Artisans and Sans-Culottes* (New York: Norton, 1969), chap. 2.

37. See: Ibid., chaps. 2, 3, 5; Rudé, *Crowd;* and Albert Soboul, *The Sans-Culottes: The Popular Movement and the Revolutionary Government, 1793–1794,* trans. Rémy Inglis Hall (New York: Doubleday [Anchor Books], 1972).

38. For an overview of the Montagnard dictatorship, see (aside from general histories of the Revolution): Soboul, *Sans-Culottes;* Richard Cobb, *Les Armées Révolutionnaires,* 2 vols. (Paris: Mouton, 1961–3); and R. R. Palmer, *Twelve Who Ruled* (Princeton, N.J.: Princeton University Press, 1941). I shall draw on these sources throughout the following discussion.

39. Jacques Godechot, "The French Revolution," in *Chapters in Western Civilization,* 3rd ed., 2 vols. (New York: Columbia University Press, 1962), vol. 2, p. 34.

40. Donald Greer, *The Incidence of the Terror During the French Revolution* (Cambridge: Harvard University Press, 1935), p. 124.

41. See Colin Lucas, *The Structure of the Terror* (New York: Oxford University Press, 1973).

42. Quoted in John Ellis, *Armies in Revolution* (New York: Oxford University Press, 1974), p. 97.

43. Sydenham, *French Revolution*, p. 187.

44. Scott, "Regeneration of Line Army."

45. See: Rudé, *Crowd,* chaps. 8–9; Moore, *Social Origins,* pp. 86–92; and Soboul, *Sans-Culottes,* especially pt. II and conclusion. Moore, in particular, emphasizes the agrarian aspect of the Montagnards' economic difficulties.

46. See: Palmer, *Twelve Who Ruled,* chaps. 11–13; and Soboul, *Sans-Culottes,* pts. III–V and conclusion. Soboul is especially excellent on the political contradictions between the popular movement and the Montagnards.

47. See Sydenham, *French Revolution,* chap. 8, "The Republic of Virtue."

48. Rudé, *Crowd,* chap. 10.

49. Clive H. Church, "The Social Basis of the French Central Bureaucracy under the Directory 1795–1799," *Past and Present* no. 36 (April 1967), p. 60.

50. Martyn Lyons, *France Under the Directory* (Cambridge: Cambridge University Press, 1975), p. 173. I have drawn broadly on chapter 11 for this paragraph.

51. See C. H. Church, "In Search of the Directory," in *French Government and Society, 1500–1850,* ed. J. F. Bosher (London: Athlone Press, 1973), pp. 261–94. Church questions the widely accepted idea that the Directory was straightforwardly a "bourgeois" regime, pointing to the tensions between Directorial politicians and the notables whose support they sought without great success. Church's approach pays much attention to the *political* structure and difficulties of the Directory, an emphasis that I find convincing and useful.

52. Lyons, *Directory,* p. 155. See also all of chap. 10.

53. Ibid., p. 154.

54. Jacques Godechot, "The Internal History of France During the Wars, 1793–1814," *The New Cambridge Modern History* (Cambridge: Cambridge University Press, 1965), vol. 9, p. 298.

55. On Napoleon's regime, see: Leo Gershoy, *The French Revolution and Napoleon* (1933; reprint ed., New York: Appleton-Century-Crofts, 1964), pp. 375–81; 451–67; F.M.H. Markham, "Napoleonic France," in *France: Government and Society,* eds. J. M. Wallace-Hadrill and John McManners (London: Methuen, 1957), pp. 188–206; and Franklin L. Ford, *Europe 1780–1830* (London: Longman, 1970), chap. 8.

56. On the difficulties of the Continental System see: Kemp, *Economic Forces,* pp. 96–104; Gershoy, *Revolution and Napoleon,* chap. 17; and Dehio, *Precarious Balance,* pp. 132–80.

57. My discussion of these military developments is synthesized from a number of sources, including most notably: S. F. Scott, "The French Revolution and the Professionalization of the French Officer Corps, 1789–1793," in *On Military Ideology,* eds. Morris Janowitz and Jacques Van Doorn (Rotterdam: Rotterdam University Press, 1971), pp. 5–56; S. F. Scott, "The Regeneration of the Line Army during the French Revolution," *Journal of Modern History* 42:3 (September 1970): 307–30; Ernest Barker, *The Development of Public Services in Western Europe* (New York: Oxford University Press, 1944), chap. 2; Theodore Ropp, *War in the Modern World,* rev. ed. (New York: Collier Books, 1962), chap. 4; Alfred Vagts, *A History of Militarism,* rev. ed. (New York: Free Press, 1959), chap. 4; and John Ellis, *Armies in Revolution* (New York: Oxford University Press, 1974), chap. 4.

58. Scott, "Professionalization," pp. 8–18.

59. On the overall changes wrought by the Revolution in the French officer corps, see Scott, "Professionalization," pp. 18ff.

60. On this point specifically, see Vagts, *History of Militarism,* p. 109.

61. Scott, "Professionalization," pp. 45–7.

62. Barker, *Development of Services,* pp. 42–3.

63. Vagts, *History of Militarism,* p. 111.

64. Quoted in Ropp, *War,* p. 116.

65. Vagts, *History of Militarism,* p. 126.

66. Gordon A. Craig, *The Politics of the Prussian Army, 1640–1945* (New York: Oxford University Press, 1955), p. 27. See also Vagts, *History of Militarism,* chap. 4. Apparently (see Vagts, p. 128) Napoleon was backing off from some of these tactical innovations by the end of his reign. But this does not change the fact that the Revolution made them possible.

67. Barker, *Development of Services,* p. 14.

68. In "Social Mobility" (Summary of Proceedings of a Conference) in *Past and Present* no. 32 (December 1965), p. 8.

69. Ibid.

70. J. F. Bosher, *French Finances, 1790–1795* (Cambridge: Cambridge University Press, 1970), p. 302.

71. Ibid., p. 313.

72. Ibid., p. 305.

73. Ibid., p. 287.

74. Ibid., p. 309.

75. Ibid., pp. 310–11.

76. Ibid., p. 288.

77. Barker, *Development of Services,* p. 14.

78. Napoleon's government is well described in: Godechot, "French Revolution," in *Western Civilization,* vol. 2, pp. 47–51; Gershoy, *Revolution and Napoleon,* pp. 348–59, 451–67; and Ford, *Europe 1780–1830,* pp. 170–88.

79. Herbert Luethy, *France Against Herself,* trans. Eric Mosbacher (New York: Praeger, 1955), pp. 18–20.

80. See Joseph Ben-David and Awraham Zloczower, "Universities and Academic Systems in Modern Societies," *Archives Européennes de Sociologie* 3:1 (1962), esp. pp. 76–80. Here France is grouped with Soviet Russia, in contrast to England and the United States, because of the highly centralized, technocratic, and state-oriented nature of the higher educational systems that emerged from the French and Russian Revolutions.

81. Godechot, "French Revolution," in *Western Civilization,* vol. 2, p. 48.

82. Ford, *Europe 1780–1830,* p. 174.

83. William McNeill, *The Shape of European History* (New York: Oxford University Press, 1974), p. 154.

84. T.J.A. LeGoff and D.M.G. Sutherland, "The Revolution and the Rural Community in Eighteenth-Century Brittany," *Past and Present* no. 62 (February 1974), p. 96. This paragraph draws on the article as a whole.

85. See especially: Paul Bois, *Paysans de l'Ouest* (Le Mans: Imprimerie M. Vilaire, 1960); Marcel Faucheux, *L'Insurrection Vendéenne de 1793* (Paris: Imprimerie Nationale, 1964); and Charles Tilly, *The Vendée* (Cambridge: Harvard University Press, 1964). See also Harvey Mitchell, "The Vendée and Counterrevolution: A Review Essay," *French Historical Studies* 5:4 (Fall 1968):

405–29; and Claude Mazauric, "Vendée et Chouannerie," *La Pensée* no. 124 (November–December 1965):54–85.

86. Le Goff and Sutherland, "Revolution and Rural Community," p. 109.

87. The outcome of the Revolution thus resembled the scheme of local government that the Old Regime had attempted to establish in 1788. See note 27 for Chapter 3.

88. Thomas F. Sheppard, *Lourmarin in the Eighteenth Century: A Study of a French Village* (Baltimore: Johns Hopkins Press, 1971), pp. 217–18. I am taking a bit of poetic license with this quote. Strictly speaking, Loumarin may not have been a "peasant village" as such, but rather a local market town. Moreover, since it was located in Provence, it already had, prior to the Revolution, an oligarchic form of government that deemphasized the role of the general assembly (see: *Loumarin,* chap. 3; and Albert Soboul, "The French Rural Community in the Eighteenth and Nineteenth Centuries," *Past and Present* no. 10 (November 1956), p. 81.). However, this only highlights the significance of the changes Sheppard notes as resulting from the Revolution. And it suggests that the loss of local solidarity and autonomy may have been even greater, by comparison, for rural communities elsewhere in France.

6. THE EMERGENCE OF A DICTATORIAL PARTY-STATE IN RUSSIA

1. The convening of the Estates-General entailed the selection of national political leaders through processes that allowed the participation of all adult, male Frenchmen. Similarly, the widespread municipal revolutions of 1789 brought to power revolutionary committees and militias which, although typically led by substantial figures in the community, nevertheless mobilized and depended upon the support of the popular, small-propertied strata (artisans, shopkeepers, journeymen, clerks, etc.) rather than merely upon the support of the privileged oligarchies that had previously dominated the cities and towns in cooperation with the royal administration. See Lynn A. Hunt, "Committees and Communes: Local Politics and National Revolution in 1789," *Comparative Studies in Society and History* 18:3 (July 1976): 321–46.

2. The "dual power" situation after the February Revolution is well described by Isaac Deutscher in "The Russian Revolution," in *The New Cambridge Modern History,* 2nd ed. (Cambridge: Cambridge University Press, 1968), vol. 12:403–32. See also: Marc Ferro, *The Russian Revolution of February 1917,* trans. J. L. Richards (Englewood Cliffs, N.J.: Prentice-Hall, 1972), chap. 6; and Oskar Anweiler, *The Soviets,* trans. Ruth Hein (New York: Pantheon, 1974), chap. 3.

3. This is how I interpret the evidence presented by Marc Ferro in *February Revolution,* chaps. 3–5.

4. Roger Pethybridge, *The Spread of the Russian Revolution* (London: Macmillan, 1972), chap. 1.

5. See the general argument of Teddy J. Uldricks, "The 'Crowd' in the Russian Revolution: Towards Reassessing the Nature of Revolutionary Leadership," *Politics and Society* 4:3 (1974):397–413.

6. See: William Henry Chamberlin, *The Russian Revolution 1917–1921*, 2 vols. (1935; paperbound reprint ed., New York: Grosset & Dunlap, 1965), vol. 1, chap. 11; and John L. H. Keep, *The Russian Revolution* (New York: Norton, 1976), pt. III.

7. See: Chamberlin: *Russian Revolution*, vol. 1, chap. 12; Paul H. Avrich, "Russian Factory Committees in 1917," *Jahrbücher für Geschichte Osteuropas* 11:2 (June 1963):164–82; and Keep, *Russian Revolution*, chaps. 5–6.

8. Marc Ferro, "The Russian Soldier in 1917: Undisciplined, Patriotic, and Revolutionary," *Slavic Review* 30:3 (September 1971): 483–512; Allan Wildman, "The February Revolution in the Russian Army," *Soviet Studies* 22:1 (July 1970):3–23; and Chamberlin, *Russian Revolution*, chap. 10.

9. Anweiler, *Soviets*, chap. 3.

10. For general background on the problems of governing after February, see: Pethybridge, *Spread;* and Paul R. Gronsky and Nicholas J. Astrov, *The War and the Russian Government* (New Haven: Yale University Press, 1929).

11. Anweiler, *Soviets*, chap. 3; and Keep, *Russian Revolution*, pts. II and III.

12. See the references cited in note 8, plus Alexander Rabinowitch, "The Petrograd Garrison and the Bolshevik Seizure of Power," in *Revolution and Politics in Russia*, eds. Alexander and Janet Rabinowitch (Bloomington, Ind.: Indiana University Press, 1972), pp. 172–91.

13. For a vivid account, see Alexander Rabinowitch, *The Bolsheviks Come to Power: The Revolution of 1917 in Petrograd* (New York: Norton, 1976), chap. 8.

14. See: Katherine Chorley, *Armies and the Art of Revolution* (1943; reprint ed., Boston: Beacon Press, 1973), pp. 195ff; and John Erickson, "The Origins of the Red Army," in *Revolutionary Russia*, ed. Richard Pipes (New York: Doubleday [Anchor Books], 1969), pp. 292–5.

15. See the section on Russia in Chapter 2 for a discussion and references on industrialization under the Old Regime. An overview is also provided in Alec Nove, *An Economic History of the U.S.S.R.* (Baltimore: Penguin Books, 1972), chap. 1.

16. Anweiler, *Soviets*, chap. 4; and Uldricks, "Crowd in Russian Revolution," pp. 410–12.

17. T. H. Rigby, *Communist Party Membership in the U.S.S.R., 1917–1967* (Princeton, N.J.: Princeton University Press, 1968), pp. 57–68; and Anweiler, *Soviets*, pp. 176–92.

18. Anweiler, *Soviets*, pp. 176–92; and Oliver H. Radkey, *The Agrarian Foes of Bolshevism: Promise and Default of the Russian Socialist Revolutionaries, February to October 1917* (New York: Columbia University Press, 1958).

19. For accounts that stress both the Bolsheviks' internal tensions and their remarkable ability to keep in touch with popular orientations, see Alexander Rabinowitch, *Prelude to Revolution: The Petrograd Bolsheviks and the July 1917 Uprising* (Bloomington, Ind.: Indiana University Press, 1968); and Rabinowitch, *Bolsheviks Come to Power*.

20. Rabinowitch, *Bolsheviks Come to Power*, chaps. 11–15 provides an excellent account.

21. Anweiler, *Soviets,* pp. 176–207.

22. See: Leonard Schapiro, *The Origin of the Communist Autocracy* (London: G. Bell and Sons, 1955), pts. I and II; and Keep, *Russian Revolution,* pts. IV and V.

23. Paul H. Avrich, "The Bolshevik Revolution and Workers' Control in Russian Industry," *Slavic Review* 22:1 (March 1963):47–63.

24. Quoted in Chamberlin, *Russian Revolution,* vol. 2, p. 79.

25. Ibid., p. 81.

26. Lazar Volin, *A Century of Russian Agriculture* (Cambridge: Harvard University Press, 1970), pp. 143–50.

27. This contrast between France and Russia is emphasized by Chorley, *Armies and Revolution,* chap. 11.

28. Bolshevik Marxist ideology helped to make these sacrifices possible for the state builders of 1918–21 because it stressed proletarian universalism, not Russian national self-assertion, as the ultimate goal of the Revolution. There was, in other words, an "elective affinity" between the objective situation and the ideology of the Party that won power and succeeded in consolidating it.

29. The one notable exception was the unsuccessful attempt of the Russian Red Army to capture Warsaw, Poland, in the summer of 1920. See Chamberlin, *Russian Revolution,* vol. 2, pp. 297–316.

30. Erickson, "Origins of Red Army," in *Revolutionary Russia,* ed. Pipes, pp. 301ff.

31. John Ellis, *Armies in Revolution* (New York: Oxford University Press, 1974), p. 174.

32. For general background see: Erickson, "Origins of Red Army," in *Revolutionary Russia,* ed. Pipes; Ellis, *Armies,* chap. 7; Chamberlin, *Russian Revolution,* vol. 2, chap. 21; and David Footman, *Civil War in Russia* (New York: Praeger, 1962), chap. 3.

33. Chamberlin, *Russian Revolution,* vol. 2, p. 29.

34. "During the Civil War between 50,000 and 100,000 officers of the old army were taken into the new Red Army . . . Perhaps as important, a little over 10,000 civil servants of the Ministry of War were absorbed, as well as the major part of the general staff and military academies of the old army." Raymond L. Garthoff, "The Military as a Social Force," in *The Transformation of Russian Society,* ed. Cyril E. Black (Cambridge: Harvard University Press, 1960), p. 329.

35. Schapiro, *Origin of Communist Autocracy,* p. 243.

36. On the Bolsheviks in the Civil War, see: Footman, *Civil War;* and Chamberlin, *Russian Revolution,* vol. 2. Chamberlin argues (and presents evidence) that although the peasants in most regions of Russia opposed both Whites and Reds, nevertheless they often resented the Whites more because the latter tried to restore landlord properties and powers in areas they occupied. The only exception was in areas where landlordism was not a problem for wealthy small farmers, as in Siberia. Another important condition for the Reds' victory was that the Western Powers, exhausted by the same world war that had triggered the Russian Revolution, did not mount serious, sustained interventions on behalf of the Whites. But, of course, Russia is so huge that enormous efforts would have been necessary.

37. On the suppression of Makhno's movement, see: Ellis, *Armies,* pp. 184–87; and Footman, *Civil War,* chap. 6.

38. Merle Fainsod, "Bureaucracy and Modernization: The Russian and Soviet Case," in *Bureaucracy and Political Development,* ed. Joseph La Palombara (Princeton, N.J.: Princeton University Press, 1963), pp. 249–53.

39. Chamberlin, *Russian Revolution,* vol. 2, p. 105.

40. See: Avrich, "Revolution and Workers' Control"; and Jeremy R. Azrael, *Managerial Power and Soviet Politics* (Cambridge: Harvard University Press, 1966), chap. 3.

41. Nove, *Economic History,* chap. 3.

42. The situation is poignantly described in Paul Avrich, *Kronstadt, 1921* (New York: Norton, 1974), chap. 1, "The Crisis of War Communism." See also Seth Singleton, "The Tambov Revolt (1920–1921)," *Slavic Review* 25:3 (September 1966):497–512.

43. Nove, *Economic History,* chap. 4.

44. Gerard Chaliand, *Revolution in the Third World: Myths and Prospects,* trans. Diana Johnstone (New York: Viking Press, 1977), p. 150.

45. Nove, *Economic History,* chap. 4, esp. pp. 94, 117–18.

46. Ibid., chap. 4, and Volin, *Century,* pp. 182–8.

47. This paragraph refers back to the arguments and references of the section on France in Chapter 3.

48. For a comparative perspective, see Gilbert Rozman, *Urban Networks in Russia, 1750–1800, and Premodern Periodization* (Princeton, N.J.: Princeton University Press, 1976), chap. 5.

49. See: Keep, *Russian Revolution,* chaps. 29–30; and D. J. Male, *Russian Peasant Organization Before Collectivization* (Cambridge: Cambridge University Press, 1971).

50. Nove, *Economic History,* pp. 105–13, and 148–51; and Volin, *Century,* pp. 182–8.

51. Sources for this paragraph are: Male, *Peasant Organization,* chap. 3; Teodor Shanin, *The Awkward Class* (New York: Oxford University Press, 1972), chaps. 9–10; Moshe Lewin, *Russian Peasants and Soviet Power,* trans. Irene Nove (Evanston, Ill.: Northwestern University Press, 1968), pt. I; and especially Thomas P. Bernstein, "Leadership and Mobilization in the Collectivization of Agriculture in China and Russia: A Comparison," Ph.D. dissertation, Department of Political Science, Columbia University, 1970 (Ann Arbor, Mich.: University Microfilms), chaps. 3–5.

52. Volin, *Century,* pp. 196–202; Lewin, *Russian Peasants,* pt. II; and E. H. Carr, "Revolution From Above: The Road to Collectivization," in *The October Revolution: Before and After* (New York: Vintage Books, 1971), pp. 95–109.

53. See: Isaac Deutscher, *The Prophet Unarmed* (New York: Vintage Books, 1959); Stephen F. Cohen, *Bukharin and the Bolshevik Revolution* (New York: Knopf, 1973), chaps. 6–9; and Alexander Erlich, *The Soviet Industrialization Debate, 1924–1928* (Cambridge, Harvard University Press, 1967).

54. Cohen, in *Bukharin,* chaps. 8–9, places considerable emphasis on the step-by-step conversion of many Party leaders to Stalin's policies.

55. Bukharin's approach would almost certainly also have required opening the Russian economy to substantial foreign investment, although during the 1930s, this might not have been successful even if attempted.

56. See Leonard Schapiro, *The Communist Party of the Soviet Union*, 2nd ed., rev. and enlarged (New York: Vintage Books, 1971), pp. 460–1; Bernstein, "Collectivization of Agriculture," chaps. 5–6; and Lewin, *Peasants and Power*, pt. III.

57. See Nove, *Economic History*, chaps. 8–9 on the accomplishments of the Stalinist industrialization drives.

58. Even Bukharin's sympathetic biographer Stephen Cohen admits that Bukharin's development strategy seriously "underemphasized the need for state intervention in both industrial and agricultural production." See *Bukharin*, pp. 208–12.

59. Nove, *Economic History*, p. 184.

60. See James R. Millar, "Mass Collectivization and the Contribution of Soviet Agriculture to the First Five-Year Plan: A Review Article," *Slavic Review* 33 (December 1974):750–66.

61. Alf Edeen, "The Civil Service: Its Composition and Status," in *The Transformation of Russian Society*, ed. Cyril E. Black (Cambridge: Harvard University Press, 1960), p. 276.

62. E. H. Carr, *Foundations of a Planned Economy, 1926–1929*, 3 vols. (New York: Macmillan, 1971), vol. 2, p. 489, table 66.

63. Warren W. Eason, "Population Changes," in *Transformation*, ed. Black, p. 73. The five-fold figure for state expansion after 1928 comes from Edeen, "Civil Service," in *Transformation*, ed. Black, pp. 276–8.

64. Zbigniew K. Brzezinski, "The Patterns of Autocracy," in *Transformation*, ed. Black, pp. 93–109.

65. See Rigby, *Party Membership*, passim.

66. Theodore H. Von Laue, *Why Lenin? Why Stalin?* 2nd ed. (Philadelphia: Lippincott, 1971), pp. 169–70, and chap. 9 generally.

67. Alexander Vucinich, "The State and the Local Community," in *Transformation*, ed. Black, pp. 207–9.

68. This paragraph draws upon: Edeen, "Civil Service," in *Transformation*, ed. Black, pp. 278–92; Raymond L. Garthoff, "The Military as a Social Force," in *Transformation*, ed. Black, pp. 329ff.; and Rigby, *Party Membership*, chaps. 3–7.

69. Merle Fainsod, *How Russia Is Ruled* (Cambridge: Harvard University Press, 1953), p. 433.

70. Nove, *Economic History*, p. 206.

71. Ibid., pp. 206–7.

72. This paragraph draws upon: Fainsod, *How Russia Is Ruled*, chap. 16; Nove, *Economic History*, pp. 181–4; and Lazar Volin, "The Russian Peasant: From Emancipation to Kolkhoz," in *Transformation*, ed. Black, pp. 306–7; and Naum Jasny, *The Socialized Agriculture of the USSR* (Stanford: Stanford University Press, 1949), pt. III.

73. Nove, *Economic History*, p. 210.

74. Ibid., pp. 179–80.

75. Ibid., pp. 238–44; and Schapiro, *Communist Party,* pp. 463–4.

76. Edeen, "Civil Service," in *Transformation,* ed. Black, p. 286.

77. Ibid., pp. 286–7.

78. Nove, *Economic History,* pp. 208–9; and Schapiro, *Communist Party,* pp. 465–7.

79. Fainsod, *How Russia Is Ruled,* p. 450.

80. For particularly telling details on this point, see Tony Cliff, *State Capitalism in Russia* (London: Pluto Press, 1974), pp. 65–81.

81. Volin, *Century,* pp. 212–31; and Nove, *Economic History,* pp. 165–76.

82. Stanislaw Swianiewicz, "The Main Features of Soviet Forced Labor," pp. 277–92 in *Russian Economic Development: From Peter the Great to Stalin,* ed. William L. Blackwell (New York: New Viewpoints, 1974).

83. Robert Conquest, *The Great Terror: Stalin's Purge of the Thirties* (New York: Crowell & Macmillan, Inc., 1973).

84. In U.S. social science during the 1950s and 1960s, it was very much the vogue to attribute postrevolutionary inequalities in the USSR to the universal "functional necessities" imposed by industrialization upon any country that undergoes it. See, for a prime example, the essays collected in Alex Inkeles, *Social Change in Soviet Russia* (Cambridge: Harvard University Press, 1968), esp. pt. III on "Social Stratification."

7. THE RISE OF A MASS-MOBILIZING
PARTY-STATE IN CHINA

1. James E. Sheridan, *China in Disintegration: The Republican Era in Chinese History, 1912–1949* (New York: Free Press, 1975), chap. 2.

2. C. Martin Wilbur, "Military Separatism and the Process of Reunification under the Nationalist Regime, 1922–1937," in *China in Crisis,* eds. Ping-ti Ho and Tang Tsou (Chicago: University of Chicago Press, 1968), vol. 1, bk. 1, p. 204.

3. Ibid., p. 205.

4. On warlordism, see, in addition to ibid.: Lucien W. Pye, *Warlord Politics* (New York: Praeger, 1971) and Hsi-sheng Ch'i, *Warlord Politics in China, 1916–1928* (Stanford: Stanford University Press, 1968).

5. See Albert Feuerwerker, *China's Early Industrialization* (Cambridge: Harvard University Press, 1958).

6. G. William Skinner, "Marketing and Social Structure in Rural China (Part II)," *Journal of Asian Studies* 24:2 (February 1965):195–228. See also the argument of Rhoads Murphey in "The Treaty Ports and China's Modernization," in *The Chinese City Between Two Worlds,* eds. Mark Elvin and G. William Skinner (Stanford: Stanford University Press, 1974), pp. 17–72.

7. Ralph L. Powell, *The Rise of Chinese Military Power, 1895–1912* (Princeton, N.J.: Princeton University Press, 1955).

8. Ch'i, *Warlord Politics in China,* p. 78.

9. See, for instance, Robert A. Kapp, "Chungking as a Center of Warlord Power, 1926–1937," in *Chinese City Between Two Worlds,* eds. Elvin

and Skinner, pp. 144–70. This was not, however, a city "milked dry" by its warlord, primarily because he also had stable access to revenues from surrounding rural areas.

10. Sources for this paragraph include: Frederic Wakeman, Jr., *The Fall of Imperial China* (New York: Free Press, 1975), pp. 253–5; Pye, *Warlord Politics,* pp. 55–7; Sheridan, *China in Disintegration,* pp. 238–9; and Hung-mao Tien, *Government and Politics in Kuomintang China, 1927–1937* (Stanford: Stanford University Press, 1972), chaps. 7–8.

11. See, above all, Philip A. Kuhn, "Local Self-Government under the Republic: Problems of Control, Autonomy, and Mobilization," in *Conflict and Control in Late Imperial China,* eds. Frederic Wakeman, Jr. and Carolyn Grant (Berkeley: University of California Press, 1975), pp. 257–98. Also see: Ernest P. Young, "Nationalism, Reform, and Republican Revolution," in *Modern East Asia: Essays in Interpretation,* ed. James B. Crowley (New York: Harcourt, Brace and World, 1970), pp. 173–8; Yuji Muramatsu, "A Documentary Study of Chinese Landlordism in Late Ch'ing and Early Republican Kiangnan," *Bulletin of the School of Oriental and African Studies* 29:3 (1966):566–99; Mark Selden, *The Yenan Way in Revolutionary China* (Cambridge: Harvard University Press, 1971), pp. 5–18; Yung-teh Chow, *Social Mobility in China* (New York: Atherton, 1966); and Morton H. Fried, *The Fabric of Chinese Society* (New York: Praeger, 1953). The last two citations are but two of many studies of Chinese local areas done between 1920 and 1940 that portray the local gentry still very much in place.

12. In his *Rebellion and Its Enemies in Late Imperial China* (Cambridge: Harvard University Press, 1970), Philip Kuhn shows how connections among groups of local gentry that were made possible by the operations of the Confucian state system allowed the creation of the armies and militias that defeated the huge mid-nineteenth-century rebellions. Achievements such as those of Tseng Kuo-fan, a high-ranking literatus who mobilized the gentry class to regional and "national" self-defense, became impossible after the fall of the Imperial regime.

13. See Hsiao-tung Fei, *China's Gentry,* ed. Margaret Park Redfield (Chicago: University of Chicago Press, 1953).

14. Wilbur, "Military Separatism," in *China in Crisis,* eds. Ho and Tsou, vol. 1, bk. 1, p. 220.

15. Robert C. North and Ithiel de Sola Pool, "Kuomintang and Chinese Communist Elites," in *World Revolutionary Elites,* eds. Harold D. Lasswell and Daniel Lerner (Cambridge: MIT Press, 1966), pp. 376–95.

16. Here I follow Wilbur, "Military Separatism," in *China in Crisis,* eds. Ho and Tsou, vol. 1, bk. 1, pp. 224–41.

17. Ibid., pp. 224–5.

18. C. Martin Wilbur, "The Influence of the Past: How the Early Years Helped to Shape the Future of the Chinese Communist Party," in *Party Leadership and Revolutionary Power in China,* ed. John Wilson Lewis (Cambridge: Cambridge University Press, 1970), p. 56. See also Jean Chesneaux, *The Chinese Labor Movement, 1919–1927,* trans. H.M. Wright (Stanford: Stanford University Press, 1968).

19. Wilbur, "Military Separatism," in *China in Crisis,* eds. Ho and Tsou, vol. 1, bk. 1, p. 242.

20. Ibid., p. 245.

21. On early Communist peasant organizing, see: Shinkichi Eto, "Hai-lu-feng – The First Chinese Soviet Government," *China Quarterly* no. 8 (October–December 1961):161–83; and no. 9 (January–March 1962):149–81; Stuart Schram, *Mao Tse-tung* (Baltimore, Md.: Penguin Books, 1967), chap. 5; and especially Roy Hofheinz, Jr., *The Broken Wave: The Chinese Communist Peasant Movement, 1922–1928* (Cambridge: Harvard University Press, 1977). The CCP's approach to rural organization during this period tended to be rather naive: Much emphasis was placed upon "preaching at" peasants, with the simple aim of getting them to join associations. On paper there were by 1927 huge memberships coordinated by district, provincial, and national CPP leaders. Mild, reformist slogans, including both antiimperialist and pro-rent-reduction appeals, were used to approach the peasants. Anxious to protect their alliance with the KMT, the CCP cadres tried to make a distinction between "bully landlords" and "patriotic landlords." The peasants, having had little direct experience with imperialism, responded most readily to the Communists' economic appeals. Few could really grasp fine distinctions between types of landlords. Nor, once aroused, were the peasants easily controlled from above. Thus the agitation by the cadres, no matter how mildly intended, worked to increase rural class tensions. But the cadres were not really prepared for rural class war. To defend themselves (and the peasants whom they had aroused) against landlords' mercenary forces, they depended completely, and with touching confidence, upon the KMT-controlled armies.

22. Wilbur, "Military Separatism," in *China in Crisis*, eds. Ho and Tsou, vol. 1, bk. 1, pp. 245–53.

23. Ibid., pp. 253–60.

24. See the endpaper maps in Elvin and Skinner, eds., *Chinese City Between Two Worlds*.

25. See note 8 for Chapter 4.

26. For the figures for China, see: Albert Feuerwerker, *The Chinese Economy, 1912–1949*, Michigan Papers in Chinese Studies, no. 1 (Ann Arbor: University of Michigan, Center for Chinese Studies, 1968), chaps. 3–5; and Chesneaux, *Chinese Labor Movement*, chap. 2. For Russia, see: Raymond W. Goldsmith, "The Economic Growth of Tsarist Russia, 1860–1913," *Economic Development and Cultural Change* 9:3 (April 1961), p.. 442; and Teddy J. Uldricks, "The 'Crowd' in the Russian Revolution," *Politics and Society* 4:3 (1974), p. 402.

27. Wilbur, "Military Separatism," in *China in Crisis*, eds. Ho and Tsou, vol. 1, bk. 1, pp. 244–5; 259–60.

28. Hung-mao Tien, *Government and Politics in Kuomintang China, 1927–1937* (Stanford: Stanford University Press, 1972), p. 180.

29. Ibid., p. 181.

30. Ibid., chaps. 5 and 6; John K. Fairbank, Edwin O. Reischauer, and Albert M. Craig, *East Asia: Tradition and Transformation* (Boston: Houghton Mifflin, 1973), pp. 787–8, 793; and Lloyd E. Eastman, *The Abortive Revolution: China under Nationalist Rule, 1927–1937* (Cambridge: Harvard University Press, 1974), chaps. 1,3,5.

31. Feuerwerker, *Chinese Economy, 1912–1949*, pp. 54–56.

32. Ibid., pp. 57–59; and Douglas S. Paauw, "The Kuomintang and

Economic Stagnation, 1928–1937," *Journal of Asian Studies* 16 (February 1957):213–20. Eastman, in *Abortive Revolution,* pp. 226–39, disagrees with Paauw's argument that the modern sector "stagnated" under the Nationalists. But he still presents a gloomy picture.

33. This paragraph draws especially upon: Tien, *Government and Politics,* pt. 1; Patrick Cavendish, "The 'New China' of the Kuomintang," in *Modern China's Search for a Political Form,* ed. Jack Gray (New York: Oxford University Press, 1969), pp. 138–86; Ch'ien Tuan-sheng, *The Government and Politics of China, 1912–1949* (Cambridge: Harvard University Press, 1950), passim; Sheridan, *China in Disintegration,* chaps. 6–7; and Eastman, *Abortive Revolution.*

34. Feuerwerker, *Chinese Economy, 1912–1949,* pp. 54, 59–62.

35. Barbara W. Tuchman, *Stilwell and the American Experience in China, 1911–45* (New York: Macmillan, 1971). On rural conditions during the wartime phase of Kuomintang rule, see Graham Peck, *Two Kinds of Time,* rev. ed. (Boston: Houghton Mifflin, 1967).

36. Mark Selden, "The Guerilla Movement in Northwest China: the Origins of the Shensi-Kansu-Ninghsia Border Region (Part I)," *China Quarterly* no. 28 (October–December 1966), p. 68.

37. Franklin W. Houn, *A Short History of Chinese Communism* (Englewood Cliffs, N.J.: Prentice-Hall, 1973), chap. 3; and Robert W. McColl, "The Oyüwan Soviet Area, 1927–1932," *Journal of Asian Studies* 27:1 (November 1967):41–60.

38. John Ellis, *Armies in Revolution* (New York: Oxford University Press, 1974), chap. 10.

39. Ying-mao Kau, *The People's Liberation Army and China's Nation-Building* (White Plains, N.Y.: International Arts and Sciences Press, 1973), pp. xxi–xxv.

40. Ibid., pp. xxv–xxvi.

41. Mark Selden, *The Yenan Way in Revolutionary China* (Cambridge: Harvard University Press, 1971), pp. 42–78.

42. Stuart Schram, *Mao Tse-tung* (Baltimore, Md.: Penguin Books, 1967), pp. 124–45; Edgar Snow, *Red Star Over China* (1938; reprint ed., New York: Grove Press, 1961), pp. 164–88; and Agnes Smedley, *The Great Road: The Life and Times of Chu Teh* (New York: Monthly Review Press, 1956), bks. 6–7. For information on still another early Red Army base, see McColl, "Oyüwan Soviet."

43. Wilbur, "Military Separatism," in *China in Crisis,* eds. Ho and Tsou, vol. 1, bk. 1, p. 260.

44. See: Ilpyong J. Kim, "Mass Mobilization Policies and Techniques Developed During the Period of the Chinese Soviet Republic," in *Chinese Communist Politics in Action,* ed. A. Doak Barnett (Seattle: University of Washington Press, 1969), pp. 78–98; and Franz Schurmann, *Ideology and Organization in Communist China,* 2nd ed. (Berkeley: University of California Press, 1968), pp. 414–16.

45. See Dick Wilson, *The Long March, 1935* (New York: Avon Books, 1973).

46. Selden, *Yenan Way,* chaps. 1–3.

47. John Israel, *Student Nationalism in China: 1927–1937* (Stanford, Cal.: Hoover Institution Publications, 1966).

48. A lively account of this "Sian Incident" is given by Edgar Snow in *Red Star Over China,* pp. 431–78.

49. Selden, *Yenan Way,* pp. 116–20.

50. Maurice Meisner, "Yenan Communism and the Rise of the Chinese People's Republic," in *Modern East Asia: Essays in Interpretation,* ed. James B. Crowley (New York: Harcourt, Brace, and World, 1970), pp. 278–9.

51. There is very little evidence for Chalmers Johnson's well-known thesis that Communist expansion during the Yenan Period was due to "peasant nationalism" rather than Communist appeals to peasants' socioeconomic interests. Most Chinese peasants were not politically aware enough (on an extralocal scale) to be "nationalist." Rather they seem to have responded favorably to the Communists whenever the latter acted to protect peasant interests – whether these were interests in greater economic security, or interests in protection against marauding armies (of whatever nationality). For arguments and evidence, see: Chalmers A. Johnson, *Peasant Nationalism and Communist Power* (Stanford: Stanford University Press, 1962); Selden, *Yenan Way,* pp. 91–3, 119–20; and Donald G. Gillin, " 'Peasant Nationalism' in the History of Chinese Communism," *Journal of Asian Studies* 23:2 (February 1964): 269–89.

52. Meisner, "Yenan Communism," in *Modern East Asia,* ed. Crowley, p. 279.

53. Selden, *Yenan Way,* chap. 4.

54. Ibid., pp. 144–61.

55. Mark Selden, "The Yenan Legacy: The Mass Line," in *Chinese Communist Politics in Action,* ed. A. Doak Barnett (Seattle: University of Washington Press, 1969), p. 102.

56. Ibid., pp. 101–2.

57. Ibid., pp. 103–4.

58. Ibid., p. 151.

59. Selden, *Yenan Way,* pp. 188–207.

60. Stuart Schram, ed., *The Political Thought of Mao Tse-tung,* rev. and enlarged ed. (New York: Praeger, 1969), pp. 316.

61. Selden, *Yenan Way,* pp. 212–29.

62. Selden, *Yenan Way,* pp. 237ff; and Franz Schurmann, *Ideology and Organization,* pp. 416ff.

63. It is worth noting that similar changes in the balance of power also apparently occurred in different ways in villages directly occupied by the Japanese. Long Bow village, described by William Hinton in his book *Fanshen* (New York: Vintage Books, 1968), was one such village. There young, poor peasants first assumed leadership roles in the intravillage underground Resistance effort. Traditional elites collaborated with the Japanese. Thus, after liberation from Japan, the "patriotic" Party workers were in a position to challenge the "traitorous" traditional elites as a prelude to promoting land reform.

64. Schurmann, *Ideology and Organization,* pp. 427–37.

65. John Gittings comments that "an essential part" of the Commu-

nists' military strategy in the Civil War with the Nationalists after 1946 "was the winning of popular support in the liberated areas . . . The winter of 1947 saw the launching of a new and more radical programme of land reform, large-scale recruitment for the coming year, and a major political and organizational overhaul of the armed forces and party." See *The Role of the Chinese Army* (New York: Oxford University Press, 1967), p. 7.

66. Schurmann, *Ideology and Organization*, pp. 431–2.

67. Franz Michael, "State and Society in Nineteenth-Century China" in *Modern China*, ed. Albert Feuerwerker (Englewood Cliffs, N.J.: Prentice-Hall, 1964), p. 58.

68. Ying-mao Kau, "Patterns of Recruitment and Mobility of Urban Cadres," in *The City in Communist China*, ed. John W. Lewis (Stanford: Stanford University Press, 1971), pp. 98–9.

69. Victor C. Funnell, "Bureaucracy and the Chinese Communist Party," *Current Scene* 9:5 (May 7, 1971), p. 6.

70. Fairbank, Resichauer, and Craig, *East Asia*, p. 896.

71. Ping-ti Ho, *Studies on the Population of China, 1368–1953* (Cambridge: Harvard University Press, 1959), p. 278.

72. The estimates are based on numbers of literati given in Michael, "State and Society," in *Modern China*, ed. Feuerwerker, p. 60, and on population estimates in Ho, *Studies*, p. 278.

73. A Doak Barnett, *Cadres, Bureaucracy, and Political Power in Communist China* (New York: Columbia University Press, 1967), pp. 428–9.

74. For general background on the Chinese Communist regime, see especially: Barnett, *Cadres and Bureaucracy*, and Franz Schurmann, *Ideology and Organization*.

75. For example, Kao Kang, a major Party leader with a strong base in Manchuria was deposed from regional power in 1953–5; see James Pinckney Harrison, *The Long March to Power* (New York: Praeger, 1972), pp. 467–8. Also, a major theme of Ezra Vogel's *Canton under Communism* (Cambridge: Harvard University Press, 1969), is the impact of central controls and programs on Canton province. And Richard Pfeffer argues that even during the Cultural Revolution, when centralized Party-state controls were weakened, regional leaders were deposed or transferred. See his "Serving the People and Continuing the Revolution," *China Quarterly* no. 52 (October–December 1972), pp. 632–3.

76. Ezra F. Vogel, "Politicized Bureaucracy: Communist China," in *Communist Systems in Comparative Perspective*, eds. Leonard J. Cohen and Jane P. Shapiro (New York: Doubleday [Anchor Books], 1974), pp. 160–70.

77. Fairbank, Reischauer, and Craig, *East Asia*, pp. 896–8.

78. A particularly insightful discussion of the Leninist and Stalinist influences on Chinese Communism is to be found in Roland Lew, "Maoism and the Chinese Revolution," in *The Socialist Register 1975* (London: Merlin Press, 1975), pp. 115–59.

79. For background on Chinese Communist consolidation and early policy initiatives in the 1950s, see: Vogel, *Canton under Communism*, pt. II; and Schurmann, *Ideology and Organization*, esp. chap. 4; pp. 371–80 in chap. 6; and pp. 438–64 in chap. 7.

80. Alexander Eckstein, *China's Economic Revolution* (Cambridge: Cambridge University Press, 1977), pp. 50–1.

81. See: Schurmann, *Ideology and Organization,* pp. 236–62; Stephen Andors, *China's Industrial Revolution* (New York: Pantheon Books, 1977), pp. 53–9; and Eckstein, *Economic Revolution,* pp. 50–4.

82. See: Eckstein, *Economic Revolution,* pp. 54–6; and C. K. Yeh, "Soviet and Communist Chinese Industrialization Strategies," in *Soviet and Chinese Communism: Similarities and Differences,* ed. Donald W. Treadgold (Seattle: University of Washington Press, 1967), pp. 327–63.

83. On the "two lines," see: Stuart R. Schram, "Introduction: the Cultural Revolution in Historical Perspective," pp. 1–109, and Jack Gray, "The Two Roads: Alternative Strategies of Social Change and Economic Growth in China," pp. 109–157, both in *Authority, Participation and Cultural Change in China,* ed. Schram (Cambridge: Cambridge University Press, 1973).

84. On pp. 305–9 of my earlier article, "Old Regime Legacies and Communist Revolutions in Russia and China," *Social Forces* 55:2 (December 1976), I mistakenly drew too close a parallel between the dynamics and trajectories of the leadership struggles in Soviet Russia after 1921 and those in Communist China after 1949.

85. See: Eckstein, *Economic Revolution,* pp. 58–63; Carl Riskin, "Small Industry and the Chinese Model of Development," *China Quarterly,* no. 46 (April–June 1971):245–73; and Jon Sigurdson, *Rural Industrialization in China* (Cambridge: Harvard University Press, 1977).

86. Sigurdson, *Rural Industrialization,* pp. 28–9.

87. On "intermediate technologies," see Jon Sigurdson, "Rural Industry and the Internal Transfer of Technology," in *Authority and Participation,* ed. Schram, pp. 199–232. On education, see: Richard D. Barendsen, "The Agricultural Middle School in Communist China," in *China Under Mao: Politics Takes Command,* ed. Roderick MacFarquhar (Cambridge: MIT Press, 1966), pp. 304–32; Pfeffer, "Serving the People," pp. 639–45; and John Gardner and Wilt Idema, "China's Educational Revolution," in *Authority and Participation,* ed. Schram, pp. 257–89. On the "barefoot doctor" program, see Victor W. Sidel and Ruth Sidel, "The Delivery of Medical Care in China," *Scientific American* 230:4 (April 1974), pp. 19–22.

88. Byung-joon Ahn, "The Political Economy of the People's Commune in China: Changes and Continuities," *Journal of Asian Studies* 34:3 (May 1975), p. 637. My discussion of the organization of collective agriculture and rural local government draws upon this article as a whole.

89. See: Ibid., pp. 657–8; Eckstein, *Economic Revolution,* pp. 206–13; and Sterling Wortman, "Agriculture in China," *Scientific American* 232:6 (June 1975):13–21.

90. On French peasants in the nineteenth century, see: Theodore Zeldin, *France: 1848–1945, Volume I: Ambition, Love, and Politics* (London: Oxford University Press, 1973), chap. 9; and Maurice Agulhon, Gabriel Désert, and Robert Specklin, *Histoire de la France Rurale,* vol. 3, *Apogée et Crise de la Civilisation Paysanne, 1789–1914* (Paris: Editions du Seuil, 1976).

91. These inequalities and the reasons for them are emphasized in

Audrey Donnithorne, "China's Cellular Economy: Some Economic Trends Since the Cultural Revolution," *China Quarterly* no. 52 (October–December 1972): 605–19.

92. Even formerly very marginal and declining areas have gained, as Richard Madsen's study of an impoverished village in Kwangtung shows. See "Revolutionary Asceticism in Communist China: Social Causes and Consequences of Commitment to the Maoist Ethos in a South China Village" (Ph.D. diss., Department of Sociology, Harvard University, April 1977).

93. For overviews see: Marianne Bastid, "Levels of Economic Decision-Making," in *Authority and Participation,* ed. Schram, pp. 159–97; and Peter Schran, "Economic Management," in *China: Management of a Revolutionary Society,* ed. John M. Lindbeck (Seattle: University of Washington Press, 1971) pp. 193–220.

94. See: Sigurdson, *Rural Industrialization,* pp. 7–10, 35–42, and chap. 3, esp. pp. 115–17; and Donnithorne, "China's Cellular Economy."

95. Andors, *Industrial Revolution,* chap. 3 and passim; and Schurmann, *Ideology and Organization,* pp. 263–308.

96. For two recent studies of the "mass line" and political mobilization in China, see: Victor G. Nee, "Community and Change in Revolutionary China" (Ph.D. diss., Department of Sociology, Harvard University, April 1977); and Charles P. Cell, *Revolution at Work: Mobilization Campaigns in China* (New York: Academic Press, 1977). The Cell book provides a survey of major campaigns and tests hypotheses about their effectiveness. Cell concludes that mass mobilization, especially for economic campaigns, *has* been an effective strategy for promoting social change in China.

97. The rationale for the "Maoist" leadership style is well presented by Martin King Whyte in "Bureaucracy and Modernization in China: The Maoist Critique," *American Sociological Review* 38:2 (April 1973):149–63; and "Iron Law versus Mass Democracy: Weber, Michels, and the Maoist Vision," in *The Logic of 'Maoism': Critiques and Explication,* ed. James Chieh Hsiung (New York: Praeger, 1974), pp. 37–61.

98. For the effects on factory management, see Andors, *Industrial Revolution,* esp. chaps. 4, 7–8, and conclusion.

99. T. H. Rigby, *Communist Party Membership in the U.S.S.R., 1917–1967* (Princeton, N.J.: Princeton University Press, 1968), chap. 6.

100. Shurmann, *Ideology and Organization,* chaps. 2–5. Explicit contrasts are drawn to the Soviet Union here and there throughout these chapters.

101. Barnett, *Cadres and Bureaucracy,* p. 430.

102. Eckstein, *Economic Recolution,* p. 303.

103. Ibid., pp. 299–301. For Russia in 1934, see Leonard Schapiro, *The Communist Party of the Soviet Union,* 2nd ed., rev. and enlarged (New York: Vintage Books, 1971), p. 465.

104. For overviews, see: Martin King Whyte, "Inequality and Stratification in China," *China Quarterly* no. 64 (December 1975): 684–711; and Pfeffer, "Serving the People," pp. 635–53.

105. Whyte, "Inequality and Stratification," pp. 695–6.

106. Ibid., p. 695.

107. Perkins, "Growth and Changing Structure," in *China's Modern Economy,* ed. in Perkins, p. 147.

108. This point is a central theme in ibid., and in Harry Magdoff, "China: Contrasts with the U.S.S.R.," *Monthly Review* 27 (July–August 1975):12–57.

109. See: Dwight H. Perkins, *Agricultural Development in China, 1368–1968* (Chicago: Aldine, 1969); and Ho, *Population: 1368–1953.*

110 G. William Skinner, "Marketing and Social Structure in Rural China (Part II)" *Journal of Asian Studies* 24 (February 1965): 195–228.

111. Fairbank, Reischauer, and Craig, *East Asia,* pp. 919–21; and Harrison, *Long March,* pp. 480–1.

112. My thinking here has been greatly influenced by Franz Schurmann, *The Logic of World Power* (New York: Pantheon, 1974), pt. II.

113. The legacy of local leadership from the land revolution is heavily stressed by Thomas Paul Bernstein, "Leadership and Mobilization in the Collectivization of Agriculture in China and Russia: A Comparison" (Ph.D. diss., Department of Political Science, Columbia University, 1970), esp. pp. 111–32, 179–200.

114. Ibid., chap. 6.

CONCLUSION

1. Lenin, "The Dual Power," originally published in *Pravda* on April 9, 1917; reprinted in Robert C. Tucker, ed., *The Lenin Anthology* (New York: Norton, 1975), p. 301.

2. See Lenin, "The State and Revolution," reprinted in *Lenin Anthology,* ed. Tucker, pp. 311–98.

3. See especially Weber on "Bureaucracy," in *From Max Weber: Essays in Sociology,* ed. and trans. H. H. Gerth and C. Wright Mills (New York: Oxford University Press, 1958), chap. 8. Lenin's and Weber's views on the state and bureaucracy are very cogently compared in Erik Olin Wright, "To Control or Smash Bureaucracy: Weber and Lenin on Politics, the State, and Bureaucracy," *Berkeley Journal of Sociology* 19 (1974–75):69–108.

4. C. Wright Mills, *The Sociological Imagination* (New York: Oxford University Press, 1959), p. 150.

5. See especially: Stanley J. Stein and Barbara H. Stein, *The Colonial Heritage of Latin America* (New York: Oxford University Press, 1970); and Walter Goldfrank, "World System, State Structure, and the Onset of the Mexican Revolution," *Politics and Society* 5:4 (1975):417–39.

6. For a succinct account of the Vietnamese Revolution that stresses these factors see John Dunn, *Modern Revolutions* (Cambridge: Cambridge University Press, 1972), chap. 5.

7. Susan Eckstein, "Capitalist Constraints on Cuban Socialist Development," mimeograph (Boston: Department of Sociology, Boston University, 1978).

8. Katherine Chorley, *Armies and the Art of Revolution* (1943; reprint ed., Boston: Beacon Press, 1973), p. 243.

9. For an excellent survey on contemporary Third World military

officer corps, their social backgrounds and modes of political involvement, see Eric A. Nordlinger, *Soldiers in Politics: Military Coups and Governments* (Englewood Cliffs, N.J.: Prentice-Hall, 1977).

10. Portugal during the mid-1970s, for a period after the coup that brought down the Salazar dictatorship, may constitute an exception to the generalization that military coups do not encourage revolts from below; nevertheless, the radical trends in Portugal have since been stopped and largely reversed. Another fascinating exception in this decade has been Ethiopia, where rebellious military officers turned to mass mobilization in a deepening assault against an archaic state and landed aristocracy, followed by mass military mobilization to assert national sovereignty in the face of an invasion from Somalia and regional succession in Eritrea. Though launched by a coup and strongly influenced from without by great power interventions, the Ethiopian Revolution has generally conformed to classic social-revolutionary patterns. Yet nothing quite like this is likely to occur again, for few if any other regimes, even nominal absolute monarchies, exhibit semibureaucratic and aristocratic features comparable to the Ethiopian Old Regime of Emperor Haile Selassie.

11. See: Dunn, *Modern Revolutions;* Eric Wolf, *Peasant Wars of the Twentieth Century* (New York: Harper & Row, 1969); Jeffery M. Paige, *Agrarian Revolution: Social Movements and Export Agriculture in the Underdeveloped World* (New York: Free Press, 1975); Susan Eckstein, *The Impact of Revolution: A Comparative Analysis of Mexico and Bolivia,* Contemporary Political Sociology Series (Beverly Hills, Cal.: Sage Publications, 1976); and Susan Eckstein and Peter Evans, "The Revolution as Cataclysm and Coup: Political Transformation and Economic Development in Mexico and Brazil," *Comparative Studies in Sociology* 1 (1978):129–55.

12. The term is that of André Gorz, and the idea is explicated in his *Strategy for Labor: A Radical Proposal,* trans. Martin A. Nicolaus and Victoria Ortiz (Boston: Beacon Press, 1967).

13. Franz Neumann, *The Democratic and Authoritarian State,* ed. Herbert Marcuse (New York: The Free Press of Glencoe, 1957), p. 264.

14. From Karl Marx and Frederick Engels, "The Communist Manifesto," reprinted in *Selected Works* (New York: International Publishers, 1968), p. 53.

15. From Karl Marx, "Critique of the Gotha Programme," excerpted in *Karl Marx: Selected Writings in Sociology and Social Philosophy,* ed. and trans. T. B. Bottomore (New York: McGraw-Hill, 1956), p. 255.

Bibliography

THIS BIBLIOGRAPHY lists the major works consulted as the arguments of the book were developed. The bibliography overlaps but does not exactly coincide with the notes. Certain articles or parts of books cited in the notes to support particular points in the text are not included here; nor have I listed works about the contrast cases, England, Prussia/Germany and Japan. The bibliography does, however, include many important books and articles that informed the overall analysis and the in-depth discussions of the French, Russian, and Chinese cases, yet which were not cited in the notes. The bibliography is organized alphabetically under four major headings:

    I.   *France: Old Regime and Revolution*

    II.   *Russia: Old Regime and Revolution*

    III.   *China: Old Regime and Revolution*

    IV.   *Theoretical and Historical Background*

In general, works that importantly influenced the arguments of Chapters 1 and 4 and the introductions to Chapters 2 and 3 are included in part IV, whereas parts I–III contain listings of the various books and articles by historians and area specialists that I consulted for each of the major case studies, including works about the Old Regimes, the events of the Revolutions, and the revolutionary outcomes.

I. FRANCE: OLD REGIME AND REVOLUTION

Acomb, Frances. *Anglophobia in France, 1763–1789*. Durham, N.C.: Duke University Press, 1950.

351

Bibliography: France

Agulhon, Maurice; Désert, Gabriel; and Specklin, Robert. *Histoire de la France Rurale*, vol. 3, *Apogée et Crise de la Civilisation Paysanne, 1789–1914*, Paris: Editions du Seuil, 1976.

Amann, Peter. *The Eighteenth-Century Revolution: French or Western?* Lexington, Mass.: Heath, 1963.

Barber, Elinor G. *The Bourgeoisie in 18th Century France*. Princeton, N.J.: Princeton University Press, 1955.

Barker, Ernest. *The Development of Public Services in Western Europe, 1660–1930*. New York: Oxford University Press, 1944.

Behrens, C.B.A. "Nobles, Privileges and Taxes in France at the End of the Ancien Régime." *Economic History Review* 2nd ser. 15 (3) (April 1963): 451–75.

The Ancien Régime. London: Harcourt, Brace and World, 1967.

Beloff, Max. *The Age of Absolutism, 1660–1815*. New York: Harper & Row, 1962.

Bernard, Leon. "French Society and Popular Uprisings Under Louis XIV." *French Historical Studies* 3: 4 (Fall 1964): 454–74.

Bien, David D. "La Réaction Aristocratique avant 1789: l'Exemple de l'Armée (à suivre)." *Annales: Economies, Sociétés, Civilizations* 29: 1 (January–February 1974): 23–48.

Bloch, Marc. "La Lutte pour l'Individualisme Agraire dans la France du XVIIIᵉ-Siècle." *Annales d'Histoire Economique et Sociale* 11: 7 (July 1930): 329–81 and 11: 8 (October 1930): 511–56.

"Sur le Passé de la Noblesse Française: Quelques Jalons de Recherche." *Annales d'Histoire Economique et Sociale* 8: 40 (July 1936): 366–78.

French Rural History: An Essay on Its Basic Characteristics. Translated by Janet Sondheimer. Berkeley: University of California Press, 1970.

Bois, Paul. *Paysans de l'Ouest: Des Structures Economiques et Sociales aux Options Politiques depuis l'Epoque Révolutionnaire dans la Sarthe*. Le Mans: Imprimerie M. Vilaire, 1960.

Bordes, Maurice. "Les Intendants Eclaires de la Fin de l'Ancien Régime." *Revue d'Histoire Economique et Sociale* 39: 1 (1961): 57–83.

Bosher, J. F. *French Finances, 1770–1795: From Business to Bureaucracy*. Cambridge: Cambridge University Press, 1970.

Bouchard, Gérard. *Le Village Immobile*. Paris: Librarie Plon, 1972.

Braudel, Fernand, and Labrousse, Ernest, eds. *Histoire Economique et sociale de la France*, vol. 2, *Des Derniers Temps de l'Age Seigneurial aux Préludes de l'Age Industriel (1660–1789)*. Paris: Presses Universitaires de France, 1970.

Brinton, Crane. *The Jacobins: An Essay in the New History*. 1930. Reprint. New York: Russell and Russell, 1961.

Bromley, J. S. "The Decline of Absolute Monarchy (1683–1774)." In *France: Government and Society*, edited by J. M. Wallace-Hadrill and John McManners, pp. 134–60. London: Methuen, 1957.

Bruun, Geoffrey. "The Balance of Power During the Wars, 1793–1814." In *The New Cambridge Modern History*, Vol. 9, pp. 250–74. Cambridge: Cambridge University Press, 1965.

Bibliography: France

Cameron, Rondo E. "Economic Growth and Stagnation in France, 1815–1914." *Journal of Modern History* 30: 1 (March 1958): 1–13.

Cavanaugh, Gerald J. "The Present State of French Revolutionary Historiography: Alfred Cobban and Beyond." *French Historical Studies* 7: 4 (Fall 1972): 587–606.

Chalmin, P. "La Désintégration de l'Armée Royale en France à la Fin de XVIIIᵉ Siècle." *Revue Historique de l'Armée* 20:1 (1964): 75–90.

Chaussinand-Nogaret, Guy. "Capital et Structure Sociale sous l'Ancien Régime." *Annales: Economies, Sociétés, Civilisations* 25: 2 (March–April 1970): 463–76.

Church, Clive H. "In Search of the Directory." In *French Government and Society, 1500–1850*, edited by J. F. Bosher, pp. 261–94. London: Athlone Press, 1973.

"The Social Basis of the French Central Bureaucracy Under the Directory 1795–1799." *Past and Present* no. 36 (April 1967): 59–72.

Clough, Shephard Bancroft. *France: A History of National Economics, 1789–1939.* New York: Octagon Books, 1964.

Cobb, Richard. "The Revolutionary Mentality in France 1793–1794." *History* 52 (1957): 181–96.

Les Armées Révolutionnaires: Instrument de la Terreur dans les Départements, Avril 1793–Floréal, An II. Paris: Mouton, 1961–3.

The Police and the People: French Popular Protest, 1789–1820. New York: Oxford University Press, 1970.

Paris and Its Provinces, 1792–1802. New York: Oxford University Press, 1975.

Cobban, Alfred. *A History of Modern France*, vol. 1, *Old Regime and Revolution, 1715–1799.* Baltimore, Md.: Penguin Books, 1957.

A History of Modern France, vol. 2, *From the First Empire to the Second Empire, 1799–1871.* Baltimore, Md.: Penguin Books, 1961.

The Social Interpretation of the French Revolution. Cambridge: Cambridge University Press, 1964.

Aspects of the French Revolution. New York: Norton: 1970.

France Since the Revolution. London: Jonathan Cape, 1970.

"Local Government During the French Revolution." In *Aspects of the French Revolution*, pp. 112–30. New York: Norton, 1970.

Crouzet, François. "Wars, Blockade, and Economic Change in Europe, 1792–1815." *Journal of Economic History* 24: 4 (December 1964): 567–88.

"England and France in the Eighteenth Century: A Comparative Analysis of Two Economic Growths." In *The Causes of the Industrial Revolution in England*, edited by R. M. Hartwell, pp. 139–74. London: Methuen, 1967.

"French Economic Growth in the Nineteenth Century Reconsidered." *History* 59: 196 (June 1974): 167–79.

Darnton, Robert. "The High Enlightenment and the Low-Life of Literature in Pre-revolutionary France." *Past and Present* 51 (May 1971): 81–115.

"In Search of the Enlightenment: Recent Attempts to Create a Social History of Ideas." *Journal of Modern History* 43 (1971): 113–32.

353

Davies, Alun. "The Origins of the French Peasant Revolution of 1789." *History* 49: 165 (February 1964): 24–41.

Davis, Ralph. *The Rise of the Atlantic Economies.* Ithaca, N.Y.: Cornell University Press, 1973.

Dawson, Philip. "The *Bourgeoisie de Robe* in 1789." *French Historical Studies* 4: 1 (Spring 1965): 1–21.

_____. *Provincial Magistrates and Revolutionary Politics in France, 1789–1795.* Cambridge: Harvard University Press, 1972.

Delbeke, Baron Francis. *L'Action Politique et Sociale des Avocats au XVIIIe Siècle.* Lowain, France: Librarie Universitaire, 1927.

Doyle, William. "The Parlements of France and the Breakdown of the Old Regime, 1771–1788." *French Historical Studies* 6: 4 (Fall 1970): 415–58.

_____. "Was There an Aristocratic Reaction in Pre-Revolutionary France?" *Past and Present* no. 57 (November 1972): 97–122.

Edelstein, Melvin. "*La Feuille Villageoise,* the Revolutionary Press, and the Question of Rural Political Participation." *French Historical Studies* 7: 2 (Fall 1971): 175–203.

Egret, Jean. *La Révolution des Notables: Mounier et les Monarchiens.* Paris: Librairie Armand Colin, 1950.

_____. "L'Aristocratie Parlementaire Française a la Fin de l'Ancien Régime." *Revue Historique* 208 (July–September 1952): 1–14.

_____. *La Pré-Révolution Française (1787–1788).* Paris: Presses Universitaires de France, 1962.

Eisenstein, Elizabeth L. "Who Intervened in 1788? A Commentary on *The Coming of the French Revolution.*" *American Historical Review* 71: 1 (October 1965): 77–103.

Faucheux, Marcel. *L'Insurrection Vendéenne de 1793: Aspects Economiques et Sociaux.* Paris: Imprimerie Nationale, 1964.

Fohlen, Claude. "France 1700–1914." In *The Emergence of Industrial Societies,* pt. 1, The Fontana Economic History of Europe, vol. 4, edited by Carlo M. Cipolla, pp. 7–75. London: Collins/Fontana, 1973.

Ford, Franklin L. "The Revolutionary–Napoleonic Era: How Much of a Watershed?" *American Historical Review* 69: 1 (October 1963): 18–29.

_____. *Robe and Sword: The Regrouping of the French Aristocracy After Louis XIV.* New York: Harper & Row, 1965.

Forster, Robert. *The Nobility of Toulouse in the Eighteenth Century: A Social and Economic Study.* Baltimore, Md.: Johns Hopkins Press, 1960.

_____. "The Noble Wine Producers of the Bordelais in the Eighteenth Century." *Economic History Review.* 2nd ser. 14: 1 (August 1961): 18–33.

_____. "The Provincial Noble: A Reappraisal." *American Historical Review* 68: 3 (April 1963): 681–91.

_____. "The Survival of the Nobility During the French Revolution." *Past and Present* no. 37 (July 1967): 71–86.

_____. *The House of Saulx-Travanes: Versailles and Burgundy, 1700–1830.* Baltimore, Md.: Johns Hopkins University Press, 1971.

Fox, Edward Whiting. *History in Geographic Perspective: The Other France.* New York: Norton, 1972.

Furet, François. "Le Catéchisme Révolutionnaire." *Annales: Economies, Sociétés, Civilisations* 26: 2 (March–April 1971): 255–89.

Furet, François, and Denis Richet. *The French Revolution.* Translated by Stephen Hardman. New York: Macmillan, 1970.

Gay, Peter. "Rhetoric and Politics in the French Revolution." *American Historical Review* 66: 3 (April 1961): 664–81.

Gershoy, Leo. *The French Revolution and Napoleon.* 1933 Reprint. New York: Appleton-Century-Crofts, 1964.

Godechot, Jacques. "The French Revolution." In *Chapters in Western Civilization,* 3rd. ed., vol. 2, pp. 1–54. New York: Columbia University Press, 1962.

Les Institutions de la France sous la Révolution et l'Empire. 2nd, rev. ed. Paris: Presses Universitaires de France, 1968.

Goodwin, A. "The French Executive Directory – A Revaluation." *History* 22: 87 (December 1937): 201–18.

"Calonne, the Assembly of French Notables of 1787 and the Origins of the Révolte Nobiliare." *English Historical Review* 61: 240 (May 1946): 202–34 and 61: 241 (September 1946): 329–77.

Goubert, Pierre. *Louis XIV and Twenty Million Frenchmen.* Translated by Anne Carter. New York: Vintage Books, 1970.

L'Ancien Régime, 2: Les Pouvoirs. Paris: Armand Colin, 1973.

The Ancien Régime: French Society, 1600–1750. Translated by Steve Cox. New York: Harper & Row, 1974.

Greenlaw, Ralph W., ed. *The Economic Origins of the French Revolution.* Lexington, Mass.: D. C. Heath, 1958.

Greer, Donald. *The Incidence of the Terror During the French Revolution.* Cambridge: Harvard University Press, 1935.

The Incidence of the Emigration During the French Revolution. Cambridge: Harvard University Press, 1951.

Gruder, Vivian R. *The Royal Provincial Intendants: A Governing Elite in Eighteenth-Century France.* Ithaca, N.Y.: Cornell University Press, 1968.

Hampson, Norman. *A Social History of the French Revolution.* Toronto: University of Toronto Press, 1963.

The Enlightenment. Baltimore, Md.: Penguin Books, 1968.

Hartmann, Louis. "Les Officiers de l'Armée Royale à la Veille de la Révolution." *Révue Historique* 100 (January–April 1909): 241–68; and 101 (March–August 1909): 38–79.

Hauser, H. "The Characteristic Features of French Economic History from the Middle of the Sixteenth to the Middle of the Eighteenth Century." *Economic History Review* 4: 3 (October 1933): 257–72.

Higonnet, Patrice L. R. "Montagne, Gironde et Plaine: Bourgeoisie Provinciale, Bourgeoisie Urbaine, Bourgeoisie Rurale." Unpublished paper. Cambridge: Harvard University, n.d.

Hoffman, Stanley, et al. *In Search of France: The Economy, Society, and Political System in the Twentieth Century.* New York: Harper & Row, 1965.

Holtmann, Robert B. *The Napoleonic Revolution.* Philadelphia: Lippincott, 1967.

Hunt, Lynn A. "Committees and Communes: Local Politics and National Revolution in 1789." *Comparative Studies in Society and History* 18: 3 (July 1976): 321–46.

Jackson, J. Hampden, ed. *A Short History of France From Early Times to 1972.* 2nd. ed. Cambridge: Cambridge University Press, 1974.

Kaplow, Jeffry. *Elbeuf During the Revolutionary Period: History and Social Structure.* Baltimore, Md.: Johns Hopkins Press, 1964.

——— "On 'Who Intervened in 1788?' " *American Historical Review* 72: 2 (January 1967): 497–502.

——— ed. *New Perspectives on the French Revolution.* New York: Wiley, 1965.

Kemp, Tom. *Economic Forces in French History.* London: Dobson Books, 1971.

Knapton, Ernest John. *Revolutionary and Imperial France, 1750–1815.* New York: Charles Scribner's Sons, 1972.

Labrousse, C. E. *La Crise de l'Economie Française à la Fin de l'Ancien Régime et au Début de la Révolution.* Paris: Presses Universitaires de France, 1943.

——— *Le Paysan Français des Physiocrates à nos Jours.* Paris: Cours de Sorbonne, 1962.

——— "The Evolution of Peasant Society in France from the Eighteenth Century to the Present." In *French Society and Culture Since the Old Regime,* edited by E. M. Acomb and M. L. Brown, pp. 44–64. New York: Holt, Rinehart and Winston, 1966.

Landes, David S. *The Unbound Prometheus: Technological Change and Industrial Development in Western Europe from 1750 to the Present.* Cambridge: Cambridge University Press, 1969.

Lefebvre, Georges. *Les Paysans du Nord pendant La Révolution Française.* Lille, France: Librairie Papeterie, 1924.

——— *The Coming of the French Revolution.* Translated by R. R. Palmer. Princeton, N.J.: Princeton University Press, 1947.

——— *Questions Agraires au Temps de la Terreur.* La Roche-sur-Yon, France: Henri Potier, 1954.

——— "The French Revolution and the Peasants." In *The Economic Origins of the French Revolution,* edited by Robert Greenlaw, pp. 73–83. Lexington, Mass.: Heath, 1958.

——— "Urban Society in the Orleanais in the Late Eighteenth Century." *Past and Present* no. 19 (April 1961): 46–75.

——— *The French Revolution.* 2 vols. Translated by Elizabeth Moss Evanson (vol. 1) and John Hall Stewart and James Friguglietti (vol. 2). New York: Columbia University Press, 1962, 1964.

——— *Etudes sur la Révolution Française.* Paris: Presses Universitaires de France, 1963.

——— "Répartition de la Propriété et de l'Exploitation Foncières à la Fin de l'Ancien Régime." In *Etudes sur la Révolution Française,* pp. 279–306. Paris: Presses Universitaires de France, 1963.

——— *The Great Fear of 1789: Rural Panic in Revolutionary France.* Translated by Joan White. New York: Pantheon, 1973.

Le Goff, T. J. A., and Sutherland, D. M. G. "The Revolution and the Rural

Community in Eighteenth-Century Brittany." *Past and Present* no. 62 (February 1974): 96–119.

Léonard, Emile G. "La Question Sociale dans l'Armée Française au XVIII Siècle." *Annales: Economies, Sociétés, Civilisations* 3: 2 (April–June 1948): 135–49.

L'Armée et ses Problèmes au XVIIIᵉ Siecle. Paris: Librarie Plon, 1958.

Le Roy Ladurie, Emmanuel. "Révoltes et Contestations Rurales en France de 1675 à 1788." *Annales: Economies, Sociétés, Civilisations* 29: 1 (January–February 1974): 6–22.

The Peasants of Languedoc. Translated by John Day. Urbana: University of Illinois Press, 1976.

Lévy-Leboyer, Maurice. "Croissance Economique en France au XIXᵉ Siècle." *Annales: Economies, Sociétés, Civilizations* 23: 4 (July–August 1968): 788–807.

Lewis, W. H. *The Splended Century: Life in the France of Louis XIV.* New York: Doubleday (Anchor Books), 1957.

Lublinskaya, A. D. *French Absolutism: The Crucial Phase, 1620–1629.* Translated by Brian Pearce. Cambridge: Cambridge University Press, 1968.

Lucas, Colin. "Nobles, Bourgeois and the Origins of the French Revolution." *Past and Present* no. 60 (August 1973): 84–126.

The Structure of the Terror: The Example of Javogues and the Loire. New York: Oxford University Press, 1973.

Luethy, Herbert. *France Against Herself.* Translated by Eric Mosbacher. New York: Praeger, 1955.

Lyons, Martyn. *France Under the Directory.* Cambridge: Cambridge University Press, 1975.

Marczewski, Jan. "Some Aspects of the Economic Growth of France, 1660–1958." *Economic Development and Cultural Change* 9: 3 (April 1961): 369–86.

"The Take-Off Hypothesis and French Experience." In *The Economics of Take-Off into Sustained Growth,* edited by W. W. Rostow, pp. 119–38. New York: St. Martin's Press, 1963.

Markham, F. M. H. "Napoleonic France." In *France: Government and Society,* edited by J. M. Wallace-Hadrill and John McManners, pp. 188–206. London: Methuen, 1957.

Martin, Kingsley. *French Liberal Thought in the Eighteenth Century.* London: Phoenix House, 1962.

Mathiez, Albert. *The French Revolution.* Translated by Catherine A. Phillips. New York: Russell and Russell, 1962.

Matthews, George T. *The Royal General Farms in Eighteenth-Century France.* New York: Columbia University Press, 1958.

Mazauric, Claude. "Vendée et Chouannerie." *La Pensée* no. 124 (November–December 1965): 54–85.

McManners, J. "France." In *The European Nobility in the Eighteenth Century,* edited by Albert Goodwin, pp. 22–42. New York: Harper & Row, 1967.

Mitchell, Harvey. "The Vendée and Counterrevolution: A Review Essay." *French Historical Studies* 5: 4 (Fall 1968): 405–29.

357

Bibliography: France

"Resistance to the Revolution in Western France." *Past and Present* no. 63 (May 1974): 94–131.

Mornet, Daniel. *La Pensée Française au XVIIIe Siècle.* Paris: Librarie Armand Colin, 1926.

Mousnier, Roland. "Recherches Sur les Soulèvements Populaires en France avant la Fronde." *Révue d'Histoire Moderne et Contemporaine* 5 (1958): 6–113.

Murphy, J., and Higonnet, P. "Les Députés de la Noblesse aux Etats Généraux de 1789." *Révue d'Histoire Moderne et Contemporaine* 20 (April–June 1973): 230–47.

Murphy, James Michael; Higonnet, Bernard; and Higonnet, Patrice. "Notes sur la Composition de l'Assemblée Constituante." *Annales Historiques de la Révolution Française* 46: 217 (July–September 1974): 321–6.

Palmer, R.R. *Twelve Who Ruled: The Year of Terror in the French Revolution.* Princeton, N.J.: Princeton University Press, 1941.

"Georges Lefebvre: The Peasants and the French Revolution." *Journal of Modern History* 31: 4 (1959): 329–42.

"Popular Democracy in the French Revolution: Review Article." *French Historical Studies* 1: 4 (December 1960): 445–69.

The World of the French Revolution. New York: Harper & Row, 1972.

Parker, Harold T. "Two Administrative Bureaus Under the Directory and Napoleon." *French Historical Studies* 4: 2 (Fall 1965): 150–69.

Patrick, Alison. "Political Divisions in the French National Convention, 1792–93." *Journal of Modern History* 41: 4 (December 1969): 421–74.

Piétri, François. *La Réform de l'Etat au XVIIIe Siècle.* Paris: Editions de France, 1935.

Ponteil, Félix. *Napoleon Ier et l'Organisation Autoritaire de la France.* Paris: Librairie Armand Colin, 1956.

Porchnev, Boris. *Les Soulèvements Populaires en France de 1623 à 1648.* Oeuvres Etrangères, no. 4. Paris: Ecole Pratique des Hautes Etudes, VI Section, Centres de Recherches Historiques, 1963.

Prestwick, Menna. "The Making of Absolute Monarchy (1559–1683)." In *France: Government and Society,* edited by J. M. Wallace-Hadrill and J. McManners, pp. 105–33. London: Methuen, 1957.

Ranum, Orest. *Paris in the Age of Absolutism.* New York: Wiley, 1968.

Reinhard, M. "Observations sur le Rôle Révolutionnaire de l'Armée dans la Révolution Française." *Annales Historiques de la Révolution Française* no. 168 (April–June 1962): 169–81.

Richardson, Nicholas. *The French Prefectoral Corps, 1814–1830.* Cambridge: Cambridge University Press, 1966.

Richet, Denis. "Croissance et Blocage en France du XVe au XVIIIe Siècle." *Annales: Economies, Sociétés, Civilisations* 23: 4 (July–August 1968): 789–97.

"Autour des Origines Ideologiques Lointaines de la Révolution Française: Elites et Despotism." *Annales: Economies, Sociétés, Civilisations* 24: 1 (January–February 1969): 1–23.

Ross, Steven T. "The Development of the Combat Division in Eighteenth-Century French Armies." *French Historical Studies* 4: 1 (Spring 1965): 84–94.

Rudé, George. *The Crowd in the French Revolution.* New York: Oxford University Press, 1959.

Revolutionary Europe, 1783–1815. New York: Harper & Row, 1966.

Paris and London in the Eighteenth Century. New York: Viking Press, 1973.

Robespierre: Portrait of a Revolutionary Democrat. New York: Viking Press, 1976.

Sagnac, Philippe. *La Formation de la Société Française Moderne.* Vol. 2. Paris: Presses Universitaires de France, 1946.

La Fin de l'Ancien Régime et La Révolution Americaine (1763–1789). Paris: Presses Universitaires de France, 1952.

Saint-Jacob, Pierre de. *Les Paysans de la Bourgogne du Nord au Dernier Siècle de l'Ancien Régime.* Dijon, France: Imprimerie Bergniaud et Privat, 1960.

Sargent, Frederic O. "Feudalism to Family Farms in France." *Agricultural History* 35: 4 (1961): 193–201.

Scott, Samuel F. "The French Revolution and the Professionalization of the French Officer Corps." In *On Military Ideology,* edited by Morris Janowitz and Jacques Van Doorn, pp. 5–56. Rotterdam, Holland: Rotterdam University Press, 1971.

"The Regeneration of the Line Army During the French Revolution." *Journal of Modern History* 42: 3 (September 1970): 307–30.

Sée, Henri. *Economic and Social Conditions in France During the Eighteenth Century.* Translated by Edwin H. Zeydel. New York: F. S. Crofts, 1931.

Shennan, J. H. *The Parliament of Paris.* Ithaca, N.Y.: Cornell University Press, 1968.

Sheppard, Thomas F. *Lourmarin in the Eighteenth Century: A Study of a French Village.* Baltimore, Md.: Johns Hopkins Press, 1971.

Soboul, Albert. "Classes and Class Struggles During the French Revolution." *Science and Society* 17: 5 (Summer 1953): 238–57.

"The French Rural Community in the Eighteenth and Nineteenth Centuries." *Past and Present* no. 10 (November 1956): 78–95.

La France à la Veille de la Révolution: Economie et Société. Paris: Centre de Documentation Universitaire, 1960.

The Sans-Culottes: The Popular Movement and Revolutionary Government, 1793–1794. Translated by Rémy Inglis Hall. New York: Doubleday (Anchor Books), 1972.

The French Revolution, 1787–1799: From the Storming of the Bastille to Napoleon. Translated by Alan Forrest and Colin Jones. New York: Vintage Books, 1975.

Sydenham, M. J. *The Girondins.* London: Athlone Press, 1961.

The French Revolution. New York: Capricorn Books, 1966.

Taylor, George V. "Types of Capitalism in Eighteenth-Century France." *English Historical Review* 79: 312 (July 1964): 478–97.

"Noncapitalist Wealth and the Origins of the French Revolution." *American Historical Review* 72: 2 (January 1967): 469–96.

"Revolutionary and Nonrevolutionary Content in the *Cahiers* of 1789: An Interim Report." *French Historical Studies* 7: 3 (Spring 1972): 479–502.

Temple, Nora. "The Control and Exploitation of French Towns During the Ancien Régime." *History* 51: 171 (February 1966): 16–34.

Thompson, J. M. *Robespierre and the French Revolution.* New York: Collier Books, 1962.

Tilly, Charles. *The Vendée: A Sociological Analysis of the Counterrevolution of 1793.* New York: Wiley, 1967.

Tilly, Louise. "The Food Riot as a Form of Political Conflict in France." *Journal of Interdisciplinary History* 2: 1 (Summer 1971): 23–57.

Tocqueville, Alexis de. *The Old Regime and the French Revolution.* Translated by Stuart Gilbert. New York: Doubleday (Anchor Books), 1955.

Treasure, G. R. R. *Seventeenth Century France.* London: Rivingtons, 1966.

Vovelle, Michel. "L'Elite ou le Mensonge des Mots." *Annales: Economies, Sociétés, Civilisations* 29: 1 (January–February 1974): 49–72.

Williams, Gwyn A. *Artisans and Sans-Culottes: Popular Movements in France and Britain During the French Revolution.* New York: Norton, 1969.

Woloch, Isser. *Jacobin Legacy: The Democratic Movement Under the Directory.* Princeton, N.J.: Princeton University Press, 1970.

Young, Arthur. *Travels in France During the Years 1787, 1788, and 1789.* Edited by C. Maxwell. Cambridge: Cambridge University Press, 1929.

Zeldin, Theodore. *France: 1848–1945,* vol. I, *Ambition, Love, and Politics.* New York: Oxford University Press, 1973.

II. RUSSIA: OLD REGIME AND REVOLUTION

Anweiler, Oskar. *The Soviets: The Russian Workers, Peasants, and Soldiers Councils, 1905–1921.* Translated by Ruth Hein. New York: Pantheon, 1974.

Avrich, Paul H. "The Bolshevik Revolution and Workers' Control in Russian Industry." *Slavic Review* 22: 1 (March 1963): 47–63.

"Russian Factory Committees in 1917." *Jahrbücher für Geschichte Osteuropas* 11: 2 (June 1963): 161–82.

Russian Rebels, 1600–1800. New York: Schocken Books, 1972.

Kronstadt 1921. New York: Norton, 1974.

Azrael, Jeremy R. *Managerial Power and Soviet Politics.* Cambridge: Harvard University Press, 1966.

Baykov, Alexander. "The Economic Development of Russia." *Economic History Review.* 2nd ser. 7: 2 (1954): 137–49.

Berdyaev, Nicholas. *The Origin of Russian Communism.* Ann Arbor: University of Michigan Press, 1960.

Bergson, Abram, and Kuznets, Simon, eds. *Economic Trends in the Soviet Union.* Cambridge: Harvard University Press, 1963.

Bernstein, Thomas P. "Leadership and Mobilization in the Collectivization of Agriculture in China and Russia: A Comparison." Ph.D. dissertation, Department of Political Science, Columbia University, 1970. Ann Arbor, Mich.: University Microfilms.

Bettelheim, Charles. *Class Struggles in the USSR, First Period: 1917–1923.* Translated by Brian Pearce. New York: Monthly Review Press, 1976.

Billington, James H. "Six Views of the Russian Revolution." *World Politics* 18 (April 1966): 452–73.

Black, Cyril E., ed. *The Transformation of Russian Society.* Cambridge: Harvard University Press, 1960.

Black, Cyril, E., et al. *The Modernization of Japan and Russia.* New York: Free Press, 1975.

Blackwell, William L. *The Beginnings of Russian Industrialization, 1800–1860.* Princeton, N.J.: Princeton University Press, 1968.

    ed. *Russian Economic Development: From Peter the Great to Stalin.* New York: New Viewpoints, 1974.

Blum, Jerome. *Lord and Peasant in Russia: From the Ninth to the Nineteenth Century.* Princeton, N.J.: Princeton University Press, 1961.

Boyd, John R. "The Origins of Order No. 1." *Soviet Studies* 19: 3 (January 1968): 359–72.

Brezezinski, Zbigniew K. "The Patterns of Autocracy." In *The Transformation of Russian Society,* edited by Cyril E. Black, pp. 93–109. Cambridge: Harvard University Press, 1960.

Carr, Edward Hallett. *The Bolshevik Revolution, 1917–1923.* 3 Vols. New York: Macmillan, 1951–68.

    Socialism in One Country, 1924–1926. 3 Vols. New York: Macmillan, 1958–64.

    "The Russian Revolution and the Peasant." *Proceedings of the British Academy* 49 (1963): 69–93.

    Foundations of a Planned Economy, 1926–1929. 3 Vols. New York: Macmillan, 1971.

    The October Revolution: Before and After. New York: Vintage Books, 1971.

Carson, George Barr, Jr. "The State and Economic Development: Russia, 1890–1939." In *The State and Economic Growth,* edited by Hugh G. J. Aitken, pp. 115–47. New York: Social Science Research Council, 1959.

Chamberlin, William Henry. *The Russian Revolution, 1917–1921.* 2 Vols. 1935. Reprint. New York: Grosset & Dunlap, 1965.

Charques, Richard. *The Twilight of Imperial Russia.* London: Phoenix House, 1958.

Chayanov, A. V. *The Theory of Peasant Economy.* Edited by Daniel Thormer, Basile Kerblay, and R. E. F. Smith. Homewood, Ill.: Richard D. Irwin, 1966.

Cherniavsky, Michael. *Tsar and People.* New York: Random House, 1969.

Cliff, Tony. *State Capitalism in Russia.* New York: Pluto Press, 1974.

Cohen, Stephen F. *Bukharin and the Bolshevik Revolution: A Political Biography, 1888–1938.* New York: Knopf, 1973.

Conquest, Robert. *The Great Terror: Stalin's Purge of the Thirties.* New York: Macmillan, 1973.

Daniels, Robert Vincent. "The Kronstadt Revolt of 1921: A Study in the Dynamics of Revolution." *American Slavic and East European Review* 10: 4 (December 1951): 241–54.

    The Conscience of the Revolution: Communist Opposition in Soviet Russia. New York: Simon & Schuster, 1969.

Deutscher, Isaac. *The Prophet Armed: Trotsky 1879–1921.* New York: Vintage Books, 1965.

    The Prophet Outcast: Trotsky 1929–1940. New York: Vintage Books, 1965.

    The Prophet Unarmed: Trotsky 1921–1929. New York: Vintage Books, 1965.

    Stalin: A Political Biography. New York: Oxford University Press, 1966.

    The Unfinished Revolution: Russia 1917–1967. New York: Oxford University Press, 1967.

    "The Russian Revolution." In *The New Cambridge Modern History,* 2nd ed., vol. 12, pp. 403–432. Cambridge: Cambridge University Press, 1968.

Dobson, Richard B. "Mobility and Stratification in the Soviet Union." *Annual Review of Sociology* 3 (1977): 297–329.

Edeen, Alf. "The Civil Service: Its Composition and Status." In *The Transformation of Russian Society,* edited by Cyril E. Black, pp. 274–91. Cambridge: Harvard University Press, 1960.

Elkin, Boris. "The Russian Intelligentsia on the Eve of the Revolution." In *The Russian Intelligentsia,* edited by Richard Pipes, pp. 32–46. New York: Columbia University Press, 1961.

Ellison, Herbert J. "Economic Modernization in Imperial Russia: Purposes and Achievements." *Journal of Economic History* 25 (December 1965): 523–40.

Emmons, Terence. "The Peasant and the Emancipation." In *The Peasant in Nineteenth-Century Russia,* edited by Wayne S. Vucinich, pp. 41–71. Stanford, Cal.: Stanford University Press, 1968.

    The Russian Landed Gentry and the Peasant Emancipation of 1861. Cambridge: Cambridge University Press, 1968.

Erickson, John. "The Origins of the Red Army." In *Revolutionary Russia,* edited by Richard Pipes, pp. 286–325. New York: Doubleday (Anchor Books), 1969.

Erlich, Alexander. *The Soviet Industrialization Debate, 1924–1928.* Cambridge: Harvard University Press, 1967.

Esper, Thomas. "Military Self-Sufficiency and Weapons Technology in Muscovite Russia." *Slavic Review* 28: 2 (June 1969): 185–208.

Fainsod, Merle. *How Russia is Ruled.* Cambridge: Harvard University Press, 1953.

    Smolensk Under Soviet Rule. Cambridge: Harvard University Press, 1958.

Feldmesser, Robert A. "Social Classes and Political Structure." In *The Transformation of Russian Society,* edited by Cyril E. Black, pp. 235–52. Cambridge: Harvard University Press, 1960.

Ferro, Marc. "The Russian Soldier in 1917: Undisciplined, Patriotic, and Revolutionary." *Slavic Review* 30: 3 (September 1971): 483–512.

Bibliography: Russia

The Russian Revolution of February 1917. Translated by J. L. Richards. Englewood Cliffs, N.J.: Prentice-Hall, 1972.

"La Naissance du Système Bureaucratique en U.R.S.S." *Annales: Economies, Sociétés, Civilisations* 31: 2 (March–April 1976): 243–67.

Field, Daniel. *Rebels in the Name of the Tsar.* Boston: Houghton Mifflin, 1976.

Fischer, George. *Russian Liberalism: From Gentry to Intelligentsia.* Cambridge: Harvard University Press, 1958.

Florinsky, Michael T. *Russia: A History and Interpretation.* New York: Macmillan, 1955.

Footman, David. *Civil War in Russia.* New York: Praeger, 1962.

Garder, Michel. *A History of the Soviet Army.* New York: Praeger, 1966.

Garthoff, Raymond L. "The Military as a Social Force." In *The Transformation of Russian Society,* edited by Cyril E. Black, pp. 323–7. Cambridge: Harvard University Press, 1960.

Gerschenkron, Alexander. "Problems and Patterns of Russian Economic Development." In *The Transformation of Russian Society,* edited by Cyril E. Black, pp. 42–72. Cambridge: Harvard University Press, 1960.

"Russian Agrarian Policies and Industrialization, 1861–1917." In *Continuity in History and Other Essays,* pp. 140–248. Cambridge: Harvard University Press, 1968.

Getzler, Israel. "Marxist Revolutionaries and the Dilemma of Power." In *Revolution and Politics in Russia,* edited by Alexander and Janet Rabinowitch, pp. 88–112. Bloomington: University of Indiana Press, 1972.

Goldsmith, Raymond W. "The Economic Growth of Tsarist Russia, 1860–1913." *Economic Development and Cultural Change* 9: 3 (April 1961): 441–75.

Golovine, Nicholas N. *The Russian Army in the World War.* New Haven: Yale University Press, 1931.

Granick, David. *The Red Executive: A Study of the Organization Man in Russian Industry.* Garden City, N.Y.: Doubleday, 1960.

Gronsky, Paul P., and Astrov, Nicholas J. *The War and the Russian Government.* New Haven: Yale University Press, 1929.

Haimson, Leopold. "The Problem of Social Stability in Urban Russia, 1905–1917." *Slavic Review* 23: 4 (December 1964): 619–42 and 24: 1 (March 1965): 1–21.

The Russian Marxists and the Origins of Bolshevism. Boston: Beacon Press, 1966.

Harcave, Sidney. *The Russian Revolution of 1905.* New York: Macmillan, 1964.

Hellie, Richard. *Enserfment and Military Change in Muscovy.* Chicago: University of Chicago Press, 1971.

Hoetzsch, Otto. *The Evolution of Russia.* London: Thames and Hudson, 1966.

Inkeles, Alex. *Social Change in Soviet Russia.* Cambridge: Harvard University Press, 1968.

Jasny, Naum. *The Socialized Agriculture of the USSR.* Stanford Cal.: Stanford University Press, 1949.

Jenkins, Joseph Craig. "Agrarian Class Structure and Peasant Revolution – Russia

1917." M.A. Thesis, Department of Sociology, State University of New York at Stony Brook, April 1974.

Karcz, Jerzy F. "From Stalin to Brezhnev: Soviet Agricultural Policy in Historical Perspective." In *The Soviet Rural Community,* edited by James R. Millar, pp. 36–70. Urbana: University of Illinois Press, 1971.

"Thoughts on the Great Problem." *Soviet Studies* 18: 4 (April 1967): 399–434.

Karpovitch, Michael. *Imperial Russia, 1801–1917.* New York: Holt, 1964.

Keep, John L. H. *The Russian Revolution: A Study in Mass Mobilization.* New York: Norton, 1976.

Keller, Theodore. "To Lead the People: Notes on the Russian Revolutionaries." *Journal of Contemporary Revolutions* 5: 3 (Summer 1973): 94–121.

Kennan, George F. "The Breakdown of the Tsarist Autocracy." In *Revolutionary Russia,* edited by Richard Pipes, pp. 1–32. New York: Doubleday (Anchor Books), 1969.

Kingston-Mann, Esther. "Lenin and the Beginings of Marxist Peasant Revolution: The Burden of Political Opportunity, July–October 1917." *Slavonic and East European Review* 50: 121 (October 1972): 570–88.

Kochan, Lionel. *The Making of Modern Russia.* Baltimore, Md.: Penguin Books, 1963.

Laird, Roy D., and Laird, Betty A. *Soviet Communism and Agrarian Revolution.* Baltimore, Md.: Penguin Books, 1970.

Lane, David. *Politics and Society in the USSR.* London: Weidenfeld and Nicolson, 1970.

The Roots of Russian Communism: A Social and Historical Study of Russian Social Democracy, 1898–1907. University Park, Penn.: Pennsylvania State University Press, 1975.

Laqueur, Walter. *The Fate of the Revolution: Interpretation of Soviet History.* London: Weidenfeld and Nicolson, 1967.

Lenin, V. I. *The Development of Capitalism in Russia.* Moscow: Progress Publishers, 1967.

Lewin, Moshe. "The Immediate Background of Soviet Collectivization." *Soviet Studies* 17: 2 (October 1965): 162–97.

Russian Peasants and Soviet Power: A Study of Collectivization. Translated by Irene Nove. Evanston, Ill.: Northwestern University Press, 1968.

Lenin's Last Struggle. Translated by A. M. Sheridan Smith. New York: Vintage Books, 1970.

Liebman, Marcel. *The Russian Revolution.* Translated by Arnold J. Pomerans. New York: Vintage Books, 1972.

Lincoln, W. Bruce. "The Genesis of an 'Enlightened' Bureaucracy in Russia, 1825–1856." *Jahrbücher für Geschichte Osteuropas* 20: 3 (September 1963): 321–30.

Longly, D. A. "Officers and Men: A Study of the Development of Political Attitudes Among Sailors of the Baltic Fleet in 1917." *Soviet Studies* 25: 1 (July 1973): 28–50.

Lyashchenko, Peter I. *History of the National Economy of Russia to the 1917*

Revolution. Translated by L. M. Herman. New York: Macmillan, 1949.

Male, D. J. *Russian Peasant Organization Before Collectivisation.* Cambridge: Cambridge University Press, 1971.

Matossian, Mary. "The Peasant Way of Life." In *The Peasant in Nineteenth Century Russia,* edited by Wayne S. Vucinich, pp. 1–40. Stanford, Cal.: Stanford University Press, 1968.

Matthews, Mervyn. *Class and Society in Soviet Russia.* New York: Walker, 1972.

McGrew, Roderick E. "Some Imperatives of Russian Foreign Policy." In *Russia Under the Last Tsar,* edited by George Stavrou, pp. 202–29. Minneapolis: University of Minnesota Press, 1969.

Menashe, Louis. "Vladimir Illyich Bakunin: An Essay on Lenin." *Socialist Revolution* no. 18 (November–December 1973): 9–54.

Mendel, Arthur P. "Peasant and Worker on the Eve of the First World War." *Slavic Review* 24: 1 (March 1965): 23–33.

Meyer, Alfred G. *The Soviet Political System.* New York: Random House, 1965.

Millar, James R., ed. *The Soviet Rural Community.* Chicago: University of Illinois Press, 1961.

———. "Mass Collectivization and the Contribution of Soviet Agriculture to the First Five-Year Plan: A Review Article." *Slavic Review* 33 (December 1974): 750–66.

Millar, James R., and Guntzel, Corinne A. "The Economics and Politics of Mass Collectivization Reconsidered: A Review Article." *Explorations in Economic History* 8: 2 (Fall 1970): 103–116.

Miller, Margaret S. *The Economic Development of Russia, 1905–1914.* 2nd ed. London: P. S. King, 1967.

Miller, Robert F. *One Hundred Thousand Tractors: The MTS and the Development of Controls in Soviet Agriculture.* Cambridge: Harvard University Press, 1970.

Moore, Barrington, Jr. *Soviet Politics – The Dilemma of Power: The Role of Ideas in Social Change.* New York: Harper & Row, 1965.

———. *Terror and Progress USSR: Some Sources of Change and Stability in the Soviet Dictatorship.* New York: Harper & Row, 1966.

Mosse, W. E. "Stolypin's Villages." *Slavonic and East European Review* 43: 101 (June 1965): 257–75.

Nettl, J. P. *The Soviet Achievement.* London: Harcourt, Brace, and World, 1967.

Nove, Alec. *An Economic History of the U.S.S.R.* Baltimore, Md.: Penguin Books, 1969.

Owen, Launcelot A. *The Russian Peasant Movement, 1906–1917.* London: P. S. King, 1937.

Pares, Bernard. *A History of Russia.* New York: Vintage Books, 1965.

Pavlovsky, George. *Agricultural Russia on the Eve of the Revolution.* London: Routledge, 1930.

Perrie, Maureen. "The Russian Peasant Movement of 1905–1907: Its Social Composition and Revolutionary Significance." *Past and Present* no. 57 (November 1972): 123–55.

Pethybridge, Roger. *The Spread of the Russian Revolution: Essays on 1917.* London: Macmillan, 1972.

Pintner, Walter M. "The Social Characteristics of the Early Nineteenth-Century Russian Bureaucracy." *Slavic Review* 29: 3 (September 1970): 429–43.

Pipes, Richard, ed. *The Russian Intelligentsia.* New York: Columbia University Press, 1961.

    Revolutionary Russia: A Symposium. New York: Doubleday (Anchor Books), 1969.

    Russia Under the Old Regime. New York: Scribner, 1974.

Pushkarev, Sergei. *The Emergence of Modern Russia, 1801–1917.* Translated by Robert H. McNeal and Tova Yedlin. New York: Holt, Rinehart and Winston, 1963.

Rabinowitch, Alexander. *Prelude to Revolution: The Petrograd Bolsheviks and the July 1917 Uprising.* Bloomington: University of Indiana Press, 1968.

    "The Petrograd Garrison and the Bolshevik Seizure of Power." In *Revolution and Politics in Russia,* edited by Alexander and Janet Rabinowitch, pp. 172–91. Bloomington: University of Indiana Press, 1972.

    The Bolsheviks Come to Power: The Revolution of 1917 in Petrograd. New York: Norton, 1976.

Radkey, Oliver H. *The Election to the Russian Constituent Assembly of 1917.* Cambridge: Harvard University Press, 1950.

    "The Socialist Revolutionaries and the Peasantry After October." In *Russian Thought and Politics,* edited by Hugh McLean, Martin Malia, and George Fischer, pp. 457–79. Cambridge: Harvard University Press, 1957.

    The Agrarian Foes of Bolshevism: Promise and Default of the Russian Socialist Revolutionaries, February to October 1917. New York: Columbia University Press, 1958.

    The Sickle Under the Hammer: The Russian Socialist Revolutionaries in the Early Months of Soviet Rule. New York: Oxford University Press, 1963.

Raeff, Marc. "The Russian Autocracy and Its Officials." In *Russian Thought and Politics,* edited by Hugh McLean, Martin Malia, and George Fischer, pp. 77–91. Cambridge: Harvard University Press, 1957.

    Origins of the Russian Intelligentsia: The Eighteenth-Century Nobility. New York: Harcourt, Brace, and World, 1966.

    Imperial Russia 1682–1825: The Coming of Age of Modern Russia. New York: Knopf, 1971.

Reed, John H. *Ten Days That Shook the World.* New York: Signet Books, 1967.

Rigby, T. H. *Communist Party Membership in the USSR, 1917–1967.* Princeton, N.J.: Princeton University Press, 1968.

Rimlinger, Gaston W. "Autocracy and the Factory Order in Early Russian Industrialization." *Journal of Economic History* 20: 1 (March 1960): 67–92.

Robinson, Geroid Tanquary. *Rural Russia Under the Old Regime.* 1932. Reprint. Berkeley: University of California Press, 1969.

Rosenberg, Arthur. *A History of Bolshevism.* New York: Oxford University Press, 1934.

Rosenberg, William G. "The Russian Municipal Duma Elections of 1917: A Preliminary Computation of Returns." *Soviet Studies* 21: 2 (October 1969): 131–63.

    Liberals in the Russian Revolution: The Constitutional Democratic Party, 1917–1921. Princeton, N.J.: Princeton University Press, 1974.

Rowney, Don Karl. "Higher Civil Servants in the Russian Ministry of Internal Affairs: Some Demographic and Career Characteristics, 1905–1916." *Slavic Review* 31: 1 (March 1972): 101–10.

Rozman, Gilbert. *Urban Networks in Russia, 1750–1800, and Premodern Periodization.* Princeton, N.J.: Princeton University Press, 1976.

Sablinsky, Walter. "The All-Russian Railroad Union and the Beginning of the General Strike in October, 1905." In *Revolution and Politics in Russia,* edited by Alexander and Janet Rabinowitch, pp. 113–33. Bloomington: University of Indiana Press, 1972.

Schapiro, Leonard. *The Origin of the Communist Autocracy.* London: G. Bell and Sons, 1955.

    The Government and Politics of the Soviet Union. Rev. ed. New York: Vintage Books, 1967.

    The Communist Party of the Soviet Union. 2nd ed., rev. and enlarged. New York: Vintage Books, 1971.

Schwarz, Solomon M. *The Russian Revolution of 1905: The Workers' Movement and the Formation of Bolshevism and Menshevism.* Translated by Gertrude Vakar. Chicago: University of Chicago Press, 1967.

Seton-Watson, Hugh. *The Decline of Imperial Russia, 1855–1914.* New York: Praeger, 1952.

    The Russian Empire, 1801–1917. New York: Oxford University Press, 1967.

Shanin, Teodor. *The Awkward Class: Political Sociology of Peasantry in a Developing Society: Russia 1910–1925.* New York: Oxford University Press, 1972.

Singleton, Seth. "The Tambov Revolt (1920–1921)." *Slavic Review* 25: 3 (September 1966): 497–512.

Sontag, John P. "Tsarist Debts and Tsarist Foreign Policy." *Slavic Review* 27: 4 (December 1968): 529–41.

Starr, S. Frederick. *Decentralization and Self-Government in Russia, 1830–1870.* Princeton, N.J.: Princeton University Press, 1972.

Treadgold, Donald W. *The West in Russia and China,* vol. 1, *Russia, 1472–1917.* London: Cambridge University Press, 1973.

Trotsky, Leon. *The Russian Revolution.* Selected and edited by F. W. Dupee. Translated by Max Eastman. New York: Doubleday (Anchor Books), 1959.

    1905. Translated by Anya Bostock. New York: Vintage Books, 1972.

Tucker, Robert C. *Stalin as Revolutionary, 1879–1929.* New York: Norton, 1974.

    ed. *Stalinism: Essays in Historical Interpretation.* New York: Norton, 1977.

Ulam, Adam B. *The Bolsheviks: The Intellectual and Political History of the Triumph of Communism in Russia.* New York: Collier Books, 1965.

Uldricks, Teddy J. "The 'Crowd' in the Russian Revolution: Towards Reassessing the Nature of Revolutionary Leadership." *Politics and Society* 4: 3 (1974): 397–413.

Venturi, Franco. *Roots of Revolution: A History of the Populist and Socialist Movements in Nineteenth Century Russia*. Translated by Francis Haskell. New York: Grosset & Dunlap, 1966.

Volin, Lazar. *A Century of Russian Agriculture: From Alexander II to Kruschchev*. Cambridge: Harvard University Press, 1970.

Von Laue, Theodore H. "Russian Peasants in the Factory, 1892–1904." *Journal of Economic History* 21 (1961): 61–80.

  Sergei Witte and the Industrialization of Russia. New York: Columbia University Press, 1963.

  "Russian Labor Between Field and Factory, 1892–1903." *California Slavic Studies* 3 (1964): 33–65.

  "The Chances for Liberal Constitutionalism." *Slavic Review* 24: 1 (March 1965): 34–46.

  Why Lenin? Why Stalin?: A Reappraisal of the Russian Revolution, 1900–1930. 2nd ed. Philadelphia: J. B. Lippincott, 1971.

Vucinich, Alexander. "The State and the Local Community." In *The Transformation of Russian Society*, edited by Cyril E. Black, pp. 191–208. Cambridge: Harvard University Press, 1960.

Vucinich, Wayne S., ed. *The Peasant in Nineteenth-Century Russia*. Stanford, Cal.: Stanford University Press, 1968.

Wade, Rex A. "The Rajonnye Sovety of Petrograd: The Role of Local Political Bodies in the Russian Revolution." *Jahrbücher für Geschichte Osteuropas* 20: 2 (June 1972): 227–40.

Walkin, Jacob. *The Rise of Democracy in Pre-Revolutionary Russia: Political and Social Institutions Under the Last Three Czars*. New York: Praeger, 1962.

Wallace, Sir Donald Mackenzie. *Russia on the Eve of War and Revolution*. New York: Vintage Books, 1961.

Watters, Francis M. "The Peasant and the Village Commune." In *The Peasant in Nineteenth-Century Russia*, edited by Wayne S. Vucinich, pp. 133–57. Stanford, Cal.: Stanford University Press, 1968.

Werth, Alexander. *Russia at War, 1941–1945*. New York: Avon Books, 1964.

Wesson, Robert G. *The Russian Dilemma: A Political and Geopolitical View*. New Brunswick, N.J.: Rutgers University Press, 1974.

Wildman, Allan. *The Making of a Workers' Revolution: Russian Social Democracy, 1891–1903*. Chicago: University of Chicago Press, 1967.

  "The February Revolution in the Russian Army." *Soviet Studies* 22: 1 (July 1970): 3–23.

Wolfe, Bertram D. *An Ideology in Power: Reflections on the Russian Revolution*. New York: Stein & Day, 1970.

Yarmolinsky, Avrahm. *Road to Revolution: A Century of Russian Radicalism*. New York: Collier Books, 1962.

Zelnik, Reginald E. *Labor and Society in Tsarist Russia: The Factory Workers of St. Petersburg, 1855–1870*. Stanford, Cal.: Stanford University Press, 1971.

"Russian Workers and the Revolutionary Movement." *Journal of Social History* 6 (Winter 1971–72): 214–34.

III. CHINA: OLD REGIME AND REVOLUTION

Ahn, Byung-joon. "The Political Economy of the People's Commune in China: Changes and Continuities." *Journal of Asian Studies* 34: 3 (May 1975): 631–58.

    Chinese Politics and the Cultural Revolution: Dynamics of Policy Processes. Seattle: University of Washington Press, 1976.

Andors, Stephen. *China's Industrial Revolution: Politics, Planning, and Management, 1949 to the Present.* New York: Pantheon Books, 1977.

Balaz, Etienne. *Chinese Civilization and Bureaucracy.* Translated by H. M. Wright. New Haven: Yale University Press, 1964.

Barendsen, Robert D. "The Agricultural Middle School in Communist China." In *China Under Mao: Politics Takes Command,* edited by Roderick Mac-Farquhar, pp. 304–32. Cambridge: M.I.T. Press, 1966.

Barnett, A. Doak. *China on the Eve of Communist Takeover.* New York: Praeger, 1963.

    Cadres, Bureaucracy, and Political Power in Communist China. New York: Columbia University Press, 1967.

    ed. *Chinese Communist Politics in Action.* Seattle: University of Washington Press, 1969.

Bastid, Marianne. "Levels of Economic Decision-Making." In *Authority, Participation and Cultural Change in China,* edited by Stuart R. Schram, pp. 159–98. Cambridge: Cambridge University Press, 1973.

Baum, Richard, with Bennett, Louise B; eds. *China in Ferment: Perspectives on the Cultural Revolution.* Englewood Cliffs, N.J.: Prentice-Hall, 1971.

Bergère, Marie-Claire. "The Role of the Bourgeoisie." In *China in Revolution,* edited by Mary C. Wright, pp. 229–95. New Haven: Yale University Press, 1968.

    "De la Chine Classique à la Chine Actuelle: Fluctuations Economiques et Révolution." *Annales: Economies, Sociétés, Civilisations* 24: 4 (July–August 1969): 860–75.

Bernstein, Thomas P. "Leadership and Mass Mobilisation in the Soviet and Chinese Collectivisation Campaigns of 1929–30 and 1955–56: A Comparison." *China Quarterly* no. 31 (July–September 1967): 1–47.

    "Leadership and Mobilization in the Collectivization of Agriculture in China and Russia: A Comparison." Ph.D. dissertation, Department of Political Science, Columbia University, 1970. Ann Arbor, Mich.: University Microfilms.

Bettelheim, Charles. *Cultural Revolution and Industrial Organization in China.* Translated by Alfred Ehrenfeld. New York: Monthly Review Press, 1975.

Bianco, Lucien. "Les Paysans et la Révolution Chine, 1919–1949." *Politique Etrangère* no. 2 (1968): 117–41.

Origins of the Chinese Revolution, 1915–1949. Translated by Muriel Bell. Stanford, Cal.: Stanford University Press, 1971.

Buck, John Lossing. *Chinese Farm Economy.* Chicago: University of Chicago Press, 1930.

Cavendish, Patrick. "The 'New China' of the Kuomintang." In *Modern China's Search for a Political Form,* edited by Jack Gray, pp. 138–96. New York: Oxford University Press, 1969.

Cell, Charles P. *Revolution at Work: Mobilization Campaigns in China.* New York: Academic Press, 1977.

Chang, Chung-li. The Chinese Gentry: Studies on Their Role in Nineteenth Century Chinese Society. Seattle: University of Washington Press, 1955.

The Income of the Chinese Gentry. Seattle: University of Washington Press, 1962.

Chang, P'eng-yüan. "The Constitutionalists." In *China in Revolution,* edited by Mary C. Wright, pp. 143–83. New Haven: Yale University Press, 1968.

Chao, Shu-li. *Rhymes of Li Yu-tsai and Other Stories.* Peking: Cultural Press, 1950.

Ch'ên, Jerome. *Mao and the Chinese Revolution.* New York: Oxford University Press, 1965.

Chesneaux, Jean. *The Chinese Labor Movement, 1919–1927.* Translated by H. M. Wright. Stanford, Cal.: Stanford University Press, 1968.

ed. *Popular Movements and Secret Societies in China, 1840–1950.* Stanford, Cal.: Stanford University Press, 1972.

Peasant Revolts in China, 1840–1949. New York: Norton, 1973.

Chesneaux, Jean; Bastid, Marianne; and Bergère, Marie-Claire. *China: From the Opium Wars to the 1911 Revolution.* Translated by Anne Destenay. New York: Pantheon Books, 1976.

Ch'i, Hsi-sheng. *Warlord Politics in China, 1916–1928.* Stanford, Cal.: Stanford University Press, 1968.

Chiang, Siang-tseh. *The Nien Rebellion.* Seattle: University of Washington Press, 1954.

Ch'ien, Tuan-sheng. *The Government and Politics of China.* Cambridge: Harvard University Press, 1950.

Chow, Tse-tung. *The May Fourth Movement: Intellectual Revolution in Modern China.* Stanford, Cal.: Stanford University Press, 1967.

Chow, Yung-teh. *Social Mobility in China.* New York: Atherton, 1966.

Ch'ü, T'ung-tsu. *Local Government in China Under the Ch'ing.* Cambridge: Harvard University Press, 1962.

Clubb, O. Edmund. *Twentieth Century China.* New York: Columbia University Press, 1964.

Cohen, Paul A. "Ch'ing China: Confrontation With the West, 1850–1900." In *Modern East Asia: Essays in Interpretation,* edited by James B. Crowley, pp. 29–61. New York: Harcourt, Brace, and World, 1970.

Crook, Isabel and David. *Revolution in a Chinese Village: Ten Mile Inn.* London: Routledge and Kegan Paul, 1959.

Diamond, Norma. "Collectivization, Kinship, and the Status of Women in Rural

China." *Bulletin of Concerned Asian Scholars, Special Issue: Asian Women* 7: 1 (January–March 1975): 25–32.

Dittmer, Lowell. *Liu Shao-ch'i and the Chinese Cultural Revolution: The Politics of Mass Criticism.* Berkeley: University of California Press, 1974.

Domes, Jürgen. *The Internal Politics of China, 1949–1972.* Translated by Rüdiger Machetzki. New York: Praeger, 1973.

Donnithorne, Audrey. "China's Cellular Economy: Some Economic Trends Since the Cultural Revolution." *China Quarterly* no. 52 (October–December 1972): 605–18.

Eastman, Lloyd E. *The Abortive Revolution: China Under Nationalist Rule, 1927–1937.* Cambridge: Harvard University Press, 1974.

Eberhard, Wolfram. *Conquerors and Rulers: Social Forces in Medieval China.* Leiden, Netherlands: Brill, 1952.

A *History of China.* 3rd ed. Berkeley: University of California Press, 1969.

Eckstein, Alexander. *China's Economic Revolution.* Cambridge: Cambridge University Press, 1977.

Elvin, Mark. *The Pattern of the Chinese Past.* Stanford, Cal.: Stanford University Press, 1973.

Elvin, Mark, and Skinner, G. William, eds. *The Chinese City Between Two Worlds.* Stanford, Cal.: Stanford University Press, 1974.

Eto, Shinkichi. "Hai-lu-feng – The First Chinese Soviet Government." *China Quarterly* no. 8 (October–December 1961): 161–83 and no. 9 (January–March 1962): 149–81.

Fairbank, John K., ed. *Chinese Thought and Institutions.* Chicago: University of Chicago Press, 1957.

The United States and China. 3rd ed. Cambridge: Harvard University Press, 1971.

Fairbank, John K.; Reischauer, Edwin O.; and Craig, Albert M. *East Asia: Tradition and Transformation.* Boston: Houghton Mifflin, 1973.

Fei, Hsiao-tung. *Peasant Life in China: A Field Study of Country Life in the Yangtze Valley.* New York: Oxford University Press, 1946.

"Peasantry and Gentry: An Interpretation of Chinese Social Structure and Its Changes." *American Journal of Sociology* 52: 1 (July 1946): 1–17.

China's Gentry: Essays on Rural-Urban Relations. Chicago: University of Chicago Press, 1953.

Fei, Hsiao-tung, and Chang, Chih-I. *Earthbound China: A Study of Rural Economy in Yunnan.* Chicago: University of Chicago Press, 1945.

Feuerwerker, Albert. *China's Early Industrialization: Sheng Hsuan-huai (1844–1916) and Mandarin Enterprise.* Cambridge: Harvard University Press, 1958.

ed. *Modern China.* Englewood Cliffs, N.J.: Prentice-Hall, 1964.

The Chinese Economy, 1912–1949. Michigan Papers in Chinese Studies, no. 1. Ann Arbor: Center for Chinese Studies, University of Michigan, 1968.

The Chinese Economy, ca. 1870–1911. Michigan Papers in Chinese Studies, no. 5. Ann Arbor: Center for Chinese Studies, University of Michigan, 1969.

Rebellion in Nineteenth-Century China. Michigan Papers in Chinese Studies,

371

no. 21. Ann Arbor: Center for Chinese Studies, University of Michigan, 1975.

Fincher, John. "Political Provincialism and the National Revolution." In *China in Revolution,* edited by Mary C. Wright, pp. 185–226. New Haven: Yale University Press, 1968.

Franke, Wolfgang. *China and the West: The Cultural Encounter, 13th to 20th Centuries.* Translated by R. A. Wilson. New York: Harper & Row, 1967.

A Century of Chinese Revolution, 1851–1949. Translated by Stanley Rudman. New York: Harper & Row, 1971.

Freedman, Maurice. *Lineage Organization in Southeastern China.* London: University of London, 1965.

Fried, Morton H. *Fabric of Chinese Society.* New York: Praeger, 1953.

Friedman, Edward. *Backward Toward Revolution: The Chinese Revolutionary Party.* Berkeley: University of California Press, 1974.

Friedman, Edward, and Selden, Mark, eds. *America's Asia: Dissenting Essays on Asian-American Relations.* New York: Vintage Books, 1971.

Gamble, Sidney D. *Ting Hsien: A North China Rural Community.* New York: Institute of Pacific Relations, 1954.

North China Villages: Social, Political, and Economic Activities Before 1933. Berkeley: University of California Press, 1963.

Gardner, John and Idema, Wilt. "China's Educational Revolution." In *Authority, Participation, and Cultural Change in Communist China,* edited by Stuart R. Schram, pp. 257–89. Cambridge: Cambridge University Press, 1973.

Gillin, Donald G." 'Peasant Nationalism' in the History of Chinese Communism." *Journal of Asian Studies* 23: 2 (February 1964): 269–89.

Warlord: Yen Hsi-shan in Shansi Province, 1911–1949. Princeton, N.J.: Princeton University Press, 1967.

Gittings, John R. *The Role of the Chinese Army.* New York: Oxford University Press, 1967.

"The Chinese Army." In *Modern China's Search for a Political Form,* edited by Jack Gray, pp. 187–224. New York: Oxford University Press, 1969.

Gray, Jack. "The Economics of Maoism." *Bulletin of the Atomic Scientists* 25: 2 (February 1969): 42–51.

"The Two Roads: Alternative Strategies of Social Change and Economic Growth in China." In *Authority, Participation and Cultural Change in China,* edited by Stuart R. Schram, pp. 109–58. Cambridge: Cambridge University Press, 1973.

Griffith, Samuel B., II. *The Chinese People's Liberation Army.* New York: McGraw-Hill, 1967.

Gurley, John. "Capitalist and Maoist Economic Development." In *America's Asia,* edited by Edward Friedman and Mark Selden, pp. 324–56. New York: Vintage Books, 1971.

Harrison, James Pinckney. *The Long March to Power: A History of the Chinese Communist Party, 1921–72.* New York: Praeger, 1972.

Hatano, Yoshiro. "The New Armies." In *China in Revolution,* edited by Mary C. Wright, pp. 365–82. New Haven: Yale University Press, 1968.

Hinton, William. *Fanshen: A Documentary of Revolution in a Chinese Village.* New York: Vintage Books, 1966.

Ho, Ping-ti. *Studies on the Population of China, 1368–1953.* Cambridge: Harvard University Press, 1959.

    The Ladder of Success in Imperial China: An Analysis of Social Mobility, 1368–1911. New York: Columbia University Press, 1962.

Hofheinz, Roy, Jr. *The Broken Wave: The Chinese Communist Peasant Movement, 1922–1928.* Cambridge: Harvard University Press, 1977.

Horn, Joshua S. *Away With All Pests: An English Surgeon in People's China: 1954–1969.* New York: Monthly Review Press, 1971.

Hou, Ching-ming. *Foreign Investment and Economic Development in China, 1840–1937.* Cambridge: Harvard University Press, 1965.

Houn, Franklin W. *A Short History of Chinese Communism.* Englewood Cliffs, N.J.: Prentice-Hall, 1973.

Hsiao, Kung-chuan. *Rural China: Imperial Control in the Nineteenth Century.* Seattle: University of Washington Press, 1967.

Hsieh, Winston. "Peasant Insurrection and the Marketing Hierarchy in the Canton Delta, 1911." In *The Chinese City Between Two Worlds,* edited by Mark Elvin and G. William Skinner, pp. 119–42. Stanford, Cal.: Stanford University Press, 1974.

Ichiko, Chūzō. "The Role of the Gentry: An Hypothesis." In *China in Revolution,* edited by Mary C. Wright, pp. 297–317. New Haven: Yale University Press, 1968.

Isaacs, Harold R. *The Tragedy of the Chinese Revolution.* 2nd rev. ed. New York: Atheneum, 1968.

Israel, John. *Student Nationalism in China: 1927–1937.* Stanford, Cal.: Hoover Institution Publications, 1966.

    "Reflections on the Modern Chinese Student Movement." *Daedalus* 97 (Winter 1968): 229–53.

Jen, Yu-wen. *The Taiping Revolutionary Movement.* New Haven: Yale University Press, 1973.

Johnson, Chalmers A. *Peasant Nationalism and Communist Power: The Emergence of Revolutionary China, 1937–1945.* Stanford, Cal.: Stanford University Press, 1962.

Karol, K. S. *China: The Other Communism.* 2nd ed. New York: Hill & Wang, 1968.

Kau, Ying-mao. *The People's Liberation Army and China's Nation-Building.* White Plains, N.Y.: International Arts and Sciences Press, 1973.

    "Urban and Rural Strategies in the Chinese Communist Revolution." In *Peasant Rebellion and Communist Revolution in Asia,* edited by John Wilson Lewis, pp. 253–70. Stanford, Cal.: Stanford University Press, 1974.

Kim, Ilpyong J. "Mass Mobilization Policies and Techniques Developed in the Period of the Chinese Soviet Republic." In *Chinese Communist Politics in Action,* edited by A. Doak Barnett, pp. 78–98. Seattle: University of Washington Press, 1969.

373

Kuhn, Philip A. *Rebellion and Its Enemies in Late Imperial China: Militarization and Social Structure, 1796–1864.* Cambridge: Harvard University Press, 1970.

"Local Self-Government Under the Republic: Problems of Control, Autonomy, and Mobilization." In *Conflict and Control in Late Imperial China,* edited by Frederic Wakeman, Jr. and Carolyn Grant, pp. 257–98. Berkeley: University of California Press, 1975.

Lampton, David M. *Health, Conflict, and the Chinese Political System.* Michigan Papers in Chinese Studies, no. 18. Ann Arbor: Center for Chinese Studies, University of Michigan, 1974.

Lee, Rensselaer, W. "The Hsia Fang System: Marxism and Modernization." *China Quarterly* no. 28 (October–December 1966): 40–62.

Lew, Roland. "Maoism and the Chinese Revolution." In *The Socialist Register 1975,* pp. 115–59. London: Merlin Press, 1975.

Lewis, John W. *Leadership in Communist China.* Ithaca, N.Y.: Cornell University Press, 1963.

ed. *Party Leadership and Revolutionary Power in China.* Cambridge: Cambridge University Press, 1970.

ed. *The City in Communist China.* Stanford, Cal.: Stanford University Press, 1971.

Lindbeck, John M., ed. *China: Management of a Revolutionary Society.* Seattle: University of Washington Press, 1971.

MacKinnon, Stephen R. "The Peiyang Army, Yuan Shih-k'ai, and the Origins of Modern Chinese Warlordism." *Journal of Asian Studies* 32: 3 (May 1973): 405–23.

Madsen, Richard. "Revolutionary Asceticism in Communist China: Social Causes and Consequences of Commitment to the Maoist Ethos in a South China Village." Ph.D. dissertation, Department of Sociology, Harvard University, April, 1977.

Magdoff, Harry. "China: Contrasts with the U.S.S.R." *Monthly Review* 27: 3 (July–August 1975): 12–57.

Maitan, Livio. *Party, Army and Masses in China.* Translated by Gregor Benton and Marie Collitti. London: New Left Books, 1976.

McColl, Robert W. "The Oyüwan Soviet Area, 1927–1932." *Journal of Asian Studies* 27: 1 (November 1967): 41–60.

"A Political Geography of Revolution: China, Vietnam, and Thailand." *Journal of Conflict Resolution* 11: 2 (June 1967): 153–67.

Meisner, Maurice. "Yenan Communism and the Rise of the Chinese People's Republic." In *Modern East Asia: Essays in Interpretation,* edited by James B. Crowley, pp. 265–97. New York: Harcourt, Brace and World, 1970.

Li Ta-chao and the Origins of Chinese Marxism. New York: Atheneum, 1973.

"Utopian Socialist Themes in Maoism." In *Peasant Rebellion and Communist Revolution in Asia,* edited by John Wilson Lewis, pp. 207–52. Stanford, Cal.: Stanford University Press, 1974.

Michael, Franz. "State and Society in Nineteenth Century China." *World Politics* 7

Bibliography: China

(April 1955): 419–33. Reprinted in *Modern China,* edited by Albert Feuerwerker, pp. 57–69. Englewood Cliffs, N.J.: Prentice-Hall, 1964.

The Taiping Rebellion: History and Documents, vol. 1, *History.* Seattle: University of Washington Press, 1966.

Milton, David, and Milton, Nancy Dall. *The Wind Will Not Subside: Years in Revolutionary China, 1964–1969.* New York: Pantheon Books, 1976.

Muramatsu, Yuji. "Some Themes in Chinese Rebel Ideologies." In *The Confucian Persuasion,* edited by Arthur F. Wright, pp. 241–67. Stanford, Cal.: Stanford University Press, 1960.

"A Documentary Study of Chinese Landlordism in Late Ch'ing and Early Republican Kiangnan." *Bulletin of the School of Oriental and African Studies* 29: 3 (1966): 566–99.

Murphey, Rhoads. "The Treaty Ports and China's Modernization." In *The Chinese City Between Two Worlds,* edited by Mark Elvin and G. William Skinner, pp. 17–72. Stanford, Cal.: Stanford University Press, 1974.

Myers, Ramon H. *The Chinese Peasant Economy: Agricultural Development in Hopei and Shantung, 1890–1949.* Cambridge: Harvard University Press, 1970.

Nee, Victor G. "Community and Change in Revolutionary China." Ph.D. dissertation, Department of Sociology, Harvard University, April, 1977.

North, Robert C., and de Sola Pool, Ithiel. "Kuomintang and Chinese Communist Elites." In *World Revolutionary Elites,* edited by Harold D. Lasswell and Daniel Lerner, pp. 319–455. Cambridge: M.I.T. Press, 1966.

Oksenberg, Michel. "Methods of Communication within the Chinese Bureaucracy." *China Quarterly* no. 57 (January–March 1974): 1–39.

Paauw, Douglas S. "The Kuomintang and Economic Stagnation, 1928–1937." *Journal of Asian Studies* 16 (February 1957): 213–20.

Parsons, James B. *Peasant Rebellions of the Late Ming Dynasty.* Tuscon: University of Arizona Press, 1970.

Peck, Graham. *Two Kinds of Time: Life in Provincial China During the Crucial Years, 1940–1941.* Rev. ed. Boston: Houghton Mifflin, 1967.

Perkins, Dwight H. *Agricultural Development in China, 1368–1968.* Chicago: Aldine, 1969.

ed. *China's Modern Economy in Historical Perspective.* Stanford, Cal.: Stanford University Press, 1975.

"Growth and Changing Structure of China's Twentieth-Century Economy." In *China's Modern Economy in Historical Perspective,* edited by Dwight H. Perkins, pp. 115–66. Stanford, Cal.: Stanford University Press, 1975.

Pfeffer, Richard. "Serving the People and Continuing the Revolution." *China Quarterly* no. 52 (October-December 1972): 620–53.

Powell, Ralph L. *The Rise of Chinese Military Power, 1895–1912.* Princeton, N.J.: Princeton University Press, 1955.

Pye, Lucien W. *The Spirit of Chinese Politics: A Psychocultural Study of the Authority Crisis in Political Development.* Cambridge: M.I.T. Press, 1968.

Warlord Politics. New York: Praeger, 1971.

Rankin, Mary Backus. *Early Chinese Revolutionaries: Radical Intellectuals in Shanghai and Chekiang, 1902–1911.* Cambridge: Harvard University Press, 1971.

Rawlinson, John L. "China's Failure to Coordinate Her Modern Fleets in the Late Nineteenth Century." In *Approaches to Modern Chinese History,* edited by Albert Feuerwerker, Rhoads Murphy, and Mary C. Wright, pp. 105–32. Berkeley: University of California Press, 1967.

    China's Struggle for Naval Development, 1839–1895. Cambridge: Harvard University Press, 1967.

Rhoads, Edward J. *China's Republican Revolution: The Case of Kwangtung, 1895–1913.* Cambridge: Harvard University Press, 1975.

Richman, Barry M. *Industrial Society in Communist China.* New York: Vintage Books, 1969.

Riskin, Carl. "Small Industry and the Chinese Model of Development." *China Quarterly* no. 46 (April–June 1971): 245–73.

    "Incentive Systems and Work Motivations: The Experience in China." *Working Papers for a New Society* 1: 4 (Winter 1974): 27–31, 77–92.

Rossanda, Rossana. "Mao's Marxism." *The Socialist Register 1971.* London: Merlin Press, 1971.

Rozman, Gilbert. *Urban Networks in Ch'ing China and Tokugawa Japan.* Princeton, N.J.: Princeton University Press, 1973.

Scalapino, Robert A., ed. *Elites in the People's Republic of China.* Seattle: University of Washington Press, 1972.

Schram, Stuart R. "Mao Tse-tung and Secret Societies." *China Quarterly* no. 27 (July–September 1966): 1–13.

    Mao Tse-tung. Baltimore, Md.: Penguin Books, 1967.

    The Political Thought of Mao Tse-tung. Rev. and enlarged ed. New York: Praeger, 1969.

    ed. *Authority, Participation, and Cultural Change in China.* Cambridge: Cambridge University Press, 1973.

Schran, Peter. "Economic Management." In *China: Management of a Revolutionary Society,* edited by John M. Lindbeck, pp. 193–220. Seattle: University of Seattle Press, 1971.

    "On the Yenan Origins of Current Economic Policies." In *China's Modern Economy in Historical Perspective,* edited by Dwight H. Perkins, pp. 279–302. Stanford, Cal.: Stanford University Press, 1975.

Schurmann, H. Franz. "Organisational Principles of the Chinese Communists." In *China Under Mao: Politics Takes Command,* edited by Roderick MacFarquhar, pp. 87–98. Cambridge: M.I.T. Press, 1966.

    "Politics and Economics in Russia and China." In *Soviet and Chinese Communism: Similarities and Differences,* edited by Donald W. Treadgold, pp. 297–326. Seattle: University of Washington Press, 1967.

    Ideology and Organization in Communist China. 2nd ed. Berkeley: University of California Press, 1968.

Schwartz, Benjamin I. "The Intelligentsia in Communist China: A Tentative Comparison." In *The Russian Intelligentsia,* edited by Richard Pipes, pp. 164–81. New York: Columbia University Press, 1961.

Chinese Communism and the Rise of Mao. New York: Harper & Row, 1967.

Selden, Mark. "The Guerilla Movement in Northwest China: The Origins of the Shensi-Kansu-Ninghsia Border Region." *China Quarterly* no. 28 (October–December 1966): 63–81, and no. 29 (January–March 1967): 61–81.

"The Yenan Legacy: The Mass Line." In *Chinese Communist Politics in Action,* edited by A. Doak Barnett, pp. 99–151. Seattle: University of Washington Press, 1969.

The Yenan Way in Revolutionary China. Cambridge: Harvard University Press, 1971.

Sheridan, James E. *Chinese Warlord: The Career of Feng Yü-Hsiang.* Stanford, Cal.: Stanford University Press, 1966.

China in Disintegration: The Republican Era in Chinese History, 1912–1949. New York: Free Press, 1975.

Shih, Kuo-heng. "The Early Development of the Modern Chinese Business Class." In *The Rise of the Modern Chinese Business Class: Two Introductory Essays,* edited by Marion J. Levy and Kuo-heng Shih, pp. 19–63. New York: Institute of Pacific Relations, 1949.

Shih, Vincent Y. C. "Some Chinese Rebel Ideologies." *T'oung Pao* 44 (1956): 150–226.

The Taiping Ideology: Its Sources, Interpretations, and Influences. Seattle: University of Washington Press, 1967.

Sidel, Victor W., and Ruth Sidel. "The Delivery of Medical Care in China." *Scientific American* 230: 4 (April 1974): 19–27.

Sigurdson, Jon. "Rural Industry and the Internal Transfer of Technology." In *Authority, Participation and Cultural Change in China,* edited by Stuart R. Schram, pp. 199–232. Cambridge: Cambridge University Press, 1973.

Rural Industrialization in China. Cambridge: Harvard University Press, 1977.

Skinner, G. William. "Marketing and Social Structure in Rural China." 3 pts. *Journal of Asian Studies* 24: 1 (November 1964): 3–43; 24: 2 (February 1965): 195–228; and 24: 3 (May 1965): 363–99.

"Chinese Peasants and the Closed Community: An Open and Shut Case." *Comparative Studies in Society and History* 13: 3 (July 1971): 270–81.

ed. *The City in Late Imperial China.* Stanford, Cal.: Stanford University Press, 1977.

Skinner, G. William and Winckler, Edwin. "Compliance Succession in Rural Communist China." In *A Sociological Reader on Complex Organizations,* 2nd ed., edited by Amitai Etzioni, pp. 410–38. New York: Holt, Rinehart and Winston, 1969.

Smedley, Agnes. *The Great Road: The Life and Times of Chu Teh.* New York: Monthly Review Press, 1956.

Snow, Edgar. *Red Star Over China.* 1938. Reprint. New York: Grove Press, 1961.

Solomon, Richard H. *Mao's Revolution and the Chinese Political Culture.* Berkeley: University of California Press, 1971.

Spector, Stanley. *Li Hung-chang and the Huai Army: A Study in Nineteenth-Century Chinese Regionalism.* Seattle: University of Washington Press, 1964.

Tan, Chester C. *Chinese Political Thought in the Twentieth Century.* New York: Doubleday (Anchor Books), 1971.

Tawney, R. H. *Land and Labour in China.* 1932. Reprint. Boston: Beacon Press, 1966.

Taylor, George E. "The Taiping Rebellion." *Chinese Social and Political Science Review* 16: 4 (1932–3): 545–614.

Taylor, Romeyn. "Social Origins of the Ming Dynasty, 1351–1360. *Monumenta Serica* 22 (1963): 1–78.

Teng, Ssu-yu. *Historiography of the Taiping Rebellion.* Cambridge: Harvard University Press, 1962.

Thaxton, Ralph. "Tenants in Revolution: The Tenacity of Traditional Morality." *Modern China* 1: 3 (July 1975): 323–58.

Tien, Hung-mao. *Government and Politics in Kuomintang China, 1927–1937.* Stanford, Cal.: Stanford University Press, 1972.

Townsend, James R. *Political Participation in Communist China.* Berkeley: University of California Press, 1969.

Treadgold, Donald W. *Soviet and Chinese Communism.* Seattle: University of Washington Press, 1967.

The West in Russia and China, volume 2, *China, 1582–1949.* Cambridge: Cambridge University Press, 1973.

Tuchman, Barbara W. *Stillwell and the American Experience in China, 1911–45.* New York: Macmillan, 1971.

Van Slyke, Lyman P., ed. *The Chinese Communist Movement: A Report of the United States War Department, July 1945.* Stanford, Cal.: Stanford University Press, 1968.

Vogel, Ezra F. *Canton Under Communism: Programs and Politics in a Provincial Capital, 1949–1968.* Cambridge: Harvard University Press, 1969.

"Politicized Bureaucracy: Communist China." In *Communist Systems in Comparative Perspective,* edited by Leonard J. Cohen and Jane P. Shapiro, pp. 160–70. New York: Doubleday (Anchor Books), 1974.

Wakeman, Frederic, Jr. *Strangers at the Gate: Social Disorder in South China, 1839–1861.* Berkeley: University of California Press, 1966.

"High Ch'ing: 1683–1839." In *Modern East Asia: Essays in Interpretation,* edited by James B. Crowley, pp. 1–28. New York: Harcourt, Brace and World, 1970

The Fall of Imperial China. New York: Free Press, 1975.

Wakeman, Frederic, Jr., and Grant, Carolyn, eds. *Conflict and Control in Late Imperial China.* Berkeley: University of California Press, 1975.

Wang, Yeh-chien. *Chinese Intellectuals and the West, 1872–1949.* Chapel Hill: University of North Carolina Press, 1966.

Land Taxation in Imperial China, 1750–1911. Cambridge: Harvard University Press, 1973.

Watt, John R. *The District Magistrate in Late Imperial China.* New York: Columbia University Press, 1972.

Whyte, Martin King. "Bureaucracy and Modernization in China: The Maoist Critique." *American Sociological Review* 38: 2 (April 1973): 149–63.

"Iron Law Versus Mass Democracy: Weber, Michels, and the Maoist Vision." In *The Logic of Maoism: Critiques and Explication,* edited by James Chieh Hsiung, pp. 37–61. New York: Praeger, 1974.

Small Groups and Political Rituals in China. Berkeley: University of California Press, 1974.

"Inequality and Stratification in China." *China Quarterly* no. 64. (December 1975): 684–711.

Whyte, Martin King; Vogel, Ezra F.; and Parish, William L., Jr. "Social Structure of World Regions: Mainland China." *Annual Review of Sociology* 3 (1977): 179–207.

Wilbur, C. Martin. "Military Separatism and the Process of Reunification Under the Nationalist Regime, 1922–1937." In *China in Crisis,* 2 vols., edited by Ping-ti Ho and Tang Tsou, vol. 1, bk. 1, pp. 203–63. Chicago: University of Chicago Press, 1968.

"The Influence of the Past: How the Early Years Helped to Shape the Future of the Chinese Communist Party." In *Party Leadership and Revolutionary Power in China,* edited by John Wilson Lewis, p. 35–68. Cambridge: Cambridge University Press, 1970.

Wilson, Dick. *The Long March of 1935: The Epic of Chinese Communism's Survival.* New York: Avon Books, 1973.

Wittfogel, Karl A. *Oriental Despotism: A Comparative Study of Total Power.* New Haven: Yale University Press, 1957.

Wolf, Margery, and Witke, Roxane, eds. *Women in Chinese Society.* Stanford, Cal.: Stanford University Press, 1975.

Wortman, Sterling. "Agriculture in China." *Scientific American* 232: 6 (June 1975): 13–21.

Wright, Mary C. *The Last Stand of Chinese Conservatism: The T'ung-Chih Restoration, 1862–1874.* Stanford, Cal.: Stanford University Press, 1957.

ed. *China in Revolution: The First Phase, 1900–1913.* New Haven: Yale University Press, 1968.

Yang, C. K. *Religion in Chinese Society.* Berkeley: Univ. of California Press, 1961.

Chinese Communist Society: The Family and the Village. Cambridge: M.I.T. Press, 1965.

"Some Preliminary Statistical Patterns of Mass Actions in Nineteenth-Century China." In *Conflict and Control in Late Imperial China,* edited by Frederic Wakeman, Jr., and Carolyn Grant, pp. 174–210. Berkeley: University of California Press, 1975.

Yang, Martin C. *A Chinese Village: Taitou, Shangtung Province.* New York: Columbia University Press, 1965.

Yang, Shang-kuei. *The Red Kiangsi-Kwangtung Border Region.* Peking: Foreign Languages Press, 1961.

Yeh, C. K. "Soviet and Communist Chinese Industrialization Strategies." In *Soviet and Chinese Communism: Similarities and Differences,* edited by Donald W. Treadgold, pp. 327–63. Seattle: University of Washington Press, 1967.

Young, Ernest P. "Nationalism, Reform, and Republican Revolution: China in the Early Twentieth Century." In *Modern East Asia: Essays in Interpretation*, edited by James B. Crowley, pp. 151–79. New York: Harcourt, Brace and World, 1970.

Young, Marilyn B., ed. *Women in China: Studies in Social Change and Feminism*. Michigan Papers in Chinese Studies, no. 15. Ann Arbor: Center for Chinese Studies, University of Michigan, 1973.

IV. THEORETICAL AND HISTORICAL BACKGROUND

Adam, Heribert. *Modernizing Racial Domination: South Africa's Political Dynamics*. Berkeley: University of California Press, 1971.

Alavi, Hamza. "Peasants and Revolution." In *The Socialist Register 1965*, pp. 241–77. London: Merlin Press, 1965.

Allardt, Erik. "Culture, Structure and Revolutionary Ideologies." *International Journal of Comparative Sociology* 12: 1 (March 1971): 24–40.

Althusser, Louis. "Contradiction and Overdetermination." In *For Marx*, translated by Ben Brewster, pp. 87–128. New York: Vintage Books, 1970.

Amann, Peter. "Revolution: A Redefinition." *Political Science Quarterly* 77: 1 (March 1962): 36–53.

Anderson, Perry. *Lineages of the Absolutist State*. London: New Left Books, 1974.
    Passages From Antiquity to Feudalism. London: New Left Books, 1974.
    Considerations on Western Marxism. London: New Left Books, 1976.

Arendt, Hannah. *On Revolution*. New York: Viking Press, 1965.

Aston, Trevor. *Crisis in Europe, 1560–1660*. New York: Doubleday (Anchor Books), 1967.

Barker, Ernest. *The Development of Public Services in Western Europe, 1660–1930*. New York: Oxford University Press, 1944.

Barraclough, G. "Universal History." In *Approaches to History: A Symposium*, edited by H. P. R. Finberg, pp. 83–109. Toronto: University of Toronto Press, 1962.

Bell, David V. J. *Resistance and Revolution*. Boston: Houghton Mifflin, 1973.

Ben-David, Joseph, and Zloczower, Awraham. "Universities and Academic Systems in Modern Societies." *Archives Européenes de Sociology* 3: 1 (1962): 45–84.

Bendix, Reinhard. *Nation-Building and Citizenship*. New York: Wiley, 1964.
    "Tradition and Modernity Reconsidered." *Comparative Studies in Society and History* 9 (1967): 292–346.

Beqiraj, Mehmet. *Peasantry in Revolution*. Cornell Research Papers in International Studies, no. 5. Ithaca, N.Y.: Center for International Studies, Cornell University, 1966.

Bittner, Egon. "Radicalism and the Organization of Radical Movements." *American Sociological Review* 28: 6 (December 1963): 928–40.

Black, Cyril E., and Thornton, Thomas P., eds. *Communism and Revolution: The Strategic Uses of Political Violence*. Princeton, N.J.: Princeton University Press, 1964.

Bibliography: Theory and History

Bloch, Marc. "Toward a Comparative History of European Societies." In *Enterprise and Secular Change,* edited by Frederic C. Lane and Jelle C. Riesmersma, pp. 494–521. Homewood, Ill.: Richard D. Irwin, 1953.

Block, Fred. "The Ruling Class Does Not Rule: Notes on the Marxist Theory of the State." *Socialist Revolution* no. 33 (May–June 1977): 6–28.

Blum, Jerome. "The European Village as Community: Origin and Functions." *Agricultural History* 45: 3 (July 1971): 157–78.

"The Internal Structure and Polity of the European Village Community From the Fifteenth to the Nineteenth Century." *Journal of Modern History* 43: 4 (December 1971): 541–76.

Borkenau, Franz. "State and Revolution in the Paris Commune, the Russian Revolution, and the Spanish Civil War." *Sociological Review* 29: 41 (1937): 41–75.

Braudel, Fernand. "European Expansion and Capitalism, 1450–1650." In *Chapters in Western Civilization,* 3rd ed., vol. 1, 245–88. New York: Columbia University Press, 1961.

Brenner, Robert. "Agrarian Class Structure and Economic Development in Pre-Industrial Europe." *Past and Present* no. 70 (February 1976): 30–75.

"The Origins of Capitalist Development: A Critique of Neo-Smithian Marxism." *New Left Review* no. 104 (July–August 1977): 25–92.

Brinton, Crane. *The Anatomy of Revolution.* 1938. Rev. and expanded ed. New York: Vintage Books, 1965.

Bukharin, Nikolai. *Historical Materialism: A System of Sociology.* Translated from 3rd Russian edition, 1921. Ann Arbor: University of Michigan, 1969.

Calvert, Peter. *A Study of Revolution.* New York: Oxford University Press, 1970.

Cammett, John M. *Antonio Gramsci and the Origins of Italian Communism.* Stanford, Cal.: Stanford University Press, 1967.

Carr, E. H. *What is History?* New York: Vintage Books, 1961.

Chaliand, Gerard. *Revolution in the Third World: Myths and Prospects.* Translated by Diana Johnstone. New York: Viking Press, 1977.

Chirot, Daniel. *Social Change in the Twentieth Century.* New York: Harcourt Brace Jovanovich, 1977.

Chorley, Katherine. *Armies and the Art of Revolution.* 1943. Reprint. Boston: Beacon Press, 1973.

Cipolla, Carlo M. *Guns, Sails, and Empires: Technological Innovation and the Early Phases of European Expansion, 1400–1700.* New York: Minerva Press, 1965.

Cohan, A. S. *Theories of Revolution: An Introduction.* New York: Halsted Press, 1975.

Cohn, Norman. *The Pursuit of the Millennium: Revolutionary Millenarians and Mystical Anarchists of the Middle Ages.* Rev. and expanded ed. New York: Oxford University Press, 1970.

Collins, Randall. "A Comparative Approach to Political Sociology." In *State and Society: A Reader,* edited by Reinhard Bendix, et al., pp. 42–69. Berkeley: University of California Press, 1968.

Conflict Sociology. New York: Academic Press, 1975.

"Some Principles of Long-Term Social Change: The Territorial Power of States." Paper presented at the Annual Meeting of the American Sociological Association, Chicago, Illinois, September 1977.

Daniels, Robert Vincent. "The Chinese Revolution in Russian Perspective." *World Politics* 13: 2 (1961): 210–30.

Davies, James C. "Toward a Theory of Revolution." *American Sociological Review* 27 (1962): 5–18.

"The J-Curve of Rising and Declining Satisfactions as a Cause of Some Great Revolutions and a Contained Rebellion." In *Violence in America,* edited by Hugh Davis Graham and Ted Robert Gurr, pp. 671–709. New York: Signet Books, 1969.

ed. *When Men Revolt and Why: A Reader in Political Violence and Revolution.* New York: Free Press, 1971.

Dehio, Ludwig. *The Precarious Balance: Four Centuries of the European Power Struggle.* Translated by Charles Fullman. New York: Vintage Books, 1962.

Deutsch, Karl W. "Social Mobilization and Political Development." *American Political Science Review* 55 (September 1961): 493–514.

Deutscher, Isaac. "The French Revolution and the Russian Revolution: Some Suggestive Analogies." *World Politics* 4: 3 (April 1952): 369–81.

DeVries, Jan. *The Economy of Europe in an Age of Crisis, 1600–1750.* Cambridge: Cambridge University Press, 1976.

Dorn, Walter L. *Competition for Empire, 1740–1763.* New York: Harper & Row, 1963.

Dunn, John. *Modern Revolutions: An Introduction to the Analysis of a Political Phenomenon.* Cambridge: Cambridge University Press, 1972.

"The Success and Failure of Modern Revolutions." In *Radicalism in the Contemporary Age,* vol. 3, edited by S. Bialer and S. Sluzar, pp. 83–114, 305–18. Boulder, Colorado: Westview Press, 1977.

Eckstein, Harry, ed. *Internal War.* New York: Free Press, 1964.

"On the Etiology of Internal Wars." *History and Theory* 4: 2 (1965): 133–63.

Edwards, Lyford P. *The Natural History of Revolution.* 1927. Reprint. Chicago: University of Chicago Press, 1970

Eisenstadt, S. N. *Modernization: Protest and Change.* Englewood Cliffs, N.J.: Prentice-Hall, 1966.

"The Social Framework and Conditions of Revolution." Forthcoming in L. Kriesberg, ed., *Research in Social Movements, Conflict and Change.* Greenwich, Conn.: J. A. I. Press.

Eisenstadt, S. N., and Azmon, Yael. *Socialism and Tradition.* Atlantic Highlands, N.J.: Humanities Press, 1975.

Ellis, John. *Armies in Revolution.* New York: Oxford University Press, 1974.

Ellwood, Charles A. "A Psychological Theory of Revolutions." *American Journal of Sociology* 11: 1 (July 1905): 49–59.

Fanon, Frantz. *The Wretched of the Earth.* Translated by Constance Farrington. New York: Grove Press, 1968.

Feierabend, Ivo K.; Feierabend, Rosalind L.; and Gurr, Ted Robert, eds. *Anger,*

Violence, and Politics: Theories and Research. Englewood Cliffs, N.J.: Prentice-Hall, 1972.

Feierabend, Ivo K.; Feierabend, Rosalind L.; and Nesvold, Betty A. "Social Change and Political Violence: Cross-National Patterns." In *Violence in America,* edited by Hugh Davis Graham and Ted Robert Gurr, pp. 606–68. New York: Signet Books, 1969.

Feldman, Arnold S. "Violence and Volatility: The Likelihood of Revolution." In *Internal War,* edited by Harry Eckstein, pp. 111–29. New York: Free Press, 1964.

Forster, Robert, and Greene, Jack P., eds. *Preconditions of Revolution in Early Modern Europe.* Baltimore, Md.: Johns Hopkins University Press, 1970.

Freeman, Michael. "Review Article: Theories of Revolution." *British Journal of Political Science* 2: 3 (July 1972): 339–59.

Friedrich, Carl J., ed. *Revolution.* New York: Atherton, 1966.

Geertz, Clifford, ed. *Old Societies and New States: The Quest for Modernity in Asia and Africa.* New York: Free Press, 1963.

Gerschenkron, Alexander. *Economic Backwardness in Historical Perspective.* Cambridge: Harvard University Press, 1962.

    Continuity in History and Other Essays. Cambridge: Harvard University Press, 1968.

Geschwender, James A. "Explorations in the Theory of Social Movements and Revolutions." *Social Forces* 42: 2 (1968): 127–35.

Gillis, John R. "Political Decay and the European Revolutions, 1789–1848." *World Politics* 22: 3 (April 1970): 344–70.

Goldfrank, Walter L. "The Causes of the Mexican Revolution." Ph.D. dissertation, Department of Sociology, Columbia University, 1973.

    "Theories of Revolution and Revolution Without Theory: The Case of Mexico." Forthcoming in *Theory and Society* 7: 1 (January–March 1979).

Goodwin, Albert, ed. *The European Nobility in the Eighteenth Century.* New York: Harper & Row, 1967.

Gorz, André. *Strategy for Labor: A Radical Proposal.* Translated by Martin A. Nicholas and Victoria Ortiz. Boston: Beacon Press, 1967.

Gottschalk, Louis. "Causes of Revolution." *American Journal of Sociology* 50: 1 (July 1944): 1–8.

Gramsci, Antonio. *Selections From the Prison Notebooks.* Edited and translated by Quintan Hoare and Geoffrey Nowell Smith. New York: International Publishers, 1971.

Greene, Thomas H. *Comparative Revolutionary Movements.* Englewood Cliffs, N.J.: Prentice-Hall, 1974.

Griewank, Karl. "Emergence of the Concept of Revolution." In *Revolution: A Reader,* edited by Bruce Mazlish, Arthur D. Kaledin, and David B. Ralston, pp. 13–17. New York: Macmillan, 1971.

Gross, Feliks. *The Revolutionary Party: Essays in the Sociology of Politics.* Westport, Conn.: Greenwood Press, 1974.

Gurr, Ted Robert. "A Causal Model of Civil Strife: A Comparative Analysis Using New Indices." *American Political Science Review* 27 (1968): 1104–24.

383

Bibliography: Theory and History

"Psychological Factors in Civil Violence." *World Politics* 20 (January 1968): 245–78.

Why Men Rebel. Princeton, N.J.: Princeton University Press, 1970.

"The Revolution–Social Change Nexus." *Comparative Politics* 5: 3 (April 1973): 359–92.

Hagopian, Mark N. *The Phenomenon of Revolution.* New York: Dodd, Mead, 1974.

Hatto, Arthur. " 'Revolution': An Inquiry Into the Usefulness of an Historical Term." *Mind* 58: (229) (January 1949): 495–517.

Hermassi, Elbaki. "Toward a Comparative Study of Revolutions." *Comparative Studies in Society and History* 18: 2 (April 1976): 211–35.

Hintze, Otto. "Economics and Politics in the Age of Modern Capitalism." In *The Historical Essays of Otto Hintze,* edited by Felix Gilbertt, pp. 422–52. New York: Oxford University Press, 1975.

"Military Organization and the Organization of the State." In *The Historical Essays of Otto Hintze,* edited by Felix Gilbert, pp. 178–215. New York: Oxford University Press, 1975.

Hobsbawm, Eric J. *Primitive Rebels: Studies in the Archaic Forms of Social Movement in the Nineteenth and Twentieth Centuries.* New York: Norton, 1965.

Bandits. New York: Delacorte Press, 1969.

"Revolution." Paper presented at the Fourteenth International Congress of Historical Sciences, San Francisco, August 1975.

Hopkins, Terence K., and Immanuel Wallerstein. "The Comparative Study of National Societies." *Social Science Information* 6: 5 (October 1967): 25–58.

Hopper, Rex D. "Revolutionary Process." *Social Forces* 28 (March 1950): 270–9.

Huntington, Samuel P. *Political Order in Changing Societies.* New Haven: Yale University Press, 1968.

Johnson, Chalmers. *Revolution and the Social System.* Stanford, Cal.: The Hoover Institution, Stanford University, 1964.

Revolutionary Change. Boston: Little, Brown, 1966.

Jouvenel, Bertrand de. *On Power: Its Nature and the History of Its Growth.* Translated by J. F. Huntington. Boston: Beacon Press, 1968.

Kautsky, John H. "Revolutionary and Managerial Elites in Modernizing Regimes." *Comparative Politics* 1: 4 (July 1969): 441–67.

Kemp, Tom. *Industrialization in Nineteenth-Century Europe.* London: Longman, 1969.

Kirchheimer, Otto "Confining Conditions and Revolutionary Breakthroughs." *American Political Science Review* 59 (December 1965): 964–74.

Kramnick, Isaac. "Reflections on Revolution: Definition and Explanation in Recent Scholarship." *History and Theory* 11: 1 (1972): 26–63.

Landes, David S. "Japan and Europe: Contrasts in Industrialization." In *The State and Economic Enterprise in Japan,* edited by William W. Lockwood, pp. 93–182. Princeton, N.J.: Princeton University Press, 1965.

Landsberger, Henry A. "The Role of Peasant Movements and Revolts in Development." In *Latin American Peasant Movements,* edited by Henry A. Landsberger, pp. 1–61. Ithaca, N.Y.: Cornell University Press, 1969.

384

Bibliography: Theory and History

ed. *Rural Protest: Protest Movements and Social Change.* New York: Barnes & Noble Books, 1973.

Langer, William L. "The Pattern of Urban Revolution in 1848." In *French Society and Culture Since the Old Regime,* edited by Evelyn M. Acomb and Marvin L. Brown, pp. 90–118. New York: Holt, Rinehart and Winston, 1966.

Laqueur, Walter. "Revolution." *International Encyclopedia of the Social Sciences,* vol. 13, pp. 501–7. New York: Macmillan, 1968.

Lasswell, Harold D., and Lerner, Daniel, eds. *World Revolutionary Elites: Studies in Coercive Ideological Movements.* Cambridge: M.I.T. Press, 1966.

Leiden, Carl, and Schmitt, Karl M. *The Politics of Violence: Revolution in the Modern World.* Englewood Cliffs, N.J.: Prentice-Hall, 1968.

Lewis, John Wilson, ed. *Peasant Rebellion and Communist Revolution in Asia.* Stanford, Cal.: Stanford University Press, 1974.

Lichtheim, George. *Marxism: An Historical and Critical Study.* 2nd ed. New York: Praeger, 1965.

Lijphart, Arend. "Comparative Politics and the Comparative Method." *American Political Science Review* 65 (September 1971): 682–93.

Lockwood, David. "Social Integration and System Integration." In *Explorations in Social Change,* edited by George K. Zollschan and Walter Hirsch, pp. 244–57. Boston: Houghton Mifflin, 1964.

Lubasz, Heinz, ed. *Revolutions in Modern European History.* New York: Macmillan, 1966.

Lukács, Georg. *History and Class Consciousness.* Translated by Rodney Livingstone. Cambridge: M.I.T. Press, 1971.

Lupsha, Peter A. "Explanation of Political Violence: Some Psychological Theories Versus Indignation." *Politics and Society* 2: 1 (Fall 1971): 89–104.

MacIntyre, Alasdair. "Ideology, Social Science and Revolution." *Comparative Politics* 5: 3 (April 1973): 321–42.

Malia, Martin. "The Escalation of European Revolution: 1640, 1789, 1848, 1917." Paper presented at the Annual Meeting of the Modern European Section of the American Historical Association, Atlanta, Georgia, December 1975.

Marx, Fritz Morstein. *The Administrative State: An Introduction to Bureaucracy.* Chicago: University of Chicago Press, 1957.

Marx, Karl, and Engels, Frederick. *Selected Works.* New York: International Publishers, 1968.

McNeill, William H. *The Shape of European History.* New York: Oxford University Press, 1974.

Migdal, Joel. *Peasants, Politics, and Revolution: Pressures Toward Political and Social Change in the Third World.* Princeton, N.J.: Princeton University Press, 1974.

Moffett, John Thurber. "Bureaucratization and Social Control: A Study of the Progressive Regimentation of the Western Social Order." Ph.D. dissertation, Department of Sociology, Columbia University, 1971.

Moore, Barrington, Jr. *Political Power and Social Theory.* New York: Harper & Row, 1965.

385

Bibliography: Theory and History

Social Origins of Dictatorship and Democracy: Lord and Peasant in the Making of the Modern World. Boston: Beacon Press, 1966.

"Revolution in America?" New York Review of Books (January 1969): 6–12.

Moore, Wilbert E. "Predicting Discontinuities in Social Change." American Sociological Review 29 (June 1964): 331–8.

Mosca, Gaetano. The Ruling Class. Edited and revised by Arthur Livingston. New York: McGraw-Hill, 1939.

Moulder, Frances V. Japan, China and the Modern World Economy: Toward a Reinterpretation of East Asian Development ca. 1600 to ca. 1918. Cambridge: Cambridge University Press, 1977.

Mousnier, Roland. Peasant Uprisings in the Seventeenth Century: France, Russia, and China. Translated by Brian Pearce. New York: Harper & Row, 1972.

Muller, Edward N. "A Test of a Partial Theory of Potential for Political Violence." American Political Science Review 66 (September 1972): 928–49.

Nagel, Ernest, ed. John Stuart Mill's Philosophy of Scientific Method. New York: Hafner, 1950.

Neumann, Franz. The Democratic and the Authoritarian State: Essays in Political and Legal Theory. Edited by Herbert Marcuse. New York: The Free Press of Glencoe, 1964.

Neumann, Sigmund. "The Structure and Strategy of Revolution: 1848 and 1948." Journal of Politics 11 (August 1949): 532–44.

Nisbet, Robert A. Social Change and History. New York: Oxford University Press, 1969

Nordlinger, Eric A. Soldiers in Politics: Military Coups and Governments. Englewood Cliffs, N.J.: Prentice-Hall, 1977.

Oberschall, Anthony R. "Rising Expectations and Political Turmoil." Journal of Development Studies 6: 1 (October 1969): 5–22.

Social Conflict and Social Movements. Englewood Cliffs, N.J.: Prentice-Hall 1973.

Overholt, William H. "Revolution." In The Sociology of Political Organization. Croton-on-Hudson, N.Y.: The Hudson Institute, 1972.

Paige, Jeffery M. Agrarian Revolution: Social Movements and Export Agriculture in the Underdeveloped World. New York: Free Press, 1975.

Palmer, R. R. "The World Revolution of the West: 1763–1801." Political Science Quarterly 69: 1 (March 1954): 1–14.

Parkin, Frank. "System Contradiction and Political Transformation." Archives Européenne de Sociologie 13 (1972): 45–62.

Parsons, Talcott. "The Processes of Change of Social Systems." In The Social System, chap. 9. New York: Free Press, 1964.

Pettee, George Sawyer. The Process of Revolution. New York: Harper and Brothers, 1938.

Polanyi, Karl. The Great Transformation: The Political and Economic Origins of Our Time. 1944. Reprint. Boston: Beacon Press, 1957.

Portes, Alejandro. "Leftist Radicalism in Chile." Comparative Politics 2: 2 (January 1970): 251–74.

386

Bibliography: Theory and History

"On the Logic of Post-Factum Explanations: The Hypothesis of Lower-Class Frustration As the Cause of Leftist Radicalism." *Social Forces* 50: 1 (September 1971): 26–44.

Rafael, Eliezer Ben. "Social Aspects of Guerilla War." Ph.D. dissertation, Hebrew University, October 1972.

Richter, Melvin. "Tocqueville's Contributions to the Theory of Revolution." In *Revolution,* edited by Carl J. Friedrich, pp. 75–121. New York: Atherton, 1966.

Riezler, Kurt. "On the Psychology of the Modern Revolution." *Social Research* 10: 3 (September 1943): 320–36.

Rosenau, James N., ed. *International Aspects of Civil Strife.* Princeton, N.J.: Princeton University Press, 1964.

Russell, D. E. H. *Rebellion, Revolution, and Armed Force: A Comparative Study of Fifteen Countries With Special Emphasis on Cuba and South Africa.* New York: Academic Press, 1974.

Russett, Bruce M. "Inequality and Instability: The Relation of Land Tenure to Politics." *World Politics* 16 (April 1964): 442:54.

Rustow, Dankwart A. "Transitions to Democracy: Toward a Dynamic Model." *Comparative Politics* 2: 3 (April 1970): 337–63.

Salert, Barbara. *Revolutions and Revolutionaries: Four Theories.* New York: Elsevier, 1976.

Scheiner, Irwin. "The Mindful Peasant: Sketches for a Study of Rebellion." *Journal of Asian Studies* 32: 4 (August 1973): 579–91.

Schorske, Carl. *German Social Democracy, 1905–1917.* New York: Wiley, 1954.

Schram, Stuart R., ed. *The Political Thought of Mao Tse-tung.* Rev. and enlarged ed. New York: Praeger, 1969.

Schurmann, Franz. "On Revolutionary Conflict." *Journal of International Affairs* 23: 1 (1969): 36–53.

The Logic of World Power. New York: Pantheon Books, 1974.

Schwartz, David C. "A Theory of Revolutionary Behavior." In *When Men Revolt and Why,* edited by James C. Davies, pp. 109–32. New York: Free Press, 1971.

"Political Alienation: The Psychology of Revolution's First Stage." In *Anger, Violence, and Politics,* edited by Ivo K. and Rosalind L. Feierabend and Ted Gurr, pp. 58–66. Englewood Cliffs, N.J.: Prentice-Hall, 1972.

Selden, Mark. "Revolution and Third World Development." In *National Liberation,* edited by Norman Miller and Roderick Aya, pp. 214–48. New York: Free Press, 1971.

Selznick, Philip. *The Organizational Weapon: A Study of Bolshevik Strategy and Tactics.* New York: McGraw-Hill, 1952.

Sewell, William H., Jr. "Marc Bloch and the Logic of Comparative History." *History and Theory* 6: 2 (1967): 208–18.

Skocpol, Theda. "A Critical Review of Barrington Moore's Social Origins of Dictatorship and Democracy." *Politics and Society* 4: 1 (Fall 1973): 1–34.

"Explaining Revolutions: In Quest of a Social-Structural Approach." In The *Uses of Controversy in Sociology,* edited by Lewis A. Coser and Otto N. Larsen, pp. 155–75. New York: Free Press, 1976.

387

Bibliography: Theory and History

"France, Russia, China: A Structural Analysis of Social Revolutions." *Comparative Studies in Society and History* 18: 2 (April 1976): 175–210.

"Old Regime Legacies and Communist Revolutions in Russia and China." *Social Forces* 55: 2 (December 1976): 284–315.

"Wallerstein's World Capitalist System: A Theoretical and Historical Critique." *American Journal of Sociology* 82: 5 (March 1977): 1075–90.

Skocpol, Theda, and Trimberger, Ellen Kay. "Revolutions and the World-Historical Development of Capitalism." *Berkeley Journal of Sociology* 22 (1977–8): 101–13.

Shanin, Theodor, ed. *Peasants and Peasant Societies.* Baltimore, Md.: Penguin Books, 1971.

Smelser, Neil J. *Theory of Collective Behavior.* New York: The Free Press of Glencoe, 1963.

Comparative Methods in the Social Sciences. Englewood Cliffs, N.J.: Prentice-Hall, 1976.

Smith, Thomas C. "Pre-Modern Economic Growth: Japan and the West." *Past and Present* no. 60 (August 1973): 127–60.

Snyder, David, and Charles Tilly. "Hardship and Collective Violence in France, 1830 to 1960." *American Sociological Review* 37 (October 1972): 520–32.

Sorokin, Pitirim A. *The Sociology of Revolution.* Philadelphia: Lippincott, 1925.

Stein, Stanley J., and Stein, Barbara H. *The Colonial Heritage of Latin America.* New York: Oxford University Press, 1970.

Stinchcombe, Arthur L. "Agricultural Enterprise and Rural Class Relations." In *Class, Status, and Power,* 2nd ed., edited by Reinhard Bendix and Seymour Martin Lipset, pp. 182–90. New York: Free Press, 1966.

"Stratification Among Organizations and the Sociology of Revolution." In *Handbook of Organizations,* edited by James G. March, pp. 169–80. Chicago: Rand McNally, 1965.

Stone, Lawrence. "Theories of Revolution." *World Politics* 18: 2 (January 1966): 159–76.

Tanter, Raymond, and Midlarsky, Manus. "A Theory of Revolution." *Journal of Conflict Resolution* 11: 3 (September 1967): 264–80.

Tilly, Charles. "Collective Violence in European Perspective." In *Violence in America: Historical and Comparative Perspectives,* edited by Hugh Davis Graham and Ted Robert Gurr, pp. 4–42. New York: Signet Books, 1969.

"Does Modernization Breed Revolution?" *Comparative Politics* 5: 3 (April 1973): 425–47.

"Town and Country in Revolution." In *Peasant Rebellion and Communist Revolution in Asia,* edited by John Wilson Lewis, pp. 271–302. Stanford, Cal.: Stanford University Press, 1974.

ed. *The Formation of National States in Western Europe.* Princeton, N.J.: Princeton University Press, 1975.

"Revolutions and Collective Violence." In *Handbook of Political Science,* vol. 3, *Macropolitical Theory,* edited by Fred I. Greenstein and Nelson W. Polsby, pp. 483–556. Reading, Mass.: Addison-Wesley, 1975.

Bibliography: Theory and History

From Mobilization to Revolution. Reading, Mass.: Addison-Wesley, 1978.

Tilly, Charles; Tilly, Louise; and Tilly, Richard. *The Rebellious Century, 1830–1930.* Cambridge: Harvard University Press, 1975.

Tiryakian, Edward A. "A Model of Societal Change in Its Lead Indicators." In *The Study of Total Societies,* edited by Samuel Z. Klausner, pp. 69–97. New York: Doubleday (Anchor Books), 1967.

Trimberger, Ellen Kay. "State Power and Modes of Production: Implications of the Japanese Transition to Capitalism." *The Insurgent Sociologist* 7 (Spring 1977): 85–98.

Revolution From Above: Military Bureaucrats, and Development in Japan, Turkey, Egypt and Peru. New Brunswick, N.J.: Transaction Books, 1978.

"A Theory of Elite Revolutions." *Studies in Comparative International Development* 7: 3 (Fall 1972): 191–207.

Tucker, Robert C. "The Political Theory of Classical Marxism." In *The Marxian Revolutionary Idea,* chap. 3. New York: Norton, 1970.

ed. *The Lenin Anthology.* New York: Norton, 1975.

Vagts, Alfred. *A History of Militarism, Civilian and Military.* Rev. ed. New York: Free Press, 1967.

Von Laue, Theodore H. *The Global City.* Philadelphia: Lippincott, 1969.

Wallace, Anthony F. C. "Revitalization Movements." *American Anthropologist* 58 (April 1956): 264–81.

Wallerstein, Immanuel. *The Modern World-System: Capitalist Agriculture and the Origins of the European World-Economy in the Sixteenth Century.* New York: Academic Press, 1974.

"The Rise and Future Demise of the World Capitalist System: Concepts for Comparative Analysis." *Comparative Studies in Society and History* 16: 4 (September 1974): 387–415.

Walzer, Michael. "Puritanism as a Revolutionary Ideology." *History and Theory* 3: 1 (1963): 59–90.

The Revolution of the Saints: A Study in the Origins of Radical Politics. New York: Atheneum, 1968.

"Regicide and Revolution." *Social Research* 40: 4 (Winter 1973): 617–42.

Weber, Max. *Economy and Society: An Outline of Interpretive Sociology.* Edited by Guenther Roth and Claus Wittich. 3 vols. New York: Bedminster Press, 1968.

Wertheim, W. F. *Evolution and Revolution: The Rising Waves of Emancipation.* Baltimore, Md.: Penguin Books, 1974.

Willer, David, and Zollschan, George K. "Prolegomenon to a Theory of Revolutions." In *Explorations in Social Change,* edited by George K. Zollschan and Walter Hirsch, pp. 125–51. Boston: Houghton-Mifflin, 1964.

Williams, E. N. *The Ancien Regime in Europe.* New York: Harper & Row, 1970

Wolf, Eric R. *Peasants.* Englewood Cliffs, N.J.: Prentice-Hall, 1966.

Peasant Wars of the Twentieth Century. New York: Harper & Row, 1969.

"Peasant Rebellion and Revolution." In *National Liberation,* edited by Norman Miller and Roderick Aya, pp. 48–67. New York: Free Press, 1971.

389

Wolin, Sheldon S. "The Politics of the Study of Revolution." *Comparative Politics* 5: 3 (April 1973): 343–58.

Wolpe, Harold. "An Examination of Some Approaches to the Problem of the Development of Revolutionary Consciousness." *Telos* no. 4 (Fall 1969): 113–44.

Wright, Erik Olin. "To Control or Smash Bureaucracy: Weber and Lenin on Politics, the State and Bureaucracy." *Berkeley Journal of Sociology* 19 (1974–75): 69–108.

Yoder, Dale. "Current Definitions of Revolution." *American Journal of Sociology* 32 (November 1926): 433–41.

Zagorin, Perez. "Theories of Revolution in Contemporary Historiography." *Political Science Quarterly* 88: 1 (March 1973): 23–52.

"Prolegomena to the Comparative History of Revolution in Early Modern Europe." *Comparative Studies in Society and History* 18: 2 (April 1976): 151–74.

Zelditch, Morris, Jr. "Intelligible Comparisons." In *Comparative Methods in Sociology,* edited by Ivan Vallier, pp. 267–307. Berkeley: University of California Press, 1971.

Index

absolutism/autocracy, 7, 27, 41, 47, 304n.4
  in China, 42, 78
  in England, 143, 294n.4
  in France, 140, 168, 178–9, 184, 202,
    207; contradictions of, 51–67
  Hohenzollern (Prussia), 104–8, 110
  in Russia, 82, 87–90 (passim), 94, 95,
    97–9, 128, 140, 227
  see also monarchy
aggregate-psychological theories, *see* theories of revolution
agriculture/agrarian economy
  and agrarian unrest, 95, 111, 150–4;
    peasant revolt, *see* peasantry
  capitalist, *see* capitalism
  Chinese: Old Regime, 48, 68–9, 110,
    147–50, 151–4, 275, 276; post-
    revolutionary, 267, 269, 270–1, 276,
    278–9
  collectivized, *see* collectivization
  English, 20, 55, 56, 118, 140, 141, 142,
    151
  French: Old Regime, 48, 54–6, 110,
    118–22, 148, 221; postrevolution-
    ary, 137, 177, 178, 191, 271
  German, 140, 146
  Japanese, 22, 103–4, 110
  "modernization" of, 89, 109
  Prussian, 106, 107, 109, 110
  Russian: Old Regime, 48, 82–3, 86–7,
    95, 103, 104, 108–9, 135; post-
    Emancipation, 89, 90, 91, 94, 109,
    128–30, 132–3, 148; postrevolution-
    ary, 137, 223–5, 228–9, 230, 278
  see also economy; land ownership
Alexander II, tsar of Russia, 85
Algeria, social revolution in, 287
Althusser, Louis, 6
America, *see* United States

American Independence, War for, 63
Anderson, Perry, 27
  Lineages of the Absolutist State, 36,
    304n.4
Angola, social revolution in, 287, 292
armed forces
  Chinese: gentry-led, 75–6; Imperial, 75–
    6, 79, 238; National Revolutionary
    Army (NRA), 243, 244, 246; "New
    Armies," 78, 79, 238; peasant/guer-
    rilla forces, 252–5, 257, 258; Red
    (People's Liberation) Army, 252–6,
    257, 258, 259, 262, 268, 272, 273,
    277; and warlordism, 80, 236, 237–
    8, 239–43, 247, 248–9, 250, 255,
    262; World War II (Nationalist), 251
  and European military competition, 50,
    52, 82, 232, 285
  French: changes in, 187, 190, 194, 195,
    196–8; conscription of (*levée en
    masse*), 188, 189, 198, 203, 204;
    under Directory, 194–5, 197, 198;
    national/revolutionary, 188, 189,
    190, 193, 198, 203, 234, 253; Old
    Regime, 54, 64–5, 67, 124, 146,
    184, 196, 197, 237, 290
  Prussian (and conscription), 105–8 (pas-
    sim), 198
  Russian, 234: Cheka, 215–16; conscrip-
    tion of, 85, 128, 211, 216, 217; Cos-
    sacks, 12, 114, 128; counterrevo-
    lutionary, 215, *see also* Russian
    Revolution; in Crimean War, 84; Im-
    perial, 82, 98, 99, 136, 138, 146,
    210, 216, 217, 237; officer corps
    (Red Army), 217, 227, 230; parti-
    sans (guerrillas), 218; Party controls
    of, 217–18, 253; Red Army, 216–
    19, 227, 230, 253; Red Guards, 211,

391

Index

armed forces (*continued*)
214, 218; in Revolution of 1905, 95, 133; soldiers as rebels, 136, 208, 209, 211, 213; White Army, 216–19 (passim); in World War I, 95–7, 133, 138–9

Austria, 94, 95–6, 136, 145, 185–7, 210
and War of the Austrian Succession (1740–48), 60

Austria-Hungary, 93, 96

autonomy, *see* peasantry; state(s)

Avrich, Paul, quoted, 206

Babeuf, F. N., 4

Barnett, A. Doak, 272
quoted, 263–4, 273

Bastille, fall of, 66

Behrens, C. B. A., quoted, 61

Belgium, 93

Bendix, Reinhard, 19
Nation-building and Citizenship, 36

Bernstein, Thomas, 278

Bittner, Egon, 170

Bloch, Marc, 36

Bolivian Revolution, 287, 291

Bolshevik Party (or Communist Party of the Soviet Union), 162, 163, 169, 206, 226, 233, 242, 291
background of leaders of, 166–7, 227, 272
basis in industry of, 192, 212, 220, 247–8
Chinese emulation of, 23–4, 247, 266, 267–8
compared to Montagnards, 192–3
coordination by, of state functions, 226–7
ideology of, 169, 170–1, 192, 338n.28
and industrial workers, 212, 213, 214, 216, 220
and peasantry, 135, 138, 216–18, 222–3, 224–5, 232, 235, 277, 278, 279
and Stalinist policies, 224–5, 230, 231, 232, 279
struggle to rule of (1917–21), 207, 212–20, 222
"transmission belt" organizations of, 227, 265
and workers' control (of industry), 214, 219
in World War I, 97, 208

Borkenau, Franz, quoted, 161, 164

Borton, Hugh, quoted, 102–3

Bosher, J. F., *French Finances*, quoted, 63–4, 199

Bourbon monarchy, *see* France, Old Regime

bourgeoisie
and "bourgeois revolutions," 7, 8; French Revolution as, 40, 41, 141, 162, 174–9, 233, 302n.84, 303n.97
development of, 7–8
in French Revolution, 51, 65–6, 174–9 (passim)

Boxer War, 76, 77

bread riots, 98, 122

Brecher, Jeremy, quoted, 17

Brenner, Robert, quoted, 142

Brinton, Crane, 33, 37
quoted, 38

Brissotins, 187, 188

Bukharin, Nikolai, 223–5
Historical Materialism, 6

bureaucracy
Chinese: Old Regime (Imperial officials), 67, 69–71, 74, 76–7, 78, 90, 152, 166, 263; revolutionary and post-revolutionary, 163, 236, 240, 249–51, 258, 263–9, 287
English lack of, 143
French: Old Regime (and "venality of office"), 52, 57–63 (passim), 107, 118, 179, 199–200, 264, 309–10n.78, *see also* France, Old Regime; revolutionary and postrevolutionary, 162–8 (passim), 176, 186, 193–5, 198–201, 204–5, 234, 236
Japanese, 101–2, 103
in Old Regimes, 47–8, 49, 161, *see also* Chinese; French, *above;* Russian, *below*
"politicized," 265
Prussian, 104–5, 107–8
Russian: Old Regime (state service), 82, 86, 87, 90, 97–8, 132, 138, 166, 226; revolutionary and postrevolutionary, 162, 206, 215, 217–20 (passim), 226–7, 229–33, 236, 271–2

Calonne, Charles Alexandre de, 64

capitalism
and capitalist agriculture: in England, 141, 151; in Russia, 83, 130, 132, 206, 221
in Marx's theory of revolutions, 7, 8
in postrevolutionary France, 162, 175–7, 179, 199–200, 205
Russian, eliminated, 227
"world capitalist system," 20–3, 54, 167
see also wealth

Carnot, Lazare, 189

Carr, E. H., 226

Catholicism, *see* Church, the

Index

Chaliand, Gerard, quoted, 220
Chamberlin, William Henry, quoted, 137, 215–16
change, as defining feature of revolution, 4–5, 288
Charles I, king of England, 141, 143
Cheka, the, 215–16
cheng-feng (Chinese reforms), 259–62, see also Communist Party, Chinese (CCP)
Chiang Hsueh-liang, 256
Chiang Kai-shek, 243, 246, 250, 251, 255 "arrest" of, 256
China, Old Regime
  agriculture/agrarian economy in, 48, 68–9, 110, 147–50, 151–4, 275, 276; and agrarian unrest, 150–4, see also peasant situation in, below
  armies of (gentry-led, Imperial, reformed/"New Armies"), see armed forces; and strategic military situation, 50, 67, 107, 238
  bureaucracy (Imperial officials) of, 67, 69–71, 74, 76–7, 78, 90, 152, 166, 263
  clans in, 148, 149, 150, 328n.1
  commerce in, 69, 73, 74, 76, 149
  compared to Prussia and Japan, 100–8 (passim)
  Confucian system in, 68, 72, 264; and literati (degree-holders), 70–1, 72, 78, 151, 239, 240, 242, 263; reforms of, 77
  cultural and political history of, 41, 67
  dominant class (gentry) in, 71–2, 81; compared to other dominant classes, 85, 88, 90, 99, 101, 102, 103, 106, 148–9, 151–2, 239; in local communities, 148–50, 236; politicization of, 78–80, 107; rebellions defeated by, 75–6, 114, 151–2, 342n.12
  economy of, 74, 76, 153, 265, 275
  foreign intrusion into, see foreign intrusion and pressures
  industry in, 74, 76–7
  land ownership in, see land ownership
  literati in, see Confucian system in, above
  peasant situation in, 48–9, 68–9, 71, 107, 148–54; impact of imperialism on, 153; and peasant-based rebellions, 74–6, 80, 107, 150–4, 294n.3, see also peasantry
  population growth in, 74, 104, 275
  regional/local power in, 74–6
  representative assemblies in, 77–9, 81; compared to Russian zemstvos, 90

and revolutionary crisis, see revolutionary crisis, emergence of
  "social banditry" in, 114, 152–3, 327n.124
  "standard marketing community" in, 69, 149
  state-structure of, 68, 69–71, 72, 73, 88, 107, 147–50, 152, 167, 173, 304n.4; after rebellions, 75; reforms in, 77–80, 81
  taxation in, 69, 74, 75, 76, 148, 150, 151, 153, 238
  and war with Japan, 76, 77, 81, 104
China, political conflicts of Revolution (1911–49)
  armies in, see armed forces
  bureaucracy during, 240, 249–51, 258
  Chinese Communist Party in, see Communist Party, Chinese (CCP)
  civil war, 257, 259, 261, 277
  dominant class (gentry) in: aftermath of 1911, 236, 239, 240–1, 247, 249; and KMT/Nationalist regime, 240; overthrown, 164, 261–2, 277–8, 285; during Second United Front, 257–8
  guerrilla warfare in, 252–5, 257, 258
  ideology in, 169–71
  industry and railroads in, 247–8
  Japanese invasions during, see Japan
  Kuomintang/Nationalists (KMT) in, 166, 167, 240, 248, 255, 263, 266; alliances with CCP, 241, 243–4, 256–9; conflicts with CCP, 242, 246, 249–51, 252, 257, 259, 261, 262, 277, 303n.99; leadership of, 239, 250; Nanking regime (1927–37), 249–50, 255; Second United Front (with CCP against Japan), 256–9; during World War II, 251
  land revolution (1940s) in, 261–2, 277–8
  leadership during, 166–7, 168, 239, 247, 252–5 (passim), 260, see also Communist Party, Chinese (CCP)
  "Long March" in, 255
  "mass line" in, 260, 272
  mass mobilization in, 246, 250, 255, 257, 259–62, 265, 268, 272, 274
  nationalism/anti-imperialism in, 78, 243–4, 246
  Nationalist regime, see Kuomintang/Nationalists (KMT) in, above
  Northern Expedition during, 244, 246, 255
  peasantry in, 238, 241; and guerrilla warfare, 252–5, 257, 258; mobiliza-

Index

China, political conflicts (*continued*)
  tion for production, 259–62; and
    peasant revolts, 113–17, 149–50,
    151, 172, 236, 239–41, 262, 279
  Red Army in, *see* armed forces
  "Revolution of 1911," 79–80; conse-
    quences compared to France (1789)
    and Russia (1917), 236–7, *see also*
    Chinese Revolution
  Soviet Union and, 243, 250
  students/intellectuals in, 239, 240, 242,
    260, 263
  taxation during, 240, 244, 249, 251,
    258
  warlords/wardlordism in, *see* armed
    forces
  Western powers/interests in, 246
China, postrevolutionary (New Regime), 3
  agriculture in: collectivization of, 267,
    270–1, 278–9; compared to French
    and Soviet, 271, 276; as dynamic
    sector, 270; Party-state support of,
    271; "teams" (villages), 270, 278
  bureaucracy in, 163, 236, 258, 263–9,
    287; and Communist regime as "po-
    liticized bureaucracy," 265
  collectivization of peasantry (as process),
    260; contrasted to Soviet, 270–1,
    278; implications of, for New Re-
    gime, 279; "participatory mobiliza-
    tion" in, 278
  compared to Chinese pre-1949 regime,
    264–5
  compared to French New Regime, 42,
    162–3, 263, 265, 271, 274
  compared to Russian New Regime, *see*
    and Soviet Union, *below*
  and Cultural Revolution, 268, 269, 272,
    273–4
  education in, 270, 274, 279
  egalitarianism in, *see* stratification pat-
    terns in, *below*
  foreign policies of, 276–7
  Great Leap Forward, 268, 272, 278
  industrialization strategies and manage-
    ment, 275, 276–7; balanced develop-
    ment, 268; First Five-Year Plan,
    267–8
  inequalities in, *see* stratification patterns
    in, *below*
  leadership in (decentralized), 271–3
  "Liuists," 268
  "Maoists," *see* Mao Tse-tung
  as Party-state, 162, 164, 265; supports
    agriculture, 271
  People's Republic established, 263
  planning procedures, 258–62, 264–5

and Soviet Union: break with, 268, 276,
    277; compared to, 42, 162–3, 263,
    265, 267–9, 270, 274, 277; influ-
    ences of, 266–9, *see also* Bolshevik
    Party
  state-building and changes, 41–2; bu-
    reaucratization and centralization,
    162–3, 236, 237, 263–9, 286–7;
    compared to other regimes, 168,
    264–5
  strategic military situation of, 237, 276–
    7, *see also* armed forces
  stratification patterns, 269; egalitarian-
    ism, 273, 274, 277; income differen-
    tials, 163, 273, 274; inequalities of
    prestige, authority, 163, 268, 273–4
  taxation in, 270
  technologies, "intermediate," 270
  urbanization controls, 269–70
Chinese Revolution (general)
  causes of, 155–7 (table)
  compared to French and Russian, 40–2,
    80–1, 147–8, 154, 155–7 (table),
    162–3, 181, 236–42 (passim), 247–
    8, 263, 266, 269, 275–9, 280, 282–
    3 (table), 303n.97
  and "democracy" versus "totalitarian-
    ism," 286
  and ideals of socialism, 287
  leadership of, 166–7, 168, 241–3
  as one process from 1911, 303n.99
  outcomes and accomplishments of, 13,
    181, 266, 269, 275, 279, 282–3
    (table), 285, 286–7
  as "Third World" revolution, 303nn.
    97, 99
  worldwide effect of, 4
Ch'ing (Manchu) Dynasty, 67, 69–70, 73–
    80 (passim), 239–40, *see also* China,
    Old Regime
Chorley, Katherine, *Armies and the Art of
    Revolution,* 65
  quoted, 289
Christianity, *see* Church, the
Chu Teh, 254
Church, Clive H., quoted, 199
Church, the
  anti-Catholicism, 193, 194, 203, 204
  Christian missionaries in China, 73, 75
  lands confiscated (France), 184, 191,
    202
  Napoleon and, 195, 202, 204
  in Russian Old Regime, 227
civil war
  Chinese, 257, 259, 261, 277
  in England, 141, 143, 181, 182, *see also*
    English Revolution

Index

Russian, 192, 216–20, 224–5, 228, 232, 253
class
  and agrarian class structure, 115–17, *see also* agriculture/agrarian economy; peasantry
  and "class struggle reductionism," 28
  conflict: peasant-landlord, *see* land ownership; peasantry; the state and, 26–31, 284, 291–2
  consciousness, 16
  dominant, *see* dominant class
  "for-itself," 15, 17
  postrevolutionary patterns of, 227–8, 231, 239–41; China, 163, 268, 269, 273–4, 277; France, 204–5; Russia, 230–1
  see also bureaucracy; wealth
Cobb, Richard, quoted, 199
Cobban, Alfred, quoted, 62, 63, 182, 330–1n.3
coercion, *see* terrorism
Colbert, Jean Baptiste, 54
collective action
  bread riots, 98, 122
  and collective violence, 10, *see also* political violence
  and group organization and resources, 13–14
  and multiple sovereignty, 11, 34
  peasant rebellion as, 115, *see also* peasantry
collective action (political conflict) theory, *see* theories of revolution
collectivization (of agriculture/peasantry)
  China, 267, 270–2, 278–9
  Russia, 223–5, 228–9, 230, 270–1, 278
colonialism/colonization
  competition in, 21
  and decolonization, 3, 290, 291
  English, 21, 60, 63
  and Imperial Russia as "semicolony," 93, *see also* European states system
  postcolonial societies, revolutions in, 288
  see also foreign intrusion and pressures; imperialism
commercialization and trade
  Chinese, 69, 73, 74, 76, 149, 240
  English, *see* England
  "free," imperialism of, 73
  French, 54–5, 56, 59, 73, 176, 221
  regional vs. national, 48
  Russian, 90, 92–3, 209
  transnational flows of, 20
  worldwide ("Great Transformation"), 4
  see also economy; industrialization
Commune, Paris, 188

communes, *see* land ownership
Communist Party, Chinese (CCP), 163, 169, 240, 291, 328n.126
  and anti-Communist campaigns (1930s), 249–51
  background of leaders of, 166–7
  Bolshevik/Russian aid to, similarities with, 23, 42, 171, 204, 243, 247, 266–9, 275, 276, 277
  bureaucratization of, 258, 264, 265
  and Cooperative Movement, 260–1
  guerrilla warfare of, 253–5, 257, 258
  ideology of, 169, 170–1, 272
  -Kuomintang alliance, 241, 243–4; and Second United Front, 256–9
  -Kuomintang conflicts, 242, 246, 249–51, 252, 257, 259, 261, 262, 277, 303n.99
  leadership in People's Republic, 263, 271–3
  and "Long March," 255
  "Maoists" versus "Liuists" in, 268–9
  and Red Army, *see* armed forces
  reforms (*cheng-feng*, 1940s), 259–62
  rural/peasant-based, 114, 153–4, 241, 242, 252, 254–7, 259, 261, 262, 270–1, 275, 277–80, 343n.21
  size of, 263
  in Yenan period (1940s), 153, 258, 345n.51
Communist Party, Russian, *see* Bolshevik Party
conjunctural analysis of revolutions, 298n.44, 320n.16
conscription, *see* armed forces
consensus, systems/value, *see* theories of revolution
conspiracy as form of political violence, 9, *see also* Gurr, Ted R.; political violence
"Constitutionalism"
  Chinese, 78, 79
  and French constitutional monarchy/reforms, 118, 144, 193
  Russian, 95, 207
Cossacks, 12, 114, 128, *see also* armed forces
Craig, Gordon, quoted, 198
Crimean War (1854–5), 83–5, 88, 90, 110
Cuba, 3, 287, 289, 318n.2

democracy
  French Revolution and, 192, 201, 234
  revolutionary ideal of, 206
  in Soviet Union, 228
  "versus totalitarianism," 286
  see also egalitarianism

Index

deprivation, *see* "relative deprivation"
Deutscher, Isaac, quoted, 95
Diaz, Porfirio, 288
discontent, mass
  and peasant revolt, *see* peasantry
  and political violence, 10, 15, 16, 17,
    19, 97–9
dominant class
  China (gentry), 71–2, 78–81, 107, 148–
    50, 236, 240–1, 247, 249, 285;
    compared to other dominant classes,
    85, 88, 90, 99, 101, 102, 103, 106,
    149, 151–2, 239; overthrown, 164,
    261–2; rebellions put down by, 75–
    6, 114, 151–2, 342n.12; during
    United Front, 257–8
  England (landed upper class), 141–4,
    149, 151, 294n.4; compared to French
    dominant class, 182, 183, 185
  France (*privilégiés*), 56–60, 64–7, 80–1,
    107, 125, 142, 145, 148, 307n.31;
    compared to other dominant classes,
    85, 99, 101, 102, 103, 106, 151, 182,
    183, 185, 239; impact of peasant re-
    volts on, 183–5, 285; privileges abol-
    ished, 118, 177, 178, 183, 184
  Japan (*daimyo, samurai*), 100, 101–3
  political leadership marginal to, 165,
    166, 167, *see also* leadership, revolu-
    tionary political
  Prussia (Junkers), 105–9, 145, 146–7,
    149, 151–2
  relationships of, to producing classes
    and imperial states, 48–9, 110, 161,
    183
  Russia (landed nobility), 85–90, 98,
    132–3, 148, 285; compared to
    other dominant classes, 85, 90, 99,
    106, 151, 239; overthrown, 164; sei-
    zure of estates of, 136–9, 209, 212,
    214, 217, 218; state support of/com-
    petition with, 26–31
Dorn, Walter, quoted, 21
Dunn, John, 290
  Modern Revolutions, 6
Durkheim, Emile, 8
Dutch War (1672–8), 54

Eckstein, Alexander, 273
  quoted, 267
Eckstein, Harry, *Internal War,* quoted, 33
Eckstein, Susan, 290
economy
  agrarian, *see* agriculture/agrarian econ-
    omy
  Chinese, 74, 76, 153, 265, 275; and
    Great Leap Forward, 268, 272, 278;

    and political consolidation of Revo-
    lution, 247–8
  English, 55–6, 61; as model, 168
  French: Old Regime, 54–6, 63–4, 66,
    120–2, 221, 265; during political
    conflict, 187, 189, 190–4; postrevo-
    lutionary, 176–7, 202–5, 221–2
  German, 93, 94, 145, 147
  Japanese, 94
  recessions in, 63, 93, 145
  Russian: Old Regime, 82–3, 85, 91,
    93–4, 99, 209, 265; during political
    conflict, 218–20, 221–5; postrevolu-
    tionary, 192, 223–5, 232, 234
  world economic structures, 20–4
  see also commercialization and trade;
    industrialization; land ownership;
    wealth
Edeen, Alf, 226
  quoted, 229–30
Edwards, Lyford, 33
  The Natural History of Revolutions, 37
egalitarianism
  Chinese Communist, 273, 274, 277
  French, 3
  Soviet Russian, 228, 231, 273; "petty
    bourgeois," 230
Ellis, John, quoted, 217
Emancipation of serfs, *see* serfdom
  and post-Emancipation agriculture, *see*
    Russia, Old Regime
England
  agriculture/agrarian economy in, 20, 55,
    56, 118, 140, 141, 142, 151
  Civil War in, 141, 143, 181, 182, *see*
    also English Revolution
  colonialism of, 21, 60, 63
  commercialization/industrialization of,
    19, 20, 21, 52, 56, 177, 186
  contrasted to France, Russia and China,
    155–7 (table)
  in Crimean War, 83–4
  dominant (landed) class in, 141–4, 149,
    151, 294n.4; compared to French
    dominant class, 182, 183, 185
  economy of: compared with France, 55–
    6, 61; as model, 168
  naval power of: versus China, 73; versus
    France, 54, 60, 63, 196
  parliamentary system of, 140, 141, 143–
    4, 181, 182–3, 294n.4
  peasantry in, 142–3, 144
  Russia (Old Regime) indebted to/as ally
    of, 93, 96
English Revolution, 113, 144
  compared to French, 141–3, 181, 183,
    185, 186

as political revolution, 140, 294n.4, 302n.84

Enlightenment, the, 51, 329nn.19, 23

Ethiopia, social revolution in, 287, 292, 350n.10

European states system, 22, 294n.3, 304n.4
and China, 68
expansion of, 4, 20–1
France and, 3, 54, 67, 186, 195, 198
and international conflicts, 185, 198
Japan and, 104
military competition within, 50, 52, 82, 232, 285
nationalism in, 195
Russia and, 81, 82, 83, 93, 94, 99, 105, 109, 110, 224, 232, 235, 277
in World War I, 95, 110
see also colonialism/colonization; foreign intrusion and pressures; imperialism

February (1917) Revolution, see Russia, political conflicts of Revolution (1917–21)

Fei Hsiao-tung, quoted, 150

feudalism, 7, 27, 304n.4
in Old Regime France, 56–7, 118, 125, 191; and "medieval rubbish," 178, 181, 184, 205

Ford, Franklin, quoted, 62

foreign intrusion and pressures, 50, 161, 285, 289
in China, 21–2, 68, 73–8 (passim), 81, 100, 110, 153, 173, 238, 242, 246, 250, 266–8
in France, 81, 100, 110, 173, 184, 188, 196
in Japan, 21–2, 100, 102, 103–4, 110
in Prussia, 105, 108, 110
in Russia, 92–3, 104, 105, 110, 173, 215, 232, 338n.36
see also colonialism/colonization; imperialism

Fox, Edward, quoted, 168

France, Old Regime, 21
absolutism in, 52, 54, 59, 64, 140
agrarian economy in, see peasant situation in, below
armed forces of, see armed forces; and strategic military situation, 50, 54, 60–4
bread riots in, 122
bureaucracy of, see parlements in, below; see also bureaucracy
commerce in, 54–5, 56, 59, 176
compared to Prussia and Japan, 100–8 (passim)

dominant class in, 56–60, 64–7, 80–1, 107, 142, 148, 183, 307n.31; compared to other dominant classes, 85, 99, 101, 102, 103, 106, 151, 182, 183, 185, 239; and "proprietary wealth," 59–60; and revolutionary political crisis, 64–7, 80–1, 99, 102, 103, 145
economy of, 54–6, 120, 220; compared to England, China, Russia, 55–6, 221–2, 265; crises in, 63–4, 66, 121–2, 202; see also finances, governmental, below
estates (social orders) in, 57–8, 59
finances, governmental, 60–4, 199–200, 202; and taxation, 55, 59, 60–4, 81, 119, 123, 124, 148
industry in, 54–6, 265
intendants in, 52, 64, 66, 120, 124, 201
parlements in, 52, 61–2, 64–6, 80, 81, 107, 182, 328n.1
pays d'etat of, 52, 64, 119
peasant situation in, 48–9, 54–5, 59, 114, 118–28, 203; agrarian economy, 48, 54–6, 110, 118–22, 148, 221
population and growth of, 54, 56, 119, 121, 126, 197–8
rents and rental claims in, see land ownership
revolutionary political crisis in, see revolutionary crisis, emergence of
seigneurial system in, 55, 58, 59, 62, 107, 119, 126
state-structure of, 52–4, 59, 87, 118, 123–6, 167, 168, 173, 178
"venality of office" in, 52, 57, 58, 59, 63, 107, 118, 179, 200, 309–10n.78, see also parlements in, above
and wars, 54, 60–2, 63

France, political conflicts of Revolution (1787–99)
armies in, see armed forces
bourgeoisie in, 51, 65
bread riots, 122
Catholic Church in, 184, 191, 193, 194, 195, 202
counterrevolution, 184–9 (passim), 191, 193, 203–4, 233–4
crisis (1787–9), 47–52, 58, 60, 62; compared to Russia (1917), 47, 137–9; effects on dominant class, 64–7; effects on peasantry, 117, 118, 121–6, 237–9
and Directory, 193–5, 197, 198, 201
dominant class in, 64–7, 125, 184; contrasted to English Revolution, 182,

France, political conflicts (*continued*)
183, 185; political polarization
within, 183, 185, 187; privileges
abolished, 118, 177, 178, 183, 184,
285
Estates-General in, 64, 65–6, 123, 182
ideology in, 169–71
leadership during, 165–8, 176, 185,
186, 188–93, 247, 253, 336n.1
liberal phases of, 183, 185, 193, 207
local government during (compared to
English Revolution), 182–3, 185
mass mobilization in, 187–93, 195
menu peuple in, 187, 193
Montagnard dictatorship ("Terror")
during, 165, 185, 188–90, 199, 247;
compared to Bolsheviks, 167, 192–3,
253
"Municipal Revolution" (1789), 66–7,
122, 124, 125, 145, 182, 336n.1
and Napoleon, *see* Napoleon I (Bonaparte)
peasant revolts (anti-seigneurial), 122–8,
137, 146, 183–5, 191, 221, 236,
239, 320n.19; compared to Russian,
137–9, 140, 221–2, 234; counterrevolutionary, 188, 189, 203–4; impact of, on dominant class, 183–5,
285
sans culottes in, 113, 142, 187–9, 190–
2, 220, 234
state-building during, 162, 165–6, 168,
178–9, 182–3, 188–9
Third Estate in, 64–6, 118, 123, 165,
166, 182, 184
and wars, impact of, 185–7
France, postrevolutionary (New Regime)
agrarian economy/society under, 177,
178, 191; compared to Chinese and
Russian, 137, 271
army of, *see* armed forces
bureaucracy in, 162, 168, 186, 193–5,
198–201
and Catholic Church, 195, 202, 204
and civil state, 178–9; bureaucratization
of, 198–201; executive controls,
182–3, 188–9; functions/activities,
202–5; legitimation, 179, 200; peasantry and, 203–5; "reach" of, 203
commerce of, 73, 176
compared to Chinese and Russian postrevolutionary regimes, 42, 137, 162–
3, 206, 233–6, 263, 265, 271, 274
departments of, 179, 180 (map)
dominant groups in, 176–7, 204–5
economic development/regulation in,
176–7, 189, 190–4, 202–5, 221–2

industrialization of, 175–7, 193, 205
land ownership in, 177, 178, 194, 204–
5, 234
Napoleon's accomplishments for, 105,
108, 195–6, 200–2, *see also* Napoleon I (Bonaparte)
social structure in, 204–5
taxation in, 179, 202, 204
and wars (and military expansion), 96,
105, 178, 185–7, 197–8
Frederick II (the Great), king of Prussia,
108
Frederick William, elector of Brandenburg,
106
Frederick William IV, king of Prussia, 145,
146, 147
French Revolution (general)
August 4, 1789, significance of, 118
as "bourgeois revolution," 40, 41, 141,
162, 174–9, 233, 302n.84, 303n.97
as bureaucratic and state-strengthening
revolution, 3, 176–7, 179, 198–200
causes of, 155–7 (table)
compared to Chinese and Russian, 40–
2, 80–1, 147–8, 154, 155–7 (table),
162–3, 181, 206, 207, 216, 233–42
(passim), 247, 263, 266, 269, 279,
280, 282–3 (table), 303n.97
compared to English, 141–3, 181, 183,
185, 186
compared to German, 144–6
and democracy, 192, 201, 234
explanations of, 51–2, 58, 65–6, 174–9
leadership of, 165–6, 168, 176
and liberalism, 40–1, 178, 183, 185,
188, 193, 201, 207, 234
outcomes and accomplishments of, 13,
126, 161–2, 163–4, 174–9, 181,
186, 195–205, 206, 234, 279, 282–
3 (table), 285–7
as social revolution, 118, 141
wars intrinsic to, 186
worldwide effects of, 3–4
frustration-aggression theories, 10, *see also*
theories of revolution
Furet, Francois, quoted, 57

German Revolution (1848), 113, 140, 164
compared to French, 144–6
liberalism in, 144, 147
Germany, 7, 167, 255, 300n.57
contrasted to France, Russia and China,
155–7 (table)
economic growth rate, 94
peasants in, 146–7
and Prussian Reform Movement, *see*
Prussia

Index

Russia opposed to, 93, 96, 99, 212, 215, 216
unification/industrialization of, 93, 105, 109, 144, 147
Gerschenkron, Alexander, quoted, 84, 177
Girondins, 166, 167, 188
Gneisenau, August Neithardt von, 108
Godechot, Jacques, quoted, 195
government, representative
  Chinese, 77–9, 81
  English Parliament, 140, 141, 143–4, 181, 182–3, 294n.4
  French, 81; Napoleon and, 201–2; National/Constituent Assembly, 182, 183–4, 200
  German (Frankfurt Parliament), 144, 145
  Russian (zemstvos), 84, 89–90, 95, 97, 99, 207, 208, 209, 227
  see also state(s)
Gramsci, Antonio, 6, 15
Great Britain, see England
Great Northern War (1700–21), 82
Greer, Donald, quoted, 189
guerrilla warfare, 287
  Chinese, 252–5, 257, 258
  counterrevolutionary, 203, 218
  as "internal war," 9
Guinea-Bissau, social revolution in, 287
Gurr, Ted R., 10, 11, 13, 16, 17, 25–6, 34
  Why Men Rebel, quoted, 9, 15
  see also theories of revolution

Haile Selassie, emperor of Ethiopia, 350n.10
Hapsburg Dynasty, 54
Hardenberg, Karl August von, 108
Hegel, Georg W. F., 40
Henry VIII, king of England, 143
Hermassi, Elbaki, quoted, 4
Hintze, Otto, quoted, 30–1
"historical" approach, 33–40, 320n.16
  and comparative historical analysis, 36–40, 43, 100
  see also theories of revolution
Hobsbawm, Eric, quoted, 18
Hohenzollern monarchy, 104–8, 110, see also Prussia
Holland, see Netherlands
Huntington, Samuel P., quoted, 163

ideologies, revolutionary, 114, 153–4, 168–71
  Bolshevik, 192, 338n.28; contradicted, 171
  Taiping (anti-Confucian), 75, 151, see also Taiping Rebellion
  totalitarian, 170
imperial state, see state(s)

imperialism
  Chinese, 67–8
  and Chinese revolutionary anti-imperialism, 78, 243–4, 246
  European, in China, see foreign intrusion and pressures
  "of free trade," 73
  French, 60, 73
  Hapsburg, 54
  Japanese, 73, 153
  Russian, 73
  U.S., in Asia, 276, 277
  see also colonialism/colonization
income differentials, postrevolutionary
  China, 163, 273, 274
  Russia, 230
  see also class
Industrial Revolution, 24, 56
industrialization
  Chinese, 74, 76–7, 247–8, 267–8, 269, 275, 276–7
  development of, 20, 21
  English, 20, 21, 56, 177
  European, military repercussions of, 82, 83
  as force for change, 4–5
  French, 54–6, 175–7, 193, 205, 265
  German, 93, 105, 109
  "imperative of," 232, 266
  Japanese, 77, 100, 101, 103–4
  Russian: Old Regime, 83, 90–4, 99, 103, 104, 110, 133, 211–2, 247, 265; during political conflict, 206, 219–20, 221–3; postrevolutionary, 192, 226–31, 232–5, 269, 276
  see also commercialization and trade; labor; modernization; technologies; urban workers
internal war as form of political violence, 9, see also Gurr, Ted R.; political violence
Italy, 7
Ivan IV (the Terrible), tsar of Russia, 82

Jacobins, Jacobinism, 163, 168–71 (passim), 196, 197, 220, 234, 242, 265, 291
  and anti-Jacobinism, 194
  Montagnard, 165–6, 188–93, 247
Japan, 167
  agrarian economy of, 22, 103–4, 110
  Chinese students in, 77
  contrasted to France, Russia and China, 155–7 (table)
  economic growth rate, 94
  foreign pressures on, 21–2, 50, 100, 102, 103–4

Japan (*continued*)
    industrialization of, 77, 100, 101, 103–4
    invades China, 73, 153, 240, 250, 251;
        and Sino-Japanese wars, 76, 77, 81,
        104, 251, 256–9, 262
    Meiji Restoration in, 100–5, 109–10,
        169–70, 300n.57
    and Russo-Japanese War, 91, 95, 104,
        133, 135
    in World War II, 266, 288
Johnson, Chalmers, 13, 15, 16, 25–6, 34,
    345n.51
    Revolutionary Change, 9; quoted, 11, 12

Kao Kang, 346n.75
Korea, 68, 73, 276
Kornilov, General L. G., 210, 211
Kuomintang Nationalist Party (KMT), *see*
    China, political conflicts of Revolu-
    tion (1911–49)

labor
    forced (in Soviet Russia), 230–1
    "free" wage, 109, 130
    unrest and strikes in Russia, 92, 95, 98,
        208
    see also unions; urban workers
Labrousse, C. Ernest, quoted, 121
land ownership
    Church lands confiscated (France), 184,
        191, 202
    communal: France (Old Regime), 120,
        121, 221; Russia (Old Regime, *obsh-
        china*), 129–30, 132, 135, 136, 139,
        209, 211, 227
    in Japan, 101
    and peasant-landlord relationships, 161;
        China, 13, 68–9, 113–17, 148–54,
        240, 241, 258, 259, 262, 277, 284,
        343n.21; England, 142–3; France,
        13, 55–61 (passim), 82–3, 85, 113–
        21, 126–7, 137, 140, 148; Prussia,
        109, 146–7; Russia, 13, 82–3, 85,
        88–9, 109, 113–17, 128, 133, 134,
        137, 140, 148, 209, 211
    by peasantry: China, 149, 254; France,
        55, 118–20, 126–7, 137, 149, 191,
        192; Russia, 135, 149, 209, 212,
        214, 216, 217, 218
    postrevolutionary: Chinese land revolu-
        tion and, 261–2, 277–8; France,
        177, 178, 194, 204–5, 234; Russia,
        137, 222, 229, (and peasant expro-
        priation) 230
    and rents: China, 148, 150, 153; France,
        56, 58, 59, 61, 80, 119–20, 126;
        Russia, 132, 135, 137
    see also wealth

Landes, David, quoted, 147
Latin America, 3
leadership, revolutionary political, 164–5,
    172–3, 287
    Chinese, 166–7, 168, 239, 247, 250,
        252–5 (passim), 260–1, 263–5,
        268, 269, 272, 278
    English, 143, 185
    French, 165–6, 168, 176, 186, 336n.1;
        Montagnard, 165, 167, 185, 188–
        93, 247, 253
    and ideologies, 168–71
    Russian, 162, 166–7, 168, 193, 206,
        207–20, 227, 230, 272
    state-building efforts of, 168, 291
    see also Bolshevik Party (Communist
        Party of the Soviet Union); Commu-
        nist Party, Chinese (CCP); state(s)
Lefebvre, Georges, quoted, 118, 123–4
legitimacy, 12, 25, 31–2, 50, 170, 179, 200
LeGoff, T. J. A., quoted, 203
Lenin, V. I., 4, 6, 171, 214, 217, 286
    quoted, 26, 47, 51, 284
    State and Revolution, 215
    and view of peasantry, 319n.12, 323n.60
Leninism, 15, 24
    in China, 4, 266
    see also Marxism-Leninism
Le Roy Ladurie, Emmanuel, 125
Leuthy, Herbert, quoted, 201–2
Levellers (England), 142, 143
Loménie de Brienne, Etienne, 64
Louis XIV, king of France, 52–3, 54, 60,
    63
Louis XVI, king of France, 63, 65, 145–6,
    185, 186
Louis Philippe, ("citizen") king of France,
    145
Louvois, Marquis de, 54
Lukács, Georg, 6, 15

McNeill, William, quoted, 202–3
Makhno, Nestor, 218
Manchu China, *see* China, Old Regime
Manchuria, 266, 275
Mao Tse-tung, 6, 254, 268, 274
    and Maoist doctrine, 15, 171, 269,
        272
    quoted, 260
Marx, Karl, 178, 284, 292, 293
    quoted, 3, 7–8, 19, 120, 174
Marxism, 8, 13, 16, 17, 19, 171, 304n.4,
    323n.60, 338n.28
    divergency within, 6
    Marxist theories debated, 34–5, 174–5
    and state autonomy and functions, 25,
        26–7, 28, 30, 31

and theory of capitalism, 56
and theory of revolution, *see* theories of
 revolution
Western, 6, 15
Marxism-Leninism, 168–71, (passim), 260,
 see also Leninism; Marxism
Meiji Restoration, *see* Japan
Mendel, Arthur, quoted, 92
Menshevik Party, 97, 167, 208, 213, 214,
 219
Metternich, Prince von, 145
Mexican Revolution, 3, 286, 287, 288, 291
Migdal, Joel S., 318–19n.6, 327–8n.126
migration, peasant, *see* peasantry
Miliband, Ralph, 27
military, the, *see* armed forces
Mill, John Stuart, *A System of Logic,* 36
Mills, C. Wright, quoted, 3, 288
modernization
 of agriculture, 89, 109
 and revolution, relationship to, 19–24
 see also commercialization and trade; industrialization; technologies
monarchy
 absolute, *see* absolutism/autocracy
 "bourgeois," 201
 Chinese, 47–51, *see also* Ch'ing (Manchu) Dynasty
 constitutional, 144, 193, 207
 English 141, 143, 144
 foreign pressures on, 50, 73, 81, 100,
  105, *see also* foreign intrusion and
  pressures
 French (Bourbon), 7, 24, 47–51, 51–67
  (passim), 68, 145, 201
 German/Prussian, 144–7
 Russian (Romanov tsars), 47–51, 82,
  84–8, 91, 95, 97–9
 upper-class conflict with, 42, 49–50
Montagnards, *see* France, political conflicts
 of Revolution (1787–99); Jacobins
Moore, Barrington, Jr., *Social Origins of
 Dictatorship and Democracy,* 6, 36
 quoted, 112
Mozambique, social revolution in, 287
"multiple sovereignty," 11, 34
"Municipal Revolution," *see* France, political conflicts of Revolution (1787–99)

Napoleon I (Bonaparte), 105, 197, 198
 and Napoleonic dictatorship, 108, 163,
  166, 181, 185–6, 193, 195–6, 200–
  2, 204, 331n.3
nation-states, *see* European states system
Netherlands, 54, 55
Neumann, Franz, quoted, 293
New Economic Policy (NEP) of Russia

during political conflict, 219–20, 221–2
postrevolutionary crisis, 223–4
Nicholas II, tsar of Russia, 91, 95, 97–9

obshchina (Russian commune, Old Regime),
 see land ownership
October (1917) Revolution, *see* Russia, political conflicts of Revolution (1917–
 21)
Offe, Claus, 27, 28
office-holding, *see* bureaucracy
Opium War, 73, 75

Paige, Jeffery, 290, 319n.11, n.12, 320n.15
Palmer, R. R., quoted, 127
Paris Commune, 188
Park, Robert, quoted, 37
parlements, see France, Old Regime
parliaments, *see* government, representative
Party-state
 Communist China as, 162, 164, 245
  (map); supports agriculture, 271
 Soviet Russia as, 162, 164, 204, 206,
  220, 222–5, 227, 229, 234; industry
  as base of, 220, 226–8, 232–3, 235
 "transmission belt" to peasantry, 227,
  265
peasantry
 autonomy of: and autonomous revolt,
  115, 116–17, 125, 138, 140, 239,
  262; Chinese, 148, 151, 152, 154;
  French, 120, 132, 204; Russian, 229,
  233
 English, 142–3, 144
 German, 146–7
 and landlords, land ownership, *see* land
  ownership
 migration of, 130, 134, 135, 152
 in Old Regimes: China, 48–9, 68–9, 71,
  74–5, 107, 148–54; France, 48–9,
  54–5, 59, 118–21, 203; Russia,
  48–9, 82–92 (passim), 128–35
 and peasant-based rebellions, 13, 31,
  112–17, 161, 285, 287, 291, 292;
  Chinese, 74–6, 80, 107, 113–17,
  149–50, 151–4, 172, 236, 239–41,
  262, 279, 294n.3; conditions for,
  156 (table); in England (absence of),
  142–4; French anti-seigneurial,
  122–8, 137, 146, 183–5, 191, 221,
  236, 239, 320n.19; French counterrevolutionary, 188, 189, 203–4; in
  Germany/Prussia (absence of), 146–
  7; and guerrilla warfare, 203, 218,
  252–5; Japanese, 102; Russian, 85,
  88, 89, 99, 113–17, 128, 132–40,
  146, 172, 206, 210, 211, 219, 221,

peasantry (*continued*)
231, 234, 236, 239, 262, 278, 279;
Russian and French compared, 137–
9, 140, 221–2, 234
during political conflicts of Revolutions:
in China (CCP and), 153–4, 252–
62, 277–8, 279–80; in France (Montagnards and), 191; in Russia (Bolsheviks and, 1917–21), 216–19,
278, 279, 338n.36
postrevolutionary (in New Regimes):
China, 270–1, 275–6, 277–80,
286–7; France, 203–5; Russia (after
1921), 220–5, 228–9, 230, 232–3,
235, 270–1, 278, 279, 286–7
Prussian, 105–9 (passim)
"social banditry" of (Chinese), 114,
152–3, 254–5, 327n.124
see also agriculture/agrarian economy;
serfdom

Perrie, Maureen, quoted, 134
Perry, Admiral Matthew, 100
Peter I (the Great), tsar of Russia, 82, 86,
87, 230
Pettee, George, 33, 37
Phillips, Wendell, quoted, 17
Plehve, Viacheslav von, 95
political conflict theories, *see* theories of
revolution
political leadership, *see* leadership, revolutionary political
political violence
defined, and major forms of ("turmoil,"
"conspiracy," "internal war"), 9
mass discontent and, 10, 15, 16, 17, 19,
97–9
see also Gurr, Ted R.
population growth
Chinese, 74, 104, 275
French, 56, 119, 121, 126
Japanese, 104
Russian, 83, 132, 220, 221, 226
Portugal, 350n.10
Potemkin Mutiny, 95
Poulantzas, Nicos, 27, 28
proletariat
development of, 8; in Russia, 88, 92
industrial, *see* urban workers
"party of," 214, 244, *see also* Bolshevik
Party (Communist Party of the Soviet
Union)
and "proletarian revolution," 41, 220,
266
proletarianization feared in tsarist Russia, 88
"will of the proletariat," 15

Prussia, 60, 167, 300n.57
armed forces in, 105–8 (passim), 198
contrasted to France, Russia and China,
155–7 (table)
dominant class (Junkers) in, 105–9, 145,
146–7, 149, 151–2
mobilizes to meet foreign competition,
50
and Prussian Reform Movement, 100,
105–9, 110, 147
in World War I, 93
see also Germany
Pugachev Rebellion (1773–5), 128

railroad(s)
Chinese, 76, 153, 247, 248 (map); 1911
reorganization of, 79, 81
French, 177
Russian: Old Regime, 83, 90, 91, 96,
212 (map), 247; during political conflicts, 208, 211–12, 218; Trans-
Siberian, 130
Rasputin, Grigori, 97
rebellions, 4
peasant, *see* peasantry
Reinhard, Marcel, quoted, 186
"relative deprivation," 9, 10, 25, 34, 115,
see also Gurr, Ted R.
religion, *see* Church, the
rents, *see* land ownership
revolution(s)
"bourgeois" versus "socialist," 8, *see
also* bourgeoisie
change as defining feature of, 4–5, 288,
294–5n.6
conjunctural analysis of, 298n.44,
320n.16
and counterrevolution, 170, 184–9, 191,
193, 203–4, 210, 215–19 (passim),
232–4, 265, 285
of 1848, 83, 113, 140, 144–7
"from above," 102, 220, *see also* Japan;
Stalin, Joseph
"general" theories of, 288, *see also* theories of revolution
"historical" approach to, 33–40,
320n.16
leadership of, *see* leadership, revolutionary political
of 1905, *see* Russia, Old Regime
peasant revolts, *see* peasantry
"proletarian," 41, 220, 266
social, *see* social revolution(s)
Third World, 41, 303nn.97, 99
urban workers and, *see* urban workers
"world-historical character" of, 4, 39,
290

Index

see also Prussia; *entries for individual revolutions*

revolutionary crisis, emergence of, 11, 12, 16, 17, 18, 26, 117, 286, 291
  in China, 47–51, 68, 79, 80–1, 99, 100, 105, 110–11, 112, 285, 290
  in France, 47–51, 52, 58, 60, 62, 64–7, 80–1, 99, 100, 105, 110–11, 112, 138, 139, 145, 185, 207, 234, 285, 290
  in Japan, 100, 109–10
  and peasant rebellion, *see* peasantry
  post-World War II, 290
  in Prussia, 109–10, 145
  in Russia, 47–51, 81, 85, 88, 91, 94, 97–9, 105, 110–11, 112, 139, 206–11, 231–2, 234, 285
  transnational relations and, 19–24
Robespierre, Maximilien de, 188, 190, 192, 193
Robinson, G. T., *Rural Russia Under the Old Regime,* 133
  quoted, 134, 135
Romanov Dynasty, *see* monarchy; Russia, Old Regime
Rousseau, Jean Jacques, 329n.23
Rudé, George, 187
Russia, Old Regime
  absolutism/autocracy in, 82, 87–90 (passim), 94, 95, 97–9, 128, 140, 227
  agriculture/agrarian life in, 48, 103, 104; and agrarian unrest, 95, 135; regional variations, 130; during serfdom, 82–3, 86–7, 108–9; following serfdom (post-Emancipation), 89, 90, 91, 94, 109, 128–30, 132–3, 148
  armed forces (Imperial, Cossacks) in, and conscription of, *see* armed forces
  bureaucracy (state service) in, 90, 97–8, 132, 138, 166, 226; recruitment for, 82, 86, 87
  compared to Japan, Prussia, France (Old Regime), 103, 104, 105, 108–9, 110, 221–2
  dominant class (landed nobility) in, 148; compared to other dominant classes, 85, 90, 99, 106, 151, 239; economic base and political power, 85–90, 98, 132–3; reaction of, to Emancipation of serfs, 106
  economy of, 82–3, 85, 91, 93–4, 99, 209, 265, *see also* industrialization (state-guided) in, *below*
  Emancipation of serfs in, 85, 88–9, 106, 108–9, 128–30, 132
  foreign investments in, 90, 92–3, 104
  foreign trade of, 90, 92–3, 209

  industrialization (state-guided) in, 90–4, 99, 103, 104, 110, 133, 211–12, 247, 265
  labor unrest, strikes, unions in, 92, 95, 98, 231
  landlord-peasant relationships in, 13, 109, 113–17, 128, 133, 134, 137, 140, 148, 209, 211; during and after serfdom, 82–3, 85, 88–9
  mir (village assembly) in, 132, 138
  obshchina (peasant commune) in, *see* land ownership
  peasant situation in, 48–9, 82–92 (passim), 128–35
  Peter the Great and, 82, 86, 87, 230
  population growth in, 83, 132
  proletariat in, 88, 92
  railroads in, 83, 90, 91, 96, 130, 211, 212 (map), 247
  representative bodies (*zemstvos*) in, 84, 89–90, 95, 99, 207, 208, 209, 227; compared to Chinese representative assemblies, 90; during World War I, 97, 209
  and Revolution of 1905, 90, 91, 93, 94–5; peasants in, 133–6
  and revolutionary crisis, *see* revolutionary crisis, emergence of
  as "semicolony" of Western Europe, 93, *see also* European states system
  state-structure of, 82, 86–8, 128, 167
  Stolypin reforms in, 130, 135, 136
  strategic military situation of, 50, 104, 224, 300n.57; before 1850, 82, 105; after 1855 (Crimean War), 84, 90; on eve of World War I, 94, 95–6
  taxation in, 82, 90, 91, 92, 128, 132, 133, 148
  and wars, domestic impact of, 237; Crimean, 83–5, 88, 90, 110; Great Northern, 82; Russo-Japanese, 91, 95, 104, 133, 135; Russo-Turkish, 90; World War I, 93–9 (passim), 104, 105, 110, 136, 138–9, 207, 209, 219, 233
Russia, political conflicts of Revolution (1917–21)
  armed forces in, *see* armed forces
  Bolshevik (Communist) Party in, 23–4, 163, 164, 204, 206, 215–20, 226–7; base of, 218, 220, 232, 278; leadership of, 162, 166–7, 193, 208, 216, 217, 219, 230; in October Revolution, 135, 138, 213–15, 219; versus political opposition, 170, 171, 207, 213–15, 217, 222; *see also* Bolshevik Party

Russia, political conflicts (*continued*)
  bureaucracy during, 162, 206, 215,
    217–20 (passim); and recruitment
    of old-regime officials, 218, 232
  Cheka (political police) in , 215–16
  Civil War, 192, 216–20, 224–5, 228,
    232, 253, 338n.36
  and counterrevolution, 210, 215, 217–
    18, 219, 232, 233–4
  dominant classes in, 98, 164, 209
  "dual power" in, 336n.2
  February Revolution, 98, 208; compared
    to France, 207; impact of, 135, 209,
    210
  ideology in, 169–71
  industrialization during, 206, 220, 221–
    3, 232; industrial workers, 92, 113,
    172, 209–14, 219, 234, *see also* ur-
    ban workers
  leadership during, 166–7, 168, 206,
    207–20, 227
  liberal-democratic goals of, 207, 209,
    214, 217, 220
  Mensheviks in, 97, 167, 208, 213, 214,
    219
  and 'New Economic Policy," 219–20
  October Revolution, 138, 207, 213–14,
    215, 219
  peasantry in, *see* peasantry
  population growth during, 220, 221
  Provisional Government in, 98–9, 136,
    138, 207–12, 213, 217
  railroads during, 208, 211–12, 218
  Red Army in, *see* armed forces
  soldiers (as rebels) in, 136, 208, 209,
    211, 213
  soviets in, 208–15 (passim), 218–19
  terror in, 215–16, 219
  trade unions in, 219
  "War Communism" during, 219, 222,
    223
  Western powers in, 215, 338n.36
  workers' control in, 209–14 (passim),
    219
  and World War I, continuing impact of,
    99, 207, 208–10, 211, 215, 216,
    217
Russia, postrevolutionary (New Regime), 21
  agrarian outcomes (of peasant revolts):
    compared to France, 137, 221–2;
    and national economy, 221–5, 232;
    Party-state and villages, 222–3
  Bukharin's policies, 223–5
  bureaucracy in, 162, 206, 215, 217–20
    (passim), 226–7, 229–33, 236, 271–2
  coercion (terror) in, 230–2, 233, 278;
    "Great Purges," 231

  compared to Chinese New Regime, 42,
    162–3, 263, 265, 267–9, 270, 274,
    277
  compared to French New Regime, 162,
    206, 234–5
  economy of, 192, 223–5, 232, 234
  industry/industrialization strategies in,
    223–5, 234, 269, 276; as base of
    Party-state, 192, 220, 226–8, 231–3,
    235; financing of, 229; "imperative
    of industrialization," 232; situation
    of workers, 228–9, 230
  inequalities in, *see* stratification patterns,
    below
  New Economic Policy (NEP) crisis,
    223–4
  peasantry under: collectivization of,
    223–5, 228–9, 230, 270–1, 278;
    1928 and after, 229, 230, 232–3,
    235, 286–7
  population growth in, 226
  Stalinist policies of, *see* Stalin, Joseph
  state-structure of, 162–3, 226–8, 232;
    party coordination in and size of,
    226; and "transmission belts," 227,
    265
  strategic military situation of, 224,
    300n.57, *see also* armed forces
  stratification patterns: income differen-
    tials, 230, 273; ranks in state admin-
    istration, 230–1; social mobility,
    227–8, 231
  trade unions in, 228
  in World War II, 233, 286
Russian Revolution (general)
  causes of, 155–7 (table), 207
  compared to Chinese and French, 40–2,
    80–1, 147–8, 154, 155–7 (table),
    162–3, 181, 206, 207, 216, 233–5,
    236–42 (passim), 247, 263, 266,
    269, 275–9, 280, 282–3 (table),
    303n.97
  and "imperative of industrialization,"
    232
  leadership of, 166–7, 168
  liberal ("February") phase of, 207–10
  "October," significance of, 213
  outcomes and accomplishments of, 13,
    161–2, 163–4, 225–33, 233–6,
    279, 282–3 (table), 285, 286–7
  peasant problem intrinsic to, 232–3
  suddenness and completeness of, 206,
    231–2
  worldwide effect of, 3, 4
Russo-Japanese War, 91, 95, 104, 133,
  135
Russo-Turkish War, 90

Index

sans culottes, see France, political conflicts of Revolution (1787–99)
Scharnhorst, Gerhard von, 108
Schurmann, Franz, 260, 261
    quoted, 236, 262
Scott, S. F., 190
Selden, Mark, 258, 260
    quoted, 259
serfdom
    Emancipation from: Baltic provinces, 130; French and English, 142; Prussian, 105, 108, 109, 147; Russian, 84, 88–9, 106, 108–9, 128–30, 132
    and rebellion, 85, 88, 116, 128
    and serf economy of Imperial Russia, 82–3, 85–8, 89, 108–9
    and serf labor in Europe, 68, 105, 108, 109, 118, 142, 147
    see also peasantry
Seven Years' War, 60, 63, 81, 108
Shanin, Teodor, 323n.60
    quoted, 112, 138
Sheppard, Thomas, quoted, 204
Siberia, 91, 130, 215
Sigurdson, Jon, quoted, 269–70
Sino-Japanese wars, *see* Japan
Skinner, G. William, quoted, 69, 149
"social banditry" (of Chinese peasants), 114, 152–3, 254–5, 327n.124
social class, *see* class; dominant class
social revolution(s)
    causes of, 155–7 (table)
    Chinese Revolution as, 164, 266
    "come, not made," 17, 18, *see also* revolutionary crisis, emergence of
    defined, 4–5, 33, 287
    French Revolution as, 118, 141, 164, 286
    German Revolution as (failed), 140, 164
    and "non-reformist reforms," 293
    outcomes of, 23, 29, 161–73, 282–3 (table)
    Russian Revolution as, 164, 231
    theories of, *see* theories of revolution
socialism
    Marxist, 171, 292, 293, *see also* Marxism
    postrevolutionary China and, 286–7
    and "socialist" versus "bourgeois" revolutions, 8, 303n.97
Socialist-Revolutionary Party, 138, 208, 213, 214
Soong, T. V., 246
South Africa, 12, 16
Soviet Regime, *see* Russia, postrevolutionary (New Regime)
Spain, 21, 288
    and War of the Spanish Succession, 54

Stalin, Joseph, 230, 286
    and "revolution from above," 220
    and Stalinist system, 171, 223, 231, 266–7, 269, 271, 272, 273, 275; Bolsheviks and, 224–5, 230, 231, 232, 279
state(s)
    as "arena," 25, 26, 29
    autonomy (potential) of, 24–32
    and class, 26–31, 284, 291–2
    coercion by, 14, 25, 26–7, 29, 32, 289
    European system of, *see* European states system
    imperial, 47–51, 304n.4, *see also* absolutism/autocracy; bureaucracy; monarchy
    international states system, 22, *see also* European states system
    office-holding (service in), *see* bureaucracy
    old-regime, *see entries for China, France, Russia*
    party and, *see* Party-state
    postrevolutionary, *see entries for China, France, Russia*
    and state-building (of new regimes), 161–73, 291–2; China, 236–7, 241–62, 266–7, 277–8; France, 182–3, 186, 188–90, 193–6, 233–6; Russia, 206, 210–20, 225, 232, 233–5; *see also* government, representative
Stein, Karl von, 108
Stilwell, General Joseph W., 251
Stolypin reforms, *see* Russia, Old Regime
strikes, *see* labor
Sun Yat-sen, 79, 243, 246
Sutherland, D. M. G., quoted, 203
Sweden, 93
    Russian war with, 82
systems/value consensus theories, *see* theories of revolution

Taiping Rebellion, 75, 151, 238, 240, *see also* peasantry
Taiwan, 276
taxation
    Chinese: during political conflict, 240, 244, 249, 251, 258; Old Regime, 69, 74, 75, 76, 148, 150, 151, 153, 238
    France: Old Regime, 55, 59, 60–4, 81, 119, 123, 124, 148; postrevolutionary, 179, 202, 204
    Prussia, 107
    by revolutionary authorities, 127
    Russia (Old Regime), 82, 90, 91, 92, 128, 132, 133, 148

Index

Taylor, George, quoted, 58, 59
technologies
    English, 56
    "intermediate," 270
    Japanese, 104
    military, 289
    in Old Regime Russia, 91, 93
    see also industrialization; modernization
terrorism
    Montagnard "Terror," *see* France, political conflicts of Revolution (1787–99)
    in revolutionary and postrevolutionary Russia, 215–16, 219, 230–2, 233, 278
    and state coercion, 14, 25, 26–7, 29, 32, 289
theories of revolution
    aggregate-psychological, 9–10, 11, 13, 115, *see also* Gurr, Ted R.
    "general," 6, 288
    and historical approach, 33–40, 320n.16
    Marxist, 4, 6, 7–8, 13, 15, 19, 26, 34–5, 292, 329n.23
    political conflict (collective action), 9, 10–11, 13, 16, 26, 27, *see also* Tilly, Charles
    and potential autonomy of the state, 24–32
    social-scientific, 5–6, 12, 34, 35, 320n.16
    and structural perspective, 14–18
    systems/value consensus, 9, 11–12, 25–6, *see also* Johnson, Chalmers
    and transnational relations, 19–24
Therborn, Göran, 27
    quoted, 28
Thermidorian Convention, 192, 193, 194, 197
Third Estate, *see* France, political conflicts of Revolution (1787–99)
Third World, 291
    Chinese experience compared to, 42, 327n.126
    military power within, 290
    nation-building revolutions of, 41, 303nn.97, 99
Tilly, Charles, 13, 15, 16, 26, 27, 34, 298n.44
    From Mobilization to Revolution, 9
    quoted, 10, 11, 126
    The Rebellious Century 1830–1930, 36
Tilly, Louise, 36
Tilly, Richard, 36
Tocqueville, Alexis de, 8, 36, 331n.5
Tokugawa Shogunate, 100–4, 110, *see also* Japan

trade, *see* commercialization and trade
trade unions, *see* labor (trade) unions (Russia)
transnational relations, 19–24, *see also* foreign intrusions and pressures
transportation difficulties (Old Regime)
    China, 69, 76
    France, 55, 56
    Russia, 83, 84, 96
    see also railroad(s)
Trotsky, Leon, 94, 217
Tseng Kuo-fan, 342n.12
Tuchman, Barbara, *Stilwell and the American Experience in China,* 251
Turkey, Russia versus, 83–4, 90, 96
turmoil as form of political violence, 9, *see also* Gurr, Ted R.; political violence

Ukraine, the, 218
unions (labor, trade)
    China, 244
    Russia, 92, 214, 219, 228, 231
United Kingdom, 94, *see also* England
United States
    Cuba and, 289
    foreign policy, 288
    imperialism in Asia, 276, 277
    intervention in Korea, 276
    Russian economy compared to, 93, 94
urban areas
    peasant migration to, 130, 134, 135, 152
    unrest in (French), 184, 185
    and urbanization control in postrevolutionary China, 269–70
urban workers
    in China, 244, 247, 268, 273–4
    in French Revolution: *menu peuple,* 187, 193; *sans culottes,* 113, 142, 187–9, 190–2, 220, 234
    insurrectionary, 112–13, 172, 285, 292
    in Russia: during Revolution, 92, 113, 172, 209–14 (passim), 219, 231, 234; postrevolutionary wages and living standards, 228–9, 230
    see also industrialization; labor

value consensus, *see* theories of revolution
value-orientations, 11–12, 13, 15, 17
Vietnam, social revolution in, 3, 287, 288, 291, 292
violence, *see* political violence
Vogel, Ezra, 265

Wallerstein, Immanuel, 22
war(s)
    China and, 73, 75, 76, 77, 81, 104, 251

France and, 54, 63, 96, 105, 178, 185–7, 198; and fiscal dilemma, 60–2

guerrilla, *see* guerrilla warfare

internal, as form of political violence, 9, *see also* Gurr, Ted R.; political violence

Russia and, 82, 83–5, 88, 90–9 (passim), 104, 105, 110, 133, 136, 138–9, 207–11 (passim), 215–19 (passim), 233, 237, 286

see also armed forces; *entries for individual wars*

"War Communism," *see* Communist Party, Russian (Bolshevik)

wealth

in China, 69, 71–2

in France, 57–9, 60, 80, 205

and income differentials, 163, 230, 273, 274

in Japan, 101–2

"proprietary," 58–9, 108

in Russia, 86–7, 138; of *kulaks*, 323n.60

see also capitalism; dominant class; land ownership

Weber, Max, 8, 286, 287, 304n.4

Whyte, Martin, quoted, 274

Wilbur, C. Martin, quoted, 244

Witte, Sergei, 94, 133

quoted, 91

Wolf, Eric, 290

Peasant Wars of the Twentieth Century, 6; quoted, 115

Wood, Gordon, quoted, 18

workers, *see* labor; peasantry; urban workers

"world time," 23, 39, 286, 288

World War I, Russia and, 93–9 (passim), 104, 105, 110, 136, 138–9, 207–11 (passim), 215–19 (passim), 233

World War II

China during, 251

economic and geopolitical shifts caused by, 21

Japan in, 266, 288

Russia and, 233, 286

Young, E. P., quoted, 78

Yuan Shih-kai, 79, 237

Yugoslavia, 287, 318n.2